P9-DMQ-506

Interest Rate (r)

10%	11%	12%	13%	14%	15%	16%	17%	18%
0.9091	0.9009	0.8929	0.8850	0.8772	0.8696	0.8621	0.8547	0.8475
0.8264	0.8116	0.7972	0.7831	0.7695	0.7561	0.7432	0.7305	0.7182
0.7513	0.7312	0.7118	0.6931	0.6750	0.6575	0.6407	0.6244	0.6086
0.6830	0.6587	0.6355	0.6133	0.5921	0.5718	0.5523	0.5337	0.5158
0.6209	0.5935	0.5674	0.5428	0.5194	0.4972	0.4761	0.4561	0.4371
0.5645	0.5346	0.5066	0.4803	0.4556	0.4323	0.4104	0.3898	0.3704
0.5132	0.4817	0.4523	0.4251	0.3996	0.3759	0.3538	0.3332	0.3139
0.4665	0.4339	0.4039	0.3762	0.3506	0.3269	0.3050	0.2848	0.2660
0.4241	0.3909	0.3606	0.3329	0.3075	0.2843	0.2630	0.2434	0.2255
0.3855	0.3522	0.3220	0.2946	0.2697	0.2472	0.2267	0.2080	0.1911
0.3505	0.3173	0.2875	0.2607	0.2366	0.2149	0.1954	0.1778	0.1619
0.3186	0.2858	0.2567	0.2307	0.2076	0.1869	0.1685	0.1520	0.1372
0.2897	0.2575	0.2292	0.2042	0.1821	0.1625	0.1452	0.1299	0.1163
0.2633	0.2320	0.2046	0.1807	0.1597	0.1413	0.1252	0.1110	0.0985
0.2394	0.2090	0.1827	0.1599	0.1401	0.1229	0.1079	0.0949	0.0835
0.2176	0.1883	0.1631	0.1415	0.1229	0.1069	0.0930	0.0811	0.0708
0.1978	0.1696	0.1456	0.1252	0.1078	0.0929	0.0802	0.0693	0.0600
0.1799	0.1528	0.1300	0.1108	0.0946	0.0808	0.0691	0.0592	0.0508
0.1635	0.1377	0.1161	0.0981	0.0829	0.0703	0.0596	0.0506	0.0431
0.1486	0.1240	0.1037	0.0868	0.0728	0.0611	0.0514	0.0433	0.0365
0.1351	0.1117	0.0926	0.0768	0.0638	0.0531	0.0443	0.0370	0.0309
0.1228	0.1007	0.0826	0.0680	0.0560	0.0462	0.0382	0.0316	0.0262
0.1117	0.0907	0.0738	0.0601	0.0491	0.0402	0.0329	0.0270	0.0222
0.1015	0.0817	0.0659	0.0532	0.0431	0.0349	0.0284	0.0231	0.0188
0.0923	0.0736	0.0588	0.0471	0.0378	0.0304	0.0245	0.0197	0.0160
0.0839	0.0663	0.0525	0.0417	0.0331	0.0264	0.0211	0.0169	0.0135
0.0763	0.0597	0.0469	0.0369	0.0291	0.0230	0.0182	0.0144	0.0115
0.0693	0.0538	0.0419	0.0326	0.0255	0.0200	0.0157	0.0123	0.0097
0.0630	0.0485	0.0374	0.0289	0.0224	0.0174	0.0135	0.0105	0.0082
0.0573	0.0437	0.0334	0.0256	0.0196	0.0151	0.0116	0.0090	0.0070
0.0521	0.0394	0.0298	0.0226	0.0172	0.0131	0.0100	0.0077	0.0059
0.0474	0.0355	0.0266	0.0200	0.0151	0.0114	0.0087	0.0066	0.0050
0.0431	0.0319	0.0238	0.0177	0.0132	0.0099	0.0075	0.0056	0.0042
0.0391	0.0288	0.0212	0.0157	0.0116	0.0086	0.0064	0.0048	0.0036
0.0356	0.0259	0.0189	0.0139	0.0102	0.0075	0.0055	0.0041	0.0030
0.0323	0.0234	0.0169	0.0123	0.0089	0.0065	0.0048	0.0035	0.0026
0.0294	0.0210	0.0151	0.0109	0.0078	0.0057	0.0041	0.0030	0.0022
0.0267	0.0190	0.0135	0.0096	0.0069	0.0049	0.0036	0.0026	0.0019
0.0243	0.0171	0.0120	0.0085	0.0060	0.0043	0.0031	0.0022	0.0016
0.0221	0.0154	0.0107	0.0075	0.0053	0.0037	0.0026	0.0019	0.0013

PRINCIPLES OF FINANCE

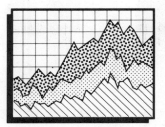

PRINCIPLES OF FINANCE

Second Edition

Robert W. Kolb
University of Miami

Ricardo J. Rodríguez
University of Miami

D. C. Heath and Company
Lexington, Massachusetts   Toronto

Address editorial correspondence to:

D. C. Heath
125 Spring Street
Lexington, MA 02173

Design: Greg Johnson
Cover design: Dustin Graphics

Cover: El Lissitzky, *Proun 99*, 1923 oil wood, 129.4 × 99 cm. Yale University
Art Gallery. Gift of the Société. El Lissitzky (1890–1941) was one of a group
of artists known as Russian Constructivists.

For permission to use copyrighted material, grateful acknowledgment is made to the
copyright holders listed on pages 799–802, which are hereby considered an extension of
this copyright page.

Copyright © 1992 by D. C. Heath and Company.

All rights reserved. No part of this publication may be reproduced or transmitted in any
form or by any means, electronic or mechanical, including photocopy, recording, or any
information storage or retrieval system, without permission in writing from the publisher.

Published simultaneously in Canada.

Printed in the United States of America.

International Standard Book Number: 0-669-27384-8

Library of Congress Catalog Number: 91-75673

10 9 8 7 6 5 4 3 2

Preface

Principles of Finance, Second Edition, is intended for a beginning course in finance. The text approaches the three traditional divisions of finance—financial instruments, investments, and corporate finance—by employing the twin concepts of value maximization and the risk/expected return trade-off throughout. One of the main innovations of the text is to provide a synoptic and integrated view of the various subdisciplines of finance, while stressing their interrelationships. Usually corporate finance texts cover financial instruments and investments in such a desultory manner as to leave introductory students thinking that the principles of finance apply to firms only. By giving financial instruments and investments separate and slightly greater treatment, this text will help the student better appreciate the universal nature of the concepts underlying investment theory and financial instruments. The orientation toward the *finance* function in this text contrasts with the accounting orientations of other texts.

Pedagogical Features of the Text

Throughout the text, three ideas are always kept in view:

- The goal of financial management is to maximize shareholder wealth;
- The financial manager confronts persistent trade-offs in the attempt to maximize shareholder wealth; and
- Finance is best understood by stressing how the various parts of the discipline form an integrated whole.

In addition to these three guiding principles, the following features should be noted:

- Completely worked-out examples are integrated throughout the text;
- Exceptionally detailed coverage is given to the time value of money;
- "Finance Today" sections appear in every chapter, highlighting the real-world applications of the material discussed in the chapter;
- "International Perspectives" sections appear in each chapter, supplementing the separate chapter on international finance;
- Numerous questions and problems are found at the ends of the chapters; and
- Answers to selected end-of-chapter problems are found at the end of the book.

Organization of the Text

The organization of *Principles of Finance, Second Edition,* reflects its integrative character. The text begins with a discussion of money in Part 1, arguing that the primary concern with money distinguishes finance from the broader field of economics. The time value of money is then brought into dramatic relief very early in the text. These concepts are given a more extensive treatment than is found in most other finance texts.

Part 2 provides a basic overview of the operation of the firm against the background of financial intermediation and the capital markets, and paves the way for a more coherent understanding of security valuation. This part concludes with Chapter 8, The Corporation and the Acquisition of Funds, which introduces the key function of the financial manager in a corporation—capital budgeting.

Part 3, Security Valuation and Capital Market Theory, explores the way in which the market values the securities issued by the corporation, while providing a more complete discussion of security valuation, portfolio construction, and capital markets than one finds in most corporate finance texts. This more conceptual approach allows students a richer understanding of the interaction between the assessment of the firm's securities by the market and the employment of those funds by the firm.

Part 4 is devoted to capital budgeting. Chapter 14 presents the basics of capital budgeting, based on the principles of security valuation. Drawing on the richer exposition of risk and capital market theory that was developed in Part 3, Chapter 15 forcefully reconsiders risk.

Part 5 puts the key ideas of finance to work by applying them to working capital management. This text treats working capital management as a problem in capital budgeting, emphasizing wealth maximization. Chapter 16 studies inventory management. Chapter 17 focuses on the management of cash and marketable securities, emphasizing the similarity between inventory and cash. Chapter 18 applies the concept of the time value of money to accounts receivable management, stressing capital budgeting. Chapter 19 considers the issue of financing seasonal working capital with short-term sources.

Part 6 presents techniques of financial analysis and planning. Chapter 20 introduces financial analysis, focusing on the interpretation of financial statements. Chapter 21 discusses financial planning. While both chapters cover the traditional topics, they both emphasize the wealth maximization criterion.

Part 7, Strategic Issues in Corporate Finance, considers those key financial decisions that are usually reserved for higher management. Chapter 22 explores capital structure and dividend policy, while Chapter 23 analyzes the decision to lease or buy, as well as the principles governing mergers.

Part 8, Futures, Options, and International Finance, relates these new financial markets to the corporate environment. Following Chapters 24 and 25, on futures and options, respectively, Chapter 26 shows how these two types of financial instruments can be employed together to reduce risk to the investor. Part 8 also contains a whole chapter on International Finance which, when combined with the "International Perspectives" boxes located throughout the text, gives *Principles of Finance, Second Edition,* unparalleled coverage of the concerns involved in international finance.

The Instructional Package

Principles of Finance, Second Edition, is accompanied by an extensive instructional package. The instructor's manual contains answers to all questions and detailed solutions to all end-of-chapter problems. It also contains a test bank with more than 1,000 multiple-choice questions, many of which are oriented toward problem-solving.

The package also includes a study guide that helps students deepen their knowledge of the topics covered in the book. The study guide includes detailed chapter outlines that emphasize key study points, numerous true/false and multiple-choice questions, and problems aimed to develop and extend the skills covered in each chapter. In addition, a set of transparencies is also available.

Acknowledgments

Writing the textbook was only one step in the complex process of bringing *Principles of Finance, Second Edition,* to life. Many colleagues have contributed greatly by reading and commenting on various sections of the book. We have benefited from the comments and criticisms provided by the following colleagues: O. B. Bautista, Central Missouri State University; Farhad F. Ghannadian, Mercer University; Michael Gombola, Drexel University; Peter Gomori, St. Francis College; Simon Hakim, Temple University; Thomas Herring, Jarvis Christian College; Surendra K. Mansinghka, San Francisco State University; Robert W. McLeod, The University of Alabama; Clair N. McRostie, Gustavus Adolphus College; Reza Rahgozar, University of Wisconsin—River Falls; Murli Rajan, University of Scranton; K. Ramakrishnan, Hofstra University; Bernard Rose, Rocky Mountain College; Charles W. Strang, Western New Mexico University; Howard R. Whitney, Franklin University.

In addition, Debbie MacInnes developed much of the ancillary material, Ana Vazquez helped in the creation of many of the "Finance Today" and "International Perspectives" boxes, and Kumar Venkataramany was brave enough to tackle the laborious and delicate task of checking the accuracy of all the math in the text. Kateri Davis, Valerie Rubler, and Diane Rubler provided valuable help in the various stages of the manuscript's production.

Before a text is written, it is difficult to imagine the numerous steps involved. The staff at D. C. Heath has been instrumental in this process. We would particularly like to thank George Lobell for his help and encouragement in this project. Stephen Wasserstein made many sound suggestions regarding organization and was extremely helpful in managing the book to its completion. In addition, Anne Starr gave the book a thorough editing and made our work much easier. Many other people at D. C. Heath contributed to the publication of this book—from the artists to the permissions staff. To all of them, our profound thanks.

Robert W. Kolb
Ricardo J. Rodríguez

Contents

■ *Chapter 7* **The Money and Capital Markets**

■ *Chapter 10*   **Preferred and Common Stock Valuation**   196

■ *Chapter 13*   **Market Efficiency**   287

PART 4   THE FIRM'S INVESTMENT DECISION   319

PART 7   STRATEGIC ISSUES IN CORPORATE FINANCE   547

■ *Chapter 22*   **Capital Structure and Dividend Policy**   549

■ *Chapter 23* **Leasing and Mergers** 594

■ *Chapter 25*   **The Options Market**   **679**

PRINCIPLES OF FINANCE

PART 1

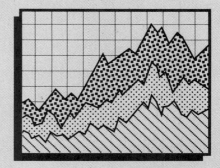

MONEY

CHAPTER 1

Introduction

This first chapter explains the relationships among the three basic areas of finance: financial institutions, investments, and corporate financial management. Each of these topics is broad enough to be treated in separate books, but one of our major goals is to stress the close connection among them.

After introducing the main areas of finance, this chapter discusses two of the most basic principles. The first is the **time value of money**—a dollar available today is worth more than a dollar available at a future date. Throughout this book we will see that the time value of money figures in virtually every financial decision.

The second basic concept is the **risk/expected return trade-off**—one must accept high risk in order to secure a high expected return, or expected profit. Unfortunately, the good (high return) comes with the bad (high risk). For example, stocks with the greatest opportunity for high returns often involve the greatest amount of risk. The risk/return trade-off will be with us throughout the book.

Even for a person not interested in finance as a career, knowledge of the subject is often valuable. First, it helps in managing one's personal finances. Second, it can influence many decisions in other areas of business, such as marketing, management, accounting, or production.

time value of money
the treatment of money that considers the time at which it will be paid or received

risk/expected return trade-off
the necessity to weigh higher expected return against higher risk

FINANCE AS A DISCIPLINE

real asset
a physical good

financial asset
a good that promises future benefits in the form of monetary payments

Finance is the branch of economics that focuses on investment in real and financial assets and their management. A **real asset** is a physical item such as a truck, land, or building. A **financial asset** is a claim for a future financial payment, such as a savings account at a bank. Financial assets generate future payments, whereas real assets alter the physical environment in some way. As we will see in detail throughout this book, finance is concerned with making wise investment decisions in both types of assets.

Real and Financial Assets, and the Finance Discipline

☞ Finance is traditionally divided into three fields: investments, corporate finance, and financial institutions and markets.

investments
the part of finance that studies how to make and manage investment in financial assets

To see how investment decisions are studied, consider the traditional division of finance into three fields: investments, corporate finance, and financial institutions and markets. We have already considered investments in financial and real assets, and this distinction matches some of the areas of the discipline. The **investments** area studies how to make and manage an investment in financial assets. For example, a share of common stock represents a fractional ownership in a corporation. If you own a share of the common stock of General Motors, you own a fraction cf all assets of GM, such as its plant and equipment, land, inventory, and all other goods it owns, including its financial assets.

corporate finance
the part of finance that considers the management of corporations

capital budgeting
the process of evaluating projects and committing funds for investment in those projects

Corporate finance considers the management of corporations, with particular emphasis on firms that invest in real capital. **Capital budgeting,** the decision to invest in real assets, is one of its most important aspects. In addition, corporate finance studies the ways in which firms acquire financial resources that allow them to invest in physical assets. For example, every corporation raises some funds by selling common stock, and may use some of the proceeds to purchase real assets, such as the plant and equipment necessary to run its business. The corporation also acquires funds by borrowing from a bank or from the public at large.

Thus far, we have considered only two of the subdisciplines of finance—investments and corporate finance. Already, however, we can see how closely connected they are. The corporation must sell stock in order to invest in equipment or manufacturing plants. Therefore, it is involved in considerations of both real and financial assets. Study in one area of finance leads to study of another.

Financial Institutions and Markets

financial institutions
firms that specialize in the sale, purchase, and creation of financial assets

The third traditional subject area of finance is called financial institutions and markets. **Financial institutions** are firms that specialize in the sale, purchase, and creation of financial assets, and they include commercial banks, savings and loan associations, and insurance companies. Their business is transforming financial assets from one form to another. As an example, consider a savings account at a bank. The saver initially gives the bank cash to hold and to use. At a later date, the saver may withdraw the original funds, plus interest. Thus the bank has transformed the original deposit into a greater amount of money.

Banks are mostly concerned with financial assets, such as savings accounts. This contrasts with the service performed by a manufacturing firm. General Motors, for example, is in the business of manufacturing automobiles. It must purchase steel and other inputs, and physically transform those materials into the finished product. To do this requires enormous investment in real assets, such as machine tools, buildings, warehouses, and research and testing facilities. The inputs and finished products are the main differences between financial institutions and manufacturing firms.

Physical assets play a relatively minor role for financial institutions. Certainly, many banks have imposing buildings, but this is not really necessary to their function. A financial institution could be run out of a small office, and in fact, some are. In contrast, for a manufacturing firm physical assets are a necessity.

A bank and a manufacturing firm both pursue profit. A bank does so by providing a valuable service to its customers and by transforming one kind of financial asset into another. Similarly, a manufacturing firm does this by effecting a transformation of material goods into a more valuable form.

stock exchange
an organization for trading stocks at the physical facility provided by the exchange

money market
the market in which securities are traded that have one year or less until maturity

In a financial market, financial assets are traded. Probably the best known of all financial markets is the stock market, led by the New York Stock Exchange. A **stock exchange** is an organized market for trading common stock. There are a number of other kinds of financial markets. For example, the **money market** is one in which debt obligations that are due for payment in less than one year are traded. In the traditional division of the finance discipline, financial institutions and markets are considered together because the institutions are the most important participants in the markets.

As noted, the different divisions of finance overlap. For example, when a manufacturing firm sells stock, all three divisions would be interested in the transaction. Corporate finance studies the raising of funds for investment in real assets. The financial manager must determine whether it will be worthwhile to sell shares and use the proceeds to make an investment in real capital. Investments studies the transaction from the point of view of the potential purchaser, who must determine whether the stock or bond provides a good expected return for the risk involved. Financial institutions and markets studies the way in which the market functions in allowing the firm to issue the stock, and might also be concerned with the kinds of financial institutions that advised the corporation in the sale.

CENTRAL CONCEPTS OF FINANCE

☞ The two most basic concepts in finance are the time value of money and the risk/expected return trade-off.

Finance, being a part of economics, relies on many of the ideas developed in economics. However, it lays special claim to the analysis of two concepts: the time value of money and the risk/expected return trade-off. These are at the core of virtually every financial decision and they overlap all three subdisciplines. Because we will meet them in virtually every chapter of this book, we introduce them here. Subsequent chapters elaborate them and make them more precise.

☞ Time value of money refers to the fact that a dollar available for use immediately is more valuable than a dollar that will become available for use in the future.

The Time Value of Money

A dollar available today is worth more than a dollar that will be available for use a year from now. This is one of the most basic principles in finance. To see why it is true, assume that the annual interest rate on savings is 7 percent, so $1 deposited today will grow to a total value of $1.07 in one year.

How Much Do I Admire Thee? Let Me Count the Returns

A group of more than 8,000 senior executives, outside directors, and financial analysts was asked to rate the largest companies—defined as those with sales of at least $500 million—in their own industry on eight attributes of reputation, using a scale of 0 (poor) to 10 (excellent). The attributes were quality of management; quality of products or services; innovativeness; long-term investment value; financial soundness; ability to attract, develop, and keep talented people; community and environmental responsibility; and wise use of corporate assets. Merck, the world's largest maker of prescription drugs, earned the highest rating of 306 major corporations for the fifth year in a row.

Spectacular profits don't guarantee a sterling reputation, as witnessed by the case of Philip Morris, whose net income rose a dazzling 28 percent over the previous year, but its ranking took a dizzying descent from number two to seventy-nine. The reason: having acquired Kraft in 1988, it has switched categories from tobacco to food. Apparently, Philip Morris's new judges in the food business didn't think much of its best-known product—cigarettes. The director of one food company put it bluntly: "Anyone in the tobacco business must be severely downgraded." Declining earnings don't burnish the image much either. Du Pont slid from number ten to thirteen after profits for the first nine months slipped 8 percent in response to slowing demand for some chemicals, textiles, and carpet fibers.

Despite these comments, it is very clear that the most admired companies tend to do very well for their investors. For example, it can be seen from the table that the most admired firms had an average annual return of between 15.82 percent and 42.16 percent during the period 1980–1990. In contrast, the corresponding returns for the least admired firms were between -30.29 percent and -12.08 percent.

Consequently, there would be no difference between receiving $1 today or $1.07 one year from now.

The time value of money concept is extremely important for virtually all financial decisions. Continue to assume an interest rate of 7 percent, and suppose you are obligated to make a tax payment either now or in one year. If you pay now, the tax will be $1,000, but if you pay in one year, it will be $1,050. Which payment would you prefer to make? This is essentially a question of the time value of money. If you pay now, you will be out $1,000 immediately. However, if you delay the payment, you could invest the $1,000 at a rate of 7 percent, and have $1,070 in one year. Out of this $1,070, you

Rank	Company	Score	Average Return, 1980–1990
MOST ADMIRED FIRMS			
1	Merck	8.86	23.62%
2	Rubbermaid	8.58	32.51
3	Procter & Gamble	8.42	22.18
4	Wal-Mart Stores	8.35	42.16
5	PepsiCo	8.19	27.62
6	Coca-Cola	8.12	28.96
7	3M	8.12	15.82
8	Johnson & Johnson	8.01	18.58
9	Boeing	7.92	16.95
10	Eli Lilly	7.90	20.49
10	Liz Claiborne	7.90	N.A.
LEAST ADMIRED FIRMS			
306	Goldome	2.83	N.A.
305	Great American Bank	2.98	N.A.
304	CrossLand Savings	3.06	N.A.
303	Wang Laboratories	3.10	−18.06
302	Meritor Savings Bank*	3.16	N.A.
301	Continental Airlines Hold†	3.33	−15.96
300	Mack Trucks‡	3.40	N.A.
299	Unisys	3.57	−13.85
298	LTV	3.81	−30.29
297	Control Data	4.00	−12.08

* Name changed from Meritor Financial Group.
† Name changed from Texas Air.
‡ Acquired by Renault Véhicules Industriels SA, October 4, 1990.

Source: Alison L. Sprout, "America's Most Admired Corporations," *Fortune*, February 11, 1991, pp. 52ff.

can pay the tax of $1,050 and still have $20 left. In this case, it is clearly better to wait before making the payment.

Another way of looking at the same problem is to calculate the amount of money that you must put aside today in order to have enough money to pay the tax of $1,050 in one year. If you take $981.31 and invest it for one year at a rate of 7 percent, the proceeds will be exactly enough to pay the bill because the interest earned will be $68.69, as shown below:

$$\text{Interest} = 0.07 \times \$981.31 = \$68.69$$

FIGURE 1.1   The Time Value of Money (interest rate = 7%)

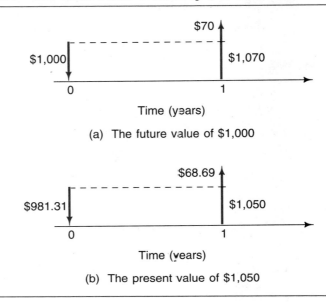

(a) The future value of $1,000

(b) The present value of $1,050

Of course, in addition to the interest you will have the original $981.31 that you invested, for a total of $1,050 that you must pay on your tax bill.

Clearly, it is better to set aside $981.31 to pay in a year, and invest that amount at 7 percent, because it costs you less money now, precisely $18.69 less. These results are shown in Figure 1.1.

In Chapters 4 and 5 we will study the time value of money much more closely. Later chapters apply the theory to many different kinds of financial problems.

The Relationship Between Risk and Expected Return

return
the percentage change in the value of an investment over a period of time

expected return
the planned or anticipated return from a risky investment

In essence, the **return** on an investment is the percentage change in the value of the investment over a period of time. If an investment involves risk, its return is uncertain at the time it is made. The **expected return** is its anticipated return.

To understand the nature of risk, consider the safest investment of all—an investment guaranteed by the Treasury of the U.S. government. The government often borrows money by selling **Treasury bills**. These are obligations that promise to pay a certain amount at a particular date in the future.

FINANCE TODAY

Clear the Court of Economists, Please

In the opinion of Judge James Zagel, the science of economics isn't just dismal, it's pseudo.

Zagel, a federal judge in Chicago, has refused to allow an economist to testify as an expert in a personal injury case. No economist, he says, can put an accurate dollar value on the life of an accident victim. "Expert" calculation, he suggests, is no better than a guess.

Economists, who agree on nothing else, have long insisted that their discipline is a science. Zagel isn't buying . "There is no unanimity on which studies ought to be considered. There is a lack of reliability," he wrote. "The risk to justice from pseudo-science is substantial." The judge even suggests that the jury's own forecasts are likely to be as accurate as that of a professional economist. Hey, maybe that's how the Bush Administration and Congress could settle their many economic disputes: Just pick 12 random citizens, and ask them.

Source: Harris Collingwood, ed., "Clear the Court of Economists, Please," *Business Week,* April 22, 1991, p. 38.

Treasury bill
a pure discount obligation of the U.S. Treasury with initial maturity of less than one year

Assume that you buy a Treasury bill that promises to pay $10,000 in one year. Considering the time value of money, you will pay less then $10,000 for this Treasury bill. In considering the risk, think of all of the possible events that could affect this payment. If the United States is conquered or if the government ceases to exist as a result of nuclear war, it is possible that the payment would not be made. Short of such calamities, however, it will be. As we will see in Chapter 3, even if the government did not have enough money to pay the $10,000, it would create the money. Because the obligations of the U.S. government are so nearly certain, Treasury bills are generally regarded as a risk-free investment.

As an example of a much riskier investment, consider the decision to build and market a new computer. The last few years have witnessed the demise of many companies in the computer industry, and this is enough to convince anyone of the great risk involved. The manufacturer cannot know with certainty how much it will cost to build the machines, or how many it will be able to sell.

☞ Because most investment is uncertain, investors seek high expected return.

Suppose that a firm with funds on hand must decide whether to invest them in Treasury bills or in a new computer project. If it invests in Treasury bills, it will receive a return of 7 percent with virtual certainty. Investment in the new computer project may lead to high returns or even to a loss. If the firm expects to earn the same return from both investments, it would be wise to choose the Treasury bills because the return is risk free. Given the different risks, why would the firm even consider the computer project? There can be only one answer—the firm must be hoping for higher returns. Because the return on this investment is risky, it is only an expected return, and the firm must make its investment decision on that basis.

☞ Normally, investments with high expected return are accompanied by high risk.

These considerations of risk and expected return lead to a general principle of great importance. Investors will make a risky investment only if they believe that the expected return justifies the risk. That is the key idea of the risk/return (or more exactly, the risk/expected return) trade-off. It is simply a fact of life that high expected return and high risk normally go together. In fact, if projects with high expected return were not of high risk, there would be little work in finance. Everyone would merely make high expected return/low-risk investments and live happily ever after. As this does not occur, virtually every investment decision involves balancing risk against expected return.

We can tie together the time value of money and the risk/return trade-off. Consider Figure 1.2, which presents the relationship in graphical form. On the vertical axis, which depicts the expected return, one point is labeled r_f, the risk-free rate. We may think of it as the rate of interest on a Treasury bill. The line connecting r_f to Q shows the relationship between expected return and risk. The fact that the line slopes upward indicates that expected return increases with risk, which is measured on the horizontal axis. Investment in a Treasury bill involves no risk, so it is located on the vertical axis. By contrast, consider a risky investment such as Q, which might depict a project like the computer. As we have seen, investors will be willing to accept a risky project only if it has enough expected return to compensate for the risk

FIGURE 1.2   The Risk/Expected Return Trade-Off

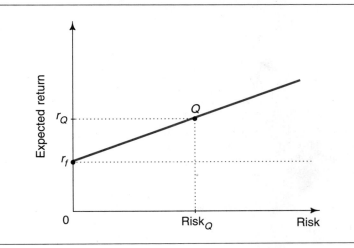

involved. The line from r_f to Q depicts the risk/return trade-off. Investing in Q gives both greater expected return (r_Q) and greater risk (Risk$_Q$) than investing in the Treasury bill, and this expected return can be divided into two parts. The first part is what the investor receives for the time value of money, and this is equal to the return r_f, what the investor could earn from a risk-free investment. Any expected return in excess of r_f is compensation for bearing risk. In our diagram, the extra return for bearing an amount of risk equal to Risk$_Q$ is $r_Q - r_f$.

Up to this point, we have said nothing about how the risk of an investment is to be measured. In fact, correctly measuring this is one of the major achievements of finance. As we will see in later chapters, very precise definitions of risk can be given. We will have occasion to return to examples like Figure 1.2 and to develop our understanding of the topic in much more detail.

BENEFITS OF KNOWLEDGE OF FINANCE

This section considers some of the ways in which knowledge of finance can be translated into direct benefits for financial and nonfinancial managers.

Careers in Finance

We can categorize careers by the areas of the discipline that we distinguished above. First, in the field of corporate finance many positions are available for those with good knowledge of the field. Some of the major decisions faced by the corporate financial manager concern capital budgeting. They are the means by which the productive resources of our society are allocated to different uses. Making wise capital budgeting decisions contributes not only to the well-being of the firm, but to the development of society as a whole.

Financial managers also play a pivotal role in raising capital for the corporation. Once capital is raised and the investment plans have been made, they are required to oversee and control the disbursement of funds.

In the investment field, a large percentage of executives have extensive training in finance. For a university graduate, a good beginning position might be as a stockbroker. A stockbroker executes orders from clients to buy and sell stocks and other securities. A good broker also advises clients on the suitability of different investment alternatives.

Today, many investments of individuals are carried out by large financial institutions, such as pension funds, in which the retirement savings of a large group of people are collected into a pool. These funds often have billions of dollars in assets available for investment.

In contrast to the more familiar commercial banks, investment banks play a central role in helping other firms administer their finance function. They are particularly important in helping the firms raise new capital. The investment banker may act as a consultant in areas such as mergers and takeovers, as well as other major transactions.

INTERNATIONAL PERSPECTIVES

A Flip-Flop in the Banking Industry

The world's economic environment is clearly changing. Throughout the 1950s and 1960s the United States was the undisputed economic champion of the world. In the 1970s things started to change, however, and the Japanese economy began to flex its muscles. At first they were dismissed as copycats and producers of lower-quality goods. No one dismisses Japan now.

Examples of the Japanese economic offensive abound. They literally wiped out the U.S. VCR industry; they all but dominate the sophisticated electronic chip industry; and they are making significant inroads in the supercomputer, high-definition television (HDTV), and many other industries. Japanese aggressiveness in the U.S. auto market reached such a level in the 1980s that they were pressured into "voluntary" quotas agreements. The list goes on, and on.

A relatively little-known indicator of Japan's rise as a world economic power is its financial strength, as reflected in its obvious number one ranking in the banking industry. The table below shows the largest commercial banks in the world for three selected years. The 1974 column reveals that not a single Japanese bank was among the ten largest in the world then. At that time, the United States had the three largest banks in the world: Bank of America, Citicorp, and Chase Manhattan. By 1985 Japan had six of the largest banks in the world. Perhaps more telling is the fact that it had the largest bank, Dai-Ichi Kangyo, even though it is not exactly a household name in the United States. In 1989, Japan's Tokai bank became a part of the prestigious list. By then, the six largest banks in the world were Japanese.

The World's Largest Commercial Banks

Bank	Country	Ranking		
		1989	*1985*	*1974*
Dai-Ichi Kangyo	Japan	1	1	11
Sumitomo	Japan	2	4	16
Fuji	Japan	3	3	17
Mitsubishi	Japan	4	5	20
Sanwa	Japan	5	6	23
Industrial Bank	Japan	6	8	22
Credit Agricole	France	7	10	8
BNP	France	8	9	4
Citicorp	United States	9	2	2
Tokai	Japan	10	14	38

In a financial institution such as a commercial bank, a college graduate may start as a loan analyst, considering requests for loans that come from firms and advising on the desirability of granting them. After a period in that position one might become a loan officer, the person who makes the decision to grant loans. Another important job is managing the bank's own investments. In a way, the finance function in a commercial bank ties together the three major areas of finance. In addition to understanding the bank itself, a loan officer has to understand the financial dimensions of other types of corporations. By the same token, the manager of the bank's investments has to understand the principles of investments.

Finance for the Nonfinancial Manager

In most business organizations, the majority of managers do not work directly in the finance area. Nonetheless, knowledge of finance is often very useful for them. Consider a marketing manager for an automobile manufacturer trying to decide what kinds of discounts and promotional incentives to offer to spur sales. One strategy is to use rebates, so perhaps a particular model might promise a $1,000 rebate per car. As an alternative, the firm might offer 0 percent financing, meaning that no interest will be charged on the car loan. Choosing between the strategies is a typical application of the time value of money. While the exact cost comparison might be performed by the finance department, the marketing manager must understand time value concepts in order to participate effectively in the decision-making process.

Personal Financial Decisions

Even outside the business world, finance training can be valuable in helping make personal financial decisions. As an example, assume that you are considering purchasing a new car, and you have found two makes that are equally attractive and have the same price. The only difference between them is that one comes with a $1,000 rebate and the other offers 0 percent financing, instead of the 10 percent that you ordinarily would have to pay. Knowledge of present value concepts can help you choose the best car.

Many retirement plans allow you to choose among various programs with different levels of risk and expected return. If you understand the risk/expected return trade-off, you will be more likely to make a wise investment decision. Another typical example involves financing a house with either a fixed rate or an adjustable rate mortgage. Equipped with knowledge of the principles of finance, you have a much better chance of making a correct decision.

SUMMARY

This chapter provided an introductory overview of the subject of finance. Finance is divided into three areas: financial institutions and markets, investments, and corporate finance. Although each of these subdisciplines has its own special areas of interest, they all make use of the same set of core concepts.

Two of these core concepts lie at the very heart of finance. The time value of money is the idea that a dollar available for use today is more valuable than one that becomes available only later. The risk/expected return trade-off states that a greater expected return is always accompanied by a higher level of risk.

Knowledge of finance can be useful for many individuals. Several different types of careers are available in the field. For nonfinancial managers, understanding the concepts can be helpful in making many decisions. Such knowledge also can help people conduct their personal financial affairs.

QUESTIONS

1. What is the difference between a real asset and a financial asset?
2. Can a financial asset involve ownership of a real asset? Explain.
3. What is capital budgeting?
4. What kinds of assets do financial institutions hold? Do they hold any real assets at all? Explain.
5. Why does money have time value?
6. What is the difference between the expected return and the return on an investment?
7. What is the normal relationship between expected return and risk?
8. Why do individuals and firms make some risky investments instead of making only risk-free investments?
9. Do U.S. Treasury bills carry some risk of default?
10. Suppose you are given the choice of receiving $10 with certainty or tossing a coin. If the coin toss results in heads you win $20, but if it results in tails you win nothing. Which alternative would you prefer? Would everyone make the same choice?
11. In the previous problem, suppose you win $30 with heads, but you must pay $10 if the coin toss results in tails. Would your choice change? Explain why or why not.

Money in the Economy

In this chapter we begin at the primordial era of finance—a world without money. Without money, there can be no financial assets and no financial investment; however, there can be real assets and real investment. Thus the economy can evolve and improve as money is introduced.

Without question, the development of a financial system is beneficial to society. For instance, the opportunity to borrow in the financial market against future income improves investors' economic status. Showing how this happens is one of the main goals of this chapter.

AN ECONOMY WITH NO EXCHANGE

☞ The most primitive economy is one that does not allow exchange of one good for another.

The most primitive economy imaginable is one that provides no opportunity to exchange one good for another. In the famous novel, Robinson Crusoe was shipwrecked on an island that was uninhabited except by a native whom Crusoe called his man Friday. Considering Crusoe and Friday as one economic unit, there was no possibility of exchanging one good for another, simply because there were no other economic units on the island. In this simple economy, it is obvious that there is no financial system.

One of the most critical economic decisions concerns consumption versus investment. Assume that a shipwrecked man, say, Robinson Crusoe, salvaged some seed corn from his ship. This corn may be eaten now, stored for future consumption, or planted to produce more corn for future consumption. Assume that this corn is the only food that Crusoe has and that it cannot be saved past the next year. Given this setting, Crusoe must decide how much to consume this year and how much, if any, to save for the next. It is clear that he must eat some now in order to stay alive, so he cannot save or plant all of it.

Figure 2.1 shows Crusoe's consumption possibilities for this period and for one year later. In Figure 2.1(a) the graph is drawn on the assumption that Crusoe cannot plant the corn, perhaps because the island is made up of volcanic lava. Although this means that Crusoe's prospects for reaching old age are slim, his decision is made easier. His problem is to allocate the existing

FIGURE 2.1   Robinson Crusoe's Consumption Opportunities

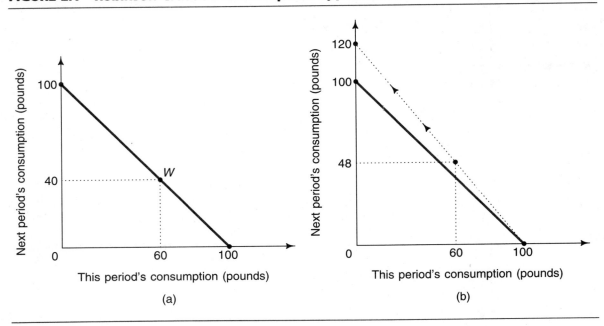

(a)

(b)

supply of corn to two periods. We assume that he has 100 pounds of corn. On the horizontal axis, Figure 2.1(a) shows his maximum consumption opportunity in the current period. If he eats all of the corn this period, he will have nothing for next year, so he will die before that time unless he is rescued from the island.

☞ Without exchange and without investment, the only economic decision is to save or to consume a good.

On the other hand, Crusoe could eat nothing this year and save all of the corn to eat next year. This is only a theoretical possibility, because we assume he will want to eat some and stay alive until next year. The extreme points on the diagonal line in Figure 2.1(a) depict these two possibilities. Of course, other allocations are also possible. If Crusoe eats 60 pounds this year and saves 40 pounds for next year, he will be at point W on the diagonal. In fact, any point on the diagonal line is attainable by choosing a different allocation of corn to the two years, as long as the sum of the allocations equals 100 pounds. The relationship between the consumption this period, C_0, and next year's consumption, C_1, depicted in the diagonal in Figure 2.1(a) is given by:

$$C_1 = 100 - C_0$$

Here, the maximum possible consumption of corn in the second period is the same as in the first—100 pounds. But wait, after wandering through the island a bit, Crusoe has found a plot of arable land. To his delight, his initially meager choices are suddenly enriched. Let us assume that the yield on planted corn is 20 percent, so planting 1 pound this year will produce 1.2 pounds next year. We will assume throughout this chapter that the returns from this investment—corn planting—are certain. This set of opportunities is shown in Figure 2.1(b) as the steeper, dashed line. For this line, the relationship between consumption now and consumption later is given by:

$$C_1 = 120 - 1.2 C_0$$

☞ In an economy with no exchange, but allowing real investment, an economic agent must decide how much to consume now and how much to invest to increase future consumption.

Figure 2.1(b) duplicates Figure 2.1(a), but it also shows the opportunities that are available from planting the corn. If all 100 pounds were planted, they would grow to 120 pounds for the next year. Therefore, the maximum possible consumption next year becomes 120 pounds, as shown by the dashed line in Figure 2.1(b). Note also that the dashed line has arrows on it indicating that corn can only be planted now to produce corn in the next period. In other words, the process is not reversible.

The important thing to notice about the chance to plant corn is that Crusoe's consumption opportunities are enriched. In Figure 2.1(a) we saw that he could eat 60 pounds this year and 40 pounds next year. If he decides to plant, he can still eat 60 pounds this year and plant the remaining 40, which will be converted into 48 pounds next year.

Notice that there is absolutely no financial system in this simple economy, and that there is no exchange of one commodity for another. The next section considers a slightly richer economy, one allowing exchange.

AN EXCHANGE ECONOMY WITHOUT MONEY

An economy without money is still a very primitive affair, much like Crusoe's. Without money, only two economic transactions are possible: one good may be exchanged for another, and real capital can be invested.

barter
the process of exchanging one physical good for another

barter economy
an economy without money

Exchanging one physical good for another is known as **barter,** and an economy without money is a **barter economy.** Before the invention of money, all exchanges were by barter.

Imagine a fisherman with a good catch of fish who needs a new sail for his boat. In a modern economy, he sells the fish for money and uses the money to buy the sail. In a barter economy he must find someone who needs fish and is willing to exchange a sail for it. Imagine the ridiculous spectacle of the man carrying fish around a village trying to exchange it for a sail. This is extremely inefficient in comparison to an economy with money. All the fisherman really wants to do is to exchange one good for another, but without money, such a simple transaction is very difficult. From this fishy story, we can note a very important point. Money makes it much easier to exchange one good for another. Instead of a direct exchange of two physical goods, a physical good can be exchanged for money, which can then be exchanged for any other physical good. Thus, money serves as a medium of exchange.

☞ In an exchange economy without money, one good may be exchanged for another or real investment can take place.

Assume now that the fisherman's catch is really spectacular, and after exchanging it for the sail he still has some fish left. Fishing is notoriously risky, and today's good catch may not be repeated for some time. To protect against those future fishless days, the man wishes to save some of the catch. This is not very easy, given the nature of fish. Unless it is dried, it cannot be stored, and this puts the fisherman in a predicament. Assuming that the fish cannot be dried, he can exchange all of the fish now for some other good that can be used immediately, he can let them go to waste, or he must exchange them now for some other good that is storable. The fisherman is worse off than Crusoe when it comes to storing a good for future use. In an exchange economy, one item can be exchanged for another, but transactions are difficult and some commodities cannot be preserved easily, so it is difficult to store value.

A MONEY ECONOMY

Recall the fisherman's three alternatives: exchange the fish for something that must be used now, let it go to waste, or exchange it for a storable commodity. Of these, the fisherman would prefer the last. To implement it, he has to find someone who can use the fish and who is willing to exchange something storable for them. Fish does not act as an effective store of value, because it spoils so quickly. Also, it does not provide an effective medium of exchange, because it is difficult to exchange for other goods with reliability. Besides, fish is smelly. The introduction of money into an economy is very useful, because it acts as an excellent **medium of exchange** and as a **store of value.**

medium of exchange
a good that can be exchanged for a variety of other goods

store of value
a good that retains its value and is easily stored, transported, and protected

Consider now the fisherman's dilemma in a money economy. He merely sells the fish and receives money, which he can exchange easily for other goods. Thus money acts as a medium of exchange that can be exchanged for a variety of other goods with ease and general acceptance. It also is an excellent store of value, since it retains its value and is easily stored. Money under the mattress certainly keeps better than fish under the mattress.

MONEY AND FINANCIAL INVESTMENT

One notable feature of this simple economy is that it does not allow for investment of money. Money functions only as a medium of exchange and as a store of value, and therefore this economy is still primitive. In this section we develop our economy by allowing for investment in financial assets, also known as lending.

As we saw, our fisherman sold his extra catch for money. Thus money functioned as a medium of exchange and as a store of value. However, without a financial system, the fisherman could only store the money in a mattress

FIGURE 2.2   Consumption Opportunities with Financial Investment

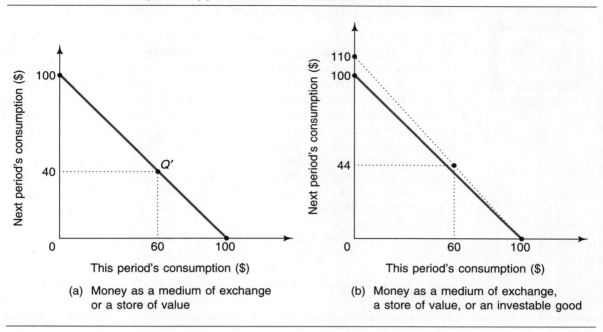

(a)   Money as a medium of exchange
      or a store of value

(b)   Money as a medium of exchange,
      a store of value, or an investable good

or cookie jar. With a financial system, he could invest it to increase its value, for example, by depositing it in a bank and letting it earn interest. This innovation makes the fisherman better off, because the investment allows him to increase future consumption.

☞ If an economy has a financial system, money can be invested to earn a return.

If there is no financial investment, money serves as a store of value, but it cannot grow, as shown in Figure 2.2(a). Consistent with the fact that we now have an economy with money, we will express the consumption opportunities in terms of dollars. Let us assume that we have an initial amount of $100.

If money serves as a medium of exchange or as a store of value but cannot be invested, Figure 2.2(a) shows our consumption opportunities. We can consume the entire $100 now, or we could save it and consume $100 in the next period. Alternatively, we could split our consumption between periods. One such alternative is shown as Q', a point at which we consume $60 in this period and $40 in the next. In fact, we can consume any amount that we wish up to $100 in the first period, and that decision determines how much will be available in the next period. Notice, however, that there is no way to invest the money. We may save $40 for the next period, but it will only be $40 after one year because the economy in Figure 2.2(a) does not allow for lending.

Will Counterfeit Bucks Stop Here?

Ulysses S. Grant is getting new threads. So are Ben Franklin and most other presidents whose faces adorn paper money. To foil counterfeiters, the Bureau of Engraving & Printing will soon print bills threaded with metallized plastic strips. Each strip, clearly visible near the Federal Reserve Board seal, will bear an imprint of the bill's denomination.

The alteration—the first in U.S. paper currency since 1957—is meant to stop such practices as bleaching out the printing on $1 bills, then reproducing them with higher values on color copiers. The thread won't reproduce, the bureau says. Neither will the words "The United States of America," which will be stamped in microprinting around the portrait.

Crane & Co. in Dalton, Mass., has won a $66.3 million supply contract and will deliver the tamper-proof paper initially for $50 and $100 bills—which may make it into wallets by summer. Eventually, $5, $10, and $20 bills will also get new threads. Only George Washington will be left out. But if evil-doers bleach $1 bills, they can't turn them into anything else.

Source: Robert Buderi, ed., "Will Counterfeit Bucks Stop Here?" *Business Week*, April 8, 1991, p. 81.

Now, however, let us assume that we have the opportunity to invest money to earn a rate of interest of 10 percent. With our original $100 available, Figure 2.2(b) shows our total consumption opportunities as the steeper, dashed line. The solid line repeats the information from Figure 2.2(a). The consumption opportunities without and with financial investment at 10 percent are shown below.

Period	Maximum Consumption with No Financial Investment	Maximum Consumption with Financial Investment
0	$100	$100
1	100	110

☞ The introduction of a financial system and financial investment improves the consumption opportunities available in an economy.

The introduction of financial investment allows a better choice of opportunities. For example, if we consume $60 right now and invest the remaining $40 at 10 percent interest, we will be able to consume $44 in the next period. Thus with the possibility of financial investment, the members of an economy are definitely better off than they would be in a more primitive economy with no financial system. Figure 2.2(b) reflects this point as well.

FINANCIAL MARKETS AND THE TRANSFORMATION OF THE INITIAL ENDOWMENT

initial endowment
the initial allocation of available wealth to specific time periods

☞ The existence of a financial system allows economic agents to transform their initial endowments to different consumption patterns.

The previous section illustrated how financial markets improve the condition of participants in the economy by allowing them to engage in financial investment. Other advantages of financial markets are also important. Let us continue to assume that the interest rate is 10 percent and consider an economic agent with a particular endowment. Specifically, let us assume that this person will receive $100 now and $100 in the next period. This is the **initial endowment**—the initial allocation of wealth to specific time periods.

With a financial system, we can change our initial endowment to one that suits us better. For example, if we wish to consume more than the $100 now, we can borrow. By contrast, if our initial endowment includes more than we want to consume in this period, we can save a portion of it to increase our consumption in the next period. This section shows how the initial endowment can be altered in ways to make a person better off. In fact, we can preview the argument of this section in a single sentence: The richer the financial system, the better the choices for people in an economy and the better off they will be.

Table 2.1 shows the consumption opportunities available with the initial endowment of $100 in this period and $100 in the next. With no financial market, money may be used as a store of value, but its value will not increase over time. Thus the maximum consumption next period is $200. This is shown in column 3 of Table 2.1.

Next, if a financial market allows only investment but no borrowing, it is possible to increase the amount of money available for consumption in the next period. With the specified initial endowment, the most the agent can consume in the current period remains at $100. This would leave $100 for the next period. As an alternative, the $100 could be saved until the next period, generating a total of $110. This, together with the next period's endowment of $100, would allow a maximum consumption of $210 in the next period. This is shown in column 4 of Table 2.1.

TABLE 2.1   Maximum Consumption Opportunities with and Without a Financial Market*

		Maximum Consumption		
Period	Initial Endowment	No Financial Markets	Investment Only	Both Borrowing and Investing
0	$100	$100	$100	$190.91
1	100	200	210	210.00

* Borrowing and lending at 10%.

FIGURE 2.3   Consumption Opportunities with Financial Investment and Borrowing

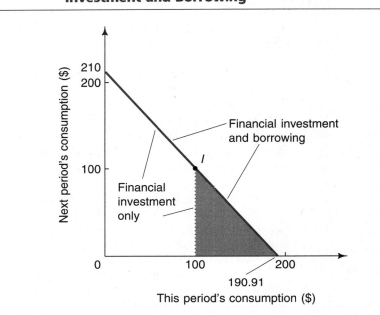

In a financial market that allows borrowing, we have another way of distributing consumption: we can borrow against our future income. If we have an endowment of $100 in this period and $100 in the next period, we could promise to pay the entire $100 to be received in period 1 and borrow an amount now that would grow into that $100 next period, or $90.91:

$$\$90.91 \times 0.10 + \$90.91 = \$100$$

In other words, we could borrow the present value of the $100 that we will receive in the next period. If we borrow $90.91 we could consume in the current period the borrowed amount plus our initial endowment of $100, for a total of $190.91.

Figure 2.3 shows the consumption opportunities with these borrowing and lending opportunities. Point I shows the initial endowment of $100 in each period. As we have already seen, if only investment is allowed, the maximum that can be consumed in the current period is the $100. This is shown by the vertical dashed line from $100 to point I. In a market with only financial investment, it is possible to reduce consumption now in order to have greater consumption opportunities later. For example, if we consume only $50 in the current period, this allows $50 to be invested, which will generate an additional $55 of consumption in the next period, for a total consumption then of $155.

☞ If the financial system allows borrowing by individuals, it improves the available consumption opportunities.

If we are allowed to borrow and have the initial endowment of $100 per period, we can achieve consumption opportunities depicted by the line from $190.91 to *I*. For example, we have seen that we could borrow against the entire $100 endowment from the next period and consume it now, together with our current endowment of $100, for a total of $190.91.

This ability to borrow makes an economic agent better off. Assume that we want to consume $130 in the current period. To do this, we would consume our initial endowment of $100 and borrow $30 against our next period's endowment. In the next period, we would have to repay $33, the $30 that was borrowed plus the 10 percent interest, and this would leave us with a consumption level of $67. This pattern is possible only if borrowing is allowed. Given that some participants in the economy will want to borrow, a well-developed financial market allows a richer set of choices that can make people better off.

The general relationship between next period's consumption in dollars, C_1, and this period's consumption in dollars, C_0, given corresponding endowments of E_1 and E_0, and a certain rate of interest, r, is given by:

$$C_1 = E_1 + (E_0 - C_0)(1 + r) \tag{2.1}$$

This expression simply states that in period 1 we can consume our endowment of E_1, plus any amount we saved in period 0, $E_0 - C_0$, as well as the interest generated by the amount saved, $(E_0 - C_0)r$. In the example just discussed, if we consume nothing this period so that $C_0 = 0$, next period we can consume a total of $210:

$$C_1 = 100 + (100 - 0)(1 + 0.10)$$
$$= \$210$$

Similarly, if we wish to leave no consumption for next period, we can consume a total of $190.91 this period:

$$0 = 100 + (100 - C_0)(1 + 0.10)$$
$$C_0 = 100 + \frac{100}{1.1}$$
$$= \$190.91$$

REAL INVESTMENT AND DIMINISHING PROFITS

In developing our imaginary economy, we considered one that provides the opportunity to make real investment, and another in which financial investment is possible. In a more robust economy, both kinds of investments would be possible.

In our previous examples we assumed that real investment earned a return of 20 percent and that financial investment earned a return of 10 percent. If an economy offers both kinds of investments, why wouldn't investors all make the same kind—the one with the higher certain return? In fact, that is exactly what they would do. In the examples we have been considering investors would all prefer to earn 20 percent on a real investment rather than 10 percent on lending. To see why actual economies have both real and financial investments we must add a bit more realism to our discussion.

Consider a firm that makes real investment, like McDonald's, of hamburger fame. In choosing a location for the first store, the firm would put it in the one with the highest return. The second store would go to the location with the second highest return, and so on. If the economy had only two kinds of investments, real investment in McDonald's earning 20 percent and financial investment earning 10 percent, then all investment would be directed toward McDonald's.

Consider what must happen to McDonald's as it saturates the market with hamburger stores. Eventually, the rate of return on the stores must fall. In the absurd case of four McDonald's at every crossroads, they cannot all be earning the same original return of 20 percent. This tendency for incremental units of physical capital to earn lower returns is called the **decreasing marginal productivity of capital.** The unit of capital employed at the margin will earn a lower return than previously employed units of capital, because investment will occur first in the uses with the highest return. This idea of a marginal return contrasts with the concept of the **average return**—the total return divided by the total investment. As the marginal productivity of capital falls, the average return on the entire investment must fall as well, because it is pulled down by the less productive units of capital that are being put into production.

decreasing marginal productivity of capital
the principle that successively employed units of capital earn a lower return, because investment occurs first in the uses with the highest returns

average return
total return divided by total investment

☞ As more and more units of real capital are invested, the marginal return on capital must fall.

Figure 2.4 graphs this decreasing marginal productivity of capital. To maintain continuity with our previous discussion, we assume that the total value available in the current period is $190.91. The slope of the curved line shows the returns to real investment. The steeper the slope of the curve, the greater is the return, so the return is highest at the bottom of the curve. The amount of investment is shown going from right to left.

To make this more concrete, consider a real investment amount of $40.91 and assume that the rate of return on this first amount of investment will be 120 percent. If this amount of investment is undertaken out of a total possible current consumption of $190.91, this leaves $150 to be consumed in the current period, and next period's consumption will increase by the proceeds of this investment. The $40.91 that is invested to earn a 120 percent return will grow to a total of $90:

$$\$40.91 + \$40.91 \times 1.20 = \$90.00$$

This possibility is graphed in Figure 2.4.

Consider now a higher level of investment. Let us assume that current consumption is restricted to $90, as shown in Figure 2.4. This leaves $100.91 available for investment, which provides for a consumption level in the next period of $160. The profit on the investment is $160 − $100.91, or $59.09.

FIGURE 2.4 The Decreasing Marginal Productivity of Capital

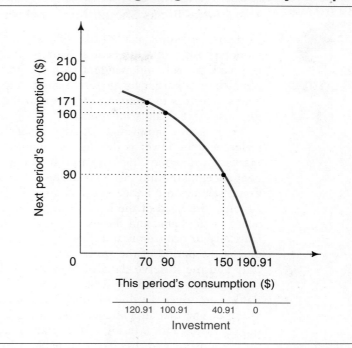

For this level of investment the average rate of return is $59.09/$100.91 = 0.59, or 59 percent. Notice that the falling rate of return is due to the diminishing marginal productivity of capital, so less is being earned on each additional unit of investment.

What happens if we restrict current consumption to $70 in order to invest $20 more, bringing our total real investment to $120.91? In that case, we have $70 of current consumption and $171 of consumption in the next period, as shown in Figure 2.4. This gives a profit on the entire investment of $50.09 and a rate of return of 41 percent.

But consider more closely what is happening as we invest that extra $20. With real investment of $100.91 we were able to consume $160 in the next period, but with an investment of $120.91 our consumption in the next period increased to only $171. We had to sacrifice $20 in this period to generate just $11 in the next period. That means that our total consumption actually fell as a result of investing that extra $20. Because we sacrificed $20 of consumption in the current period, we actually had a loss in total consumption of $9 ($11 increase in the next period minus $20 sacrificed in this period). So the return on our $20 of additional investment was − $9/$20, or −45 percent.

INTERNATIONAL PERSPECTIVES

The Central Banks Should Cry Freedom

In theory, it should make little difference whether a government sets fixed monetary rules that the central bank is told to obey, or whether the central bank is made independent with the prime goal of price stability. In practice, it is harder for governments to repeal the independence of central banks than it is to tamper with rules, so independence provides more credible insurance against inflation.

Experience shows that the freer a central bank is from government interference, the lower is the rate of inflation. A study by Alberto Alesina of Harvard University* ranks central banks according to an index of independence, taking into account characteristics such as the formal institutional relationship between the central bank and the government (e.g., who appoints the head of the bank), the presence of government officials on the board of the bank, and the existence of rules forcing the central bank automatically to print money to finance budget deficits. The least independent during the period of the study (1973–86)—and they included the Bank of Italy and the Reserve Bank of New Zealand—are given a value of one; the most independent—Germany's Bundesbank and the Swiss National Bank—are given a value of four. The countries whose central banks had a rating of one had an average inflation rate of 12.5 percent over the period; the countries with a rating of four had an average rate of 4 percent. Moreover, countries with freer central banks also tended to have lower rates of unemployment. This fits the theory that policy credibility allows inflation to be defeated at a smaller cost in terms of lost growth and jobs.

* Alberto Alesina, "Politics and Business Cycles in Industrial Democracies," *Economic Policy* no. 8, April 1989.

Source: "The Good Central Bankers' Guide," *The Economist*, March 2, 1991, p. 72.

Table 2.2 presents the actual dollar return, plus the average and marginal returns for each level of investment. As the table shows, if we invest just $10.91, we will have a total of $28 next period, for an average return of 157 percent and a marginal return of 120 percent. Notice that the marginal return is less than the average return. This is always the case as long as the marginal return is falling, as in our example. In fact, for investment amounts above $70.91, the marginal return actually becomes negative. This means that an additional $10 of investment will produce less than $10 in the next period. Even with negative marginal returns, the average return of the entire investment can still be positive, due to the profits earned on previous investments.

TABLE 2.2   Average and Marginal Returns on Real Investment

Amount Invested	Return	Average Return	Marginal Return*
$ 10.91	$ 28	157%	120%
20.91	50	139	110
30.91	71	130	90
40.91	90	120	80
50.91	108	112	30
60.91	121	99	20
70.91	133	88	10
80.91	144	78	−20
90.91	152	67	−20
100.91	160	59	−40
110.91	166	50	−50
120.91	171	41	−60
130.91	175	34	

* Percentage return on next $10 of investment.

If we examine Figure 2.4, can we decide how much should be invested? It is tempting to say that real investment should stop as soon as the marginal return becomes negative, but this is not the case. Unfortunately, in the situation of Figure 2.4 we cannot say anything definite about how much investment should be undertaken. To answer this question, we must take the final step of considering real and financial investments together.

REAL AND FINANCIAL INVESTMENTS

We noted that investors always prefer an investment with higher returns in a situation of certainty. But we saw how the marginal returns on real investment change, depending on how much investment is made. This leads to important interactions between real investment and the financial market. In this section, we merge the real investment analysis of the preceding section with a simple financial market in which the rate of interest is 10 percent. Figure 2.5 shows the real investment opportunities of Figure 2.4, but includes the initial endowment of $100 in each period. The straight line shows the different consumption opportunities that are available by transacting in the financial market.

By combining real and financial investments, new and better consumption opportunities are available due to the high initial returns on real investment. For example, if we borrow against next period's endowment of $100, we will obtain $90.91 of investable funds right now. This means that immediate consumption could be left at $100, in accordance with the initial endowment, and $90.91 can be devoted to real investment. This $90.91 would generate a

FIGURE 2.5   Financial and Real Investment Opportunities

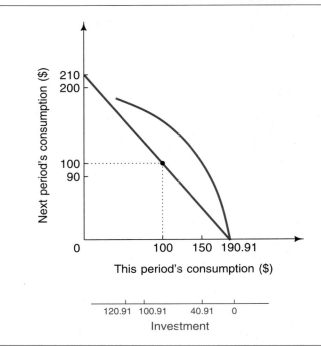

67 percent average return, as shown in Table 2.2, and a total consumption opportunity of $152 in the next period. By making this real investment, next period's consumption is increased by $52.

☞ An economy should undertake all real investment with marginal returns in excess of the financial market rate of return.

How much real investment should be undertaken? Since we can lend money at 10 percent in the financial market, we will not make any that has a return of less than 10 percent. Examining Table 2.2, we see that the marginal return hits that level with an investment of $70.91. If we invest more than that, we earn a return less than 10 percent. Therefore, we should put no more than $70.91 in real investment. That leaves a maximum consumption opportunity of $120 in the current period.

But what if we wish to consume more than $120 right now? Does that mean we should invest less than $70.91? Recall that in addition to lending in the financial market at a rate of 10 percent, we can also borrow at 10 percent. This suggests the following strategy: borrow at 10 percent in order to invest at a rate greater than 10 percent. If we look again at Table 2.2, we see that all real investment up to $70.91 has a marginal rate of return in excess of 10 percent, so we should place exactly $70.91 in real investment.

Figure 2.6 shows the optimal amount of real investment as point Q^* on the opportunity curve for real investment. Notice how the real investment

**FIGURE 2.6   The Interaction of Real and Financial
Investment Opportunities**

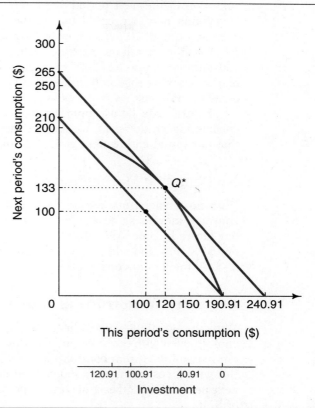

This period's consumption ($)

Investment

opportunities enrich the consumption opportunities. With real investment of $70.91, consumption of $120 is allowed in the current period and $133 is allowed in the next period.

We can think of Q^* as representing our new initial endowment if we undertake our real investment opportunities. But what if we do not like this initial endowment? What if we do not want to consume $120 now and $133 in the next period? Perhaps we want to consume more now. Notice that Figure 2.6 has a straight line passing through Q^* with a slope that shows the opportunities in the financial market, represented by the ability to borrow and lend at 10 percent. We can use the financial market to alter our consumption patterns by borrowing and lending, but now, due to the real investment opportunities, we are at a higher level of consumption.

With our position at Q^* ($120 of consumption now and $133 in the next period), we can change our consumption pattern. If we want to consume everything in the next period, we could lend our $120 in the financial market at 10 percent, and this would give us $132 ($120 × 1.1) of additional consumption in the next period, for a total of $265. If we wanted to consume everything now, we could borrow next period's available consumption of $133 at a rate of 10 percent, which would yield an additional $120.91 ($133/1.1). Combined with our existing $120, this would give a maximum of current consumption equal to $240.91. In our example, the existence of a financial market working together with attractive real investment opportunities combines to make the economy better off.

To conclude, let us summarize the different economies that we have been considering. In doing so, we assume that the interest rate is 10 percent and that our initial endowment is $100 in this period and $100 in the next.

No Financial Market and No Real Investment

With no financial market and no real investment opportunities, we cannot consume more than $100 now because we have no way to borrow against our future income. Also, if there is no financial market, we can merely store our $100 now and add it to our consumption for next period, making a total of $200 maximum consumption in the next period.

Lending, No Borrowing, and No Real Investment

With the possibility of lending, we can improve our range of consumption choices, even with the same initial endowment. Because there is no borrowing, our maximum current consumption is still the $100 of our initial endowment. But with investment, our $100 current endowment can generate $110 in the next period. This gives a maximum possible consumption in the next period of $210.

Lending, Borrowing, and No Real Investment

If we borrow against our future income, we can consume a maximum of $190.91 in the current period—our current period's endowment plus the present value of our next period's endowment. On the other hand, if we lend everything until the next period, we can consume $210 then.

Lending, Borrowing, and Real Investment

If real investment is possible and there is a financial market, we will undertake all real investment with a marginal return greater than the rate of return available in the financial market. In our example, this investment gave a consumption opportunity shown as Q^* in Figure 2.6. Using the financial market for borrowing and lending, we now have a maximum current consumption of $240.91 and a maximum consumption in the next period of $265. Of the

**FIGURE 2.7   Summary of Consumption Opportunities in
Economies of Increasing Complexity**

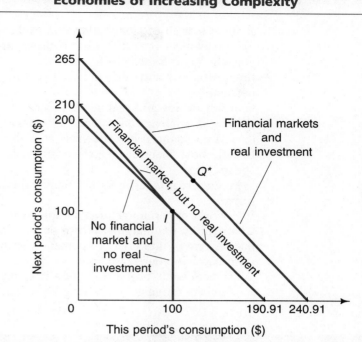

three cases, we are best off with both a financial market and real investment opportunities.

All of these opportunities are summarized in Figure 2.7, where the initial endowment is indicated as *I*. People are better off the better their consumption opportunities.

SUMMARY

In this chapter, we assumed that there was no risk in investment. We considered an economy with no money or financial system and saw that the opportunities for investment and for altering consumption patterns were very limited. By introducing money and gradually making the economy more complex, we noted that the well-being of individuals in the economy is enhanced by the existence of a financial system.

With a well-developed financial system, it is possible to take better advantage of opportunities for real investment. As a consequence, the financial system and financial investment work together with real investment to improve the conditions of all participants in the economy.

QUESTIONS

1. Assume that an economy allows no exchange or investment. If your initial endowment is $1,000, what is the maximum lifetime consumption you can have? Explain.
2. In an economy without a financial system, what kinds of exchanges are possible?
3. Contrast money and real goods as suitable stores of value.
4. Explain how money in an economy makes economic agents better off, even if no financial investment is possible.
5. Explain how financial investment improves the condition of economic agents.
6. Why does real investment normally exhibit diminishing marginal returns?
7. In a world of certain returns on both real and financial investments, what will be the marginal return on real investment? Assume that the market rate of interest is 10 percent and that the economy is in equilibrium. Explain your reasoning.
8. What's the value of the slope of a line such as the one in Figure 2.3?
9. Explain the rationale underlying Equation 2.1.

PROBLEMS

Use this information to answer all of the following problems. Interest rates are 10 percent, and you have an initial endowment of $1,000 in the current period and $1,000 in the next period.

1. What is your maximum immediate consumption opportunity?
2. What is your maximum consumption opportunity for the next period?
3. How would you invest or borrow to have a consumption level of $1,500 right now? What would be your consumption in the next period?
4. How would you invest or borrow to have a consumption level of $1,500 in the next period? What could you consume right now?
5. Draw a graph of your maximum consumption opportunities and show your consumption level for both periods if you consume $1,500 now.
6. If real investment pays 12 percent, what is your maximum possible consumption right now? Assume that borrowing is not possible.
7. If real investment pays 12 percent, what is your maximum possible consumption right now? Assume that borrowing is possible.
8. If real investment pays 12 percent, what is your maximum possible consumption in the next period? Assume that borrowing is not possible.

9. If real investment pays 12 percent, what is your maximum possible consumption in the next period? Assume that borrowing is possible.

10. Assuming that real investment pays 12 percent, draw a graph of your maximum consumption opportunities and show your consumption level for both periods if you consume $1,500 now.

11. Comparing your answers to Problems 5 and 10, how much more can you consume in the next period if you have the real investment opportunities?

The Time Value of Money

time value of money
the principle that $1 received today has a greater value than $1 received in the future

This chapter introduces the most important concept in finance—the time value of money. The **time value of money** refers to the principle that $1 received today has a greater value than $1 received in the future. This simple idea is the driving force for many financial decisions.

In this chapter we analyze the time value of single payments. For example, we want to understand how $1,000 deposited in a bank account grows to a greater sum in the future In the next chapter we will study the time value of a series of payments. The ideas developed there will rely heavily on a thorough understanding of the concepts discussed in this chapter.

SIMPLE INTEREST

simple interest
interest computed on the assumption that any interest does not itself earn interest

principal
the base amount used in calculating future value

Suppose a customer walks into a bank and deposits $1,000 in a savings account that earns an interest rate of 6 percent per year. How much will this depositor have in two years if the account earns simple interest? We compute **simple interest** by assuming that interest does not itself earn interest. Equivalently, to compute the amount of interest earned during any period, we must always use the same base amount, or principal. The original deposit of $1,000 is the **principal**. The depositor receives this principal again at the end of the investment period, plus all interest earned. For this deposit, the value of the account after two years will be equal to the sum of the principal and the interest earned over those years. The interest earned in the first year is $1,000 × 0.06 = $60. Similarly, in the second year the account earns another $60, since with simple interest the principal never changes. Consequently, the value of the account at the end of two years is $1,000 + $60 + $60 = $1,120.

In general, if P is the principal, r is the rate of interest, and n is the amount of time the principal earns interest, the total dollar amount of interest (i) is calculated with the following formula:

$$i = P \times r \times n \tag{3.1}$$

The total amount the depositor has at the end of n years equals the original deposit (P) plus the interest earned (i). Since the total interest earned can be found by using Equation 3.1, the value of the account after n years of earning simple interest is:

$$\text{Value after } n \text{ years} = P + i$$
$$= P + P \times r \times n$$
$$= P(1 + r \times n) \tag{3.2}$$

In the example, the bank account earns simple interest for two years. After this time its value equals the prinicipal plus the simple interest. This gives a total of $\$1{,}000(1 + 0.06 \times 2) = \$1{,}120$, the same result as above.

COMPOUND INTEREST

compound interest
compounding method in which interest earns interest

Generally, we calculate interest as **compound interest,** not simple interest. In this case the principal and interest received earn interest in later periods. Equivalently, the accumulated amount at the end of a period becomes the principal used to compute the interest earned over the next period.

In the bank deposit example, suppose the account pays interest in the second year on both the principal and the first year's interest. Since we know that the account earns $\$60$ interest during the first year, its value at the end of that year is $\$1{,}060$. This $\$1{,}060$ becomes the new principal for the second year, which will earn 6 percent interest over that year. Thus, the value of the account after two years is:

$$\text{Value after 2 years} = \text{value after 1 year} + \text{interest in year 2}$$
$$= \$1{,}060 + \$1{,}060 \times 0.06$$
$$= \$1{,}060(1.06)$$
$$= \$1{,}000(1.06)(1.06)$$
$$= \$1{,}000(1.06)^2$$
$$= \$1{,}123.60$$

Consider a deposit of P dollars. If this deposit is held for n years and earns r percent per year, it will be worth:

$$\text{Value after } n \text{ years} = P(1 + r)^n \tag{3.3}$$

☞ Interest may be calculated as either simple interest or as compound interest.

Comparing the two ways of computing interest, we see that the value of the account after two years of simple interest is $\$1{,}120.00$. With annual compounding, it is $\$1{,}123.60$. The difference of $\$3.60$ between the two methods is due to the 6 percent interest earned in the second year on the first year's $\$60$ interest when using compound interest: $\$3.60 = \$60 \times 0.06$. This highlights the difference between simple interest and compound interest. In simple interest, interest earned previously does not itself earn interest. With compound interest, interest earned in previous periods becomes part of the principal that earns interest in later periods.

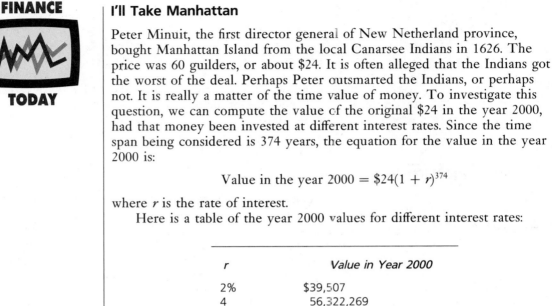

FINANCE TODAY

I'll Take Manhattan

Peter Minuit, the first director general of New Netherland province, bought Manhattan Island from the local Canarsee Indians in 1626. The price was 60 guilders, or about $24. It is often alleged that the Indians got the worst of the deal. Perhaps Peter outsmarted the Indians, or perhaps not. It is really a matter of the time value of money. To investigate this question, we can compute the value of the original $24 in the year 2000, had that money been invested at different interest rates. Since the time span being considered is 374 years, the equation for the value in the year 2000 is:

$$\text{Value in the year 2000} = \$24(1 + r)^{374}$$

where r is the rate of interest.

Here is a table of the year 2000 values for different interest rates:

r	Value in Year 2000
2%	$39,507
4	56,322,269
6	69,920,550,000
8	75,979,390,000,000
10	72,623,220,000,000,000

It's hard to know how much Manhattan is worth today, and it is difficult to say how much the Indians could have earned on the $24. To understand the kind of value that the computations reflect, however, assume that in the year 2000 the world's population will be 6.5 billion and that the money is to be distributed equally among each of its inhabitants. Under these assumptions, each person would receive about $11 if the original money had been invested at 6 percent, $11,689 if it had been invested at 8 percent, and $11,172,800 if it had been invested at 10 percent.

EXAMPLE 3.1

An investor deposits $500 in a bank account. What will be the value of the account after three years if it earns 9 percent simple interest?

$$
\begin{aligned}
\text{Value after 3 years} &= P(1 + r \times n) \\
&= \$500(1 + 0.09 \times 3) \\
&= \$635
\end{aligned}
$$

What will be the value of the account after three years if it earns 9 percent interest, compounded annually?

$$\text{Value after 3 years} = P(1 + r)^3$$
$$= \$500(1.09)^3$$
$$= \$647.51$$

PRESENT VALUE AND FUTURE VALUE

present value
the value of a payment if the payment were made immediately

future value
the value of the payment if the payment were made in the future

☞ Present values and future values are related mathematically by the interest rate and the amount of time between the present and future payment.

The **present value** of a future payment is the value of that payment if it were made immediately. The **future value** of a payment made today is the value of that payment if it were made at some time in the future.

The present value of the bank account is $1,000. If the owner deposits the funds at 6 percent for two years, compounded annually, the account will be worth $1,123.60 after two years. That is the future value of the $1,000 deposit in two years and with an interest rate of 6 percent.

The interest rate and the amount of time between the present and future payments tie the present and future values together mathematically. Let the present value be denoted by PV and the future value by FV. Then the general relationship between future values and present values is:

$$FV = PV(1 + r)^n \tag{3.4}$$

EXAMPLE 3.2

A bank customer deposits $150 in an account for five years with an interest rate of 12 percent. What is the future value of this $150 at the end of the five years?

Using the basic relationship in Equation 3.4, we have:

$$FV = PV(1 + r)^n = \$150(1.12)^5 = \$264.35$$

Equation 3.4 is the basic relationship of the time value of money. We will use it throughout this book to compute a multitude of extremely important relationships. It is truly a fundamental equation in finance.

EXAMPLE 3.3

Evelyn goes to a loan shark and borrows $1,000 for five years at an interest rate of 80 percent per year with annual compounding. What is the future value of the loan after five years?

$$FV = PV(1 + r)^n = \$1,000(1.80)^5 = \$18,895.68$$

Obviously, Evelyn has a problem waiting for her, particularly if she does not understand how compound interest works. Evelyn is a tough negotiator, however.

What will she owe if she convinces the loan shark to forget the annual compounding and to do her the favor of lending her the $1,000 for five years at 80 percent simple interest?

$$\text{Total debt after 5 years} = P(1 + r \times n)$$
$$= \$1,000(1 + 0.80 \times 5)$$
$$= \$5,000$$

In this case, Evelyn will only owe $5,000 in five years. All of the difference between the $18,895.68 and the $5,000 debt is due to the interest earned on interest with annual compounding.

FUTURE VALUES AND THE FREQUENCY OF COMPOUNDING

☞ Other things being equal, the more frequently interest is compounded, the faster money will grow.

The more frequently interest is compounded, the faster the present value grows. To illustrate this principle, let us compute the future value after one year of an initial investment of $1,000 at 12 percent annual interest, compounded semiannually. With semiannual compounding, we add the interest earned in the first half-year to the principal, and the total becomes the new principal that will earn interest in the second half-year. Since the annual interest rate is 12 percent, the interest rate for one half-year is 6 percent. This means that the value of the account after the first half-year is $1,060 = \$1,000(1 + 0.12/2)$. When this amount of $1,060 earns interest for the second half-year, it grows to $1,123.60 = \$1,060(1 + 0.12/2)$. We can see that the value of the $1,000 initial investment with semiannual compounding is $1,123.60 after one year.

A more direct way to calculate future value is to reason that the $1,000 is being invested for two periods of six months each, and the rate of interest per period is 6 percent. Thus stated, this becomes a future value problem where the interest rate is 6 percent per period and the number of periods is two. More generally, if there are m compounding periods per year, the value of PV dollars at the end of n years, with an r percent annual interest rate, is given by:

$$FV = PV\left(1 + \frac{r}{m}\right)^{mn} \tag{3.5}$$

Table 3.1 shows how the frequency of compounding affects the future value of $1,000 at the end of one year with an interest rate of 12 percent. Notice that the difference between the daily and continuous compounding of $1,000 is only three cents after one year. This is a rather surprising result, in view of the fact that continuous compounding occurs every single instant. In contrast, daily compounding occurs just once every 86,400 seconds.

Figure 3.1 illustrates the effect of compounding over a ten-year period with a 12 percent interest rate. With simple interest, the $1,000 grows to

TABLE 3.1   Future Values and the Frequency of Compounding

Frequency	m	Future Value of $1,000
Annual	1	$1,120.00
Semiannual	2	1,123.60
Quarterly	4	1,125.51
Monthly	12	1,126.83
Daily	365	1,127.47
Continuous*	∞	1,127.50

* With continuous compounding the value of m is infinite, so we cannot use Equation 3.5. Instead, the formula for continuous compounding is $FV = PVe^{rn}$, where $e = 2.718281828\ldots$ is the base of the natural logarithms.

FIGURE 3.1   The Effects of Compounding on Future Value

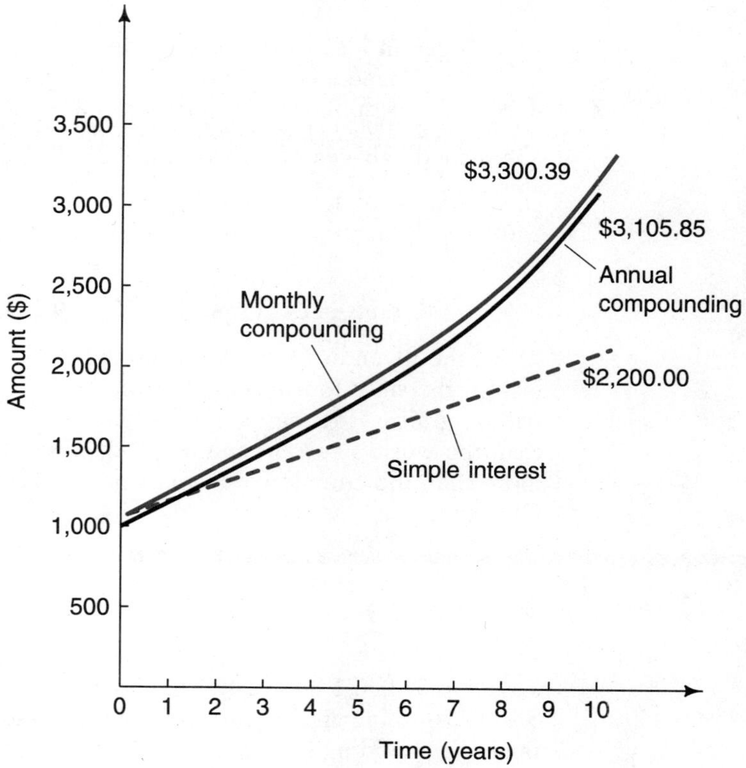

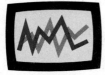

FINANCE

TODAY

The Ultimate Checkmate!

A colorful legend surrounds the invention of chess, a game that is believed to have originated in India around the seventh century A.D., after evolving from the Indian game Chaturanga. It is said that in those days, the local ruler became enamored with the new game of chess and, as a gesture of gratitude, decided to let its inventor choose any prize, no matter how expensive. Without hesitating, the inventor humbly laid a chess board in front of the local ruler, and requested that a single grain of wheat be put on the first of the board's sixty-four squares, two grains of wheat on the next square, four grains on the third square, and so on, doubling the number of grains on each successive square. Once the board had been filled with grains of wheat according to this procedure, the inventor would consider the prize paid in full. Hardly containing his laughter after listening to what seemed like a trivial request, the ruler immediately ordered his assistants to comply with the inventor's modest wishes. To the ruler's chagrin, it soon became apparent that the inventor was not so humble after all.

To get an idea of the magnitude of the prize requested by our shy inventor, we can analyze this story as a time value of money problem. Indeed, we can think that the investor was demanding a "wheat growth rate" of 100 percent per square. For example, the second square required $1(1 + 1.00) = 2 = 2^1$ grains; the third square required $2(1 + 1.00) = (1 + 1.00)^2 = 2^2$; for the fourth square, the number of grains would be 2^3; and so on. Therefore, for the last square, the number of grains needed would be:

$$\text{Grains in 64th square} = 2^{63} = 9{,}223{,}372{,}000{,}000{,}000{,}000$$

Thus, the inventor of chess was asking for about 9.2 million trillion grains just on the sixty-fourth square of the board, give or take a few thousand trillion grains. How big is this number of grains? It is much, much more than the world's current annual production of wheat. In fact, it is much more than the cumulative amount produced in all of recorded history. Checkmate!

$2{,}200 = \$1{,}000(1 + 0.12 \times 10)$. Figure 3.1 also shows the future value of the \$1,000 assuming annual compounding and monthly compounding. With annual compounding and an interest rate of 12 percent, the future value of the \$1,000 is \$3,105.85 after ten years. With monthly compounding, the \$1,000 grows to \$3,300.39 over that time.

THE EFFECTIVE RATE OF INTEREST

effective rate of interest
the annually compounded
rate of interest that is
equivalent to an annual
interest rate that is compounded more than once
per year

As we have already noted, the more frequently we compound, the faster the present value grows. The **effective rate of interest** (r_e) is the annually compounded rate of interest that is equivalent to an annual interest rate compounded more than once per year. This last annual rate is known as the nominal, or stated, rate of interest. The effective rate and the nominal rate of interest are equivalent whenever they both generate the same future value. This indicates that in order to find the effective rate of interest, all we have to do is to solve the following equation:

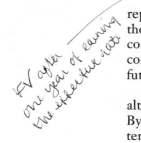

$$(1 + r_e) = \left(1 + \frac{r}{m}\right)^m \quad \rightarrow \text{FV after compounding} \tag{3.6}$$

FV after one year of earning the effective rate

We can interpret Equation 3.6 as follows. The left side of the equation represents the future value after one year of a present value of $1 earning the effective rate of interest, whereas the right side is the future value of $1 compounded for m periods at a rate of r/m per period. Since m periods constitute one year, the equation expresses the requirement that both of these future values must be equal.

The effective rate of interest is very useful for comparing investment alternatives having different interest rates and different compounding intervals. By comparing the effective rate of interest on each alternative, we can determine the best investment.

EXAMPLE 3.4

You plan to invest $10,000 for one year and you have the chance to invest it at 12 percent annual interest, compounded monthly. Alternatively, you could invest the funds at an annual rate of 12.25 percent compounded semiannually. What is the effective rate of interest of each alternative?

For the investment at 12 percent annual rate compounded monthly, the monthly rate of interest is 1 percent. An investment of $1 at 1 percent per period over twelve periods will have a future value of:

$$FV = \$1(1.01)^{12} = \$1.1268$$

We invested $1 at the beginning and received $1.1268 at the end of the year. Therefore, the effective rate of interest of 12 percent nominal interest, compounded monthly, is 12.68 percent. We could also obtain the effective rate by directly solving Equation 3.6. Substituting the values in the example and solving for r_e gives 12.68 percent also.

Using Equation 3.6 for the investment at 12.25 percent compounded semiannually we have:

$$(1 + r_e) = \left(1 + \frac{0.1225}{2}\right)^2 = 1.1262$$

Solving for r_e gives an annual effective rate of interest of 12.62 percent.

TABLE 3.2   Future Value of $1

n	1%	2%	3%	4%
1	1.0100	1.0200	1.0300	1.0400
2	1.0201	1.0404	1.0609	1.0816
3	1.0303	1.0612	1.0927	1.1249
4	1.0406	1.0824	1.1255	1.1699
5	1.0510	1.1040	1.1593	1.2167

Future Value Tables

As an alternative to the calculations of future values of single payments with the future value formula, this book includes a future value table in the Appendix. Table 3.2 reproduces a portion of the table to indicate how it should be used.

Suppose you want to know the future value in three months of $2,000 with an interest rate of 2 percent per month. Table 3.2 indicates that the future value of $1 invested at 2 percent per period for three periods is 1.0612. This is the future value factor for 2 percent and three periods. Since we are concerned with the future value of $2,000, and not of $1, we simply multiply the future value factor by $2,000 to get the desired future value: $2,000 × 1.0612 = $2,122.40.

Note that the interest rate used in the table is not necessarily an annual rate. Similarly, the number of periods is not necessarily expressed in years. In our example, we used monthly rates and periods expressed in months. The important rule to remember is that the time periods should always be expressed in units consistent with the interest rate. If each period is one month, the interest rate must be expressed as a monthly rate.

It will be useful to develop some shorthand notation for the future value factors. We will use the notation $FV(r, n) = (1 + r)^n$. With this notation, we can write the future value factor for 2 percent per period and three periods as $FV(2, 3) = (1 + 0.02)^3 = 1.0612$.

Note that although the future value table can be useful, it cannot solve all future value problems because it only has integer interest rates and integer periods. Therefore, it cannot solve a problem involving an interest rate of 8.5 percent per period for 4.3 periods. In such cases, the formulas discussed previously must be used.

Present Value

As sums invested now have future values, payments scheduled for the future have a present value. By an algebraic manipulation of Equation 3.4, we can derive an expression for the present value:

$$PV = \frac{FV}{(1 + r)^n} \tag{3.7}$$

Assume that a wealthy uncle promises you a gift of $1,000 in one year. Current interest rates are 10 percent. The $1,000 you will receive has a present value lower than $1,000 because you could invest less than $1,000 today at 10 percent and end up with $1,000 one year from now. This argument is the essence of the time value of money: money has a time value because we can use it to earn interest.

The present value for the payment the uncle promised is the sum that would make you exactly as well off today as the $1,000 payment to be received in one year. So, the present value of next year's $1,000 payment is the amount you must invest now in order to have $1,000 in one year. We can compute the present value today of $1,000 in one year with a 10 percent interest rate by using Equation 3.7. In this case, the future value is $1,000, the interest rate is 10 percent, and the time until the future payment is one year. The present value is then:

$$PV = \frac{\$1,000}{1 + 0.10} = \$909.09$$

With interest rates at 10 percent per year, the present value of next year's $1,000 is $909.09. We can verify this conclusion by showing that investing $909.09 for one year at 10 percent has a future value of $1,000: $909.09(1.10) = $1,000.

In an important sense, future values and present values are two sides of the same coin. This is clear from considering the close relationship between Equation 3.4 for future values and its rearrangement to give Equation 3.7 for present values.

EXAMPLE 3.5

If interest rates are 13 percent per year, what is the present value of $1,630.47 to be paid in four years?

$$PV = \frac{\$1,630.47}{(1 + 0.13)^4} = \$1,000.00$$

Thus, we see that $1,000 is exactly the amount we would have to invest now at 13 percent, to generate a future value of $1,630.47 in four years.

Present Value Tables

As there are tables of future values, there are also tables of present values. They, too, reflect values of $1. Table 3.3 presents a portion of the more complete present value table found in the Appendix.

Let the notation $PV(r, n)$ represent the present value factor for an interest rate of r percent per period and n periods. For example, $PV(3, 4)$ is the present value factor for 3 percent and four periods. From Table 3.3, $PV(3, 4) = 0.8884$. Notice that future value factors are always greater than 1 and present value factors are always less than 1. When using the present value tables, remember

TABLE 3.3   Present Value of $1

n	1%	2%	3%	4%
1	0.9901	0.9804	0.9709	0.9615
2	0.9803	0.9612	0.9426	0.9245
3	0.9706	0.9424	0.9151	0.8889
4	0.9610	0.9239	0.8884	0.8547
5	0.9515	0.9058	0.8625	0.8218

that the present value factors assume a future value of $1. When the future value is an arbitrary amount FV, the present value is given by $PV = FV \times PV(r, n)$.

EXAMPLE 3.6

Compute the present value of $3,500 to be received in four periods, for an interest rate of 3 percent.

We have already seen that the present value factor is $PV(3, 4) = 0.8884$. Since this is the present value of $1, we need only multiply this factor by $3,500 to find the total present value, so $PV = \$3,500 \times 0.8884 = \$3,109.40$.

SOLVING FOR AN UNKNOWN INTEREST RATE

On occasion, financial managers and investors must deal with a time value of money problem in which the present and future values are known, as well as the time between them, but not the interest rate that connects those values. For example, many bonds require a payment now and return a specified larger payment at some future date, but the implicit interest rate the bond earns is not stated, so it must be computed separately.

There are several ways to solve such problems. Today, financial calculators can do the job easily. A second technique is to solve the problem directly. We can also use present value or future value tables. To solve the problem directly, we must find the interest rate from the present value equation. If the time between the present and future values is n, this requires essentially isolating the term containing r and taking the nth root on both sides of the equation. The expression for r is then:

$$r = \left(\frac{FV}{PV}\right)^{1/n} - 1 \tag{3.8}$$

EXAMPLE 3.7

Mr. Willie Himan, a fast-talking salesman, comes into your office and offers a great deal that pays $10,000 in six years. He says that the price you must pay today is only $8,375. To know whether this is an attractive deal, you must calculate the interest rate that your investment would earn.

We may solve this problem directly by applying Equation 3.8:

$$r = \left(\frac{\$10,000}{\$8,375}\right)^{1/6} - 1 = 0.03$$

Thus, we see that the fantastic deal earns 3 percent on your investment.

EXAMPLE 3.8

Before you can throw Mr. Himan out the door, he improves the offer by cutting the price of the deal. Now Willie says he will give you the $10,000 six years from now for only $7,677.50 today. What interest rate does the deal now offer?

We will solve this problem using the future value tables. We first find the future value factor. Since the future value is $10,000 for an investment of $7,677.50, the future value factor is:

$$FV(r, 6) = \frac{\$10,000}{\$7,677.50} = 1.3025$$

This factor is not found in the future value table in the Appendix. The value we seek lies between $FV(5, 6) = 1.3401$ and $FV(4, 6) = 1.2653$. Therefore, the interest rate is between 4 and 5 percent. Because our future value factor is about half-way between, the interest rate on the deal must be about 4.5 percent. The exact interest rate is 4.5033 percent, so interpolation gave us an excellent approximation in this case.

SOLVING FOR THE NUMBER OF PERIODS

Sometimes the financial manager has to know how long it will take for a certain amount invested today to grow to a certain value, given that it earns a known rate of interest. For example, a pension fund manager may have $300 million to invest today to meet future pension needs. The manager might want to know how long it would take for that money to grow to the $1 billion needed to meet the firm's obligations. The analytical solution is derived from the relationship between present and future value, Equation 3.4. Solving that expression for n gives:

$$n = \frac{\ln\left(\dfrac{FV}{PV}\right)}{\ln(1 + r)} \tag{3.9}$$

In this formula, we use the natural logarithm, but any logarithm measure, such as base 10 logarithms, would work equally well. The only restriction is that the logarithms used in the numerator and denominator must use the same base.

INTERNATIONAL PERSPECTIVES

Money for Nothing

[Nicaraguan] shoppers knew what was coming. In a burst of desperation buying, they emptied store shelves of anything that was for sale. Merchants knew too. Many of them closed their doors, preferring to be stuck with rotting merchandise rather than the worthless currency known derisively as "piggies." When the government of President Violeta Barrios de Chamorro officially devalued the cordoba [in March 1991] to a stratospheric 25 million to the dollar, most Nicaraguans were simply glad the waiting was over.

The long-rumored shock therapy illustrated the . . . government's failure to stabilize a chaotic economy. Inflation, which [in 1990] topped 13,000 percent, is still out of control. To soften the devaluation's blow, most salaries were tripled and Chamorro promised not to fire any employees on the bloated state payroll.

[In April and May 1991], new gold cordobas worth 5 million old cordobas, or 20¢ each, . . . [replaced] the piggies as legal paper tender. Chamorro publicly set fire to a small mountain of worn-out cordobas that had already been exchanged, then went shopping at a Managua supermarket armed with a supply of the new currency.

Chamorro's advisers [knew what was] at stake. [Said] the President's son-in-law Antonio Lacayo: "If this plan fails, the government will have to go." The opposition Sandinista National Liberation Front's response: "They might as well start packing." The Sandinistas should know: their mishandling of the economy helped sweep Chamorro into power.

Source: "These Piggies Went to Market," *Time,* March 18, 1991, p. 61.

EXAMPLE 3.9

If you earn an annual rate of interest of 10 percent compounded annually, how many years will it take for your money to double?

Since you wish to double your money, we can assume that you start out with $1, and after n years you will have $2. Substituting these numbers and the 10 percent interest rate in Equation 3.9, we compute the value of n:

$$n = \frac{\ln\left(\dfrac{\$2}{\$1}\right)}{\ln(1 + 0.10)} = \frac{0.69315}{0.09531} = 7.27 \text{ years}$$

To approximate the time required to double money, we can use the "72 rule." We calculate the required time as the ratio 72/r, where r is a percentage.

In the example, the rule would give 72/10 = 7.2 years, for a very good approximation.

SUMMARY

This chapter introduced the time value of money. The central idea is that $1 received today is worth more than $1 received in the future because we can invest money to earn an interest rate.

Interest can be calculated in many ways. We began by considering simple interest, and then learned how to calculate compound interest. With compounding, we add interest earned in one period to the principal and this total becomes the new principal for the following period. In other words, with compound interest, interest earns interest. In addition, the more often we compound interest, the greater will be the effective rate of interest.

We have seen how to calculate present values and future values and we can compute them directly through the use of formulas, using a financial calculator, or by using present value and future value tables. We also learned how to compute an unknown interest rate if we know the present value, the future value, and the length of time between the two. Finally, we learned how to find the number of periods between a present and future value, given the interest rate. This chapter considered only individual payments. In many finance applications, an investment involves a series of payments. The next chapter explores the present and future values of series of payments.

QUESTIONS

1. For a present value today, will the future value be greater or smaller the higher the rate of interest? Why?
2. For a present value today, will the future value be greater or smaller the longer the time until the future value is to be received? Why?
3. For a given future payment, will the present value be greater or smaller the higher the rate of interest? Why?
4. For a given future payment, will the present value be greater or smaller the longer the time until the future payment is to be made? Why?
5. Would you rather earn 10 percent for a year or an effective interest rate of 10 percent? Explain.
6. If you are borrowing $10,000, would you rather pay 10 percent simple interest or 10 percent compounded daily? Why?
7. If you are lending $10,000, would you rather receive 10 percent simple interest or 10 percent compounded daily? Why?
8. If you are investing funds, would you prefer a longer or a shorter compounding interval? Why?

9. Can you compute all possible future values using a future value table?
10. Explain what it means to find a present value for a future date.

PROBLEMS

1. What is the future value of a $10,000 investment if it earns 10 percent simple interest for one year?
2. What is the future value of a $10,000 investment if it earns 15 percent simple interest for two years?
3. What is the future value of a $10,000 investment if it earns 10 percent simple interest for five years?
4. What is the future value of a $10,000 investment if it earns 10 percent interest, compounded quarterly, for one year?
5. What is the future value of a $25,000 investment if it earns 15 percent compounded quarterly for six quarters?
6. Using the future value table, compute the future value of an investment of $30,000 invested for three years at 12 percent simple interest.
7. Using the future value table, compute the future value of an investment of $30,000 invested for three years at 12 percent compounded semiannually.
8. Using the future value table, compute the future value of an investment of $30,000 invested for three years at 12 percent compounded quarterly.
9. Using the future value table, compute the future value of an investment of $30,000 invested for three years at 12 percent compounded monthly.
10. What is the present value of a payment of $50,000 to be received in four years if the discount rate is 15 percent? What discounting period should be used for this computation? Why?
11. What is the present value of a payment of $50,000 to be received in four years if the discount rate is 15 percent, assuming semiannual discounting?
12. What is the present value of a payment of $50,000 to be received in four years if the discount rate is 15 percent, assuming quarterly discounting?
13. What is the present value of a payment of $50,000 to be received in four years if the discount rate is 15 percent, assuming discounting every two months?
14. Using the present value table, compute the present value of a payment of $100,000 to be received in eight years if the discount rate is 16 percent.
15. Using the present value table, compute the present value of a payment of $100,000 to be received in eight years if the discount rate is 16 percent, assuming semiannual discounting.

16. Using the present value table, compute the present value of a payment of $100,000 to be received in eight years if the discount rate is 16 percent, assuming quarterly compounding.

17. What is the effective rate of interest on a loan if the stated rate is 14 percent and the principal is compounded monthly?

18. What is the effective rate of interest on a loan if the stated rate is 14 percent and the principal is compounded semiannually?

19. You want to borrow money to be repaid in two years. Moon Bank offers you a loan rate of 13 percent with annual compounding. Venus Bank offers you the same two-year loan at a stated rate of 12.284 percent but with monthly compounding. Which loan would you prefer?

20. Amerilast Bank uses quarterly compounding for its loans and offers you a nominal rate of 12 percent. What simple interest rate on a one-year loan could you get that would be equivalent to the quarterly loan?

21. Using the future value table, make the best estimate that you can for the future value of $10,000 in ten periods with an interest rate of 4.5 percent. Compute the same problem by calculator. How close were you to the exact answer when you used the table?

22. Using the present value table, make the best estimate that you can for the present value of $10,000 in ten periods with an interest rate of 4.5 percent. Compute the same problem by calculator. How close is your answer to that in the table?

23. Your Uncle Buck will pay you $1,000 in five years. What will be the present value of that future payment in two years, assuming an 11 percent discount rate?

24. One year from now, you tell Uncle Buck that he should keep his money. In present value terms, how much did that rashness cost you?

25. Uncle Buck gives you a choice of $500 now or $1,000 in four years. What interest rate would make you indifferent between this present value and future value?

26. You are a hard bargainer, and convince Uncle Buck to agree to change the terms to $1,200 in three years or $600 now. What interest rate does this imply? Which would you choose if you could invest at 20 percent annual interest?

27. You can pay a tax of $150 now or $175 in one month. What interest rate does this choice imply? What choice should you make if you can earn 11 percent for one month in your savings account?

28. Suppose you can skip your $150 tax payment now and pay tax of $200 in one year, plus a penalty of $20. What interest rate must you earn to make it worthwhile to do this?

29. Your company is excited about a new research project that will take eight years to complete. At that time, the created technology should be worth $1 million. By the end of year four the value of the technology will be obvious, as will the ultimate success of the research. Consequently, your firm plans to sell rights to the technology at that time. If

interest rates are 12 percent, what should the present value of the technology be at year four?

30. Exactly how long does it take for money to double if you earn 5 percent annual interest? What if you earn 15 percent? Compare the exact answers to those given by the 72 rule.

31. How long does it take for money to triple if you earn 7 percent annual interest?

32. Wonderland, Inc., offers an investment with a 100 percent annual interest rate. If Alice decides to invest, how long will it take for her money to grow to 64 times her initial investment?

33. In the previous problem, suppose Alice has a goal of achieving a certain amount of money at the end of seven years. How long will it take her to reach half of her goal?

34. Investment A will quadruple your money in the same amount of time that investment B will triple it. Find the functional relationship between the two implicit interest rates. (For example, the relationship might be expressed as $r_A = 2r_B$.)

35. Many people like to complain about how expensive mailing a letter has become. They cite that in 1939 it cost only three cents to mail a first-class letter, whereas in 1991 it cost 29 cents—almost ten times more! Find the average annual postal inflation rate over that 52-year period. Are those complaints really justified?

36. In 1654 Archbishop James Ussher of Ireland announced the results of his quest to pinpoint the moment of creation. Somehow, he concluded that the event took place on October 26, in the year 4004 B.C., at precisely 9:00 A.M. Assuming that Ussher's estimation is correct, what has been the average annual population growth rate throughout the history of humankind? To simplify, assume that exactly 6,000 years have gone by since the creation, that the first two people—Adam and Eve—were also created at that time, and that the current world population is 5.5 billion.

37. The overall global population growth rate is 1.74 percent per year, and the world's population is 5.5 billion. How many years will it take for the population to double? To triple?

38. Continuing with our population analysis, is the current population growth rate of 1.74 percent high or low by historical standards? (*Hint:* When would our earliest ancestors have lived?)

39. Nigeria's annual population growth rate is 3.4 percent. At this rate, how long will it take for the number of Nigerians to double?

40. Assume that Nigeria currently has a population of 120 million and a population growth rate of 3.4 percent, while the rest of the world grows at 1.7 percent. How many years would it take for the population of Nigeria to equal half the world's population? Recall that the entire world currently has a population of 5.5 billion.

41. What does population growth have to do with the time value of money anyway?

CHAPTER 4

The Time Value of a Series of Payments

In Chapter 3 we introduced the principles of the time value of money and studied their application to single payments. This chapter shows how we can value a stream of payments by extending the time value of money concepts for single payments. We begin by analyzing an infinite stream of payments (paradoxically, this is the easiest stream of all to value) and proceed with the valuation of a finite stream of payments.

Many finance applications focus on a series of payments. For example, the typical home mortgage runs for 360 equal monthly payments, and car loans generally require monthly payments for four or five years. We study how to solve problems such as these in this chapter.

PERPETUITIES

perpetuity
an infinite series of equal payments made at regular intervals

A **perpetuity** is an infinite stream of equal cash flows occurring at regular intervals. For example, if a savings account has a current balance of $20,000 and earns an interest rate of 12 percent compounded annually, the depositor (and the depositor's heirs) can enjoy a yearly cash flow of $2,400 forever, as long as the original $20,000 is left in the account.

An infallible rule in valuing any stream of payments is to value each of the component cash flows, and then add the individual values. Given that with perpetuities we must value an infinite number of cash flows, it is perhaps surprising that these are the easiest to value.

☞ The present value of a perpetuity is just the ratio of the periodic payment over the discount rate.

We assume that the first payment of the perpetuity occurs one year from the present. In principle, to find the present value, PV, of a perpetuity paying C each period with an interest rate of r percent per period, we must evaluate the summation of the individual present values:

$$PV = \frac{C}{(1 + r)} + \frac{C}{(1 + r)^2} + \cdots$$

Fortunately, this infinite summation adds up to the following simple formula:[1]

$$PV = \frac{C}{r} \qquad (4.1)$$

[1] Finding the value of the infinite summation requires knowledge of geometric series. A geometric series, S, is a summation of the form $S = 1 + x + x^2 + x^3 + \ldots$, which adds up to $S = 1/(1 - x)$. Such summations are useful in finance and many other disciplines. The formula tells us, for example, that in the limit the sum $1 + \frac{1}{2} + \frac{1}{4} + \frac{1}{8} + \ldots$ adds up to 2.

☞ The present value of a perpetuity is always located one period before the first cash flow.

The perpetuity formula in Equation 4.1 gives the present value one period before the first payment. Thus, to find the present value of a perpetuity at time $t = 0$, the first payment must occur at time $t = 1$. Similarly, if the first payment of a perpetuity occurs at time $t = 19$, Equation 4.1 gives the present value of the perpetuity as of time $t = 18$.

EXAMPLE 4.1

Find the present value of an investment that promises to pay $2,500 each year, forever, when the interest rate is 12 percent.

Using Equation 4.1, the present value is:

$$PV = \frac{\$2,500}{0.12}$$

$$= \$20,833.33$$

The following section shows that by using the perpetuity formula, we can easily value other types of cash flow streams.

ANNUITIES

annuity
a series of equal cash flows made at regular intervals

An **annuity** is a finite series of equal cash flows made at regular intervals. A car loan with 48 equal monthly payments is a typical annuity. As with perpetuities, finding the value of an annuity requires valuing the individual payments and adding them.

Calculating the value of an annuity is a common problem of finance. Consider an individual who decides to save $1,000 per year for the next three years and makes the first payment exactly one year from today. Taking the present time as time 0, the payment stream appears as in the following time line:[2]

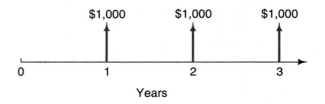

simple annuity
an annuity with the first cash flow occurring one period from now

Notice that in this three-year annuity the first payment occurs one period from the present, which makes it a **simple annuity.** If the individual were

---

[2] In a time line, an arrow pointing upward indicates a cash inflow, an arrow pointing downward indicates a cash outflow, and the horizontal position of the arrows indicates the time at which the cash flows occur.

annuity due
an annuity with the first cash flow occurring immediately

to make the first payment immediately, this would be an **annuity due.** For a three-year annuity due, the payment stream would look as follows:

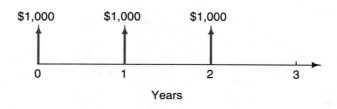

It is important to distinguish between a simple annuity and an annuity due. Notice that in our examples they both have three payments, and only the timing of the cash flows distinguishes them. In this book, if we speak of an annuity without qualification, we are discussing a simple annuity.

The Present Value of an Annuity

Often we can either pay for a service now or pay installments over time. For example, a two-year contract for a service might allow the buyer to pay $1,500 now. Alternatively, the buyer might pay $850 one year from now and another $850 two years from today. Which payment plan is better? When we must pay for a service, the basic rule is to choose the payment with the lowest present value.

☞ The present value of an annuity is the present value of all future payments that make up the annuity.

We can calculate the present value of an annuity by treating the payments as a collection of individual payments. We simply compute the present value of the individual payments and add them to find the present value of the annuity. To see how this works, let us calculate the present value of an annuity of $850 for two years with a 15 percent rate of interest:

$$PV = \frac{\$850}{1.12} + \frac{\$850}{(1.12)^2}$$

$$= \$850\left(\frac{1}{1.12} + \frac{1}{(1.12)^2}\right)$$

$$= \$850(1.6900)$$

$$= \$1,436.54$$

With a present value of $1,436.54, the purchaser should take the deferred payment plan and invest the $1,500 that is freed at 12 percent.

This was a simple calculation; we would not be so anxious to compute the present value of a 50-payment annuity. Therefore, it is convenient to have a table of present value factors for annuities. This calculation requires three pieces of information: payment, interest rate, and number of periods. Table 4.1 provides some present value factors for annuities. A more complete table is found in the Appendix.

TABLE 4.1   The Present Value of an Annuity of $1, PA(r, n)

Period (n)	Interest Rate (r)			
	1%	2%	3%	4%
1	0.9901	0.9804	0.9709	0.9615
2	1.9704	1.9416	1.9135	1.8861
3	2.9410	2.8839	2.8286	2.7751
4	3.9020	3.8077	3.7171	3.6299
5	4.8534	4.7135	4.5797	4.4518

The final term in parentheses in the above calculation is the present value factor for a two-period annuity with a 12 percent rate of interest. We define $PA(r, n)$ as the present value factor for an annuity with an r percent rate of interest per period and with n periods. In our example, $PA(12, 2) = 1.6900$. Note that the present value factor assumes a periodic payment of $1, so if we want to find the present value of an annuity with a different payment, we simply multiply the amount of the payment by the annuity factor:

$$PV = C \times PA(r, n) \tag{4.2}$$

EXAMPLE 4.2

Your Aunt Julia knows that you are a finance student and decides to test your knowledge. She offers you a choice of an $1,100 gift right now or the payment of $100 per month for 12 months beginning one month from now. If interest rates are 1 percent per month, which should you choose?

To decide, you must compare the present values of the two gifts. Clearly, the present value of the lump sum is $1,100, so we only need to find the present value of the 12 monthly payments. These constitute an annuity of 12 periods, with an interest rate of 1 percent per period. Therefore the present value of the annuity is:

$$PV = C \times PA(1, 12)$$
$$= \$100 \times 11.2551$$
$$= \$1,125.51$$

Because the present value of the stream of payments is greater, you would prefer the monthly payments, assuming Aunt Julia is reliable.

As an alternative to the present value table, we can find an explicit formula for calculating the present value of an annuity. This could be accomplished in essentially the same way as was done for perpetuities. However, rather than using brute-force mathematics, we will derive the annuity formula by using some financial intuition plus our knowledge of the perpetuity formula.

FIGURE 4.1 An Annuity as the Difference of Two Perpetuities

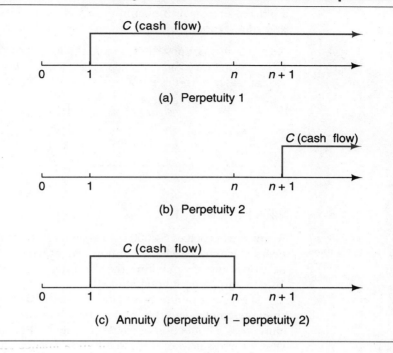

(a) Perpetuity 1

(b) Perpetuity 2

(c) Annuity (perpetuity 1 – perpetuity 2)

☞ An annuity can be valued as the difference of two perpetuities.

Figure 4.1 shows that an n-year annuity is just the difference of two perpetuities, with first cash flows at time $t = 1$ and time $t = n + 1$, respectively. It follows that the present value of an annuity is just the difference of the present values of its two component perpetuities. Thus, using Equation 4.1 we have:

$$PV = \frac{C}{r} - \frac{C}{r}(1 + r)^{-n}$$

☞ The present value of an annuity is always located one period before the first cash flow.

The n-year discount factor in the second term arises because for the perpetuity that starts at time $t = n + 1$, Equation 4.1 gives the present value at time $t = n$. Thus, it is necessary to bring the present value of the second perpetuity down to time $t = 0$. Rearranging results in the formula for the present value of an annuity:

$$PV = C\left[\frac{1 - (1 + r)^{-n}}{r}\right] \tag{4.3}$$

☞ The present value factor of an annuity, PA(r, n), is always less than the number of its component cash flows, n.

Comparing Equations 4.3 and 4.2, it is clear that the present value annuity factor for r percent and n periods, PA(r, n), is equal to:

$$PA(r, n) = \left[\frac{1 - (1 + r)^{-n}}{r}\right] \tag{4.4}$$

EXAMPLE 4.3

Find the present value annuity factor for an interest rate of 12.73 percent and nine years.

Note that it is not possible to compute this annuity factor using the present value table, since it only contains integer values for r. Nevertheless, using Equation 4.4 we can easily solve this problem:

$$PA(12.73, 9) = \left[\frac{1 - (1.1273)^{-9}}{0.1273} \right]$$

$$= 5.1836$$

The Future Value of an Annuity

☞ The future value of an annuity is the future value of all of the individual payments that make up the annuity.

A saver who places $1,000 into a savings account for each of the next three years, starting one year from now, might wonder how much the account will be worth just after making the third deposit. Assume that the account earns 10 percent, compounded annually.

We can compute the value of the account by considering each of the single payments and the interest they will earn by year three. This treats the annuity as a collection of single payments. The graph on the time line below shows the essence of the calculation.

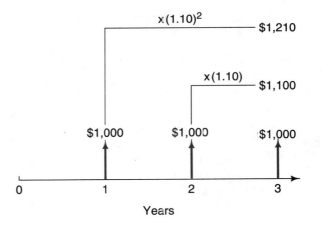

In the graph, the $1,000 at time $t = 1$ earns interest for the next two years at 10 percent. The cash flow at $t = 2$, however, can earn interest for only one year, and the final $1,000 does not earn any interest at all. We can now calculate the total future value of the three payments by simply adding the

TABLE 4.2   The Future Value of an Annuity of $1, FA(r, n)

	Interest Rate (r)			
Period (n)	1%	2%	3%	4%
1	1.0000	1.0000	1.0000	1.0000
2	2.0100	2.0200	2.0300	2.0400
3	3.0301	3.0604	3.0909	3.1216
4	4.0604	4.1216	4.1836	4.2465
5	5.1010	5.2040	5.3091	5.4163

individual future values:

$$FV = \$1{,}000(1.10)^2 + \$1{,}000(1.10) + \$1{,}000$$
$$= \$1{,}000[(1.10)^2 + (1.10) + 1]$$
$$= \$1{,}000(3.3100)$$
$$= \$3{,}310$$

Just as we did with the present value, we can construct a table for the future value of an annuity. Notice from our example that the future value at year three of a three-year simple annuity with a 10 percent rate of interest would be 3.3100 times the $1,000 payment. The 3.3100 is the future value factor of the annuity. We can collect all of these future value factors and put them into a table, as in Table 4.2 for an annuity of $1. A more extensive table is found in the Appendix.

☞ The future value factor of an annuity, FA(r, n), is always greater than the number of its component cash flows, n.

We will use the notation FA(r, n) to denote the future value factor of an annuity with a periodic interest rate of r percent and with n periods. Thus, in our example, FA(10, 3) = 3.3100.

The general expression for the future value of an annuity is:

$$FV = C \times FA(r, n) \tag{4.5}$$

EXAMPLE 4.4

An investor plans to save $1,500 per year for 25 years as a retirement fund and expects to earn 12 percent per year on all invested funds. Using the table for the future value of an annuity, calculate how much the investor will have at the end of 25 years.

To calculate the solution using the table, we have to find the factor and multiply it by the periodic contribution. The future value table in the Appendix shows that the factor is FA(12, 25) = 133.3338. The complete solution is:

$$FV = \$1{,}500 \times FA(12, 25)$$
$$= \$1{,}500 \times 133.3338 = \$200{,}000.70$$

Immediately after making the last deposit in 25 years, the investor will have $200,000.70 in the retirement fund.

Just as we did with the present value, we can find a formula for the future value of an annuity. This can be done in several ways. One way is to realize that the future value at time n can be calculated by finding its present value at $t = 0$ and compounding that present value for n periods. In other words:

$$FV = PV \times (1 + r)^n$$

Since we already know the formula for the present value, we simply multiply that expression by the n-year compound factor. Assuming the periodic payment is $\$C$ and the interest rate is r, we have:

$$FV = C\left[\frac{(1 + r)^n - 1}{r}\right] \tag{4.6}$$

Equation 4.6 provides much more flexibility than the future value table, since it is also valid for fractional interest rate values.

EXAMPLE 4.5

Find the future value of a five-year simple annuity with a $375 yearly payment with an interest rate of 7.4 percent per year.

Using the formula for the future value of an annuity, Equation 4.6, we have:

$$FV = \$375 \; \frac{(1.074)^5 - 1}{0.074}$$

$$= \$375(5.7968) = \$2,173.80$$

SOLVING FOR AN UNKNOWN INTEREST RATE

Many life insurance companies sell annuities, particularly to retirees. We can pay a lump sum now to receive an annuity, for example, of $10,000 for 10 years. If the price of this annuity were $61,450, would it be attractive? The answer depends on the implied interest rate. This section shows how to find the interest rate in such cases.

We start from the basic relationship for the present value of an annuity, Equation 4.2:

$$PV = C \times PA(r, n)$$

In our example, we know all the elements in this equation except the interest rate. Rearranging terms we have:

$$PA(r, n) = \frac{PV}{C} \tag{4.7}$$

Substituting the known values into Equation 4.7 gives:

$$PA(r, 10) = \frac{\$61,450}{\$10,000}$$

$$= 6.1450$$

To find the interest rate this annuity implies, we have to find the 6.1450 factor in the 10-year row of the present value of an annuity table in the Appendix. In this case, it lies in the column for 10 percent. Therefore, the price charged for the annuity implies an interest rate of 10 percent.

This implied interest rate has a specific meaning. If you could invest the $61,450 at 10 percent per period, you would just be able to make the payments on the annuity and have nothing left at the end of the ten years.

EXAMPLE 4.6

A four-year annuity of $1,200 costs $3,700 today. What is the implied rate of interest?

To solve this problem we substitute the known values into Equation 4.7:

$$PA(r, 4) = \frac{\$3,700}{\$1,200} = 3.0833$$

To finish the problem, we look for the 3.0833 factor in the row for four periods in the present value of an annuity table in the Appendix, and read the interest rate from the column heading. However, the value 3.0833 does not appear in the row for four periods. The closest values we find are PA(11, 4) = 3.1024 and PA(12, 4) = 3.0373. Therefore, the table cannot be used to determine the exact interest rate in this case, but we can be sure that it lies between 11 and 12 percent.[3]

For an annuity, no general formula can compute the value of the interest rate r when all other variables are known. Financial calculators can find the interest rate, but only because they use trial-and-error methods, and it takes much longer than finding any of the other time value of money variables, as you can readily verify.

SOLVING FOR AN UNKNOWN ANNUITY PAYMENT

Suppose you want to convert $1 million that you have in the bank into a seven-year annuity. With an interest rate of 8 percent, how large can each annuity payment be? To determine this, we can rearrange the terms in

---

[3] Using a financial calculator, the actual rate is 11.29 percent.

FINANCE

TODAY

Home, Sweet Home: Part I

The standard home mortgage calls for 360 monthly payments of equal amounts over 30 years, which constitutes a simple annuity. Consider a fairly typical mortgage of $100,000, and assume that the stated rate of interest is 12 percent. This mortgage requires payments of $1,028.61 each month. Many lenders use a rule of thumb requiring that the payment be no more than 28 percent of the homeowner's before-tax income. For this mortgage, a monthly income of $3,673.61 ($1,028.61/0.28), or an annual income of $44,083, would be required. For this homeowner, the $100,000 will earn 1 percent interest, or $1,000, during the first month the mortgage is owed. Consider the homeowner's position after one month (one payment of $1,028.61):

Payment	Interest	Principal Payment	Balance Owed
$1,028.61	$1,000.00	$28.61	$99,971.39

Only $28.61, or less than 3 percent of the $1,028.61 payment, actually went toward repaying the loan. This means that during the life of the loan, the homeowner will pay a total of $370,299.60, including interest of $270,299.60. The interest paid is 2.7 times the principal amount.

Faced with these facts, which are normal for home mortgages, consider the effect of differences in interest rates on the size of the payment and, therefore, a person's ability to afford a home with a $100,000 mortgage, as shown in the first three columns of the table below. As interest rates change, the monthly payment changes dramatically. For example, if interest rates fall as low as 8 percent, the monthly payment is only $733.76 and

Equation 4.2 to solve for the payment C:

$$C = \frac{PV}{PA(r,\ n)} \tag{4.8}$$

We can use Equation 4.8 to find the maximum annuity that the $1 million will support. In our example, $PA(8,\ 7) = 5.20637$. Thus,

$$C = \frac{\$1,000,000}{5.20637} = \$192,072.40$$

The problem can be interpreted as follows. If we invest the $1 million at 8 percent and withdraw $192,072.40 at the end of each of the next seven years, the last withdrawal will leave a 0 balance in the account. Table 4.3

the required annual income is only $31,447. This is almost one-third less than our original example of 12 percent interest. On the other hand, if interest rates are as high as 16 percent, the monthly payment is $1,344.76 and the required annual income is $57,633.

Another way to see the effect of interest rates on homeowners is to consider how much mortgage a given income can support. The last column of the table shows the maximum mortgage that a $40,000 annual income can sustain for different interest rates. Looking at the problem this way gives another picture. It shows, in effect, how the quality of the house you can afford is affected by interest rates. With an interest rate of 8 percent, a $40,000 income can support a mortgage of $127,198. If interest rates are 16 percent, the maximum mortgage is $69,405. It is clear from these calculations that the prevailing mortgage rates can dramatically affect your standard of living.

Interest Rate	Monthly Payment for a $100,000 Mortgage	Income Required to Pay a $100,000 Mortgage	Maximum Mortgage for $40,000 Income
8%	$ 733.76	$31,447	$127,198
9	804.62	34,484	115,996
10	877.57	37,610	106,354
11	952.32	40,814	98,006
12	1,028.61	44,083	90,737
13	1,106.20	47,409	84,373
14	1,184.87	50,780	78,771
15	1,264.44	54,190	73,814
16	1,344.76	57,633	69,405

TABLE 4.3   How $1,000,000 Supports an Annuity
($r = 8\%$; $n = 7$ years)

Time	Payment	Interest	Principal Reduction	Balance
0	N.A.	N.A.	N.A.	$1,000,000.00
1	$192,072.40	$80,000.00	$112,072.40	887,927.60
2	192,072.40	71,034.21	121,038.19	766,889.41
3	192,072.40	61,351.15	130,721.25	636,168.16
4	192,072.40	50,893.45	141,178.95	494,989.21
5	192,072.40	39,599.14	152,473.26	342,515.95
6	192,072.40	27,401.28	164,671.12	177,844.83
7	192,072.40	14,227.59	177,844.81	0.02

illustrates this solution in more detail. Each year some of the payment goes to pay the remaining principal and some goes to pay interest. At the beginning, a large portion goes for interest, but that becomes smaller as time progresses and the principal is repaid. Since the sum of interest and principal totals $192,072.40, the principal portion of the annuity increases each year. Finally, at the end of the seventh year the debt is completely paid, except for a negligible rounding error that may occur.

EXAMPLE 4.7

Joe's parents have given him an amount sufficient to generate 50 monthly payments of $500 for a college education, knowing that Joe can earn an interest rate of 1 percent per month in his savings account. However, Joe decides to spend $4,598 of that money on a used car right away. What monthly payment can the remaining amount generate over the next 50 months?

First, we find the required lump sum payment, to the nearest dollar:

$$PV = C \times PA(1,\ 50)$$
$$= \$500 \times 39.1961 = \$19,598$$

After buying the car, Joe has $15,000 left in his savings account. We can now find the monthly payment using Equation 4.8:

$$C = \frac{\$15,000}{PA(1,\ 50)}$$

$$= \frac{\$15,000}{39.1961} = \$382.69$$

Obviously, Joe is going to be living on a tight budget and hope the car does not break down.

THE NUMBER OF PERIODS OF AN ANNUITY

In some cases, both the amount available to fund an annuity and the size of the annuity payments are fixed. For example, assume a retiree has $85,000 and needs $10,000 per year to live. If annual interest rates are 9 percent, how long will the funds last? We can solve this problem by using Equation 4.2, the basic relationship for the present value of an annuity:

$$PV = C \times PA(r,\ n)$$

In this case, we have all the necessary values except the number of periods that the annuity will last. Substituting these known values gives:

$$\$85,000 = \$10,000 \times PA(9,\ n)$$

Isolating the unknown annuity factor, we obtain:

$$PA(9, n) = \frac{\$85,000}{\$10,000} = 8.5000$$

To find the solution, we consult the present value of an annuity table in the Appendix and search in the 9 percent column for the factor that equals 8.5000. In the table we find $PA(9, 16) = 8.3126$ and $PA(9, 17) = 8.5436$. Therefore, we conclude that funds will be available for 16 years, with a little money left over.

We can find the exact number of periods until money runs out by recalling that the present value of an annuity is also given by Equation 4.3. Solving this expression for the number of periods, n, gives:

$$n = \frac{\ln\left(\dfrac{C}{C - PV \times r}\right)}{\ln(1 + r)} \tag{4.9}$$

Applying Equation 4.9 to the retiree problem gives:

$$n = \frac{\ln\left(\dfrac{\$10,000}{\$10,000 - \$85,000 \times 0.09}\right)}{\ln(1 + 0.09)}$$

$$= \frac{1.44817}{0.08618} = 16.80 \text{ years}$$

EXAMPLE 4.8

Returning to Joe, our college student who really needs a car, consider this possible solution to his lack of funds: purchase the car, leaving $15,000 in the college account, go to school spending $500 a month until the money runs out, and then beg his parents for more. By that time, graduation might be near and Joe hopes his parents will be willing to kick in some more money. If interest rates are 1 percent per month, how long will this $500 annuity last?

Using Equation 4.9 we have:

$$n = \frac{\ln\left(\dfrac{\$500}{\$500 - \$15,000 \times 0.01}\right)}{\ln(1 + 0.01)}$$

$$= \frac{0.35667}{0.00995} = 35.85 \text{ months}$$

Joe can plan on using his persuasion skills in less than three years.

FINANCE

TODAY

Home, Sweet Home: Part II

Prospective homeowners usually have the option of choosing a combination of mortgage rate and points. The higher the mortgage rate, the lower the points, where one point is equal to 1 percent of the initial mortgage amount. Thus, if a $100,000 mortgage calls for a payment of two points at the time of closing, the borrower must pay $2,000 at that time.

Faced with various rate/points alternatives, which one should the future homeowner choose? In intuitive terms, it shouldn't make much difference in a sophisticated home mortgage market—if one of the alternatives is clearly superior, all borrowers would choose it, and the others would vanish quickly. Conversely, banks would probably design the various combinations in such a way that they are roughly equivalent. To study this conjecture, consider an $80,000 mortgage, and assume that the homeowner will stay in the house for five years and has an annual cost of money of 12 percent. Furthermore, assume that when the house is sold the homeowner will receive a cash flow equal to the accumulated equity in the house. In other words, the price of the house in five years will be the same as today's price. The homeowner pays the points at the time of closing on the loan, makes 60 equal monthly payments, and in 60 months will receive the cash from the equity in the house. Notice that we are disregarding the down payment, because it will be the same regardless of which alternative is chosen.

The table below gives the present values for three alternative rate/points strategies from the point of view of the homeowner.

Rate/Points	Payment	Points	Equity*	PV(PMT + equity)[†]	PV(total)[†]
10.25/2	$716.88	$1,600	$2,615.82	$30,787.49	$32,387.49
10.00/3	702.06	2,400	2,740.24	30,052.77	32,452.77
9.50/5	672.68	4,000	3,007.60	28,584.82	32,584.82

* The equity accumulated in the house is equal to $80,000 minus the present value of all remaining payments.
[†] The homeowner's annual discount rate is assumed to be 12 percent, or 1 percent per month.

As the last column of the table indicates, the range in total present values for the alternatives considered is relatively small—about $200. Thus, the analysis suggests that in an efficient mortgage market, one alternative has little advantage over another. In practice, the amount of the advantage will vary according to the homeowners' cost of money.

VALUING AN ANNUITY DUE

We previously noted that an n-year simple annuity makes its first payment one year from the present, whereas an n-year annuity due makes its first payment immediately. However, both have n payments. This section shows how to value annuities due.

We could derive the formulas for an annuity due in a similar manner as we did for simple annuities. Instead, we will use our knowledge of the formulas for simple annuities and some financial reasoning.

Suppose the first cash flow of the annuity due occurs now, at time $t = 0$. Then, the present value of an n-year annuity due of $\$C$ with an annual interest rate of r percent may be found by recognizing that it becomes an n-year simple annuity when viewed from time $t = -1$. Metaphorically, if you look into the future while standing at time $t = -1$, you see n equal payments, the first one at $t = 0$. This means that at time $t = -1$, the present value of the annuity due is equal to the present value of an n-year simple annuity. Since we are interested in the present value of the annuity due at time $t = 0$, not at time $t = -1$, we compound the value of the simple annuity for one period, from $t = -1$ to $t = 0$, to obtain its present value at time $t = 0$. All this means that:[4]

$$PV_{\text{annuity due}} = PV_{\text{simple annuity}} \times (1 + r) \qquad (4.10)$$

The future value of an n-year annuity due as of time $t = n$ is found using a similar reasoning. Since we now know that an n-year annuity due that starts at $t = 0$ is equivalent to an n-year simple annuity with its origin at $t = -1$, it follows that the future value of the n-year annuity due at time $t = n - 1$ is equal to the future value of the n-year simple annuity, also at time $t = n - 1$. To find the future value of the annuity due at time $t = n$, all we have to do is compound the future value of the simple annuity for one more period. This implies that the future value of an n-year annuity due at time $t = n$ is:

$$FV_{\text{annuity due}} = FV_{\text{simple annuity}} \times (1 + r) \qquad (4.11)$$

☞ The value of an annuity due equals the value of the equivalent simple annuity, compounded for one period.

Notice from Equations 4.10 and 4.11 that, whether we are finding the present value or the future value of an annuity due, the same basic formula applies: to find the value of an annuity due just compound the value of the equivalent simple annuity for one period.

EXAMPLE 4.9

Compute the present and future values of a five-year annuity due, with 8 percent annual interest rate and a $300 yearly payment.

---

[4] There is at least another way we could find the expression relating the present values of both types of annuities. Consider the cash flows from $t = 1$ to $t = n - 1$ as an $(n - 1)$-year simple annuity. Find the present value of this annuity and add the payment at $t = 0$ to get the total value of the annuity due.

First, we compute the present and future values of the equivalent simple annuity. Using the formulas derived previously, we have:

$$PV = \$300 \times PA(8, 5) = \$300 \times 3.9927 = \$1,197.81$$

Similarly, the future value of the same simple annuity is:[5]

$$FV = \$300 \times FA(8, 5) = \$300 \times 5.8666 = \$1,759.98$$

It is now an easy matter to determine the present and future values of the annuity due using Equations 4.10 and 4.11:

$$PV = \$1,197.81(1.08) = \$1,293.63$$
$$FV = \$1,759.98(1.08) = \$1,900.78$$

An alternative way to obtain the future value of the annuity due is to compound its present value at 8 percent for five years:

$$FV = \$1,293.63(1.08)^5 = \$1,900.78$$

In general, the present and future values of a given annuity due are related through the following expression:

$$FV_{\text{annuity due}} = PV_{\text{annuity due}} \times (1 + r)^n \qquad (4.12)$$

More important than memorizing this or any other formula is to understand the reasoning behind it. Equation 4.12 follows from the fact that we can substitute the annuity due for a single cash flow at time $t = 0$ equal to the present value of the annuity. To obtain the future value of this single cash flow at time n, we know from Chapter 3 that we must compound it for n years at the appropriate interest rate, r.

THE PRESENT VALUE OF A GROWING PERPETUITY

growing perpetuity
an infinite stream of regular cash flows growing at a constant rate

A **growing perpetuity** is an infinite stream of regular cash flows that grow at a constant rate each period. If the cash flow growth rate is g percent per period, and the cash flow at time t is denoted by D_t, then we have the following relationship:

$$D_t = D_{t-1}(1 + g) \qquad (4.13)$$

As with any cash flow stream, the present value of a growing perpetuity is just the sum of the present values of the individual cash flows. Thus, using

[5] Recall from the previous discussion that the present value of the simple annuity is located at time $t = -1$. Similarly, the future value of the simple annuity is located at time $t = 4$.

Equation 4.13 we have:

$$PV = \frac{D}{(1 + r)} + \frac{D_2}{(1 + r)^2} + \frac{D_3}{(1 + r)^3} + \cdots$$

$$= \frac{D_1}{(1 + r)} + \frac{D_1(1 + g)}{(1 + r)^2} + \frac{D_1(1 + g)^2}{(1 + r)^3} \cdots$$

$$= \frac{D_1}{(1 + r)}\left[1 + \frac{1 + g}{1 + r} + \left(\frac{1 + g}{1 + r}\right)^2 + \cdots \right]$$

The infinite summation in brackets is a geometric series that adds up to $(1 + r)/(r - g)$. Using this expression and simplifying gives the desired formula for a growing perpetuity:

$$PV = \frac{D_1}{r - g} \tag{4.14}$$

Two important facts should be remembered when using the growing perpetuity formula. First, the cash payment to be used in the numerator is next period's payment, D_1. Second, the formula can be used only when the discount rate is strictly greater than the cash flow growth rate. That is, it is valid only when $r > g$.

EXAMPLE 4.10

The cash flow generated by Boone Enterprises is expected to grow at a rate of 5 percent per year, forever. Next year's cash flow is expected to be $45,000. If the annual discount rate for Boone is 14 percent, find Boone's current value.

We are given next year's cash flow and the discount rate is greater than the growth rate, so we can use the growing perpetuity formula. A direct application of Equation 4.14 gives:

$$PV = \frac{\$45,000}{0.14 - 0.05} = \$500,000$$

THE PRESENT VALUE OF A GROWING ANNUITY

growing annuity
a finite stream of regular cash flows growing at a constant rate

A **growing annuity** is a finite stream of regular cash flows that grow at a constant rate each period. Just as an annuity can be viewed as a truncated perpetuity, a growing annuity can be thought of as a truncated growing perpetuity. This links the valuation of a growing annuity to the value of a growing perpetuity. The derivation follows in a parallel fashion to our derivation of the annuity formula from the perpetuity formula.

INTERNATIONAL PERSPECTIVES

LDC Debt Rescheduling: Less Is More

Many less developed countries (LDCs) are in big trouble; they don't seem to be able to pay their debt obligations on time. After the shock of Mexico's debt repayment suspension in August 1982, many banks started to look for ways to make debt rescheduling that would not overburden the LDCs.

The arrangement through which countries reschedule existing loans into the future is called a multi-year restructuring agreement, or MYRA. A good example was the Mexican MYRA signed in March 1985.* Under this agreement, a $5 billion loan made by 526 commercial banks in 1983 was restructured along with 52 previous loans totaling $23.6 billion. Basically, these 53 loans were repackaged into a new "loan." At the same time, a number of other contractual terms, such as interest rates, were also changed. We now show that, contrary to popular belief, the lenders accepting the restructuring can still reap benefits, even when the interest rate on the new loan is lowered.

Consider a country that currently ($t = 0$) has a loan outstanding from an international banking syndicate. The face value of the loan is $100 million, with a maturity of two years and $50 million in principal payment amortization (A) due in each of the next two years. The loan rate is 10 percent, and the interest charges are represented by I. If the discount rate for the banks is 8 percent, then:

$$PV_0 = \frac{50 + 10}{1.08} + \frac{50 + 5}{1.08^2} = \$102.71 \text{ million}$$

Now suppose that soon after the loan is made, the LDC unexpectedly finds these repayment terms and dates burdensome and asks the banks for a MYRA to avoid defaulting on the original loan. Let us assume that the

---

☞ A growing annuity can be valued as the difference of two growing perpetuities.

The present value of an n-year growing annuity can be found by referring to Figure 4.2. There, it is graphically seen that the growing annuity can be decomposed into the difference of two growing perpetuities: one with the first cash flow at time $t = 1$, minus the other with its first cash flow at time $t = n + 1$. This means that the present value of the growing annuity at $t = 0$ is the difference of the present values of the two growing perpetuities:

$$PV = \frac{D_1}{r - g} - \frac{D_{n+1}}{r - g}(1 + r)^{-n}$$

Since cash flows grow at a rate of g percent per period, we have $D_{n+1} = D_1(1 + g)^n$. Using this result and rearranging gives the formula for a

banks agree to a new amortization schedule of four years, beginning in Year 3. Thus, the country will pay $25 million in each of those four years.

Assume that the LDC will keep up interest payments on the original $100 million even during the grace period, but that the interest rate is lowered from 10 percent to 9 percent. Those who just analyze interest rate spreads might argue that this is a concession that will ease the borrower's burden. However, this is not a foregone conclusion; it actually depends on the present value of the new deal compared to the present value of the old deal.

The last part of the restructuring deals with the administrative costs involved in a MYRA, which are passed on to the borrower. Assume that this fee is $1 million. Thus, the present value of the restructured loan is:

$$PV_R = 1 + \frac{9}{1.08} + \frac{9}{1.08^2} + \frac{25 + 9}{1.08^3} + \frac{25 + 6.75}{1.08^4} + \frac{25 + 4.5}{1.08^5} + \frac{25 + 2.25}{1.08^6}$$

$$= \$104.63 \text{ million}$$

Although it looks as if the bank has made a concession by cutting the interest rate on the loan, the effects of the fee, the grace period, and the revised amortization schedule, as well as the bank's discount rate, combine to increase the present value of the loan from the bank's perspective. The present value framework clearly shows that the financial burden of the MYRA may be favorable to the lender even when the lender lowers the interest rate on the loan.

* See "MYRA Makes the Years Roll By," *Euromoney*, October 1985, p. 29.

Source: Anthony Saunders and Marti Subrahmanyam, "LDC Debt Rescheduling: Calculating Who Gains, Who Loses," *Federal Reserve Bank of Philadelphia Business Review* November/ December 1988, pp. 13–23; reproduced in *The International Finance Reader*, edited by Robert W. Kolb (Miami: Kolb Publishing Co., 1991), pp. 107–116.

growing annuity:

$$PV = \frac{D_1}{r - g}\left[1 - \left(\frac{1 + g}{1 + r}\right)^n\right] \tag{4.15}$$

Equation 4.15 is valid not only when $r > g$, but also when $r < g$. This is in contrast to the growing perpetuity formula, which is valid only for $r > g$. However, Equation 4.15 cannot be used in the special situation in which $r = g$.[6] In that case, to find the present value of the growing annuity we have

[6] This should be clear by noting that when $r = g$, we would have to divide by 0, which is never allowed. Alternatively, we would have an expression of the form 0/0, which is indeterminate. (0/0 is not 0, nor is it 1.)

FIGURE 4.2 A Growing Annuity as the Difference of Two Growing Perpetuities

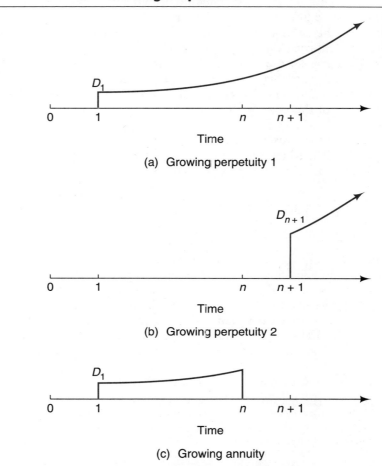

(a) Growing perpetuity 1

(b) Growing perpetuity 2

(c) Growing annuity

to make use of the foolproof method of adding all the present values of the individual cash flows. This gives:

$$
\begin{aligned}
\text{PV} &= \frac{D_1}{(1+r)} + \frac{D_2}{(1+r)^2} + \cdots + \frac{D_n}{(1+r)^n} \\
&= \frac{D_1}{1+r}\left[1 + \frac{1+g}{1+r} + \cdots + \left(\frac{1+g}{1+r}\right)^{n-1}\right]
\end{aligned}
$$

Since $r = g$ by assumption, each term in brackets is equal to 1. Since there are n such terms within the brackets, the formula for a growing annuity when the discount rate equals the cash flow growth rate is given by:

$$PV = \frac{D_1 n}{1 + r} \tag{4.16}$$

EXAMPLE 4.11

Ruth works at Rey Burger and expects her annual salary to grow steadily at 5 percent per year for the next 10 years, when she plans to retire. Her current salary, which has just been paid, is $30,000. If Ruth can earn 12 percent on her investments, what is the present value of her remaining salaries?

First, we have to compute next year's salary. Since it will be 5 percent greater than this year's salary, then $D_1 = \$30,000 \times 1.05 = \$31,500$. Since $r > g$, to compute the present value of the growing annuity we use Equation 4.15:

$$PV = \frac{\$31,500}{0.12 - 0.05}\left[1 - \left(\frac{1.05}{1.12}\right)^{10}\right] = \$213,992.79$$

What would be the present value of Ruth's future salaries if she earns only 5 percent annually on her investments?

In this case $r = g$, so we must use Equation 4.16:

$$PV = \frac{\$31,500 \times 10}{1.05} = \$300,000$$

We can interpret these present values as follows. If Ruth can earn 12 percent on her money, with $213,992.79 invested today she could withdraw annual amounts equal to her future salaries and have nothing left after the tenth withdrawal. If she earns only 5 percent, however, she must invest $300,000 today to be able to make annual withdrawals equal to her future salaries and have nothing left over at the end. In effect, the lower rate of interest must be compensated by investing a greater amount now.

SUMMARY

In this chapter we covered the time value of a series of payments. We began by calculating the present value of a perpetuity. Then we differentiated between simple annuities and annuities due, and noted that the only difference between them is the timing of the payments.

We learned how to calculate the present and future values of both simple annuities and annuities due. We also discussed the techniques for determining how large an annuity a given lump sum finances over a specified period. We then learned how to calculate the number of periods a given lump sum lasts if it pays a specific annuity amount, and showed how to find the payment necessary to generate a given annuity.

Finally, we discussed the valuation of growing perpetuities and growing annuities. The latter are very useful in dealing with problems relating to the typical lifetime earnings pattern.

QUESTIONS

1. What happens to the present value of a perpetuity as the interest rate grows larger?
2. If the present value of a perpetuity at time $t = 0$ is $200, what is its present value at $t = 2$? At $t = 5$? At $t = 100$? Explain.
3. What happens to the present value of an annuity as the interest rate gets larger?
4. What happens to the future value of an annuity as the interest rate gets larger?
5. Consider two annuities for six periods with an interest rate of 11 percent. One annuity is for $100 and the other is for $200. What can you say about the present value of the two annuities?
6. Consider two annuities for six periods with an interest rate of 11 percent. One annuity is for $100 and the other is for $200. What can you say about the future value of the two annuities?
7. Which will have a greater present value, other things being equal, an annuity due or a simple annuity? Explain.
8. Which will have a greater future value, other things being equal, an annuity due or a simple annuity? Explain.
9. Explain how to find the present value of an annuity if you do not know any of the principles about valuing annuities.
10. Show that $PA(r, n) < n$, for any positive value of r.
11. Write the formula for a growing perpetuity in terms of the current cash flow, not next year's cash flow.
12. Why is it absurd to use the formula for a growing perpetuity when the growth rate is greater than the discount rate?
13. We provided a formula for the present value of a growing annuity. However, no formula for the future value of a growing perpetuity was given. Nevertheless, the future value can be found by a simple adaptation of the present value formula. Explain how this may be done.

PROBLEMS

1. Find the future value of an annuity with a payment of $55 per period, five periods, and an interest rate of 7.5 percent.
2. Find the future value of an annuity with a payment of $20 per period, four periods, and an interest rate of 10.5 percent.
3. Find the present value of an annuity with a payment of $55 per period, five periods, and an interest rate of 7.5 percent.

4. Find the present value of an annuity with a payment of $515 per period, two periods, and an interest rate of 17.5 percent.
5. Find the future value of an annuity due with a payment of $55 per period, five periods, and an interest rate of 7.5 percent.
6. Find the future value of an annuity due with a payment of $20 per period, four periods, and an interest rate of 10.5 percent.
7. Find the present value of an annuity due with a payment of $55 per period, five periods, and an interest rate of 7.5 percent.
8. Find the present value of an annuity due with a payment of $515 per period, two periods, and an interest rate of 17.5 percent.
9. Calculate the present value of an annuity factor for three periods and an interest rate of 13.5 percent.
10. Calculate the future value of an annuity factor for four periods and an interest rate of 9.5 percent.
11. Would you prefer to make four annual payments of $100 or five annual payments of $85 if the interest rate is 12 percent?
12. Would you prefer to receive four annual payments of $100 or five annual payments of $85 if the interest rate is 12 percent?
13. Your life insurance agent offers you an annuity of $1,000 that you will receive every year for the next 12 years if you pay $3,498 now. What interest rate does this imply?
14. Your life insurance agent offers you an annuity of $1,000 to be paid every year for 12 years, but the first payment will be paid 4 years from today. If the interest rate is 7 percent, how much should this annuity cost today?
15. You received $100,000 as a signing bonus from your first employer. You plan to use this money to buy a 20-year annuity at a rate of 12 percent. How much will you receive each year?
16. For the same $100,000 with an interest rate of 12 percent, how long will your annuity run if you require $20,000 per year as your payment?
17. Consider the following cash flows:

Year	Cash Flow
1	$1,500
2	900
3	600
4	600

Find the present value of this cash flow stream, assuming an interest rate of 8 percent.
18. A bond with 10 years until maturity pays an annual coupon of $90 and will also pay $1,000 at maturity. What is the price of the bond if the interest rate is 11 percent?

19. A bond with 10 years and 1 minute until maturity has a par value of $1,000 and pays an annual coupon of $90. (In other words, it has a total of 11 coupon payments remaining, the first to be paid immediately.) What is the price of the bond if the interest rate is 11 percent?

20. If you put $2,000 every year in your savings account earning 12 percent, how long will it be before you have $50,000?

21. If you put $2,000 in your savings account every year and it earns only 8 percent each year, how long will it be before you have $50,000?

22. Congratulations, you have just won $10 million in the lottery! However, the actual payment will be made in 20 equal annual installments, the first one to be received immediately. In present value terms, how much have you really won, assuming that you can earn 7 percent per year on your money?

23. Continuing with the lottery problem, suppose the lottery organization can invest its funds at an annual rate of 12 percent. How much money must it set aside in order to pay your prize? In other words, how much money does the $10 million prize really cost them?

24. Jose Cangordo, a famous baseball player, has just signed a five-year contract for a total of $25 million. Cangordo will receive equal annual payments, starting one year from now. Included in the total figure is an immediate signing bonus of $2 million. If he can earn 10 percent on his money, how much is this deal worth today?

25. If you save 10 percent of your salary every year, and your salary increases by 6 percent annually, how many times your current salary will you have at the end of 20 years? Assume that you earn 8 percent annual interest over the entire period.

26. You currently have $20,000 in your savings account. One year from today you withdraw $2,000. Each year thereafter you withdraw 5 percent more than the previous year, for a total of 10 withdrawals. How much money is left in the savings account just after the final withdrawal? Assume 10 percent interest.

27. Construct a table (called an amortization schedule) to determine the amount of interest and principal you will pay if you take out a $2,500 loan with your banker. The annual interest rate on the loan is 15 percent, and it should be paid in four equal annual installments.

28. If you pay $300 per month on a loan with a 12 percent nominal annual interest, how many dollars of the very last installment go to pay the principal?

29. You make equal annual payments on a loan. If the interest portion of your last payment is one-fifth of the entire payment, what is the interest rate on the loan?

30. Find an expression for the present value today of a perpetuity paying $C each year, starting n years from today, if the discount rate is r percent.

31. Carmen Fleure wants to be remembered as a charitable person. To that effect, she wants to build a trust account by depositing $10,000

each year for the next few years, starting one year from now. The account is to pay $10,000 to charity in perpetuity, starting one year after her last annual contribution. Show that the only way in which this can be done is if the interest rate on the account (r) and the number of deposits she makes (n) are related as follows: $(1 + r)^n = 2$.

32. A gold mine is being depleted in such a way that the cash flow it generates each year is 4 percent lower than the previous year. If the mine is expected to generate $200,000 next year, how much is it worth today? Assume an interest rate of 13 percent.

33. Find an expression for the present value of a growing perpetuity with the first cash flow occurring n years from today.

34. A perpetual subscription to *Newstimes* magazine costs $250 (such subscriptions have actually been offered by some magazines in the past). A yearly subscription costs only $25. Whichever route you choose, you will subscribe immediately. If you are indifferent as to the two alternatives, what is your annual rate of interest? Disregard inflation.

35. Insulating your home costs $5,000, but it will save you 200 kilowatt-hours (kWh) of energy each month. Each kWh currently costs $0.10, but the cost per kWh is rising each month. If you earn 1 percent per month on your money, what is the minimum monthly inflation rate that makes insulating a smart investment? Assume the savings from insulating last forever.

36. A car dealer offers 0 percent financing on a new car with a price tag of $15,000. However, a down payment is required, and you must pay in 24 equal monthly payments. If the dealer can normally earn 1 percent per month on its money, how much down payment is required so that the 0 percent financing gimmick is equivalent to a cash discount of $1,000 on the car?

37. Show that the present value of a growing perpetuity grows at the same rate as the cash flow growth rate, g. In other words, show that $PV_t = PV_{t-1} \times (1 + g)$.

PART 2

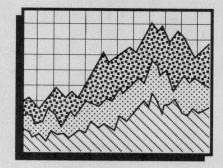

THE BUSINESS ENVIRONMENT AND FINANCIAL INTERMEDIATION

CHAPTER 5

Forms of Business Organizations and the Tax Environment

This chapter begins with a discussion of three forms of business organizations—sole proprietorships, partnerships, and corporations. Although we focus mainly on corporations, a survey of the other two types will allow us to compare their advantages and disadvantages.

We then review taxation and discuss the different tax rules that apply to individuals and to corporations. Tax rules are critically important, as they affect the decision-making process of individuals and business firms alike.

BUSINESS ORGANIZATIONS

This section discusses the three major business organizations in the United States. Each has advantages and disadvantages.

Sole Proprietorship

sole proprietorship
a business owned by a single individual

As the name implies, a **sole proprietorship** is a business owned by a single individual. These firms range from gardening services to drugstores, and are limited in size only by the wealth of the owner. Most tend to be small, relative to major corporations, but their size is compensated by their large numbers in the economy. Sole proprietorships make up about 80 percent of the businesses in the United States; however, they make only about 10 percent of business sales. Perhaps the reason is that many of the successful ones eventually become corporations.

☞ A sole proprietorship is easy to begin, but it subjects the proprietor to unlimited liability.

Sole proprietorships have several special advantages and disadvantages, as summarized in Table 5.1. One advantage is that control rests in the hands of a single individual, making it easy to decide on, and set a course for, the firm. In addition, this person receives all of the profits.

Another advantage is that a sole proprietorship is easy to create, and does not require the much higher level of legal effort that goes into creating a corporation. The business is also easy to dissolve. Because it has no other claimants to its profits, it may simply be shut down and the creditors paid, with the owner going off with any remaining funds. A final advantage stems from tax treatment. For tax purposes, all proceeds are treated as the owner's personal income and therefore are taxed only once at the personal level. As we will see later, corporations sometimes must pay taxes at the levels of the firm and of the individual stockholder.

FINANCE TODAY

Smoke, Mirrors, and Taxes

It should be easy to figure out how much a company pays in federal taxes, right? Well, maybe. Consider the case of General Motors a few years ago. Tax Analysts, a research group, figured that GM had a negative federal tax burden of $1.9 billion on U.S. profits of $307 million in 1987, for an effective rate of minus 633 percent. A rival corporate-tax watcher, the Nader-backed Citizens for Tax Justice, said GM qualified for a $742 million refund, on profits of $2.4 billion, for a tax rate of minus 31 percent. GM itself said it paid $73 million in 1987.

Calculating effective corporate tax rates is a messy business. Messy, but politically important. Congress toughened corporate minimum taxes in 1986 because companies like General Electric and General Dynamics weren't paying some people's idea of a "fair" share.

But tax burdens are as much a matter of interpretation as of accounting facts. Corporate taxes are surrounded by a lot of confusion, which is compounded by the fact that corporations don't release their tax returns. They do, however, publish tantalizing details about their tax bills in footnotes to their income statements. From these footnotes it is possible to make intelligent guesses about actual taxes paid. Tax Analysts also got help from some unpublished GM data.

What can an outsider do? For starters, you can ignore the "provision for income taxes" that appears on the income statement. That number bears little relation to the size of the check sent to the IRS. For one thing, it includes state and foreign income taxes. For another, it includes money set aside for taxes that will be due in later years but that relate to profits made this year. For example, if GM takes fast depreciation on its tax return, it will lower its tax payments this year but have less depreciation—

unlimited liability
the principle that holds an owner of a business responsible for losses exceeding the value of the firm

The most important disadvantage of a sole proprietorship is **unlimited liability**. Because the firm is treated as the personal possession of the owner, its obligations also are those of the owner. In other words, the business and its owner cannot be separated from a legal perspective. If the business fails, leaving large debts, the creditors may be able to seize the owner's personal assets even if they were never used in the business. Because of its small size

TABLE 5.1   Advantages and Disadvantages of Sole Proprietorships

Advantages	Disadvantages
Ownership of all profits	Unlimited liability
Easy to create and to dissolve	Small size
Tax savings	Difficulty acquiring new funds

and therefore higher taxes—in a later year. GM handles this by reporting in its provision for income taxes the amount it pays immediately plus an additional sum for deferred taxes. The deferred taxes aren't sent to Washington right away; they are tucked away in a reserve.

Now turn to the footnotes. General Motors reported that its current federal tax for 1987 was minus $1.3 billion, meaning it got the equivalent of a refund for that amount. This figure does not include any of the reserves for deferred taxes. Furthermore, it doesn't necessarily equal the bottom line on GM's tax return, but it comes closer than the provision for income taxes number in the income statement.

The current figure seems like a good one to use for true taxes paid, but different groups using the same footnotes come up with different numbers for effective tax rates. One reason is the GM finance subsidiary that finances cars. Citizens for Tax Justice included that subsidiary's results in its tax numbers, but Tax Analysts did not. General Motors' annual report does not, although GM did file a consolidated return with the finance subsidiary. Thus, the $1.3 billion refund probably appears nowhere on GM's tax return, on which the car operations and the finance subsidiary are lumped together.

Why didn't Tax Analysts report GM's tax burden as minus $1.3 billion, the figure in the footnotes? In essence, there were some tax savings that could reasonably have been assigned either to tax year 1987 or to an earlier year. Tax Analysts decided to assign them to 1987. So what is the $73 million figure that GM reported as its true tax burden for 1987? Well, the company refuses to say just what the number represents or how it was calculated.

Source: Laura Saunders, "One Company's Taxes," *Forbes,* January 9, 1989, p. 298.

a sole proprietorship faces difficulty growing. Even with good growth opportunities, it requires additional funds. For example, the owner of a restaurant with one location might wish to establish a second restaurant, but may not have money available to do so. Thus, the only source of additional funds will be loans, but many lenders are hesitant to lend too much to a single individual, even if that individual is running a successful business. This difficulty can often limit the growth and the success of a sole proprietorship.

Partnership

partnership
an organization of two or more persons for the purpose of engaging in business

A **partnership** is an organization of two or more persons for the purpose of engaging in a particular line of business. It is a common organization for a small business, although some very large firms are partnerships. For example, large accounting and investment banking firms often have more than 100 partners.

TABLE 5.2   Advantages and Disadvantages of Partnerships

Advantages	Disadvantages

Easy to attract talent and wealth
Incentive of future ownership to
   outstanding employees
Easy to grow and expand
Chance for better credit standing
	The firm dissolves with the death of
	   a partner
	Hard to withdraw funds
	Opportunity for dispute and ill will
	   among partners

general partner
a partner with unlimited liability

limited partnership
a partnership with one or more limited partners

limited partner
a partner with limited liability, usually taking no active role in the management of the firm

Partners are either general or limited partners. A **general partner** bears unlimited liability for the firm's obligations. If the business has only general partners, each one bears unlimited liability. A **limited partnership** has at least one **limited partner,** an individual who invests in the firm but is specially designated as having limited liability. The most that a limited partner can lose from the partnership is the amount invested. Usually, a limited partner takes no active role in managing the partnership. Every partnership must have at least one general partner, so that some individual always has unlimited liability for the firm's performance.

The partnership has several advantages and disadvantages, summarized in Table 5.2. One advantage is that it can bring the talents and wealth of more than one individual to the business. Banks and other potential creditors may be more willing to lend money to it than they would be to a sole proprietor. In addition, a partnership may expand by offering partner status to other individuals, such as particularly good employees. This provides a way for the firm to grow and motivation for employees to excel in their work.

On the other hand, when a partner dies or leaves, the partnership is legally dissolved. This can be particularly troublesome in partnerships with only two people. In some cases, it can even mean that the firm must use its assets to pay the beneficiaries of the deceased partner. It also may be difficult to withdraw wealth from the partnership. Finally, antagonistic disputes often arise among partners over their respective contributions. In short, there is some truth to the television image of once-friendly partners going at each other's throats.

The Corporation

corporation
a business owned by stockholders that has a special legal status similar to that of a person

☞ Most large businesses are corporations.

A **corporation** is a business owned by stockholders with a legal status similar to that of a person, since it can make contracts, own property, sue, and be sued. Most important, it is legally different from its owners, and this has important implications for owners' liability. Although only about 15 percent of businesses in the United States are corporations, they account for about 85 percent of all sales made. There is no limit to the size of a corporation, and some are worth billions of dollars. Table 5.3 presents the 25 largest corporations in the United States, ranked by sales. As the table indicates, a high sales volume does not necessarily mean that a firm is profitable.

TABLE 5.3   The Largest U.S. Industrial Corporations

Rank	Name	Sales (millions of dollars)	Profits (millions of dollars)
1	General Motors	$126,017	$(1,986)
2	Exxon	105,885	5,010
3	Ford Motor	98,275	860
4	IBM	69,018	6,020
5	Mobil	58,770	1,929
6	General Electric	58,414	4,303
7	Philip Morris	44,323	3,540
8	Texaco	41,235	1,450
9	E. I. Du Pont de Nemours	39,839	2,310
10	Chevron	39,262	2,157
11	Chrysler	30,868	68
12	Amoco	28,277	1,913
13	Boeing	27,595	1,385
14	Shell Oil	24,423	1,036
15	Procter & Gamble	24,376	1,602
16	Occidental Petroleum	21,947	(1,695)
17	United Technologies	21,783	751
18	Dow Chemical	20,005	1,384
19	USX	19,462	818
20	Eastman Kodak	19,075	703
21	Atlantic Richfield	18,819	2,011
22	Xerox	18,382	243
23	Pepsico	17,803	1,077
24	McDonnell Douglas	16,351	306
25	Conagra	15,518	232

Source: Fortune 500 listing, *Fortune*, April 22, 1991. © 1991 The Time Inc. Magazine Company. All rights reserved.

board of directors
a group of individuals responsible for the operations of a corporation

inside director
a member of the board of directors who is also a member of top management

outside director
a member of the board of directors who is not employed by the corporation

Ultimate control of each corporation rests with the stockholders. Usually each share of stock has one vote, so shareholders have influence that is proportional to their ownership of stock. The **board of directors** is a group of individuals responsible for the company's operation. A director may be either an inside director or an outside director. An **inside director** is a member of the board of directors who is also a member of top management; usually, this is the president of a company. An **outside director** is a member of the board but is not part of the corporation's management. Many corporations choose leading citizens as their outside directors and pay them for that service.

The board of directors appoints the top officers and also is responsible for the firm's overall conduct. Until a few years ago, being an outside director of some corporations did not necessarily involve much beyond attending a few meetings each year and collecting the fee. Recently, however, the move has been toward greater responsibility on the part of all outside directors. Since some attempts have been made to sue directors for the actions of the

Those Little White Lies

For decades we have made the most fundamental and far-reaching economic decisions on the basis of that supposedly magic number, the bottom line. We are making a big mistake. Reported earnings have become virtually worthless in terms of their ability to tell us what is really going on at a company. At least part of the blame must go to the accountants who, in their well-meaning attempts to cure abuses, have in many cases made it even easier for companies to hide the ball.

Take Prime Motor Inns, until recently the world's second-largest hotel operator. In 1989 Prime reported a healthy net income of $77 million, up nearly 15 percent from the year before. In September 1990 it filed for Chapter 11 bankruptcy.

What happened? Could the bankruptcy filing have been foreseen? Prime's problem was that it didn't have enough cash coming in. Much of its reported 1989 bottom line came from selling hotels. But outside financing for those sales had dried up, and Prime had to finance many of those deals itself, leaving it without enough cash to pay its debt service, including debt for the properties it had "sold." According to banking consultants Financial Proformas, Inc., Prime had a $15 million cash outflow from operations in 1989—the year it reported a $77 million profit.

Prime has had plenty of company over the years. Penn Central, Crazy Eddie, Miniscribe, and more than a few savings and loan associations all reported impressive earnings and still went bankrupt. As with hairdos and hemlines, fads in accounting come and go. In the 1920s accountants devoted their skills to inflating asset values (shades of the 1980s!). In the 1960s the focus was on revenues. In the 1980s the big problem was banks and savings and loans overstating the value of their assets.

Today, net income is making a comeback. So are what Berkshire Hathaway Chairman Warren Buffett likes to call "white lies," aimed at making reported profits look better than they really are.

One popular white lie is the so-called big bath method of suddenly cleansing balance sheets of past sins, after years of insisting that everything

---

firm, corporations must often provide their directors with insurance against suits from disgruntled stockholders or consumers.

The corporate organization offers important benefits, chief among which is the limited liability of the owners. Stockowners may lose up to the full value of the stock, but cannot lose more. In other words, their liability is limited to the amount of invested funds. In the event of bankruptcy, this is extremely important, because stockholders need not fear losing other property. As noted above, the unlimited liability of a sole proprietor or a partner means

☞ Corporations allow investors to have limited liability and a way to withdraw investment without hurting the firms.

is just fine. Why can it take management so long to own up to the problems? Because the accounting rules are vague. They say only that companies must write down the assets as soon as management realizes that the assets are "permanently impaired." Plenty of room for interpretation there. Warns accounting expert Lee Seidler, "If push comes to shove, and the chairman wants a nickel more per share, any good controller knows where to find it."

Oil companies are champions of income smoothing. One of their favorite methods: simply add to (or delay adding to) reserves for future environmental cleanups.

Look how well it works. Amoco Corporation announced in July 1990 that it had an extraordinary gain of $471 million in the second quarter from settling claims dating from Iran's seizure of the company's assets in the late 1970s. The company simultaneously added $477 million to its reserves for environmental damage. Texaco had a $362 million gain last year from selling a stock interest in a subsidiary. In the same quarter, it booked a $355 million charge for future environmental programs.

Where did all this subjective judgment about the shape of the bottom line start? Go no farther back than the seventeenth-century trading companies like the East India Company, chartered by Queen Elizabeth I in 1600 and one of the first joint stock companies. Initially, the company distributed all profits (if any) at the end of each spice-trading voyage. But in 1661 the company's governor announced that future distributions would consist of periodic dividends paid out of retained earnings.

All of a sudden, measuring profits was a job for the accountants, who had to start making judgment calls. In short, trading companies like the East India Company introduced accrual accounting, the bottom line, and most of the bookkeeping problems we face today.

Source: Dana Wechster Linden, "Lies of the Bottom Line," *Forbes*, November 12, 1990, pp. 106ff.

that a business failure could cost these individuals some of their personal wealth, in addition to what they invested in the business.

A second major benefit of the corporation is the ability to enter and withdraw investment from the firm. As we will see in later chapters, stocks are traded in a very active market, at least for larger firms. Stockholders who no longer desire to maintain ownership may sell their stock in the stock market. Similarly, a new investor can become a part owner by buying stock.

The fact that transfer of ownership is so simple makes it easy for a corporation to attract capital. Investors may confidently buy shares knowing that the commitment is not permanent; when they wish to sell, the stock market provides an easy means for them to do so. Also, because ownership is through shares of stock, it is relatively easy for a corporation to expand. New funds can be raised by issuing new shares.

Of course, a corporate organization has some disadvantages. First, each corporation must have a charter granted by a state government. Although it need not be extremely expensive, creating a corporation is usually more expensive and difficult than creating a sole proprietorship or a partnership. For very small businesses, these expenses can be large enough to make incorporation impractical.

Because corporations are legal entities, they come under a considerable amount of government regulation. It is more severe for some firms and some industries than for others. Corporations with widely held or publicly traded securities are subject to rigorous reporting standards, and must make public annual reports of their business activities. The requirement of public reporting makes privacy difficult. Privacy of investment activities can be very important for some firms, particularly those involved in research and development of new products.

Workers often lack genuine interest in the success of a corporation, especially when they earn fixed wages. As a result, corporations often have difficulty motivating their employees.

double taxation
the taxation of corporate earnings distributed as dividends twice: first as corporate income and then as individual income

Another big disadvantage stems from the fact that corporations are subject to **double taxation**. That is, their earnings are taxed first at the corporate level and again when they are paid to stockholders in the form of dividends. Relative to a sole proprietorship or a partnership, this can be a serious disadvantage. Table 5.4 shows the effect that double taxation can have on the after-tax profits paid to owners. Consider $100 of before-tax profits made by either a sole proprietorship or a partnership, and the same $100 profit made by a corporation. If the corporation must pay corporate income tax of 30

TABLE 5.4   The Effect of Double Taxation on Corporate Profits

	Sole Proprietorship or Partnership	Corporation
Profits before business taxes	$100.00	$100.00
Corporate tax at 30%	N.A.	−30.00
Profits after business taxes	100.00	70.00
Personal income tax at 28%	−28.00	−19.60
After-tax receipts by owners	72.00	50.40

The calculations in this table assume that all profits are paid to the owners. The individual tax rate is assumed to be 28 percent.

TABLE 5.5 Advantages and Disadvantages of Corporations

Advantages	Disadvantages
Limited liability	More expensive
Potentially long life	Increased regulatory burden
Easy to transfer ownership	Lack of secrecy
Easy to attract new capital	Difficulty in motivating employees
Ability to grow	Double taxation

percent, this leaves only $70 to pay to shareholders. This compares with the full $100 that will be paid to the owners of the sole proprietorship or partnership, which must pay only their personal income tax, assumed to be 28 percent. On an after-tax basis, the sole proprietorship or the partnership delivers $72 of the $100 original profit to its owners, but the corporation delivers only $50.40.

subchapter S corporation
a corporation with up to 25 stockholders that elects to be treated as a partnership for tax purposes

Because double taxation may be particularly troublesome, a provision has been made to avoid this burden, but it is open only to small corporations. A **subchapter S corporation** has no more than 25 stockholders and elects to be treated as a partnership for tax purposes. Thus its earnings are taxed only as personal income, but it enjoys the limited liability feature of a regular corporation. Table 5.5 summarizes the advantages and disadvantages of the corporate form of ownership.

TAXES

The Tax Reform Act of 1986 instituted sweeping changes in the structure of tax rates and dramatically altered the taxation of income from securities investing. Keep in mind that the tax laws change with some frequency, so some of the ones described in this section may already have changed. Consequently, it is more important to understand how to work with, say, tax schedules than to memorize the various brackets and rates contained in those schedules.

Individual Tax Rates

Once taxable income is calculated, the taxpayer must still calculate the tax to be paid. Table 5.6 presents the tax rates applied to individuals and couples for 1991. Taxable personal income consists of all income from wages and investments, adjusted for various factors. For instance, interest paid on a home mortgage and certain allowances for dependents may be subtracted.

Once the taxable income is known, Table 5.6 can be used to compute the tax due. For example, assume that a couple is filing jointly and has a

FINANCE

TODAY

The Honor System Is Alive and Well

Prisoners have been given charge in their own prisons, and condemned men forced to dig their own graves. Now the Internal Revenue Service is asking U.S. taxpayers to audit their own returns. In an experimental program, the IRS will send letters to 2,000 taxpayers in New England and up-state New York with incomes between $50,000 and $100,000, asking them to correct suspected errors on their 1989 returns.

The letters will point out items the IRS questions. If you'd rather not audit yourself, the IRS will conduct a regular audit. If you find you erred, you're supposed to report it and pay the appropriate penalty and interest. And if you conclude that you're in the right, try to persuade the IRS.

If the experiment works, next year the IRS may ask filers to do self-audits without telling them which items are being questioned. The bottom line is saving money: if people are as hard on themselves as the IRS is, paying agents to go after them doesn't make much sense.

Source: "Look into Your Heart and Pay," *Time*, March 18, 1991, p. 69.

taxable income of $60,000. Using the table, we can see that the tax would be $5,100 plus 28 percent of all income above $34,000. The computation is:

$$\text{Tax} = \$5,100 + 0.28(\$60,000 - \$34,000)$$
$$= 5,100 + 7,280$$
$$= \$12,380$$

TABLE 5.6   Personal Federal Income Tax Schedule for 1991

Taxable Income	Tax Rate	Starting Tax
INDIVIDUALS		
$ 0–$20,350	15%	$ 0.00
20,350–49,300	28	3,052.50
49,300+	31	11,158.50
MARRIED COUPLES FILING JOINTLY		
0–34,000	15	0.00
34,000–82,150	28	5,100.00
82,150+	31	18,582.00

This table is for illustration purposes. Various modifications may apply for some taxpayers.

TABLE 5.7   Federal Tax Rates for Corporations for 1991

Taxable Income	Tax Rate	Starting Tax
$ 0–$50,000	15%	$ 0.00
50,000– 75,000	25	7,500.00
75,000–100,000	34	13,750.00
100,000–335,000	39	22,250.00
335,000+	34	$113,900.00

marginal tax rate
the tax rate to be applied to the next dollar of income

For this couple, the tax paid on each additional dollar of income, or the **marginal tax rate,** equals 28 percent; however, their **average tax rate** is 20.63 percent ($12,380/$60,000). As the table shows, the highest marginal rate for personal taxes is 31 percent. State or local income tax would be in addition to federal tax.

average tax rate
the total tax divided by total income

Corporate Tax Rates

Table 5.7 presents the federal income tax schedule for corporations. As are individuals, corporations are subject to many adjustments in figuring taxable income. Some of the most important of these are the adjustments for interest expenses and for depreciation.

Depreciation

☞ Depreciation expenses generate tax savings by reducing the amount of income subject to taxation.

The tax laws assume that the value of assets decreases over time. To reflect this decrease, accounting rules allow firms to reduce the value of some assets by a certain amount each year. This reduction can be subtracted from their income as a depreciation expense for that year. The ability to treat the normal wear and tear on an asset as an expense has major tax consequences for firms.

The two basic ways to calculate the depreciation expense are the straight-line depreciation method and the modified accelerated cost recovery system (MACRS). The straight-line depreciation method begins by calculating the **depreciable value**
the cost of an asset minus the expected salvage value

depreciable value of the asset; that is, the cost minus the expected salvage value. The **straight-line depreciation** expense is the depreciable value divided by the number of years in the depreciation period. For example, if the initial cost of an airplane is $10 million, and if it will have a salvage value of $1 million after 10 years of service, the airplane's depreciable value is $9 million. With a 10-year life, the straight-line depreciation expense would be $900,000 for each of the 10 years.

straight-line depreciation
a technique in which the depreciation expense is the same each period

In general, if an asset has an initial cost of I, has a salvage value of SV, and is to be depreciated over a period of n years, then the yearly depreciation,

FINANCE TODAY

Child Abuse

Honesty is the best policy—especially when you have no alternative. That would seem to be the conclusion of millions of U.S. taxpayers. In 1988, 8.7 million of them claimed a tax credit for child-care expenses, but in 1989 only 6 million did so. Could it be that in just a year 2.7 million taxpayers stopped paying for child care? Not likely. A better explanation: in the interim a law took effect requiring parents who claimed such tax breaks to identify their day-care providers. Suddenly, if the IRS wanted to check out your claim, it could.

"We are fairly certain that there was a major impact because of this new provision of the law," says an IRS spokesman, politely sidestepping the more pointed conclusion that some children previously cited as dependents existed only in the imagination of resourceful 1040 filers. Estimated windfall to the U.S. Treasury from the stricter rule: more than $1.2 billion.

Source: "Is This Kid for Real?" *Time*, February 25, 1991, p. 67.

D, using the straight-line depreciation method, is given by the following formula:

$$D = \frac{I - SV}{n} \tag{5.1}$$

Applying Equation 5.1 to the airplane example, we obtain the same yearly depreciation as before:

$$D = \frac{\$10,000,000 - \$1,000,000}{10}$$

$$= \$900,000$$

To compute the depreciation expenses for an asset using the MACRS requires knowledge of the depreciable life of the asset, the depreciable value of the asset, and the appropriate MACRS percentages for each year of the asset's life. In discussions of depreciation, it is customary to assume that the asset is acquired in period 0. It is assumed that an asset is placed in service at midyear, so the first year's depreciation is only half the normal amount. To reflect this convention, we assume throughout this text that the first depreciation expense is at period 1. The rules allow for switching to straight-line depreciation at any time. The depreciable life of assets other than buildings can be 3, 5, 7, 10, 15, or 20 years. Table 5.8 gives the depreciation percentages for each class of property that we will consider, and reflects switching to straight-line at the time that makes the depreciation as fast as possible. Under

TABLE 5.8   Depreciation Rates Under MACRS

	Recovery Period		
Year	Three Years	Five Years	Seven Years
1	33.33%	20.00%	14.29%
2	44.45	32.00	24.49
3	14.81	19.20	17.49
4	7.41	11.52	12.49
5		11.52	8.93
6		5.76	8.93
7			8.93
8			4.46

This table is for illustration purposes. Other categories also exist.

the MACRS rules, the full price of an asset is depreciated with no allowance for salvage value.

EXAMPLE 5.1

A contractor buys a pickup truck for $17,000. A pickup truck is classified as five-year property. What are the depreciation expenses generated by the truck for each year?

The depreciation is calculated as shown below.

Year	MACRS	Depreciation Expense	Accumulated Depreciation
1	20.00%	$3,400.00	$ 3,400.00
2	32.00	5,440.00	8,840.00
3	19.20	3,264.00	12,104.00
4	11.52	1,958.40	14,062.40
5	11.52	1,958.40	16,020.80
6	5.76	979.20	17,000.00

Capital Gains and Losses

An increase in the price of a security during the time it is held is a capital gain, and a decrease in price is a capital loss. Capital gains and losses may be either realized or unrealized. They are realized when an investor sells a security. Also, for the most part, only realized capital gains and losses give rise to tax consequences, although there are some exceptions. In essence, they are treated as additions to or subtractions from taxable income.

Soak the Poor?

Revenge is a dish best served cold—and on White House china. While drafting its recently submitted budget, the Bush Administration secretly proposed that the IRS target its stringent audits not on wealthy individuals and companies (whose lawyers can often stall a case for years) but on middle- and lower-income taxpayers (who generally pay up without protest and provide immediate revenue). IRS Commissioner Fred Goldberg rejected the cash-now plan, calling it "no-good tax policy." But his request to spend an additional $76 million to catch rich tax cheats was pared down to a puny $6 million. Could it be that the President remembers the pain of coughing up to the taxman? He was furious when an IRS audit in 1984 forced him to pay nearly $200,000 in taxes, interest, and penalties on the sale of an $843,000 house in Houston. In 1988 George Bush ridiculed Michael Dukakis' plan to catch more tax avoiders and railed against "putting an IRS agent in every kitchen." What he really meant, it seems, is that he didn't want a taxman in every boardroom.

Source: David Ellis and Sidney Urquhart, "White House to IRS: Hands Off the Rich," *Time,* April 1, 1991, p. 15.

Taxes on the Firm's Securities

Because the goal of the financial manager is to maximize shareholders' wealth, the manager must be aware of the taxes that investors face. Investing in securities gives rise to taxable income from two major sources: cash flows from owning the securities (dividends or interest received) and changes in the value of the securities (capital gains or losses). Historically, these two kinds of incomes have been treated quite differently, as the tax rate on capital gains has been lower than that on dividends or interest. After the Tax Reform Act of 1986, however, that differential was eliminated.

☞ Interest is treated as ordinary income for tax purposes.

Taxation of Interest Received   Interest received by individuals or corporations, whether it be on long-term bonds, money market accounts, or bank accounts, is taxable income. An important exception is the interest received on tax-exempt municipal debt obligations, which remains free of federal income taxation. Both individuals and corporations simply add 100 percent of any interest income to other taxable income in computing their taxes.

Taxation of Dividends   The full amount of dividends received by individuals is taxable. For corporations owning securities in other firms, 80 percent of the dividends received are tax exempt. The remaining 20 percent is added to other taxable income.

The New Spirit in Tax Policy

Since the Tax Reform Act of 1986, the tendency has been to eliminate tax-sheltering provisions of the law for both individuals and corporations. For individuals, the deductibility of consumer interest, such as credit card interest, was phased out starting in 1987; by 1991 none of that type of interest was deductible. Also, only 80 percent of meal and entertainment expenses are deductible, whereas in the past they were fully deductible. (The proverbial 3-martini lunch thus becomes a watered-down 2.4-martini lunch for tax purposes, although we strongly suspect its alcoholic potency remains intact!)

SUMMARY

This chapter introduced the major forms of business organization in the United States and explored their advantages and disadvantages. Among other points, proprietorships dominate in terms of number of entities, but for dollar investment, earnings, and sales, the corporation is by far the most important form. In this text we focus on the corporation.

Taxation affects all businesses and individuals. This chapter discussed the tax environment that economic agents must confront in the United States.

QUESTIONS

1. How does a limited partner differ from a general partner?
2. What is the difference between limited and unlimited liability?
3. What kinds of investors have limited liability?
4. What kinds of investors have unlimited liability?
5. What is an inside director?
6. Explain the concept of double taxation.
7. What kinds of business firms are subject to double taxation?
8. What is a subchapter S corporation? What tax advantages does it have over a regular corporation?
9. Is depreciation itself a cash flow? How does depreciation generate a cash flow?
10. What methods are permitted for depreciation?
11. How does the taxation of dividends differ between corporations and individuals?
12. What is a capital gain?

PROBLEMS

1. A corporation has $100 in before-tax income that it plans to use to pay dividends. Assume that the corporation is in the 34 percent tax bracket and the investor receiving the dividend is in the 28 percent tax bracket. How much after-tax income does the investor receive?

2. An investor receiving dividends from Debussy, Inc., retains $4 per share after paying personal taxes. The investor is in the 28 percent tax bracket. If the corporate tax rate is 34 percent and Debussy pays out all its profits as dividends, how much pretax profit did Debussy make per share?

3. An item of three-year property costs $1,500. What is the yearly depreciation schedule for this property under the MACRS method?

4. A seven-year property item costs $150,000. Under MACRS, what is the depreciation expense for this item in year 3?

5. A firm in the 34 percent tax bracket just purchased a seven-year machine for $250,000. What is the effect of depreciation on the firm's tax bill in year 6 under both straight-line and MACRS depreciation?

6. Using the rates in Table 5.7, compute the tax bill for a corporation with $350,000 taxable income.

7. Compute the average corporate tax rate corresponding to the upper limit income of each bracket in Table 5.7, and compare it to the corresponding marginal tax rate.

8. Using the straight-line method, find the annual depreciation of a piece of equipment with a five-year useful life, an initial cost of $8,000, and an expected salvage value of $1,500.

9. An asset has a salvage value equal to its annual depreciation. If its cost is $2,000 and it has an eight-year life, find its annual depreciation using the straight-line method.

10. An industrial compressor has a current book value of $2,000. Four years from now its book value will be $800. If the compressor initially cost $4,000, how many years has it been in use? Assume straight-line depreciation.

11. Consider a hypothetical individual tax schedule in which the amount of tax paid is proportional to the square of taxable income. Show that the average tax rate is proportional to taxable income.

12. In the previous problem, show that the marginal tax rate—the amount of tax paid on the next dollar of taxable income—is also (approximately) proportional to taxable income.

13. Now consider another hypothetical individual tax schedule in which the amount of tax paid is proportional to the square root of taxable income. What is the relationship between the average tax rate and the level of taxable income?

14. If the average tax rate is always equal to the marginal tax rate, what is the relationship between taxable income and the amount of taxes owed?

The Role of Financial Intermediaries

financial intermediary
a firm acquiring funds from one group of investors and making them available to another economic unit

This chapter explores the nature of financial intermediaries and their role in the economy. A **financial intermediary** is a firm that acquires funds from one group of investors and makes them available to another economic unit. The financial intermediary plays a vital role in the economy by channeling funds from surplus to deficit spending units. In the process, it issues securities to their owners and creditors in exchange for funds. The funds they acquire are "repackaged" and provided to other economic units. For providing this service, the intermediary charges a fee in the hope of making a profit.

In repackaging or restructuring financial obligations, the intermediary alters the obligations in many ways. For example, a bank accepts small deposits and guarantees their safety. The funds thus acquired may be bundled together to provide a large risky loan to a commercial firm. In channeling these small and virtually risk-free deposits to a large risky loan, the intermediary provides a valuable service to the depositors, the borrower, and the economy as a whole. There are many types of financial intermediaries, such as commercial banks, savings and loan firms, insurance companies, and pension funds.

INTERMEDIARIES IN THE ECONOMY

We saw in Chapter 2 that the existence of a financial system provides great benefit to individuals in the economy, since with a financial market people can alter consumption patterns. By borrowing, for example, future consumption opportunities can be transformed into present consumption opportunities. Similarly, commercial banks borrow from their depositors and lend money to other economic units.

TYPES OF INTERMEDIATION

☞ Mismatches between the needs of users and suppliers of funds give rise to the need for financial intermediaries.

To understand the role of intermediation, consider first an economy with only manufacturing firms and individual savers, and no intermediaries. The manufacturing firm needs large amounts of funds available for a protracted period of time to invest in risky real goods. Individual savers have small amounts of money that they may need on short notice, and may be unwilling

TABLE 6.1   Mismatch in Needs Between Firms and Savers

Firms	*Individual Savers*
Need large amounts of funds	Have small amounts to invest
Need long-term commitments	Need ready access to funds
Projects involve high risk	Prefer low-risk investments
Superior knowledge of project's payoffs and risk	Less knowledge of firm's investment opportunities

to accept the level of risk involved in a manufacturing venture. Table 6.1 summarizes the mismatch between these needs. Given their very different situations, it may be inefficient for firms to acquire funds directly from individuals. Figure 6.1(a) highlights this inefficiency, where a large borrower attempts to acquire funds directly from many small savers.

FIGURE 6.1   Size Intermediation

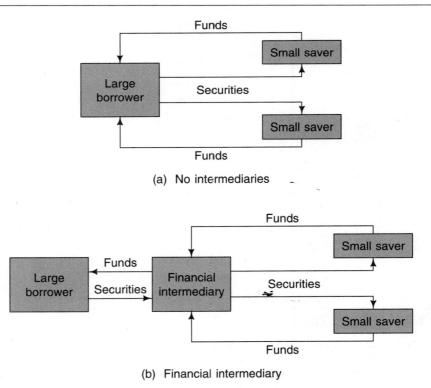

(a) No intermediaries

(b) Financial intermediary

To highlight just one of the mismatches, consider a firm that seeks funds to build a chemical plant with a construction time of 5 years, and plans to repay those funds over the next 30 years. Small savers may wish to earn a return on their savings, but may also wish to have quick access to those funds for unexpected medical expenses, education needs, and so on. Figure 6.1(b) shows how a financial intermediary, such as a commercial bank, can play a useful role in the economy by stepping between the firm and the individual savers. It eliminates the mismatches by performing four types of intermediation: size intermediation, maturity intermediation, risk intermediation, and information intermediation.

☞ Intermediaries help to resolve discrepancies of size of funds, maturity of commitment, risk level, and information between users and suppliers of funds.

Size Intermediation

surplus

In our economy, households tend to be surplus spending units whereas firms tend to be deficit spending units. Economic efficiency requires that funds flow from surplus to deficit units and that the deficit units pay a return to the surplus units. Large firms have a large appetite for funds, but households, as the major surplus spending units, are small individually. This creates a size mismatch between them. An intermediary can gather funds from households efficiently and combine these small amounts into larger packages that are attractive to the firms.

☞ The need for size intermediation arises from the fact that an individual supplier of funds can normally supply only a small portion of the needs of a user of funds.

In the process of providing this service, the intermediary strives to make a profit by borrowing from the surplus spending units at a lower rate and providing funds to deficit spending units at a higher rate. The difference between these rates is the **spread.** From it the intermediary must pay the cost of gathering and disbursing funds, and must pay its own investors a return for providing funds to the intermediary.

spread
the difference between the buying and the selling price for a trader

Maturity and Liquidity Intermediation

Mismatches exist not only in the size of surplus and deficit spending units, but also in the time horizons and liquidity needs of funds. In our earlier example, we considered a firm planning to build a chemical plant with a horizon of 30 years between the acquisition and final repayment of funds. Very few households can commit money for such a long time. The need to bridge the time preferences of surplus and deficit spending units provides an opportunity for the financial intermediary.

☞ Time intermediation helps to resolve the maturity preferences of suppliers and users of funds.

By developing a pool of many contributors of small amounts of funds, the intermediary amasses the amount desired by the chemical firm and solves the problem of size intermediation. However, because the pool of funds is created by attracting many small contributors, the intermediary can also resolve the time mismatch. Some early contributors may withdraw their funds before the project is completed, but the intermediary can provide continuous financing to the firm over the entire time by attracting new contributors to replace them.

INTERNATIONAL

PERSPECTIVES

Drug Dealers Need Banks, Too

Drug dealing is one of the largest cash businesses of all time. After all, no one wants to write a check to a drug dealer and few drug dealers accept checks anyway. Where does the cash go and how does it get there?

Banks are required by law to report all deposits exceeding $10,000, so one way to avoid detection is for drug dealers to keep their transactions small. However, that is not possible for really large dealers. As a consequence, they attempt to launder their money so that it appears legitimate.

Foreign countries with stringent laws favoring bank secrecy play a large role in making drug money appear legitimate. Cash is flown out of the United States on private jets and deposited in a foreign bank. The funds are eventually sent to the United States through legal channels, to be invested there in American stocks and bonds, or in other legal investment media.

U.S. banks accepting such deposits really have no way of knowing whether the money is derived from legitimate sources. As the Justice Department's representative states: "Banks can wind up warehousing drug money in an account of another institution and not even realize it."*

While some banks unwittingly hold drug money on deposit, there is little doubt that some banks cooperate with drug traffickers. John Lawn, head of the Drug Enforcement Administration, said: "Based on investigations we and the FBI have been in, I would have to say that there is definitely complicity in the banking community in at least some aspects of international narcotics trafficking. In general, there has been a reluctance among banks to cooperate with the law enforcement community in these matters."* In fact, not all of the lack of cooperation comes from private banks. Currently, cash flows into the United States from Latin America. Every day planes from Latin America land in Miami to unload millions of dollars in small denomination bills. It then becomes the job of the Federal Reserve to manage the circulation of the newly introduced cash. One Miami Fed official says: "We don't care where the money comes from. Finding out is not our business. Our job is simply to keep money in circulation, period."*

* All quotes from Allan Dodds Frank, "See No Evil," *Forbes*, October 6, 1986.

Without an intermediary, not only would the chemical firm have to acquire funds from many small contributors, it would have to continue to find new contributors to replace those that withdraw their money over time. If the financial intermediary can step between the ultimate surplus spending units and the chemical firm to manage this time mismatch more efficiently, it can make a profit. Because they specialize, intermediaries are often more efficient than other types of firms in acquiring funds from small surplus units and making a large package available to a deficit spending unit for extended periods.

Risk Intermediation and Risk Pooling

☞ Intermediaries help to alleviate different risk preferences between suppliers and users of funds.

Intermediaries also act to resolve mismatches in the risk preferences of surplus and deficit spending units. The level of risk of the chemical plant project may be too high for many surplus spending units. As a consequence, the surplus units will not invest directly in the firm. By acquiring funds at one risk level and lending them at a higher level, the financial intermediary has an opportunity to make a profit by intermediating this risk mismatch.

Banks accept deposits from individuals and guarantee to repay those deposits with interest. In fact, the federal government backs these promises in many cases. Therefore, we may regard many commercial bank deposits as risk free, so banks can lend these funds to firms desiring to invest in a risky project. If the chemical firm attempted to raise funds directly from the risk-averse surplus spending units, it would have difficulty guaranteeing the level of safety that the surplus units demand. Financial institutions can provide the risk intermediation service much more efficiently than nonspecializing firms.

The difference between the risk of its deposits and its loans is a major contributing factor to the size of the spread the bank is able to earn. The risk level of deposits is fixed effectively because of government guarantees. In this environment, banks have an incentive to adopt a risky posture by making riskier loans with higher rates of interest.

Information Intermediation

☞ Intermediaries are expert at gathering and evaluating information about users of funds, so they can help remedy the lack of information confronting many suppliers of funds.

If the spread that the bank earns varies directly with the risk difference between its deposits and its loans, why don't depositors make the risky loans themselves and capture the higher rate of interest? There are two basic reasons, one of which we have already seen. That is, many depositors are risk averse and prefer the safety of government-guaranteed bank deposits. The second reason is that making risky loans requires information about the actual extent of the risks and about the borrower's willingness and ability to pay as promised. Gathering the relevant information about borrowers requires capital, effort, and expertise. From one perspective, we may view financial institutions as information intermediaries.

For example, assessing the risk of a chemical plant is difficult. To do a good job requires knowing the company's financial position in detail, knowing the structure of the chemical industry, and projecting future demand and supply for the chemical being produced. Because of their limited resources, individuals are in a poor position to gather such information, a fact that provides an opportunity for a specialist in information processing.

In many cases, financial institutions can assess information much more efficiently than individuals, due to their larger scale, their corresponding ability to amortize fixed costs associated with the information-gathering process, and their specialization in financial matters. For an individual investor with just $10,000 to invest, a thorough investigation of the chemical firm's prospects is not feasible. By contrast, a financial institution may be prepared to lend $10 million to the chemical firm. Accordingly, it can afford to devote, say, $10,000 to determining the wisdom of making the loan. In many instances, the bank has a continuing relationship with a large borrower, so it will already have a high level of knowledge about it. In summary, financial institutions are better information processors than individuals for three major reasons:

1. They deal with larger sums, so they can commit more resources to information collection and evaluation.
2. Because of continuing relationships with prospective borrowers, they already have much of the information.
3. They specialize in risk evaluation and other financial matters that individuals do not possess.

DIVERSIFICATION

diversification
the allocation of funds to a variety of investment opportunities in order to reduce risk

Financial institutions offer another service in addition to intermediation. **Diversification** is the allocation of investable funds to a variety of investment opportunities in order to reduce risk. As we will see in more detail in Chapters 11 and 12, by dividing funds among a variety of different opportunities, it is possible to reduce dramatically the amount of risk in the investment as a whole. For a small investor, it is not easy to achieve the risk-reduction benefits of diversification. For example, a person with $1,000 to invest would find it difficult to invest $100 in ten different projects.

☞ Intermediaries make the benefits of diversification available to suppliers of funds.

Financial intermediaries, however, make it easy for such individuals to reap the benefits of diversification. They collect funds from a number of investors and pool them, and because the size of the pool is large, it can be invested in a variety of opportunities. Then each of the contributors has, in effect, a share of the diversified investment portfolio.

investment company
a firm that pools funds from investors and uses them to buy a portfolio of securities, with each investor owning a fraction of those shares proportional to the investment

Another popular kind of financial intermediary that provides diversification is the **investment company.** An investment company, such as a mutual fund, collects funds from a variety of investors and uses the proceeds to buy securities such as stocks and bonds. Each of the contributors owns a fraction of the entire portfolio that is created. This provides very efficient diversification for even the smallest investor. For example, with an investment of only $1,000, an investor can own a fraction of an investment company's portfolio that may include hundreds of securities.

We note that the diversification service provided by an investment company or other financial intermediary is not the same service as risk intermediation discussed earlier. In risk intermediation, the financial intermediary bears a higher level of risk and issues claims to its depositors, for example, at a lower level of risk. In providing a diversification service, an investment company merely collects funds from individuals and invests them more efficiently. The contributors still bear the entire risk, but the amount is reduced due to diversification.

THE INTERMEDIARY AS A BUSINESS

We have seen that the financial intermediary performs five important services that are summarized in Figure 6.2. Funds flow from surplus spending units to the financial intermediary. In return, the surplus spending units hold direct claims against the intermediary. Usually, these claims are for small amounts, highly liquid, and of low risk. In addition, they are on the intermediary as a whole, so they are indirect claims on a diversified portfolio of investments.

☞ As a business enterprise, the financial intermediary acquires funds from ultimate suppliers and transforms the characteristics of those funds to make them more attractive to their users.

For its part, the intermediary raises its own capital by selling stock and by issuing bonds. It then accepts funds from the surplus spending units, but it alters the characteristics of the funds. After transforming the funds, it makes them available to deficit spending units, usually business firms that require long-term commitments of large amounts of money. The ultimate providers of funds, the surplus spending units, hold a direct claim against the financial intermediary, and they also hold an indirect claim against the deficit spending units through the intermediary. In short, the financial intermediary pays

FIGURE 6.2 **The Role of the Intermediary in the Flow of Funds**

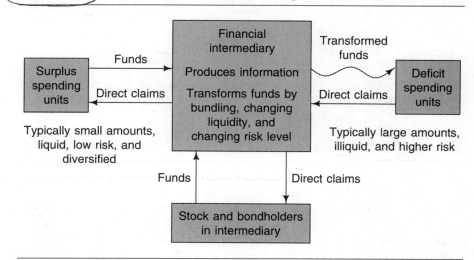

surplus spending units one rate of return, transforms the funds it collects, and charges the deficit spending units a higher rate for using the funds. This difference between the rates constitutes the intermediary's spread. Part of this spread is earned by bundling the funds and changing their liquidity, and part of it is compensation for the fact that funds provided to the deficit spending unit are of a higher risk level than those acquired from surplus spending units.

DISINTERMEDIATION

disintermediation
the process of direct contact between surplus and deficit spending units, leaving out the financial intermediary

It would be tempting for the surplus and deficit spending units to get together to eliminate the intermediary. By providing funds without it, the surplus units might receive a higher rate for their funds and the deficit units might be able to acquire their needed money at a lower rate. This process of direct contact between surplus and deficit spending units is known as **disintermediation.** For example, many large industrial firms raise short-term funds directly from small surplus spending units. Similarly, many industrial firms own financing companies. As a typical example, General Motors owns the General Motors Acceptance Corporation (GMAC), specializing in automobile financing. A buyer who purchases a GM automobile can acquire financing from a bank or directly from GMAC. Today, the increasing tendency is to leave the bank out of the process entirely.

TYPES OF FINANCIAL INTERMEDIARIES

A complex economy such as that of the United States has many different kinds of financial intermediaries. It is customary to separate them as depository and nondepository.

Depository Institutions

☞ There are four types of depository institutions: commercial banks, savings and loans, savings banks, and credit unions.

The four types of depository institutions are commercial banks, savings and loans, savings banks, and credit unions. Of these, commercial banks are the largest by far.

Commercial Banks Banks play a critical role in the creation of money by accepting deposits and issuing loans in amounts far greater than their deposits. The extent to which they can create money is governed by the reserve requirements that are administered by the Federal Reserve Board. Today's commercial bank is a complex enterprise offering a diversity of services.

consumer loans
loans made to individuals

The classic functions of commercial banks are to accept deposits and to grant loans. A large part of their business comes from **consumer loans,** which are made to individuals. One of the most visible forms of consumer lending is through credit cards such as Visa and MasterCard.

TABLE 6.2   Consolidated Balance Sheet for All U.S. Commercial Banks as of December 31, 1990

ASSETS	Amount (billions of dollars)	LIABILITIES AND NET WORTH	Amount (billions of dollars)
Investment securities	$ 602.8	Total deposits	$2,359.4
Trading account assets	22.0	Borrowings	545.6
		Other liabilities	265.0
Interbank loans	201.5	Net worth	220.4
Commercial and industrial loans	656.8		
Real estate loans	830.6		
Individual loans	387.1		
Other loans	230.3		
Total cash assets	221.6		
Other assets	237.7		
Total	**$3,390.4**	**Total**	**$3,390.4**

Source: *Federal Reserve Bulletin*, March 1991, Table 1.25.

trust services
the service of managing funds for individuals and businesses that ~~have~~ entrusted their funds to the trust department of a bank or other financial institution

Banks also offer payment services. For example, funds held in a checking account may be disbursed by writing checks. In addition, commercial banks offer **trust services.** The trust department of a bank manages money for individuals and businesses that have entrusted their funds to the bank. It might oversee all monthly payments for some customers, manage their stock and bond portfolios, and execute leases on their behalf. For these services the customers would pay a fee to the trust department. In addition, the trust department often plays an important role in managing the estate of a deceased person.

Table 6.2 presents the aggregated balance sheet for all U.S. commercial banks. The total assets are about $3.4 trillion, with total loans being about $2.3 trillion. The rest of the assets are held in securities (about $500 billion) or in cash assets (about $200 billion). About $2 trillion of these assets are financed by deposits or by borrowing. Here the borrowing would consist primarily of long-term bonds that the bank issues in the securities market.

money center banks
the very largest commercial banks such as Citibank, Chase Manhattan, and Manufacturers Hanover

Regulation of Commercial Banking   The United States today has over 10,000 commercial banks. They range from the very largest **money center banks** in New York, such as Citibank, Chase Manhattan, and Manufacturers Hanover, to extremely small banks in small towns. Because of their critical importance in creating money and in stimulating general economic activity, they are all subject to regulation.

What's in a Name?

Some of Wall Street's best-known company names are biting the dust, victims of the latest wave of consolidation and reorganization in the U.S. securities industry.

It's almost enough to make some people shed a tear. "In a way you lose the tradition and history of an industry when you eliminate some of the oldest names," says Jeffrey Schaefer, research director at the Securities Industry Association. "It's beating down a beaten industry. It's too bad."

To see how much Wall Street is changing, dig out an old ad for a security offering and count the brokerage firms that aren't around anymore. It gives new meaning to "tombstone," the nickname for those plain, slab-style ads. For example, of the 47 brokerage firms listed in a 1969 tombstone ad for a stock offering by American Motors Corporation, only one company (McDonald & Co.) remains. American Motors itself has been absorbed by Chrysler.

The latest to go was Bache, a nearly 100-year-old name on Wall Street, which the former Prudential-Bache Securities, Inc., purged this week. It's now just Prudential Securities, Inc., to emphasize its ties to its parent, Prudential Insurance Co. of America. Out went the namesake of Jules Bache, grandson of an officer who fought under Napoleon.

"Certain names have franchise value," says Samuel Hayes, a Harvard Business School professor. "And in the case of certain names that have bitten the dust," including Hutton and Bache, "obviously they've lost their franchise value."

More names—some great, some not—are expected to vanish as Wall Street continues remaking itself. And even survivors are fiddling with names.

Merrill Lynch & Co., for example, no longer uses its full, unwieldy moniker, Merrill Lynch, Pierce, Fenner & Smith, Inc., even though that's still the legal name of Merrill's broker-dealer unit.

The goals of regulation are to provide a safe and competitive banking system. To some extent, they naturally conflict. For example, in competitive industries, some firms fail. So if banking is regulated in a way to make banks compete and thereby provide banking services at a low cost to the public, the number of banking failures will increase. If too many banks fail, the public will lose faith in the safety of the system. From these straightforward considerations, it is apparent that successful regulation requires balancing these inconsistent goals.

dual regulatory system
a system of bank regulation at both federal and state levels

The United States employs a **dual regulatory system**—a system of regulation at both federal and state levels. The first level of regulation stems

Merrill Lynch is responsible for the death of the once-respected Wall Street name White, Weld & Co., which the firm briefly kept alive after acquiring White, Weld in the 1970s. It was eventually dropped. "Too clumsy," a spokesman says.

"Company names are very emotional subjects," says Alan Siegel, chairman of Siegel & Gale, Inc., corporate-identity consultants, who has worked with Merrill, CS First Boston, Inc., Prudential Insurance, and other financial firms. Working with big-ego investment bankers has taught Mr. Siegel that "the name and reputation of the firm and the image they're projecting is very critical."

Usually, descendants aren't around to complain when old names die. But when Drexel Burnham Lambert, Inc., collapsed last year, the Burnhams weren't thrilled.

"If your name is on the door, it doesn't make you feel good to see what happened," says Jon Burnham, 55-year-old son of the man who founded Burnham & Co. in 1935, which was later merged into Drexel. Mr. Burnham's family put their name on a new door, Burnham Securities, Inc.

No firm has more old, dead names in its closet than Shearson Lehman Brothers, Inc., a unit of American Express Co. Shearson has legal rights to dozens of old names, such as E. F. Hutton and Kuhn Loeb & Co., that it acquired in the 1970s and 1980s.

Now, Shearson is reviving a name. Last year, it was called Shearson Lehman Hutton. It dropped Hutton and added Brothers to emphasize the "Lehman Brothers" part of its heritage. It even plays down the Shearson name. "We're still changing signs around here," says one executive.

Source: William Power, "Name-Dropping on Wall Street, No Longer What It Used To Be," *The Wall Street Journal*, February 22, 1991, p. C1.

from the fact that every bank must have a charter, which can be either a national or a state charter. Only nationally chartered banks can use the word "national" in their names. So the First National Bank of Podunk has a national charter. Currently, about 5,000 commercial banks hold national charters. Also, national banks sometimes have names followed by the letters "N.A.," indicating a national association. All other banks hold charters from a state banking regulatory commission.

Every national bank is subject to the regulations of the Comptroller of the Currency, and they are examined by the Comptroller's office at least once a year. An examiner may choose a loan at random and examine its payment history to determine whether the bank accurately reports the quality of that loan. All national banks must also be members of the Federal Reserve System; in addition, many state chartered banks join the System voluntarily. The System is empowered to examine all member banks.

The Federal Deposit Insurance Corporation (FDIC) is involved in commercial bank regulation as well. As its name implies, it insures deposits. About 98 percent of all commercial banks are members of the FDIC and pay a fee for membership. In return, the FDIC guarantees the safety of all deposits up to the current maximum of $100,000, in case the bank collapses. In the early 1990s, the reserves of the FDIC have been dwindling dangerously due to a severe crisis in the banking industry.

State banking commissions grant charters to state banks. Because almost all banks are members of the FDIC, they are subject to examination by both the FDIC and the state banking commission. To conserve resources, the FDIC and the state banking commission usually cooperate in examining state banks.

Unit Banking and Branching   Under the terms of the McFadden Act of 1927, no bank could open a branch office across state lines. The law held that, regardless of the source of its charter, the expansion of banking offices within a state should be controlled by state law. In a **unit banking state,** each bank may have only one office. For many years Texas and Illinois were classic unit banking states. At the other end of the spectrum, some states have long allowed unrestricted **statewide branching.** For example, in New York and North Carolina, branches may be opened anywhere in the states. As a middle ground, some states allow **restricted branching.** In this case, a bank might be allowed to open a branch within a certain distance from an existing office or might be allowed to open a certain number of branches in a given year.

Some states have restricted branching in the belief that keeping banks small will stimulate competition and restrict the economic power of banks. Others maintain that liberal branching provides greater convenience to customers, and allows banks to achieve a scale that will be more efficient, thereby making it possible to reduce the cost of their services.

Holding Companies and Interstate Branching   To skirt restrictions on opening branches, a new corporate entity was created. The **bank holding company** is a nonbank corporation that owns one or more commercial banks. Commercial banks are not permitted to engage in certain business activities, for example, to assist corporations in selling new securities. This restriction is a key element of the Glass–Steagall Act. However, these restrictions do not apply to holding companies, which were formed for two principal reasons.

First, a multibank holding company can obtain some of the benefits of branch banking. For example, it might be able to achieve a greater scale and provide services to its constituent banks more efficiently than would be possible

---

unit banking state
a state in which each bank may have only one office

statewide branching
the practice of allowing banks to establish branch offices anywhere within a given state

restricted branching
the practice of allowing banks to establish branch offices only under certain restrictions

bank holding company
a nonbank corporation owning one or more commercial banks

for a single bank. Second, a one-bank holding company could enter other lines of business prohibited to commercial banks, such as travel agency or life insurance. Bank holding companies must register with the Federal Reserve System, which controls their acquisition of, and entry into, nonbank fields of commerce.

We are today witnessing a growing trend toward types of business activities that closely approximate interstate banking. For example, Citicorp, the holding company for Citibank, has been allowed to purchase chains of savings and loan associations in both California and Florida. This gives Citicorp a network of depository institutions in a number of states, which is a close approximation to interstate banking. In the near future, we can expect more movement in that direction.

Savings and Loan Associations   Savings and loans are either stock associations or mutual associations. In a stock association, depositors are creditors, just as they would be in a commercial bank. In a mutual association, the depositors are owners. Both associations are subject to the reserve requirements of the Federal Reserve Board, just as are commercial banks.

Table 6.3 presents the aggregated balance sheet for all U.S. savings and loan associations (S&Ls). The S&Ls have long been committed to providing mortgage financing. In fact, most of them were created for that specific purpose, as reflected in the balance sheet of Table 6.3. Notice also that the total assets of all S&Ls are much smaller than the total assets of commercial banks, given in Table 6.2. Furthermore, in recent years the S&L industry has experienced a general shrinking, with financial losses accumulating to the point at which it is facing its greatest crisis ever. Notice, for example, that S&Ls as a group have no net worth. The careful reader will also observe that the individual accounts don't add up to the total of $1,140,300 million; maybe the "Other"

TABLE 6.3   Aggregated Balance Sheet for U.S. Savings and Loan Associations as of August 31, 1990

	Amount (millions of dollars)		Amount (millions of dollars)
ASSETS		**LIABILITIES AND NET WORTH**	
Mortgages	$ 677,217	Savings capital	$ 864,800
Mortgage-backed securities	155,499	Borrowed money	219,500
Commercial loans	20,100	Other	N.A.
Consumer loans	53,200	Net worth	0
Cash and investment securities	152,700		
Other	N.A.		
Total	**$1,140,300**	**Total**	**$1,140,300**

Source: Federal Reserve Bulletin, March 1991, Table 1.37.

TABLE 6.4   Aggregated Balance Sheet for U.S. Savings Banks as of July 31, 1990

ASSETS	Amount (millions of dollars)	LIABILITIES AND NET WORTH	Amount (millions of dollars)
Mortgages	$327,330	Savings capital	$432,387
Mortgage-backed securities	78,033	Borrowed money	119,998
Commercial loans	19,815	Other	9,508
Consumer loans	33,308	Net worth	22,373
Cash and investment securities	71,795		
Other	45,996		
Total	**$587,521**	**Total**	**$587,521**

Source: Federal Reserve Bulletin, March 1991, Table 1.37.

accounts, with their N/A balances (whatever "not available" really means) are being used as financial black holes. In fact, some analysts would probably not be surprised if net worth actually turned out to be negative.

Mutual Savings Banks   In the United States, savings banks are concentrated geographically in the Northeast. The depositors are owners of the banks, not merely creditors.

Table 6.4 presents aggregate balance sheets for U.S. savings banks. As with S&Ls, they attract most of their funds in the form of savings deposits and use those funds to invest in mortgages.

Credit Unions   A credit union is a depository institution accepting deposits only from members. The members must meet specific qualifications, such as working for a particular employer. For example, many universities have a credit union open to their employees. Credit unions offer savings and checking-type accounts. In addition, they make loans to their members for automobiles and home mortgages, as well as other personal loans. Many also issue credit cards to members.

Credit unions are exempt from federal and state income taxation. They are chartered by state agencies and by the National Credit Union Administration. There are approximately 20,000 of them in the United States.

Pension Funds

☞ The pension fund is a pool of funds managed to provide retirement income for its members.

An important financial institution for most employed people is the pension fund, which is a pool of money devoted to providing retirement income for its members. Pension funds may be either public or private. The public ones are managed by government agencies and include social security as well as the retirement programs of state and local governments. Private pension funds are operated by nongovernment units, such as employers.

Pension funds may also be classified as funded or unfunded. In a **funded pension plan** the sponsor of the plan authorizes a trustee to manage the assets in a way to provide future benefits for its members. In an **unfunded pension plan,** the sponsor has obligations but has not yet put aside any specific funds for meeting them. Many funded plans are only partially funded, or underfunded; that is, only some portion of the necessary money has been placed under the control of the trustee.

The major piece of federal law regulating private pension funds is the Employee Retirement Income Security Act of 1974 (ERISA), which governs the conditions under which a worker qualifies for coverage and stipulates minimum funding requirements. A Pension Benefit Guaranty Corporation guarantees the payment of at least a portion of promised benefits.

A problem with many pension plans is serious underfunding. For the government plans, this may be because they rely on the government's taxing authority to provide funds as necessary. Private pension funds have no taxing authority, so their underfunding is a very serious matter. If they go bankrupt, their employees may not receive their pensions or may receive only a fraction of the promised amount.

The money actually under the control of pension funds is invested in long-term securities such as stocks and bonds. Because the participants in the plan are, on average, relatively young, the obligations of the plan, on average, will become due for payment in the very distant future.

Insurance Companies

Insurance companies may be classified as providing either life or casualty insurance, with some writing policies in both areas. A casualty insurance firm might insure a house against fire, a driver against accidents, and an individual against health-related expenses. Insurance companies are financial intermediaries because they collect a large pool of funds from the premiums they charge for their coverage. Their liabilities are, on average, in the distant future, so they must employ those funds to earn enough to pay future claims. The principal liabilities of insurance companies are these future claims, and their assets are the investments they hold now to earn enough to make the future payments.

Focusing on the life insurance industry, Table 6.5 shows how companies distribute their assets across different investment opportunities. Their total assets were about $1.3 trillion at the end of 1989; the vast majority were invested in financial instruments such as bonds and stocks, with a mix of roughly 80 percent and 20 percent, respectively.

funded pension plan
a pension plan in which the sponsor places assets under the management of a trustee to manage in a way to provide future benefits for employees covered by the plan

unfunded pension plan
a pension plan in which the sponsor has obligations but has not yet put aside any specific funds for meeting them

FINANCE TODAY

Buying a Little Insurance Insurance

For most of us, choosing an insurance policy is about as much fun as having our teeth cleaned. Too often, we make the decision on the basis of an agent's sales pitch. But with the balance sheets of many insurers becoming increasingly shaky, that could spell disaster.

Unlike savings-and-loan depositors, you can't count on Washington to bail you out should your insurance company fail. Policyholders must depend on state guaranty funds—pools underwritten by assessments on insurers—to pay claims. These funds typically reimburse up to $100,000. That's a comfortable three times more than the average death benefit, though it may not fully cover you. Even if it does, when an insurer collapses, the funds can take a year or two to pay out, usually in one lump sum. And while guaranty funds for property casualty insurance exist in all states and the District of Columbia, there are no guaranty funds for life and health policies in Colorado, Louisiana, New Jersey, or D.C. If you're caught without a guaranty fund, you'll be just another creditor in a liquidation proceeding—and you may wait many years.

To avoid such unpleasantries, do some sleuthing about a prospective insurer's financial stability before you take out a policy. First, see if the company is currently in trouble. Many state insurance departments answer questions from the public about the financial stability of carriers.

How do you spot an insurer who is not in trouble but may be eventually? "You can't rely on the regulators for that," says Joseph M. Belth, an Indiana University insurance professor. He recommends A. M. Best Co., an Oldwick (N.J.) firm that publishes detailed analyses of insurers' financial condition. *Best's Insurance Reports*, which most libraries carry, provides letter ratings, from A+ (superior) to C− (fair). Many insurers are too small or too shaky to be rated. Also, check to see whether an insurer is on Best's "watch list" of companies whose financial condition has recently deteriorated; their ratings may soon be downgraded (see the table). The watch list is published periodically in the monthly magazine *Best's Review*.

Professor Belth synthesizes data from numerous sources in his own newsletter every September. For a copy, send $10 to *Insurance Forum*, Box 245, Ellettsville, Ind. 47429.

Checking out your prospective insurer can itself be some of the best insurance you'll ever get.

Insurers to be Wary of?*

Company	Home State	Assets (millions of dollars)
LIFE INSURANCE		
American Merchants	Minn.	$ 25.3
Atlantic & Pacific Life	Ga.	14.1
Mountain States Life	Colo.	13.5
PROPERTY-CASUALTY		
American Indemnity	Tex.	105.6
American Fire & Indemnity	Tex.	10.0
American Indemnity Lloyds	Tex.	0.5
Atlantic Casualty	N.C.	21.6
Coronet Insurance	Ill.	181.6
Cotton States Mutual	Ga.	112.0
Farmers Casualty	Iowa	14.4
Merchants & Businessmens	Pa.	21.6
Mid-Plains Insurance	Iowa	3.4
Texas General Indemnity	Tex.	10.1
Universal Insurance	N.C.	9.3

* Companies on A. M. Best's "watch list" rated B+ or below whose financial condition has worsened during 1990. Further deterioration could result in a ratings downgrade, although that has not happened yet.

Source: A. M. Best Co.

Source: Larry Light, "Buying a Little Insurance Insurance," *Business Week*, December 10, 1990, p. 207.

TABLE 6.5   Distribution of Life Insurance Company Assets as of December 31, 1989

	Amount (millions of dollars)
ASSETS	
Government securities	$ 77,297
Bonds and stocks	764,521
Mortgages	254,215
Real estate	39,908
Policy loans	57,439
Other assets	106,376
Total	**$1,299,756**

Source: Federal Reserve Bulletin, March 1991, Table 1.37.

Investment Companies

closed-end investment company
an investment company that issues a number of shares at creation, allows those shares to trade in the market and issues no new shares over the life of the company

mutual fund
a type of investment company that pools investments from individuals to purchase a portfolio and gives to investors fractional ownership of the created portfolio; a mutual fund also redeems investors' shares at the net asset value of the shares

☞ Investment companies intermediate the size and diversification requirements of their investors.

Investment companies have one of two forms, **closed-end investment companies** or **mutual funds,** depending on how they accept funds. A closed-end company accepts funds only at its creation, and these make up the firm's investment base. A mutual fund is always ready to receive money from new investors, and uses them to expand its portfolio. Given these characteristics, it is perhaps not surprising that the most successful type of investment company by far is the mutual fund.

Investment companies are essentially a phenomenon of the twentieth century. Overall, their growth has been very strong. Figure 6.3 shows that they have increased their size by a factor of more than 100 since 1950, with the most spectacular growth occurring in the 1980s. By contrast, the growth of closed-end companies' assets has been modest.

The preference for mutual funds must be due to the way the funds are invested. In fact, mutual funds have the natural advantage in growth, since they are open ended. Their ability to continue to receive money at any point makes growth substantially easier. Individual closed-end companies, once established, can grow in asset size only through successful investment of the original funds, and this segment of the industry can grow only through the creation of additional closed-end companies.

In both mutual funds and closed-end companies, investors purchase shares that entitle them to a fraction of the assets of the company. The total assets minus the liabilities constitute the net asset value. The net asset value per share is simply the total net asset value of the company divided by the number of shares outstanding. In a closed-end company, the number of shares is constant; for a mutual fund, the number may increase or decrease.

One of the most important benefits of investment companies is the fact that they provide a ready-made, diversified portfolio for the small investor.

FIGURE 6.3   The Growth of Mutual Funds

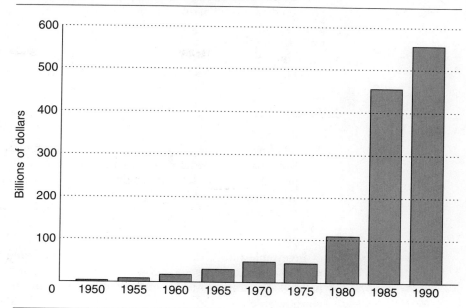

Such an individual may not have enough funds to construct a portfolio of 20 to 30 stocks without incurring relatively large transaction costs. If the investor wants to hold 20 stocks and the average price is $25 per share, the person would need $50,000 to avoid trading in odd lots. (An **odd lot** is a number of shares that is not an even multiple of 100. Odd lot trades are subject to high transaction costs.) For many investors, that is too large an amount to commit to the stock market.

The second clear benefit is the clerical and management function. To manage a portfolio of 20 stocks is a time-consuming task involving much bookkeeping. The investment company achieves important economies of scale in this function, to the benefit of the individual investor.

A third possible benefit, and one that is often claimed by investment company managers, is the provision of professional investment advice. One of the key rationales for using professional money managers is to capitalize on their presumably greater knowledge of the market. However, it is not clear that investment companies really succeed in providing this benefit to their clients.

odd lot
a set of shares of one company with a number different from a multiple of a round lot (usually 100 shares)

☞ Investment companies provide a ready-made portfolio for the investor.

☞ Most financial institutions develop an asset portfolio to match their liabilities.

Money Market Mutual Funds

Without doubt, one of the most important features in the development of mutual funds has been the emergence of the money market mutual fund that holds money market securities. Money market securities are debt securities issued with original maturities of up to one year. Usually, they are issued by very creditworthy borrowers, such as the federal government and prestigious firms. From their inception in 1974, money market mutual funds have come to dominate the market. Many people prefer them as a substitute for checking or savings accounts because the yields are often better than what banks offer. Today, however, banks also offer money market accounts.

SUMMARY

This chapter examined the role of financial intermediaries in a modern economy. In particular, intermediaries raise funds from surplus spending units and provide them to deficit spending units. Because surplus and deficit units have different needs for funds, intermediaries change the characteristics of the funds acquired from surplus units to make them more attractive to deficit units.

The typical surplus spending unit is a household with a small amount of investable funds, the need for liquidity, and strong aversion to risk. The typical deficit unit needs a commitment of funds for a long period of time in large amounts, with the understanding that the investment may involve considerable risk. Financial intermediaries provide a service by intermediating the surplus and deficit units' needs. In doing so, they attempt to raise funds at one rate and to employ them at a higher rate. In the case of a bank, the difference between the two rates constitutes the spread.

The United States has a variety of financial intermediaries, including several kinds of depository institutions, pension plans, insurance companies, and investment companies. The second part of this chapter considered some of their most important features.

QUESTIONS

1. Explain how a financial institution functions as a time intermediary.
2. Explain how a financial institution functions as a size intermediary.
3. How does a financial intermediary act to intermediate risk?
4. What role does the capital of the intermediary play in risk intermediation?
5. Why are financial institutions better information gatherers and processors than the typical suppliers of funds?
6. How does an intermediary offer the service of diversification?
7. Explain how and why some suppliers and users of funds seek to avoid intermediation.

8. Explain how the dual system of bank regulation functions.
9. Why are there one-bank holding companies?
10. Explain how a pension fund can be over- or underfunded.
11. What kind of maturity management strategy would you recommend for the assets of a life insurance company? What effect would that have on the riskiness of the insurance company?
12. What kinds of assets do life insurance companies prefer?
13. Among bonds and stocks, which do insurance companies seem to prefer? Why do you think this is the case?
14. Why do you think mutual funds have vastly outgrown closed-end investment companies?
15. What do you think are the main reasons for the deep S&L crisis of the late 1980s and early 1990s?

CHAPTER

7

The Money and Capital Markets

money market
the market for securities that have one year or less until maturity

bond market
the market for debt obligations with original maturities of more than one year

stock market
the market in which ownership claims on firms are traded

This chapter explores the institutional features of the money, bond, and stock markets in the United States. The **money market** is the market for debt securities issued with original maturities of up to one year. The maturity of a security is the time remaining until the last payment. The **bond market** is the market for debt securities originally issued with maturities longer than one year.

For most people, the **stock market,** where ownership claims on firms are traded, represents the focus of the securities markets. Television's nightly newscasts frequently report the day's developments in the stock market, but feature no other security reports on a regular basis. By contrast, the debt market receives relatively little attention. Part of the reason for this is the fact that bonds are not traded with the activity of stocks. Together, the stock and the bond markets constitute the capital market— the market for long-term commitments of investable funds.

SECURITY RETURNS

Investors who buy securities hope to earn positive returns. The return on a security for a given period equals the change in price of the security plus any payments made by the security during the time period divided by the amount originally paid for the security:

$$\text{Return} = \frac{\text{security's price change} + \text{payments from security}}{\text{original price paid}}$$

dividend
a cash payment made to the owner of a share of stock

coupon payment
the periodic payment made by coupon bonds

For a share of stock, the periodic payments are called **dividends.** For a debt instrument, the periodic payments are called interest payments or **coupon payments.** Therefore, for a share of stock, the return in a given period is:

$$\text{Stock return} = \frac{\text{change in stock price} + \text{cash dividends}}{\text{original stock price}}$$

For example, an investor might purchase a share of Gulf Oil for $70, hold it for six months, and sell it for $76. Also, assume that the share paid a dividend

FINANCE TODAY

The Ideal Pin-Up Stock

Playboy CEO Christie Hefner has a nettlesome problem—too many share-holders. Ever since *Playboy* went public in 1971, collectors attracted more by leggy blondes than by stocks and bonds have been buying single shares in *Playboy*. Reason: The stock certificates picture 1971 Playmate Willy Rey in the buff.

Hefner has announced a recapitalization plan that would force all 14,000 single-share stockholders, half the total, to sell their shares back to *Playboy*. This would save $100,000 annually in mailing and other expenses. Relax, single-shareholders. *Playboy* will send you another Willy "certificate" to replace the one you'll surrender and about $13, the current value of your share. Stockholders with a bigger stake will get new certificates. These will still portray a female, but one who's fully clothed.

Hefner also wants to issue a new class of non-voting shares that would enable her to raise money in the equity markets without diluting father Hugh's 71 percent voting stake. She would use the money to advance a diversification program. Short term, the real cash is in licensing the bunny logo, which in 1989 earned $5.7 million pretax. *Playboy* had an overall op-erating loss of $3.4 million.

But sometimes the logo is even too much for Hefner. She says those bunny air fresheners that dangle in so many cabs sully *Playboy's* image. So she has barred further production.

Source: "Hefner Dresses Up Her Stock," *Fortune*, June 18, 1990.

of $2.40 during this period. The return for that share over the six months is:

$$\text{Stock return} = \frac{\$6 + \$2.40}{\$70} = 0.12 = 12\%$$

For a debt instrument, the return on the investment is given by:

$$\text{Bond return} = \frac{\text{bond price change} + \text{coupon payments}}{\text{original bond price}}$$

For example, an investor who buys a bond for $940 and later sells it for $900 has a loss on the price change of the bond. However, if we assume that the bond made a coupon payment of $60 during this period, its return is:

$$\text{Bond return} = \frac{-\$40 + \$60}{\$900} = \frac{\$20}{\$900} = 0.022 = 2.2\%$$

Many debt instruments, such as those issued in the money market, do not have coupons. For them, the entire return comes from a change in price.

The return equation for these zero coupon securities is the same as the bond return equation, but the coupon payment is 0.

THE MONEY MARKET

marketable security
a financial obligation that can be converted into cash immediately with little reduction in its value

Cash earns no interest. Although it is advisable to have some cash available, firms and investors should avoid holding excess amounts. Because of the difficulty in anticipating future needs, however, companies and investors sometimes find themselves with excess cash available for short-term investment. The instruments of the money market, or **marketable securities,** act as a substitute for cash and as a medium for short-term investment. Their great advantage is that they can be converted into cash rapidly, yet earn interest.

Investment in the financial market normally provides a lower return than a firm is able to earn through investments in its own line of business. For example, commercial banks can earn a higher return by making loans than by investing in money market securities. For banks, however, funds are held in marketable securities in anticipation of depositors' withdrawals or to service short-term demand for loans. Because of these differences in returns, most firms do not want to invest in marketable securities on a long-term basis. Frequently, however, they will use marketable securities as a short-term investment medium.

☞ Many firms use marketable securities to manage seasonal fluctuations in the amount of cash available.

There are three basic motivations for investing in marketable securities. The first, difficulty predicting cash needs exactly, has been mentioned. Second, many firms have seasonal cash fluctuations, and might have an excess amount of cash for a short period, such as one month. They can invest the excess cash for one month in marketable securities. Third, firms often know in advance that they will soon need a large amount of cash. For example, a bank loan may be coming due for payment. In this case, they might accumulate the necessary funds over a period of time before the repayment and invest them in marketable securities on a short-term basis.

Money Market Instruments

☞ Governments, banks, and corporations all issue and invest in money market securities.

Whatever the reason for investment in marketable securities, many different types are available. Governments, banks, and corporations all issue and invest in money market securities.

Treasury Bills   One of the most important kinds of securities in the money market is the Treasury bill, or T bill. These are obligations of the U.S. Treasury issued with maturities of up to 52 weeks. They have a minimum denomination of $10,000 and go up from that minimum in increments of $5,000.

Currently, more than $500 billion worth of T bills are outstanding, with billions of dollars traded every day. As such, T bills represent one of the most important instruments of the money market. Because they are instruments issued by the Treasury, they are fully guaranteed by the U.S. government. Due to their great safety, they have the lowest yields of all marketable securities.

T bills are zero coupon securities, or **pure discount securities,** debt instruments that have no coupon. They have a stated **par value** or **face value,** such as $10,000, but sell for a lower price, say for $9,500. The difference between the par value and the price is the **discount,** $500 in our example.

pure discount security
a debt instrument paying no coupons, but which pays its par value on maturity

Commercial Paper Commercial paper consists of short-term, unsecured debt obligations of the largest and most creditworthy industrial and financial firms. By law, the initial maturity cannot exceed 270 days. Commercial paper, like the T bill, is a pure discount security. Some big issuers of commercial paper are the finance subsidiaries of American auto makers, such as General Motors Acceptance Corporation, and the major money center banks of New York, such as Citibank.

par value or **face value**
for a pure discount bond, the amount that is promised to be paid on maturity; for a coupon bond, the principal amount of the bond

discount
for a debt security, the difference between the promised future payment and the price

Certificates of Deposit As we have seen, banks acquire funds by accepting deposits and by borrowing money in other ways. One of the most important of these is certificates of deposit, or CDs, which may be either negotiable or nonnegotiable. A **negotiable instrument** is a security that can be sold and transferred from one party to another. Small nonnegotiable CDs are often held by individual investors. Large CDs, of $100,000 or more, are negotiable and are an important part of the money market. For a firm buying a CD, the purchase is very much like putting money into an interest-bearing bank account. The main differences are that the denomination is fixed and that the CD comes due for payment at a specific time.

negotiable instrument
a security that can be sold and transferred from one party to another

Eurodollars A **Eurodollar** is a dollar-denominated bank deposit held in a bank outside the United States. A Eurodollar CD is a dollar-denominated CD issued by a bank outside the United States.[1] The CD component is the most important part of the Eurodollar market. Many foreign banks issue Eurodollar CDs to attract dollar-denominated funds, and many investors prefer Eurodollar CDs to domestic CDs since they pay a somewhat higher rate of interest because they are generally somewhat riskier. The greater risk arises from the fact that the issuing banks are not as tightly regulated as U.S. banks. Accordingly, they must pay more to attract funds. On the other hand, since they escape the cost of tighter regulation, they are also able to pay the higher rate the market demands.

Eurodollar
a dollar-denominated bank deposit held outside the United States

To a large extent, the Eurodollar market was created by U.S. banking regulation. Virtually all bank deposits in the United States pay to be insured by the FDIC, an arm of the U.S. government. For banks outside the United States, the insurance requirements are normally less stringent, so the banks avoid some of this cost. All U.S. banks are subject to reserve requirements, and the higher these are, the more restricted the banks are in the amount

---

[1] In addition to Eurodollars, one sometimes hears mention of Asian dollars and petrodollars. As defined here, these would be components of the Eurodollar market as well. Asian dollars are dollar-denominated deposits held in Asian-based banks, and petrodollars are dollar-denominated deposits generated by oil-producing countries.

Wild Days on the Street

For the first time in the history of the New York Stock Exchange (NYSE), more than 100 million shares were traded on August 18, 1982, with exactly 132,681,120 shares being traded. In 1985, the average daily trading volume exceeded 100 million shares for the first time. Today, it is common for more than 200 million shares to trade in a single day, and the daily average is about 160 million shares.

The following table lists the largest-volume trading day of each year in the NYSE during the 1980s.

Busiest Trading Day of the Year at the NYSE

Date	Shares (thousands)
October 16, 1989	416,396
June 17, 1988	343,949
October 20, 1987	608,149
December 19, 1986	244,293
December 5, 1985	181,027
August 3, 1984	236,565
January 6, 1983	129,411
November 4, 1982	149,385
January 7, 1981	92,881
November 5, 1980	84,297

All of these annual record days strain the system for recording and reporting transactions. The exchanges never seem to be quite able to modernize their procedures as quickly as their volume grows. For instance, on October 20, 1987, the market essentially overheated and trading had to stop to catch its breath. No wonder, since that was the day following the infamous " Black Monday," when the Dow Jones Industrial Average suffered a demoralizing 508-point drop, the worst in the market's history.

they can lend. These regulatory differences create important cost differences between U.S. banks and their foreign competitors, and they also create significant risk differences. Therefore, banks taking Eurodollar deposits must pay a higher interest rate than would be paid by a domestic U.S. bank.[2]

---

[2] For more on Eurodollar CDs and the importance of U.S. banking regulation in their creation, see Joseph F. Sinkey, Jr., *Commercial Bank Financial Management* (New York: Macmillan, 1983), pp. 585–587.

The graph depicts the average, high, and low daily volumes from 1950 to 1989. Clearly, the volume growth during that period has been truly spectacular. Perhaps it is not surprising to find that with higher average daily volumes comes a greater volume volatility. In other words, as the dispersion between high and low daily volumes increases, the average volume increases. This statistical behavior goes by the unfriendly name of heteroskedasticity.

Average, High, and Low Volume Days in the New York Stock Exchange

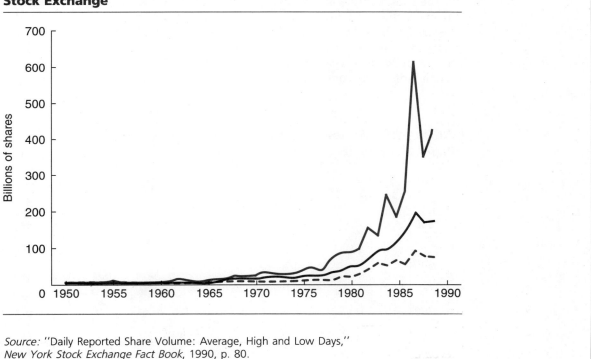

Source: "Daily Reported Share Volume: Average, High and Low Days," *New York Stock Exchange Fact Book*, 1990, p. 80.

Banker's Acceptances   The banker's acceptance is a money market instrument used mainly in financing international trade. It is a draft against a bank ordering the bank to pay some specified amount at a future date. When the bank accepts that obligation, and stamps the draft "accepted," it creates a banker's acceptance. The bank undertakes this obligation because the drawer of the draft (analogous to the writer of a check) has made arrangements with the bank for that service. Once the banker's acceptance is created, it is ready for investment as a marketable security.

In international trade, few firms are willing to ship goods on open account, as is often done domestically. Because companies in two different countries may not know each other so well, and may not have strong measures of recourse against those who default on their obligations, it is very useful for banks to come into play. Assume that a small U.S. firm wishes to import from a foreign supplier. It is much easier for the foreign supplier to trust the name of a respected American bank than the unknown importer. The creation of a banker's acceptance means that the bank is committed to making the specified payment, even if the importing firm defaults, thus giving the foreign supplier an added measure of safety. The original obligation of the American importer still remains, so banker's acceptances are normally "two-name paper"; that is, the bank and the firm for whom the acceptance was created are obligated to make the payment. Thus a banker's acceptance is a very safe security. Figure 7.1 shows the growth of the commercial paper and banker's acceptances markets in recent years. As indicated, the value of outstanding acceptances has actually decreased, whereas the commercial paper market not only is much larger, but continues to expand steadily.

FIGURE 7.1   Growth of Banker's Acceptances and Commercial Paper Markets (total value outstanding)

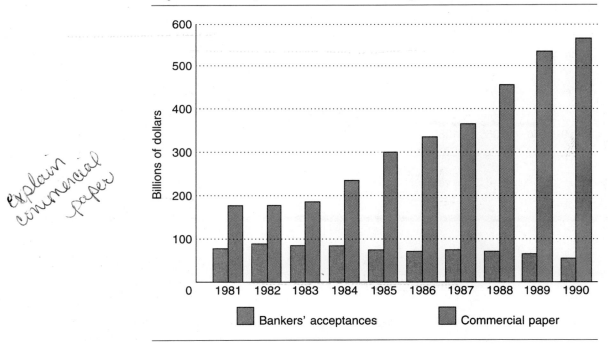

Source: Federal Reserve Bulletin, various issues.

repo
short for repurchase agreement, which arises when one party sells a security to another party with an agreement to buy it back at a specified time and at a specified price

overnight repo
repo agreements that are just for one day

Repurchase Agreements   Repurchase agreements, or **repos,** arise when one party sells a security to another party with an agreement to buy it back at a specified time and at a specified price. The difference between the sale and repurchase prices defines the interest rate. Repos are useful mainly for very short-term financing, the great majority being for just one day. Because of this, they are often called **overnight repos.**

By buying a security, with a commitment to resell it the next day at a slightly higher price, a corporation puts its excess cash to work. The desire for this kind of transaction has led to the creation of the repo market. Most of the securities used in the repo market are U.S. government securities.

Risks in Marketable Securities

default risk
the chance that one or more promised payments on a security will be deferred or missed altogether

interest rate risk
the risk that a security's value will change due to a change in interest rates

liquidity risk
the risk that a marketable security cannot be converted easily into cash

Although marketable securities are short-term instruments, they carry some risk. First, **default risk** is the risk that the obligation will not be paid as promised. U.S. Treasury issues are free of default risk, but instruments such as CDs and commercial paper carry a slight chance of default. In the early 1970s, for example, Penn Central stunned the financial market when it defaulted on its commercial paper.

A second kind of risk is **interest rate risk,** the chance that the security's value will change due to a change in interest rates. When interest rates rise, the prices of debt obligations fall, as does the value of a marketable security. However, short-term securities, such as those that firms would purchase as marketable securities, are affected relatively little by changes in interest rates. A rise in interest rates results in some fall in prices, and a drop causes an increase.

A third risk associated with all marketable securities is **liquidity risk,** the chance that the security cannot be converted easily into cash. Sometimes, markets are disrupted and the liquidity of securities is impaired. For example, if a firm holds a CD of a bank undergoing reorganization, there may be some delay before the CD can be converted to cash. Again, these risks are relatively low.

Yield Relationships in the Money Market

☞ Money market instruments differ in their risk levels and offer different yields to compensate for those risk differences.

The different risk factors enumerated above are present in marketable securities to different degrees, and are reflected in interest rates. Normally, T bills offer the lowest rate since they have the best backing. Commercial paper and banker's acceptances typically have rates that are very close, with commercial paper issued by top industrial corporations having a slightly lower yield. For both, the yield lies below that of CDs. The difference between commercial paper and CD rates reflects the greater creditworthiness of the best industrial corporations, in comparison with banks.

A banker's acceptance offers a lower return than CDs because it is two-name paper, which gives the lender an added margin of security. Finally,

FIGURE 7.2   Money Rates

MONEY RATES

Friday, April 12, 1991

The key U.S. and foreign annual interest rates below are a guide to general levels but don't always represent actual transactions.

PRIME RATE: 8¾%–9%. The base rate on corporate loans at large U.S. money center commercial banks.

FEDERAL FUNDS: 5½% high, 4⅞% low, 4⅞% near closing bid, 5% offered. Reserves traded among commercial banks for overnight use in amounts of $1 million or more. Source: Babcock Fulton Prebon (U.S.A.) Inc.

DISCOUNT RATE: 6%. The charge on loans to depository institutions by the New York Federal Reserve Bank.

CALL MONEY: 7½% to 8½%. The charge on loans to brokers on stock exchange collateral.

COMMERCIAL PAPER placed directly by General Motors Acceptance Corp.: 5.75% 30 to 149 days; 5.80% 150 to 270 days.

COMMERCIAL PAPER: High-grade unsecured notes sold through dealers by major corporations in multiples of $1,000: 5.875% 30 days; 5.90% 60 days; 5.90% 90 days.

CERTIFICATES OF DEPOSIT: 5.77% one month; 5.78% two months; 5.82% three months; 5.95% six months; 6.40% one year. Average of top rates paid by major New York banks on primary new issues of negotiable C.D.s, usually on amounts of $1 million and more. The minimum unit is $100,000. Typical rates in the secondary market: 5.90% one month; 5.95% three months; 6.05% six months.

BANKERS ACCEPTANCES: 5.73% 30 days; 5.72% 60 days; 5.72% 90 days; 5.73% 120 days; 5.74% 150 days; 5.74% 180 days. Negotiable, bank-backed business credit instruments typically financing an import order.

LONDON LATE EURODOLLARS: 5 15/16% – 5 13/16%

one month; 6% – 5⅞% two months; 6 1/16% – 5 15/16% three months; 6⅛% – 6% four months; 6¼% – 6⅛% five months; 6¼% – 6⅛% six months.

LONDON INTERBANK OFFERED RATES (LIBOR): 6% one month; 6⅛% three months; 6 5/16% six months; 6¾% one year. The average of interbank offered rates for dollar deposits in the London market based on quotations at five major banks. Effective rate for contracts entered into two days from date appearing at top of this column.

FOREIGN PRIME RATES: Canada 10.50%–10.75%; Germany 10.50%; Japan 8.25%; Switzerland 11.13%; Britain 12%. These rate indications aren't directly comparable; lending practices vary widely by location.

TREASURY BILLS: Results of the Monday, April 8, 1991, auction of short-term U.S. government bills, sold at a discount from face value in units of $10,000 to $1 million: 5.60% 13 weeks; 5.68% 26 weeks.

FEDERAL HOME LOAN MORTGAGE CORP. (Freddie Mac): Posted yields on 30-year mortgage commitments for delivery within 30 days. 9.42%, standard conventional fixed-rate mortgages; 6.50%, 2% rate capped one-year adjustable rate mortgages. Source: Telerate Systems Inc.

FEDERAL NATIONAL MORTGAGE ASSOCIATION (Fannie Mae): Posted yields on 30 year mortgage commitments for delivery within 30 days (priced at par). 9.36%, standard conventional fixed rate-mortgages; 7.20%, 6/2 rate capped one-year adjustable rate mortgages. Source: Telerate Systems Inc.

MERRILL LYNCH READY ASSETS TRUST: 5.94%. Annualized average rate of return after expenses for the past 30 days; not a forecast of future returns.

Source: Wall Street Journal, April 15, 1991. Reprinted by permission of *Wall Street Journal*, © 1991 Dow Jones & Company, Inc. All Rights Reserved Worldwide.

Eurodollar CDs pay a greater rate than domestic CDs because of their greater risk. While these relationships normally prevail, occasional exceptions exist. One good source of information about current rates of marketable securities is the column "Money Rates," which appears daily in the *Wall Street Journal*. A sample is shown in Figure 7.2.

THE BOND MARKET IN THE UNITED STATES

The U.S. bond market can be divided according to the three major types of issuers—the federal government, corporations, and municipalities. Each has distinguishing characteristics, including maturity, tax status, and risk level. Consequently, it is easiest to focus on them separately.

The Market for U.S. Government Bonds

☞ The U.S. government is the world's single largest debtor, with outstanding federal securities exceeding $3 trillion.

The U.S. government is the world's single largest debtor, with debt exceeding $3 trillion. Figure 7.3(a) shows the growth in net federal debt since 1950. In spite of the increasing trend, the amount of outstanding debt relative to gross national product (GNP) actually declined from the 1950s to 1980, although it has sloped upward since then, as shown in Figure 7.3(b). Of this outstanding debt, the most important part is U.S. Treasury debt.

FIGURE 7.3   Net Federal Debt

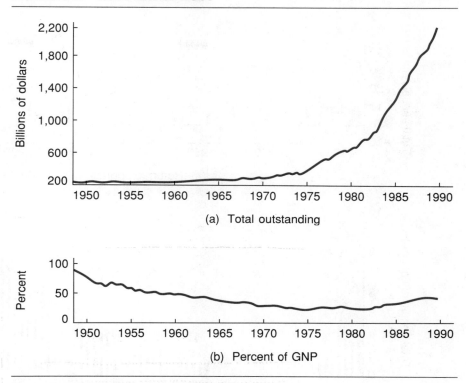

(a) Total outstanding

(b) Percent of GNP

Source: Federal Reserve Historical Chart Book, 1989, p. 49.

Treasury Debt

☞ The three principal
kinds of U.S. Treasury obligations are Treasury bills,
notes, and bonds.

The three principal kinds of U.S. Treasury obligations are bills, notes and bonds. We discussed T bills above, so the focus here is on the longer-maturity issues. Treasury notes and bonds are alike in the structure of their payment streams, and differ only in their maturity. The notes have original maturities of between 1 and 10 years, whereas Treasury bonds are usually issued for much longer maturities, usually in the range of 20 to 30 years. Quotations for various federal issues are carried daily in the *Wall Street Journal* and other major newspapers.

coupon bond
a bond making a series
of regular payments,
called coupon payments,
throughout its life

Treasury notes and bonds are **coupon bonds**—bonds that make regular payments over their life and that return their face value on maturity. Most have semiannual coupon payments. Figure 7.4 presents the year-by-year percentage returns for both bills and bonds. Notice that the investor in bills has never had an actual loss in any given year, because T bills mature in one year or less and they have always been paid as promised. The investor in Treasury bonds has been stung on occasion, however. Even though all pay-

FIGURE 7.4 Yearly Total Returns on Treasury Bonds and Bills

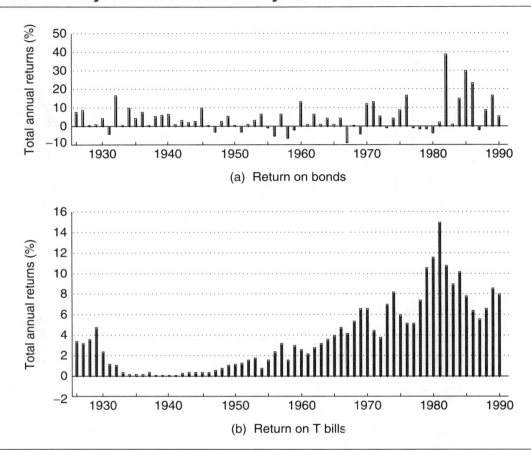

(a) Return on bonds

(b) Return on T bills

Source: © *Stock, Bonds, Bills, and Inflation: 1991 Yearbook*, Ibbotson Associates, Chicago, (annually updates work by Roger G. Ibbotson and Rex A. Sinquefield). All rights reserved.

ments have been made as promised, an investor could still have a loss in a given year, because the dollar return on holding a Treasury bond for a given year is composed of the interest payments received plus any price change in the bond itself. In the years of losses shown in Figure 7.4, the fall in the bond price exceeded the interest income, giving a net loss on the holding. For the entire period 1926–1990, $1,000 invested in T bills at the outset would have grown to $10,430. The same $1,000 invested in Treasury bonds would have grown to $17,400 over the same period.

inflation
the change in the general
price level over time

To evaluate the success of an investment, we must also consider **infla-tion**—the change in the general price level over time. If we divide the terminal

FINANCE TODAY

Where Pennies Still Count

A 29-cent stamp is irritating enough. Couldn't they have made it an easier 30 cents? Pennies are bothersome—not like 20 years ago when a stamp cost 8 cents, the best seat to a Broadway show cost $15, and money was money. Or was it? Adjusted for inflation, yesterday's prices weren't always a bargain (see the table).

In February 1991, the price of a first-class stamp, which is good for an ounce of content, represented a 45 percent increase in inflation-adjusted terms over the 1971 price. Postmaster General Anthony M. Frank says that postal productivity helps keep prices down: The post office delivered 218,614 pieces of mail per employee last year, vs. 123,443 in 1971. But Frank, CEO of First Nationwide Bank—a successful San Francisco S&L—until 1988, knows the value of small change. He pushed for a 30-cent stamp. He quotes the saying "Penny wise, pound foolish," and adds, "The current increase may be called penny foolish." The independent Postal Rate Commission clearly disagreed.

Prices: What's Up, What's Down

	1971 Price	Price in 1991 Dollars	1991 Price	Change
UP				
Levi's jeans	$ 6.98	$ 23.56	$ 38.00	61%
First-class stamp	0.06	0.20	0.29	45
Toyota Corolla	2,145.00	7,239.00	9,618.00	33
Broadway musical	15.00	50.62	60.00	19
Hershey Bar (1 oz.)	0.07	0.24	0.26	8
DOWN				
Salmon (1 lb.)	0.98	3.31	2.95	−11
Disneyland (for 4)	7.80	127.57	100.00	−22
Sirloin steak (1 lb.)	1.45	4.89	3.65	−25
Los Angeles *Times*	0.10	0.34	0.25	−27
Milk (half gallon)	0.58	1.96	1.39	−29

Source: Sally Solo, "Where Pennies Still Count," *Fortune,* February 25, 1991.

value of the investments by the change in the price level over the same period, we get a dollar amount that indicates how much purchasing power the proceeds from the investment would have. In other words, if you invest for a year and earn 10 percent, but the price level goes up 10 percent during the year, you have the same purchasing power at the end of the investment period as you had at the beginning. The investor who put $1,000 into T bills in 1926 and kept it invested would have had $1,400 in purchasing power in 1990. The persistent T bond investor would have enjoyed a greater increase, as a $1,000 investment in 1926 would have grown to a purchasing power of $2,400. Clearly, over this period, the rate of return on Treasury securities was only slightly greater than the inflation rate.

The Corporate Bond Market

☞ Private corporations issue bonds as a source of long-term funding for their investment plans.

Corporate bonds are issued by private corporations as a source of long-term funding. The issuer promises to make a series of payments on specified dates. For many investors, estimating the chance that the promise will be kept is extremely important. To aid them in making that assessment, services are available that rate the quality of various bonds.

☞ Bond prices change as a result of changes in both interest rates and the prospects of the issuing firm.

The ratings are designed to measure default risk—the chance that one or more payments on the bond will be deferred or missed altogether. We already considered default risk in connection with money market securities, but in the bond market default risk is more important because of the extremely long time until bonds are repaid. Table 7.1 presents the ratings of the two principal services. In general, they follow each other very closely.

The differences in yields of various bonds are due largely to differences in their risk. Figure 7.5 shows the yield relationship between top-quality and lower-quality corporate bonds.

TABLE 7.1   Bond Rating Categories

Moody's	Standard & Poor's
Aaa	AAA
Aa	AA
A	A
Baa	BBB
Ba	BB
B	B
	CCC-CC
Caa	
	C
Ca	
	DDD-D
C	

FIGURE 7.5   Long-Term Bond Yields

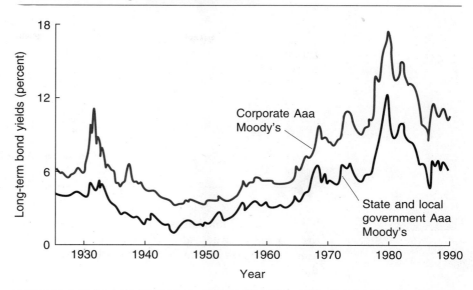

Source: Federal Reserve Historical Chart Book, 1989, p. 97.

The Municipal Bond Market

municipal bond
a debt obligation issued by a state or local governmental agency that is usually free from federal taxation and also from certain state and local taxes

☞ Because of their tax exemption, municipal bonds are of greater relative value to investors with high marginal tax rates.

A **municipal bond** is a debt security issued by a government or government agencies other than those associated with the federal government. Almost all municipal bonds are exempt from federal income taxation, a key feature that distinguishes them from other bonds and gives them greater relative value to investors with high marginal tax rates. Such investors can obtain the same after-tax return from a relatively low-yielding municipal bond or a higher-yielding taxable bond. For bonds of like risk and maturity, the rational investor prefers the one that gives the higher after-tax return. Table 7.2 presents taxable yields and their equivalent tax-exempt yield for investors in different tax brackets. As the table shows, the higher the tax rate, the greater should be the preference for tax-exempt securities. Given the after-tax equivalences, it is not surprising that market yields for tax-exempt securities are lower than those of risk-equivalent taxable securities. An investor in the 30 percent marginal tax bracket would be equally happy with a municipal bond yielding 7 percent or a taxable bond yielding 10 percent, assuming the other variables are comparable.

In addition to exemption from federal taxation, some municipal bonds are exempt from income taxation by the state and municipality in which they were issued. In spite of the fact that the municipal bond market is huge in total size, exceeding the size of the corporate bond market, it is not very

TABLE 7.2   **Taxable and Tax-Exempt Equivalent Yields**

	Marginal Tax Rate			
Taxable Yield	20%	30%	40%	50%
8%	6.4	5.6	4.8	4.0
10	8.0	7.0	6.0	5.0
12	9.6	8.4	7.2	6.0
14	11.2	9.2	8.8	7.0
16	12.8	11.2	9.6	8.0

The entries show the equivalent tax-exempt yields to the taxable yields in the leftmost column for various tax rates.

liquid market
one in which an asset can be sold easily for a price that approximates its true value

liquid. A **liquid market** is one in which an asset can be sold easily for a price that equals its true value. This illiquidity results from the fact that many municipal issues are small, and from the desire of investors to keep the issues they buy.

The Bond Contract

bond contract or **bond indenture**
a legal document stating in precise terms the promises made by the issuer of a bond and the rights of the bondholders

trustee
for a bond issue, the agent charged with the responsibility of protecting the rights of the bondholders and monitoring the performance of the issuer to ensure that his promises are kept

first mortgage bond
a bond offering to the bondholders the first claim against specific pieces of property owned by the corporation in the event of default

The **bond contract,** or **bond indenture,** is a legal document precisely stating the promises made by the bond issuer and the rights of the bondholders. For all corporate bonds issued in interstate commerce with an issue size above $5 million, the Trust Indentures Act requires that a trustee be established. The **trustee** has the responsibility of protecting the rights of the bondholders and ensuring that the issuer's promises are kept. The trustee is usually a bank that is financially independent from the issuer.

In addition to specifying the amount and timing of payments made to bondholders, the bond indenture contains numerous covenants. Among the most important of these are the portions defining the security that the issuer is offering and the specification of how the bond is to be retired. Bondholders naturally desire the greatest security possible for their investment, other things being equal, leading some issuers to back bonds by mortgages on specific corporate assets. For example, an issuer could offer a fleet of vehicles or a production plant as security. In the event of default, the trustee would be empowered to seize the specified assets in order to recoup the investment of the bondholders. Such bonds may be either first mortgage bonds or have some inferior status, such as second or third mortgage. A **first mortgage bond** gives the bondholders first claim on assets specified in the mortgage. In the event of a default or bankruptcy, those assets are used to repay the bondholders. Clearly, the first mortgage is the best kind of security.

In addition to mortgage bonds, some firms offer security under slightly different arrangements. For those without sufficient physical assets, it is customary to pledge financial assets. Bonds secured by financial assets are known as **collateral trust bonds.**

collateral trust bonds
bonds secured by financial assets

Bonds with no specific pledge of particular assets are **debentures,** which are often used by financially strong corporations. When they are issued after mortgage bonds are already outstanding, they have an inferior claim on the assets of the corporation. In addition to straight debentures, **subordinated debentures** are unsecured bonds that have an inferior claim to other outstanding debentures. They are said to be junior to the original debentures.

debenture
a bond with no specific pledge of particular assets as security

First mortgage bondholders have the strongest claim on the assets and common stockholders have the weakest. Without any specific security pledged to them, debentures may seem a very risky kind of investment. But bond contracts for debentures, as well as for mortgage bonds, often have certain restrictive covenants that protect bondholders by restricting the behavior of the issuer. For example, a firm might be required to maintain a certain level of current assets relative to current liabilities, or it may be prohibited from issuing additional debt until outstanding debt is retired. Another restrictive covenant might constrain the amount of dividends paid to common stockholders. These restrictions enhance the safety of the bond investment, and the trustee has the responsibility for ensuring that the issuer complies with them. The contract also specifies how the bond is to be retired, and there are many different ways of doing this.

subordinated debenture
a debenture that has a claim that is inferior to other outstanding debentures

Many bonds are **callable bonds.** That is, the issuer has the right to call them, paying them at a price stipulated in the bond contract. Issuers have an incentive to call their existing bonds if the prevailing interest rate is lower than the coupon rate being paid on the bonds. Usually the issuer is not permitted to call bonds for a certain period of time after issue. Also, the price the issuer must pay, the **call price,** usually gives a premium to the bondholder. Often, only a portion of a bond is called, and the particular bonds to be called are selected at random and published by serial number in the financial press.

callable bond
a bond that may be retired at the discretion of the issuer, usually subject to certain constraints

call price
the price the issuer must pay to retire a callable bond when it is called

Callable bonds are often retired through a **sinking fund,** which allows for the orderly and gradual retirement of bonds prior to the maturity date. The sinking fund may operate in two basic ways. The trustee may use its resources to purchase bonds in the open market, or the fund may provide for retirement of a certain portion of the bonds on a redemption date. In such a case, specific bonds are called to be surrendered on a certain date.

sinking fund
a fund set aside by the bond issuer for the orderly retirement of bonds

THE MARKET FOR COMMON STOCK

common stock
equity capital that has been contributed by parties outside the corporation

A share of **common stock** is a security representing an ownership interest in a corporation. Ownership is shared among all of the holders of common stock, with the percentage depending on the portion of stock owned. These shares are traded in the stock market. As owners of a firm, the holders of common stock have certain rights and responsibilities.

Common Stock Rights and Responsibilities

As owners of the corporation, shareholders have certain privileges and responsibilities. Because it represents an ownership claim, common stock constitutes a **residual claim** on the firm's assets and proceeds. The claim is residual, because it is on the value of the firm after other claimants have been satisfied. For example, owners of bonds are entitled to receive their promised payments before the stockholders receive their money. In this sense, stockholders are the last in line to enforce their claims; however, they can justifiably claim everything in the firm once the other claimants have been satisfied.

It is clear that common stockholders have the riskiest position of all claimants. In spite of this, common stock has important risk-limiting features, such as limited liability. **Limited liability** means that the shareholder cannot lose more than the amount invested.

Although the stock is owned, the only cash flow from the shares is the cash dividend. Many firms, particularly new ones and those in financial distress, pay no dividends.

Owners of common stock vote on major matters pertaining to the operation of the firm, usually at the time of the annual meeting. Typically, shareholders vote on issues that have been carefully defined by management with an eye toward securing the desired outcome. As an example, they are often asked to vote on new directors for the corporation, with a slate of nominees previously picked by management.

In the normal event, management can direct the course of most corporate elections. One important tool for doing so is the **proxy,** a statement giving another party the right to vote one's shares. Generally it is impossible for most shareholders actually to appear at the meeting to cast their votes, so they empower some other party to vote for them by giving them a proxy. Management can solicit these proxies from indifferent shareholders or those who cannot attend the meeting, and in so doing naturally acquire a great deal of voting power. Often it has an even more effective means of amassing voting power. That is, shareholders who fail to return their proxy forms are considered to have conferred their proxies to management by default. Given the normal apathy of many shareholders, this arrangement virtually guarantees effective control of voting.

On occasion, however, real disputes arise, causing serious dissention and making the voting issue important. Dissident shareholders might try to unseat management or change fundamental managerial policies. To do so, they have to acquire voting rights themselves by gaining proxies. This leads to a **proxy fight,** the struggle to gain voting rights from shareholders who will not be attending the annual meeting.

Sometimes, owners of common stock receive stock dividends or stock splits. These generate no cash flows, so they are substantially less important than cash dividends. A stock dividend occurs when a firm creates additional shares and gives them to current shareholders. A stock split is similar. This distribution of new shares is a **stock dividend** when the increase in shares

residual claim
a claim that is to be satisfied only after other claims, such as that of the common stockholders of the firm

limited liability
the principle that stockholders' financial liabilities are limited to the value of their stock

☞ Common stockholders have the riskiest position of all claimants against a firm.

proxy
a statement giving another party the right to vote one's shares

proxy fight
the struggle to gain voting rights from shareholders who will not be attending the annual meeting

stock dividend
the distribution of new shares to existing stockholders, when the amount of increase in the number of shares is 25 percent or less

FINANCE TODAY

The Stock Market According to Dave Barry

The way this works is, you find yourself a reputable stockbroker (defined as "a stockbroker who has not been indicted yet"), and you give him some money. He keeps some for himself and uses the rest to buy you a stock that he got a Hot Tip on and Recommends Highly, although of course he keeps his own personal money in a mayonnaise jar. Next you spend a lot of time trying to keep track of your stock by frowning at the newspaper financial listings, which look like this:

	Up	Odds	RBI	VCR	Low Tide	East
Gmrh	34	4–3	23	$349	3:43	One spade
Sodm	12	8–1	8(e)	45% off	IRT #2	No trumps

You also spend a lot of time listening to radio and TV "financial analysts" who clearly have no idea what the stock market is going to do next, but are absolutely brilliant at coming up with creative explanations as to why it did whatever it just did. ("Stocks were off sharply today in response to rumors that the July unemployment figures have been eaten by goats.") Eventually you start to notice that your "can't miss" stock is not performing up to expectations, as evidenced by the fact that the newspaper is now listing it on the comics page. Finally you tell your broker to sell it, which he does, taking another chunk of the proceeds for himself and paying the balance to you out of one of those bus-driver-style change dispensers. Then he's off to the golf course, to pick up some more Hot Tips for you.

Source: Dave Barry, *Dave Barry Turns 40* (New York: Crown Publishers, Inc., 1990), pp. 112–113.

stock split
the distribution of new shares to existing stockholders, when the amount of increase in the number of shares is greater than 25 percent

is 25 percent or less. The distribution of shares is a **stock split** when the percentage increase exceeds 25 percent.

To see how this works, assume that a stockholder owns 100 shares of a stock trading at $80, and the corporation decides on a 20 percent, or a five-for-four, stock dividend. Thus the stockholder has 120 shares, and the question becomes how much they are worth. Other things being equal, the decision to have a stock dividend generates no cash flow for the firm or investor. As such, it should have no impact on the firm's value. This means that the shares should fall in value by an amount proportional to the dividend. The original market value of the 100 shares was $8,000. After the stock dividend, there are 120 shares. Since, by assumption, nothing has happened to alter the firm's cash flows, the wealth of the stockholder should be unchanged. This means that the 120 shares should still have a total value of $8,000, or a price of $66.67 per share.

Because a stock dividend or a stock split by itself cannot change the basic operations of the firm or its future cash flows, it should not have any impact on the firm's value.[3] Notice, however, that a stock dividend or split with the cash dividend per share held constant does mean that the stockholder's cash dividend is increased. In the preceding example, assume that the original cash dividend was $0.20 per share. This means that the annual dividend originally received was $20 per year. If that cash dividend is maintained at $0.20 per share but the number of shares is increased to 120, the annual cash dividend will be increased to $24 on the holding.

Common stockholders may also have a right to maintain their current fractional ownership of the firm, called a **preemptive right.** It means that a stockholder may buy a fraction of any new issues of shares to maintain the same fractional ownership of the firm.

Organization of the Stock Market: The Secondary Market

The stock market can be divided into the **secondary market** for existing securities, and the **primary market** for new securities. We focus here on the secondary market, and the next chapter considers the primary market. The secondary market consists of organized stock exchanges and a dealer market called the over-the-counter market.

A **stock exchange** is an exchange with a trading floor where all of the trading of stocks takes place under rules created by the exchange. In the United States, the organized exchanges share many features, largely because the smaller exchanges have patterned themselves after the New York Stock Exchange.

Organized Stock Exchanges in the United States The major stock exchanges in the United States are the New York Stock Exchange (NYSE), the American Stock Exchange (ASE), and the Pacific Stock Exchange (PSE). Smaller exchanges are located in Denver, Chicago, Philadelphia, and Boston. Within the United States, the dominance of the NYSE is truly dramatic, with the majority of all shares traded on exchanges being traded there. Only firms meeting certain minimum requirements are eligible for listing on the NYSE. The exchange imposes requirements in the form of earning power, total value of outstanding stock, and number of shareholders. Smaller firms trade on other exchanges or in the over-the-counter market.

General Organizational Features of Stock Exchanges A stock exchange is a voluntary organization formed by a group of individuals to provide an

preemptive right
the right of common stockholders to buy new shares before the shares are offered to others

secondary market
the market for the exchange of existing financial claims

primary market
the market for the original issuance of securities

stock exchange
an organization for trading stocks, in which the trading takes place under rules created by the exchange at the physical facility provided by the exchange

☞ There is a secondary market for the trading of already existing securities, and a primary market for the selling of newly created securities.

---

[3] The classic study of the impact of stock splits on share prices, "The Adjustment of Stock Prices to New Information," by Eugene Fama, Lawrence Fisher, Michael Jensen, and Richard Roll, *International Economic Review*, 10, 1969, pp. 1–20, concludes that stock splits have no effect on the value of the underlying shares.

institutional setting in which common stock and other securities can be bought and sold. Usually, the stock exchange is a nonprofit corporation that exists to further the financial interest of its members. Members participate through the ownership of seats on the exchange. Seats can be bought and sold like other assets, and their price depends mainly on the volume of trading and the price level of stocks. The exchange formulates and enforces certain rules designed to govern trading activity. Only members or their representatives are allowed to trade on the exchange. In that sense, they have a monopoly position, because all orders to buy or sell securities on a given exchange must flow through a member.

One of the key regulations imposed by the exchange concerns restrictions on the place and time at which trading may occur. Each stock exchange allows trading only on its floor and only during approved hours. The floor of an exchange is an actual physical location to which orders are transmitted for execution.

Some of the people working on the floor are employed by the exchange, whereas others trade stocks for themselves, hoping to make a profit. In addition, there are **brokers** on the floor, individuals who receive orders from the public, execute the orders, and charge a commission for this service. Examples of some of the largest brokerage firms are Merrill Lynch, Salomon Brothers and Paine Webber.

broker
a person who executes orders to buy or sell for a client

The Specialist System   Each security traded on an exchange has a **specialist** assigned to it who stands ready to trade at least 100 shares of a stock. In addition, the specialist keeps a record of all orders awaiting execution in the stock.

specialist
on a stock exchange, the member assigned to make a market in a given security, including holding shares in inventory and keeping a record of all orders awaiting execution

Specialists have the responsibility of making a market in a given security. As such, they must maintain an inventory of the security and stand ready to buy or sell shares on order from other members of the exchange or public. This requires considerable capital investment and involves taking a risk position in the stock. As compensation, the specialist expects to make a profit on each share of stock traded.

bid-ask spread
the difference between the price at which one is willing to sell (asked price) and the price at which one is willing to buy (bid price)

The specialist maintains a **bid-ask spread**, offering to buy shares at the lower bid price and to sell them at the asked price. The specialist is free, within certain limits, to set both prices. In a certain sense, the ideal situation would be to set them so that the number of buy orders exactly balanced the number of sell orders. This would leave the inventory at a constant level, and the specialist would make a gross profit equal to the bid-ask spread on the purchase and subsequent sale of each security.

However, the life of the specialist is not so easy. New information reaches the market on a random basis and influences stock prices. A specialist who does not respond to the new information, and who leaves the bid and ask prices as they were, will soon have orders on only one side of the market. In addition, other traders outside the exchange may sometimes have more information than the specialist. Finally, the specialist is under the surveillance of the exchange to ensure that the bid-ask spreads are not too wide.

Stalking the Elusive Trigger

"The sharp drop in U.S. stock prices in October 1987 gave birth to at least one industry—the production of explanations for the crash. Among the most popular are those related to the U.S. market's institutional structure and practices—computer-assisted trading, portfolio insurance, the organized exchange specialists, concurrent trading in stock index futures, margin rules, and the absence of 'circuit breakers' such as trading suspensions and limitations on price movements. . . .

The debaters seem to accept without question that the arrangements in place during October were somehow related to the event. Yet there is virtually no evidence to support such a view. If the institutional structure of the U.S. market had been the sole culprit, the market would have crashed even earlier. There must have been an underlying 'trigger.' . . . [Various possibilities have been suggested,] but no one has been able to substantiate the underlying cause of the October market decline. [Whatever the trigger, it seems to have manifested itself throughout the world.]

. . . During the entire calendar year 1987, stock market performance varied widely across major countries. The table below gives the total percentage change in the major stock price index for each of 23 countries, in both local-currency and U.S.-dollar terms.* The best performer in dollar terms was Japan (+41.4 percent), the worst performer New Zealand (−23.8 percent). The local-currency results, however, are quite different from the dollar-denominated results. For example, Mexico had a 5.5 percent dollar-denominated return in 1987, but was up 158.9 percent in local currency!

The wide disparity in 1987 returns is typical, [given that] the intercountry correlations were mostly positive, but moderate in size, in the period mid-1981 through September 1987. Indeed, correlations above 0.5 are relatively rare, and there are only two above 0.7 (Canada–United States and Malaysia–Singapore). These modest correlations are in marked contrast to the usual correlation found between any two well-diversified portfolios within the same country. Randomly selected portfolios of U.S. stocks, for example, generally have correlations above 0.9 when there are 50 or more issues included in each portfolio.

The table also reports total percentage market movements for each country during the month of October 1987. They are all negative! This alone is a cause of wonder. During the whole period of data availability (calendar years 1981 through 1987, inclusive), October 1987 is the *only* month when all markets moved in the same direction, but in that month every stock fell, and most fell by more than 20 percent.

In October Austria, the world's best-performing country, experienced an 11.4 percent local-currency decline, and Japan declined 12.8 percent, but the currencies of both countries appreciated significantly against the

* The data source was Goldman, Sachs & Co., *FT-Actuaries World Indices*, various monthly editions. The indexes are the most widely followed in each country. A complete list of each country is contained in Goldman, Sachs & Co., *Anatomy of the World's Equity Markets*.

dollar. The worst performer, Hong Kong, had the same result in both local currency and in U.S. dollars, −45.8 percent. The rank of the United States improves considerably (from eleventh to fifth) when the results are expressed in local currency, because the dollar depreciated against most countries during October.

Given the generally low correlations between countries, the uniformity during October 1987, even in local-currency units, is all the more striking. There seems to have been an international trigger that swamped the usual influences of country-specific events. If only we could find it."

Stock Price Index Percentage Changes in Major Markets (calendar year 1987 and October 1987)[a]

	Local Currency		U.S. Dollars	
	1987	October	1987	October
Australia[b]	−3.6	−41.8	4.7	−44.9
Austria	−17.6	−11.4	0.7	−5.8
Belgium	−15.5	−23.2	3.1	−18.9
Canada[b]	4.0	−22.5	10.4	−22.9
Denmark	−4.5	−12.5	15.5	−7.3
France	−27.8	−22.9	−13.9	−19.5
Germany	−36.8	−22.3	−22.7	−17.1
Hong Kong	−11.3	−45.8	−11.0	−45.8
Ireland	−12.3	−29.1	4.7	−25.4
Italy	−32.4	−16.3	−22.3	−12.9
Japan	8.5	−12.8	41.4	−7.7
Malaysia	6.9	−39.8	11.7	−39.3
Mexico[b,c]	158.9	−35.0	5.5	−37.6
Netherlands	−18.9	−23.3	0.3	−18.1
New Zealand[b]	−38.7	−29.3	−23.8	−36.0
Norway	−14.0	−30.5	1.7	−28.8
Singapore	−10.6	−42.2	−2.7	−41.6
South Africa[b]	−8.8	−23.9	33.5	−29.0
Spain	8.2	−27.7	32.6	−23.1
Sweden	−15.1	−21.8	−0.9	−18.6
Switzerland	−34.0	−26.1	−16.5	−20.8
United Kingdom	4.6	−26.4	32.5	−22.1
United States	0.5	−21.6	0.5	−21.6

[a] Annual average dividend yields are generally in the 2 to 5 percent range except for Japan and Mexico, which have average dividend yields less than 1 percent.
[b] The currencies of these countries depreciated against the dollar during October 1987.
[c] Mexico is the only country whose currency did not appreciate against the dollar during 1987.

Source: Richard Roll, "The International Crash of October 1987," Financial Analysts Journal, September/October 1988, pp. 19–35.

Order Flow to the Exchange Orders can be initiated from virtually anywhere, but they must be traded through a member of the exchange such as a brokerage firm. The customer may contact the broker by telephone to place an order, and the broker then communicates the order to the brokerage firm's representatives on the floor of the exchange. The representatives give the order to a floor broker, who executes it with another floor broker or with the specialist for the stock in question.

The price and amount of the transaction will be recorded and placed into the reporting system of the exchange, and the original customer will be notified of the outcome of the transaction. This entire process takes only a few minutes. Usually, the customer can place the order and receive confirmation during a brief telephone call. Final settlement for a stock transaction occurs five business days after the transaction is made, and the customer is expected to have the necessary funds on deposit with his broker by that time, including the commission that must be paid to the brokerage firm for making the transaction.

The Over-the-Counter Market Relative to the NYSE, the over-the-counter (OTC) market receives little attention. This is really an oversight, since trading on this market has been growing faster than trading on organized exchanges, even the NYSE. Furthermore, recent and future advances in computer technology will probably benefit the OTC market more than the organized exchanges because of the structural differences between them.

The OTC market differs from organized exchanges in two important ways. First, it has no central trading floor where all trading activity takes place. Instead, it is made up of many people in diverse locations linked by electronic communication. Second, it does not use specialists. Instead, it has a number of **market makers**—firms and individuals who make a market in particular stocks.

market makers
traders who trade for their own account in specific securities

☞ The OTC market has no central trading place and does not use specialists.

In a sense, these differences are embodied in the name "over-the-counter." This nickname comes from the fact that participants in the market were originally thought to be like retailers who kept a supply of shares and sold them to buyers across the counter, just as one might buy a bolt of cloth in a general store. In important respects, this system continues today, with a number of market makers for each security. The privilege of trading in the OTC is granted by the National Association of Securities Dealers (NASD) based on financial soundness and qualification examinations. Only a member of the NASD is allowed to trade on the OTC market.

Margin Trading and Short Sales

margin trading
the practice of trading securities using borrowed funds to finance a portion of the transaction

As with almost every good in today's economy, it is also possible to purchase shares on credit. If one wishes to invest in stocks in an amount exceeding the cash available to pay for them, one can buy the shares on margin. In **margin trading,** one borrows some of the share price from the brokerage

broker's call rate
the rate charged by banks for loans to brokerage houses on loans secured with securities

initial margin
in margin trading for securities, the percentage of the value of securities that one can borrow

maintenance margin
in the stock market, the minimum fraction of the traded shares' value that must be on deposit with the broker

margin call
the demand from a broker for an investor to deposit additional margin funds with the broker

firm, which itself borrows money at the **broker's call rate,** the rate charged by banks for loans to brokerage houses on loans covered by securities. With the combination of the investor's own funds and the loan, the shares can be purchased. The broker holds them as collateral for the loan. Since the Great Depression, the percentage that one can borrow has been regulated by the Federal Reserve Board Regulation T and is called the **initial margin.**

The advantage, and potential disadvantage, of margin trading is the greater leverage that it gives the investor. Assuming that 50 percent of the invested funds are borrowed, the investor realizes the full gain or loss on the shares, while buying only one-half of them. To make this more concrete, consider a simple example in which one buys 1,000 shares trading at $100 each, invests $50,000 of personal funds, and borrows the other $50,000 at 10 percent from the broker. After one year, assume that the shares have risen in value to $115, so the value of the entire block of shares is $115,000. The investor could then sell the shares and pay the broker $55,000 in principal and interest. This would leave a profit of $10,000 on the original investment of $50,000, or a 20 percent return. Without margin trading, the investor would have earned only 15 percent.

It must also be noted that with a margin account, any fall in share prices amplifies any detrimental impact on the investor's fortunes. For example, imagine that the share price fell from $100 to $80 per share. After one year the value of the 1,000 shares would be $80,000. Since the broker must still be paid $55,000, this leaves only $25,000 for the investor. In this case, a 20 percent drop in the share price causes a 50 percent loss for the investor.

In addition to the initial margin, the broker imposes a **maintenance margin** requirement. When share prices fall, the value of the shares serving as the collateral for the broker deteriorates and the broker can require additional cash funds from the investor. This demand for more cash is known as a **margin call.** The investor must pay the broker the new funds, or the broker is authorized to sell the shares, keep the money owed to him, and return the excess to the investor.

Before October 1929 there were no margin restrictions whatsoever, and it had become customary for investors to borrow 100 percent of the share value from brokers. This practice allowed investors of very limited resources to assume enormous positions in the market, which was wonderful in that time of consistently rising prices. Because of the extreme percentage of borrowed funds, however, any drop in prices would quickly result in margin calls from the broker, and investors who were overextended often found it impossible to meet the calls. The broker would then sell the shares at whatever price the market would bear.

In this way a deadly spiral could develop. The drop in share prices would generate margin calls, which many investors could not meet. Thus many shares came on the market to be sold by brokers, which depressed prices even further and, of course, led to new margin calls. This spiral of falling stock prices and margin calls played an important role in the market crash

FINANCE TODAY

Three Short Stories

Many investors think of buying a certain stock when they believe it has the potential to appreciate in value. However, you can also make money if you believe the stock will be a loser. In this case, instead of buying the stock, you short-sell it. Selling short means that you sell a stock you don't even own; rather, you simply borrow the stock from your broker and immediately sell it.

How do you spot either good or bad stocks? One way is to open your eyes the next time you go to the mall, or buy a car, or go to a restaurant. That's what Peter Lynch, the idol of Wall Street who has now retired from the enormously successful Fidelity Magellan Fund, was proud of doing. He used his common sense and his positive everyday experiences to find great stock picks.

You can read all about it in his *One Up on Wall Street*. Lynch liked the doughnuts at Dunkin' Donuts and bought the stock. He liked the beds at La Quinta Motor Inns and his wife liked the L'eggs pantyhose made by Hanes. Lynch's fund bought the stocks. In these cases and many others, the results were spectacular investment returns.

What if, as a consumer, you don't like the merchandise? Your doughnuts are stale, perhaps. Or your mattress is lumpy. Despair not. These experiences can be turned into profitable short sales. Sadly for the world, but happily for people who sell borrowed shares in the hope that the shorted stocks will go down, there are as many idiotic business concepts as good ones, and as many shoddy products as outstanding ones. So the next time you're really angry at a product, or a salesman blatantly lies to you, think about shorting the company's stock.

You can think of this approach as the "Clint Eastwood short." In his *Dirty Harry* films, Eastwood was invariably confronted with rude, annoying people whom he would eventually blow away. This outlet for frustration is illegal in the United States, but short-selling is not (although it is in many other countries). Here are three short stories, as told by journalist Frederick E. Rowe, Jr.:

Story Number One. Several years ago I took my family to dinner at a Fuddruckers. At the time Fuddruckers was a very popular company on Wall Street, a "concept" stock. You could tell it was a concept stock because the financials were so bad. The company had a lot of debt and had paid through the nose for dubious locations as it grew rapidly. The earnings were paltry and many other financials were out of proportion to everything but management's promises.

When my family and I arrived, the restaurant, which was huge, was deserted. The entire staff was in the kitchen entertaining themselves with a radio. They ignored us. After much pleading, we were eventually served some undercooked meat. At the end of the meal the waiter disappeared after I handed him the money. More pleading to other members of the staff produced my change. Before leaving, we had a few other hassles.

I went to the office the next day and shorted the stock at $5\frac{1}{2}$. I covered, like a coward, at 2. Dirty Harry probably would have hung in there. Fudd-ruckers finally reorganized, with the successor stock last quoted at 56 cents.

Story Number Two. In 1987 Sears, Roebuck sent around a couple of representatives to talk about putting polyvinyl siding on our clapboard guest house. Actually, the salesmen worked for a company called AMRE, a Sears licensee. They seemed like a couple of characters out of that 1987 comedy about siding salesmen, *Tin Men.* Their bid seemed ridiculously high. I protested. "Tell you what," one said, "you just sign here and we'll throw in storm windows free."

I didn't sign up, but I did read AMRE's annual report. It told me that at AMRE, materials and labor represented about one-third of sales. A general contractor marks up materials and labor maybe 25 percent. These people were marking them up almost 200 percent. A bull in the stock tried to be patient with me, saying "You don't understand. This is not a general contracting company. This is a telemarketing company. Do you realize that of the people who contract for AMRE's siding, more than 90 percent sign up on the first meeting?" I understood why. Nearly everyone who bothered to get a second bid would never consider using AMRE. I shorted AMRE at $11 (adjusted for a subsequent split). It's now trading at half that. I've been mad and I've made money, and making money is better.

Story Number Three. Sometimes my retaliatory shorts backfire. I once had the unpleasant experience of putting Viadent toothpaste in my mouth. The active ingredient is sanguinarine, a substance derived from the blood-root plant and believed to be effective in preventing all sorts of gum problems caused by plaque and tartar. It also tastes like garbage.

Again, I sent off for financials for producer Vipont Pharmaceutical. In terms of price to sales, price to earnings and price to book value, the stock seemed absurdly overvalued. I had a few friends test the product. One friend convinced me that a short sale had merit. He said to me, "People are not going to put a product in their mouths which smells bad, tastes bad, and is brown."

I shorted Vipont at $15. But Colgate–Palmolive's decision not long ago to acquire Vipont at $14 left a bitter taste in my mouth.

Do you have the makings of a successful short-seller? You have to have a lot of staying power and a thick skin. Short-sellers are not well liked. A frequent complaint about short-sellers is that they see all glasses as half-empty and never as half-full. Nonsense. A lot of those glasses are *empty.*

Source: Frederick E. Rowe, Jr., "Don't Get Mad, Go Short," *Forbes,* June 25, 1990, pp. 244–245.

of 1929, and was largely responsible for the onset of the Great Depression. It was in response to this danger that the Federal Reserve Board received authorization to regulate initial margin.[4]

Normally, one thinks of stock transactions as following a pattern of buying shares and eventually selling them. In a **short sale,** however, one sells shares that one does not own, with the intention of buying them back later at a lower price. Simple financial advice has always been to buy low and sell high. Short selling reverses this to sell high and buy low.

short sale
the sale of a borrowed security executed in the hope that the price of the security will fall

Many times, selling what is not yours can lead to a jail term. In the stock market, however, it is a recognized and legitimate form of trading when one anticipates a drop in the price of a stock. To execute a short sale, one has the broker borrow shares from another investor and sell them in the market. The broker has a ready supply of shares to borrow, since they are held for customers in street name. That is, customers simply leave the shares they own in the custody of the broker. The broker is authorized to loan them by the agreement that opens the brokerage account.

It should be recognized that short selling essentially involves trading on margin, since the seller takes a position in the market without putting up the full value of the transaction. Also, the seller must make any dividend payments to the lender of the shares. These complications make it clear that investors engaging in short selling must have a thorough understanding of these intricacies and a clear agreement with their broker.

Market Indices

☞ Market indices provide a useful way of summarizing and conceptualizing the vast array of information generated by the continuous buying and selling of securities.

Market indices provide a useful way of summarizing the vast array of information generated by the continuous buying and selling of securities. At the same time, however, their use presents new problems. First, many different indices compete for attention. Second, they differ in construction and interpretation. There are indices for almost all kinds of instruments. This section focuses exclusively on the two best known.

The most widely cited market index of any type is the Dow Jones Industrial Average. Yet, as a gauge of the entire market, it is extremely limited, reflecting price movements of only 30 of the largest industrial concerns listed on the NYSE. These are the mammoth firms, such as General Motors, Exxon, and IBM, which account for most of the market's activity. For example, IBM stock often accounts for about 25 percent of the market's daily trading volume. The firms included in the Dow Jones Industrial Average vary from time to time as the economy changes, but they are always 30 of the largest and most powerful. Each of these 30 "blue chip" stocks receives an equal weight in the index.

The Dow Jones Industrial Index is quoted each day in the *Wall Street Journal*. This is not surprising, given that the *Journal* is published by Dow

---

[4] For the classic tale of these events, see John Kenneth Galbraith, *The Great Crash.*

FIGURE 7.6   The Dow Jones Averages

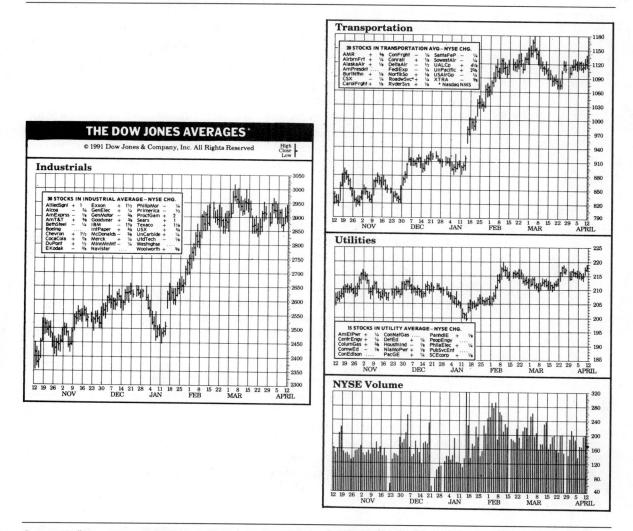

Source: Wall Street Journal, April 15, 1991. Reprinted by permission of Wall Street Journal, © 1991 Dow Jones & Company, Inc. All Rights Reserved Worldwide.

Jones, Inc. Figure 7.6 shows the presentation from the *Journal*. For each day of trading, a vertical line shows the high and low reached for the index that day.

☞ The S&P 500 Index and the Dow Jones Industrial Average are two of the best-known stock market indices.

The S&P 500 Index is a broader market index composed, as the name implies, of 500 stocks from several industries. Of these, 400 are industrial firms, 40 are utilities, 40 are financial institutions, and 20 are transportation companies. These stocks account for more than 80 percent of the market value of all stocks listed on the NYSE, although a few OTC-traded firms are included. Another feature of the S&P 500 index is that each stock is weighted according to the market value of its outstanding shares. For example, IBM receives a weight of almost 4 percent, reflecting the fact that the market value of its shares is about 4 percent of the entire value of the S&P 500 firms.

This broader inclusion of firms, and the weight of each firm by its market value, makes the S&P 500 a better gauge of activity on the NYSE than the Dow in the eyes of most experts. In addition, it is very important because many professional money managers have their performance monitored with it as the standard of comparison. The idea is that, with equal risk, a talented manager should be able to earn at least as much on a managed portfolio as is earned by the unmanaged portfolio of 500 stocks that makes up the S&P 500.

SUMMARY

This chapter explored the money, bond, and stock markets. Securities in these markets represent an incredible diversity of maturities, cash flow patterns, and risk levels. In addition, the markets vary widely in the exact manner in which transactions are consummated.

Debt instruments of great safety and very short maturities are traded in the money market. Longer-term debt instruments with higher risk are traded in the bond market. Bonds are issued by a diversity of issuers with different risk levels and payment streams. The stock market trades ownership claims for corporations. Because the stockholder can be paid only after other claimants of the firm are satisfied, stocks represent the riskiest type of investment. Nonetheless, they vary widely in their riskiness, and some are safer than some bonds.

The blizzard of trading that occurs every day in the stock market generates a need for summary information about the performance of the market. Several indices provide those data. This chapter concluded with a brief examination of two of the most important ones—the Dow Jones Industrial and the S&P 500.

QUESTIONS

1. Why is stock ownership a residual claim on the firm?
2. Can a securities market function without a specialist?
3. What are the main differences between the OTC market and an organized securities exchange?
4. Assume that you own 130 shares of a stock trading at $14. If the firm has a 4 percent stock dividend, what is the stock price after the dividend? How has your wealth changed?
5. Which entity is the largest issuer of securities in the world?

6. How might the fees charged by investment bankers for risk bearing be related to the creditworthiness of the issuer, the issuer's general reputation, and the current stability of financial markets?

7. Why does the federal government issue only debt and no equity?

8. How much cash does IBM receive if an investor buys a share for $120 on the secondary market?

9. What are the three principal classes of bond issuers?

10. What are the three principal kinds of U.S. Treasury debts?

11. In spite of the fact that T bills and T bonds have experienced virtually identical returns over the recent past, T bonds seem to have had a greater variance of returns. Does this violate the basic idea of a trade-off between expected return and risk? Why or why not?

12. What do the bond ratings provided by firms such as Standard & Poor's and Moody's attempt to measure?

13. The contract between a corporation and its bondholders often restricts the dividends that the firm can pay to stockholders. What is the purpose of this kind of provision?

14. Why do firms issue callable bonds? Other factors being equal, should a callable or a noncallable bond have a higher yield to maturity? Why?

15. In the money market, there is a well-established relationship among yields on different types of instruments. What do these yield differences reflect?

16. Even within a given class of securities, such as certificates of deposit, there are well-established yield relationships. Assume that bank A has traditionally had a yield on its CDs one-half of a percentage point lower than the yield on those of bank B. If that difference became smaller, how would you interpret the change?

The Corporation and the Acquisition of Funds

Many goals are possible for an organization such as a corporation. This chapter argues that the goal should be to maximize the wealth of its present owners, which is equivalent to maximizing the price of the firm's common stock. This definition gives a central role to the finance function within the corporation and allots a key role to the financial manager. It also provides a backdrop against which we can explore the issuance of new securities in the primary market.

THE COST-BENEFIT PRINCIPLE OF VALUE CREATION

All of us make decisions every day. Implicit in each one is the belief that the chosen course of action will be valuable. In a very general sense, we can say that value is created when the benefits of a decision exceed its costs. This cost-benefit principle applies to any type of rational behavior. For example, it explains why some drivers choose to exceed the maximum highway speed limit. For them, the benefits of excessive speeding, such as arriving at their destination earlier, exceed the costs associated with the chance of being stopped by the police, including a speeding ticket, a higher insurance premium, and loss of time on the road and possibly in court. Of course, many drivers believe the expected costs of speeding are high compared to the benefits, and so they obey the speed limit.

The cost-benefit principle also applies in finance: a financial manager will go ahead with a decision when the perceived benefits exceed its associated costs. For example, if an automobile firm invests in a new plant to build its latest model, it must believe that the future benefits, say, net cash generated, will exceed the cost of building and operating the plant. Whenever the benefits of a decision exceed its costs, value has been created by virtue of that decision. Thus, the decision to build a new automobile plant is expected to increase the overall value of the company. This simple and intuitive principle is extremely powerful, and we use it throughout this text.

Broadly speaking, financial value is created through the influence of just a few variables, the most important of which are cash flow, time, and risk. If all other variables are held constant, higher cash flows give rise to higher value. Similarly, value is greater when cash flows are received sooner as well as when the risk associated with the cash flow decreases. In practice, these three variables are interrelated and should be considered simultaneously when assessing the value created by a financial decision. It is a potentially grave mistake to emphasize one at the expense of the others. For example, it is a common fallacy to argue that one investment is better than another because it is expected to produce a greater cash flow. Such a statement is actually meaningless without considering both the timing and the riskiness of the expected cash flows.

THE GOAL OF THE FIRM

The general objective of the firm to maximize its value is accomplished by making decisions in which the benefits exceed the costs. Although this general concept is intuitive and clear, the practical way of maximizing firm value is less obvious. We have noted that any strategy leading to the creation of value must simultaneously take into account cash flow, time, and risk, and we use this as our guideline in evaluating the desirability of three potential ways to increase the value of the corporation: maximize size, maximize accounting profits, and maximize the stock price.

Maximizing Size

A firm that is too small cannot operate efficiently. For example, it might be unable to buy raw materials in quantities big enough to get the cheapest price. On the other hand, firms that are too large can suffer from inefficiencies, because managers may have difficulty obtaining information in time to act effectively. Furthermore, firms that grow too quickly may suffer growing pains that can be fatal; that is, rapid growth may create excessive risk.

Although maximizing firm size is at least intuitively consistent with maximizing the firm's cash flow, it disregards both the time and the risk components of value creation. Thus, it cannot by itself be an appropriate goal for corporations.

Maximizing Accounting Profits

accounting profits
the earnings reported on the firm's financial statements

☞ Maximizing accounting profits does not serve as a suitable goal for the firm because it does not say *which* accounting profits should be maximized, and does not consider risk.

By **accounting profits** we mean the earnings reported in the company's income statement based on accounting rules. However, they are not always the most economically meaningful measure of firm performance and value. In particular, they are not the same as cash flow. In fact, a firm that reports accounting losses may have generated a positive cash flow.

The financial manager should care more about cash flow than profits, because cash is used to pay dividends to stockholders, interest to bondholders, wages to employees, and accounts payable to suppliers. Since profits usually differ from cash flow, maximizing them does not completely take into account one of the essential variables involved in creating financial value. Nor does it consider the time dimension of value creation. For example, which period's

A Taxonomy of Bears and Bulls

Financial Bears come in four general subspecies:

The Intrinsic Value Bear believes stocks should sell for what they are truly worth. These bears find it bothersome when stocks sell for excessive multiples of book value, earnings, and sales. Short-selling is an outlet for their frustrations. Intrinsic Value Bears have done well lately but will be crushed in a serious bull market, when extreme valuations become even more extreme.

Debt Bears see things more narrowly. They believe that the extravagant use of debt is wrong. While cash flows may fluctuate, debt is eternal. It does not go away. These bears have also enjoyed a great success lately, as many of the monuments to financial leverage built in the last decade have collapsed.

Then there's a third subspecies. "I'd like to work for the Securities & Exchange Commission but they can't afford me" Bears delight in exposing frauds and hype artists. As the current bear market has dragged on, frauds and hypes have become harder to find. These bears will remain in hibernation until the next bull market.

Closely related to the above subspecies is the Chip on the Shoulder Bear. He or she thinks: "Cocky, arrogant, rich-for-the-moment jerks deserve a taste of humility." Donald Trump was an easy target. These bears have had plenty of opportunity to gloat as the financial heroes of the 1980s have mostly toppled.

Whatever their specialty, bears generally don't make as much money as bulls. One of Wall Street's oldest adages is "You don't find bears living in Fifth Avenue mansions." The world, after all, belongs to optimists. Bears are more likely to drive Volvos and own cats than to drive Mercedes and own golden retrievers. Their brows are generally furrowed. They are tense, and they tend to have trouble with easy lay-ups, short putts, and simple volleys to the open court. Truth is elusive.

For successful bulls, "Truth is virtue" has little relevance. Bulls generally accept the world as it is, not as they think it ought to be. A couple of examples:

Truth Is a Lie Bulls—George Soros, according to many people, is "the world's most successful money manager." I don't know if that can be proven, but Soros was kind enough to share his philosophies with us in his book *The Alchemy of Finance*. In it he says economic history is a never-ending series of episodes based on falsehoods. Lies, not truths, represent the path to big money. The object is to recognize the trend whose premise is false, ride that trend, and step off before it is discredited.

Finance Is Only a Game Bulls know that investing is something not to be taken seriously. The better players have a knack for recognizing new games very early or even inventing new games. Finance Is Only a Game Bulls have more fun. They are relaxed. They radiate confidence. They will make that slippery, downhill six-footer to beat you—and then laugh.

Source: Frederick E. Rowe, Jr., "Why Bears Drive Volvos," *Forbes*, January 21, 1991, p. 120.

accounting profits should be maximized? Maximizing short-run accounting profits can often be accomplished by hurting the firm's future prosperity. For instance, a pharmaceutical house could easily increase this year's accounting profits by eliminating its current research and development expenses. Since these expenses are usually assumed to help increase future sales, the company would appear to benefit now only to suffer later, perhaps irreversibly. Smart investors will not be fooled by such tricks, and in this example the value of the pharmaceutical firm is likely to decrease, even as accounting profits and short-term cash flows increase.

Furthermore, maximizing accounting profits is unsuitable because it does not consider risk. In every period, the manager faces different strategies with different risk levels. In most circumstances, those with the highest expected accounting profits are subject to the greatest risk. If we simply try to maximize expected accounting profits, we will ordinarily choose the riskiest strategies; however, we have seen that high risk leads to a lower firm value.

Maximizing Stock Price

☞ The corporation should be managed to maximize the price of the stock, which is equivalent to maximizing shareholder wealth.

☞ The goal of maximizing shareholder wealth accurately evaluates the impact of cash flows, timing, and risk, which are the main variables in the creation of value.

The third method takes into account all of the essential variables involved in value creation. Thus, we argue that the corporation should be managed to maximize the price of its stock, which is equivalent to maximizing the shareholders' wealth.

As discussed previously, investors are more interested in cash flow than in accounting profits. If they perceive that the firm will generate substantial cash flow in the future, they will demand the stock in greater quantities, thus increasing its price. Furthermore, if the cash flow is to be received sooner rather than later, the stock price will also increase, because a dollar today has a greater value than the same dollar tomorrow. Finally, if the firm's strategy is too risky for the expected rewards, investors will sell their shares and the price of the stock will fall. In the remainder of this book we take the maximization of shareholder wealth or, equivalently, the maximization of stock price as the proper goal of the firm.

THE ROLE OF THE FINANCIAL MANAGER

The head of finance is usually a vice president for finance or the chief financial officer, who normally reports directly to the president or the chief executive officer.

Normally, the vice president for finance draws support mainly from the treasurer and the controller. The controller bears prime responsibility for those areas usually associated with accounting, such as preparing the firm's financial statements and budgets, planning and paying taxes, and payroll operations. Figure 8.1 shows how the main areas of finance are divided between the treasurer and the controller.

FIGURE 8.1   Organization of the Finance Function Within a Corporation

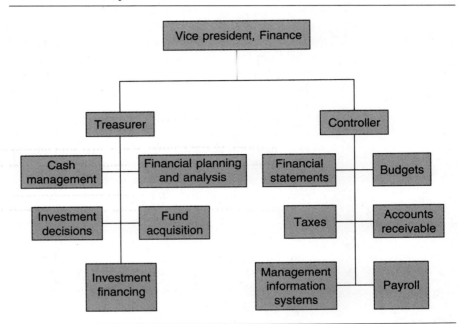

ACQUISITION AND EMPLOYMENT OF FUNDS

☞ The basic task of the finance function is the acquisition and employment of funds.

The basic task of the finance function is to acquire and employ funds. By making wise decisions in these areas, the financial manager adds to the wealth of the firm's shareholders.

The firm raises funds by selling ownership interest to stockholders or by borrowing money. Acquiring these funds is costly, since the firm must compensate the suppliers of funds. The funds raised become the pool of investable funds that are committed to attractive investment projects the firm has available. These projects are undertaken because they are expected to add value for the firm.

If the investment projects are successful, they generate more funds, which can be used in only two ways. First, the firm must return a portion of them to the capital market contributors of the original investable funds. This is the payment the investors receive for committing their resources. Second, the firm retains the remaining funds to increase the amount that can be invested for future projects.

THE ISSUANCE OF NEW SECURITIES

primary market
the market for the original issuance of securities

When most people think of buying or selling securities, they think first of the large stock Exchanges, such as the New York Stock Exchange, discussed in the preceding chapter. However, the securities traded on the NYSE are being traded on a secondary market, one for existing securities. Before securities reach the secondary market they must be issued by corporations or governments. This initial offering takes place in the **primary market**—the market for new securities. The primary market is much less visible than the secondary market, but it is crucial to the world of finance.

investment bank
a firm specializing in helping governments and firms issue new securities

☞ The investment banker aids corporations and governments in the initial distribution of securities.

An **investment bank** specializes in helping governments and firms issue new securities. In the United States, investment banking has been kept almost totally distinct from the more familiar commercial banking by the Glass–Steagall Act. Instead of accepting deposits, as does the commercial bank, the investment banker aids corporations and governments by acting as a consultant and helping distribute the securities, and often bears considerable risk in the process.

The Primary Market: Size and Scope

preferred stock
a security issued by corporations with features of both equity and debt

We can distinguish new issues in the primary market by the type of issuer and the type of security being issued. The basic issuers are governments and corporations. The securities may be bonds, common stock, or preferred stock. A **preferred stock** is a cross between a bond and common stock. A share normally pays a fixed amount, as bonds do, but the firm makes the payments only if enough funds are available, as is the case with common stock. Of these types of securities, only corporations issue common and preferred stock. Since stock, particularly common stock, represents an ownership claim on the issuing entity, governments cannot issue it.

public offering
the issuance of a new security that is offered for sale to the public at large

private placement
the selling of an entire security issuance to a single buyer or small consortium of buyers, without the issue ever being made available to the public

Private Placements Versus Public Offerings   There are two types of offerings, public and private. In a **public offering** the issuer offers the security to the public at large, giving any investor the right to purchase a portion of the new issue. The entire process of issuance is governed by regulations of the Securities and Exchange Commission (SEC). As an alternative, many companies prefer to make a **private placement** in which the issuer sells an entire bond issue to a single buyer, or to a small consortium of buyers, but never makes it available to the public. There are several advantages to private placements. For a corporation, the process escapes the attention of the SEC and thus avoids rigorous and costly rules imposed by the Commission on publicly issued securities. Another advantage is the avoidance of public disclosure of its business plans. The SEC requires considerable disclosure in any public offering. For a firm in an industry where protecting secrets is important, such as high technology or defense, this can be very undesirable.

The buyers of private placements tend to be large institutions with plenty of cash, such as insurance companies. They realize certain advantages from these transactions. Usually, privately placed bonds pay a little more interest than publicly offered bonds because their cost is lower. For large investors, even a small interest rate differential can be important. The buyers also have an important disadvantage. They cannot sell the bond, since it has never undergone the scrutiny required for a public offering. The buyers therefore sacrifice liquidity to obtain the higher rate of interest.

Although common stocks generally attract more investor attention than the bond market, the primary stock market is really quite small compared to the primary bond market. However, stocks trade much more frequently than bonds on the secondary market. It is the degree of activity in trading in the secondary market that makes stocks the main focus of financial market analysts.

☞ The largest issuer of securities in the world is the U.S. government.

The largest issuer of securities in the world is the U.S. government. In addition, state and local governments issue municipal bonds. The size of this market is also very large, almost equaling the total issuance of securities by corporations.

The Process of Issuing Securities

☞ The investment banker normally fulfills three functions for the corporation in the process of issuing a new security: consulting, forming a distribution network, and bearing risk involved.

The development of a good relationship with an investment banker is very important to the financial management of corporations. Most firms attempt to maintain a close working relationship with one or two investment bankers with whom they can be in regular contact as their financing needs develop. Investment bankers normally fulfill three functions for the corporation in the process of issuing a new security: consulting, forming a distribution network, and bearing risk involved in the issuance of the new security.

The Investment Banker as Consultant

prospectus
a legal document describing a planned security and the operating and financial condition of the issuing entity

To the firm planning to issue a security, the investment banker acts as a consultant in preparing the necessary registration and informational material, timing the issuance, and setting the sale price for the security. One of the important requirements is the formal disclosure of the firm's financial condition and plans, which is contained in the **prospectus,** a legal document required by the SEC. The investment banker often plays an important advisory role in creating the prospectus.

The prospectus includes a report of the firm's financial condition, the names of the principal officers, and their holdings in the firm. It also must give information about the firm's line of business and its plans for future expansion. This information must be detailed and highly accurate. Since the firm offers the securities for sale through the prospectus, any error in the document could make the firm liable for investors' losses. Consequently, the prospectus is usually written by the firm's legal staff in legal prose. Other authors usually include top management of the issuing firm and specialists in prospectus writing. Also, some of the expertise usually comes from the investment banker.

All firms would prefer to issue their securities when they will receive a high price for them. The ideal time to issue stocks would be when the secondary stock market is at a peak, and for bonds, when interest rates are very low. Investment bankers often advise firms on this issue of timing. Another crucial aspect of timing concerns commercial policy; for example, firms often issue securities after the announcement of a successful new product.

why ?

Pricing the new securities is very important as well. Since investment bankers know the primary market, they should be in a good position to give advice on this. The goal is to set the highest price that will allow all of the issue to sell quickly (an issue that sells out rapidly is said to go "out the window"). If the price is too low, the issue will sell out virtually immediately, but will not bring the firm as much cash as it could have had it been priced properly. On the other hand, an issue that is priced too high will not be sold promptly (these are said to be "sticky issues"). The investment banker helps the issuing firm avoid both of these pricing mistakes.

lead bank
the primary member in a consortium of investment banks attempting to sell a new security

The Distribution Network The typical structure of the distribution network is shown in Figure 8.2. The issuing corporation creates the security and passes it to the lead bank and the syndicate members. The **lead bank** is the

FIGURE 8.2 Organization of the Distribution Network

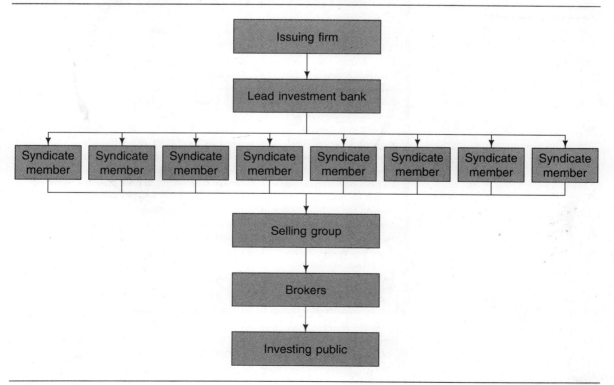

syndicate member
an investment banking firm that assists in the flotation of a security

flotation
the initial sale of a security

investment bank with primary responsibility for issuing a security. The **syndicate member** is another investment banking firm that commits itself to assisting in the flotation of a given security. The **flotation** is the initial sale of the security. From the numerous members of the syndicate, the securities are distributed to members of the **selling group**—the investment houses that

FIGURE 8.3 A Typical Tombstone

This announcement constitutes neither an offer to sell nor a solicitation of an offer to buy these securities. The offering is made only by the Prospectus, copies of which may be obtained in any State from such of the undersigned and others as may lawfully offer these securities in such State.

New Issue   April 11, 1991

1,100,000 Shares

 **LXE**

Common Stock

Price $9.50 Per Share

The Robinson-Humphrey Company, Inc.   A. G. Edwards & Sons, Inc.

Bear, Stearns & Co. Inc.	The First Boston Corporation	Alex. Brown & Sons Incorporated
Dillon, Read & Co. Inc.	Donaldson, Lufkin & Jenrette Securities Corporation	Goldman, Sachs & Co.
Hambrecht & Quist Incorporated	Lazard Freres & Co.	Lehman Brothers
Merrill Lynch & Co.	PaineWebber Incorporated	Prudential Securities Incorporated
Robertson, Stephens & Company		Smith Barney, Harris Upham & Co. Incorporated
Wertheim Schroder & Co. Incorporated		Dean Witter Reynolds Inc.
William Blair & Company	J. C. Bradford & Co.	Dain Bosworth Incorporated
Kemper Securities Group, Inc.	Oppenheimer & Co., Inc.	Piper, Jaffray & Hopwood Incorporated
Wheat First Butcher & Singer Capital Markets	Raymond James & Associates, Inc.	Van Kasper & Company
Advest, Inc.	Arnhold and S. Bleichroeder, Inc.	Robert W. Baird & Co. Incorporated
Brean Murray, Foster Securities Inc.	The Chicago Corporation	Cowen & Company
Crowell, Weedon & Co.	Equitable Securities Corporation	Ferris, Baker Watts Incorporated
Furman Selz Incorporated	Interstate/Johnson Lane Corporation	Janney Montgomery Scott Inc.
Ladenburg, Thalmann & Co. Inc.	C.J. Lawrence Inc.	McDonald & Company Securities. Inc.
Morgan Keegan & Company, Inc.	Neecham & Company, Inc.	Parker/Hunter Incorporated
Pennsylvania Merchant Group Ltd	Ragen MacKenzie Incorporated	Scott & Stringfellow Investment Corp.
Seidler Amdec Securities Inc.	Stephens Inc.	Stifel, Nicolaus & Company Incorporated
Sutro & Co. Incorporated	Tucker Anthony Incorporated	Wedbush Morgan Securities
Williams Securities Group, Inc.		L.H. Alton & Company

Source: Wall Street Journal, April 15, 1991. Reprinted by permission of *Wall Street Journal*, © 1991 Dow Jones & Company, Inc. All Rights Reserved Worldwide.

selling group
the group of investment bankers who help sell newly issued securities

are participating to a smaller degree in the distribution process. Only when the securities reach the brokers is contact with the public possible. The brokers are in direct contact with their customers, who are the final investors in the securities.

Officially, it is only through the prospectus that securities can be offered for sale. For that matter, only investors who have received a copy of the prospectus are allowed to buy the securities. Securities are often announced, however, in the *Wall Street Journal* with advertisements such as the one shown in Figure 8.3, which is known as a "tombstone," due to its size, shape, color, and contents. It announces the firm making the issue, the price, the number of securities, and the members of the syndicate. Notice the disclaimer, "This announcement is neither an offer to sell nor a solicitation of an offer to buy any of these securities. The offer is made only by the Prospectus. . . ." Because of the strict regulations on security issuance, such an obvious advertisement to sell securities has to say that it is not offering securities for sale.

To illustrate the process of issuing a security, consider a firm making a fairly large issue ($20–50 million), with the corporation receiving $100 per share of common stock, as shown in Table 8.1. As the security flows through the network of intermediaries, each layer tacks on its profit margin. By the time it reaches the public, its final price may well be 6 percent or more above the amount received by the corporation. The prices shown in Table 8.1 assume the security flows through the entire chain; however, this is not true of all of the shares of stock in the issue. For example, the lead bank also markets the shares through its own internal distribution network. The difference between the price paid by the final investor and the amount the issuing firm receives is known as the **spread**.

spread
the difference between the buying and the selling price for a trader; in the futures market, the difference in price between two futures contracts

The Service and Cost of Risk Bearing Forming the distribution network described above and marketing securities are parts of the retailing function, but the compensation that investment bankers receive is not only for acting as retailers. In many offerings, these individuals also bear a great deal of risk because they actually buy the securities from the issuing firm and then try to sell them to the public at a profit. The spread constitutes the compensation for this risk-bearing service as well as the distribution cost.

TABLE 8.1 Typical Distribution Process in a Common Stock Issuance

Recipient	Price per Share
Corporation	$100.00
Lead investment bank	101.25
Other syndicate members	103.00
Selling group members	104.50
Brokers making sales directly to the public	106.00

This Noble House Doesn't Trust the Proletariat

Jardine Matheson, Hong Kong's most noble trading house, is pondering the future. "We need to begin," says its general counsel, Mr. Greg Terry, "by recognizing the special reality of Hong Kong. In 1997 Hong Kong will become a special administrative region of the People's Republic of China. This has important implications."

Quite so. Jardine Matheson's solution is to demand that it and other corporate giants—those incorporated overseas, listed on a recognized foreign exchange, and having either shareholders' funds of over HK$4 billion ($513 million) or post-tax profits of over HK$400 million—be exempted from Hong Kong's securities regulations. Otherwise, the alternative may be "to delist from the Hong Kong market, with possible damaging effects to Hong Kong as a whole." Since Jardine accounts for up to 14 percent of the market's capitalization, the threat is not to be taken lightly.

Britain's Keswick family, which controls the Jardine group, has bitter memories of 1949, when the company was forced to leave its assets behind in Shanghai. In 1984, as Britain was negotiating the eventual handover of Hong Kong to China, Jardine reacted by switching its domicile to Bermuda. A third of Hong Kong's 296 listed companies have since followed suit and are legally incorporated in either Bermuda or the Cayman Islands. In theory, the balmy islands offer protection from China's putative worst.

Practice might prove otherwise for companies that have their physical assets in Hong Kong and only a grass plate overseas. The Securities and Futures Corporation (SFC), Hong Kong's energetic market regulator, is preparing to exempt multinationals such as IBM, Sony, and Shell from local regulations. A secondary listing in Hong Kong would provide only a small market for these companies' shares, but would be attractive to local investors. But why, the SFC wonders, should it exempt companies—like Jardine—that have most of their assets in Hong Kong? A foreign passport, argues the SFC, should not mean exemption from investor-protection laws any more than from traffic laws.

The SFC is ready to allow at least one long-standing Jardine demand, for Hong Kong–listed companies to be able to buy back their own shares (something the Keswicks might also want to do without launching a full bid). That would help soothe the Keswicks' underlying fear: that after 1997, corrupt concert parties will thwart even the toughest regulators and take over the family jewels. Delisting, of course, would remove that fear entirely.

Source: "A Share in the Colony," *The Economist,* December 8, 1990, p. 88.

TABLE 8.2   Spread Size by Size and Type of Issue

Size of Issue (millions of dollars)	Spread	
	Common Stock	Bonds
< $0.5	11.3%	7.4%
0.5–0.9	9.7	7.2
1.0–1.9	8.6	7.0
2.0–4.9	7.4	4.2
5.0–9.9	6.7	1.5
10.0–19.9	6.2	1.0
20.0–49.9	4.9	1.0
≥ 50.0	2.3	0.8

Source: From Securities and Exchange Commission data as found in *Foundations of Financial Management, Fifth Edition,* by Stanley B. Block and Geoffrey A. Hirt (Homewood, IL: Richard D. Irwin, Inc., 1989), p. 449. Reprinted with permission.

These services demand a high level of compensation. Corporations pay their investment bankers in two ways.[1] First, they typically pay out-of-pocket expenses for consulting services, legal fees, and document preparation. Second, the securities are offered at a price that allows the investment bankers, and all other members of the distribution network, to make a profit.

When an investment banking syndicate actually buys the securities from the issuing corporation, it acts as an **underwriter.** The price the corporation receives must be low enough to allow the syndicate to distribute the securities to the public at a profit. The spread constitutes the gross margin for the distribution network, but in an issue that is underwritten, a large portion of it is compensation for risk bearing.

The prices of Table 8.1 are fairly representative, but the spread depends on the size of the issue and the kind of security that is under consideration. As Table 8.2 shows, it is typically lower for debt issues than for issues of common stock. Furthermore, as a percentage of the proceeds, it is smaller for larger issues. For very small issues, the flotation costs become extremely expensive. In addition to the spread, the issuing firm pays certain out-of-pocket expenses, as mentioned above, and although smaller than the spread, they add significantly to the total flotation costs. For small issues, total flotation costs approach 20 percent; for the largest issues, they can be less than 3 percent. The issuing firm must make at least the total flotation cost on the investment being financed by the security issuance in order to get back to

underwriter
an investment bank that buys an entire issue of securities from the issuing firm and assumes the risk of selling them

---

[1] This section focuses only on the process for corporations. Governments and their agencies operate somewhat differently. Many are required by law to offer securities under a process of competitive bidding, rather than through an underwriting system. The U.S. government issues securities through its own special media, including Federal Reserve Banks and U.S. government security dealers.

zero. For the securities investor this is also sobering, since it indicates just how much profit the firm must make before the investor could expect a positive return.

shelf registration
the single registration with the Securities Exchange Commission of a planned security allowing for both the postponement of issuance and for issuance of multiple securities

Shelf Registration   One of the most significant developments in the primary security markets in recent years has been the advent of **shelf registration.** The high costs of issuing securities have been deemed necessary by regulators, notably the SEC, to protect the investing public and to maintain a smoothly functioning primary market. Requiring issuers of securities to go through lengthy procedures to guarantee full disclosure and to seek representation by investment bankers for every issue is undoubtedly very expensive.

As an experiment to determine whether such costs could be reduced, the SEC, under its Rule 415, first permitted shelf registration on a temporary basis, and since January 1, 1984, as a permanent technique for issuing a security. This allows firms to register with the SEC one time, and then to offer securities for sale through agents and through the secondary markets for a period of two years after the registration. The rule applies to both stocks and bonds. This appears to offer corporations two chief advantages. First, corporations can reduce the expense of offering securities by avoiding too numerous registrations. Also, they can avoid the fixed price system of the investment bankers, as discussed above. Not surprisingly, the investment banking community lobbied very hard against the adoption of Rule 415.

The second advantage arises from the greater flexibility the firms achieve in timing an offering. Before shelf registration, the final go/no-go decision had to be made about three to six weeks before the actual offering was to take place. With security markets exhibiting radical fluctuations, issuing firms can now take advantage of favorable market conditions by issuing quickly under the provisions of shelf registration.

SUMMARY

In this chapter we began by considering the cost-benefit principle of value creation, which guided the discussion of the appropriate goal of the firm. The proper goal of the firm is to maximize shareholder wealth or, equivalently, maximize the firm's stock price. This goal defines the role of the financial manager in acquiring funds in the primary market. In this framework, we considered the flotation of securities in the primary market. The key role of the investment banker and of the entire distribution process was considered. In addition, the costs of bringing a new security to market were discussed.

QUESTIONS

1. What is the goal of financial management?
2. How does an increase in the amount of cash flow affect value?
3. How does an increase in the timing of the cash flows affect value?

4. How does an increase in the risk of the cash flows affect value?

5. Based on your answers to the previous three questions, write at least two alternative possible equations to describe the functional relationship between value and its component variables. The equations may or may not be accurate, but must reflect the general effect of each variable on the firm's value.

6. Comment on the following statement by a financial manager: The stockholders in my firm look at the income statement I generate. Naturally, they want to see large earnings. Because my job is to keep the stockholders satisfied, I give them what they want—I strive to maximize net income.

7. Explain the differences, if any, between maximizing shareholder wealth and maximizing the price of the stock.

8. Comment on the following claim: Maximizing stock price is a very nice goal, except it neglects risk. The true goal of financial management should be to maximize stock price, subject to a given level of risk.

9. Why is the acquisition and employment of funds the main decision made by the financial manager? To what does this decision owe its special importance?

10. What information is in a prospectus?

11. Will a small or a large issue of securities have higher percentage flotation costs? Why?

12. If you were the president of a software firm trying to raise funds for the introduction of Bugbuster, a revolutionary new product for personal computers, what considerations would be important to you in choosing between a public offering and a private placement? Why?

PART 3

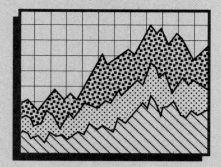

SECURITY VALUATION AND CAPITAL MARKET THEORY

161

Bond Valuation

This chapter builds on the discussion of the bond and money markets presented in Chapter 7 and explores the relationships among the key variables of bond pricing: maturity, coupon rate, and rate of interest. It also introduces factors that determine the level of interest rates. This chapter discusses the term structure, which expresses the relationship between maturity and bond yields, and can be graphed as a yield curve.

Thus far, we have focused almost exclusively on bonds that are free of default risk—the risk that payments on a bond will not be made as promised. Differences in default risk give rise to the risk structure of interest rates—the relationship between the yields of different securities as a function of their risk level. Risk levels change over time, and so do the yield differences or risk differentials of bonds from different classes. The bond manager must understand the reasons for those differences. In fact, one of the manager's most important tasks is choosing the correct level of default risk.

THE BOND PRICING FORMULA

pure discount bond or **zero coupon bond**
a bond that makes no payments between its issue and maturity date

coupon bond
a bond making a series of regular payments, called coupon payments

Firms issue corporate bonds as pure discount bonds or as coupon bonds. A **pure discount bond,** or **zero coupon bond,** makes no intermediate payments between its issue date and its maturity date. A **coupon bond** makes a series of regular coupon payments throughout its life. This section shows how to value both kinds using the time value of money concepts presented in Chapters 3 and 4.

Pure Discount Instruments

A pure discount bond promises to pay a certain amount at its maturity. The promised future payment is its **par value,** or **face value.** The difference between the par value and the lower selling price is the **bond discount.** The

par value or **face value**
for a pure discount bond, the amount paid at maturity; for a coupon bond, the principal amount of the bond

equation for the price of a pure discount bond is:

$$P = \frac{C}{(1 + r)^n} \tag{9.1}$$

where

P = the price of the instrument

C = the cash flow to be paid at the maturity of the bond

r = the annualized yield to maturity on the bond

n = the time in years until the bond matures

bond discount
for a bond with a market price less than par value, the par value minus the bond's price

As an example, consider a pure discount bond that matures in five years and has a face value of $1,000. If its interest rate is 12 percent, its price must be $567.43:

$$P = \frac{\$1,000}{(1.12)^5} = \$567.43$$

Coupon Bonds

Most corporate bonds are coupon bonds. Typically, they make coupon payments semiannually and the principal is repaid at maturity. The fact that coupons are paid semiannually makes the valuation of these bonds somewhat more complex, but the value is always the present value of all future payments that the bonds will make.

The promised payments consist of two parts. First is a series of equal coupon payments, so they constitute an annuity. Second, the principal, equal to the par or face value, must be paid on the date the bond matures. Consider a newly issued 30-year coupon bond with a face value of $1,000 and a coupon rate of 8 percent of the face value. The coupon payment will be $80 per year, or $40 semiannually. This bond promises 60 semiannual coupon payments of $40 and a $1,000 payment at the end of 30 years. Its price will equal the present value of all of these payments, and is expressed in the **coupon bond pricing formula:**

coupon bond pricing formula
an expression summarizing the price of a coupon bond as a function of its coupon, maturity, and discount rate

$$P = C \times \text{PA}(r, n) + F(1 + r)^{-n} \tag{9.2}$$

☞ Most corporate bonds are coupon bonds that make semiannual payments and repay the principal at maturity.

As an example, consider a coupon bond with a face value of $1,000, a yield of 13 percent, that pays a semiannual coupon of $60, and matures in one year. With this information, the bond pricing formula can be applied as follows:

$$P = \$60 \times \text{PA}\left(\frac{13}{2}, 2\right) + \$1,000\left(1 + \frac{0.13}{2}\right)^{-2}$$

$$= \$109.24 + \$881.66 = \$990.90$$

Notice that we used a discount rate of $13/2 = 6.5$ percent, and two periods, because the periodic payments are semiannual. In general, the units for the interest rate and the number of periods should be consistent. Thus, if payments had been monthly, we would have used a monthly discount rate.

Even if many payments remain to maturity, the price of the bond can be calculated by treating the coupon payments as an annuity and by treating the return of principal as a single payment. Consider a bond with a face value of $1,000 and a coupon rate of 10 percent that matures in 25 years and that has a yield to maturity of 12 percent. This bond will make 50 coupon payments of $50 and a final payment on the maturity date of $1,000.

According to the bond pricing formula, the price of the bond must equal the present value of the annuity of coupon payments plus the present value of the face value. Thus, we have:

$$\text{Bond price} = \$50 \times \text{PA}(6, 50) + \$1,000(1.06)^{-50}$$
$$= \$788.09 + \$54.29$$
$$= \$842.38$$

For simplicity, we will assume from now on that coupons are paid annually, unless stated otherwise.

THE APPROXIMATE YIELD TO MATURITY FORMULA

If we know the bond's price, coupon payments, face value, and maturity, we may want to compute its yield to maturity. Unfortunately, it is impossible to find a general formula for the yield to maturity of coupon bonds. Therefore, calculators rely on trial-and-error methods, which require a starting guess obtained from an approximate YTM formula such as the one presented below. This formula is useful when programming a computer to calculate the exact YTM by iteration. The approximate formula is:[1]

coupon payment +

$$\text{YTM} \approx \frac{C + \dfrac{(F - P)}{n}}{\dfrac{(F + 2P)}{3}} \quad \left(\text{weighted average of being \& ending price}\right) \tag{9.3}$$

The approximate formula has an intuitive interpretation. Indeed, the numerator is the sum of the coupon payment and the average annual capital gain, and the denominator is a weighted average of the beginning and ending bond prices. Thus, the approximate <u>yield to maturity</u>, like many other rate of return measures, <u>is just the ratio of the average annual cash flow over the average price.</u>

To evaluate the performance of the yield approximation formula, consider a bond maturing in five years and paying a 10 percent annual coupon with

[1] For a derivation of Equation 9.3, see Ricardo J. Rodriguez, "The Quadratic Approximation to the Yield to Maturity," *Journal of Financial Education,* Fall 1988, Vol. 17, pp. 19–25.

J. P. Morgan's Myopia

Many factors affecting bond prices are not explicitly reflected in the bond equation itself, such as the protective covenants in the bond indenture agreement. In a bond covenant, the firm places restrictions on its behavior in order to induce investors to buy bonds. The goal in creating the covenant should be to place restrictions that will attract bond investors, but that will not handcuff the company. Normally, great care is taken to make sure that the restrictions on the firm's conduct will not become burdensome. For example, if the bond indenture restricts the firm's right to issue new debt too severely, it may later have difficulties raising new capital to undertake attractive investment opportunities. Firms occasionally place themselves under restrictions that later prove very unpleasant.

In 1896 J. Pierpont Morgan helped to reorganize the bankrupt Northern Pacific Railroad Company, which today is owned by Burlington Northern, Inc. (BNI). The reorganization effort included the issuance of new, very long-term bonds. Because the firm was attempting to come back after bankruptcy, the bondholders were very skeptical and demanded particularly stringent safeguards. Shortly after the Civil War, Congress had granted tremendous amounts of land to the railroad. The bond covenant issued in 1896 required that every cent from those land holdings be spent on the railroad business. For the bondholders, this made the bonds very attractive because new money would be pumped into the railroad, thus helping to keep the firm out of another bankruptcy.

These restrictive covenants on the operating policy of the railroad eventually came back to haunt the management of BNI. Since the early decades of the twentieth century, the railroad industry has been in decline. With the railroad industry in ill health, BNI would like to commit capital to more lucrative businesses. However, the bonds do not mature until 1997 and 2047, and the restrictions in the covenants apply until the bonds are retired. The land covered by the bonds consists of 1.9 million acres of land and 2.4 million acres of mineral rights. In addition, the land includes terminals and railyards in urban areas. The bond covenant also prohibits the company from selling its railroad business. As one observer viewed the

a face value of $1,000. If it has a price of $1,059.12, its yield to maturity is exactly 8.5 percent. The approximate yield to maturity formula gives a close estimate of 8.48 percent:[2]

[2] Prior to the availability of this approximate formula, a similar one was used. The only difference between them is that the denominator of the traditional formula is $(F + P)/2$, rather than $(F + 2P)/3$. You can verify that the traditional formula gives a YTM of 8.56 percent for the example. The result of this example is typical, since Equation 9.3 provides a better estimate of YTM in most realistic cases.

issue, "To put all those earnings into the railroad, BNI would have to gold-plate the rails."

The bonds maturing in 1997 have a 4 percent coupon rate, while the bonds maturing in 2047 carry a 3 percent coupon rate. Because the coupon rates are so far below market rates, the bonds would normally sell at a deep discount from their par values of $1,000. To escape the stricture of the bond indenture, BNI offered to pay all bondholders a price greater than the market value of the bonds—$390 for each 3 percent bond and $535 for each 4 percent bond.

Another peculiarity of the bond indentures on these two bonds is that *all* bondholders must approve any change in the bond covenant. If a single bondholder owning only one bond did not agree, BNI could not escape the requirement to put all of the funds generated by the lands into the railroad business. However, if BNI is successful in retiring all of the bonds, it is released from the bond covenant.

Because the bond covenant requires that *all* bondholders must approve any change in the indenture of the bond, some investors attempted to force BNI to pay a very high price for the bonds. This tactic was feasible because freedom from the restrictions on the use of the funds would be very valuable to BNI. The firm countered this move by getting the bond trustees to agree to free the resource earnings, which would make it easier for BNI to live with the bonds. The bondholders then responded by suing BNI and asking the court that the firm pay at least $1,000 for each bond.

Because of this mess, the name of J. P. Morgan is not very fondly remembered around BNI today. The plight of BNI emphasizes the fact that financial managers must pay careful attention to bond indenture provisions. The indenture should offer prospective bondholders enough security and safeguards to make the bonds attractive, but they cannot be allowed to hamper the business strategy of the firm.

Source: Gelvin Stevenson and Brenton Welling, "Burlington Northern Tries to Break Its Bonds," *Business Week*, June 10, 1985.

$$\text{YTM} \approx \frac{\$100 + \dfrac{(1{,}000 - \$1{,}059.12)}{5}}{\dfrac{(\$1{,}000 + 2 \times \$1{,}059.12)}{3}}$$

$$= \frac{\$100 - \$11.82}{\$1{,}039.41}$$

$$= 8.48\%$$

BOND PRICE, COUPON RATE, AND YIELD TO MATURITY

par bond
a bond with a market price equal to its par value or face value

premium bond
a bond with a market price greater than its par or face value

discount bond
a bond with its price below its par or face value

We can distinguish among bonds according to their price. A **par bond** has a current price equal to its face value. Most bonds sell at or near par value when they are issued. A **premium bond** sells for more than its face value. A **discount bond** sells for less than its face value.

The following is a set of useful relationships between the price of a bond, its coupon rate, and its yield to maturity:

If YTM > CR, then $P < F$ *Price < Face Value*

If YTM = CR, then $P = F$

If YTM < CR, then $P > F$ *Price > Face Value*

For example, suppose that a bond has a coupon rate of 12 percent and a yield to maturity of 14 percent. These relationships tell us that the bond has to sell at a discount. It should be noted that the relationships work in both directions. Thus, if a bond is selling for $900 and has a coupon rate of 12 percent, the above relationships state that its yield to maturity has to be greater than 12 percent. Although the inequalities don't give us the exact value of, say, the yield to maturity, they provide a quick estimate and may serve to check our results. Of special importance is the equality relationship, since it tells us immediately that if the bond is selling at par, the yield to maturity is exactly equal to the coupon rate, without the need to perform any calculation. Notice that none of the three relationships requires knowledge of the bond's maturity (n). In other words, they are true regardless of maturity.

Actually, a better set of relationships compares the yield to maturity with the bond's current yield, instead of the coupon rate. The current yield is the ratio of the bond's coupon to its current price. The new set of relationships is:

If YTM > CY, then $P < F$

If YTM = CY, then $P = F$

If YTM < CY, then $P > F$

The relationships using the current yield provide better information than the ones using the coupon rate. To see this, consider the bond selling for $900 with a coupon rate of 12 percent. Using the first set of relationships we saw that the yield to maturity must be greater than 12 percent. With the new set of relationships we can say that the yield to maturity has to be greater than the bond's current yield; that is, we must have YTM > 13.33 percent ($120/$900). Both relationships are true, but the one using the current yield is closer to the true yield to maturity. The relationship among yield to maturity, coupon rate, and current yield for both premium and discount bonds is shown in Figure 9.1.

FIGURE 9.1   Relationship Among Coupon Rate, Current Yield, and Yield to Maturity

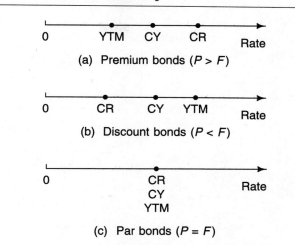

(a) Premium bonds ($P > F$)

(b) Discount bonds ($P < F$)

(c) Par bonds ($P = F$)

EXAMPLE 9.1

A 10-year, 10 percent coupon bond is currently selling for $800. Find the current yield and the exact YTM. Assume the bond pays coupons annually.

Since the coupon rate is 10 percent, the annual coupon payments are $100 (0.10 × $1,000). The current yield is then $100/$800 = 12.5 percent. Because the bond sells at a discount, we know that the YTM will be greater than the coupon rate. In fact, it will be greater than the current yield of 12.5 percent. The exact YTM is 13.81 percent. We verify that for this discount bond: CR < CY < YTM (10% < 12.5% < 13.81%), in agreement with Figure 9.1.

THE TIME PATH OF BOND PRICES

At maturity, the price of a bond must equal the face value. This means that a premium bond's price will generally be falling over its life, even if interest rates do not change. By the same token, the price of a discount bond must rise, reaching the face value by the maturity date. To illustrate the time path of bond prices, assume that interest rates are constant at 10 percent. Figure 9.2 shows the paths that the prices of three bonds must follow over time. Bond 1 is a 20-year, 12 percent coupon bond; bond 2 is a 20-year, 10 percent coupon bond; and bond 3 is a 20-year, 8 percent coupon bond. Since we

FIGURE 9.2 Bond Price Paths with a Constant Interest Rate

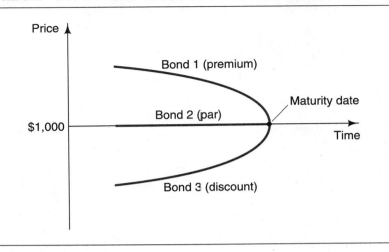

assume that interest rates remain constant at 10 percent, bond 1 will be a premium bond, so its price falls over time until, at maturity, its price equals its face value. Bond 2 has a coupon rate equal to the yield of 10 percent. As a consequence, it trades at a price equal to its face value over the entire period. Bond 3, with a coupon rate less than its yield to maturity, sells at a discount, and its price must rise toward the par value over time.

BOND PRICES AND THE LEVEL OF INTEREST RATES

interest rate risk
the risk that a security's value will change due to a change in interest rates

It is essential to understand the ways in which the prices of bonds with different characteristics respond to changes in the market rates of interest. The effect of a given change in interest rates on the price of a bond depends on three key variables: the bond's maturity, its coupon rate, and the level of interest rates at the time the rates change. **Interest rate risk** is the risk that a bond's price will change due to a change in interest rates. As we will see, bonds vary considerably in their interest rate risk.

This section develops five principles that explain how the price of a given bond will change in response to a sudden change in interest rates. The principles were proved rigorously by Burton Malkiel in a now famous article.[3] Here they are illustrated rather than proved.

[3] See Burton G. Malkiel, "Expectations, Bond Prices, and the Term Structure of Interest Rates," *Quarterly Journal of Economics*, May 1962, pp. 197–218.

INTERNATIONAL PERSPECTIVES

Japanese Zeroes

Investors in the United States and other nations are anxious to reduce their tax liabilities, although the tax codes they face are often different. A zero coupon bond must sell at a discount, with the difference between the par value and the purchase price generating the return on the investment.

Under Japanese law, capital gains are exempt from taxation, but interest income is taxed as ordinary income. These rules provide the Japanese with a perfectly legal way to avoid taxes. By simply investing in zero coupon bonds, all returns from the bond would be tax-exempt.

The exploitation of this strategy in the early 1980s swept Japan like brushfire. The Ministry of Finance, however, did not appreciate the effect it had on tax revenues. Eventually, the Ministry solved the problem by prohibiting the purchase of zero coupon bonds by individuals, thereby ending a very attractive tax avoidance scheme.

Why should there be a distinction of treatment for capital gains versus ordinary income in either the U.S. or Japanese tax laws? The philosophical foundation for the differential treatment stems from the belief that investors who contribute capital to business are providing a valuable service to society. In an effort to stimulate capital investment that contributes substantially to the economic growth of a nation, many tax codes give preferential treatment to capital gains.

Part of the difference in the growth rates of the United States, Japan, and other countries must be attributed to the different incentive schedules facing investors. The fact that Japan has no tax on capital gains makes its economic philosophy crystal-clear. By contrast, in the United States, long-term capital gains receive less favorable treatment. Furthermore, there seems to be a cyclical outburst of arguments to do away with preferential capital gains treatment altogether as a prerogative of the rich. In fact, the Tax Reform Act of 1986 eliminated the preferential treatment of capital gains in the United States. These differential attitudes may help to explain the different paths that the economies of the United States and Japan have taken.

PRINCIPLE 1: Bond prices move inversely with interest rates.

☞ Bond prices move inversely with interest rates.

Figure 9.3 illustrates the price of a 20-year, 12 percent coupon bond as a function of the interest rate. For example, using the bond pricing formula of Equation 9.2, the price of this bond when the interest rate level is 10 percent is $1,171.60. If interest rates drop suddenly from 10 to 8 percent, the new price would be $1,392.73, as shown in the figure. This illustrates the first principle. Conversely, an increase in interest rates creates a decrease in the price of the bond.

FIGURE 9.3   Relationship Between Bond Price and Discount Rate

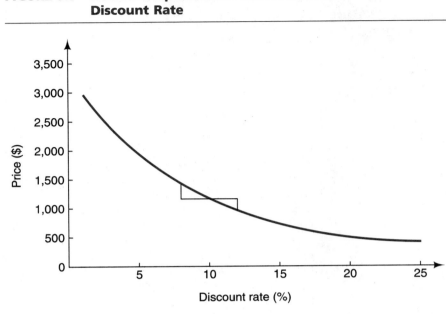

PRINCIPLE 2: **For a given bond, the increase in price caused by a decrease in interest rates is greater in magnitude than the decrease in price caused by a corresponding increase in interest rates.**

☞ The capital gain caused by a given fall in rates is greater than the capital loss caused by an increase in rates of the same size.

Principle 2 is also illustrated in Figure 9.3. It is clear from the figure that when the interest rate rises from 10 to 12 percent, the price change is lower than the increase in price the bond experiences when the interest rate decreases from 10 to 8 percent. Geometrically, Principle 2 states that the slope of the bond price curve becomes less negative as the interest rate increases.

PRINCIPLE 3: **The longer the maturity of the bond, the more sensitive is its price to a change in interest rates.**

☞ The longer the maturity of a bond, the greater its price sensitivity to a change in interest rates.

Figure 9.4 illustrates the sensitivity of coupon bonds to a drop in interest rates from 10 to 8 percent as a function of the maturity of the bonds. All bonds in the figure are 12 percent coupon bonds. Clearly, as maturity increases, so does the sensitivity of bond price changes. As an example, a 20-year bond would experience a 19.14 percent price increase under the assumptions of Figure 9.4, whereas a 10-year bond would increase its price by only 13.09 percent.

FIGURE 9.4 Relationship Between Bond Price Change and Maturity

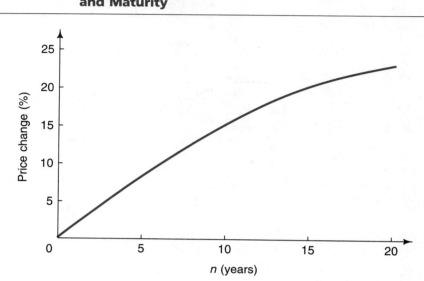

PRINCIPLE 4: The price sensitivity of bonds increases at a decreasing rate with maturity.

☞ The price sensitivity of bonds increases with maturity, but at a decreasing rate.

According to Principle 4, the difference in sensitivity between a 15-year and a 10-year bond will be smaller than the difference in sensitivity between a 10-year and a 5-year bond, because the sensitivity is increasing at a decreasing rate. This feature is also shown in Figure 9.4. Although the sensitivity of the bond's price always increases as the maturities get longer, it does so at a decreasing rate. A curve that increases at a decreasing rate is said to be concave. Geometrically, Principle 4 states that the slope of a sensitivity curve, such as the one in Figure 9.4, decreases with maturity.

PRINCIPLE 5: The lower the coupon rate on a finite maturity bond, the more sensitive is its price to a change in interest rates.[4]

☞ The lower the coupon rate on a bond, the greater its price sensitivity to a change in interest rates.

Just as longer-maturity bonds are more sensitive to changes in interest rates, so are low-coupon bonds, holding other factors constant. This is due to the fact that bonds with low coupons return less of their value early in their lives through the payment of the higher coupons, relative to high-coupon bonds. In this sense, a

---

[4] For perpetual bonds, also known as consols, the sensitivity of prices to changes in interest rates is independent of the bond's coupon, and depends solely on the initial interest rate level.

FIGURE 9.5   Relationship Between Bond Price Change and Coupon Rate

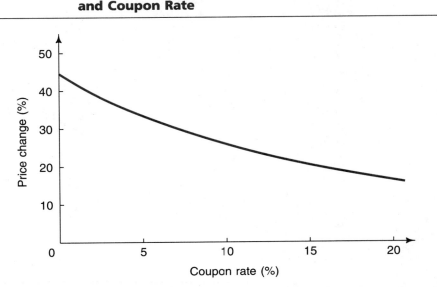

low-coupon bond can be thought of as having a "longer" maturity than a high-coupon bond. This principle is illustrated in Figure 9.5, which graphs the percentage price changes of 20-year bonds with various coupon rates when interest rates fall from 10 to 8 percent. As should be expected, the most sensitive coupon rate of all is the zero coupon rate of a pure discount bond. As the graph of Figure 9.5 shows, a drop in yields from 10 to 8 percent causes a price increase of 44.34 percent for a 20-year zero coupon bond.

These five principles summarize the ways in which changes in interest rates affect the prices of bonds. We turn now to the factors that determine the level of interest rates.

THE LEVEL OF INTEREST RATES

In discussing interest rates it is customary to speak of their overall level, term structure, and risk structure. Because the level of and changes in rates are so crucial to price changes of individual bonds, this section focuses on the level of interest rates. Term structure and risk structure are considered later in this chapter. Because we address risk later, our discussion here focuses on risk-free bonds, so we will consider the level of interest rates on U.S. Treasury obligations.

The Nominal Rate of Interest

nominal rate of interest
an interest rate reflecting only the promised dollar payments without reference to the expected purchasing power of the payments

☞ The rate on a bond free of default risk depends on the *expected* inflation rate and the real rate of interest.

Yields on debt securities are quoted as a **nominal rate of interest.** That is, a rate that takes account only of the promised dollar payments without reference to the expected purchasing power of the payments. For example, a one-year loan of $100 at a nominal rate of 12 percent returns $112. To understand the determinants of the nominal rate of interest, which is in fact the market rate of interest, it is customary to break it down into its components. Since the work of Irving Fisher,[5] it has become customary to express the nominal rate on a default-free security as being composed of "the real rate of interest" and the "expected rate of inflation." For any single period, this relationship can be expressed as follows:

$$(1 + r) = (1 + r^*) [1 + E(I)] \qquad (9.4)$$

nominal   *real rate of interest*   *expected rate of inflation over the period.*

where r = the nominal rate of interest
r^* = the real rate of interest
$E(I)$ = the expected rate of inflation over the period

The Real Rate of Interest and the Expected Inflation Rate

real rate of interest
the expected change in purchasing power necessary to induce investors to postpone consumption

When investors buy bonds it is uncertain what will happen to inflation over the bonds' lives. However, it seems clear that investors will demand some increase in the purchasing power of their funds. This leads to a definition of the **real rate of interest**—the expected increase in purchasing power necessary to induce the investor to postpone consumption.

To continue using the example of a one-year bond investment with a nominal rate of 12 percent, the investor will not be pleased if the inflation rate during that period is 14 percent because it will mean a reduction in purchasing power over the year. Although the initial investment will increase in value by $12, what $100 would buy at the outset of the investment will require $114 at year's end. The purchasing power of an investment can be found by using Equation 9.5, assuming the rate of inflation and the rate of return for the period are known:

$$\text{Purchasing power} = \frac{C(1 + r)}{C(1 + I)} = \frac{(1 + r)}{(1 + I)} \qquad (9.5)$$

initial investment   *rate of interest*   *actual inflation rate over the investment period.*

where C = the initial investment
r = the rate of interest
I = the actual inflation rate over the investment period

[5] Irving Fisher, *The Theory of Interest* (New York: A. M. Kelley, Publishers, 1965). This classic was originally published in 1930.

FINANCE TODAY

A Tale of Two Credit-Rating Agencies

These are the best of times for Moody's and Standard & Poor's (S&P), the two American companies that dominate the world business of rating government and corporate debt. They earn their bread by reckoning up for investors the risk of default. When defaults proliferate, as they do during and after recessions, the two firms wield enormous clout in financial markets.

Their duopoly is not secure. Their chief American competitors, Fitch and Duff & Phelps, are redoubling efforts to win business. In Europe, where credit ratings are not yet universal, the two face competition from IBCA, a decade-old specialist in bank credit. Investment banks too are starting to publish opinions on credit just as they do on equities. But no one is about to oust Moody's and S&P as market leaders.

Several trends have boosted the credit raters' importance:

- **Recession.** The world's economic downturn has triggered a rash of defaults in commercial paper and long-term debt, particularly by unrated issuers. In 1990, Moody's reckons, companies defaulted on $22 billion of bonds, the highest nominal figure in 20 years. That has prompted investors to demand ratings from more issuers of debt and to take the ratings more seriously.

- **Cross-border finance.** Not long ago European companies could issue paper on the strength of their names alone; domestic investors would buy, believing that famous companies do not go bust. Now some have—and foreign investors, less credulous anyway, are more careful than they used to be. Less-known companies certainly will not get cash from them without ratings, preferably from the two top firms.

- **Financial innovation.** Asset-backed debt, hybrid securities and the like are not new, but they are appearing more often. Banks are issuing a stream of securities backed by mortgages, credit-card receivables, and other assets stripped off their balance sheets. The rating of such "structured financings" is the fastest-growing segment of the raters' business.

- **Regulation.** Regulators are increasingly relying on ratings to measure and control risks undertaken by the institutions they oversee. America's Securities and Exchange Commission, for example, recently restricted money-market funds' investments in low-rated commercial paper.

Normally, issuers invite, and pay, the agencies to rate their debt (though Moody's, to the irritation of more than one issuer, has sometimes rated debt uninvited). They are often aghast at the results. At worst, a poor rating can put a company out of business. At the least, it is likely to drive up the cost of borrowing. That happened in early 1991 when S&P and Moody's downgraded some of Chrysler's debt. The American car maker had guaranteed an issue of $1.1 billion of debt with interest rates linked to its credit ratings. When the ratings fell, its interest bill jumped by $38 million a year. Upgraded companies can save correspondingly. The market's obsession with credit ratings has spawned a sideline for investment banks: advising clients how to spruce up their presentations to the rating agencies.

Poor ratings are especially bad for banks and other financial companies. Because of their low ratings, some of America's biggest banks pay more for short- and long-term funds than do their industrial customers. They can no longer lend at a profit to well-rated corporate borrowers. The business goes to stronger banks.

Issuers wish Moody's and S&P were not so powerful: more competition among credit-raters might limit the damage caused by one bad rating. Institutional investors, the main users of the ratings, share that wish. The head of bond research at one large American institution calls the concentration of power in Moody's and S&P dangerous. Both do a good job, he says, but "I would rather see more judgments out there in the market."

Some investors complain that Moody's and S&P were slow to recognize the financial deterioration of American banks and of certain state governments. Some think the agencies' analysts risk becoming too friendly with the companies they rate. More cogently, some observe that these analysts track the credit quality of up to 35 companies apiece, and are paid significantly less than equity analysts on Wall Street.

The second-tier agencies hope to exploit these feelings. Duff & Phelps, a Chicago-based company, recently merged with a competitor, and now claims to rate nearly three-quarters of corporate bonds publicly issued in America. Fitch was acquired by new owners in 1989 and promptly raided senior executives from Moody's and S&P. In Europe, IBCA recently began rating debt issued by British industrial companies. Robin Monro-Davies, its chief, says that IBCA intends to become a full-fledged rater of European debt. With only 26 analysts, mostly banking specialists, it still has far to go.

Some second-tier agencies have adopted a kind of ratings *machismo* that promises investors harsher verdicts than those handed down by Moody's and S&P. Fitch recently published tough criteria for rating bond insurers, companies that use their financial clout to secure triple-A ratings for bonds issued by local governments and other issuers. Fitch reckons that not all bond insurers deserve the top rating; those that do, it believes, suffer because investors do not trust the triple-As assigned to the insured debt by Moody's and S&P. The agency plans to assign its own ratings to bond insurers.

(continued)

Moody's and S&P try to stay above this fray. The principles of credit rating are immutable, they insist; their credit opinions are never swayed by the judgments of others. This is hard to believe, but impossible to disprove. Yet the top two do not feel as smug as they may sound. Investors say that both have improved their services since they started to face serious competition. And though Moody's and S&P rate nearly all big debt issues in America, they are not taking Europe for granted. S&P has expanded largely through joint ventures and acquisitions. It owns half of a French rating agency, ADEF, and all of Nordisk, a Swedish firm. Its overseas staff has risen three-fold in the past five years, to 75 analysts. Moody's says a quarter of its staff is non-American. It rates four-fifths of Eurocommercial paper and two-thirds of longer-term Eurobonds.

Competitors could challenge Moody's and S&P more easily if the two leaders made more mistakes. They do not make many. In 20 years only one company with an investment-grade rating from Moody's has defaulted on long-term debt—Manville, a single-A company that went bankrupt voluntarily to protect itself from asbestosis lawsuits. A New Zealand finance company, DFC, defaulted on its commercial paper in 1989 while still carrying a prime rating by S&P. The agency says it relied on a government commitment to provide liquidity, but the government reneged.

Moody's and S&P sell reams of information on the companies they rate, but say little about themselves. Although the collapse of the junk-bond market cut business in 1990, both agencies make money. But, both being owned by larger companies—Moody's by Dun & Bradstreet; S&P by a publishing firm, McGraw-Hill—they need not disclose their financial details, and do not. Lucky folk, they do not need credit ratings.

Source: The Economist, March 30, 1991, p. 80.

In our example,

$$\text{Purchasing power} = \frac{\$100(1.12)}{\$100(1.14)} = \frac{\$112}{\$114} = 0.9825$$

The investor earns a negative real rate of return, because purchasing power has been reduced to 98.25 of the original purchasing power. Thus, the investor has really lost 1.75 percent, despite the fact that the investment yielded 12 percent in nominal terms.

Having defined the real rate as the expected change in purchasing power necessary to induce investment, the next question becomes, what level of real rates are possible and what do investors demand? We considered this same issue under another guise in Chapter 2. Refer to Figure 2.6 (p. 29), which shows the relationship between real and nominal interest rates and the marginal productivity of capital. As we discussed in Chapter 2, real investment will be undertaken just so long as its return exceeds the return on investment in bonds. In Figure 2.6 this point is Q^*, where the slope of the production curve is tangent to the slope of the capital market line.

This production opportunity curve expresses the rate at which a unit of physical capital can be transformed into more units of capital, so it is a real rate of interest. Notice that it does not reflect inflation, because real goods do not lose their purchasing power: an ear of corn will always be worth one ear of corn. Therefore, the slope of the capital market line in Figure 2.6 expresses the real rate of interest. If inflation is expected, the nominal rate of interest must exceed the real rate by the expected inflation. Even in the face of expected inflation, investors will evaluate opportunities based on real, not merely nominal, returns.

In the securities markets, the investor always faces uncertain future prospects. Given a stated nominal rate on some investment, a great deal of uncertainty exists about what portion of that rate should be attributed to expected real returns or to expected inflation. Presumably, the expected real return is never negative. If that is a reasonable assumption, it is apparent that investors are often disappointed. On numerous occasions the realized real rate of return on T bills has, in fact, been negative. Figure 9.6 presents the nominal and real returns from 1926 through 1990 for investment in Treasury bills, as well as the annual inflation rates over the period. Although the nominal return was positive every single year, the real return was negative in some years. If we assume that investors make investments only when the expected real return is positive, then some investors' expectations were clearly wrong during this period.

Although Treasury bills returned 3.67 percent compounded annually over 1926 to 1990 in nominal terms, they returned only 0.5 percent in real terms. Thus, it must be acknowledged that the real rate is not very important in determining the nominal interest rate. Instead, the nominal rate is mainly made up of the expected inflation rate. This is seen by noting that the annual average rate of inflation was 3.1 percent over the past 65 years.[6]

☞ The nominal interest rate mainly consists of the expected inflation rate.

However, the experience shown in Figure 9.6 is clearly from the past and reflects actually achieved returns and experienced inflation rates. It cannot be emphasized strongly enough that the nominal rate of interest depends on the expected rate of inflation, not the actual rate. Quoted interest rates pertain to investment over some future time period. As such, they cannot depend on the actual inflation rate to be sustained during the investment period, since that is not known. Instead, expected inflation is the key component.

[6] For T bills, nominal annual returns ranged from 14.7 percent in 1981 to a low of 0.0 in 1938. In real terms, the greatest annual return was 12.55 percent in 1932, and the lowest was −15.07 in 1946. Inflation rates ranged from a high of 18.2 percent in 1946 to a low of −10.3 in 1932.

FIGURE 9.6 Returns on Treasury Bills

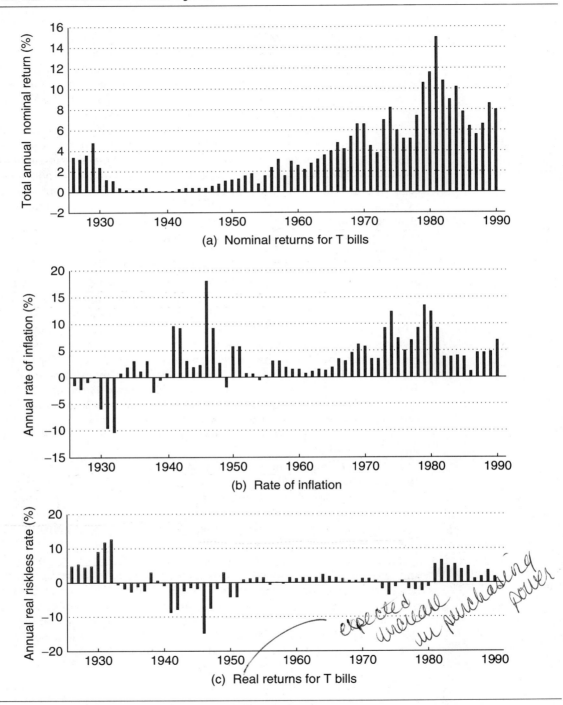

(a) Nominal returns for T bills

(b) Rate of inflation

(c) Real returns for T bills

expected increase in purchasing power

Source: © *Stocks, Bonds, Bills, and Inflation, 1991 Yearbook*, Ibbotson Associates, (annually updates work by Roger G. Ibbotson and Rex A. Sinquefeld). All rights reserved.

THE TERM STRUCTURE OF INTEREST RATES

It is not unusual to find that short-term bills have low yields, whereas long-term bonds have much higher yields. At first glance, this is very strange. Both have equal backing by the U.S. Treasury, so they have the same level of default risk. In fact, the essential differences between them are their maturities. This difference in yields, due solely to differences in maturities, is described by the yield curve, or the term structure of interest rates. Naturally, this gap in yield is of prime importance to the bond portfolio manager. It appears that the manager should accept the higher yields of the long-term bonds, but this easy solution is not necessarily correct, as it leaves out the important considerations associated with the term structure of interest rates.

The term structure of interest rates is the relationship between the term to maturity, or time left until maturity, and the yield to maturity for bonds that are similar in all respects except their maturities. Because yield curve analysis explores the differences in yields arising strictly from differences in maturities, the bonds used in the analysis should be as similar as possible in other respects. For example, they should be similar in their risk level and should have the same call provisions, sinking fund characteristics, and tax status.

These requirements for similarities are cumbersome, because it is difficult to find a pool of bonds that meet all of those conditions. For this reason, it is customary to focus on the term structure of Treasury securities, which all have the same level of default risk and tend to be alike in their tax status and other features. Also, since they are lowest in risk, the Treasury yield curve provides the basic yield curve to which the yields of other securities can be related. This section therefore focuses on the Treasury yield curve, shown in Figure 9.7.

The yield curve in the figure is approximately flat. At other times, it may take on different shapes. For example, Figure 9.8 shows yield curves for high-grade corporate bonds for various years. Even within a very short period from 1979 to 1982 it is possible to note violent swings in their shape and in the level of rates as well. The shape of the yield curve is very important, because it contains information about the expected future course of interest rates. Developing this understanding of yield curves first requires knowledge of forward rates.

Forward Rates

forward rate
a rate of interest for a period in the future implied by spot rates

spot rate
a rate of interest on a security at a given moment

Forward rates of interest are rates for future time periods implied by currently available spot rates. A **spot rate** is a yield prevailing at a given moment on a security. With a set of spot rates, it is possible to calculate forward rates for any intervening time period.

For convenience, let us introduce the notation that a bond yield expressed as $r_{x,y}$ is the rate for the period beginning at time x and ending at time y. The present is always time $t = 0$, so a bond yield covering any time span

FIGURE 9.7 **Yield Curve for Treasury Securities**

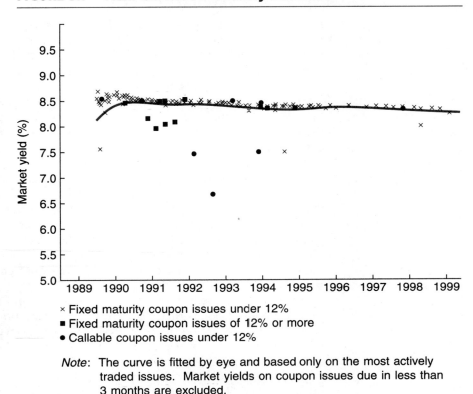

× Fixed maturity coupon issues under 12%
■ Fixed maturity coupon issues of 12% or more
● Callable coupon issues under 12%

Note: The curve is fitted by eye and based only on the most actively traded issues. Market yields on coupon issues due in less than 3 months are excluded.

Source: Treasury Bulletin, September 30, 1989, p. 55.

beginning at $t = 0$ is a spot rate. For example, $r_{0,5}$ would be the spot rate for an instrument maturing in five years. If the time covered by a particular rate begins after $t = 0$, it is a forward rate. The forward rate to cover a period beginning two years from now and extending three years to time $t = 5$ would be $r_{2,5}$ in our notation.

Principle of Calculation for Forward Rates   Forward rates are calculated on the assumption that returns over a given period of time are all equal, no matter which maturities of bonds are held over that span of time. Taking a five-year period as an example, this principle implies that forward rates can be calculated over the five years on the assumption that all of the following strategies would earn the same return over that period: buy the five-year bond and hold it to maturity; buy a one-year bond and, when it matures, buy another one-year bond, following this procedure for the entire five years;

☞ Forward rates give important information about the future course of interest rates.

FIGURE 9.8 Yield Curves of Various Shapes

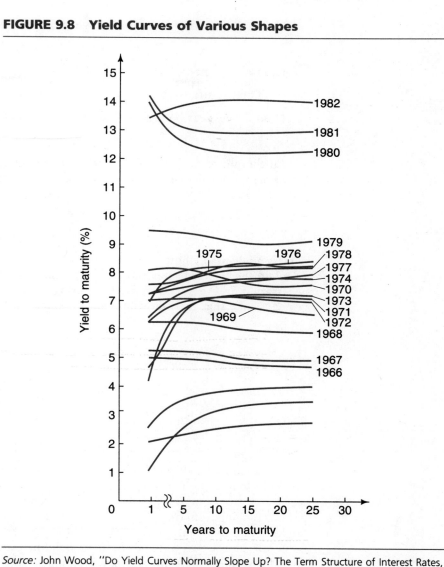

Source: John Wood, "Do Yield Curves Normally Slope Up? The Term Structure of Interest Rates, 1862–1982," *Economic Perspectives*, Federal Reserve Bank of Chicago, July/August 1983, p. 18.

or buy a two-year bond and, when it matures, buy a three-year bond and hold it to maturity.

According to this principle of calculation, holding bonds of any maturity over these five years would give exactly the same return. Notice that this is not a prediction of returns, but is an assumption used to calculate forward rates. In terms of the notation being used in this chapter, these three strategies can be expressed as follows:

Hold one five-year bond for five years:

$$\text{Total return} = (1 + r_{0,5})^5$$

Hold a sequence of one-year bonds:

$$\text{Total return} = (1 + r_{0,1})(1 + r_{1,2})(1 + r_{2,3})(1 + r_{3,4})(1 + r_{4,5})$$

Hold a two-year bond followed by a three-year bond:

$$\text{Total return} = (1 + r_{0,2})^2(1 + r_{2,5})^3$$

Furthermore, the forward rates shown above can be calculated by applying the principle of calculation, which says that those total returns should all be equal. Thus, we have:

$$(1 + r_{0,5})^5 = (1 + r_{0,2})^2(1 + r_{2,5})^3$$
$$= (1 + r_{0,1})(1 + r_{1,2})(1 + r_{2,3})(1 + r_{3,4})(1 + r_{4,5})$$

To understand how the principle of calculation makes it possible to calculate the forward rates shown here, some values for the spot yields are necessary. For Treasury securities maturing in one, two, three, four, and five years, assume that the following yields obtain:

	Spot Rates	*Maturity*
$r_{0,1}$	0.080	1 year
$r_{0,2}$	0.088	2
$r_{0,3}$	0.090	3
$r_{0,4}$	0.093	4
$r_{0,5}$	0.095	5

These are all spot yields consistent with an upward-sloping yield curve, since the longer the maturity of the bond, the greater the yield. As we will see, this set of spot rates also implies a number of forward rates to cover periods ranging from time $t = 1$ to $t = 5$. An investor with a five-year horizon might hold a five-year bond, with a yield of 9.5 percent. However, there are numerous alternative ways of holding a bond investment over the same time period. Consider the third strategy mentioned above in which the investor might hold a two-year bond followed by holding a three-year bond. Right now, at $t = 0$, it is impossible to know what the yield will be on the three-year bond to cover the time period from $t = 2$ to $t = 5$. This rate cannot be known with certainty until time $t = 2$ actually arrives.

At time $t = 0$, however, it is possible to calculate a forward rate to cover the time span from $t = 2$ to $t = 5$. As shown above, the principle of calculation implies:

$$(1 + r_{0,5})^5 = (1 + r_{0,2})^2(1 + r_{2,5})^3$$

Using the spot rates given above, we have:

$$(1.095)^5 = (1.088)^2(1 + r_{2,5})^3$$

Now the only unknown is the forward rate, so the equation can be solved for $r_{2,5}$:

$$(1 + r_{2,5}) = \sqrt[3]{\frac{1.5742}{1.1837}} = 1.0997$$

$$r_{2,5} = 9.97\%$$

The forward rate implied by this set of spot rates to cover the period from year 2 to year 5 is 9.97 percent. Given the relevant spot rates, it is possible to calculate any forward rate. Notice that nothing has been said so far about how the forward rates are to be interpreted. Different theories of the term structure interpret forward rates in somewhat different ways; however, all of them give important information about the future course of interest rates.

Theories of the Term Structure

Three theories of the term structure have received the greatest attention: the pure expectations theory, the liquidity premium theory, and the market segmentation theory. The first two use forward rates as a key element, and both can be stated by their interpretation of those rates.

☞ The pure expectations theory asserts that forward rates equal expected future spot rates.

The Pure Expectations Theory This theory states that forward rates are unbiased estimators of future interest rates. Equivalently:

Forward rates = expected future spot rates

The theory claims that, on average, today's forward rate equals the spot rate that will actually occur in the future. Of course, the actual rate that occurs may be higher or lower than expected, but the theory's claim holds.

The rationale is that many bond investors will switch their funds to any maturity strategy that is seen to offer the highest yield. However, this means that all maturity strategies must have the same expected return in equilibrium. In other words, after all of the maturity switching has stopped and equilibrium has been achieved, there must be an equal expected return for any investment horizon, no matter what maturities of instruments are held over that horizon.

Now the stage is set to see how the pure expectations theory ties together forward rates and expected future spot rates. Suppose an investor has a five-year bond yielding 9.5 percent per year over the five years. According to the theory, an investor with a five-year horizon holding a two-year bond and planning to follow that with holding a three-year bond must be expecting to earn the same 9.5 percent annual return over the entire period. However, the yield to maturity on the two-year bond is only 8.8 percent. The investor who earns 8.8 percent for the first two years of a five-year holding period must earn much more in the last three years in order to have a 9.5 percent rate of return over the whole period. If this is true, then the following relationship must hold:

$$1.095^5 = (1.088)^2(1 + x)^3$$

where x = the expected yield on the three-year bond from period $t = 2$ to $t = 5$. Solving this equation for x gives:

$$(1 + x) = \sqrt[3]{\frac{1.5742}{1.1837}}$$

$$x = 9.97\%$$

Notice that this expected interest rate for the three-year bond is exactly equal to the forward rate for the same bond calculated above. This is the crux of the argument for the pure expectations theory. If expected returns from all maturity strategies are to be the same, forward rates must necessarily equal expected future spot rates. This equality follows logically from the view that all maturity strategies have the same expected return over any given holding period. If enough investors do not care about the maturity of the instruments they hold and merely go after the highest expected return, they will ensure that all different maturity strategies have the same expected return and they will force the major conclusion of the pure expectations theory to be true.

☞ The liquidity premium theory maintains that forward rates exceed expected future spot rates by the amount of the liquidity premium.

The Liquidity Premium Theory   In many ways, the liquidity premium theory resembles the pure expectations theory. At least they both see the problem similarly. The liquidity premium theory states that forward rates are upwardly biased estimators of expected future spot rates; that is, the estimates are too high:

Forward rates > expected future spot rates

As explained above, the pure expectations theory must be true if enough bond investors care only about returns, regardless of maturity. The liquidity premium theorists acknowledge this, but reject the claim that numerous investors are indifferent about the maturities of the bonds that they hold. They assert that bondholders greatly prefer to hold short-term rather than long-term bonds. Short-term bonds have less interest rate risk, as we saw earlier in this chapter. The fact that they will not change dramatically in price as interest rates change makes them more attractive than long-term bonds to many investors. According to the liquidity premium theory, short-term bonds are so much more attractive that investors are willing to pay more for them than for long-term bonds. This extra amount that they are willing to pay is the liquidity premium.

The willingness of investors to pay a liquidity premium for short-term bonds also implies that the yields will be lower than those on long-term bonds, other things being equal. Another way of saying the same thing is to notice that long-term bonds must provide a greater return than short-term bonds to induce investors to commit their funds to them.

If yields on short-term bonds are lower than those on long-term bonds in the normal event, the total return from investing in the former will be less than the total return from investing in the latter even when the two are pursued over the same time interval. According to the key claim of the liquidity premium theory, the expected rate of return on a succession of one-year bonds must be less than the expected rate of return on a long-term bond, when the two are pursued over the same horizon.

Both the pure expectations and liquidity premium theories follow logically from their respective beliefs about the preferences and behavior of bond market participants. The basic disagreement between them turns on whether bondholders prefer short-term to long-term instruments. Before examining the evidence about the term structure theories, we must consider one more theory.

The Market Segmentation Theory   Unlike the previous two theories, this one is not expressly stated in terms of forward rates. Rather, it takes a more institutional approach. According to this theory, the yield curve that exists at any one time reflects the actions and preferences of certain major participants in the bond market. To a large extent, the market is dominated by large financial institutions, with each kind having strong maturity preferences stemming from the business it pursues. Commercial banks, for example, have relatively short-term liabilities in the form of demand deposits and certificates of deposit (CDs). As a consequence, they prefer to invest in relatively short-term bonds. Life insurance companies, by contrast, have their liabilities falling due far in the future on the death of policyholders. Correspondingly, they prefer long-term bonds. Casualty insurers, such as those writing auto and home insurance, have liabilities that fall due in the medium term, so they favor medium-maturity bonds.

These preferences of different types of institutions arise from the nature of their businesses, and a desire to match the maturity of their assets and liabilities to control risk. Therefore, the institutions tend to trade bonds only in their respective maturity ranges. For example, to induce a bank to invest in long-term bonds, the bonds must pay an attractively higher yield in comparison to the short-term bonds that banks prefer. This leads directly to the segmented markets hypothesis, which states:

> The yield curve is determined by the interplay of supply and demand factors in different segments of the maturity spectrum of the bond market. Financial institutions with strong maturity preferences occupy those different segments and effectively cause the bond market to splinter into different market segments based on maturity.

It must be stressed that, according to the market segmentation theory, also known as the preferred habitat theory, the institutions have preferred maturity ranges, but the preference is not absolute. In reality, if interest rates

☞ The market segmentation theory maintains that the shape of the yield curve is determined by the strong maturity preferences of different types of financial institutions.

in a maturity range that is not the natural habitat of a certain industry become sufficiently attractive, it is likely the firms in that industry will strongly consider investing in that range.

SUMMARY

This chapter began by examining the bond pricing formula and the way bond prices respond to changes in interest rates. The principles discussed show that (1) bond prices move inversely to interest rates, (2) a given drop in interest rates causes a larger capital gain than the capital loss caused by the same size increase in rates, (3) long-term bonds are more sensitive to interest rate changes than short-term bonds, (4) the sensitivity of bond prices to interest rate changes increases at a decreasing rate with respect to maturity, and (5) bonds with large coupons are less sensitive to interest rate changes than those with small coupons.

With bond prices being so sensitive to changes in interest rates, it is important to understand the basic factors that influence interest rates. We saw that the nominal or market rate of interest for a risk-free bond equals the real rate of interest plus the expected rate of inflation.

The yield curve, or the term structure of interest rates, expresses the relationship between yield to maturity and term to maturity for bonds of the same risk level. Because bond yields differ by maturity, understanding these relationships is important to the bond manager. The manager must understand the opportunities and risks inherent in pursuing higher yields, which leads to an exploration of theories of the term structure. These theories generally concur in assigning a very important role to expectations of future interest rates in the explanation of the term structure.

QUESTIONS

1. Why must the price of a bond converge to its par value at maturity? Is this true of pure discount bonds and coupon bonds? Under what conditions might the price not converge to the par value?
2. Evaluate the following claim: An investor should never buy a premium bond. It has a built-in capital loss due to the fact that its price must converge to its par value. This means that the return will be adversely affected.
3. What are the three key variables that influence bond pricing?
4. Assume that you are a money manager with a large stock of cash that you will be investing in bonds. You anticipate a strong upward movement in interest rates in general. What do your beliefs imply about the kinds of bonds you will select for investment, particularly with respect to maturity and coupon?

5. Consider three 8 percent coupon bonds with 10-, 15-, and 20-year maturities. Which is the most sensitive to a change in interest rates? What do we mean by saying that one bond is more "sensitive" than another to changes in interest rates? Is the difference in sensitivity between the 10- and 15-year bonds the same as the difference in sensitivity between the 15- and 20-year bonds?

6. What is the relationship between the nominal and market rates of interest?

7. Evaluate the following argument: Over the past year, inflation has been quite high. Because interest rates depend on the real rate of interest and the inflation rate, interest rates now should be quite high.

8. What market forces exist to make the real rate of interest equal to the marginal productivity of physical capital in a riskless environment?

9. How would you form an estimate of the market's expectations of future inflation?

10. Why should the nominal rate of interest exceed the expected rate of inflation?

11. What are the three major theories of term structure?

12. In examining the yield curve, why should you use bonds of the same risk level?

13. How could differences in tax status among bonds used in yield curve analysis affect the analysis?

14. Liquidity premium theorists would maintain that it is normal for the yield curve to slope upward. Are there instances in history of flat or downward-sloping yield curves?

15. How would the pure expectations theory and the liquidity premium theory explain a downward-sloping yield curve?

16. You can choose between holding five successive one-year T bills and holding one five-year bond for five years. According to the liquidity premium theory of the term structure, which should have the greater expected return? Why? How would the pure expectations theory differ?

17. For the liquidity premium theory to be true, investors must have preferences for short-term bonds. How does the market segmentation theory make use of the idea that investors have different maturity preferences? Are these theories really the same?

18. In our discussion of bond pricing, we have seen that long-maturity bonds have considerable price risk because their prices can move a great deal in response to a change in interest rates. How does this price risk differ from default risk?

19. Two bonds are identical in all respects, except in their maturities. Each bond's coupon rate also happens to be equal to its yield to maturity. A friend of yours reasons that the bond with the larger maturity must have the greater price, simply because it will provide more coupon payments. What do you think?

20. Explain the intuition for the approximate yield to maturity formula.

PROBLEMS

1. Consider a five-year pure discount bond with a face value of $1,000 that yields 10 percent compounded annually. What is its price? What will its price be if interest rates suddenly rise to 11 percent? What will its price be if interest rates suddenly fall to 9 percent? Are the capital gain and loss the same?

2. What is the price of a three-year 8 percent annual coupon bond yielding 11 percent and having a face value of $1,000? Assume annual compounding.

3. For the bond in Problem 2, assume that interest rates suddenly rise to 13 percent. Compute the new price of the bond by discounting the cash flows at the new rate.

4. A two-year bond is yielding 15 percent and a one-year bond is yielding 11 percent. What is the forward rate for a bond to cover the second year? Does the yield curve slope upward in this case?

5. Consider the following rates for bonds of differing maturities:

Maturity	Yield
5 years	14%
4	13
3	12
2	11
1	10

Compute all possible forward rates. (*Note:* There are ten forward rates to calculate.)

6. Using the data in Problem 5, what would be the interest rate forecast of a pure expectations theorist for one-year rates three years from now? How would the forecast of the liquidity premium theorist differ?

7. What is the price of a pure discount bond maturing in three years if the interest rate is 0.25 and the bond has a face value of $100,000?

8. A bond pays a semiannual coupon of 12 percent on a face value of $1,000 and matures in three years. If it has a yield of 15 percent, what is its price?

9. A bond pays a semiannual coupon of 12 percent on a face value of $1,000 and matures in three years. If it has a yield of 9 percent, what is its price?

10. A bond pays a semiannual coupon of 12 percent on face value of $1,000 and matures in three years. If it has a yield of 12 percent, what is its price?

11. Review the results of the last three problems. What can you say about the relationship between bond prices and yields? Be specific.
12. A bond with a coupon rate of 10 percent is currently selling at par. Find its yield to maturity.
13. A bond with annual coupon payments of $120 has a yield to maturity of 12 percent. Find its price.
14. If a bond sells at $975 and has a coupon rate of 8 percent, what is the most you can say about its yield to maturity? (For example, you might be able to say that the YTM of the bond is less than 40 percent.)
15. If a bond sells at $1,200 and has a coupon rate of 11 percent, what is the most you can say about its yield to maturity?
16. Under what conditions will the approximate yield to maturity formula give the exact value of the yield to maturity?

APPENDIX: DURATION AND IMMUNIZATION STRATEGIES

DURATION

Duration, a concept first developed by Frederick Macaulay, is a single number for a bond that summarizes all of the various factors that affect the bond's price sensitivity to changes in interest rates.[1] Intuitively, duration measures the economic life of a bond, as opposed to its legal life, or maturity. It depends on three key variables: term to maturity, the coupon rate, and yield to maturity. Duration D is given by Equation A9.1:

$$D = \frac{\sum_{t=1}^{n} t \times \frac{C_t}{(1 + r)^t}}{P} \qquad (A9.1)$$

where P = the bond's price
C_t = the cash flow from the bond occurring at time t
r = the yield to maturity
n = the bond's maturity

As an example of how to calculate duration, consider a five-year bond paying an annual coupon of 10 percent, with a yield to maturity of 14 percent and a par value of $1,000. The price of this bond would be $862.69. Table A9.1 sets out the cash flows and shows the calculation of this bond's duration, which is 4.10 years.

---

[1] See F. R. Macaulay, *Some Theoretical Problems Suggested by the Movements of Interest Rates, Bond Yields, and Stock Prices in the United States Since 1856* (New York: Columbia University Press, 1938).

TABLE A9.1   The Calculation of Duration

	Years				
t	1	2	3	4	5
C_t	$100.00	$100.00	$100.00	$100.00	$1,100.00
$C_t(1 + r)^{-t}$	87.72	76.95	67.50	59.21	571.31
$tC_t(1 + r)^{-t}$	87.72	153.90	202.50	236.84	2,856.55

$$D = \frac{87.72 + 153.90 + 202.50 + 236.84 + 2,856.55}{862.69} = 4.10 \text{ years}$$

An alternative equation expresses duration as the negative of elasticity of the bond's price with respect to a change in the discount factor $(1 + r)$:

$$D = -\frac{\dfrac{\Delta P}{P}}{\dfrac{\Delta(1 + r)}{(1 + r)}} \tag{A9.2}$$

Being essentially an elasticity measure, duration gives a single measure of the way in which the bond price changes for a change in the discount factor $(1 + r)$. This becomes clear when Equation A9.2 is rearranged to give Equation A9.3:

$$\Delta P = -D\frac{\Delta(1 + r)}{(1 + r)}P \tag{A9.3}$$

To see how this works, consider the bond we used previously to compute duration. It was a five-year, 10 percent annual coupon bond yielding 14 percent and with a duration of 4.10 years. If yields drop from 14 to 12 percent, the bond's price will increase, and the amount of the increase can be found by using Equation A9.3:

$$\Delta P = -4.10 \times \frac{-0.02}{1.14} \times \$862.69 = \$62.05$$

With this change in price, the new price should be the old price plus the price change:

$$\text{New price} = \$862.09 + \$62.05 = \$924.14$$

This can be confirmed by applying the bond pricing formula to this bond, using the new yield of 12 percent:

$$P = \$100\text{PA}(12, 5) + \$1,000 \times 1.12^{-5} = \$927.90$$

According to the bond pricing equation, the new price is $927.90, which is not the same as the new price of $924.14 obtained by using the duration price change equation. There are two reasons for this. First, any such calculation may have some rounding error. Second, the duration price change formula uses concepts derived from calculus, and they will hold exactly only for infinitesimal changes in the variables.

Much of the importance of duration stems from the fact that it provides such a convenient summary measure of the three key variables determining bond price movements: the coupon rate, the maturity of the bond, and the level of interest rates. This means that investors can compare the price movement sensitivities of different bonds simply by comparing their durations.

PORTFOLIO IMMUNIZATION TECHNIQUES

Although it is difficult to accept the proposition that the future of interest rates cannot be forecast, increasing numbers of bond portfolio managers agree. If one gives up the hope of forecasting interest rates, active bond portfolio management has little appeal. If the manager does not know how to alter a portfolio to take advantage of an expected shift in interest rates because there is no good reason to expect one shift rather than another, active portfolio management has no useful role.

As bond managers have increasingly accepted this perspective, passive strategies have become more popular, particularly a set of techniques known as portfolio immunization. A bond portfolio is immunized if its investment result is not sensitive to a change in interest rates. In recognition of an inability to predict interest rates, many managers are finding that it makes sense to protect their portfolios from undesirable effects due to these changes by immunizing them. We consider just one technique—bank immunization.

In the simplest possible form of bank immunization, a commercial bank borrows money by accepting deposits and uses those funds to make loans. The portfolio of deposits and the portfolio of loans may both be viewed as bond portfolios, with the deposit portfolio constituting the liability portfolio and the loan portfolio constituting the asset portfolio. One of the most serious problems in commercial banking is the fact that the deposit portfolio has a very short duration, since most deposits can be withdrawn on very short notice. By contrast, the loan portfolio consists of obligations to provide funds for longer periods, since banks make commercial and consumer loans and also provide mortgage financing. We considered this kind of portfolio difference in our discussion of intermediation in Chapter 6.

The top half of Table A9.2 shows the position of Simple National Bank, which holds a deposit portfolio and liability portfolio with book and market values of $1,000 each. The duration of the liability portfolio is one year, and that of the asset portfolio is five years. Assume for the sake of simplicity that the interest rate earned on both is 10 percent. With different durations, the

TABLE A9.2   The Balance Sheet of Simple National Bank

ASSETS		LIABILITIES	
Loan portfolio	$1,000	Deposit portfolio	$1,000
Portfolio duration	5 years	Portfolio duration	1 year
		Owner's equity	$0
Interest rate	10%	Interest rate	10%
Loan portfolio	$909	Deposit portfolio	$982
		Owner's equity	−$72
Interest rate	12%	Interest rate	12%

bank has considerable interest rate risk. As we saw in Chapter 9, if interest rates fall, all bond values will rise, so the value of both portfolios will rise as well. But the asset portfolio is about five times as sensitive to a change in interest rates as the liability portfolio because its duration is five times as long. If interest rates rise, however, all bond values fall, and the asset portfolio will fall in value much more than the liability portfolio will.

To see the effect of these fluctuations on the bank, assume that interest rates rise from 10 to 12 percent on both portfolios. For Simple National Bank, the change in the value of the deposit portfolio with a one-year duration will be, according to Equation A9.3:

$$-1\left(\frac{0.02}{1.10}\right)\$1,000 = -\$18.18$$

For the loan portfolio, the same change in rates creates a much larger drop in value:

$$-5\left(\frac{0.02}{1.10}\right)\$1,000 = -\$90.91$$

The effects on the bank are shown in the bottom half of Table A9.2. Because the duration of the asset portfolio was so much greater, the effect of the rise in rates caused its value to drop much more. Starting from a position of no owner's equity, the bank moved to a position of negative equity, or technical insolvency.

By careful management of its liabilities and assets, the bank might have been able to achieve the immunized position shown in the top half of Table A9.3, where both the asset and liability portfolios have a duration of three years. Then, with the same shift in rates from 10 to 12 percent, each portfolio would have the same change in value, since the durations are the same. With the value of both portfolios falling by the same amount, the owner's equity would be unchanged, as the bottom half of Table A9.3 shows. The bank is immunized against a change in interest rates, because the change in rates leaves its equity position unchanged.

TABLE A9.3   The Immunized Balance Sheet of Simple National Bank

ASSETS		LIABILITIES	
Loan portfolio	$1,000	Deposit portfolio	$1,000
Portfolio duration	3 years	Portfolio duration	3 years
		Owner's equity	$0
Interest rate	10%	Interest rate	10%
Loan portfolio	$945	Deposit portfolio	$945
		Owner's equity	$0
Interest rate	12%	Interest rate	12%

It must be noted that perfect immunization is very difficult for many financial institutions to achieve. Due to the nature of commercial banking, which involves accepting short-term deposits and making longer-term loans, it is hard to make the durations of the two portfolios equal. However, managing the gap in the durations can help to offset the effects of changes in interest rates. In fact, virtually every bank in the United States has an asset/liability management committee. The committee plays a crucial role in the management of the bank, and the duration structure of the two sides of the bank's balance sheet is one of the most important issues it addresses.

CHAPTER 10

Preferred and Common Stock Valuation

This chapter examines the second major segment of the capital market—preferred and common stock. Preferred stock is a hybrid security, sharing features of both bonds and common stock. The discussion of preferred stock is followed by a more detailed consideration of common stock.

Much work in finance is directed toward studying the trade-off between risk and expected return. Common stock provides a laboratory for such study, and this chapter also focuses on its features that create value and risk. The chapter concludes with a brief discussion of the relationship between the risk an investor bears with different kinds of securities and the return the firm must expect to pay for different kinds of long-term financing.

PREFERRED STOCK

Preferred stock is normally issued with a stated par value. Payments made on preferred stock are called dividends and are usually expressed as a percentage of the par value. With a $100 par value and a 6 percent dividend, the annual dividend on a share would be $6.

In many respects, the dividend on a preferred stock is similar to the coupon payments made on a corporate bond; however, important differences exist between preferred stock and corporate bonds. First, preferred stock never matures. In the normal course of events, the firm will make payments of preferred dividends forever. Second, because preferred stock never matures, the purchaser never receives a return of the par value. Third, unlike the case of corporate bonds, if the firm misses a scheduled payment on preferred stock, the firm has not defaulted, and the preferred stockholder has no immediate legal remedy against the corporation.

cumulative preferred stock
a type of preferred stock requiring that any dividend payments that the firm misses must be paid later, as soon as the firm is able, and before common stockholders receive dividends

Most preferred stock is cumulative. With **cumulative preferred stock** any dividend payments that the firm misses must be paid later, as soon as possible. In fact, the agreement between the firm and the preferred stockholders typically requires that no dividends be paid to common stockholders until all late payments to preferred stockholders have been made.

This cumulative feature offers partial protection to the preferred stockholders. If a firm must temporarily suspend dividend payments, there is still

☞ Preferred stock is a hybrid security with features of both bonds and common stocks.

a fair chance that the payments will be made later. Even in such a case, however, the preferred stockholder loses the use of the money from the time the payment was scheduled to the time it is finally made. These features of no maturity, no return of principal, and no default when a payment is missed combine to make preferred stock riskier than a bond issued by the same corporation.

Like many bonds, some preferred stock is callable. The issuing firm can require the preferred stockholders to surrender their shares in exchange for a cash payment known as the call price. The amount is specified in the agreement between the stockholders and the firm.

Usually preferred stockholders, like bondholders, are not allowed to vote on matters of concern to the firm. This contrasts with common stockholders who have the right to vote to choose management and on a number of other decisions. On occasion, the contract allows preferred stockholders to vote, but usually that is only when the firm is in serious financial difficulty.

Advantages and Disadvantages of Financing with Preferred Stock

Like virtually any financing method, preferred stock financing has its own advantages and disadvantages. Probably the greatest advantage is its flexibility. If a payment on a bond is missed or delayed, the firm is technically bankrupt. As we have seen, this is not the case with preferred stock financing. At worst, the firm may have to make up missed preferred dividend payments.

☞ Issuing preferred stock does not dilute management control of the firm, and missing preferred stock dividend does not constitute default.

The second major advantage also stems from its flexibility. By issuing preferred stock, the corporation secures financing without surrendering voting control. This freedom from worry over bankruptcy when a dividend is missed, coupled with the fact that no control of the firm is surrendered, explains the attractiveness of preferred stock.

Preferred stock also has certain disadvantages: interest payments on a bond are made from the firm's before-tax income, but dividend payments to preferred stockholders are made from after-tax earnings. This is a very important distinction, because it has great bearing on the actual after-tax cost of the two financing methods.

☞ Preferred stock dividends must be paid from the firm's after-tax earnings, so preferred stock financing provides no tax shelter for the firm.

To see the importance of before-tax versus after-tax payments, consider a firm in the 34 percent tax bracket that must pay $1,000 interest to its bondholders and $1,000 in dividends to its preferred stockholders. To make a $1,000 interest payment takes only $1,000 of before-tax earnings, because the interest expense is deductible for tax purposes. For the preferred stock, the firm must pay taxes on all earnings before paying dividends. To generate the same $1,000 on an after-tax basis, the firm must have $1,515 in before-tax earnings. After the government takes its 34 percent tax, the firm will be left with the $1,000 to pay the preferred stockholders. Therefore, it must weigh the advantages of the greater flexibility of preferred stock financing against its potentially higher cost.

Reverse Splits and the Average Investor

Most stock dividends or splits increase the number of shares outstanding. In some cases, however, the stock split can be arranged to reduce the number of shares. In such a case, the split is called a reverse split.

On occasion, a reverse split can be very harmful to the minority stockholders, those stockholders who hold only a small portion of the firm's shares. When this happens, the ownership position of the stockholders and their alleged preemptive rights become virtually worthless. Consider the case of Metropolitan Maintenance Co., a janitorial services firm in Nutley, N. J., with recent sales of $16 million per year and about 175 shareholders. Metropolitan imposed a 1-for-3,000 reverse split on its shareholders. For every 3,000 shares turned in, a shareholder got 1 new share. For fractions of the needed 3,000 amount, shareholders received cash. A shareholder holding 2,000 shares, for instance, would receive only cash, and would have no remaining ownership interest in the firm. To make matters worse, it turned out that only two shareholders had more than 3,000 shares—the president and executive vice president. After the smoke cleared, these two individuals owned the entire firm. Further, some allege that the amount paid to the stockholders for their old shares was too small. As one stockbroker summarized the situation: "That's a ripoff of the shareholders. There's no other way to define it."

In the Metropolitan Maintenance case, there are really two issues—the squeezing out of the smaller shareholders and the compensation paid. Little can be said about the squeeze-out: after the reverse split, there were only two stockholders. The compensation paid is another matter. Shareholders of fractional shares received a per share rate of $37, which was considerably less than the book value of $72 per share. In the year before

The Valuation of Preferred Stock

☞ The value of a share of preferred stock equals the present value of all future dividends from the share.

As is the case for all investments, the value or price of a share of preferred stock equals the sum of the present values of all cash flows that will come from the stock. Because preferred stock is scheduled to make equal payments forever, it may be treated as a perpetuity for valuation purposes:

$$P = \frac{D}{r} \tag{10.1}$$

where P = the price of the preferred share
D = the dividend payment from the preferred share
r = the discount rate appropriate to the preferred share

In this valuation formula, the payments are known, because the dividend is given by the par value and the dividend rate on the shares. The rate of

the reverse split, the firm's earnings were $5.93 per share and were still climbing at the time of the reverse split.

How did the firm decide on a $37 per share price? The decision was reached by the firm's board of directors, a three-man board, including (you guessed it) the president and vice president. After deciding that the shares were worth $37, the board hired a financial consulting firm for $7,500 that confirmed the value of the shares at $37. Everything was conducted with the appearance (at least) of propriety. In a formal communication to the shareholders regarding the value of the firm's shares at $37, the firm disclosed "the opinion of the board of directors must be considered in light of the fact that the board is controlled by Messrs. Rockwell and McDougald, who constitute two of the company's three directors." As *Forbes* summarized matters, "Nobody can complain about inadequate disclosure."

While the experience at Metropolitan Maintenance may be an extreme case, it is not an isolated instance of freezing out the smaller shareholders. Warren National Corp., an Ohio Savings and Loan, recently conducted a 1-for-16 reverse split that will leave three shareholders. In another case, Surgical Appliance Industries of Cincinnati conducted a 1-for-50,000 split which will leave two shareholders.

The shareholder is the theoretical owner of the firm in whose benefit the firm is supposed to be operated. However, matters do not always work that way and the presumed rights of shareholders are not always respected. This is particularly problematic for minority shareholders of small companies, such as the ones discussed here.

Source: Robert McGough, "Squeeze Play," *Forbes*, November 19, 1984.

discount, r, is the rate of return required by the preferred stockholders, and depends on the risk assigned to the preferred stock.

As an example, consider a share of preferred stock with a par value of $100 that pays an 8 percent annual dividend. If the discount rate for this share is 12 percent, the preferred stock would be worth:

$$P = \frac{\$8}{0.12} = \$66.67$$

COMMON STOCK

Of the three major types of long-term financing—debt, preferred stock, and common stock—common stock is the most fundamental. No corporation can exist without it because it represents an ownership interest.

☞ The common stock-holders are the owners of the firm, and management has the duty to promote their interest by maximizing the stock price.

Holders of common stock commit their funds and assume the last place claim on the value of the firm in hope of securing substantial profits. While the stock is owned, the only cash flow from the shares is the cash dividend. Many firms, particularly new ones and those in financial distress, do not pay dividends. Dividends are so crucial for common stock that they play a key role in determining the value of shares.

Common Stock Quotations

Figure 10.1 shows a portion of the quotations taken from the *Wall Street Journal* for stocks listed on the New York Stock Exchange. The first two columns show the high and low prices over the last 52 weeks. It is customary for stock quotations to be given in eighths of dollars, so a price of $20\frac{3}{8}$ is $20.375 per share. The third column contains the company's name, and the fourth shows the firm's yearly dividend in dollars.

Column 5 shows the dividend yield on a share, which is equal to the annual dividend divided by the current price. Column 6 shows the P/E ratio, equal to the price divided by the year's earnings. This P/E ratio is a widely used measure of the growth potential of the firm's stock price. In column 7,

dividend yield

yearly dividend

FIGURE 10.1   Common Stock Quotations

Source: Wall Street Journal, April 15, 1991, p. C3. Reprinted by permission of Wall Street Journal, © 1991 Dow Jones & Company, Inc. All Rights Reserved Worldwide.

the number of shares traded is shown in hundreds. The next three columns are the high, low, and closing prices for the day being reported. The final column, headed "Net Chg.," is the change in the share's price from the close of trading on the preceding day to the close on the day being reported.

The Dividend Valuation Model

The stock prices reported in the *Wall Street Journal* emerge from the action of the marketplace, in which traders are always revising their opinions about what stocks are worth. We know that the value of any investment depends on the future cash flows generated by the investment, the timing of those cash flows, and the rate of discount that is applied to them. The discount rate, in turn, depends on the riskiness of the investment, as we will see in the next two chapters.

In the case of most bonds, the timing of the cash flows is quite clear, since the cash flows are promised to be paid on certain dates. The only ones that come from a share of stock are the dividends paid by the firm. The timing of the dividend payments is not always so clear. Some firms pay no dividends, but hope to do so in the future. Each year, some firms that have paid dividends for many years fall on hard times and either reduce or eliminate their dividends. For example, in December 1990 Citicorp, the largest bank holding company in the United States, unexpectedly announced a sharp reduction in dividends. Since they are not contractually obligated payments, their timing becomes much more a matter of prediction and speculation than is the case with bond coupon payments.

Because of this greater speculative element in the amount and timing of dividend payments, risk assessment for equity securities is a great concern. This perceived riskiness of shares is reflected in the discount rate applied to the firm's dividend stream. In the case of stocks, the value of a share can be expressed by the following equation, which we will call the **dividend valuation model:**

dividend valuation model
a stock valuation model that expresses the value of a share as the present value of all future dividends to come from the share

$$P = \sum_{t=1}^{\infty} \frac{D_t}{(1 + r)^t} \tag{10.2}$$

Equation 10.3 gives an alternative expression of Equation 10.2:

☞ The present value of a share of common stock equals the present value of all future dividends.

$$P_0 = \frac{D_1}{(1 + r)} + \frac{D_2}{(1 + r)^2} + \frac{D_3}{(1 + r)^3} + \frac{D_4}{(1 + r)^4} + \cdots \tag{10.3}$$

where P_0 = the price of the share at time t

   D_t = the expected dividend to be paid at time t

   r = the discount rate appropriate to the riskiness of the expected dividends

capital gain or **capital loss**
the gain or loss in the value of an asset over an investment period

☞ The dividend valuation model reflects dividends directly and potential capital gains indirectly

Equation 10.2 states that the current stock price (P_0) equals the sum of the present values of all future expected dividends (D_t) when those dividends are discounted at the stockholder's required rate of return (r). This implies that the value of a share is determined solely by the present value of the cash flows to come from owning the stock.

Equation 10.2 appears to neglect **capital gains,** profits due to a change in the price of an asset. This problem is only apparent, however, as the following discussion shows.

The Dividend Valuation Model and Capital Gains   According to the dividend valuation model the only cash flows that matter to an investor in common stock are the expected dividends. Yet many investors buy stocks for the expected capital gains. In fact, many buy stocks that pay no dividends, with the plan to sell them later for a profit. This behavior is quite rational, as shown in Table 10.1, which presents the division of total common stock returns between capital appreciation and dividends for the years 1980–1990. As the table shows, capital gains constituted the majority of the total returns for 7 of the 11 years.

If the dividend valuation model were really saying that these capital gains did not matter to an intelligent investor, then so much the worse for the model. The investor would be wise to pocket the capital gains and ignore the model. However, the model does not ignore capital gains, but treats them indirectly, through their relationship to dividends.

To see how it takes account of capital gains, consider a stock that pays a dividend annually. An investor might buy such a stock and plan to hold it for three years. In this case the cash flows that would come to the investor

TABLE 10.1   The Division of Common Stock Returns Between Capital Appreciation and Dividends

Year	Capital Appreciation	Dividends
1980	25.77%	5.73%
1981	−9.72	4.89
1982	14.78	5.50
1983	17.27	5.00
1984	1.39	4.56
1985	26.34	5.10
1986	14.63	3.74
1987	2.03	3.64
1988	12.41	4.17
1989	27.26	3.85
1990	−6.56	3.36

Source: Stocks, Bonds, Bills and Inflation 1991 Yearbook™, Ibbotson Associates, Chicago (annually updates work by Roger G. Ibbotson anc Rex A. Sinquefeld). All rights reserved.

would consist of the three annual dividends to be paid during the time the stock is held, plus the value of the share when it is sold. In terms of the dividend valuation model, the value of such a share would be:

$$P_0 = \frac{D_1}{(1 + r)} + \frac{D_2}{(1 + r)^2} + \frac{D_3}{(1 + r)^3} + \frac{P_3}{(1 + r)^3} \qquad (10.4)$$

In this case, P_3 is the value of the share when it is sold three years after purchase, right after the third dividend is paid. An investor with the planned three-year holding period would be looking forward to receiving three dividends and would be hoping for a capital gain over the three years equal to $P_3 - P_0$.

At first glance, Equation 10.4 appears to contradict the dividend valuation model of Equation 10.2 because it contains the term for the price at the end of the third year, P_3. This is only an apparent discrepancy, because the value of the share in three years depends on the future dividends expected to be paid to shareholders from that time forward. In other words, the value of the share in the third year (P_3) depends on the dividends to be paid in subsequent years, D_4, D_5, and so on:

$$P_3 = \frac{D_4}{(1 + r)} + \frac{D_5}{(1 + r)^2} + \frac{D_6}{(1 + r)^3} + \frac{D_7}{(1 + r)^4} + \cdots \qquad (10.5)$$

Equation 10.5 is just like Equation 10.2 or 10.3, except that the subscripts denoting the timing of the dividends are changed to reflect the fact that the value of the share is being measured at the end of the third year instead of at time 0. If Equation 10.5 is substituted into Equation 10.4, the result is exactly the same as the original version of the dividend valuation model, namely Equation 10.3.

☞ Capital gains reflect the increase in the present value of future dividends.

This discussion shows that the anticipated capital gain over the three years that the stock is to be held is due to the changing valuation of the future dividends. So even if capital gains are not explicitly shown in the dividend valuation model of Equation 10.2, they are reflected implicitly. Another way of seeing that the value of a share depends on the expected future dividends is to reflect upon the following question: how much is a share of stock worth, assuming that everyone knows with certainty that it will absolutely never pay a dividend? Investing in such share would be investing in something that will never generate any cash flows. If the investment will generate no cash flows, it has no value, and its price should be 0. To this, one might object that the share is not being purchased for dividends (since there are none), but for prospective capital gains. The hope is to buy the stock now and sell it for a higher price to someone else. However, under the assumption that everyone knows that the stock will never pay a dividend, no one should be willing to pay anything for it. With no buyers, its price will remain 0, and there will be no capital gains.

☞ A share of common stock guaranteed to never pay a dividend should be worth 0.

The hope of selling such a share for a capital gain is based on what is known as the greater fool theory.[1] To pay something for a stock that promises never to pay a cent in dividends is very foolish. To try and make money by buying the stock and selling it for a profit to someone else depends on finding someone who is a "greater fool" than the original purchaser.[2]

The Indefinite Future of Dividends   Another apparent problem with the dividend valuation model of Equation 10.2 is the possibly infinite number of dividends populating the right-hand side of the equation. If one wishes to apply the model in actual practice, how is it possible to sum the present value of all those dividends?

We have already seen in the case of preferred stock that the solution is very straightforward if the dividends are constant. As shown in Equation 10.1, the price is merely equal to the payment divided by the discount rate. This formula applies because the preferred stock can be seen as a perpetuity, as discussed in Chapter 4. However, if the dividends change over time, as occurs with common stock, no such easy solution is possible.

Even if the dividends are not constant, there is still a way to apply the model and to avoid the pitfall of trying to add a potentially infinite number of dividends. Most firms that are successful hope to be able to pay increasingly large dividends as time progresses. If the dividends grow at a regular rate, g, the dividend valuation model can be greatly simplified. In such a case, the dividend in the second year equals the dividend in the first year plus the growth in dividends, or:

$$D_2 = D_1(1 + g)$$

Similarly, the dividend in the third year is given by:

$$D_3 = D_2(1 + g)$$
$$= D_1(1 + g)(1 + g)$$
$$= D_1(1 + g)^2$$

growth rate
the rate at which a firm's dividends grow

In this case, knowing the value of the dividend D_1 provides enough information to calculate the value of all subsequent dividends. For this special case of a constant **growth rate** in dividends, the dividend valuation model is

---

[1] See Burton Malkiel's excellent book, *A Random Walk Down Wall Street* (New York: W. W. Norton and Company, 1991), for a very interesting and amusing discussion of the greater fool theory.

[2] Throughout history, there have been various episodes in which the greater fool theory has actually come to life. The classic example is the tulip bulb craze of the seventeenth century. People were willing to buy tulip bulbs at ever increasing prices in the belief that the bulbs would fetch even greater prices later on. Eventually, bulb prices exceeded the price of gold, ounce for ounce. A few years later, the greatest fool of all must have been found, because the tulip bulb craze juggernaut suddenly crashed.

mathematically equal to:

$$P_0 = \frac{D_1}{r - g} \tag{10.6}$$

constant growth model
a stock valuation model, consistent with the dividend valuation model, that can be applied when dividends grow at a constant rate

☞ If dividends are assumed to grow at a constant rate, the dividend valuation model can be simplified to the constant growth model.

This is known as the **constant growth model.** The essential technique employed to reach this result is to calculate the value of an infinite sum. There are several assumptions behind this simplification of the model:

1. The dividends grow each year at the constant growth rate, g.
2. The dividends grow at the rate g forever.
3. The growth rate, g, is less than the discount rate, r.

Clearly, Equation 10.6 is a simplification of reality. Nevertheless, it is useful because it provides a way of dealing with the problem of a potentially infinite series of dividends. To see how this simplified version of the dividend valuation model can be applied, consider a stock that you expect will pay $1.20 in dividends one year from now. You believe that such an investment should pay a return of 17 percent, and you expect that the long-term growth rate for dividends will be 3 percent. According to Equation 10.6, the share would be worth $8.57, as shown below:

$$P_0 = \frac{\$1.20}{0.17 - 0.03} = \$8.57$$

The value of a share of stock is highly sensitive to the discount rate or cost of capital, r, and the expected long-term growth rate in dividends, g. This sensitivity is reflected in Table 10.2, which shows the value of a share as given by Equation 10.6, assuming an initial level of dividends of $1 per share. For example, the table shows that the share might be worth as much as $50.00, with a cost of capital of 12 percent and a growth rate in dividends of 10 percent. Alternatively, it could be worth as little as $5.00 if the cost of capital is 20 percent and dividends are not expected to grow.

TABLE 10.2   Share Values for Stocks Paying $1 in Initial Dividends with Different Growth Rates and Different Discount Rates

				r			
g	8%	10%	12%	14%	16%	18%	20%
0%	$12.50	$10.00	$ 8.33	$ 7.14	$ 6.25	$ 5.56	$ 5.00
2	16.67	12.50	10.00	8.33	7.14	6.25	5.56
4	25.00	16.67	12.50	10.00	8.33	7.14	6.25
6	50.00	25.00	16.67	12.50	10.00	8.33	7.14
8	—	50.00	25.00	16.67	12.50	10.00	8.33
10	—	—	50.00	25.00	16.67	12.50	10.00

INTERNATIONAL PERSPECTIVES

Stakeholders

Despite the bravest efforts by management thinkers to make their subject more complicated—and thus to appear more scientific—the simplest questions often cause the fiercest debates in boardrooms, bars, and the pages of business journals. The simplest of all is: in whose interest should a company be run?

In principle, the answer should be equally simple: in the interest of the shareholder–owners, of course. This answer is complicated only by a practical observation that a firm's directors, acting as the shareholders' agents, often see their interests as different from those of the owners. Intervention by shareholders, either directly or through takeover bids, is therefore aimed at keeping managers' behavior aligned with shareholders' interests. Until, that is, a new notion cropped up: that companies should be run in the interests not just of shareholders but of a wider group of "stakeholders," including employees, suppliers, customers, and neighbors.

This fashionable idea has obvious attractions to directors keen to find excuses for poor profits or a low share price. And it provides an argument against hostile takeovers: they breach the trust that stakeholders place in the firm and so may prove counterproductive. But does the idea mean anything? At worst, it is motherhood: companies will prosper if they are nice to the people in and around them.

There is, however, another reason for this interest in stakeholders. Like many of today's fashionable business nostrums, its origins lie in an attempt to learn from Japan. Lifetime employment, close relations with suppliers, low dividends for shareholders—all these famed features of Japanese business suggest a concern for stakeholders rather than share-

The Dividend Valuation Model and Irregular Dividend Patterns It might appear that the dividend valuation model still has an insurmountable difficulty. On the one hand, Equation 10.2 has an infinite number of dividend payments to consider. On the other hand, the only workable version of the model, presented in Equation 10.6, seems to hold only for the extremely improbable case of a dividend that grows at a constant rate forever. The model is really much more flexible than that, as this section shows.

Historically, many of the best buys in the stock market have been shares that paid no dividends. In fact, many of the supergrowth firms are likely to pay no dividends early in their lives. One challenge for the dividend valuation model is its applicability to such firms. Actually, the model can be applied quite directly to such shares. For a stock paying no current dividends, it simply says that the future dividends are the cash flows that are worth worrying about.

holders, and they are associated with long-term investment, another fashionable idea. Indicated action: copy them.

The trouble is that emulators have a distorted view of quite what it is they are copying. At one extreme, the mistake is to assume that an emphasis on stakeholders is oriental far-sightedness. At the other extreme, the error is to assume that Japan's methods are rooted in its culture.

According to a book by Carl Kester of the Harvard Business School,* the raw truth is simpler. The Japanese emphasis on stakeholders is rooted in economics. There is nothing mystical or cultural about it. Big Japanese industrial groups have evolved into coalitions of commercial interest, including banks, leasing companies, insurers, manufacturers, parts suppliers, distributors, and others.

The point that Western admirers ignore, however, is that these stakeholders are bound together in a conventional way. They own shares in each other. In other words, in these groups there is no difference between the interests of stakeholders and shareholders.

What, then, is in the interest of the stakeholding owners? Shareholders in Japanese firms get low dividends, so the payoff cannot be there. Large capital gains do compensate owners for low dividends. But Mr. Kester argues that stakeholding owners benefit in other ways: their shareholding gives them a privileged right to provide credit, say, or insurance, or to supply parts or handle distribution. In other words, business flows their way.

* W. Carl Kester, *Japanese Takeovers: The Global Contest for Corporate Control* (Cambridge: Harvard Business School Press, 1991).

Source: "Stakes, Shares and Digestible Poison Pills," *Economist*, February 2, 1991.

This can be made clear by considering an example. Imagine a new small firm that is launching successful new products in the computer industry. All of its profits are being put back into new investment, so it has no money available to pay the shareholders a dividend. Currently, many such firms are operating in the microcomputer industry, and without doubt, some of them will emerge successful.

Consider an imaginary firm, Prune Computer, that pays no current dividend. According to the dividend valuation model, the price range must be based on the expected dividends that will come later. After serious investigation, you expect that Prune will not pay any dividends for the next three years, due to the need to reinvest all profits in new product development and to market existing products. In the fourth year, however, you anticipate that Prune will be able to pay a dividend of $1.50 per share, and that dividend payments will grow at a long-term rate of 10 percent. On an investment as risky as this, you feel that you must demand a rate of return of 18 percent. How much is Prune worth, given these assumptions?

Here is the expected dividend stream for Prune for the next 10 years:

$$D_1 = \$0$$
$$D_2 = \$0$$
$$D_3 = \$0$$
$$D_4 = \$1.50$$
$$D_5 = \$1.65$$
$$D_6 = \$1.82$$
$$D_7 = \$2.00$$
$$D_8 = \$2.20$$
$$D_9 = \$2.42$$
$$D_{10} = \$2.66$$

To apply the dividend valuation model, a two-step procedure is necessary. First, there is a period beginning with the fourth year in which the dividend pattern of Prune Computer matches the requirements of the model. According to the model, the value of the shares at time 3 must be given by the following expression:

$$P_3 = \frac{\$1.50}{0.18 - 0.10} = \$18.75$$

Thus, three years from now the price of a share of Prune should be $18.75. However, what is really of interest is the price of Prune at time $t = 0$. To convert the price at year 3 into the current price, the value of Prune Computer at year 3 must be discounted back to the present at Prune's appropriate discount rate:

$$P_0 = \frac{\$0}{(1.18)} + \frac{\$0}{(1.18)^2} + \frac{\$0}{(1.18)^3} + \frac{\$18.75}{(1.18)^3}$$

$$= \$11.41$$

Notice that this example is really just like Equation 10.4 above, except that there are no dividends to consider in the first three years for Prune.

Another case is one in which there are irregular dividend payments in the near term. Industries, and the firms in them, often go through a cycle of growth. Normally, the growth is more rapid at the beginning, and then settles down to a lower long-term rate.

As an example of such a firm, consider the imaginary mobile phone company Cellular Technodynamics. At the end of 1991 you forecast the following dividend stream: for 1992 you expect a dividend of $1.40, for 1993, $1.95, for 1994, $2.80, and then a long period of growth at 10 percent. These dividends are shown in the following table:

Year	Dividend	Year	Dividend
1992	$1.40	1996	$3.39
1993	1.95	1997	3.73
1994	2.80	1998	4.10
1995	3.08	1999	4.51

Even for such an irregular flow of dividends, the dividend valuation model applies. The dividend stream for Cellular Technodynamics can be broken into two parts, the part with the regular growth rate of 10 percent and the earlier period of rapid growth. Clearly, the dividend discount model can handle the period of regular growth. Assuming a stockholder's required return of 16 percent, the price of a share of Cellular Technodynamics at the end of 1994, after paying the $2.80 dividend, is given by:

$$P_{1994} = \frac{\$3.08}{0.16 - 0.10} = \$51.33$$

According to the dividend valuation model, the price of the shares at the end of 1994 is expected to be $51.33. It remains only to take account of the value of the earlier dividend payments and the fact that a price must be calculated for the present, which is the end of 1991. The value of Cellular Technodynamics depends on the dividends received in the years before the dividend becomes smooth, plus the value of the shares at the time the dividend growth rate becomes constant.

$$P_{1990} = \frac{\$1.40}{(1.16)} + \frac{\$1.95}{(1.16)^2} + \frac{\$2.80}{(1.16)^3} + \frac{\$51.33}{(1.16)^3}$$
$$= \$1.21 + \$1.45 + \$1.79 + \$32.88 = \$37.33$$

Notice that the price expected for the end of 1994 must also be discounted back to the present. Also, the dividend to be paid at the end of 1994 and the value of the shares in 1994 are both discounted back for three years. The assumption here is that the $51.33 expected value of the shares at the end of 1994 is the value immediately after the 1994 dividend has been paid.

These examples make clear the flexibility of the dividend valuation model. With minor adjustments, it can handle most realistic situations, such as those for firms with initially irregular dividend streams, or even for those firms paying no current dividends.

The Dividend Valuation Model and Earnings   Thus far the entire emphasis has been on dividends. Yet the reader of the financial press knows that market professionals pay great attention to earnings reports and the earnings prospects of different firms. It is not surprising that an intimate link is present between earnings and dividends, which is reflected in the dividend valuation model.

Throwing the Fox Out of the Henhouse

Chrysler Corp's bland announcement [in March 1991] that it was dropping five of its 18 directors in order to "improve efficiency and effectiveness as well as reduce cost" didn't fool industry observers. The unusual pedigree of one of those directors—Owen Bieber, president of the United Auto Workers union—signaled other, less technocratic motives. Most bets are that the willful U.A.W. boss, a board member since 1984, was dropped because of his frequent opposition to management, led by its equally willful chairman, Lee Iacocca. "There were a lot of 17-to-1 votes," Bieber said. . . .

There was also more than a little friction. Bieber had routinely voted against raises for top executives. In 1989 Chrysler management enraged the union boss by concealing from him plans to close a Detroit plant.

Bieber's removal from the board . . . marks the end of an experiment in union-management cooperation, which began with the appointment of the U.A.W.'s then president, Douglas Fraser, during Chrysler's dark days of 1980. Chrysler's board shuffle also sparked talk that the troubled company was streamlining itself for a merger with a foreign car company. Possible suitors: Honda, Fiat, and Mitsubishi. Whatever Iacocca decides to do, he will have one less dissenting vote to worry about.

Source: "Shuffling the Chrysler Board," *Time,* March 25, 1991, p. 51.

The earnings that a firm generates have three, and only three, outlets according to accounting convention. They must be paid in taxes, paid as dividends, or retained for further investment in the firm. For corporations in the United States, Figure 10.2 shows how profits have been divided among these uses. Clearly, profits have been quite variable. The strong tendency has been toward a greater level of total dividends in the economy, even though the amount of dividends paid has varied considerably over time.

The dividend valuation model recognizes the very close relationship between earnings, E, and dividends, D, by applying the accounting convention mentioned above. Focusing now just on after-tax earnings, every dollar of earnings a firm achieves either goes to retained earnings or is paid as a cash dividend. The portion retained can be represented as a percentage, b. The remainder of the dollar of earnings, $1 - b$, the firm pays in cash dividends. Firms that always pay a fixed percentage of their earnings follow what is called a **constant payout policy.** Their dividends are always a fixed fraction of earnings.

constant payout policy
the policy of paying a fixed percentage of firm earnings as dividends in each period

For a firm with a constant payout policy, knowing the level of earnings is enough to tell the level of dividends. In a given year t, the dividend is

FIGURE 10.2   The Allocation of Corporate Profits

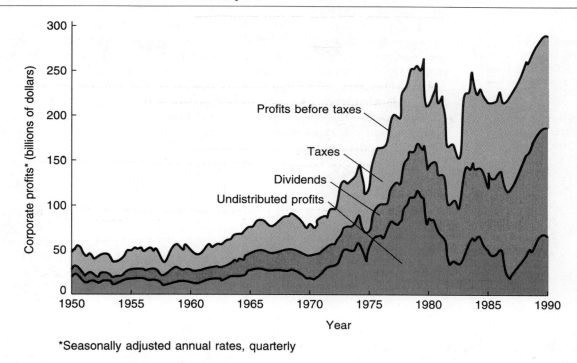

*Seasonally adjusted annual rates, quarterly

Source: *Federal Reserve Historical Chartbook,* 1990, p. 60.

given by the following expression:

$$D_t = (1 - b)E_t$$

Estimating the dividend payments to be made is the same problem as estimating the future earnings stream. For example, consider a well-established firm growing at its long-term growth rate of $g = 4$ percent. Next year's earnings are expected to be $3.60 per share, and the firm follows the practice of paying 60 percent of its earnings in dividends. Furthermore, assume that the required rate of return, or the cost of capital, for the firm's shares is 14 percent. How much is the firm worth? The dividend valuation model provides an easily calculated answer:

$$P_0 = \frac{D_1}{r - g} = \frac{(1 - b)E_1}{r - g} = \frac{(1 - 0.4)\$3.60}{0.14 - 0.04} = \$21.60$$

Growth Stocks and the P/E Ratio

The financial manager knows that, other things being equal, <u>causing earnings to grow</u> will help the stock price. Whereas some managers may become obsessed with earnings, the clever ones know that increasing earnings is important only because of their effect on the share price.

The stocks of firms expected to enjoy a rapid increase in earnings are known as **growth stocks.** For example, Genentech and other genetic engineering firms are typical growth stocks. Genentech is a leader in its field and is actively developing new products. At the outset, it had high hopes, an ambitious research program, literally no dividends, and virtually no earnings. Nonetheless, its stock price has been relatively high throughout its life.

One measure of the height of the stock price is known as the **price/earnings, or P/E, ratio,** which is defined as the ratio of the stock price to the firm's annual earnings:

growth stocks
stocks expected to enjoy a rapid increase in earnings or value

price/earnings ratio or **P/E ratio**
the price of a share of stock divided by its earnings per share

$$P/E \ ratio = \frac{stock \ price}{current \ annual \ earnings}$$

Some firms have a high P/E ratio, which usually indicates the prospect of rapid future growth in earnings. Typically, growth stocks also have high P/E ratios. Figure 10.3 shows how the earnings/price ratios have varied over most of this century. The P/E ratios are the inverse of the E/P ratios. Thus, an E/P ratio of 12 percent in the figure corresponds to a P/E ratio of 8.33.

FIGURE 10.3   Earnings/Price Ratios

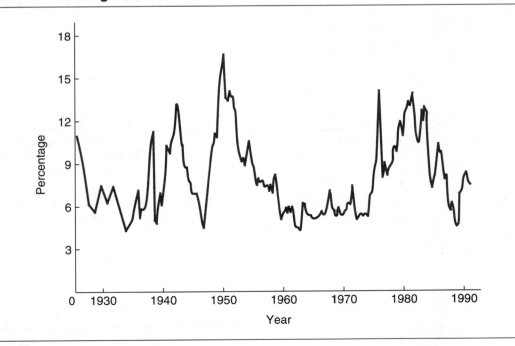

Source: Federal Reserve Historical Chartbook, 1990, p. 95.

P/E Ratios in the United States and Japan

The rapid rise in Japanese share prices during the mid-1980s made the price/earnings ratio in Japan much higher than that in the United States. Many of the findings that Japanese firms faced lower required returns on equity during this period were based on this fact.

There are both theoretical and empirical difficulties in using price/earnings ratios or, more accurately, their reciprocal (earnings/price ratios) to describe required returns. One theoretical objection is that certain specific conditions must be met for the earnings/price ratio to be equal to the current required return. That is, if required equity returns change over time, then the earnings/price ratio equals an average of current and future required returns, minus the expected growth rate of earnings. Today's required return is equal to the earnings/price ratio only if the required return is constant over time. A second difficulty is that the observed earnings/price ratios reflect the stock market's expectation of future corporate growth. Therefore, a low earnings/price ratio could result from optimistic growth expectations, rather than from low costs of equity finance. The following table shows the great difference in P/E ratios between the United States and Japan.

Price/Earnings Ratios for the United States and Japan, 1975–1990

Year	United States	Japan
1975	11.8	25.2
1976	11.2	22.0
1977	9.1	19.3
1978	8.2	21.5
1979	7.5	16.6
1980	9.6	17.9
1981	8.2	24.9
1982	11.9	23.7
1983	12.6	29.4
1984	10.4	26.3
1985	15.4	29.4
1986	18.7	58.6
1987	14.1	50.4
1988	12.9	54.3
1989	14.8	53.7
1990	15.9	36.6

Source: French and Poterba (1991a, Table 6). U.S. price/earnings ratios are taken from Standard & Poor's 500 index of actively traded stocks; Japanese ratios are from the Nomura Research Institute's 350 index of actively traded stocks.

Source: James M. Poterba, "Comparing the Cost of Capital in the United States and Japan: A Survey of Methods," *Federal Reserve Bank of New York Quarterly Review*, Winter 1991, p. 25.

INTEREST RATES, INFLATION, AND STOCK PRICES

In Chapter 9 we saw that the nominal rate of interest on a default-free bond depends on the real rate of interest and the expected rate of inflation. Of the two, the real rate of interest is the smaller component, so this discussion focuses mainly on the relationship between inflation and stock returns.

Real returns are the relevant returns for measuring investment success because they measure changes in purchasing power. These changes indicate the change in consumption opportunities, and investors are ultimately interested in improving their consumption opportunities.

☞ Although ownership of common stock gives title to real assets, it does not provide total protection against inflation.

Inflation is particularly important for common stocks because, apparently, investing in common stocks should protect an investor against its ravages. A share of common stock represents fractional ownership of the earning power and the physical assets of a corporation. In periods of inflation, these assets should also increase in nominal value, just as prices of goods and services of all types rise. If that is so, the value of the common stock should also rise in tandem with the general price level. While this theory seems reasonable, it does not always work out. Table 10.3 presents the results for the five years of highest and lowest inflation rates for the years 1926–1990. During the five years with the highest inflation, the average real return on common stocks was −12.23 percent. By contrast, in the low inflation years, the real return on common stocks was 4.58 percent. This gives reason to favor low inflation environments rather than high inflation environments. Thus it seems that common stock investment does not provide perfect protection against inflation.

TABLE 10.3   Nominal and Real Common Stock Returns in Years of High and Low Inflation

High-Inflation Years				Low-Inflation Years			
Year	Nominal Stock Returns	Inflation	Real Stock Returns	Year	Nominal Stock Returns	Inflation	Real Stock Returns
1946	−8.07%	18.16%	−26.24%	1932	−8.19%	−10.30%	2.11%
1979	18.44	13.31	5.13	1931	−43.34	−9.52	−33.82
1980	32.42	12.40	20.02	1930	−24.90	−6.03	−18.87
1974	−26.47	12.20	−38.67	1938	31.12	−2.78	33.90
1941	−11.59	9.72	−21.31	1927	37.49	−2.08	39.57
		Average	−12.23			Average	4.58

Average for All Years 1926–1990
Nominal Stock Returns: 10.1%
Inflation: 3.1%
Real Stock Returns: 7.0%

Source: © *Stocks, Bonds, Bills, and Inflation 1991 Yearbook*™, Ibbotson Associates, Chicago (annually updates work by Roger G. Ibbotson and Rex A. Sinquefeld). All rights reserved.

Formal studies have evaluated the effects of inflation on stock returns, and most of them tend to support the more casual evidence offered by Table 10.3. Whether the inflation is anticipated or unanticipated, it seems to have a strong negative impact on stock returns, both nominal and real. In general, it is one of the stock investors' worst enemies. Even when high inflation is anticipated, real stock returns tend to suffer. Things are worse, however, when inflation is not anticipated, because real stock returns are typically negative during such periods.

RISK AND THE REQUIRED RATE OF RETURN

We have now surveyed the principal instruments of the capital market and discussed the valuation principles that apply to bonds, preferred stock, and common stock. Each represents a different source of financing and each has its own particular characteristics. One of the major differences among them is the risk that the owner takes in giving money to the firm in exchange for promises of future cash flows.

☞ Common stock is the riskiest of the securities that a firm issues, and it must therefore have the highest expected return in order to attract investors.

Investors demand greater compensation for bearing greater risk. For instance, we noted that the owner of a first mortgage bond has a more secure position than the holder of the same firm's debenture. In general, all of the bondholders have a less risky position than holders of stock, and preferred stockholders bear less risk than common stockholders. The differences in risk levels are reflected in the different rates of return that these various securities earn. Figure 10.4 presents this general relationship in schematic form. The

FIGURE 10.4 The Basic Relationship Between Risk and Return for Different Kinds of Securities

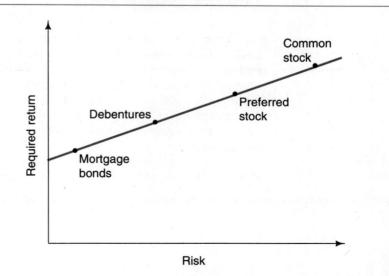

FINANCE TODAY

Frictional Tales

The hyperactive trading portfolios of some investment letters remind me of the perpetual motion machines of crackpot inventors. They look great on paper, but they don't work. Both are predicated on the myth of frictionless motion—and both are hopelessly unrealistic.

On Wall Street, friction takes the form of trading costs. One cost, of course, is the commission on a trade. But there's another, less visible factor that influences results. The adviser recommends a stock at 24, but when you go to buy it, you have to pay $24\frac{1}{2}$ or even 25. This is because a marketmaker has tacked on a spread and/or because other investors following the same recommendation are competing for a limited number of shares.

There is good evidence of just how unrealistic it is to evaluate a paper portfolio without allowing for transaction costs. Simply compare the performance results claimed by various letters with the performances as calculated by the *Hulbert Financial Digest*. The numbers are sometimes wildly divergent.

Most letter publishers do not include these trading costs in their calculations. I do. The *HFD* docks a hypothetical portfolio 2 percent round-trip (that is, for selling a stock and reinvesting the proceeds in other stocks). And the *HFD* executes all trades at the prices prevailing when the typical subscriber receives the advice in the mail or over a hotline.

A good illustration of how much frictional loss investors suffer is provided by Mark Leibovit's *Volume Reversal Survey.* This letter's model portfolio is hyperactive: Its portfolio turnover rate for the single month of August was over 300 percent. Ignoring commissions, Leibovit calculates his gain from the beginning of 1987 through August 1990 as a compound annual 16 percent. *HFD*, in contrast, figures a 21 percent annual loss.

A similar lesson emerges from portfolios that actively trade commodity futures contracts, even though discount commissions are smaller for commodities than for stocks. Consider the commission-free performance calculated by the *Futures Hotline/Bond Fund Timer* for its model portfolio of commodity futures contracts. For the first three quarters of 1990, this service reports a loss of 55 percent. Taking commissions into account, the *HFD* reports a loss of 65 percent—almost identical to the 66 percent loss reported by a *Forbes* reader who wrote to describe his experiences following this service.

But commissions are not the only drag on advisers' perpetual motion portfolios. A more subtle factor is that subscribers almost invariably receive less favorable executions than the adviser assumes in evaluating his own record. How much larger is this factor?

A dramatic illustration is provided by Louis Navellier's *MPT Review*. Over the 33 months through 1990's third quarter, Navellier reports that his *$200,000 Conservative* portfolio gained an amount that equates to a compound annual 40 percent, far outpacing the Wilshire 5000's total return of 10 percent. Significantly, however, Navellier's calculations do not take commissions into account, and they assume that each month's transactions take place at the end of the month—as opposed to a week or so later, when subscribers receive their issues of his advisory letter in the mail and are actively competing with one another for the shares Navellier recommends.

So let's look at Navellier's results after adjusting for transaction costs and allowing for real-world execution of orders. Taking both commissions and more realistic prices into account, the *HFD* reports a 27 percent compound annual return over the same 33 months—very similar to the 25 percent gain that a *Forbes* reader wrote to say he had achieved over this period by following Navellier's advice. In short, the real-world performance, while still impressive, is only about two-thirds as good as the frictionless paper gain that Navellier reports.

Commissions and poor executions aren't the only obstacles to profitably translating an adviser's recommendations into practice, however. Another occurs when an adviser recommends a security with low trading volume, making it difficult or impossible for lots of subscribers to act on the recommendation. This problem arose in October 1987, for example, when Martin Zweig recommended that subscribers to his *Zweig Forecast* purchase an out-of-the-money index put option. It turned out to be a very profitable trade, but the closed-end fund Zweig had set up to follow his investment strategy (the Zweig Fund, traded on the New York Stock Exchange) did not purchase the put, since the fund was so large that it would have overwhelmed the market for this particular option.

The investment moral of these case studies? It's that trading is costly. It is so costly that the average investor is almost guaranteed to lag the market unless he or she follows a long-term investment strategy. The other moral is simply this: Take with a whole spoonful of salt any letter's claim to earth-shattering results for its followers.

Source: Mark Hulbert, "Why the Brokers Own Yachts," *Forbes*, January 21, 1991, p. 119.

basic principle is clear—the greater the risk, the greater must be the return to encourage investors to commit their funds. The next two chapters take a detailed look at the relationship between risk and expected return.

For common stock, much of its required return may come from its growth potential in the form of a capital gains yield. This is seen by reorganizing the constant growth model to solve for the required rate:

$$r = \frac{D_1}{P_0} + g \tag{10.7}$$

The first term on the right-hand side of Equation 10.7 is the dividend yield of the stock. We saw that this ratio is quoted in the *Wall Street Journal* each day.[3] However, the second term is not quoted. It is the capital gains yield. To see why the dividend growth rate is exactly the same as the capital gains yield, note that, by definition, the capital gains yield is given by the expression:

$$\text{Capital gains yield} = \frac{P_1 - P_0}{P_0} \tag{10.8}$$

Also, from the constant growth model, next year's price is equal to:

$$P_1 = \frac{D_2}{r - g}$$

$$= \frac{D_1(1 + g)}{r - g} = P_0(1 + g)$$

Thus, the stock's price grows at the same rate as dividends grow. From these equations we have:

$$\text{Capital gains yield} = g$$

This reasoning shows that, quoted or not, the firm's dividend growth rate is a component of the required rate of return on the stock. The higher the growth rate, the higher its relative importance to the firm's overall rate of return.

As an example, consider a firm that is expected to pay a dividend of $2 in one year, has a current price of $50, and is expected to experience a long-term growth rate of 6 percent each year. Then, the required rate of return on this stock is:

$$r = \frac{2}{50} + 0.06$$

$$= 0.04 + 0.06 = 10\%$$

In this example, most of the return of the stock is expected to come from capital gains, as has been historically the case in the real world.

---

[3] Actually, the dividend yield quoted is D_0/P_0. The error is usually not substantial.

SUMMARY

This chapter examined two major elements of the capital market—preferred stock and common stock. Preferred stock is a hybrid security, with features of both corporate bonds and common stock. It normally pays a fixed dividend rate, similar to the coupon rate on a corporate bond. However, unlike most corporate bonds, it has no maturity date, so the dividends are intended to be paid forever. The fact that it does not mature means that the firm need never repay the par value of the stock.

Preferred stock provides the firm with a flexible financing alternative, because the dividend payments are not contractually obligated (as they are with most bonds) and preferred stockholders do not normally have voting rights (as do common stockholders). This advantage of flexibility is partially offset by the fact that dividends must be paid from the firm's after-tax earnings. Interest payments on bonds, by contrast, are paid from before-tax earnings.

Common stock is the one kind of financing common to all corporations, because its ownership represents ownership in the corporation. The corporation need not sell preferred stock or bonds, but must sell common stock. Common stockholders are entitled to receive dividends as a return on their investment. However, because they receive dividends only after the other claimants of the firm are satisfied, there is no assurance that they will actually be paid. Of all of the financing instruments issued by a corporation, common stock is the riskiest.

The value of both preferred and common stock, like the value of any investment, equals the sum of the present values of all of the expected cash flows. In the case of preferred stock, the flows are stated as a fixed dollar amount, so preferred stock may be valued as a perpetuity. In the case of common stock, the matter is more complicated, because the dividends may not currently exist, or if they do, they may grow yet larger. For those periods when dividends are growing at a constant rate, they may be valued with the constant growth model.

QUESTIONS

1. A new firm makes a 100 percent believable commitment to never pay dividends. What should the price of its shares be worth? Why?
2. Respond to the following claim: The dividend valuation model is worthless as a guide to stock prices because it completely neglects capital gains.
3. Why do many new firms pay no dividends? Does this imply that their share prices should be 0? Why or why not?
4. React to the following criticism: The dividend valuation model is not very useful because it can be applied only to firms having smoothly growing dividends. For example, it cannot be applied to firms that

might experience a period of rapidly and erratically growing dividends.

5. How would you respond to the following attack on the dividend valuation model? The model assumes that dividends grow at a constant rate g forever. This is obviously unrealistic, so it cannot be applied in practice.

6. In terms of the dividend valuation model, why does a firm with a higher growth rate of dividends have a higher discount rate?

7. If a firm cuts its dividend, should its price fall according to the dividend valuation model?

8. Consider a firm that announces a very attractive new investment opportunity and also announces that it is eliminating its dividend in order to finance the new investment. What should happen to the stock price according to the dividend valuation model?

9. What similarities are there between preferred stock and a regular corporate bond?

10. What are the similarities between preferred and common stock?

11. Other things being equal, which kind of preferred stock should be more valuable, regular or cumulative? Explain.

12. Which should be more valuable, a bond with an infinite life having a par value of $100 and a 6 percent coupon, or a share of preferred stock with a par value of $100 and a 6 percent dividend rate? Explain.

13. What is the preemptive right held by the common stock owners?

14. Why does the P/E ratio appear in the stock market quotations?

15. Explain how the P/E ratio is affected by the dividend payout ratio, the firm's growth rate, and the firm's required rate of return, other things being equal.

16. Explain how the firm's growth rate is likely to be related to its dividend payout policy. What does this explain about the payout policies of many high-growth firms?

17. The *Wall Street Journal* quotes the dividend yield of a stock. Is this the stock's required rate of return?

18. Why is a stock's dividend growth rate the same as its capital gains yield, according to the constant growth model?

PROBLEMS

1. Consider a firm that pays a dividend in the next period of $0.70 and that has a growth rate of 11 percent for the next four years. What are the dividends for these periods? Assume that the firm will never pay any dividends beyond the fifth year. According to the dividend valuation model, what should be the price of this share? The discount rate is 15 percent.

2. For a share paying a dividend in the coming period of $1.20, with a

long-term growth rate of 4 percent and a cost of equity capital of 10 percent, what is the share price according to the dividend valuation model?

3. For the previous share, what happens as the growth rate accelerates and other factors are held constant? Graph the share price as a function of the difference between the cost of equity capital (10 percent) and the growth rate, as the growth rate increases.

4. You estimate that a firm will have the following dividends for the next three periods: $1.17, $1.44, $1.88. After these, you expect dividends to grow at a long-term rate of 3 percent. What is the share price according to the dividend valuation model? What would it be if the long-term growth rate were 5 percent rather than 3 percent? The discount rate is 10 percent.

5. A fully mature firm follows the policy of paying 60 percent of its earnings in dividends, and these earnings have been growing at the long-term growth rate of 4 percent. Further increases in earnings are expected to remain at the 4 percent level as well. If the earnings in the current period are $1.20 per share, what is the value of this share according to the dividend discount model, assuming a 12 percent cost of equity capital?

6. For the firm in Problem 5, assume that the payout ratio is 100 percent rather than 60 percent. What does this imply about the growth rate and what should be the value of the share?

7. For a share of preferred stock with a discount rate of 11 percent and an annual dividend of $6, what should its price be?

8. What should the price of a preferred share be if the appropriate discount rate is 13 percent and the annual dividend is $6?

9. Hard Times, Inc., is expected to skip its annual preferred dividend payments of $9 for the next three years. However, it is expected to resume its normal payment pattern starting four years from now. At that time, the three delayed dividends will also be paid in full. If the required rate on the preferred stock is 12 percent, find the current price of the preferred stock.

10. Assume that Hard Times must pay 10 percent interest, compounded annually, on any delayed preferred dividends. What is the current preferred stock price in that case?

11. A firm has a constant payout policy of paying 40 percent of earnings as a cash dividend, and next year's earnings are projected at $1.40. If the long-term growth rate in earnings is 6 percent and the firm's cost of capital is 11 percent, what should this share be worth?

12. If a stock will pay a $3 dividend in one year, is currently selling for $42, and has a long-term dividend growth rate of 3.5 percent, what is its required rate of return?

13. A share of common stock is currently worth $60. Dividend payments from this stock are expected to grow at 6 percent forever. What do you expect the price of this stock to be in five years?

14. The stock price of Lya's Creations is expected to double in five years. What is Lya's long-term dividend growth rate?

15. Microtech has decided not to pay any dividends on its common stock for the next six years, to devote all its resources to R&D. In year 7 it will pay a dividend of $4.50 per share, and each year thereafter it will increase its dividend by 3 percent. If the required rate on Microtech stock is 17 percent, what is its current stock price?

16. The Fortyniner gold mine is being depleted rapidly. In fact, each year it generates 10 percent less earnings for its common stockholders. Given this depressing state of affairs, all the earnings are paid to the stockholders. Earnings for the year just finished were $8 per share, and the corresponding dividends were just paid. If investors require 18 percent return from Fortyniner's stock, what is its current stock price? What will its price be in two years?

17. Yo-Yo Cellos, Inc., is experiencing a period of very fast growth. Yo-Yo expects to increase its earnings by 12 percent annually for the next 10 years. After that period, earnings will increase by 5 percent forever. Next year's earnings are expected to be $12 per share. If the annual discount rate is 10 percent, what is Yo-Yo's current price?

CHAPTER 11

Risk and the Required Rate of Return

Thus far we have largely neglected the risk component of value creation so that we could focus on the valuation of cash flow streams through time. In this chapter we introduce the concepts of risk and return. High risk normally accompanies high expected returns.

Given techniques for measuring risk and expected return, we can analyze the ways to combine securities to form portfolios. A portfolio is a collection of securities held by a single investor. As this chapter explains in detail, one of the main incentives for forming portfolios is diversification —the allocation of investable funds to a variety of securities in order to reduce risk.

THE PRINCIPLES OF RISK AND RETURN

This section introduces the basic concepts of risk and return, which are used extensively throughout this chapter and the next. The risk/return trade-off constitutes the foundation of portfolio theory.

Expected Return

random variable
a variable whose outcome
is uncertain

Suppose you have the opportunity to invest $1 in Bernoulli Research Corporation. If the outcome of this risky investment is favorable, you receive $4; but if it is unfavorable, the project generates no cash and you lose your $1 investment. Thus, the net payoff, or simply payoff, is either $3 or −$1. The outcome will be known almost immediately, so you can disregard the time value of money. Because the payoff of this project is uncertain, it is a **random variable.** Also assume that the probability of each outcome is 50 percent. Before investing your precious dollar, you want to quantify the amount you would expect to earn and how much risk you would be taking with this venture.

probability distribution
a list of all possible
outcomes of a random
variable, with their
respective probabilities

With the information given, we can obtain a probability distribution of the possible payoffs. A **probability distribution** is a list of all possible outcomes with their respective probabilities. For this investment, the probability distribution is given in Table 11.1. This same information about the probability distribution of payoffs is presented graphically in Figure 11.1.

TABLE 11.1   Probability Distribution of Payoffs for Bernoulli Research Corporation

Outcome	Probability	Payoff
Favorable	0.50	+$3
Unfavorable	0.50	−1

Of course, if the investment is made only once, you will either win $3 or lose $1. Of more interest is knowing how much you can expect to earn or lose on average if you make a similar investment repeatedly. In this example, basic intuition says that you should win $3 half the time and lose $1 the other half. This suggests that the expected payoff, E(payoff), can be found as follows:

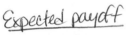

$$E(\text{payoff}) = (\$3) \times 0.5 + (-\$1) \times 0.5 = \$1$$

In general, if a random variable r can have n possible outcomes r_i, where $i = 1, 2, \ldots, n$, and each outcome has probability p_i, then the expected value of r is given by:

$$E(r) = r_1 p_1 + r_2 p_2 + \cdots + r_n p_n \tag{11.1}$$

We can write this summation more compactly as follows:

$$E(r) = \sum_{i=1}^{n} r_i p_i \tag{11.2}$$

FIGURE 11.1   Probability Distribution of Payoffs for Bernoulli Research Corporation

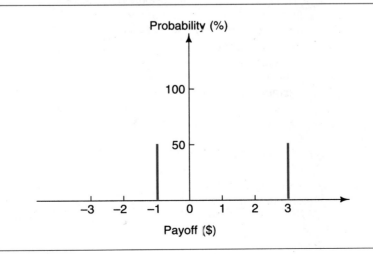

We also note the basic fact that the sum of all the probabilities must add to 1. This must always hold because we know with certainty that one of the possible outcomes will be observed. In our notation, we have:

$$\sum_{i=1}^{n} p_i = 1 \tag{11.3}$$

Variance and Standard Deviation

A casual definition of the riskiness of a random variable is the possibility that the actual outcome will differ from the expected outcome. Intuitively, the greater the difference, the greater the riskiness of the random variable. In other words, the notion of risk is associated with the dispersion of possible outcomes.

A common way to measure the dispersion of any random variable, r, around its mean is to calculate its variance, σ^2, as follows:

$$\sigma^2 = [r_1 - E(r)]^2 p_1 + [r_2 - E(r)]^2 p_2 + \cdots + [r_n - E(r)]^2 p_n \tag{11.4}$$

or, using the compact notation,

$$\sigma^2 = \sum_{i=1}^{n} [r_i - E(r)]^2 p_i \tag{11.5}$$

For Bernoulli Research, the variance is equal to:

$$\sigma^2 = [3 - 1]^2 \times 0.5 + [-1 - 1]^2 \times 0.5 = 4$$

Notice that if the unit for the random variable is dollars, the unit for the variance is dollars squared, making the variance awkward to interpret. Because of this difficulty, an alternative measure of risk, the **standard deviation,** is often used. The standard deviation of a random variable is the square root of its variance, and is denoted by σ. Thus, the standard deviation is defined by the following relationship:

$$\sigma = \sqrt{\sigma^2} \tag{11.6}$$

standard deviation
the square root of the variance of a random variable

☞ Risk can be measured as the variance or standard deviation of returns for an investment.

The standard deviation measures the dispersion of a random variable around its mean. Both it and the expected return are expressed in the same units. For the $1 investment in Bernoulli, the standard deviation of the random payoffs is $2. The standard deviation gives a range of values around the mean that are likely to occur more frequently. Since Bernoulli has an expected payoff of $1, the standard deviation of $2 indicates that we can expect most payoffs to be between −$1 ($1 − $2) and $3 ($1 + $2). In fact, in this example the standard deviation gives the entire range of possible payoffs: −$1 and $3.[1]

Both the variance and standard deviation measure risk as distance from the mean. With these measures, the greater the chance of getting a result far

---

[1] This is not generally the case. For example, if the payoffs conformed to a normal distribution, they would fall within one standard deviation of the mean payoff about two-thirds of the time.

FIGURE 11.2   The Dispersion of Returns for Assets A and B

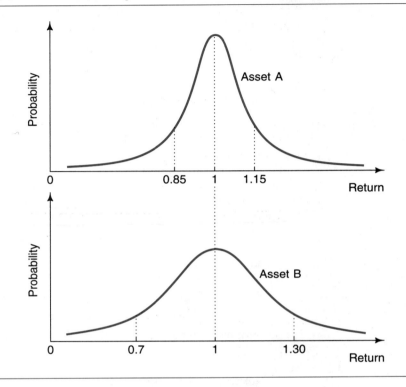

away from the mean, the greater the risk of a particular investment. Figure 11.2 illustrates this difference graphically, showing the probability distribution of returns for two hypothetical assets with normally distributed returns.

The expected return for each of the assets is 1. The difference between the assets lies in the risk each involves. Since the payoffs on both are normally distributed, about 68 percent of the total area under each curve lies within one standard deviation of the mean. For asset A the standard deviation of returns is 0.15, and for asset B it is 0.30.

Asset A has a 68 percent chance of getting a return between 0.85 and 1.15, and asset B between 0.70 and 1.30. This means that the chance of getting very large or very small returns from asset B is higher. When considering risk, most investors want to avoid extremely low returns. Using the normal distribution table in the Appendix we find that, for asset A, the probability of getting a return of less than 0.7 is 2.25 percent;[2] however, for asset B it is

_____

[2] In general, with a normal distribution, the probability of obtaining a return at least two standard deviations away from the mean is just about 4.5 percent. Since there are two tails in the distribution, this leaves 2.25 percent for each tail.

TABLE 11.2 Probability Distribution of Payoffs from Combining Bernoulli and Binomial

Bernoulli	Binomial	Probability	Bernoulli Payoff	Binomial Payoff	Combined Payoff
Favorable	Favorable	0.25	$ 1.50	$ 1.50	$ 3.00
Favorable	Unfavorable	0.25	1.50	−0.50	1.00
Unfavorable	Favorable	0.25	−0.50	1.50	1.00
Unfavorable	Unfavorable	0.25	−0.50	−0.50	−1.00

15.87 percent. Obviously, asset B is much riskier than asset A because it has a much greater chance of low returns.

To continue our example, suppose that you have found another firm, Binomial Software, that offers the same payoff distribution as Bernoulli Research. At this point you wonder if there is any benefit in investing only $0.50 in Bernoulli and the other $0.50 in Binomial. After all, they look exactly alike in terms of their payoff probability distributions. Of course, by splitting your investment equally in each firm, you will also split your payoffs, so you receive a payoff of only $1.50 from each firm if its outcome is favorable, and you lose only $0.50 for each firm with an unfavorable outcome.

independent investments
investments for which the outcome of one does not influence the outcome of the other

Assume that Bernoulli and Binomial are **independent investments**. This means that the outcome of one will not influence the outcome of the other. Because their payoffs are independent, the probability distribution of the combined investment consists of four equally likely outcomes, as shown in Table 11.2.

Under the new combined probability distribution of returns, you have a 50 percent chance of receiving a $1 payoff. Also, the probability of each extreme outcome, $3 and −$1, has been reduced to 25 percent. Figure 11.3 depicts the probability distribution for the combined investment in Bernoulli and Binomial.

Knowing the probability distribution of this combined investment strategy, we can compute its expected payoff using Equation 11.1:

$$E(\text{payoff}) = (\$3.00 \times 0.25) + (\$1.00 \times 0.25) + (\$1.00 \times 0.25)$$
$$+ (-\$1.00 \times 0.25)$$
$$= \$1.00$$

We can see from this example that dividing your money into two identical independent investments provides the same expected payoff as putting all the money into one of them. Now consider what happens to the risk of the combined investment. Is it possible that it is also unaltered? To answer this question we compute the variance of the combined investment using

FIGURE 11.3   Probability Distribution of Payoffs from Combining Bernoulli and Binomial

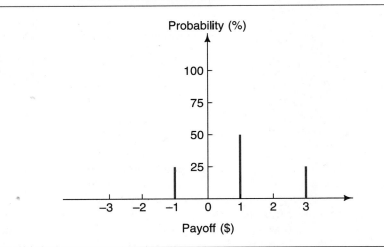

Equation 11.4:

$$\sigma^2 = [(3-1)^2 \times 0.25] + [(1-1)^2 \times 0.25] + [(1-1)^2 \times 0.25]$$
$$+ [(-1-1)^2 \times 0.25]$$
$$= 2.00$$

We find that the variance from investing equally in Bernoulli and Binomial is just half the variance of investing the entire $1 in Bernoulli alone. Since the variance is a measure of risk, the combined investment is less risky than investing entirely in only one of the firms.[3] Most important, no cost is associated with this risk reduction because the expected payoff is unchanged.

Knowing the variance, we compute the standard deviation of the two firm investment strategy, using Equation 11.6:

$$\sigma = \sqrt{2} = \$1.41$$

This simple example with two independent identical investments illustrates the following general result. By investing in equal proportions in n identical independent projects, the expected payoff will be the same as that of investing all the money in only one of the projects. However, the overall standard deviation from the n project investment is lower than that from the single investment. If σ_1 is the standard deviation of the single investment and

---

[3] Of course, this is not a surprising result if you believe in the saying, Don't put all your eggs in one basket.

σ_n is the standard deviation of the n project investment, then:

$$\sigma_n = \frac{\sigma_1}{\sqrt{n}} \qquad (11.7)$$

This means that in the case of Bernoulli and Binomial, it is not necessary to calculate the standard deviation of the two-project investment directly from the definition, as we did. Rather, since we already calculated that the standard deviation of each of the two identical independent projects is $2, we can use Equation 11.7 directly:

$$\sigma_2 = \frac{\$2}{\sqrt{2}} = \$1.41$$

This is exactly the same result we found before.

Covariance

covariance
a statistic that measures the tendency of two variables to change together

Intuitively, **covariance** measures the tendency of a pair of random variables to move together. Equivalently, it measures the connection between two random variables. For example, because tall people tend to weigh more than short people, we can say that height and weight have a positive covariance. In finance, when interest rates increase unexpectedly, the stock market index tends to decrease. This means that interest rates and the market index have a negative covariance. Knowledge of the behavior of one random variable helps predict the behavior of the other variable with some degree of accuracy. Thus, higher future interest rates would likely lead to a decline in the stock market index, other things being equal.[4] Another example is tossing two coins. We know from casual observation and intuition that the outcome from tossing one coin does not affect the outcome of the other coin toss. This is another way of saying that the coin tossing outcomes—heads or tails—are independent. For pairs of independent random variables we expect the covariance to be 0, since they are not connected.

To formalize these ideas, suppose two random variables, x and y, have n possible combined outcomes, labeled $i = 1, 2, \ldots, n$. When combined outcome i occurs, the value of x is x_i and the value of y is y_i. Assume that the probability that outcome i occurs is p_i. Let the expected values of x and y be $E(x)$ and $E(y)$, respectively. Then the covariance between these two random variables is defined as follows:

$$\begin{aligned}
\text{cov}(x, y) = {} & [x_1 - E(x)][y_1 - E(y)]p_1 \\
& + [x_2 - E(x)][y_2 - E(y)]p_2 + \cdots \\
& + [x_n - E(x)][y_n - E(y)]p_n
\end{aligned} \qquad (11.8)$$

[4] Unfortunately, too frequently other things are not equal. For example, interest rates could increase at the same time that the earnings of many firms increase. In that case, it is very hard to say what will happen to the stock market index.

FINANCE

TODAY

More Carriers Needed

Although two random variables may be found to have a high correlation coefficient, it does not automatically mean that one of them is responsible for the other. In other words, if two variables are correlated, one is not necessarily the cause of the other. A very amusing example of this important fact was presented by Helmut Sies of the University of Dusseldorf in a letter to *Nature*.

Sies suggested an explanation "that every child knows makes sense" for the long decline in the birthrate in West Germany. He simply presented two curves depicting the number of newborn babies, and another showing the number of pairs of brooding storks in West Germany. As the figure below illustrates, there is clearly a remarkable correlation between the stork population and the number of newborn babies. But have the Germans heard about the birds and the bees?

Storks Versus Babies

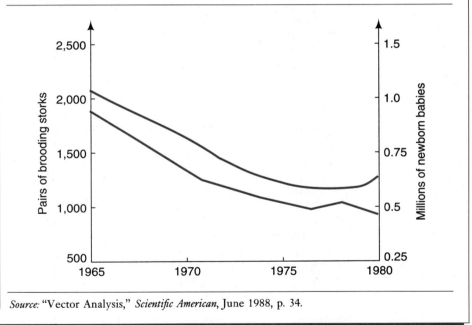

Source: "Vector Analysis," *Scientific American*, June 1988, p. 34.

Using the compact notation, we can write:

$$\text{cov}(x, y) = \sum_{i=1}^{n} [x_i - E(x)][y_i - E(y)]p_i \qquad (11.9)$$

With this definition, we can compute the covariance between the payoffs of Bernoulli Research and Binomial Software, using the data in Table 11.2:[5]

$$
\begin{aligned}
\text{cov}(x, y) &= [1.50 - 0.5][1.50 - 0.5]0.25 + [1.50 - 0.5][-0.50 - 0.5]0.25 \\
&\quad + [-0.50 - 0.5][1.50 - 0.5]0.25 \\
&\quad + [-0.50 - 0.5][-0.50 - 0.5]0.25 \\
&= (1 - 1 - 1 + 1)0.25 \\
&= 0.00
\end{aligned}
$$

This computation tells us that there is no covariance between the two identical firms. This should not be surprising, since we already know that the two investments are independent of each other and, therefore, do not covary.[6]

It is useful to note that the variance is just the covariance of an asset with itself. For example, the covariance of asset x with itself is, according to Equation 11.9:

$$\text{cov}(x, x) = \sum_{i=1}^{n} [x_i - E(x)][x_i - E(x)]p_i = \sum_{i=1}^{n} [x_i - E(x)]^2 p_i$$

$$= \sigma_x^2 \qquad (11.10)$$

Thus, the covariance is a more general concept than the variance, since the latter is just a special case of the former.

Another useful property of the covariance is that the order of the variables is irrelevant in its computation. Thus,

$$\text{cov}(x, y) = \text{cov}(y, x) \qquad (11.11)$$

These properties will be useful when we discuss multiple-asset portfolios.

Correlation Coefficient

The covariance is a useful measure of the amount of connection between two random variables. However, it has two major disadvantages. First, it is not bounded. It may be any number, however large or small. Second, the numerical value of the covariance depends on the units used to measure the random variables. For example, the actual numerical value of the covariance between height and weight varies depending on whether they are measured in inches and pounds, or in centimeters and kilos. These problems make

---

[5] Notice that whereas the expected payoff of the combined investment is $1, the expected payoff of each investment considered separately is $0.50.

[6] It is always true that if two random variables are independent they have a 0 covariance. However, a 0 covariance does not necessarily imply independence of the random variables.

INTERNATIONAL PERSPECTIVES

The Correlation Matrix

You probably realize that to get adequate diversification, you need to spread your money around various types of investments. But which categories should you hold, and in what amounts? The American Association of Individual Investors in Chicago has put together a chart that provides some answers. It shows how well certain assets correlate with one another—that is, whether they tend to move in the same direction. The chart uses data for various asset classes, from 1973 through 1989.

The chart measures these relationships in terms of "correlation coefficients." A coefficient approaching 1.00 indicates that two investments move together very closely and thus don't deliver much in the way of diversification. However, a negative coefficient, especially one nearing −1.00, shows that two assets tend to go in opposite directions. A coefficient at or around 0.00 signifies that there's no relationship to the movement of two assets. For example, as the AAII chart indicates, long-term corporate and government bonds tend to move in opposite directions to gold. Conversely, the two categories of bonds correlate closely with each other. Blue-chip stocks in the Standard & Poor's 500 tend to move in tandem with small stocks (as measured by the NASDAQ composite index), but less so with equities traded in London, Tokyo, or other foreign markets represented by the Europe–Australia–Far East (EAFE) index.

"The implications of the behavior of these categories for portfolio diversification are fundamentally profound and simple," writes John Markese, executive vice president and director of research for the AAII. "If you do not have meaningful positions in large and small domestic common stocks, international common stocks, fixed-income securities, and real assets, your portfolio is probably not well-diversified and you are taking on needless portfolio risk." Markese emphasizes that people nearing retirement shouldn't put too much faith in bonds, despite their low perceived volatility. "The correlation matrix, especially relating to bonds, will hopefully shock you into maintaining a well-balanced portfolio with common stocks, short-term fixed-income securities, and real assets."

---

comparisons of covariances difficult. It is very hard to say if the degree of connection between interest rates and the stock market index is stronger than the degree of connection between height and weight among people.

Fortunately, the problem can be solved through the ingenious trick of dividing the covariance of two random variables by the product of their standard deviations. It is a remarkable fact that by performing this operation the resulting number will always be between −1 and +1. This is true regardless of whether the variables are measured in pounds, kilos, dollars, annual rate of return, or any other unit. This number between −1 and +1 is called the **correlation coefficient** between the two random variables, and

correlation coefficient
a statistic that measures the tendency of two variables to change together in which the value must fall between −1 and +1

**Correlation Matrix of Investment Categories
(based on annual returns from 1973–1989)**

	1. S&P 500	2. NASDAQ Composite	3. London Index	4. Tokyo Index	5. EAFE Index	6. Long-Term Corporate Bonds	7. Long-Term Government Bonds	8. Gold	9. Single-Family Homes
1. S&P 500	1.00								
2. NASDAQ Composite	0.90	1.00							
3. London Index	0.63	0.57	1.00						
4. Tokyo Index	0.52	0.41	0.31	1.00					
5. EAFE Index	0.56	0.52	0.44	0.69	1.00				
6. Long-Term Corporate Bonds	0.54	0.38	0.33	0.33	0.28	1.00			
7. Long-Term Government Bonds	0.4	0.25	0.11	0.28	0.23	0.93	1.00		
8. Gold	(0.37)	(0.24)	(0.48)	(0.55)	(0.30)	(0.43)	(0.25)	1.00	
9. Single-Family Homes	(0.25)	0.01	0.04	(0.46)	(0.29)	(0.56)	(0.55)	0.51	1.00

Source: "Retirement Outlook," *Personal Investor,* January 1991.

it measures their degree of connection. In general , the correlation coefficient between two random variables x and y is given by the following formula:[7]

$$\rho(x, y) = \frac{\text{cov}(x, y)}{\sigma_x \sigma_y} \tag{11.12}$$

For Bernoulli and Binomial, we found that the covariance between their payoffs is 0. It follows from Equation 11.12 that their correlation coefficient is also 0, confirming that the two investment payoffs have no connection.

[7] When there is no possible confusion, we will simply write ρ instead of $\rho(x, y)$.

The correlation coefficient is essentially a scaled covariance, where the scaling process forces the correlation to fall between −1 and +1. If it exceeds 0, the two variables tend to move in the same direction when they change. For example, knowing that Valerie is taller than Ana, our best guess would be that Valerie also weighs more than Ana. A negative value for the correlation coefficient indicates that the two variables tend to move in opposite directions. Thus, if interest rates fall, we can expect the stock market to go up. If the correlation between two variables is 0, they have no connection.

RISK AND RETURN IN THE NEW YORK STOCK EXCHANGE

In this section we apply the concepts of risk and return to the recent history of the New York Stock Exchange. Figure 11.4 shows the yearly rate of return on common stocks for the period 1926–1990. The largest return, 53.99 percent,

FIGURE 11.4 Yearly Rates of Return on Common Stocks, 1926–1990

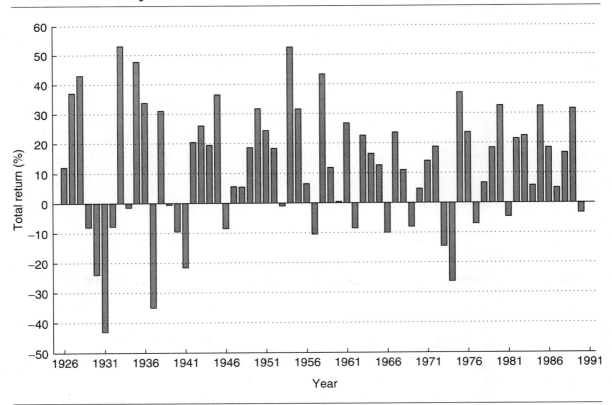

Source: © *Stock, Bonds, Bills, and Inflation, 1991 Yearbook*™, Ibbotson Associates, Chicago (annually updates work by Roger G. Ibbotson and Rex A. Sinquefeld). All rights reserved.

FIGURE 11.5   Frequency Distribution of Yearly Rates of Return on Common Stocks

```
                                        1988
                              1990      1986
                              1981      1979
                              1977      1972           1989
                              1969      1971  1983 1985
                              1962 1987 1968 1982 1980
                              1953 1984 1965 1976 1975
                              1946 1978 1964 1967 1955
                              1940 1970 1959 1963 1950
                    1973 1939 1960 1952 1961 1945
                    1966 1934 1956 1949 1951 1938 1958
               1974 1957 1932 1948 1944 1943 1936 1935 1954
      1931 1937 1930 1941 1929 1947 1926 1942 1927 1928 1933
   |    |    |    |    |    |    |    |    |    |    |    |    |
  -60  -50  -40  -30  -20  -10   0   10   20   30   40   50   60   70
                            Rate of return (%)
```

Source: © *Stock, Bonds, Bills, and Inflation, 1991 Yearbook*™, Ibbotson Associates, Chicago (annually updates work by Roger G. Ibbotson and Rex A. Sinquefeld). All rights reserved.

occurred in 1933; and the smallest, −43.44 percent, came two years earlier, in 1931. Obviously, this was a period of great volatility in the market, after the great crash in October 1929. It is also clear that years of gains occurred about twice as often as years of losses; in fact, common stock had 20 years of losses and 45 years of positive returns. Perhaps the most striking feature is the great tendency for radical swings from one year to the next, corroborating the belief that investing in the stock market is very risky, especially in the short term.

For common stocks, the geometric mean rate of return over the entire period was 10.1 percent, and the standard deviation of those returns was 20.8 percent. These statistics provide a convenient way of summarizing a great deal of information. Figure 11.5 presents the same information as Figure 11.4, but in the form of a frequency distribution of the yearly rates of return over the period chosen. The figure also shows which years produced returns in a certain range. For example, it confirms that for 1931 the return on common stocks was between −40 and −50 percent; the most frequent annual rate of return range was 10 to 20 percent; and the second most frequent range was actually negative—between 0 and −10 percent. All of these statistics reinforce a very simple, but sobering, fact: investing in the market may be very profitable in the long run, but it is also very risky in the short run.

We can also ask if a given year's return has any influence over the following year's return. We can answer this question by computing the correlation coefficient between the returns of consecutive years.[8] If a relatively bad year is likely to follow a bad year, and a good year tends to follow a good year, then the correlation would be positive. If bad years tend to follow good years, and vice versa, the correlation would be negative. The computation on the annual data for common stocks for 1926–1990 gives a correlation coefficient of 0.00, so we must conclude that no connection exists between the returns on common stocks over consecutive years.

PRINCIPLES OF PORTFOLIO ANALYSIS

For the discussion that follows, we make some simplifying assumptions about markets and investor psychology. Although the assumptions themselves are not necessarily realistic, markets behave very much as if they were true.

First, we assume that the securities markets operate with no transaction costs, such as commissions and taxes. This is the assumption of "frictionless markets." Second, we assume all investors have free access to all relevant information about securities. Third, we assume that investors appraise the available information similarly, so investors have identical estimations about the risk and expected return of securities. This means that investors have "homogeneous expectations." Fourth, we assume that investors care about only the risk and expected return characteristics of securities, and that they seek higher expected returns and avoid risk. Finally, we assume that all investors have a one-period time horizon.

The Goals of Investing

☞ We assume that investors desire higher expected returns and lower risk.

We assume that investors desire only the monetary benefits of investing. For example, they do not value bragging at cocktail parties about the number of IBM shares they own, or showing off their one share of Playboy stock. Second, we assume investors prefer more wealth to less. This is known as the "non-satiation" principle. Finally, we assume investors are risk averse. That is, they prefer to avoid risk where possible. This does not mean that they refuse to undertake risk, but that they demand an expected return commensurate with it.

These last two assumptions, which describe most people quite well, point out the essential tension that characterizes securities investment. The investment opportunities that seem to offer the greatest increase in wealth tend to be the riskiest, so investors typically must trade off a benefit—higher return—against a cost—riskiness. Thus we can state the goal of investors in the following equivalent ways:

1. For a given level of risk, investors desire the highest expected return possible,
2. For a given expected return, investors desire the least possible risk.

---

[8] This is called serial correlation, since it pertains to a single series of data points.

TABLE 11.3   Historical Returns for Assets A and B

Year	Asset A	Asset B
1987	0.18	0.14
1988	0.15	0.09
1989	−0.13	0.02
1990	0.05	−0.03
1991	0.14	0.07
Mean	0.078	0.058
Variance	0.0127	0.0034
Standard deviation	0.1127	0.0582

Risk and Expected Return Space

Table 11.3 presents data for two risky assets. We use these data to illustrate the idea of a risk/expected return space. Although investors focus on the **expected return** and **variance,** it is customary to estimate future expected returns by past mean returns. In Table 11.3, the expected return of security A is 7.8 percent and that of security B is 5.8 percent. Security B also has a smaller level of risk as measured by the variance or the standard deviation. An investor considering securities A and B faces a risk/return trade-off.[9] The trade-off arises because to get the higher expected return for investing in A rather than in B, the investor must also accept the greater risk of security A. It is not clear whether all investors would prefer asset A over asset B, since each decision variable considered separately indicates that the investors must choose a different security.

When an investor can absolutely prefer asset X to asset Y, we say that asset X dominates asset Y. Figure 11.6 illustrates the idea of dominance by showing four securities in risk/return space. The arrow points to the preferred direction for all investors, because they all like greater expected returns and they all wish to avoid risk. Given our assumptions, any investor would prefer security C to security E, because C offers greater expected returns and they share the same level of risk. Similarly, every investor prefers security C to security D, because although they offer the same level of expected returns, C has less risk. Also, every investor would prefer security C to security F, because C offers both greater expected return and less risk. By a similar reasoning, all investors prefer security E to security F and D to F.

These preferences we have been observing help us to formulate a definition of **dominance** for any pair of securities: Security X dominates security Y if security X has the same or greater expected return and the same or lower risk level as security Y.

expected return
for a risky investment, the expected return is the planned or anticipated return from the investment

variance
a measure of dispersion for any random variable

☞ Every investment opportunity can be located in risk/expected return space.

dominance
a security dominates another if it provides a risk return combination that is preferred by all risk-averse investors

---

[9] The reader should bear in mind that, properly speaking, this is a risk/*expected* return trade-off. However, we customarily speak simply of the risk/return trade-off.

FIGURE 11.6   Dominance in Risk/Expected Return Space

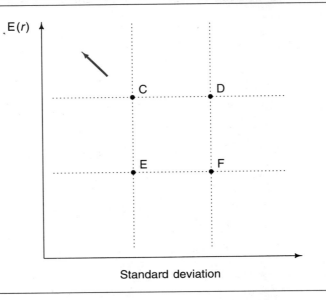

Standard deviation

Using this dominance rule in Figure 11.6, security C dominates D because C has the same expected return and a lower risk. Similarly, D dominates F because D has a greater expected return and the same risk. Also, C dominates F because C has both a greater expected return and a lower risk. Note that the dominance relationship is transitive: because C dominates D and D dominates F, it follows that C dominates F.

Sometimes, however, it is not possible to say in advance that all investors would prefer one security to another. If we compare D and E in Figure 11.6, some investors might prefer E whereas others could reasonably prefer D. Their preferences depend on their willingness to accept additional risk to capture additional expected returns. The choice depends on the individual investor's risk/return trade-off. Equivalently, it depends on the investor's degree of risk aversion. In this case, neither security dominates the other because the dominance rule stated above does not hold for D and E.

TWO-ASSET RISKY PORTFOLIOS

We use the simplest possible risky portfolio, a two-asset portfolio, to illustrate diversification and the building of portfolios. The expected return of a two-asset portfolio depends on the expected returns of the individual assets and the relative percentage of funds invested in each, as described below.

The Expected Return of a Two-Asset Risky Portfolio

The expected return of a portfolio consisting of assets A and B is:

$$E(r_P) = w_a E(r_a) + w_b E(r_b) \tag{11.13}$$

where w_i = percentage of funds, or weight, committed to asset $i = a, b$
    $E(r_i)$ = the expected return on asset i, where $i = a, b,$ or P[10]

Notice also that we must have:

$$w_a + w_b = 1 \tag{11.14}$$

Equation 11.14 implies that we can express one of the weights in terms of the other. In other words, both weights cannot vary freely, since they must add up to 1.

To illustrate the central ideas behind two-asset risky portfolios, we use the data for securities A and B given in Table 11.3. Suppose their proportions in the portfolio are 70 percent and 30 percent, respectively. Substituting the appropriate values in Equation 11.13 gives:

$$E(r_P) = 0.7 \times 0.078 + 0.3 \times 0.058 = 0.072$$

As this calculation illustrates, the expected return of a two-asset portfolio is a simple weighted average of the expected returns of the individual assets.

The Risk of a Two-Asset Portfolio

The risk of a portfolio may also be measured by the variance and standard deviation. The same basic formula for the variance presented in Equation 11.5 is also valid, since a portfolio may be viewed as just another asset. However, if we already have the expected return and the variance of assets A and B, as well as the covariance between them and their weights, Equation 11.5 can be transformed into the following expression:

$$\sigma_P^2 = w_a^2 \sigma_a^2 + w_b^2 \sigma_b^2 + 2 w_a w_b \, \text{cov}(r_a, r_b) \tag{11.15}$$

We previously discussed how to calculate the covariance in terms of the possible combined returns of the random variables and the probabilities associated with those returns. When dealing with returns, the past returns for each asset during each period are used to calculate the covariance of returns. In this case, equal probability is assigned to each period. For example, if data from 20 past periods for two stocks are used to calculate the covariance, each period is assigned a 5 percent probability. With this clarification, we can use Equation 11.9 to compute the covariance between assets A and B. This

[10] Any portfolio of assets can be considered to be an asset in itself. In particular, we can find the portfolio's expected return and variance, just as we would find them for any individual asset.

operation results in a covariance of 0.0044, which, in addition to our other information, is enough to compute the variance and standard deviation of a two-asset portfolio composed of securities A and B:

$$\sigma_P^2 = 0.7^2 \times 0.0127 + 0.3^2 \times 0.0034 + 2 \times 0.7 \times 0.3 \times 0.0044$$
$$= 0.0084$$

Using Equation 11.6, the standard deviation of returns for this portfolio is 0.0915, or 9.15 percent. Because the standard deviation has the same units as the original variable, it is more intuitively meaningful than the variance.

We can also express the variance of a two-asset portfolio using the correlation coefficient, ρ, instead of the covariance. The formula is:[11]

$$\sigma_P^2 = w_a^2 \sigma_a^2 + w_b^2 \sigma_b^2 + 2 w_a w_b \sigma_a \sigma_b \rho \tag{11.16}$$

Risk, Covariance, and Correlation

☞ Covariance or correlation of returns among individual assets is the prime determinant of a portfolio's risk.

The risk of a portfolio depends mainly on the covariance or correlation between its assets, as well as the riskiness of the assets. We can illustrate this fact for a two-asset risky portfolio. Consider securities A and B and assume they have the following risk/return characteristics.

	A	B
E(r)	0.10	0.18
σ	0.08	0.22
w	0.40	0.60

Notice that, although it greatly affects the risk of a portfolio, the correlation between two securities has no effect on the return. This is clear from Equation 11.13, the expression for the expected return, since the correlation coefficient is not present. In the case of our portfolio made up of A and B, the expected return is:

$$E(r_P) = 0.4 \times 0.10 + 0.6 \times 0.18 = 0.148$$

To see how the correlation of returns determines the risk of a portfolio, we consider two special cases. The first arises when the correlation between the assets equals 1, the case of perfect positive correlation. The second arises when the correlation equals −1, the case of perfect negative correlation.

Correlation = +1 If the correlation coefficient equals 1, the last term in Equation 11.16 becomes $2w_a w_b \sigma_a \sigma_b$. In this special case, the expression for

[11] To obtain this version of the formula, note that from Equation 11.12 we have cov(a, b) = $\rho \sigma_a \sigma_b$.

**FIGURE 11.7   Possible Risk/Return Combinations of A and B
When $\rho = 1$**

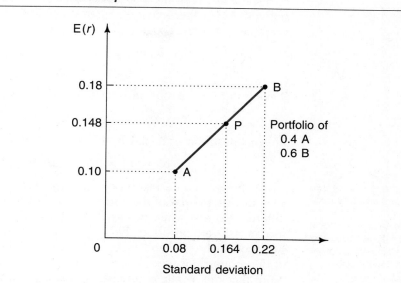

the variance is a perfect square:[12]

$$\sigma_P^2 = w_a^2\sigma_a^2 + w_b^2\sigma_b^2 + 2(w_a\sigma_a)(w_b\sigma_b)$$
$$= (w_a\sigma_a + w_b\sigma_b)^2$$

Taking the square root on both sides of this perfect square, we obtain:

$$\sigma_P = w_a\sigma_a + w_b\sigma_b \qquad (11.17)$$

When the correlation coefficient equals 1, the risk of the portfolio depends only on the risk of the individual assets and on the proportion of each one. For the portfolio of A and B, assuming perfect positive correlation, the standard deviation is:

$$\sigma_P = 0.4 \times 0.08 + 0.6 \times 0.22 = 0.164$$

☞ For a two-asset portfolio with a correlation coefficient equal to $+1$, its standard deviation is a weighted average of the standard deviations of the two assets.

Other weights would give portfolios of different risk levels. In fact, if we construct different portfolios of A and B by choosing different weights, we can find the locus of all possible portfolios of A and B in risk/return space.

Figure 11.7 shows the position of A and B in risk/return space. It also shows portfolio P made up of 40 percent A and 60 percent B. Notice that when the correlation between A and B is $\rho = 1$, all possible portfolios lie on the straight line between A and B.

---

[12] Recall from your high school algebra that $(a + b)^2 = a^2 + b^2 + 2ab$.

Correlation $= -1$ The second special case arises when the correlation coefficient between the two assets equals -1. In this case, the last term in Equation 11.16 becomes $-2w_a w_b \sigma_a \sigma_b$. Once again, the expression for the variance is a perfect square:

$$\sigma_P^2 = w_a^2 \sigma_a^2 + w_b^2 \sigma_b^2 - 2(w_a \sigma_a)(w_b \sigma_b)$$
$$= (w_a \sigma_a - w_b \sigma_b)^2$$

Taking the square root on both sides of this expression gives:

$$\sigma_P = w_a \sigma_a - w_b \sigma_b \qquad (11.18)$$

For our portfolio of A and B, the standard deviation is:

$$\sigma_P = 0.4 \times 0.08 - 0.6 \times 0.22 = 0.10$$

☞ If the returns of two assets are perfectly negatively correlated, it is possible to form a portfolio with 0 standard deviation by choosing the appropriate portfolio weights.

Although the derivation of the two special cases considered thus far is very similar, the risk of the portfolios can be quite different. The most striking difference is that when two assets are perfectly negatively correlated we can form a risk-free portfolio. This is because the two terms on the right side of Equation 11.18 tend to cancel each other. By making an appropriate choice of the proportions of each asset in the portfolio, they will cancel completely. Note that this result is impossible when the assets are perfectly positively correlated.

To find the proportions of each asset that lead to a risk-free portfolio, we can see from Equation 11.14 that $w_b = 1 - w_a$. Using this expression in Equation 11.18 and solving for w_a we get:

$$w_a = \frac{\sigma_b}{\sigma_a + \sigma_b} \qquad (11.19)$$

Similarly, the proportion of asset B required for a risk-free portfolio is:

$$w_b = \frac{\sigma_a}{\sigma_a + \sigma_b} \qquad (11.20)$$

In our example, the proportion of asset A required to form a risk-free portfolio is:

$$w_a = \frac{0.22}{0.08 + 0.22} = 0.73$$

Since we require 73 percent of the investment in asset A, the remaining 27 percent should be allocated to asset B. These are the only weights that result in a risk-free portfolio of assets A and B.[13]

---

[13] We can check these proportions by calculating the standard deviation of the portfolio. The calculation is: $\sigma_p = 0.73 \times 0.08 - 0.27 \times 0.22 = -0.001$. The small discrepancy from 0 is due to rounding error when computing the portfolio weights.

FIGURE 11.8   Possible Risk/Return Combinations of A and B When $\rho = -1$

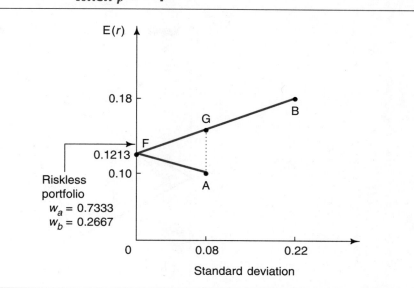

Figure 11.8 shows the possible portfolio combinations we can construct from A and B when $\rho = -1$. The line from B to the vertical axis and from there to A defines the risk/return possibilities, which include a risk-free portfolio, F. Figure 11.8 also illustrates the idea of dominance introduced earlier. By combining A and B in the correct amounts, we can form a portfolio at point G on the line between B and F. Portfolio G dominates asset A because G has the same level of risk but offers greater expected return. In fact, some portfolio on the line from F to B will dominate any portfolio on the line from A to F. Because A is dominated, no investor should hold A alone.

Correlation Between -1 and $+1$ Thus far we have considered two extreme cases, $\rho = +1$ and $\rho = -1$. Because the correlation coefficient must lie within this range, the extremes define the entire realm of risk/return possibilities we can form using securities A and B. However, for most security pairs the correlation of returns between them lies at neither extreme.

☞ In general, the lower the correlation between assets, the greater the risk reduction potential when those assets form a portfolio.

Most security pairs are positively correlated. Figure 11.9 shows the portfolio possibilities between A and B for a correlation of 0.7. This value is typical of the correlations found in the marketplace. The line from B to A indicates the possible portfolios with perfect positive correlation, and the broken line from B to F to A indicates the possibilities with perfect negative correlation.

FIGURE 11.9   Possible Risk/Return Combinations of A and B When $\rho = 0.7$

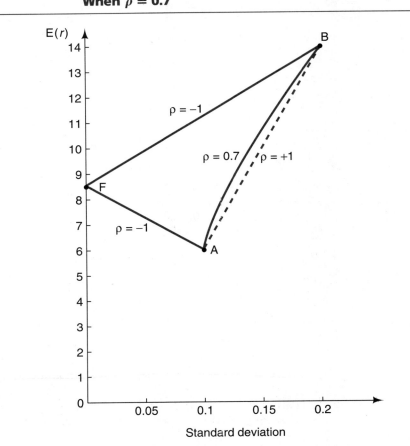

MULTIPLE-ASSET PORTFOLIOS

All of the basic ideas introduced in the context of two-asset portfolios hold when we allow investors to construct portfolios of many assets. The formulas for the expected return and risk of a portfolio with many assets are essentially the same, only somewhat lengthier. In general, the expected return for an n-asset risky portfolio is:

$$E(r_p) = \sum_{i=1}^{n} w_i\, E(r_i) \tag{11.21}$$

FINANCE

TODAY

Tough Times? Yippee!

During periods of economic distress, investors invariably clamor for recession-proof plays. Jack Laporte, president of the T. Rowe Price Horizon Fund, believes that he has found a real gem—a stock that isn't just recession-proof but actually benefits from economic slumps: Payco American.

Payco is a little-known collection agency that operates nationwide through 37 offices that are equipped with a computer-aided collection system. Not surprisingly, savvy investors such as Laporte have been scooping up Payco shares, which have climbed since early November from $9\frac{1}{2}$ to 12. He expects the stock to hit 20 in the next 12 to 18 months.

Laporte notes that as the number of unpaid bills increases, Payco's business expands. "Payco is one of the few pure plays in the recession," says Laporte. He estimates that earnings will leap to 70¢ a share in 1991 from an estimated 55¢ last year and 41¢ in 1989. Revenues are also expected to soar—to $120 million to $125 million in 1991 from an estimated $107 million in 1990 and $95.7 million in 1989. Payco has "extraordinarily strong cash flow," says Laporte, which he estimates will grow to $2 a share in 1991 from $1.50 in 1990.

Because the company's share of the debt-collection business is on the rise, Laporte believes that Payco should be attractive to one of the big financial companies and may soon become a takeover target.

Source: Gene G. Marcial, "Tough Times? Yippee!" *Business Week*, January 14, 1991, p. 4.

and the variance of an n-asset portfolio is given by:

$$\sigma_P^2 = \sum_{i=1}^{n} \sum_{j=1}^{n} w_i w_j \, \text{cov}(i, j) \tag{11.22}$$

Although the expression for the variance of a multiple-asset portfolio seems menacing, a simple way to make it operational uses the so-called **covariance matrix method.** It consists of forming an $n \times n$ matrix containing a total of n^2 cells. Each cell is filled using the same simple general expression. Once the matrix is full, we compute the variance of the portfolio by simply adding the values of all the cells.

To illustrate, consider the two-asset portfolio. From Equation 11.15, we know that the formula for its variance is:

$$\sigma_P^2 = w_a^2 \sigma_a^2 + w_b^2 \sigma_b^2 + 2 w_a w_b \, \text{cov}(r_a, r_b)$$

We can express the right-hand side of this expression in a different way by using the covariance matrix method. The key is to realize that the last term of this formula is really the sum of two equal terms. This means that we can

covariance matrix method
a general method for finding the variance of any n-asset portfolio

☞ A portfolio, like a single asset, can be located in risk/expected return space and can be treated as a single asset for constructing more complicated portfolios.

think of the variance formula as having four terms. These can be arranged in a 2×2 matrix, as follows:

	1	**2**
1	$(w_a \sigma_a)^2$	$w_a w_b \, \text{cov}(a, b)$
2	$w_b w_a \, \text{cov}(b, a)$	$(w_b \sigma_b)^2$

Each cell in the covariance matrix may be denoted by $c(i, j)$, where the first index (i) always indicates the row and the second index (j) indicates the column in the matrix. In this two-asset example we have $c(2, 1) = w_b w_a \, \text{cov}(b, a)$ and $c(1, 2) = w_a w_b \, \text{cov}(a, b)$. Since we know from Equation 11.11 that $\text{cov}(a, b) = \text{cov}(b, a)$, it follows that $c(2, 1) = c(1, 2)$. Whenever $c(i, j) = c(j, i)$, a matrix is said to be symmetric. A very useful implication is that with a symmetric matrix, we can avoid computing nearly half the matrix cells. Fortunately, all covariance matrices are symmetric.

In the general case of an n-asset portfolio, each cell of the covariance matrix can be filled using the following simple formula:

$$c(i, j) = w_i w_j \, \text{cov}(i, j) \qquad (11.23)$$

It is important to note that Equation 11.23 is also valid for the cells along the main diagonal, since the covariance of any asset with itself is equal to the variance of that asset, as noted in Equation 11.10. For example, in the two-asset case we can fill cell $c(1, 1)$ using the general formula in Equation 11.23, as follows:

$$c(1, 1) = w_1 w_1 \, \text{cov}(1, 1) = (w_1 \sigma_1)^2$$

A similar computation gives $c(2, 2) = (w_2 \sigma_2)^2$.

The Dramatic Effects of Diversification

☞ Diversification can reduce investment risk dramatically.

The full power of the covariance matrix method is unleashed when we analyze the effects of diversification on the variance or standard deviation of a portfolio, as the number of assets in the portfolio increases. As a first example, consider the variance of a portfolio of n identical and independent assets. Equation 11.7 stated without proof that if the variance of each individual asset is σ_1^2, and the same amount is invested in each asset, so that $w_i = 1/n$ for each asset i, then the variance of that portfolio is:

$$\sigma_n^2 = \frac{\sigma_1^2}{n}$$

We will now use the covariance matrix method to give a simple proof of this formula. Since there are n assets, we must fill an $n \times n$ matrix. Because the

FINANCE TODAY

A Crash Course in Portfolio Analysis

West Texas State University seems to have shot itself in the foot doing business with its benefactor, the erstwhile corporate raider T. Boone Pickens. Beginning in 1987 Pickens and his company, Mesa Limited Partnership, made a series of donations to the Amarillo-area school eventually totaling $500,000. For that and other gifts, the grateful folks at WTSU dubbed their business school the T. Boone Pickens College of Business.

Turns out that university regents promptly invested the entire $500,000 back into Mesa. Pickens was then on the school's Board of Regents. Texas state auditors recently criticized the school for not disclosing what the auditors called a "related-party transaction." The vice chairman of the regent said the board bought into Mesa because it was a good income producer and in hopes of encouraging further donations from Pickens. But when WTSU finally bailed out of Mesa, the school had a capital loss of $217,000. Even counting in Mesa's once-hefty dividends, the school lost $42,000 of the half-million-dollar gift. And that doesn't include what it could have made by simply sticking the money into T-bills.

The vice chairman of WTSU says Boone never solicited the Mesa investment, and that Pickens "did more for the school than anyone in its history." One thing he apparently did not do was encourage the regents to take a course on portfolio diversification at the Pickens school.

Source: "Thanks, Boone," *Forbes*, November 26, 1990.

assets are independent, $\text{cov}(i, j) = 0$ for $i \neq j$. Also, since the covariance of an asset with itself is the variance of that asset, we have $\text{cov}(i, i) = \sigma_1^2$ for $i = 1, 2, \ldots, n$. This means that the matrix for n identical independent assets will look as follows:

	1	**2**	**3**	$\cdots$	$n-1$	n
1	$(\sigma_1/n)^2$	0	0	$\cdots$	0	0
2	0	$(\sigma_1/n)^2$	0	$\cdots$	0	0
3	0	0	$(\sigma_1/n)^2$	$\cdots$	0	0
$\cdots$	$\cdots$	$\cdots$	$\cdots$	$\cdots$	$\cdots$	$\cdots$
$n-1$	0	0	0	$\cdots$	$(\sigma_1/n)^2$	0
n	0	0	0	$\cdots$	0	$(\sigma_1/n)^2$

**FIGURE 11.10   The Effect of Diversification for
Independent Assets**

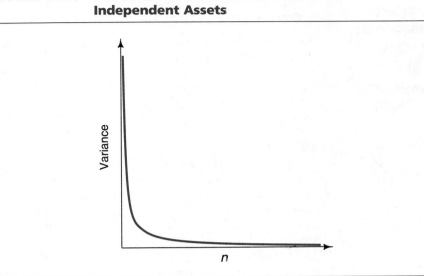

We know that the variance of the portfolio is the sum of all the cell entries in the matrix. Since there are only n equal non-0 entries, all of them along the main diagonal, the variance is equal to:

$$\sigma_n^2 = n \times \left(\frac{\sigma_1}{n}\right)^2 = \frac{\sigma_1^2}{n}$$

This equation, which is the square of Equation 11.7, shows that as the number of identical independent assets in the portfolio increases, the risk of the portfolio decreases. This is illustrated in Figure 11.10. For a large number of independent assets, the portfolio variance eventually becomes negligible. For example, according to Equation 11.7, spreading the investment among 100 identical and independent assets will reduce the variance of the portfolio to only 1 percent of the variance of each asset.

As a second application of the covariance matrix method, consider another portfolio of n stocks. As in the previous example, all stocks have the same variance, σ_1^2, and the same weight, $w_i = 1/n$. In this portfolio, all pairs of distinct assets are positively correlated, with the same correlation coefficient, ρ, for all possible pairs. We are interested in computing the effect that the number of assets, n, has on the portfolio variance. In particular, is it possible to reduce the portfolio risk to a negligible amount by incorporating more and more stocks in the portfolio? To answer this question, we construct the covariance matrix.

Assessing Country Risk

The table below ranks the highest- and lowest-risk countries, given the economic and political fallout from the Gulf crisis. Compare these scores to the rankings for the same countries in 1989, before Iraq's invasion of Kuwait on August 2, 1990.

For investors and companies seeking to invest abroad, evaluating country risk is clearly essential. Although politically unstable countries typically offer attractive interest rates, this correlation does not necessarily guarantee a flood of funds to the high-yield (but also high-risk) country. The real question is: Is the high yield enough to compensate for the additional risk that would be taken?

Country Risk Rankings, 1989–1990
(before and during the Gulf crisis)

Rank		Country	Rating (0–100)		
1990	1989		1990 (during)	1990 (before)	1989
1	3	West Germany	92.1	94.1	93.0
2	1	Japan	91.9	93.4	95.0
3	N.A.	Luxembourg	91.1	91.5	N.A.
4	10	Austria	89.9	90.7	88.0
4	8	Netherlands	89.9	90.1	89.0
4	6	France	89.9	91.1	90.0
7	1	Switzerland	87.6	88.1	95.0
8	8	Sweden	87.4	88.4	89.0
9	10	Finland	86.2	86.5	88.0
10	6	Canada	85.8	86.3	90.0
11	4	USA	85.7	88.4	92.0
124	120	Lebanon	19.6	19.6	17.0
125	109	Guyana	19.4	19.6	25.0
125	109	Uganda	19.4	19.6	25.0
127	109	Ethiopia	19.3	19.5	25.0
128	N.A.	Namibia	18.9	18.9	N.A.
129	101	Iraq	18.4	22.3	28.0
130	117	Liberia	17.3	17.3	21.0
131	N.A.	Nicaragua	14.5	14.5	N.A.
131	119	Sudan	14.5	17.3	18.0
133	108	Mozambique	13.6	13.6	26.0

Source: Hania Forham, "Country Risk and the Gulf Crisis," *Euromoney*, September 1990, pp. 87–88.

Since all pairs of distinct assets have the same correlation, ρ, each off-diagonal cell will have a value of:

$$c(i, j) = \left(\frac{1}{n}\right)\left(\frac{1}{n}\right)\text{cov}(i, j) = \left(\frac{\sigma_1}{n}\right)^2 \rho$$

Similarly, since the correlation coefficient between an asset and itself is always $\rho = 1$, each entry in the diagonal cells is equal to $c(i, i) = (\sigma_1/n)^2$. With this information, we can fill all the cells in the covariance matrix, which looks as follows:

	1	2	3	$\cdots$	$n-1$	n
1	$(\sigma_1/n)^2$	$(\sigma_1/n)^2\rho$	$(\sigma_1/n)^2\rho$	$\cdots$	$(\sigma_1/n)^2\rho$	$(\sigma_1/n)^2\rho$
2	$(\sigma_1/n)^2\rho$	$(\sigma_1/n)^2$	$(\sigma_1/n)^2\rho$	$\cdots$	$(\sigma_1/n)^2\rho$	$(\sigma_1/n)^2\rho$
3	$(\sigma_1/n)^2\rho$	$(\sigma_1/n)^2\rho$	$(\sigma_1/n)^2$	$\cdots$	$(\sigma_1/n)^2\rho$	$(\sigma_1/n)^2\rho$
$\cdots$	$\cdots$	$\cdots$	$\cdots$	$\cdots$	$\cdots$	$\cdots$
$n-1$	$(\sigma_1/n)^2\rho$	$(\sigma_1/n)^2\rho$	$(\sigma_1/n)^2\rho$	$\cdots$	$(\sigma_1/n)^2$	$(\sigma_1/n)^2\rho$
n	$(\sigma_1/n)^2\rho$	$(\sigma_1/n)^2\rho$	$(\sigma_1/n)^2\rho$	$\cdots$	$(\sigma_1/n)^2\rho$	$(\sigma_1/n)^2$

It remains to add all the entries to get the portfolio variance. We can simplify the summation by noting that there are two distinct types of terms. There are n equal diagonal terms, and $(n^2 - n)$ equal off-diagonal terms, so the variance of a portfolio of n correlated assets is:

$$\sigma_n^2 = n \times \left(\frac{\sigma_1}{n}\right)^2 + (n^2 - n) \times \left(\frac{\sigma_1}{n}\right)^2 \times \rho$$

$$= \frac{\sigma_1^2}{n}(1 - \rho) + \sigma_1^2\rho \tag{11.24}$$

Equation 11.24 demonstrates the important result that with n identical correlated assets it is not possible to eliminate risk completely, except in the special case of two assets with perfect negative correlation ($\rho = -1$).[14] Since the second term of Equation 11.24 is not affected by the number of assets in the portfolio, the minimum possible variance of the portfolio is $\sigma_1^2\rho$. This shows that in practical investment situations where pairs of assets are positively correlated, there is a limit to diversification. No matter how hard we try, we

[14] This case was already considered as one of the extreme cases for two-asset portfolios.

FIGURE 11.11   The Effect of Diversification for Assets with Pairwise Correlation of $\rho = 0.7$

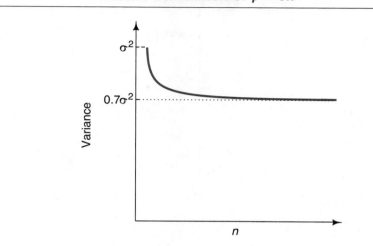

will be unable to eliminate risk completely. Figure 11.11 graphs the variance for a portfolio of n stocks, where each pair of stocks has a correlation coefficient of 0.7. In this example, an investor can avoid at most 30 percent of the risk of a single stock.

The Efficient Set and the Efficient Frontier

In a market with many securities, the final result of portfolio building is likely to look like Figure 11.12 in risk/return space. The points on the interior of the curve represent individual assets, while the curve running from L to H represents the ultimate portfolios that the investor can create from the many individual assets available in the marketplace. Certain portfolios on the curve from L to H are dominated, such as those on the curve from L to MR. However, all of the portfolios which lie on the line from H to MR are not dominated. The **efficient set** is the set of all assets and portfolios that are not dominated. The **efficient frontier** is the graphical representation of the the elements of the efficient set. In Figure 11.12, the efficient frontier is line from H to MR.

Since all investors desire higher expected returns and wish to avoid risk, they will invest in portfolios that belong to the efficient set. This desire is reasonable, because any other portfolio will be dominated by one on the efficient frontier.

efficient set
the set of all portfolios and securities that are not dominated by any other

efficient frontier
the graph in expected return/risk space of all nondominated securities and portfolios

FIGURE 11.12   The Efficient Frontier with Many Assets

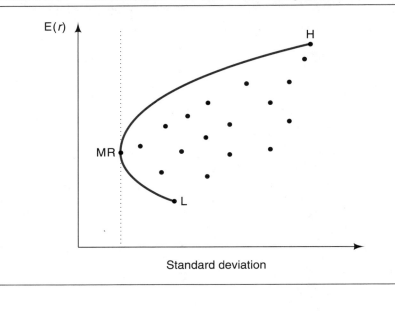

INVESTORS' PREFERENCES

Even though we have assumed that investors prefer higher expected returns and seek lower risk, we still do not know which portfolio a given investor will prefer. We do know that it will be one of the portfolios on the efficient frontier, such as that depicted in Figure 11.12. However, a multitude of portfolios are available to choose from.

It is not possible to say which of the many risky portfolios on the efficient frontier an investor will prefer because each investor may have personal preferences regarding risk and return. For example, it is possible to imagine an aggressive investor seeking additional expected return and willing to bear considerable risk to get it. Another may be determined to avoid risk to a greater extent, and might be willing to forgo additional expected return to escape risk. To see the effect of different preferences and life situations, contrast a 70-year-old retiree and a 35-year-old yuppie. Investment income is probably a very important component in the retiree's consumption income. Accordingly, the investment strategy cannot be too risky. For the yuppie, who has a high yuppie income, a riskier strategy might be preferred. The yuppie can afford the temporary setbacks that might come from a high-risk investment strategy, thanks to an income from employment that is large enough to meet basic needs.

These differences in investor preferences can be illustrated graphically in the return/risk space of Figure 11.13 for two hypothetical investors. Con-

FIGURE 11.13   Utility Curves for Conservative and Aggressive Investors

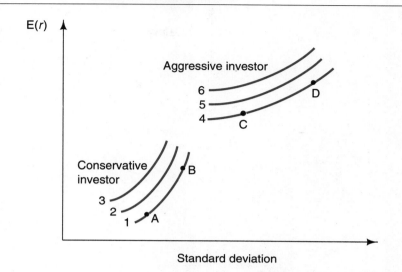

sider first the set of curves for the conservative investor. They are constructed so that each individual line represents different combinations of expected return and risk that are equally attractive. In curve 1, for example, the conservative investor would be indifferent between positions A and B; A offers less expected return than B, but it also involves less risk. This is called an **indifference curve** because the investor is indifferent among all of the different opportunities that lie on it. The aggressive investor, for example, would be indifferent between positions C and D.

For each investor, a set of curves is constructed in a way that expresses different levels of satisfaction, or utility. The conservative investor would find all the points on curve 2 equally attractive, but would prefer to be at any point on curve 2 than to be at any point on curve 1. In terms of the graph, this individual would prefer to be on the highest obtainable curve, and the same is true for the aggressive investor.

It may not be possible, however, for these investors to reach the higher curves. The attainment of any position on any of the indifference curves depends on the investment opportunities that are available in the marketplace. Given a set of preferences that is implied by the utility curves, and given information about the investment opportunities that the investors have available to them, it is then possible to determine which investment opportunities will actually be chosen.

Figure 11.14 puts together the preferences of the conservative and aggressive investors from Figure 11.13 and the investment opportunities from

indifference curve
a line connecting points, usually in expected return/risk space, that are equally preferred by an investor

☞ Investors differ in the degree of risk aversion, and this difference influences the portfolios that they choose.

FIGURE 11.14 Investment Preferences and Attitudes Toward Risk

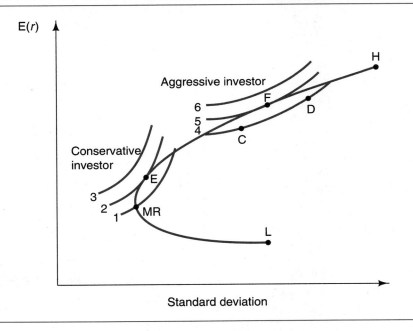

Figure 11.12. The efficient set, shown on the curve from H to MR, indicates the best opportunities available to investors. The conservative investor may achieve a point on indifference curve 2 by holding the portfolio E. The aggressive investor will hold portfolio F to obtain a position on indifference curve 5. An investor will do best by holding a portfolio on the efficient frontier that is just tangent to an indifference curve.

Both the conservative and aggressive investors choose portfolios that lie on the efficient frontier, but have different risk and return characteristics. These choices are consistent with their attitudes toward risk and return. The fact that the slope on the conservative investor's indifference curves is steeper reflects a greater degree of conservatism. The more nearly horizontal slope of the aggressive investor's indifference curves indicates a greater willingness to accept risk. These different attitudes are shown in Figure 11.15.

For these two investors, consider the additional expected return represented by X and X', respectively, that they hope to obtain from taking on an additional risk Y. The aggressive investor is willing to accept a lower incremental amount of expected return than the conservative investor, for the same amount of increase in risk, Y. Because $X > X'$, the aggressive investor

FIGURE 11.15   Indifference Curves and the Variety of Attitudes Toward Risk

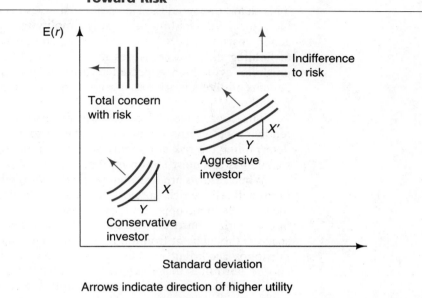

Standard deviation

Arrows indicate direction of higher utility

must be relatively less risk averse, whereas the conservative investor is relatively more risk averse.

Figure 11.15 also shows two extreme positions. The horizontal indifference curves reflect a total indifference to risk. An investor with such indifference curves is said to be risk neutral, because a given level of expected return is the only factor that determines the utility that the investor receives. The horizontal indifference curves indicate that the risk-neutral investor obtains the same level of satisfaction as long as the expected return does not change, even if faced with wildly different risk levels.

The vertical indifference curves reflect a total concern with risk. In this case, the level of expected return does not affect the utility received by the investor. Rather, the total concern is with risk. The horizontal and vertical indifference curves are clearly extremes, and are not intended to represent actual investors in the real world. Both show that there is no concern whatsoever with a risk/return trade-off. Instead, the total concern is with expected return for the risk-neutral investor, and with risk for the risk-abhorrent investor. More realistic indifference curves are those shown for the conservative and aggressive investors. As long as the lines are not vertical or horizontal, there is some trade-off between risk and return.

SUMMARY

This chapter adopted the viewpoint that investors are concerned with achieving return and avoiding risk. Using simplifying assumptions, such as 0 transaction costs, free access to information, and no taxes, it analyzed the effects of holding different securities in portfolios. Assuming that investors desire portfolios with high expected return and low risk, we saw the important benefits of diversification that arise from combining individual securities into portfolios.

The covariance and correlation of returns, both of which measure the tendency of returns on two investments to move together, are crucial in determining the risk of the portfolio. In fact, the tendency of returns to move together is the most important determinant of portfolio risk.

When returns are less than perfectly positively correlated, forming portfolios will reduce risk, but not completely. In a market with many risky assets, many investment opportunities will not be dominated. The nondominated opportunities constitute the efficient set and may be graphed in risk/return space as the efficient frontier. Individual investors may choose different risky portfolios according to their attitudes toward risk. Risk-tolerant investors choose portfolios that offer high expected returns and high risk, and conservative investors choose portfolios with lower expected returns and lower risks.

QUESTIONS

1. In this book, we generally assume that investors dislike risk. If a particular investor liked both risk and high expected returns, what kinds of opportunities would that person find in the financial marketplace?
2. In terms of risk and return, what are the goals of investing?
3. The standard deviation and variance consider outcomes that are both above and below the mean return. Someone might argue that this makes them poor measures of investment risk, because the only risk of concern to an investor is the chance that the result might be below the mean. How could you respond to this criticism?
4. Why do investors diversify?
5. Which is important to the investor's decision as we have defined it, return or expected return?
6. Security A has an expected return of 14 percent and security B has an expected return of 12 percent. Is this enough information to determine whether A dominates B?
7. If security A has an expected return of 14 percent and a standard deviation of returns of 20 percent, and security B has an expected return of 12 percent and a standard deviation of returns of 19 percent, does A dominate B? Why or why not?

8. Your broker tells you that it is important to diversify because doing so will increase your expected returns, even if you diversify by randomly selecting stocks. What do you think?

9. Your broker tells you that the standard deviation of returns for a portfolio depends only on the standard deviations of the individual securities and the amount of funds invested in each. What should be your response? Why?

10. Why was the correlation coefficient invented, given that the covariance already measures the connection between two variables?

11. What is the relationship between the covariance of returns and the correlation of returns?

12. You were always very proud of your one-stock portfolio, but after reading this chapter, you are somewhat embarrassed and hastily add a second stock. Your broker recommends you choose yet another stock because the one you added has a high covariance with the original stock. However, your broker does not know the standard deviation of either stock's returns. What should you do? Why?

13. Securities C and D have returns with a correlation coefficient of -0.9. Can you combine them to form a risk-free portfolio?

14. Your new broker is helping you form a new portfolio and recommends that you select from 30 stocks that, according to the research department, lie on the efficient frontier. What should you do? Why?

15. Your second new broker says that no individual stock could ever lie on the efficient frontier. Is this correct? Why or why not?

16. In the case of a portfolio of many risky assets, why does the efficient frontier not go below the minimum risk investment opportunity?

17. Why is the covariance between assets A and B the same as the covariance between assets B and A?

18. Why is the covariance a more general concept than the variance?

19. Can the variance of a random variable be computed without knowledge of the expected value of that random variable?

20. Is it possible to have three or more assets with all possible pairs of assets having negative correlation? Explain.

PROBLEMS

1. Over three years an investor earns returns of 8 percent, 11 percent, and 15 percent. What is the arithmetic mean for these annual returns over the three-year period?

2. An investor undertakes a series of one-year investments starting with $700. After the first year the investment is worth $784; after two years it is worth $878.10; after three years it is worth $983.40; finally, after four years it is worth $1,101.50. Calculate the arithmetic mean yearly rate of return.

3. For a five-year period, a stock portfolio had the following rates of return: −15 percent, 23 percent, 11 percent, −3 percent, and 37 percent. What was the arithmetic mean rate of return and the variance of the returns?

4. Mr. Diversey held a portfolio with three stocks. He invested 20 percent of his funds in stock A, 45 percent in stock B, and 35 percent in stock C. The rates of return were: for A, 13 percent; for B, −5 percent; and for C, 9 percent. What was the rate of return for the entire portfolio?

5. Security X has an expected return of 0.25 and a standard deviation of returns of 0.20. Security Y has an expected return of 0.18 and a standard deviation of returns of 0.18. Plot the two securities in risk/return space. Does one dominate the other?

6. Using the data of the previous problem, what is the expected return of a portfolio with 30 percent invested in security X and 70 percent invested in security Y?

7. Over three years, security Q had returns of 10 percent, 14 percent, and −3 percent. For the same three years, security R had returns of 12 percent, 10 percent, and 5 percent. What is the variance and standard deviation of returns for these two securities? What is the covariance of returns between them? What is the correlation of returns?

8. Consider a portfolio with 40 percent of the funds invested in security Q from the preceding question, and with 60 percent invested in security R. What is the variance of returns for this two-asset portfolio?

9. Security V has expected returns of 13 percent and a standard deviation of 20 percent, and security W has expected returns of 5 percent and a standard deviation of 13 percent. If the two securities are perfectly negatively correlated, what proportion of your money would you put in each to have a 0 risk portfolio? What would be the expected return of the portfolio?

10. Starting with the compact definition of the variance of a random variable, show that the variance of a portfolio is given by Equation 11.15.

11. Show that the correlation coefficient of an asset with itself is always 1.

12. You combine assets A and B and the resulting portfolio is risk free. The variance of asset B is four times larger than the variance of asset A. Also, the expected returns of A and B are 10 percent and 18 percent, respectively. Find the expected return on the portfolio.

13. You are considering investing $6 in two identical and independent projects with a probability p of a favorable outcome. Only one other outcome—unfavorable—is possible. If you invest all your money in one of the projects and the outcome is favorable, the payoff is $10; and if it is unfavorable, the payoff is −$6. On average, you expect the payoff from each project to be 0. What is the probability of a favorable outcome?

14. You combine two risky assets in equal proportions. If both assets have the same variance and the resulting portfolio has a variance equal to

25 percent of the variance of each one, what is the correlation between the assets?

15. Assets A, B, and C form a portfolio. The proportions are 25 percent, 25 percent, and 50 percent, respectively. The correlation is $\rho = 0.5$ for the three possible pairs of assets. The variances are equal to 100 for all three assets. Find the standard deviation of this portfolio.

16. Show that if all assets in a portfolio are perfectly positively correlated, and if they all have the same variance and the same weight, then diversification has no benefit. In other words, the variance of the entire portfolio is equal to the variance of the individual assets.

chapter 12

The Market Price of Risk

This chapter shows how the presence of the risk-free asset greatly increases the investor's opportunities and how it makes virtually all investors better off than they would be in a market with only risky assets. It also shows how the introduction of the risk-free asset gives rise to a market standard against which other investment opportunities can be compared. We examine the **separation theorem,** which states that all investors should hold the same portfolio of risky assets, no matter how risk tolerant or averse they may be. This leads to an exposition of the capital asset pricing model (CAPM), a general model that expresses the equilibrium rate of expected return for an asset as a function of its inherent risk characteristics.

Although the assumptions employed in this chapter to construct the model simplify reality, they allow us to improve our understanding of the ways in which securities are priced. Also, as we will see in the next chapter, security prices actually behave in a way that is highly consistent with the picture presented in our simplified model.

separation theorem
the theorem that asserts that the choice of the portfolio of risky assets is separable from the choice of the risk level to be borne

THE RISK-FREE ASSET

By definition, the risk-free asset has no default risk. Because we consider a one-period model, the risk-free asset is certain to pay its expected return. As we discussed in Chapter 11, the expected return of a two-asset portfolio is given by:

$$E(r_P) = w_a E(r_a) + w_b E(r_b) \qquad (12.1)$$

where w_i = percentage of funds committed to asset $i = a, b$
$E(r_i)$ = the expected return on asset i, for $i = a, b, P$

☞ For the risk-free asset, both its variance of returns and its covariance or correlation of returns with any other asset are 0.

We denote the return of the risk-free asset as r_f. The expected return of a portfolio composed of the risk-free asset and the risky asset j is just the weighted average of the two expected returns. As before, the weights are the percentage of funds committed to the two assets. Since the risk-free asset has no default risk, we have $E(r_f) = r_f$ and the expected return for the portfolio is:

$$E(r_P) = w_f r_f + w_j E(r_j) \qquad (12.2)$$

Similarly, the equation for the variance of a two-asset portfolio given in Chapter 11 is applicable, so we have:

$$\sigma_P^2 = w_f^2 \sigma_f^2 + w_j^2 \sigma_j^2 + 2 w_f w_j \operatorname{cov}(f, j) \qquad (12.3)$$

For the risk-free asset, $\sigma_f^2 = 0$ and $\operatorname{cov}(f, j) = 0$. These facts simplify the evaluation of Equation 12.3, since its first and third terms are 0. Consequently, the variance of a two-asset portfolio that includes the risk-free asset will be:

$$\sigma_P^2 = w_j^2 \sigma_j^2 \qquad (12.4)$$

From this, the standard deviation of the portfolio is:

$$\sigma_P = w_j \sigma_j \qquad (12.5)$$

☞ The standard deviation of a two-asset portfolio that includes a risk-free asset depends only on the standard deviation of the risky asset and the proportion of funds invested in the asset.

To illustrate these principles, consider a portfolio made up of the risk-free asset f and a risky portfolio j. The table below gives the relevant data for f and j:

	f	j
E(r)	0.10	0.17
σ	0.00	0.21
w	0.45	0.55
cov(f, j)	0.00	

In this case, the expected return for the portfolio is found using Equation 12.2:

$$E(r_P) = 0.45 \times 0.10 + 0.55 \times 0.17 = 0.1385$$

☞ In risk/expected return space, portfolios composed of the risk-free asset and a risky asset will always lie on a straight line running between the two assets.

and the standard deviation of the portfolio is found from Equation 12.5:

$$\sigma_P = 0.55 \times 0.21 = 0.1155$$

Figure 12.1 shows the risk-free asset, f, the risky portfolio, j, and the combined portfolio, P, in risk/return space. We can achieve any point on the line between f and j by constructing a portfolio containing only those assets. Each point along the line corresponds to a different weight combination.

CHOOSING THE BEST RISKY PORTFOLIO

In the example illustrated by Figure 12.1, we combined risky portfolio j with the risk-free asset f to form portfolio P. However, investors may prefer to combine other risky portfolios with f. In fact, this section shows that rational

FIGURE 12.1   Combining the Risk-Free Asset *f* with Risky Portfolio *j*

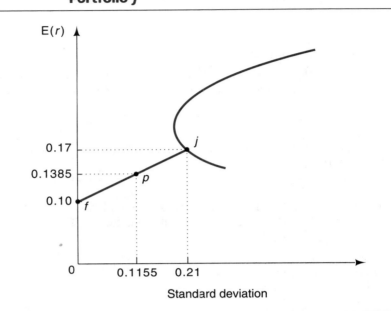

investors will all choose the same particular risky portfolio to combine with the risk-free asset.

No matter what an investor's risk preferences might be, investing in risky portfolio *j* is never optimal. To see why, consider Figure 12.2, which shows assets *f, j,* and another risky portfolio, *k.* Just as we could combine *f* and *j* to achieve portfolios on the line *f j,* we can combine *f* and *k* to achieve portfolios on the line *f k.* However, every portfolio on the line *f j* is dominated by some portfolio on the line *f k.* Consequently, every investor would prefer to hold *k* rather than *j.*

From this comparison, it is clear that we should move up the curve beyond *k* to find even better risky portfolios. This process ceases when the line from *f* to the risky portfolio is just tangent to the efficient frontier. Figure 12.3 shows this portfolio of risky assets, *M.*

☞ The introduction of the risk-free asset changes the efficient frontier, improving the opportunities available to investors.

Notice that the efficient frontier has been changed by the introduction of the risk-free asset. The new efficient frontier runs from *f* to *M* to *Z.* Any portfolio not lying on the line *f MZ* will be dominated. Thus, the introduction of the risk-free asset means that all of those risky portfolios lying on the curve to the left of *M* are not on the efficient frontier and no investor will hold any risky portfolio on that portion of the curve, because a better portfolio is available by combining *f* and *M.*

FIGURE 12.2 Combining the Risk-Free Asset _f_ with Risky Portfolio _j_ and with Risky Portfolio _k_

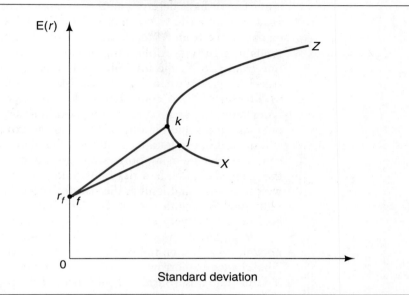

FIGURE 12.3 Combining the Risk-Free Asset _f_ with the Optimal Risky Portfolio _M_

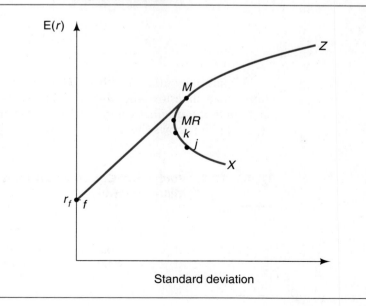

BORROWING AND LENDING

Thus far we have determined that investors seek portfolios on the line fMZ. How can we trade to create such portfolios? To construct portfolios that lie on the curve from M to Z, the investor need only invest 100 percent of all funds in a risky portfolio on that curve. To build portfolios that lie on the line from f to M, the investor must combine the risky portfolio M and the risk-free asset. We can think of the risk-free asset as a Treasury bill. Investing in Treasury bills is equivalent to lending to the government, so portfolios lying between f and M are lending portfolios since they involve some holding of stocks and some lending of funds to the government.

In addition to lending portfolios, there are also borrowing portfolios. We can construct them by borrowing funds and investing them, in addition to the original capital, in a risky portfolio. Because we assume perfect markets, we can borrow and lend at the risk-free rate, r_f. Of course, in the real world, individual investors cannot do that, but many institutional investors can borrow at rates very close to the risk-free rate.

We already know that it is efficient for the investor to hold any risky portfolio that lies on the curve from M to Z when no borrowing is available. The chance to borrow at a rate r_f improves the investor's opportunity set. To illustrate this, consider the following example, using the data given below.

	Asset	
	f	*M*
E(*r*)	0.10	0.23
σ	0.00	0.18

Assume an initial wealth of $1,000. To create a borrowing portfolio, consider an investor who borrows $750 at $r_f = 10$ percent. The borrowed funds plus the original capital of $1,000 are invested in the risky portfolio M. Table 12.1 shows the different portfolios with their expected returns and

TABLE 12.1 Portfolios Constructed from the Risk-Free Asset *f* and Risky Portfolio *M*

w_f	w_M	E(r_p)	σ_p
0.5	0.5	0.165	0.09
0.0	1.0	0.23	0.18
−0.75	1.75	0.3275	0.3150

standard deviations. We computed these expected returns and standard deviations using the formulas given above.

Assume that risky portfolio M actually earns the expected return in the period under analysis. Using the information in Table 12.1, the value of the portfolio at the end of the period will be $1,750 \times 1.23 = \$2,152.50$. At the end of the period, the investor must also repay the $750 loan plus 10 percent interest, or $825. After the risky portfolio earns the 23 percent return and the investor repays $825, $1,327.50 remains. The investor has then earned $327.50 on the original capital of $1,000. This implies a 32.75 percent annual rate of return. As this example shows, borrowing increases the expected return on the original capital, from 23 percent without borrowing to 32.75 when $750 is borrowed.

Although borrowing at r_f to invest in a risky portfolio increases the expected return, it also has the undesirable effect of increasing risk. To see how, assume the risky portfolio M earns a return one standard deviation above or below its expected return. We compute the returns on the borrowing portfolio for these two cases.

If the risky portfolio earns one standard deviation less than its expected return, it earns $0.23 - 0.18 = 0.05$, or 5 percent. Thus the borrowing portfolio will be worth $1.05 \times \$1,750 = \$1,837.50$. From this amount the investor must pay the debt of $825, leaving $1,012.50. This gives a return of only 1.25 percent on the original capital. If the return on the risky portfolio is one standard deviation above the expected return, the risky portfolio will earn $0.23 + 0.18 = 0.41$, or 41 percent. In this case, it will be worth $1.41 \times \$1,750 = \$2,467.50$ at the end of the period. From these proceeds, the investor repays $825, leaving $1,642.50. On the initial capital of $1,000, the investor earns a hefty return of 64.25 percent.

An alternative way of obtaining the same results is through the use of Equations 12.2 and 12.5, as follows:

$$E(r_P) = -0.75 \times 10\% + 1.75 \times 23\% = 32.75\%$$
$$\sigma_P = 1.75 \times 18\% = 31.5\%$$

☞ Leverage increases both the expected return and the risk of an investment.

The above discussion illustrates the general principle that the use of borrowing, or financial leverage, increases both the expected returns and the variability of returns. Figure 12.4 shows the result of borrowing funds at r_f to invest in portfolio M. In the example just considered, we found that the expected return of the leveraged portfolio was 32.75 percent and the standard deviation was 31.50 percent. Figure 12.4 shows this leveraged portfolio, S. Notice that portfolio S falls on the straight line joining f and M. In fact, all leveraged portfolios fall on that line.

Before we introduced borrowing to invest in a risky portfolio, the efficient frontier ran from f to M to Z. Borrowing changes the efficient frontier. For example, consider portfolio V, which lies on the curve between M and Z.

FIGURE 12.4 Portfolio Possibilities with Borrowing and Lending—The Capital Market Line

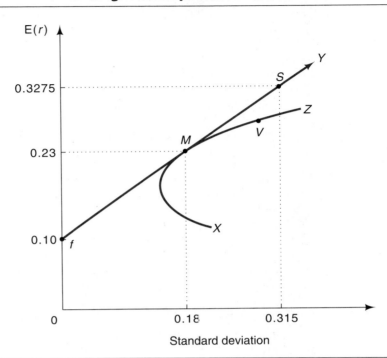

Formerly, portfolio V was in the efficient set. Now a borrowing portfolio lying between M and S dominates V.

☞ The only risky portfolio that is not dominated is M, the market portfolio.

There is only one risky portfolio that is not dominated, and that is M. Therefore, all investors will hold M as their risky portfolio, although they may differ in the proportion of funds they invest in it. Some will invest a portion of their funds in M and lend some funds at the risk-free rate. Bolder investors might borrow some funds and invest the proceeds in M along with their original capital. Others might even prefer to hold risky portfolio M in isolation. However, all investors who hold any of their funds in risky assets will put those funds exclusively in portfolio M. Investing in another risky portfolio is irrational.

☞ Investors can choose investment opportunities lying anywhere on the capital market line by allocating the correct proportion of funds to the market portfolio and to the risk-free asset.

How well does this discussion of borrowing at the risk-free rate and investing in M fit with reality? Some borrowers have very low borrowing costs that approximate the risk-free rate, but they cannot borrow an unlimited amount of funds at that rate. Also, the Federal Reserve Board limits the amount of borrowing for securities investment with its margin requirements. In practice, then, investors cannot achieve unlimited leverage. In Figure 12.4, there are practical limits to how far to the right of M the investor can go on the line fMS.

INVESTOR UTILITY AND THE RISK-FREE ASSET

As shown in Figure 12.4, the introduction of a risk-free asset creates a new range of investment options for investors. Now it is possible to select a portfolio that dominates the one an investor would have selected from just the set of risky assets. This means that all investors will be able to reach a higher utility curve than would be possible without the existence of the risk-free asset, regardless of their degree of risk aversion.

☞ If investors can invest in risky assets and the risk-free asset, almost all of them will be able to reach a higher indifference curve than would be possible through investing in risky assets alone.

Figure 12.5 repeats the investment opportunities shown in Figure 12.4, but includes the utility curves of two investors. For the one whose utility curves are numbered 1 through 4, there has been a dramatic increase in utility. With only a universe of risky assets, this investor would have chosen portfolio T on the efficient frontier of risky assets. With the risk-free asset, however, this same investor could hold portfolio U on the line fMY. This point will be preferred to portfolio T because U provides a higher utility.

A second set of utility curves is numbered 5 through 8. For this investor the preferred portfolio is M, which happens to be both on the line fMY and

FIGURE 12.5   Investor Utility Possibilities with the Introduction of the Risk-Free Asset f

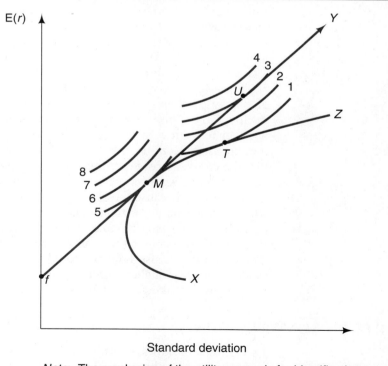

Standard deviation

Note: The numbering of the utility curves is for identification only. It does not imply any ordering.

☞ Every investor who chooses to hold some risky asset will hold portfolio *M*, the market portfolio.

on the efficient frontier for risky assets considered alone. This investor will choose portfolio *M* whether the risk-free asset exists or not, because its existence does not affect the investor's utility. For all investors, however, the introduction of the risk-free asset increases the investment choices that are available. Almost all investors will be helped by it because they will be able to find an investment combination that gives them a higher level of satisfaction, or utility, by combining the risk-free asset with a risky portfolio.

THE MARKET PORTFOLIO AND THE SEPARATION THEOREM

So far we have seen that all investors who commit any funds to risky securities will invest in portfolio *M* in Figure 12.4. Therefore, it is important to understand the characteristics of this special portfolio *M*.

market portfolio
a portfolio in which each asset available in the market is included in proportion to its market value

We argue that it is the market portfolio. The **market portfolio** includes every risky security in the marketplace, with a weight proportional to its market value. Accordingly, it is a value-weighted portfolio. For example, if the total market value of IBM's shares were $4 billion and the market value of all securities were $100 billion, then IBM would have a weight of 4 percent in the market portfolio.

We can see that portfolio *M* must be the market portfolio from reflecting on the following two facts. First, we know all investors hold *M* as the risky component of their portfolio. Second, we know that someone owns each security available in the market. There are simply no securities floating around without owners. Because all risky securities have an owner and all investors have the same risky portfolio, each investor must hold all possible risky securities. This is the same as saying that all investors hold the market portfolio.

Because all investors who hold risky assets hold portfolio *M*, the choice of a risky portfolio is separate from the choice of a particular portfolio on the line *f MY*. This is the famous separation theorem: the financing decision—whether to borrow or lend, and how much—is separate from the choice of investing in a portfolio of risky assets. To see this point in another way, note that the choice of risky portfolio *M* is separate from the decision concerning how much expected return to seek and how much risk to bear. This is clear in Figure 12.4, because the investor can attain any point along the line *f MY* while holding only portfolio *M* as the portfolio of risky assets. By holding portfolio *M* and lending at the risk-free rate, the investor can reduce the riskiness of the combined portfolio at the cost of reducing the expected return. The investor can also hold portfolio *M* and borrow money at the risk-free rate to achieve a higher expected return than the return of *M*, but only at the expense of taking additional risk.

THE CAPITAL MARKET LINE

As Figure 12.4 shows, investors can attain any point on the line *f MY*. Each one chooses a combination of the risky portfolio *M* and the risk-free asset *f*. Since they can move only along line *f MY*, that line represents the trade-off

capital market line
a line expressing the equilibrium relationship between expected return and risk for well-diversified portfolios

between risk and return available in the capital market. Consequently, it is known as the **capital market line** (CML). Because the CML slopes upward, it shows graphically that the acquisition of greater expected return requires that the investor accept more risk. The slope of the CML is the rate at which an investor can exchange expected return and risk.

From algebra, we know that the equation of a straight line is:

$$y = mx + b$$

where y = the value on the vertical axis
m = the slope of the line
x = the value on the horizontal axis, and
b = the intercept on the y axis

In Figure 12.4 line fMY intercepts the vertical axis at f, so $b = r_f$. Also, the slope of a line equals the change in vertical distance over the change in horizontal distance, or the "rise over run." In our case, the slope is found by noting that if the investor bears no risk, the return is r_f; if the investor accepts risk equal to σ_m, the expected return is r_m. Thus, if an investor increases risk from 0 to σ_m, the expected return increases from r_f to $E(r_m)$. From this information, the slope of the CML is:

$$\text{Slope of CML} = \frac{E(r_m) - r_f}{\sigma_m} \qquad (12.6)$$

Now we can express the CML as an equation. Consider any portfolio j on the CML with an expected return of $E(r_j)$ and a risk of σ_j. Using the general equation of a straight line and applying it to portfolio j, we have:

$$E(r_j) = \frac{E(r_m) - r_f}{\sigma_m} \sigma_j + r_f \qquad (12.7)$$

We often write this equation in the equivalent form:

$$E(r_j) = r_f + \frac{\sigma_j}{\sigma_m} [E(r_m) - r_f] \qquad (12.8)$$

☞ The expected return on a well-diversified portfolio depends on the risk-free rate, the risk of the portfolio relative to the risk of the market portfolio, and the market price of risk.

To apply this equation, consider a situation in which $r_f = 10\%$, $E(r_m) = 17\%$, $\sigma_m = 24\%$, and $\sigma_j = 34\%$. With these values we can calculate the expected return of portfolio j, which lies on the CML:

$$E(r_j) = 0.10 + \frac{0.34}{0.24} [0.17 - 0.10] = 0.1992$$

Note that the expected return of portfolio j (19.92%) exceeds the expected return of the market portfolio (17%) because j has higher risk.

RISK AND EXPECTED RETURN FOR INDIVIDUAL SECURITIES

☞ The CML pertains only to well-diversified portfolios.

The CML is important because it expresses the relationship between the risk and expected return of a portfolio consisting of a mix of the market portfolio and the risk-free asset. The slope of the CML reveals how much extra return investors obtain for each extra unit of risk they bear. Therefore, the slope gives the market price of risk for fully diversified portfolios. It is important to note that the CML pertains only to well-diversified portfolios, since every portfolio on the line contains the fully diversified market portfolio.

☞ For investors with the opportunity to hold portfolios, the only relevant risk of a security is the contribution it makes to the riskiness of the portfolios.

Another important relationship, the security market line (SML), expresses the expected return of an individual security as a function of its relevant risk. But what is the relevant risk for each security in the market portfolio? We know it cannot be the variance of the security, since part of that variance can be diversified away when the security is part of a portfolio. We also know all investors hold the market portfolio of risky assets. Therefore, the only relevant risk of an individual security is the risk it contributes to the overall risk of the market portfolio. It is also clear that the risk of the market portfolio arises from some aggregation of the relevant risks of its component securities. We define **beta** to be the relevant risk of individual securities.

beta
a measure of the systematic risk of a given security relative to the market as a whole

☞ Beta measures the systematic risk of an individual asset or portfolio.

Beta

In the preceding chapter we examined the behavior of multiple-asset risky portfolios. We saw that the overall riskiness of a portfolio depended on the correlation or covariance between all pairs of assets. We also introduced the covariance matrix method to facilitate the computation of the variance of any portfolio, including the variance of the market portfolio. After all, the market portfolio is nothing but a multiple-asset portfolio, albeit a very large one. The computation of its variance will reveal the contribution of each component security to its overall risk. Each security's contribution is its beta.

If there are n risky assets in the market, and w_i is the ratio of the value of asset i to the value of the market, then the variance of the market portfolio, σ_m^2, is the sum of all the entries in the following covariance matrix:

	1	2	$\cdots$	n
1	$(w_1\sigma_1)^2$	$w_1w_2\,\text{cov}(1, 2)$	$\cdots$	$w_1w_n\,\text{cov}(1, n)$
2	$w_2w_1\,\text{cov}(2, 1)$		$\cdots$	$w_2w_n\,\text{cov}(2, n)$
3	$w_3w_1\,\text{cov}(3, 1)$	$w_3w_2\,\text{cov}(3, 2)$	$\cdots$	$w_3w_n\,\text{cov}(3, n)$
$\cdots$	$\cdots$	$\cdots$	$\cdots$	$\cdots$
n	$w_nw_1\,\text{cov}(n, 1)$	$w_nw_2\,\text{cov}(n, 2)$	$\cdots$	

If we sum across each row of the matrix, and recall that $\text{cov}(i, i) = \sigma_i^2$, we obtain the following expression:

$$\begin{aligned}
\sigma_m^2 = w_1[&w_1 \, \text{cov}(1, 1) + w_2 \, \text{cov}(1, 2) + w_3 \, \text{cov}(1, 3) \\
&+ \cdots + w_n \, \text{cov}(1, n)] \\
+ w_2[&w_1 \, \text{cov}(2, 1) + w_2 \, \text{cov}(2, 2) + w_3 \, \text{cov}(2, 3) \\
&+ \cdots + w_n \, \text{cov}(2, n)] \\
+ w_3[&w_1 \, \text{cov}(3, 1) + w_2 \, \text{cov}(3, 2) + w_3 \, \text{cov}(3, 3) \\
&+ \cdots + w_n \, \text{cov}(3, n)] \\
+ \cdots& \\
+ w_n[&w_1 \, \text{cov}(n, 1) + w_2 \, \text{cov}(n, 2) + w_3 \, \text{cov}(n, 3) \\
&+ \cdots + w_n \, \text{cov}(n, n)]
\end{aligned} \tag{12.9}$$

We can simplify the terms in brackets by noting that for any random variables y, x_1, and x_2 the covariance can be expressed as:

$$\text{cov}(y, a_1 x_1 + a_2 x_2) = a_1 \, \text{cov}(y, x_1) + a_2 \, \text{cov}(y, x_2) \tag{12.10}$$

where a_1 and a_2 are arbitrary numbers. This distinctive property of the covariance can be extended to any number of random variables.

Now recall that the market portfolio is a weighted average of the individual securities, where the weight for security i is w_i. With this fact and the covariance property stated in Equation 12.10, we see that the first term in brackets in Equation 12.9 is equal to the covariance of security 1 with the market, the second term in brackets is the covariance of security 2 with the market, and so on. Thus, Equation 12.9 can be rewritten as:

$$\sigma_m^2 = w_1 \, \text{cov}(1, m) + w_2 \, \text{cov}(2, m) + \cdots + w_n \, \text{cov}(n, m) \tag{12.11}$$

Finally, we multiply and divide the right-hand side of Equation 12.11 by the variance of the market, σ_m^2, to get:

$$\sigma_m^2 = \sigma_m^2 \left[w_1 \frac{\text{cov}(1, m)}{\sigma_m^2} + w_2 \frac{\text{cov}(2, m)}{\sigma_m^2} + \cdots + w_n \frac{\text{cov}(n, m)}{\sigma_m^2} \right] \tag{12.12}$$

Equation 12.12 suggests that we define the beta of asset i as follows:[1]

$$\beta_i = \frac{\text{cov}(i, m)}{\sigma_m^2} \tag{12.13}$$

With this definition of beta, we can rewrite Equation 12.12 as:

$$\sigma_m^2 = \sigma_m^2 [w_1 \beta_1 + w_2 \beta_2 + \cdots + w_n \beta_n] \tag{12.14}$$

---

[1] It is sometimes useful to express the beta of an asset in an alternative form, based on the identity $\text{cov}(i, m) = \sigma_i \sigma_m \rho_{i,m}$:

$$\beta_i = \frac{\sigma_i}{\sigma_m} \rho_{i,m}$$

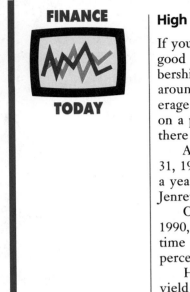

High Yield, Low Risk?

If you think that a seat on the American Stock Exchange (Amex) is as good as a load of junk, you may be overestimating its value. Buy a membership of the exchange, lease it out, and your investment return will be around 30 percent—ten percentage points higher than the yield on the average junk bond. The yield at the New York Stock Exchange (NYSE) is on a par with the junk market. The difference is that, by leasing out a seat, there is little of a junk bond's risk.

At the Amex, where 473 of the 900 seats are leased, a sale on October 31, 1990, was for $52,000. Amex seats were then leasing for around $18,000 a year, which is a staggering yield of 31.7 percent. Donaldson Lufkin & Jenrette's index of high-yield bonds stands at 21 percent.

Of the NYSE's 1,366 seats, 581 are leased. A seat sold on October 18, 1990, went for $295,000. The price for a leased membership was at that time $54,000–60,000 a year, so the mid-price gives a current yield of 19.3 percent.

High-yield bonds are not called junk for nothing. If an investment yield matches that of a junk bond, what do you think that says about the investment? Seat prices have collapsed since highs (in 1987) of $1.15 million at the NYSE and $400,000 at the Amex. Now that the bear circus is in town, it seems that the only ringside seats are the cheap ones.

Source: "Sliding Seats," *Economist*, November 10, 1990, p. 102.

This expression shows that the overall risk of the market portfolio, σ_m^2, is the weighted average of the betas of the individual component securities. It follows that a security's beta measures its contribution to the risk of the entire portfolio. This is the result we were seeking.

As a direct corollary of Equation 12.14, the weighted average of all the betas in the market portfolio is equal to 1:

$$\sum_{i=1}^{n} w_i \beta_i = 1 \tag{12.15}$$

Equivalently, the beta of the market portfolio is $\beta_m = 1$, a result that provides a standard against which we can measure other securities or portfolios. Thus, a security or portfolio with a beta greater than 1 is defined as **aggressive** because it has more risk than the market portfolio. A security or portfolio with a beta less than 1 is **defensive** because it has less risk than the market portfolio.

Figure 12.6 presents the actual distribution of betas for firms in the stock market for the period 1926–1985. The figure contains several interesting features. First, it shows that the distribution of betas is skewed to the right, indicating that most firms tend to be defensive. Second, almost all firms have

aggressive portfolio
a portfolio with a beta greater than 1

defensive portfolio
a portfolio with a beta less than 1

FIGURE 12.6   Frequency Distribution of Betas for the Period 1926–1985

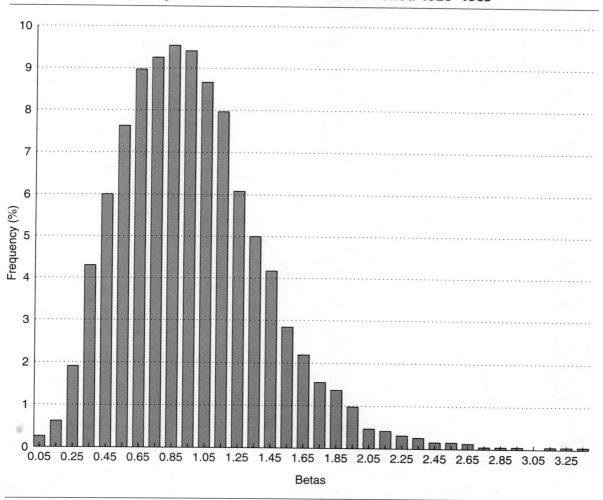

Source: "The Regression Tendencies of Beta: A Reappraisal," by Robert W. Kolb and Ricardo J. Rodríguez, from *The Financial Review*, May 1989. Reprinted by permission.

positive betas. Based on the definition of beta in Equation 12.13, a negative beta for an asset indicates a negative correlation between the asset and the market. Figure 12.6 shows that such firms are very rare. Third, the figure confirms that the average risk of all firms in the market is 1.

Beta and the Characteristic Line

☞ Beta is the slope of the characteristic line.

In practice, the beta of an asset is calculated by fitting a straight line between the points representing the returns on the asset and the market. To illustrate, Figure 12.7 shows the relationship between the returns of IBM and the market

FIGURE 12.7   The Characteristic Line for IBM

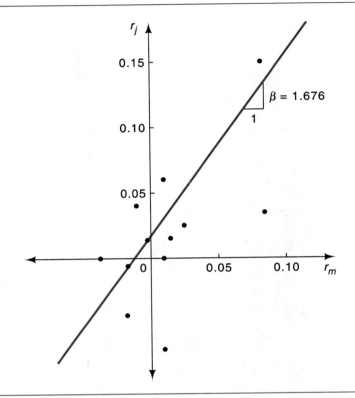

portfolio over a certain 12-month period.[2] Each dot in the figure corresponds to the returns earned by IBM and the S&P 500 index, a proxy for the market portfolio, on a particular month.

By plotting the return pairs for any security and the market portfolio, we can see the relationship between the returns on the security and the returns on the market. The characteristic line of Figure 12.7 summarizes this relationship. The **characteristic line** is chosen by regression analysis to provide the best fit for the pattern of dots in the graph.

characteristic line
a line showing the relationship between returns for a given security or portfolio and a market index

The regression equation, or the equation for the characteristic line, for some security i is:

$$r_{it} = \alpha_i + \beta_i r_{mt} + \varepsilon_{it} \qquad (12.16)$$

where $r_{it} =$ the return on the ith security in the tth period
$r_{mt} =$ the return on the market portfolio in the tth period
$\alpha_i =$ the parameter for the intercept term (alpha)
$\beta_i =$ the parameter for the slope coefficient (beta)
$\varepsilon_{it} =$ a random error term assumed to have a 0 mean

---

[2] In practice, it is customary to use 60 monthly data points to calculate betas.

alpha
the intercept of the
characteristic line

Using historical data, we estimate the parameters in the regression equation, α_i and β_i. In Figure 12.7 the characteristic line for IBM has an intercept at 0.0171 and a slope of 1.676. The intercept, α_i, is the **alpha** and the slope of the characteristic line, β_i, is the beta. Beta measures the risk of a security relative to the market. For IBM, the measured beta during this period was 1.676. We can interpret this beta by saying that when the market return increases by 1 percent, we expect the return on IBM to increase by 1.676 percent. Similarly, when the market return decreases by 1 percent, we expect IBM's return to fall by 1.676 percent. Therefore, in this example, IBM is riskier than the market.

☞ The beta of the market portfolio must always equal 1.

The beta of any security or portfolio is relative because it measures risk relative to the market portfolio. In particular, if we think of the market portfolio as a security and plot its returns against the market portfolio, we obtain an intercept of $\alpha_m = 0$, and a slope of the characteristic line of $\beta_m = 1$. This slope of 1 is consistent with our finding in the previous section that the market portfolio has a beta of 1. Figure 12.8 illustrates this result.

The reason that beta can be found in practice by using linear regression techniques is that the slope of any regression of a variable y against another variable x is given by:

$$\text{Slope of regression line} = \frac{\text{cov}(x, y)}{\sigma_y^2}$$

This expression becomes identical to the beta of an asset x with respect to the market, if m is substituted for y. Thus, finding the slope of the regression line of an asset against the market is exactly the same as finding its beta.

FIGURE 12.8   The Characteristic Line for the Market Portfolio

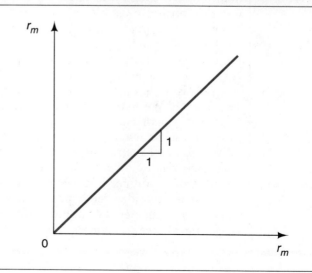

INTERNATIONAL PERSPECTIVES

International Capital Asset Pricing

One of the key features of the capital asset pricing model is the important role assigned to the market portfolio. The theory asserts that rational investors will seek to hold a portfolio of risky assets that is a miniature of the market portfolio. Because of this, it becomes very important to identify the market portfolio correctly. In practice, most analysts have used the U.S. stock market portfolio to approximate the market portfolio. In theory, however, it appears that the real market portfolio is a world market portfolio. In this portfolio, all risky assets in the world would be included in proportion to their contribution to total world wealth.

It is already a simplification to pretend that only stocks are relevant, and to use stock market portfolios to act as surrogates for all other assets. In particular, using only stocks tends to neglect the two greatest categories of world wealth—human capital and real estate. However, to restrict the market portfolio to only domestic stocks is even worse. Here we will consider only the extent to which the world stock market might be the best portfolio to consider and we will leave aside the greater question of whether it is important to include other assets besides stocks.

Part of the reason for restricting attention to just the U.S. stock market has been the belief that capital markets across international boundaries are segmented. A "segmented market" is a market in which capital cannot move freely from one part of the market to another, and as we will see, this has important implications for investors' ability to diversify fully. If the equity markets of the world are segmented by various kinds of restrictions on the movement of capital or relevant information across national boundaries, it may be that a different capital asset pricing model would hold for each country. In other words, with segmented markets, the expected return of a security would depend only on the beta of that security when it is measured against the market portfolio from the same country. On the other hand, if international equity markets are not segmented, then the expected return of a security should depend on the beta of that security when it is measured against the world market portfolio.

This issue has great implications for the question of international diversification. We have seen that poorly diversified portfolios have a risk level that is higher than necessary for their expected returns, and that this situation can be remedied by further diversification. In particular, by committing some of their funds to international investment, investors can reduce their risk by diversifying beyond their national boundaries.

Markets can differ in the extent to which they are segmented. For example, if we consider geographical segmentation, the market for residential housing is segmented, because it is difficult to move the goods from one geographical area to another. The U.S. stock market is not geographically segmented at all, because capital can be shifted from one location to another very easily. If capital markets are "strictly segmented" it will be impossible to diversify abroad. However, if capital markets are "weakly segmented," there may be even greater potential gains to international diversification. A market might be weakly segmented if there are difficulties in moving capital or in acquiring information about activities in other market segments.

The table shows the betas of domestic stock portfolios when the returns from domestic markets are regressed against the world market portfolio. In other words, each of the complete domestic equity markets from a foreign country was regressed against the world market portfolio to measure its beta. Notice the extreme diversity of betas, from the lows of 0.08 and 0.1 for Spain and Denmark, to the high of 1.1 for the United States. In fact, only the United States had a beta greater than 1.

More important, however, is the relationship between beta and the expected returns on the portfolios. Using the betas for the domestic portfolios shown above, financial analyst Donald R. Lessard calculated the

The Standard Deviations and Betas of National Stock Markets

Country	Standard Deviation of Returns	Beta
Australia	16.1	0.51
Austria	13.0	0.26
Belgium	11.4	0.55
Canada	12.3	0.95
Denmark	11.5	0.10
France	17.1	0.50
Germany	19.4	0.86
Italy	21.6	0.50
Japan	18.4	0.49
Netherlands	14.8	0.94
Norway	16.0	0.21
Spain	12.7	0.08
Sweden	13.6	0.46
Switzerland	18.6	0.96
U.K.	15.8	0.61
U.S.A.	12.5	1.10
World	10.6	1.00

Note: Betas for each national stock market are measured against the world market portfolio.

(continued)

expected return for each of the domestic portfolios and then compared these to the risk-equivalent world portfolio, which is constructed of the world-equity portfolio and the risk-free asset in proportions to match the risk of the domestic portfolio. For each of the countries there would have been a gain in expected return by holding the world portfolio rather than just the domestic portfolio. This is the additional expected gain that could be realized by holding the world portfolio instead of the domestic portfolio, and it could be achieved without any additional risk beyond that which was already present in the purely domestic portfolio.

The figure presents this same information graphically. Here the risk-free rate is taken as 6 percent in accordance with Lessard's analysis, and the world market portfolio has an expected return of 10 percent. For example, we find that Austria has a standard deviation of returns of 13 percent and an expected return of 7.04 percent. By comparison, investing in the world portfolio and using leverage to bring the risk level to 13 percent in order to match Austria's would have an expected return of 10.92 percent. For its risk level, an investment in Austria's market would be underperforming the market by 3.88 percent per annum. Similarly, an investment in any of the other countries would also be earning a lower return for its level of risk than the return that could be achieved by investing in the world market portfolio.

This indicates that there are substantial advantages to be gained from international diversification and the magnitude of these advantages depends upon the investor's home country. We have already seen that there are dramatic risk reduction possibilities. Now, we also see a way to quantify the shortfall in expected return that comes from holding poorly diversified portfolios. In this case, the poorly diversified portfolios are thoroughly diversified domestically, but do not take advantage of international diversification. Also, as shown in the figure below, the advantages to international diversification differ across countries. In the figure, the United States is almost on the world capital market line, so there is relatively little benefit for the U.S. investor to diversify internationally. The situation is very different for an Austrian investor, because the Austrian domestic portfolio lies well below the world capital market line. Even though the benefits to the U.S. investor from international diversification are small, they are still significant. The importance of international diversification for U.S.

The Expected Return of a Security

Portfolios on the capital market line only have systematic risk. In other words, they are perfectly diversified because they are composed of the market portfolio of risky assets. However, for individual securities and smaller portfolios, we still have to know the factors that determine their expected returns.

The World Capital Market Line and Purely Domestic Portfolios

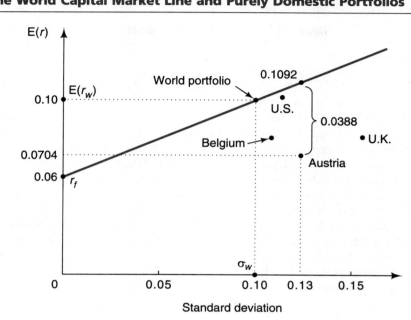

investors has been emphasized by a recent strong trend in the United States toward international diversification.

The principle is clear. The investor who holds a portfolio of only a few stocks is not taking advantage of the domestic diversification opportunities that are available. Likewise, the investor who diversifies thoroughly but uses only the domestic market is not taking advantage of the opportunities for international diversification. Both investors are earning a lower rate of return for a given level of risk than they could achieve by holding the world market portfolio.

Source: Donald R. Lessard, "World, Country, and Industry Relationships in Equity Returns: Implications for Risk Reduction Through International Diversification," *Financial Analysts Journal,* January–February 1978, pp. 2–8.

☞ A well-diversified portfolio has little nonsystematic risk.

We know that two parts compose the risk of an individual security: systematic and nonsystematic risk.[3] It is reasonable to suppose that the expected return of a security depends on its risk level. However, unlike a

[3] The same holds true for portfolios that are not fully diversified. For this reason, we speak of single securities in this section, but the argument holds equally well for portfolios that are not fully diversified.

☞ According to capital market theory, only systematic risk is compensated by additional expected return.

perfectly diversified portfolio, a single security has diversifiable risk remaining. Recall that we assume markets are perfect, so investors can diversify without cost. By doing so, only the systematic risk of the security will remain. Because of this, only nondiversifiable risk receives compensation in the market. The market will not reward investors for bearing unnecessary, diversifiable risk.

Another way to see the same point is to consider the risk-bearing function in society. Many social benefits arise only after someone is willing to take considerable risk. Drilling for oil is a clear example, since it involves considerable risk but, if successful, provides valuable energy for society (and valuable cash for the driller). Investors who bear these risks deserve compensation from society for the service they render. However, it is not necessary to reward investors who bear unnecessary risks. The investor who holds a single security, or who drills a single oil well, bears both systematic and nonsystematic risk. Only the bearing of systematic risk serves society, because the rest is easily diversifiable.

☞ The expected return for a security or portfolio includes compensation for the passage of time and for bearing systematic risk.

For an individual security, the expected return includes compensation for the passage of time in the form of the risk-free rate. It also includes a reward for bearing systematic risk, as measured by beta. So the expected return of an individual security should equal the risk-free rate, plus an additional amount for the bearing of systematic risk. The security market line expresses this relationship between expected return and risk.

THE SECURITY MARKET LINE

☞ According to the capital asset pricing model, the expected return of a security depends on the risk-free rate, the systematic risk of the security (measured by beta), and the market price of risk.

The SML expresses the central idea of the capital asset pricing model (CAPM): the expected return of a security increases linearly with risk, as measured by beta. This relationship is shown in Figure 12.9.

We can derive the SML using the knowledge we have already acquired. By definition, the risk-free asset has 0 risk and a return of r_f. We also know that the market portfolio has a beta of 1 and its expected return is $E(r_m)$. It is also clear from our previous discussion that $E(r_m) > r_f$, since risk bearing should be compensated in the market. The greater the risk, the greater the expected return. This means that the SML will be upward sloping and will pass through the points corresponding to the risk-free asset and the market portfolio. However, this does not guarantee that the SML will be a straight line, as the CAPM claims. By this definition, the SML could be an upward sloping curve. We now show why it must be a straight line.

Consider security A in Figure 12.10, which lies below the SML and has a beta of 0.5. It is dominated by portfolio C on the SML, which combines the risk-free rate and the market portfolio in equal proportions. Since it is dominated by C, no investor would hold security A. As a result, the return of A would have to increase until it equaled the return of C. Only then would A become as attractive to investors as C. This shows that, in equilibrium, no security can lie below the SML.

Now consider security B located above the SML in Figure 12.10. Combining B with the risk-free security to achieve a beta of 1 generates portfolio

FIGURE 12.9   The Security Market Line

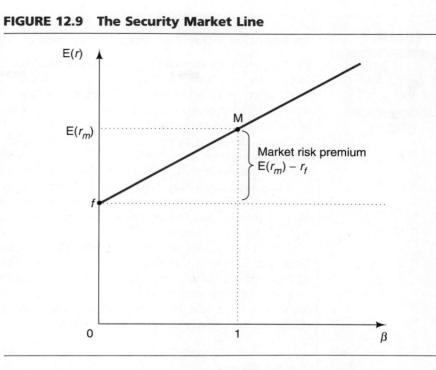

FIGURE 12.10   Why the Security Market Line Is Straight

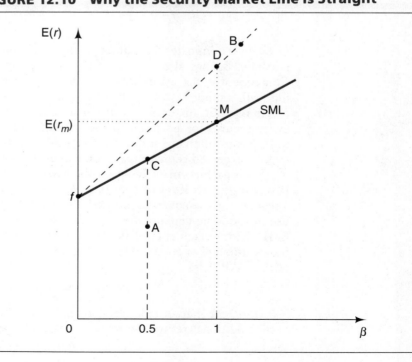

FINANCE

TODAY

An Incentive a Day Can Keep Doctor Bills at Bay

Paying people to stay healthy may sound like an impractical way to control health care costs, but benefit consultant Hay/Huggins reports that that's what a handful of employers are doing. They provide employees with financial incentives if they meet certain "wellness" criteria, such as not smoking and maintaining normal weight.

Typically, such incentives take the form of either lower premium contributions required from employees or higher benefits. Baker Hughes Inc., a Texas drilling-and-tool company, figures it has saved $2 million annually by charging nonsmoking employees $120 less a year for health insurance. Adolf Coors Co. says it has saved $3.2 million a year by offering its employees incentives to meet weight, smoking, blood pressure, cholesterol, and other health criteria.

Other companies rewarding healthy lifestyles include U-Haul, Control Data, and Southern California Edison. To avoid charges of unfairness and discrimination, some companies provide cost savings to employees actively involved in improving their health, even if they don't meet wellness guidelines. The rule, Hay/Huggins advises, should be "Don't include anything that isn't under the employee's control."

Source: Gene Koretz, "An Incentive a Day Can Keep Doctor Bills at Bay," *Business Week,* April 29, 1991, p. 22.

D. Since D dominates the market portfolio, no investor would hold the market portfolio. But we already know that all investors hold the market portfolio. Consequently, the assumption that B, or any other security, can lie above the SML cannot be true in equilibrium.

In equilibrium, each security or portfolio lies on the SML. This includes every security or portfolio in the market, even the market portfolio. The SML has its intercept at the risk-free rate, and its upward slope indicates the greater expected return that accompanies higher levels of beta.

With each security lying on the SML, each security is receiving compensation for its level of beta risk. We can express the expected return for a security by the equation for the SML. To find the equation, we again make use of the basic equation for a straight line, $y = mx + b$, noting that for the SML the intercept is the risk-free rate and the slope is found by comparing the coordinates of points M and f. It is then easy to see that the basic equation of the CAPM is:

$$E(r_i) = r_f + [E(r_m) - r_f]\beta_i \tag{12.17}$$

Here, the market risk premium is $E(r_m) - r_f$. The market risk premium is the additional return the investor expects to earn by holding the market portfolio rather than the risk-free asset. It is also equal to the slope of the SML.

THE CAPITAL MARKET LINE AND THE SECURITY MARKET LINE

☞ The CML holds only for fully diversified portfolios, whereas the SML pertains to all portfolios and to individual securities.

To complete our discussion of the CAPM, we compare the CML and the SML to see how they are mutually consistent. Figure 12.4 presents the CML and Figure 12.9 shows the SML. The two differ as follows:

1. The risk measure for the CML is the standard deviation, a measure of total risk. The risk measure for the SML is beta, a measure of systematic risk.
2. In equilibrium, only fully diversified portfolios lie on the CML, whereas individual securities will plot below the CML. For the SML, in equilibrium, all securities and all portfolios fall exactly on the SML.

Because the graph of the CML measures risk by the standard deviation, it shows the total risk of the individual securities and portfolios in risk/return space. However, we know that some risk of a security is not relevant to determining expected return. All individual securities embody some non-systematic risk. This portion does not contribute to their expected return, so individual securities do not lie on the CML.

Figure 12.9 uses beta as the risk measure. Since beta measures only systematic risk, the expected returns of securities fully reflect that risk, so each security lies exactly on the SML when the market is in equilibrium. The graph of the SML reveals nothing about the total risk of the individual securities; it reflects only the systematic risk measured by beta.

SUMMARY

In this and the preceding chapter we traced the main outlines of capital market theory. We assumed that security markets are perfect, that investors have full information about the pricing of securities, and that they all evaluate information similarly. Using these assumptions, we derived the main result of the CAPM. This result states that the expected return of any security or portfolio increases linearly with its risk, as measured by beta. This relationship is described by the security market line, SML.

QUESTIONS

1. Why do the weights committed to different securities in a portfolio have to sum to 1?
2. If we put $1,000 in an investment with a standard deviation of 0.2 and $1,000 in an investment with a standard deviation of 0.1, what is the

standard deviation of the resulting portfolio? Can the question be answered with the information provided? Explain.

3. On what factors does the risk of a two-asset portfolio depend?
4. Of all investment opportunities, assume that one has the highest expected return. Can it ever be dominated? Explain.
5. What is the difference between the efficient set and the efficient frontier?
6. Evaluate the following claim: Diversification reduces risk, but only at the expense of reducing expected return.
7. What interpretation does beta have for a stock with a beta equal to 1?
8. If a stock has a beta of 1, does that mean that it has the same standard deviation as the market?
9. Why do some industries tend to have high or low betas?
10. For what risk factors do investors demand compensation?
11. What is the market risk premium?
12. What is the separation theorem?
13. You know that asset A has the same risk as the market. If the returns on A and the market are both 12 percent, can you determine the risk-free rate? What's going on here?
14. If the risk of asset A is twice the risk of asset B, does it follow that the expected return of A is twice the expected return of B? Explain.
15. You know that the standard deviation of Generalized Motors is lower than the standard deviation of the market, and that GM has a positive correlation with the market. Can the stock of GM be aggressive? Explain.
16. If the risk-free rate increases 2 percent and the market risk premium remains the same, what happens to the expected return of defensive and aggressive stocks?
17. If the risk-free rate increases by 3 percent and the expected return on the market remains the same, what happens to the expected return of defensive and aggressive stocks?

PROBLEMS

Security A has an expected return of 0.15 and a standard deviation of 0.2. Security B has an expected return of 0.1 and a standard deviation of 0.15. Use this information to solve Problems 1 through 5.

1. If the correlation between securities A and B is 0.8, what is the expected return of a portfolio with half of the funds invested in each security?
2. What is the standard deviation of the portfolio in Problem 1?
3. If 30 percent of the funds are put in security A, what is the expected return of the portfolio made up of A and B?
4. What is the standard deviation of the portfolio in Problem 3?

5. The correlation between security C and the market is 0.8. If the standard deviation of security C is 0.2 and the standard deviation of the market is 0.17, what is the beta of security C?

6. Solve Problem 5, except assume that the standard deviation of security C is 0.14.

7. Solve Problem 5, except assume that the standard deviation of security C is 0.17.

8. The current risk-free rate is 12 percent, the expected return on the market is 0.18, and security D has a beta of 1.2. According to the CAPM, what is the expected return on security D?

9. Security E has a beta of 1. If the risk-free rate of interest is 10 percent and the market risk premium is 8 percent, what is the required rate of return on security E according to the SML equation?

10. A reputable firm, Muskrat Manor, is considering expanding its food franchising operation by opening another store to sell its smash hit food product, Muskrat McNuggets. Already operating 157 stores nationwide, the firm knows that the beta of these previous projects is 1.2. With risk-free interest rates at 12 percent, and assuming the standard market risk premium of 8.9 percent, what required rate of return should be applied to the new store project?

11. If Muskrat Manor goes ahead with the new store, it expects sales of $1 million per year, with total costs of $800,000 per year, all stated on an after-tax basis. The project should last 20 years. Investment for the new store would be $800,000. Using the information from the previous problem, should they open the new store?

12. Muskrat Manor is considering a bold addition to the menu at its stores—hamburgers. In spite of the fact that this is a new product for them, the firm believes that it is relatively low risk and assigns a beta of 0.9 to the project. With the standard market risk premium of 8.9 percent and a risk-free rate of 11 percent, what should be the required rate of return for the hamburger project?

13. For Muskrat's hamburger project, considerable investment costs are involved, including market testing, promotion, and necessary equipment. All of this investment should cost about $15 million. However, the firm believes that the hamburger might catch on. It estimates nationwide sales at $30 million per year, with total costs of $24 million, all on an after-tax basis. Using the data from the previous problem, should Muskrat sell hamburgers?

Use the following data in solving Problems 14 through 16. Current risk-free interest rates are 11 percent. The standard market risk premium of 8.9 percent applies.

14. Sursum Corda, Inc., is considering a project that will generate after-tax annual cash flows of $300,000 for five years. The beta of the project is 0.8. The investment cost for the project is $900,000. Should the firm undertake the project?

15. Lacrimosa, Inc., is considering a project that will generate after-tax cash flows of $300,000 for five years. The beta of the project is 1.3. The investment cost for the project is $850,000. Should the firm undertake the project?

16. Draw a graph of the SML and locate the projects of Problems 14 and 15 on the graph.

17. If IBM has the same variance as the market, and the correlation between the two is 0.7, what is IBM's beta?

18. Asset A has a beta of 0.7 and asset B has a beta of 1.3. The expected rates of return are 10 percent and 14 percent, respectively. Find the risk-free rate of return.

19. Frisky Foods, Inc., has a beta of 0.8 and an expected return of 13 percent. If Double Whammy Mfg. has a beta of 1.6 and the risk-free rate is 9 percent, what is the expected return on Double Whammy? Under what circumstance would the answer be 26 percent? Is this realistic?

CHAPTER 13

Market Efficiency

An efficient market responds well and quickly to new information, which is very important for the issue of market equilibrium. Whereas the capital asset pricing model (CAPM) states what the equilibrium relationship between expected return and risk should be, the entire theory would be worthless for practical application if markets never reached equilibrium. If the market is not efficient, there is no reason to think that the CAPM actually works.

The close conceptual relationship between the CAPM and the efficient market hypothesis (EMH) means that they cannot be tested independently of one another in many instances. Tests of the EMH try to establish whether markets process new information in a way that makes prices move quickly toward the new equilibrium. To evaluate that, however, one must have some conception of where the equilibrium lies. Since that is specified by the CAPM, the two theories are tied together. Despite the difficulties in separating the CAPM and the EMH, a number of empirical tests have been conducted that are quite revealing. Together, they provide a very good indication of the adequacy of the CAPM and the efficiency of the financial markets.

In recent years, a number of controversies have arisen surrounding the CAPM. Some question the entire CAPM framework. In addition, a number of market anomalies have been discovered that apparently violate either the CAPM or the EMH.

THE EFFICIENT MARKET HYPOTHESIS

operationally efficient market
a market that performs well in executing orders

informationally efficient market
a market in which prices respond quickly to new information

The EMH is one of the central ideas in modern finance. A market may be operationally efficient or informationally efficient. It is **operationally efficient** if it works smoothly, with limited delays. For example, orders can be transmitted from all parts of the world to a market rapidly and accurately, and those orders can be executed and confirmed quickly.

A market may be operationally efficient, however, without being informationally efficient. That would be one in which orders are handled smoothly, but with prices adjusting only slowly to new information. A market is **informationally efficient** if its prices fully reflect all available information at all times. The EMH and our discussion pertain only to this kind of efficiency.

In this definition, the words "fully reflect" are very important. If market prices fully reflect a set of information, it means that they have already completely adjusted to levels in accordance with the information. This also implies that that information cannot be used to create a trading strategy to beat the market, because if prices already have completely adjusted to reflect the information, it cannot be used to advantage in trading. All available information has already been processed by investors and, consequently, is reflected in the market prices.

☞ Different versions of the efficient market hypothesis can be specified by considering different information sets.

Since this definition specifies that a market is efficient with respect to some body of information, it means that we can develop different versions of the EMH by specifying different information sets. It has become traditional to distinguish three versions of the EMH[1]: weak form efficiency, semistrong form efficiency, and strong form efficiency.

Weak Form Efficiency

☞ A market has weak form efficiency if its prices fully reflect all historical price and market data.

A market is weakly efficient if its prices fully reflect the information contained in all historical market data. These include the complete history of market prices, volume figures, and other similar information. If markets are weakly efficient, all such information is useless for directing a trading strategy. Analysis of this kind of information is known as technical analysis, so if the market is weakly efficient, technical analysis is without validity, at least from the point of view of trying to make money.

☞ If the weak form of the EMH is correct, technical analysis cannot improve investment performance.

Technical analysis claims that information is still to be gleaned from analyzing the historical market record. For example, various techniques exist that purportedly signal when to buy or sell a given stock, based on the past behavior of that stock's price. The EMH states that this cannot occur in an efficient market, since the stock's current price already incorporates whatever information past prices may provide. Because all the information has already been harvested, nothing is to be gleaned.

Semistrong Form Efficiency

☞ A market has semistrong form efficiency if its prices fully reflect all public information.

A market has semistrong efficiency if its prices at all times fully reflect all public information. Public information includes all published reports, such as those found in newspapers, the financial press, and government publications and announcements, as well as television and radio news reports and investigative reports. Public information also includes all historical market data. Hence, the semistrong version of the EMH is more general than the weak version.

[1] See Eugene F. Fama, "Efficient Capital Markets: A Review of Theory and Empirical Work." Reprinted in James Lorie and Richard Brealey, *Modern Developments in Investment Management* (New York: Praeger Publishers, 1972), pp. 109–161.

FINANCE

TODAY

Maybe the Market Isn't So "Efficient" After All

Is there a way for small investors to beat the market? Yes, say two Stanford professors. And what's more, they have the profits to prove it. Myron S. Scholes and Mark A. Wolfson show that investors can win by buying shares in companies that offer their stockholders a discount to purchase additional shares. Scholes and Wolfson started out by investing a meager $7,000 of their own money in 1984. But that quickly escalated. In total, including borrowed money, they put in some $3.6 million between 1984 and 1988.

They invested in 30 companies, all offering discount dividend reinvestment or stock purchase plans at an average discount of 5.2 percent from current prices. Most of the companies were banks, with a smattering of real estate and utility companies. The professors earned a net profit of $421,000. If they had invested similar sums in the Salomon Brothers Bank Stock Index (since their portfolio was heavily weighted toward bank stocks), they would have made a profit of only $182,600.

Besides making money, the professors had another reason for the exercise: To test the efficient-market theory. That axiom of modern-day finance holds that the stock market is such an "efficient" processor of information that investors cannot systematically profit from available information. But their calculations show a way of consistently beating the market by using public information.

Some caveats are in order, though. Investing in discount stock purchase plans takes time, since each corporation has differing rules and companies tend to open and reopen the programs depending on their capital needs. The professors also wryly note that they had no fun putting together a 20-page, single-spaced typed schedule of capital gains and losses on their 1985 tax returns. But that's a lot better than documenting straight losses.

Source: Christopher Farrell, "Maybe the Market Isn't So 'Efficient' After All," *Business Week*, October 30, 1989.

Strong Form Efficiency

☞ A market has strong form efficiency if its prices fully reflect all information.

A market has strong form efficiency if its prices fully reflect all information, both public and private. Private information is that generated by government officials or corporate insiders that has not yet been made public. For example, members of the Federal Reserve Board often have access to private information. Imagine a meeting of the board in which new guidelines for the conduct of monetary policy are adopted. Until these are revealed to the public, the board members are the only ones privy to that valuable information. As another example, imagine a company that makes a major oil find but has not announced it. Before the discovery is published, some employees of the corporation have access to that private information.

The strong form version of the EMH states that even this private information is already reflected in stock prices. The most important consequence of this claim, if true, is that such information could not be used to generate a trading profit that beats the market. As its name implies, the strong form efficiency claim is very strong indeed.

RELATIONSHIPS AMONG THE THREE FORMS OF MARKET EFFICIENCY

Figure 13.1 shows how the information sets for these three versions of the EMH are related. The weak form says that financial markets are efficient with respect to a minimum core of information—historical market data—represented by the small interior circle in the figure. The semistrong form claims that markets reflect the minimum core of information plus any other type of public information. The strong form says that all of the information in the large circle is reflected in market prices, including all public information, which in turn includes all market-related data.

FIGURE 13.1 Information Sets and Different Versions of the EMH

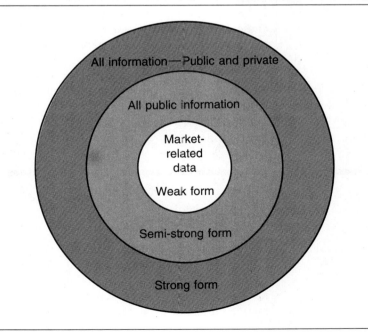

These relationships mean that any refutation of the weak form will also invalidate both the semistrong and strong versions. If the market is not efficient with respect to market-related information, it cannot be efficient with respect to all public information, and, in fact, it cannot be efficient with respect to all information.

☞ If the weak form efficiency hypothesis is false, so are the semistrong and strong forms.

The truth of the weak form of the EMH is a necessary condition for the truth of the other two versions. It is not, however, a sufficient condition, because the weak form could be true, and the semistrong and strong versions could be false. Similarly, the truth of the semistrong version is a necessary, but not sufficient, condition for the truth of the strong version. By contrast, if the strong version is true, the semistrong and weak ones must be true; that is, the truth of the strong form is a sufficient condition for the truth of the other two.

THE PRACTICAL CONSEQUENCES OF THE EMH

☞ If the market is efficient with respect to some information set, that information is not useful for devising a superior investment strategy.

If the different versions of the EMH are true, this has extremely important implications for actual market conduct. If the weak form is true, for example, it means that all market-related data are already reflected in security prices, so they cannot be useful for directing a trading strategy. The selling of charts of past price movements of securities is a multimillion-dollar business in the United States, and customers buy such charts largely to help them formulate better investment strategies. If the weak form of the EMH is true, the charts are worthless and the money spent on them is wasted, to the extent that they are to be used for improving investment performance. In short, if the weak version of the EMH is true, technical analysis is useless.[2]

fundamental analysis
the search for superior performing securities based on the examination of publicly available information

If the semistrong form is true, it has equally important practical consequences. **Fundamental analysis** is a method of searching for lucrative securities using publicly available information in the hope of beating the market. It typically focuses on the financial statements of a corporation to determine the fundamental value of the firm, regardless of the price path its stock might have followed. However, if the semistrong version of the EMH is true, this and all other publicly available information is already incorporated into stock prices. As a consequence, analysis of this information would be as effective as reading tea leaves.

Currently, numerous laws are on the books regarding the appropriate use of privileged information for securities market trading. Transgressors of these laws are occasionally discovered and even imprisoned, as the Wall Street scandals featuring Ivan Boesky and Michael Milken, among others,

---

[2] The chart business is busy diversifying into home computer software that will allow owners of personal computers to down-load price histories from a central data management source and to construct charts through the client's own computer. An immediate implication for investors that could be drawn from the truth of the weak form efficient markets hypothesis is that investment in such services is wasted money.

have illustrated. If the strong form of the EMH is true, such laws are unnecessary, as attempts to use even inside information are pointless because all of this information would already be reflected in security prices. On the other hand, if the strong form is not true, the laws have a much better claim to validity and may be worthy of strict enforcement.

THE CONNECTION BETWEEN THE CAPM AND THE EMH

An intimate connection exists between the CAPM and the EMH. Essentially, the CAPM specifies the market standard for the relationship between risk and expected return, and empirical tests of the EMH look for instances in which that specified relationship is violated.

As an example, consider the fact that some stocks trade on both the New York and Pacific stock exchanges, and assume for the moment that there are no transaction costs. During parts of the day, both exchanges are open and engage in active trading of the same securities. Across the country, traders follow the activity on both exchanges. Now assume that a particular stock trades for $105 in New York and for $100 on the Pacific exchange. A trader could simultaneously buy the stock on the latter and sell it on the former, which would be riskless and would require no capital. The trades would be riskless because they would be simultaneous; they would require no capital because they would be concluded at the same time. The result would be an

arbitrage opportunities transactions that yield a certain profit without investment

☞ The presence of arbitrage opportunities is inconsistent with equilibrium pricing.

arbitrage profit of $5 per share. A market that allows **arbitrage opportunities** is performing very poorly. In a real sense, the presence of arbitrage opportunities means that money is lying around that no one is willing to pick up.

It is also apparent that the presence of arbitrage opportunities is inconsistent with equilibrium pricing. In our example, the price differential of $5 will surely attract interest. Traders will buy the stock on the Pacific exchange for $100 and sell it in New York for $105, and will continue to perform this operation as long as the price differential subsists. These transactions will generate excess demand for the stock at a price of $100 on the Pacific exchange, because everyone will want to buy at that price. Similarly, everyone will be trying to sell the stock for $105 in New York, creating an excess supply. With excess demand on the Pacific exchange, the price must rise; and with excess supply on the New York exchange, the price must fall. In fact, only when the two prices are equal can there be any equilibrium.[3]

With well-developed securities markets one expects to find arbitrage opportunities never or very rarely. As a consequence, most potential violations

---

[3] Remember we assumed away transaction costs for purposes of this example. With transaction costs, a slight difference in the price of the stock on the two exchanges could persist if the transactions costs eroded the potential profits arising from the price discrepancy. For example, if the total transaction cost to exploit the arbitrage opportunity were $1 per share, there could be a persistent price differential of $1 or less. The moment the price differential exceeded $1, there would be an arbitrage opportunity again, and traders would have a strong profit incentive to trade in the way we described.

FIGURE 13.2   The SML with Securities Not in Equilibrium

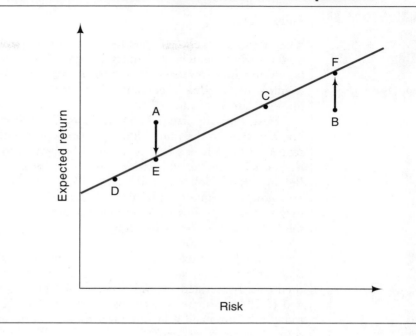

of the CAPM and the EMH are difficult to identify. Figure 13.2 shows an historical relationship between risk and return, with the line being consistent with the SML. If we think of the line as expressing the predicted trade-off between risk and return, securities C and D are exactly consistent with the theory. Securities A and B, however, are not.

If we rule out chance or errors in our estimation procedures as an explanation for the deviations of securities A and B from the theoretically correct risk and return relationship, only two other explanations are possible. First, it could be that the market is not responding to the relevant information about securities A and B. In other words, the market may be inefficient. This is similar to the presence of arbitrage opportunities discussed above. An investor could purchase security A and receive a greater level of return than the market should allow, according to the CAPM. For the same level of systematic risk, the investor should only be receiving a return like that of security E. If A's returns are always above the line representing the appropriate trade-off between risk and return, the market may be inefficient.

A second possible explanation for A being above and for B being below the prescribed level of return for their levels of risk could be that the CAPM does not give the correct risk-return relationship in the market. It may be that systematic risk is not really important at all and that the CAPM is completely false. Alternatively, it may be that returns depend on other factors besides systematic risk, and that the CAPM does not give a complete ex-

INTERNATIONAL PERSPECTIVES

Tulip Mania

The first extensively documented speculative bubble in Europe seems to be the early seventeenth-century Dutch frenzy for tulip bulbs. At its peak, family fortunes were squandered for a single bulb. It can serve as a perfect example of the great speculative frenzies that have come since, including those in our own time.

First, the tulip itself. The name may come from the Turkish word *dulban*, a turban. In the mid-sixteenth century, travelers in Turkey had been struck by the flower's beauty and had brought it to Vienna; it soon attracted wide notice, and within a few years was grown in Germany, then Belgium, then Holland. In the late 1570s it reached England, where the new flower became popular in court circles. By the early seventeenth century in France, tulips were immensely fashionable, and the early traces of the later madness could be seen.

Cultivated tulips occasionally produce striking mutations, caused by a virus, which enhance their speculative interest. A grower would anxiously scan his garden for such a "break," as it was called. The beautiful bloom, then called "rectified," could expect ready buyers, who would propagate and resell it at higher prices, just as the sire of a Kentucky Derby winner today can command a huge figure from a stud farm. In fact, the perfect tulips became "breeders."

By the early 1620s excitement over tulips and their mutations had reached Holland, and the rarest specimens were selling for thousands of florins. By degrees, the madness spread from a handful of enthusiasts to permeate the whole of Dutch society. Soon virtually all houses had their tulip fields, filling every inch of Holland's available surface.

Originally, sales occurred over the winter. A speculator might take some specimens and a supply of bulbs to one of the inns frequented by the confrerie of tulip traders. There he could exchange his "Admiral Tromp," purchased for five hundred florins, plus another two hundred florins in cash for a "General Bol," which he would hope to sell within the week for a thousand. By 1634 every level of society had succumbed to this excitement, from laborers to the nobility, and soon deals were being conducted all year round, for delivery the following spring. What we call put and call options on the value of the tulips were invented and widely traded. Often the speculator had no intention of actually acquiring possession of what he had bought; rather, he expected to resell his contract promptly at a profit to some later enthusiast. This was called "trading air."

Tulips in seventeenth-century Holland presented even more problems than commodities today, since there was no member firm to stand behind the contract, and whoever finally did take delivery of a particular bulb could not even be sure of receiving what the contract specified, until it actually bloomed. To cope with this activity, new laws were promulgated and special tulip notaries were created.

As the frenzy mounted, other economic activity slowed, and prices mounted giddily. Estates were mortgaged to permit their owners to participate in the constant rise of tulip prices; new buying power pushed prices up further. One "Viceroy" bulb sold for four oxen, eight pigs, twelve sheep, four loads of rye and two of wheat, two hogsheads of wine and four barrels of beer, two barrels of butter and half a ton of cheese, together with a quantity of house furnishings. A "Semper Augustus"—with vertical red and white stripes over a bluish inner hue—sold for about twice that value in cash, plus a carriage and horses. The Dutch became convinced that not only other Dutch speculators but also foreigners would pay ever-rising prices. Indeed, at one point a single rare bulb was given in France as full payment for a successful brewery.

One story illustrates the temper of those days. A shoemaker of The Hague, in the little plot that almost every Dutch household by this time had dedicated to tulip raising, finally managed to grow a black flower. He was visited by some growers from Haarlem, to whom he sold his treasure for 1,500 florins. Immediately one of them dropped it to the floor and stamped on it until it was ground to pulp. The cobbler was aghast. The buyers explained that they, too, possessed a black tulip, and had destroyed his to protect the uniqueness of their own. They would have paid anything: 10,000 florins, if necessary. The heartbroken cobbler is said to have died of chagrin.

But the day of reckoning inevitably came. When these crazy price levels finally cracked, the entire economic life of Holland crumbled. Lawsuits were so numerous that the courts could not handle them. Many great families were ruined, fine old merchant firms were thrown down, and it was years before commercial life in Holland recovered.

Source: John Train, *Famous Financial Fiascos* (New York: Clarkson N. Potter, Inc., 1985), pp. 9–12.

planation of the factors that generate returns. Furthermore, even if systematic risk is the only relevant factor, expected return may not be linearly related to systematic risk, as the CAPM assumes; for example, it may be related to the square of its systematic risk.

The most important point to see here, however, is that attempts to test the EMH or the CAPM turn out to be joint tests of both theories. As just explained, given persistent occurrences of securities like A or B, the problem could be with either the CAPM, the EMH, or both. From the empirical tests, we probably will not be able to tell where the difficulty lies.

PERFORMANCE MEASUREMENT AND BEATING THE MARKET

Implicit in the discussion of the relationship between the EMH and the CAPM is the idea that the CAPM provides a measure of normal performance. As we have developed the explanation of the CAPM we have stressed that it expresses the equilibrium level of expected returns for a given level of risk, and that this relationship can be depicted graphically be the SML, as shown in Figure 13.2. If the SML expresses the normal level of performance that can be expected by an investor, we have already observed that this level can be achieved by holding the market portfolio in conjunction with the risk-free asset.

As a consequence, any special efforts at investment analysis must focus on attempts to find securities like A or B in Figure 13.2. Security A offers too much return for its level of risk and security B offers too little. If investors could successfully identify such securities, they would want to buy those like A and sell ones like B. When the other participants in the market realized that the securities were mispriced, market forces would be exerted to move them to their right level of return for their respective levels of risk. In the case of security A, many traders would want to buy it. This increase in buying interest would drive A's price up and its return down, until A offered the correct level of return for its level of risk. In the figure, A would be purchased until it came to occupy the same point as security E. Analogously, security B's price is too high for its level of risk, and investors would sell it out of their portfolios or would even sell it short. This selling pressure would drive down the price of B, thereby raising its return. This process would continue until B's price was low enough so that its return is the same as the return of security F, which has the same risk level.

☞ The goal of investment analysis is to find securities that lie above or below the security market line.

☞ A superior investment performance is one that gives returns that are high relative to risk.

Thus we see that the goal of investment analysis must be to find securities that do not fall on the SML, and to trade to exploit those opportunities. The analyst who finds securities consistently lying off of the SML will perform better than the market. In other words, to beat the market an analyst must consistently find investment opportunities with an excessively high or low return for their level of risk. Within the CAPM framework, beating the market requires that the securities lie either above or below the SML.

Since the CAPM expresses a relationship between expected return and risk, it can often be difficult to validate an analyst's superior performance. In

FINANCE

TODAY

The Infallible Forecaster

Jim L. had a full-time job in the daytime, but with assets that consisted only of a phone, patience, and an easy way of talking, he managed to parlay a nighttime sideline into an ill-gotten fortune. The routine went like this.

Jim would phone, say, Mrs. Smith and quickly assure her that, no, he didn't want her to invest a single cent. "Never invest with someone you don't know," he preached. But he said he would like to demonstrate his firm's "research skill" by sharing with her the forecast that so-and-so a commodity was about to experience a significant price increase. Sure enough, the price soon went up.

A second phone call to Mrs. Smith didn't solicit an investment either. Jim simply wanted to share with her a prediction that the price of so-and-so a commodity was about to go down. "Our forecasts will help you decide whether ours is the kind of firm you might someday want to invest with," he added. As predicted, the price of the commodity subsequently declined. By the time Mrs. Smith received a third call, she was a firm believer. She not only wanted to invest but insisted on it—with a big enough investment to make up for the opportunities she had already missed out on.

What Mrs. Smith had no way of knowing was that Jim had begun with a calling list of 200 persons. In the first call, he told 100 that the price of so-and-so a commodity would go up and the other 100 were told it would go down. When it went up, he made a second call to the 100 who had been given the "correct forecast." Of these, 50 were told the next price move would be up and 50 were told it would be down.

The end result: Once the predicted price decline occurred, Jim had a list of 50 persons eager to invest. After all, how could they go wrong with someone so obviously infallible in forecasting prices? But go wrong they did, the moment they decided to send Jim a half million dollars from their collective savings accounts.

Source: "Investment Swindles: How They Work and How to Avoid Them," National Futures Association, 1987, pp. 9–10.

any given year, some analysts will do better than others just by chance. As a consequence, the mere report of a very good year on an investment portfolio should not earn too much respect from us. We would want to know how much risk was involved, and also how consistently the analyst had been able to turn in a good performance. If an analyst recommends a high beta portfolio in a year when the market happens to go up, it would be no surprise to find that the portfolio actually performed well. To be truly successful, the analyst's track record must be sufficiently good and sufficiently long to minimize the possibility that the record was produced by chance.

THE RANDOM WALK HYPOTHESIS AND MARKET EFFICIENCY

random walk hypothesis a hypothesis stating that successive returns are independent, which implies that future security prices are totally unpredictable from past security prices.

The concept of market efficiency is often linked to the **random walk hypothesis,** which, when applied to securities, asserts that successive returns are independent. This implies that the correlation between one period's return and the next period's return is 0. In other words, knowledge of a given period's return is not useful in predicting the following period's return. In addition, the hypothesis asserts that the probability distribution of returns in all periods is identical. This implies, for example, that the chance of observing a 10 percent return is the same in every period.

A full explication of the random walk hypothesis would be very mathematical, but we can get a good idea of the properties of a variable that followed a random walk by considering the following example. In a now

FIGURE 13.3   Randomly Generated Artificial Price Changes

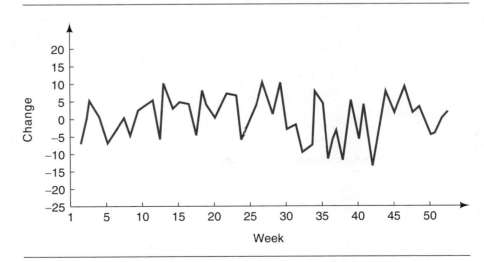

Source: Harry V. Roberts, "Stock Market 'Patterns' and Financial Analysis: Some Methodological Suggestions," *Journal of Finance,* March 1959, pp. 1–10.

FIGURE 13.4 Changes in an Artificial Price Level Generated by Random Price Changes

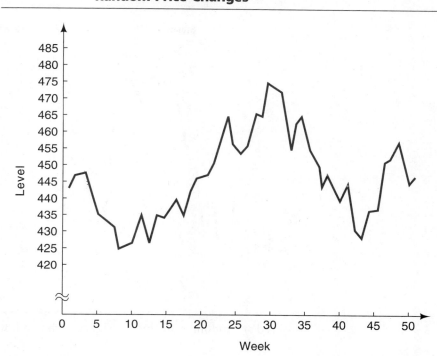

Source: Harry V. Roberts, "Stock Market 'Patterns' and Financial Analysis: Some Methodological Suggestions," *Journal of Finance*, March 1959, pp. 1–10.

famous article,[4] a table of random numbers was used to generate a series of price changes, assuming that these changes started from an initial level of 450. In other words, changes from that initial value were created by selecting random numbers and applying those changes to the variable that started at 450, with this process continuing for 52 simulated weeks (Figure 13.3). We should not be surprised at the lack of pattern in the changes. After all, they were generated at random. However, as Figure 13.4 shows, when they were applied to an initial assumed price level of 450, they appear to have generated some strong patterns. For example, from about week 12 to week 28, there appears to have been a very strong bull market. The point is that price changes that are really random can generate changes in price levels that appear to have important trends.

[4] Harry V. Roberts, "Stock Market 'Patterns' and Financial Analysis: Some Methodological Suggestions," *Journal of Finance*, March 1959, pp. 1–10.

FIGURE 13.5   The Dow Jones Industrial Average Weekly Closing, December 30, 1955–December 28, 1956

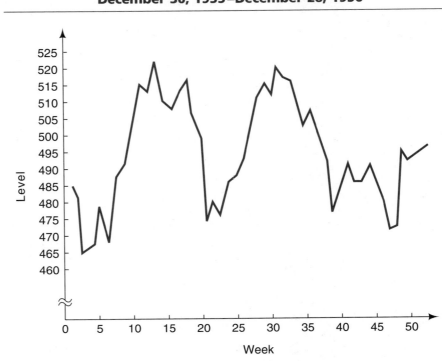

Source: Harry V. Roberts, "Stock Market 'Patterns' and Financial Analysis: Some Methodological Suggestions," *Journal of Finance,* March 1959, pp. 1–10.

When investors look at the history of security prices, they frequently claim to detect strong trends. An example of this is given in Figure 13.5, which shows the weekly closing level of the Dow Jones industrial average for one year. Notice the strong patterns, similar to those in Figure 13.4. However, if we examine the changes in the weekly level for the same period, shown in Figure 13.6, they seem to be quite random, just like the ones generated for Figure 13.3. For anyone believing in examining price trends to forecast future prices, this should be very disturbing news.

It must also be acknowledged, however, that security prices do not appear to follow a random walk. Tests indicate small but statistically significant departures from randomness; however, as we shall see, this does not rule out market efficiency. Even if slight statistical regularities exist in the movements of security prices, they might not be strong enough to give rise to a profitable trading strategy. This means that the market may be efficient even if security prices do not, strictly speaking, follow a random walk. It is important to realize that the random walk hypothesis is based on statistics, whereas the EMH is

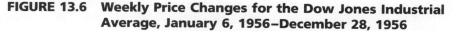

FIGURE 13.6   Weekly Price Changes for the Dow Jones Industrial Average, January 6, 1956–December 28, 1956

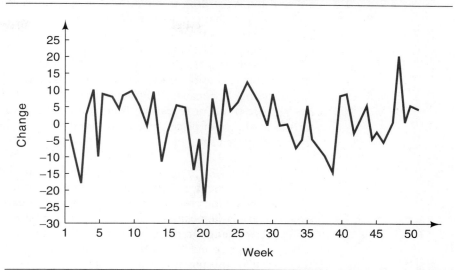

Source: Harry V. Roberts, "Stock Market 'Patterns' and Financial Analysis: Some Methodological Suggestions," *Journal of Finance,* March 1959, pp. 1–10.

based on economics. Essentially, if we wish to refute the EMH we must discover rules for trading to beat the market. In refuting the random walk hypothesis, we refute only statistics, but we do not show that markets are inefficient. This distinction is elaborated below.

TESTS OF EFFICIENT MARKETS AND PRICING MODELS

This section reviews some efforts to test the CAPM and the EMH. These hypotheses have been tested for many different kinds of financial markets, the most famous being conducted for the stock market. The discussion is divided along the lines of the three versions of the EMH.

Tests of Technical Trading Rules

In its purest form, technical analysis focuses on patterns of securities prices and on measures of market mood or investor behavior. The strategies that focus on market mood consider matters such as the level of insider trading activity, the behavior of the odd lot trader, volume indicators, and other nonprice indicators. Briefly, active net buying by corporate insiders would be a buy signal because it means that the group with the best information is buying. The idea here is to follow the knowledgeable investors. The odd lot trader trades shares in amounts fewer than a round lot, which is usually 100 shares. This kind of trading usually incurs higher transaction costs and is the province of participants with little capital who, after all, cannot even afford a round lot. According to technical analysis, these are the least sophisticated traders in the market, so the odd lot theory suggests that one should do exactly the opposite of what they do. Heavy net buying by odd lot traders is a sell signal to the informed trader, according to this view.

The technical trading techniques that focus on price patterns have received more attention from researchers than strategies focusing on market mood, probably because they are more specific in their prescriptions. Following that trend in research, three techniques have been employed to test for the existence of price patterns in stock prices: serial correlation tests, runs tests, and filter tests.

Serial Correlation Tests   If price changes behaved in regular ways from one day to the next, it seems that an investor could learn the regular rules for their behavior and use that information to earn fantastic returns. For example, if a large positive price change in one period is likely to be followed by a similar change in the next period, a smart trader could buy a stock after it had a big price increase and then capture the next big price increase. One way to test for this possibility is to examine stock returns to determine whether any such rules are valid.

The examination of successive returns for a single security over time focuses on serial correlation.[5] A simple way to consider serial correlation is to plot a security's returns on a pair of axes such as those shown in Figure 13.7, where the horizontal axis refers to the return in period t and the vertical axis refers to the return in period $t + 1$. For example, if the returns on some stock in four successive periods were 10, 12, -2, and 5 percent, we could plot the points $(10, 12)$, $(12, -2)$, and $(-2, 5)$ in a graph such as those in Figure 13.7. These points would plot on the northeast, southeast, and northwest quadrants, respectively.

The graph in Figure 13.7(a) shows how the points would plot if there were no correlation of returns between one period and the next. Positive returns would sometimes be followed by positive returns, leading to a point being plotted in the northeast quadrant. However, some positive returns would be followed by a negative return in the next period. This pair would be plotted in the southeast quadrant. Similarly, negative returns would be followed by either positive or negative returns in approximately the same proportion. If there were no correlation between returns in successive periods, the graph would be a circular cloud of points, as in Figure 13.7(a).

---

[5] Serial correlation differs from "contemporaneous correlation." When we discussed diversification in Chapter 11, we were concerned with the tendency of two or more securities to have the same kinds of returns in the same period. Now the focus is on the relationship between the returns in different periods for the same security.

FIGURE 13.7 Possible Patterns of Correlated and Uncorrelated Securities Returns

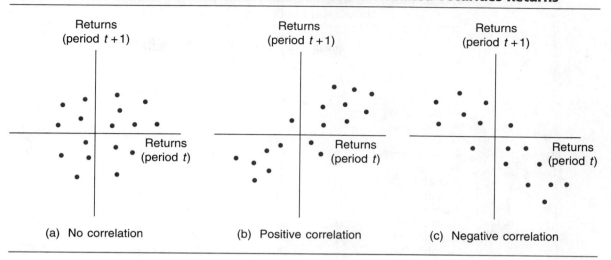

(a) No correlation   (b) Positive correlation   (c) Negative correlation

If there were positive correlation between successive returns, the graph would appear as shown in Figure 13.7(b), with returns in one period followed by returns of the same sign in the next. In this case, most pairs of successive returns would tend to lie in the northeast and the southwest quadrants. Similarly, if returns were negatively correlated, most of the plotted points would lie in the southeast and the northwest quadrants, as shown in Figure 13.7(c).

Even if no correlation were found between returns in contiguous periods, a nonzero correlation might still be possible between returns in noncontiguous periods. For example, if there were a correlation of returns between one day and the trading day four days earlier, this could be useful information. In such a case, we say that there would be a correlation of "lag four." Table 13.1 considers this possibility and reports calculated correlation values for stock returns when the lag is 1, 4, 9, and 16 days. It shows all of the Dow Jones industrial average stocks and finds correlations that are very low. Theoretically, if these correlations were 0, it would not be possible to devise a strategy of using high returns in one period to tell the investor what to do in another. Practically, if the correlations are close to 0, it would be pointless to try to use such information. For practical purposes, the correlations shown in Table 13.1 are essentially 0.

Having seen the evidence of Table 13.1, it is not surprising that a graph of actual market values looks like Figure 13.8, which graphs the points corresponding to returns in successive months for the U.S. stock market for the

TABLE 13.1   Serial Correlation Coefficients for Dow Jones Industrial Stocks

Stock	Differencing Interval (days)			
	1	4	9	16
Allied Chemical	0.017	0.029	−0.091	−0.118
Alcoa	0.118*	0.095	−0.112	−0.044
American Can	−0.087*	−0.124*	−0.060	0.031
AT&T	−0.039	−0.010	−0.009	−0.003
American Tobacco	0.111*	−0.175*	0.033	0.007
Anaconda	0.067*	−0.068	−0.125	0.202
Bethlehem Steel	0.013	−0.122	−0.148	0.112
Chrysler	0.012	0.060	−0.026	0.040
DuPont	0.013	0.069	−0.043	−0.055
Eastman Kodak	0.025	−0.006	−0.053	−0.023
General Electric	0.011	0.020	−0.004	0.000
General Foods	0.061*	−0.005	−0.140	−0.098
General Motors	−0.004	−0.128*	0.009	−0.028
Goodyear	−0.123*	0.001	−0.037	0.033
International Harvester	−0.017	−0.068	−0.244*	0.116
International Nickel	0.096*	0.038	0.124	0.041
International Paper	0.046	0.060	−0.004	−0.010
Johns Manville	0.006	−0.068	−0.002	0.002
Owens Illinois	−0.021	−0.006	0.003	−0.022
Procter & Gamble	0.099*	−0.006	0.098	0.076
Sears	0.097*	−0.070	−0.113	0.041
Standard Oil (Calif.)	0.025	0.143*	−0.046	0.040
Standard Oil (N.J.)	0.008	0.109	−0.082	−0.121
Swift & Co.	−0.004	−0.072	0.118	−0.197
Texaco	0.094*	−0.053	−0.047	−0.178
Union Carbide	0.107*	0.049	−0.101	0.124
United Aircraft	0.014	−0.190*	−0.192*	−0.040
U.S. Steel	0.040	−0.006	−0.056	0.236*
Westinghouse	−0.027	−0.097	−0.137	0.067
Woolworth	0.028	−0.033	−0.112	0.040

* Coefficient is twice its computed standard error.

Source: From "Efficient Capital Markets: A Review of Theory and Empirical Work" by Eugene F. Fama in *The Journal of Finance* XXV No. 2, May 1970. Copyright © by The American Finance Association. Reprinted by permission.

FIGURE 13.8   Serial Correlation for the U.S. Stock Market Using Monthly Returns for the Period 1951–1990

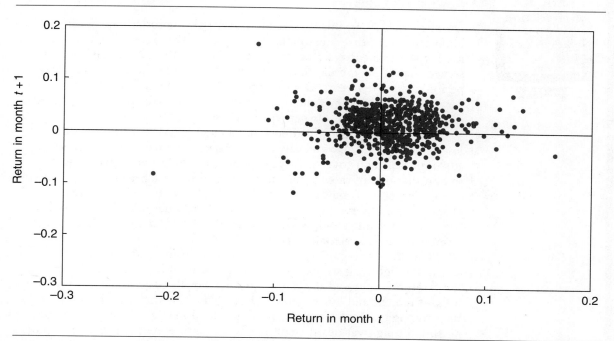

Source: © *Stocks, Bonds, Bills, and Inflation: 1991 Yearbook*™, Ibbotson Associates, Chicago (annually updates work by Roger G. Ibbotson and Rex A. Sinquefeld).

☞ Security prices appear to exhibit statistically significant serial correlation, but it is not strong enough to allow profitable trading strategies.

period 1951–1990. As it clearly indicates, the returns show very little correlation from one period to the next.

Most studies have found small but statistically significant positive correlations. These are not large enough to allow a profitable trading strategy, however, because the transaction costs would be too large. As a consequence, these studies indicate that the random walk hypothesis is probably false, but they do not provide evidence against the EMH. The reasons for this are clear when we consider the results of a runs test.

Runs Tests   Whereas the tests for serial correlation reflect the size of the individual returns, runs tests examine the tendencies for losses or gains to be followed by further losses or gains without regard for their size. They are often performed by examining a time series of returns for a security and testing whether the number of consecutive price gains (or the number of consecutive price drops) shows a pattern. If we represent a price gain by a + and a price drop by a −, the price movements of a security will be a series of + and − signs. For example, one possible series might look like this: + + + − + + + − + + + − + + + − + + + − ....

Against All Odds

On many occasions, this or that forecaster gains notoriety for predicting an important event that subsequently comes true. For example, a handful of market analysts correctly predicted the crash of 1987. It has also been observed that a few mutual funds have been top performers each year over a period of, say, ten years. Does this prove that some people truly have a "crystal ball" that allows them to forecast or to anticipate a rally in a particular stock? Perhaps. Or perhaps it is just a matter of chance.

If you throw a coin 10 times, the odds of getting all heads is very low—just 1 in 1,024. Similarly, if you observe the performance of, say, 1,000 mutual funds over a 10-year period, it would not be too surprising to find that one of those funds outperformed the market in each of the 10 years. The point is that even very improbable events may occur by mere chance if the observed sample is large enough. The following account, more than a century old, is a rather bizarre reminder that even extremely improbable events actually happen.

"On the evening of April 25 last [1891], during a violent thunderstorm, the lightning struck the lightning rod until it came to a defective insulator, then entered the house, striking Mr. Roode about half an inch back of the ear and burning its way through the entire length of his body, then through a wool mattress, splitting a hard maple bedstead, afterward passing through various parts of the house until it reached the water pipe. Mr. Roode regained consciousness and is on the road to recovery. His body is now so heavily charged with electricity that he can impart to anyone an electric shock equal to that received from a powerful battery."

Source: "50 and 100 Years Ago," *Scientific American*, May 1991, p. 14.

☞ There appear to be more runs in security prices than one would expect by chance, but not enough to allow profitable trading strategies.

If the price changes for a security had this pattern of three gains followed by a loss, repeated over and over, it would lead to a simple trading strategy consisting of buying the security at the close of a day with a loss, holding it for three days, and selling it at the close of the third day. Of course, we would not really expect actual price movements to follow such a rigid and simple pattern. If they followed any rule, however, it would be useful to know it and to try to form a strategy to take advantage of it.

To test for this possibility, researchers perform a runs test to determine whether the sequence of price gains and losses is similar to that generated by chance. This is like testing to determine whether the sequence could have been generated by tossing a coin. If we let heads represent a gain and tails represent a loss, what is the probability that the gains and losses could have been generated by coin flipping? If the sequence is random, it is useless to try to find patterns, just as it is useless to try to predict whether the next coin toss will be heads or tails by examining past tosses.[6]

Runs tests for the stock market found significant departures from randomness in stock price runs. In particular, the tendency was for gains to follow gains and for losses to follow losses. A trader might be able to use knowledge of this tendency to generate a simple profitable trading strategy: buy after a price rise and sell after a loss.

In summation, it is reasonable to believe that stocks show a tendency to experience runs in a way that is not entirely consistent with chance, but that is not enough to show that the market is inefficient. It must also be possible to devise a strategy that beats the market. Departures from randomness may be *statistically significant,* but that does not mean that they are *economically significant;* and it is economic significance that is important for the issue of market efficiency.

For a trader with absolutely no transaction costs, it would be possible to trade using the simple rule given above. However, every trader, even an exchange member, has some transaction costs. When even the lowest of these are taken into account, the prospective profits from the runs rule disappear. We must conclude that runs tests have found only statistically significant, and not economically significant, departures from randomness, and they are not large enough to allow anyone to make a supernormal return, so they do not count against market efficiency.

☞ Filter rules generate trading profits, but not enough to cover transaction costs and leave a profit.

Filter Tests   The last kind of technical trading rule we consider is a filter rule, which is as follows:

> If the daily closing price of a security rises at least *x* percent, buy the security and hold it until its price moves down at least *x* percent from a subsequent high. At that point, sell the security short and maintain the short position until the price rises at least *x* percent above a subsequent low.

Different filter rules can be specified by choosing different values for the filter *x.* Table 13.2 presents some of the key results of examining this rule. Testing filters of different sizes, ranging from $x = 0.5\%$ to $x = 20\%$, it was found that the filter rules could generate positive returns on a consistent basis, if transaction costs were ignored. These returns ranged from 4.3 to 11.5 percent per year. One problem with this technique is that it calls for very frequent trading. The third column of Table 13.2 shows the number of transactions that would be generated by following the filter strategy. The final column shows the total returns if transaction costs are taken into account. Even

---

[6] A common misconception is to say that if a coin has come up heads many times in a row, the next toss is more likely to result in tails. Actually, if the coin is fair, both outcomes are equally likely each time it is tossed, regardless of previous outcomes.

TABLE 13.2 Average Annual Rates of Return from Filter Rules, 1957–1962

Value of Filter x	Return with Trading Strategy	Total Transactions with Trading Strategy	Return with Trading Strategy After Commissions
0.5%	11.5%	12,500	−103.6%
1.0	5.5	8,700	−74.9
2.0	0.2	4,800	−45.2
4.0	0.1	2,000	−19.5
6.0	1.3	1,100	−9.4
8.0	1.7	700	−5.0
10.0	3.0	400	−1.4
20.0	4.3	100	3.0

Source: "Filter Rules and Stock Market Trading" by E. F. Fama and M. E. Blume, from *Journal of Business*, January 1966. Reprinted by permission of the University of Chicago Press.

assuming very low transaction costs, the apparent profits are turned to losses in almost every case. Only the 20 percent rule generates a positive return after commissions, but it is only 3 percent, and the investor could beat that return with a risk-free bond.

These three kinds of tests of technical trading rules agree in finding no workable rules, and many more such tests have broadly consistent findings. In general, researchers have been unable to find any compelling evidence that technical analysis works, but that is not to say that it is worthless. There are many possible kinds of technical trading strategies and to make the case against technical analysis airtight would require testing all of them. However, whereas technical trading rules have not been absolutely proved not to work, we have very little reason to believe that they do. In a way, testing them is like looking for a needle in a haystack: we may not be able to find the needle, but this does not mean that it doesn't exist. Similarly, as we continue looking without finding a successful rule, it does not mean that no such rule exists. However, after continued diligent and unsuccessful searching it becomes reasonable to doubt the presence of a needle, at least a large one. The continued absence of evidence in favor of technical trading rules justifies skepticism about the value of technical analysis.

Tests of the Semistrong Form of Market Efficiency

The semistrong form of the market efficiency hypothesis maintains that security prices at all times reflect all publicly available information. Thus, it should be impossible to use any public information to direct a trading strategy that earns more than the equilibrium risk-adjusted rate of return stipulated by the CAPM.

Stock Splits   One implication of the semistrong version of the EMH is that it should be impossible to earn supernormal returns by responding quickly to new public information. In effect, the public announcement of information should be so well anticipated by the market that security prices will have adjusted to their new equilibrium level even before it is made.

Occasionally, firms change the number of shares outstanding through a stock split or a stock dividend. This involves no cash flow to the investor, as it simply adjusts the total number of shares outstanding. Because dividends and splits differ only in their accounting treatment and have the same economic significance, we use the terms interchangeably in the discussion that follows.

Stock splits do tend to follow periods of unusually good performance by stocks, and seem to be a predictor of greater expected future earnings and dividends. Also, firms apparently use them to signal improved circumstances to the marketplace, and they are often quickly followed by increases in cash dividends as well. Based on a study of 940 splits, Figure 13.9 shows the risk-

FIGURE 13.9   Relative Performance for 940 Firms with Stock Splits

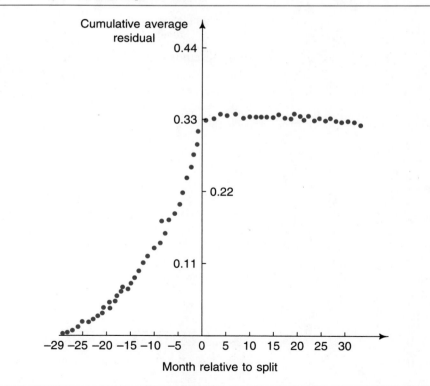

Source: Eugene F. Fama, Lawrence Fisher, Michael C. Jensen, and Richard Roll, "The Adjustment of Stock Prices to New Information," *International Economic Review,* February 1969, pp. 1–21.

adjusted relative performance of the sample relative to the market as a whole. The sample period consisted of 30 months before and 30 months after the split. The rising line prior to the announcement of the split, which is month 0, shows that these firms, on average, did 33 percent better than other securities of comparable risk. By the time of the split, however, all of the relatively superior performance had been achieved, as revealed by the fact that the line is almost flat after the announcement date; that is, the announcement of the split had no effect on the market. To the extent that it was good news, or was associated with good news, the market had anticipated it and gave no reaction to the announcement itself.

Although the split may not be important to investors, the fact that it tends to accompany announcements of changing cash dividends is important. When the sample of 940 firms was divided into those that had increases and those that had decreases in cash dividends, after the stock split the market's expectation about increases in cash dividends was apparent. Figure 13.10

FIGURE 13.10   Relative Performance for Firms with Stock Splits Followed by Increased Cash Dividends

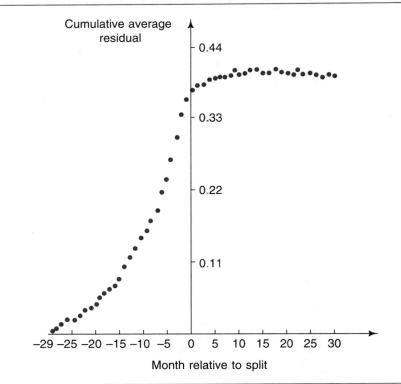

Source: Eugene F. Fama, Lawrence Fisher, Michael C. Jensen, and Richard Roll, "The Adjustment of Stock Prices to New Information," *International Economic Review*, February 1969, pp. 1–21.

FIGURE 13.11   **Relative Performance for Firms with Stock Splits Followed by Decreased Cash Dividends**

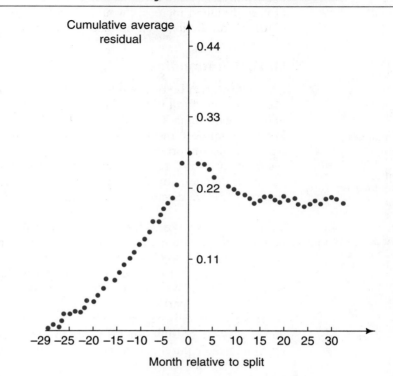

Source: Eugene F. Fama, Lawrence Fisher, Michael C. Jensen, and Richard Roll, "The Adjustment of Stock Prices to New Information," *International Economic Review*, February 1969, pp. 1–21.

shows the relative performance for firms increasing dividends. Notice the slight increase after the split announcement, which is consistent with the view that the dividend increase was almost fully anticipated. Actually, increasing the cash dividend did very little to help the stock's performance. By contrast, a dividend decrease had a deleterious effect on relative performance, as shown in Figure 13.11. For firms that announced a split but had a dividend decrease, the stock price was well under the market norm.

These results have important implications for the EMH. An investor who bought every stock that announced a split would not enjoy any performance that was better than the market norm, as shown by Figure 13.9. The market appears to be efficient with respect to the public information embodied in the split announcement. If the investor could find out in advance about the split by using privileged information, it does appear that superior returns could be earned. This finding has implications for the strong form of the EMH, which is discussed below. Finally, if an investor could tell which of the splitting stocks would have cash dividend increases, it would be possible to buy only those and earn a superior return. In other words, the early detection of cash dividend increases would be useful. However, no evidence suggests that such predictions can be made on a consistently successful basis.

Market Anomalies

market anomalies
actual behavior of the market that cannot be explained by current capital market theory

Although a great body of evidence is broadly consistent with the CAPM and the semistrong form of the EMH, recent evidence has accumulated that is at variance with them. Collectively, these disquieting discoveries are becoming known as **market anomalies**—apparent inconsistencies that appear to contradict some important features of the CAPM. This contradiction may be resolved by future research, but whether or not market anomalies can be resolved, they are currently important in the development of capital market theory. Here we discuss two of them.

☞ Market anomalies are important because they reveal potential errors in capital market theory.

The Day of the Week Effect   Considerable recent attention has been devoted to the difference in daily returns on many securities, depending on which day of the week is under examination. Nothing in the CAPM or the EMH indicates that returns on Thursday should be different from those on, say, Tuesday or Wednesday, but a great deal of evidence shows that they are different. In particular, Friday returns are generally high and Monday returns are generally negative. These differences are persistent and substantial, and it may be possible for investors to earn a return that beats the market by timing their purchases to take advantage of them.[7]

The day of the week effect suggests that either the semistrong EMH is not true or that the CAPM is not true, or both. If the CAPM is the correct pricing relationship in the market, the EMH must be false, because it appears that prices do not adjust correctly to reflect all available information. If the EMH is true, the CAPM must be false, because additional risk factors not recognized by the CAPM must be operational.

Earnings Reports   Another market anomaly concerns the market's response to announcements of quarterly earnings. With the forecast of next period's earnings, researchers look for large deviations in either direction from the forecast earnings. By buying stocks with especially favorable announcements and by selling those with unfavorable announcements, several studies have shown that traders can beat the market, even including transaction costs. If the market is efficient with respect to these announcements and the CAPM gives the correct pricing relationship for risk and return, it would be impossible to react to the announcements in a way that gave a supernormal return.

---

[7] Although Fridays tend to produce high returns, Friday the 13ths have produced statistically negative returns, even without including the near-panic drop of 190 points on the Dow Jones index that occurred on Friday, October 13, 1989. We might call this apparent anomaly the superstition effect.

The Semistrong Form of Market Efficiency and Fundamental Analysis

☞ If the semistrong form of the EMH is correct, fundamental analysis cannot improve investment performance.

Despite the questions raised by these market anomalies, a great preponderance of evidence remains in favor of the efficiency of the securities markets in the semistrong sense. Furthermore, among researchers a consensus seems to be emerging that these anomalies should be interpreted as a challenge to the CAPM and not to market efficiency. If the semistrong version of the EMH is accepted, it has strong implications for fundamental analysis. Essentially, fundamental analysis would be worthless as a technique for improving security returns.

Tests of the Strong Form of Market Efficiency

☞ If the strong form of the EMH is correct, even corporate insiders have no special information that could improve investment performance.

If the strong form of the efficient markets hypothesis is true, no information is valuable for directing a securities investment program, because all information has already been reflected in securities' prices. However, the best evidence clearly indicates that the strong form is false. Two tests of strong form efficiency examine the investment performance of corporate insiders and the returns earned by stock market specialists. It must be emphasized that trading on the basis of inside information is generally illegal.

Corporate Insiders   Corporate insiders often have access to potentially valuable information regarding the investment prospects of their firms before it is given to the general public. This raises the possibility that they could use it to earn returns in excess of the risk-adjusted norm. That appears to be exactly what occurs.

Considerable anecdotal evidence shows that insiders are able to make lots of money by trading on their privileged information. Generally, these stories come to public attention only in connection with court cases. Almost surely, the most exciting and juicy stories never see the public light because the illegal trading is never detected.

In addition to anecdotal evidence, more formal evidence exists. Corporate insiders are required to report their trading activity to the SEC within two weeks of the trade, and the SEC publishes this information in its "Official Summary of Insider Trading." Studies of this document reveal that insiders consistently earn more than would be expected in a strong form efficient market.

Market Specialists   Stock exchange specialists hold a book showing the orders that are awaiting execution at different prices as well as an inventory in the specialized stocks. If there are a large number of buy orders at $50 and the current price is $55, the specialists can be fairly confident that the price will not fall below $50, at least in the short run. This kind of privileged information is very valuable, according to studies of returns. Indeed, specialists

FINANCE TODAY

Insider Foresight?

One argument used by bulls these days is that the smart money is buying. Corporate insiders have been buying a lot more of their companies' shares than they have been selling. Defined by the securities laws as a company's officers, directors, and large stockholders, these insiders presumably know what is going on in their companies, so their buying is a tip-off that stocks are cheap. Don't be persuaded by their argument.

As evidence, look at the performance of an advisory letter that bases its recommendations on insider buy-and-sell decisions reported to the SEC. The letter, entitled *The Insiders,* is edited by Norman Fosback and Glen Parker out of their Institute for Econometric Research in Fort Lauderdale, Florida. Over the nearly six years from January 1985 through the third quarter of 1990, the stock recommended in *The Insiders* gained an average annual 4.9 percent, well below the S&P 500's 13.5 percent.

Nor is the experience of Fosback and Parker unique. The *Hulbert Financial Digest* tracked another insider letter whose performance lagged the market until it was discontinued. This other service, entitled *Insider Indicator,* was started in the early 1970s by Shannon Pratt of Portland State University, the co-author of the original academic study that showed that outside investors could beat the market by following the lead of corporate insiders. Alas, there seems to be a considerable gap between discovering a market "anomaly" like this and profiting from it. Over the period from January 1985 to August 1987, Pratt's letter did even worse than Fosback's and Parker's. At that point *Insider Indicator* was folded into Fosback's letter.

What prevented these letters from capitalizing on the anomaly? One reason may be that this apparent market inefficiency was in large part a different sort of market anomaly in disguise—namely, the tendency of small companies and low price/earnings companies to do well. Alas, the small-cap and low-P/E strategies, whatever their validity over the long pull, haven't worked in recent years. Another problem: Too many may be trying to follow the insiders' leads, and in the process are discounting away what used to be a way of earning above-market returns.

There's another reason to suspect that the insider anomaly may be a lot weaker today than it was in prior decades. In the 1970s the market was mostly bearish, and an insider who fought the tape to buy anyway was presumably highly confident that he was buying value at a discount. The

1980s, in contrast, were mostly bullish. Today's inside buyer may be simply another investor caught up in the euphoria of the moment. Consider: In late 1988 John Reed, Citicorp's chief executive, bought $1 million worth of his company's stock at 25. Citicorp is now trading at half that level. A year ago ten insiders at the Bank of New England bought shares of the bank's stock at prices between 14 and 19. Recent price: $1\frac{1}{8}$.

Fosback and Parker also use insider trades to create a signal on the overall market's direction. In each week's issue of *The Insiders*, they compute the percentage of all insider open market transactions that are purchases, and compare a five-week average of those percentages with the historic average buying level of 35 percent. (The average buying level is low because so many insider trades consist of sales of stock accumulated through stock option plans.) Any percentage above 35 percent—right now it is 74 percent—is supposed to be bullish.

The timing performance of this indicator leaves much to be desired, however. To be sure, as Fosback and Parker are quick to point out, the last time the signal was as bullish as today's 74 percent reading was one month after the 1987 crash. That was a great call, coming just before a 1,200-point rise in the Dow industrial average. But the call is somewhat vitiated by the indicator's not having turned bearish before the crash. (It became less bullish in the summer of 1987, but had returned to solidly bullish territory right before the crash.) Furthermore, the signal was bearish during much of 1983, 1985, and 1986, good years to be owning stocks.

The weak link in the bulls' argument is their belief that insiders' behavior in the aggregate is a good market timing indicator. Even if it were still true that corporate insiders often have valuable insight into their own companies' prospects, it doesn't necessarily follow that their aggregate behavior tells us anything about where the market as a whole is going. Academic studies bear out this point. Professors Wayne Lee and Michael Solt at Santa Clara University have discovered no correlation between the market's overall direction and the ratio of insider buying to selling.

In short, if you want to be bullish now, don't try to justify it on the basis of insider trading.

Source: Mark Hulbert, "Insider Trading," *Forbes,* December 24, 1990, p. 162.

appear to average returns of about 100 percent on their invested capital, which is clearly much more than the risk-adjusted norm. Almost all studies of strong form efficiency reach the same conclusion. Securities markets are not strong form efficient.

CHALLENGES TO THE CAPITAL ASSET PRICING MODEL

Given the apparently damaging evidence suggesting that markets cannot be semistrong efficient if the CAPM expresses the correct relationship between risk and return, it is not surprising that important challenges have arisen to the CAPM. This section discusses two of the most important of these. First, Richard Roll challenged the CAPM regarding the validity of its measurements and the issue of whether the model is truly testable as a scientific hypothesis. The second challenge has arisen in the form of an alternative theory of capital asset pricing, the arbitage pricing theory.

Roll's Critique

In theory, the market portfolio used in the CAPM should include all assets in the world in proportion to their value. In practice, most tests use a stock index limited to U.S. firms, and neglect any direct inclusion of the world's two largest asset categories, human capital and real estate. Furthermore, it appears that there is no hope of being able to construct an adequate index of the true market portfolio, due to the practical difficulties of measuring and properly weighing the returns on all of the different asset categories for all the countries of the world.

Richard Roll has pointed out the consequences of this.[8] All important implications of the CAPM require that the market portfolio be efficient in the sense of not being dominated by some other portfolio, as discussed in Chapter 11. However, since we cannot observe the market portfolio, due to the measurement problems mentioned above, we have no way to test its efficiency. This means that all other tests of the CAPM must have uncertain results, since we must always be uncertain about the market portfolio. Furthermore, even if the index used in practice is quite good, there can still be problems. As Roll has shown, even if two indices have a 0.95 correlation, they could give different answers in issues of performance evaluation. To date, Roll's critique has not been answered, and it presents one of the major outstanding problems for the CAPM.

Arbitrage Pricing Theory

Given the present difficulties of the CAPM, it is not surprising that an alternative theory has emerged. It is called the arbitrage pricing theory (APT).

---

[8] See Richard Roll, "A Critique of the Asset Pricing Theory's Tests," *Journal of Financial Economics*, March 1977.

It was created by Stephen Ross,[9] who maintains that there can be a number of risk factors that are priced in the market. If these factors do not affect the expected return of a security, there will be arbitrage opportunities. If we are willing to assume that there should be no unexploited arbitrage opportunities, Ross is able to show that we can express the expected return of a security as a function of the risk-free rate and a number of different factors. The arbitrage pricing model is represented by the following expression:

$$E(r_j) = r_f + \gamma_1 F_1 + \gamma_2 F_2 + \ldots + \gamma_n F_n$$

This equation says that the expected return on security j, $E(r_j)$, equals the risk-free rate, r_f, plus some number of risk factors, $\gamma_1 \ldots \gamma_n$, times the price of each unit of that type of risk, $F_1 \ldots F_n$.

It is also possible to view the CAPM as a special case of the APT. If there happens to be one significant factor, and if that factor happens to be systematic risk, then the APT would boil down to the CAPM.

SUMMARY

Until the last few years it was fairly easy to summarize the evidence on the CAPM and efficient markets. Only recently have market anomalies been discovered and the CAPM come under attack. Today, we can still be quite confident that securities markets in the United States are efficient in the weak sense and inefficient in the strong sense.

This chapter stressed the intimate relationship between evaluating a market's efficiency and relying on a pricing model. Market anomalies may be interpreted as calling either the pricing model or the market's efficiency into question. Currently, most researchers believe that they constitute a more severe challenge to the CAPM than they do to semistrong market efficiency. Faced with this uncertain situation, what should the investor do? The bulk of evidence still favors semistrong market efficiency. None of the studies that have found anomalies have provided evidence of gross or widespread inefficiencies. Furthermore, these apparent anomalies may be entirely due to faults in the pricing models, rather than to failure of semistrong efficiency.

If the market is efficient in the semistrong sense, investors should hold a well-diversified portfolio in order to eliminate unsystematic risk. In addition, they should not pay for research that attempts to beat the market. Also, if it is not really possible to analyze public information successfully, there is little reason for active trading. A policy of active trading would be appropriate if investors believe it is possible to identify underpriced securities. In a semistrong efficient market, this should not be possible. Consequently, trading should be oriented toward buy-and-hold strategies.

[9] See Stephen Ross, "The Arbitrage Theory of Capital Asset Pricing," *Journal of Economic Theory*, December 1976.

1. What is the difference between operational efficiency and informational efficiency?
2. How are the three traditional versions of the efficient market hypothesis distinguished?
3. If you find conclusive evidence that you can beat the market consistently by charting past stock prices, which version of the EMH would you disprove?
4. If a worker in the U.S. Patent Office learns about new products before they are announced publicly, is this worker able to use this information to beat the market? If the worker could beat the market using that information, which version of the EMH would that disprove?
5. It is often said that the EMH and the CAPM are tested jointly. Why?
6. Hot Stock, Inc. is trading at this moment for $6 on the NYSE and for $6.75 on the Pacific exchange. What exact transactions would you make to earn an arbitrage profit?
7. If you earned more than the S&P 500 for five years in a row, can you conclude that you beat the market?
8. What is the relationship between the random walk hypothesis and the efficient market hypothesis? Is the random walk hypothesis true?
9. What is a market anomaly and why might it be important?

PART 4

THE FIRM'S INVESTMENT DECISION

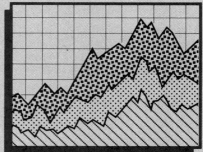

CHAPTER 14

Capital Budgeting

In the preceding chapters we considered investment opportunities from the point of view of the investor and found that securities markets are generally efficient. With this chapter we return to a consideration of firms engaging in real investment. The most crucial problem facing any firm is how to invest in real assets. Consequently, we begin by considering the implication of capital market theory for real investment.

Capital budgeting is the allocation of funds for real investment. The decision to build or expand a factory is a typical capital budgeting problem. Investing in a given project depends on the value of the investment relative to the present value of the cash flows that will come from the project. This is how benefits are compared to costs. Consequently, the goal of capital budgeting is to select projects with cash flows that are worth more than their cost in present value terms and thus create value for the firm.

In capital budgeting analysis, some problems occur so frequently that they have names. This chapter considers five that the financial manager is likely to face. The first arises when two projects compete for the same resources or for some other reason both cannot be undertaken. They are called mutually exclusive projects. Second, sometimes managers are confronted with so many attractive projects that they do not have funds available to invest in all of them. The allocation of funds among a set of projects requiring more financing than is available is known as capital rationing. Third, managers often have to choose the best time to replace a machine of the same type that is now operating. They are said to face the machine replacement problem. Fourth, it is often the case that two machines produce the same good, but do it in different ways. The typical choice is between a high-priced machine that lasts a long time and a cheap one that wears out quickly. This is a classic case of projects with different lives. Finally, an investment project can have a positive net present value if undertaken immediately, but it may become even more attractive later, creating a problem of investment timing.

capital budgeting
the allocation of investment funds to long-term real assets

SECURITIES INVESTMENT AND REAL INVESTMENT

In Chapters 11 through 13 we explored the world of securities in detail. Figure 14.1 summarizes our basic conclusions:

1. The appropriate measure of risk is beta, a measure of systematic risk.
2. The required return on an investment increases linearly with beta, because investors must be compensated for bearing systematic risk.
3. The securities market is highly efficient, so individual securities and portfolios lie on the security market line (SML).

We also know a great deal about the corporation and its management:

1. The corporation issues securities in the securities markets. The SML of Figure 14.1 indicates the return investors require for a given level of risk.
2. The manager should maximize the wealth of the firm's owners or, equivalently, maximize the share price.
3. The market for investment in real goods is not efficient. In essence, the ability to undertake some real investment opportunities requires market position and power. For example, it is very hard for an individual to compete with IBM in introducing a new computer.
4. It is reasonable to undertake real investment only if its return exceeds the return available in the securities market for the same risk level.

FIGURE 14.1   The Security Market Line and Real Investment

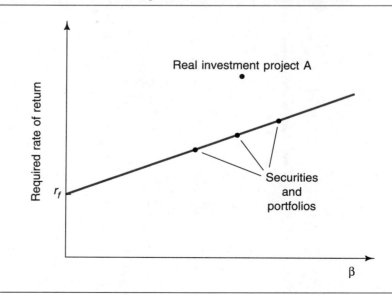

We can now put together these conclusions about the securities market and the corporation to understand the task of the financial manager in committing funds to real investment.

☞ In capital budgeting, the financial manager creates wealth for shareholders by undertaking projects whose expected returns exceed required returns.

Each firm has a certain pool of funds available for investment. If those funds are invested in projects that generate cash flows with the same present value, the firm's wealth will not increase. Instead, the firm has merely exchanged funds in one form for funds in another form of equal value.

net present value (NPV) the present value of cash inflows from a project minus the present value of the investment costs

In capital budgeting, the manager seeks projects whose cash flows have a greater present value than the invested funds. This difference between the present value cash flows and the investment is the project's **net present value** (**NPV**):

$$NPV = PV \text{ of cash flows} - PV \text{ of investment}$$

Equivalently, we have:

$$NPV = -I + \sum_{t=1}^{n} \frac{C_t}{(1 + r)^t} \tag{14.1}$$

positive net present value project a project with a present value of cash flows that exceeds the present value of the investment

Projects whose present value of cash flows exceeds that of the cost of the investment have **positive net present value.** When the firm undertakes such projects it increases the shareholders' wealth by the amount of the positive NPV. Consider investment project A in Figure 14.1, lying above the SML. Since its expected return exceeds the required return given by the SML, it has a positive NPV and the firm should undertake it.

☞ The amount of wealth created by a project is equal to its NPV.

☞ The securities market is efficient, but the market for real investment is not.

Here is the key point of all financial management. The securities market is efficient, but the market for real investment is not. In an efficient market, the expected return equals the required rate of return. In capital budgeting, the financial manager creates wealth for shareholders by undertaking real investment projects with expected returns exceeding required returns; in other words, by finding projects whose present value of cash inflows exceeds investment cost. It is only because the market for real investment is inefficient that capital budgeting can succeed.

Firms must seek out investment projects in which they can earn positive NPVs. This chapter explains how to analyze such projects.

TECHNIQUES FOR EVALUATING CASH FLOWS

In this section we cover several approaches for evaluating cash flow streams. We begin with a brief discussion of some traditional measures and their inadequacies. We then turn to techniques based on present value concepts that are the main focus of the chapter.

To make our discussion concrete, let us consider an investment that requires the following cash flows. At the outset, time $t = 0$, the investment is $2,500. After this the project generates cash flows according to the following schedule:

Year	Cash Flow
0	−$2,500
1	+1,500
2	+1,700
3	+1,000
4	+1,000
5	+1,000

The Payback Period

payback period
the time in a project's life at which the investment cost is recovered, or paid back, from its cash flows

The **payback period (PP)** has long been a very popular criterion for capital budgeting, largely due to its simplicity. It is the time it takes for the positive cash flows to equal the amount of the investment. Equivalently:

$$0 = -I + \sum_{t=1}^{PP} C_t \tag{14.2}$$

For this example the payback period is the time until the positive cash flows equal $2,500. This does not happen in the first year, when the cash flow is only $1,500; but by the end of the second year, the accumulated operating cash flow is $3,200. Therefore, the payback period falls somewhere between years 1 and 2. Assuming that the operating cash flows come in evenly across time, the payback period is 1.5882 years.[1] The payback rule is to prefer projects with a short payback period.

☞ The payback criterion completely neglects cash flows that occur after the payback period.

However, the technique has serious drawbacks. First, it neglects cash flows that occur after the payback period. According to the payback criterion, all of the following cash flow patterns are equally desirable:

Year	Original Cash Flow	Pattern A	Pattern B	Pattern C
0	−$2,500	−$2,500	−$2,500	−$2,500
1	+1,500	+1,500	+1,500	+1,500
2	+1,700	+1,700	+1,700	+1,700
3	+1,000	0	0	0
4	+1,000	0	0	0
5	+1,000	+1,000	0	−1,000

[1] After one year we still need $1,000 to pay back the investment of $2,500. Since during the second year we will receive $1,700, the fraction of that year required for the payback is $1,000/$1,700 = 0.5882.

☞ The payback criterion does not consider the timing of cash flows except to determine the payback period.

Cash flow patterns A, B, and C have exactly the same payback period as our original cash flows. Therefore, they are equally desirable according to the payback criterion. However, anyone would have good reason to prefer some of these patterns over others. First, we would all prefer the original cash flows to pattern A, because we get an extra $1,000 in each of years 3 and 4 and the same cash flow in year 5. Payback ignores that difference. Second, we would prefer A to B because it gives us an extra $1,000 in year 5. However, according to the payback criterion, A and B are equally desirable. Third, we would prefer B to C. The two are identical in years 0 through 4, but C provides a cash outflow of $1,000 in period 5. The payback period criterion neglects all of these important differences and therefore cannot be a useful guide to making investment decisions. In short, it ignores cash flows beyond the payback period.

A second important problem with the payback criterion is that it disregards the timing of the cash flows. For example, consider our original cash flows and pattern D:

Year	Original Cash Flow	Pattern D
0	−$2,500	−$2,500
1	+1,500	+1,500
2	+1,700	+1,700
3	+1,000	0
4	+1,000	0
5	+1,000	+3,000

Their payback period is identical, so they are equally attractive, according to the payback criterion; however, the original cash flows are definitely better than those of pattern D. In spite of the fact that the cash flows have the same total, the original ones are received earlier than those in D. Due to the time value of money, we would always prefer the original cash flows.

The Discounted Payback Period

discounted payback period
a variation of the payback period that incorporates time value of money concepts

The payback period disregards the time value of money. The **discounted payback period (DPP)** addresses this shortcoming. It is the time until the present value of the positive cash flows equals the amount of the investment. The appropriate discount rate for the project is used to calculate the DPP. The DPP involves solving the following formula:

$$0 = -I + \sum_{t=1}^{DPP} \frac{C_t}{(1 + r)^t} \tag{14.3}$$

For our example, the discounted payback is slightly greater than two years, since we have:

$$-69.44 = -2,500 + \frac{1,500}{1.20} + \frac{1,700}{1.20^2}$$

The DPP can be appreciated more clearly by graphically representing the process of searching for it. This is done by plotting the NPV of the project, assuming that it is after the first cash flow, the second cash flow, and so on. Figure 14.2 illustrates this process for our project. There we see that for $t = 0$ the NPV is $-\$2,500$, for $t = 2$ it is $-\$69.44$, and for $t = 5$ it is $\$1,393.39$. The DPP is at the point at which the graph crosses the horizontal axis.

Accounting-Based Profitability Measures

A number of accounting-based profitability measures can be used in capital budgeting analyses. In essence, each one divides some measure of accounting profits by some measure of investment. For example, the return on investment (ROI) is usually calculated by dividing after-tax accounting profits by the investment.

FIGURE 14.2   The Discounted Payback Period

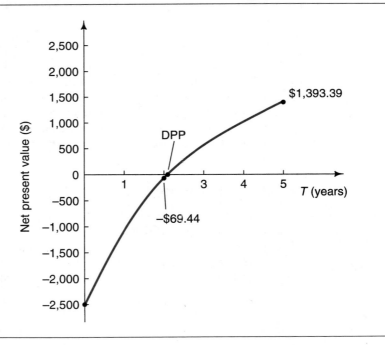

☞ Accounting measures of return on investment typically focus on accounting profits, not cash flow, and fail to consider any profits except for those of a single year under analysis.

All of these methods have serious flaws. First, they focus on accounting profits rather than on cash flow. We have seen that the value of any investment depends on the present value of its cash flows. Cash flow can be spent or reinvested, accounting profits cannot. Second, these measures consider only the profits of one year. As a consequence, they are unable to deal with situations in which competing projects have different lives, or with projects whose profits change from period to period. This means that they cannot adequately consider the timing of cash flows or projects with uneven cash flows. As is the case with the payback method, the methods are greatly inferior to the present value techniques, which are the focus of the rest of this chapter.

NET PRESENT VALUE

☞ If the NPV is positive when the cash flows are discounted at the appropriate discount rate, accept the project.

Earlier in this chapter we introduced the principle of NPV for evaluating an investment's cash flows. Here we explore the computation of the NPV and other related measures based on present value concepts. These principles can be illustrated using the original cash flows shown above. We assume that the appropriate discount rate is 20 percent. For our original cash flows we have the following table:

Year	Original Cash Flow	Present Value
0	−$2,500	−$2,500.00
1	+1,500	1,250.00
2	+1,700	1,180.56
3	+1,000	578.70
4	+1,000	482.25
5	+1,000	401.88

The sum of the inflows in years 1 through 5 is $3,893.39, and the present value of the investment is $2,500. Applying Equation 14.1, we have:

$$\text{NPV} = \text{PV of cash flows} - \text{PV of investment}$$
$$= \$3,893.39 - \$2,500$$
$$= \$1,393.39$$

Undertaking this project adds $1,393.39 to the firm's wealth. If the project had a negative NPV, we would reject it because the investment cost is higher than the present value of the cash inflows. The basic NPV rule is:

NPV RULE
If the NPV is positive when the cash flows are discounted at the appropriate discount rate, accept the project.

FINANCE

TODAY

Financing from Crib to Dorm

In 1985, Duquesne University began selling zero-coupon bonds, called Children's Receipts of Inflation-adjusted Benefits or CRIBs, redeemable for tuition at Duquesne in 1999. Four years of tuition at Duquesne beginning in 1999 were selling then for $5,593. Duquesne officials estimated that four years of tuition in 1999 would cost $51,912, assuming a 6 percent inflation rate over that period. Based on that assumption, the purchasers of future tuition in 1985 for a payment of $5,593 would receive a very healthy 17.25 percent annual rate of return.

Where else could parents get a 17.25 percent return? In fact, if it seems to be such a good deal for the parents, how can it be a good deal for Duquesne? There must be some strings attached. First, if the child dies, is not admitted, or does not want to go to Duquesne, the school will refund only the initial payment the parent made. Second, if the scholar flunks out, Duquesne refunds nothing. But if the student enrolls in Duquesne, has a 2.5 average, and transfers to another university, Duquesne will pay the tuition at the other school, up to the amount of Duquesne's tuition.

There are some obvious problems with the concept. Admissions offices may be pressured to accept marginally acceptable students who have prepaid. Alternatively, a student may have an acceptable academic record, but might prefer to go to some other university. With tuition prepaid at Duquesne, parents are likely to pressure the student to go there.

In spite of the complications, CRIBs can be considered to be the kind of investment that one can make now or later. The CRIB could be purchased for a child born today, or the parents could wait to buy the bond later. As the child gets older, the cost of the tuition bond must go up,

INTERNAL RATE OF RETURN

internal rate of return (IRR)
the discount rate that equates the present value of all project and investment flows to 0

☞ If the IRR is greater than the appropriate discount rate, accept the project.

For any set of cash flows, the **internal rate of return (IRR)** is defined as the discount rate that makes their NPV equal to 0. In general, to find the IRR of a sequence of cash flows, we can use trial and error, a financial calculator, or a computer. The formula used to solve for the IRR is:

$$0 = -I + \sum_{t=1}^{n} \frac{C_t}{(1 + \text{IRR})^t} \qquad (14.4)$$

We can find the IRR of our original project by forcing the NPV to equal 0 and finding the discount rate; this discount rate is the IRR. In our example,

because Duquesne will have the money for a shorter period before enrollment.

In other words, you can look at the problem of timing an investment with a positive NPV. In order to do so, you must make some more simplifying assumptions. Let us assume that interest rates do not change, so the price of a bond for tuition to begin at a fixed point in the future goes up at a rate of 17.25 percent per year. Let us also ignore the fact that parents will learn more about the child's abilities and interests as the child matures. With these assumptions, matters are fairly clear. Assuming that a rate of 17.25 percent is attractive for an investment of this risk level, the bond should be purchased now. Waiting will not change anything because we have assumed away changing interest rates and new information.

If you are a little more realistic and consider the problem actually faced by a prospective CRIBs purchaser, things become much more complex. If interest rates and expected inflation change, it may be better to wait to purchase the bond. Even more important, if you buy a bond for a newborn child, it is a very risky investment. Perhaps the child is simply not college material, and the entire investment will be lost. If you wait until the child is older and you can assess the abilities of the child, then the investment becomes much less risky. For example, if your kid is six years old, reads nuclear physics books, and has Duquesne stickers all over her bedroom, then the investment starts to look very good. At any rate, the investment is a very complex one and it is not at all easy to say when is the best time to make the investment.

Source: Lawrence Minard, "The CRIBs Age," *Forbes*, November 18, 1985.

the IRR is 46.48 percent, because discounting the original cash flows at that rate gives a net present value of 0:

$$\text{NPV} = -\$2,500 + \frac{\$1,500}{1.4648} + \frac{\$1,700}{1.4648^2} + \frac{\$1,000}{1.4648^3} + \frac{\$1,000}{1.4648^4} + \frac{\$1,000}{1.4648^5}$$

$$= -\$2,500 + \$1,024.03 + \$792.30 + \$318.17 + \$217.21 + \$148.29$$

$$= 0$$

Notice that this project has a cash outflow in period 0 followed by a series of cash inflows, so there is just one change of sign in the sequence, between period 0 and period 1. A project with only one sign change in the

normal project
a project with only one change of sign in the sequence of cash flows

sequence of cash flows is called a **normal project.** It is important to note that normal projects have only one IRR. However, if the sign changes more than once, there could be more than one positive IRR. In general, the maximum possible number of positive IRRs for a project is equal to the number of sign changes in the cash flows. The possibility of multiple IRRs is discussed in the next section.

When the project is normal and the IRR is greater than the appropriate discount rate, the NPV will always be positive. Thus, we can use the IRR to decide whether to accept a project according to the following basic rule:

IRR RULE
If the IRR is greater than the appropriate discount rate, accept the project.

To illustrate this rule, consider again the original cash flows. We assumed that their appropriate discount rate was 20 percent and found that the IRR was 46.48 percent. Because the IRR exceeds the appropriate discount rate, we would accept the project. Following the IRR rule gives the same accept-reject decision as the NPV rule.

THE NPV PROFILE

NPV profile
a graphical technique representing the NPV of a project for various discount rates

An extremely useful tool for analyzing capital budgeting problems is the **NPV profile.** It is a graphical representation of the NPV of a project for various discount rates. For a normal project, it is downward sloping. Figure 14.3 shows the NPV profile for the original cash flows. The shape of this graph is typical

FIGURE 14.3   The NPV Profile for the Original Cash Flows

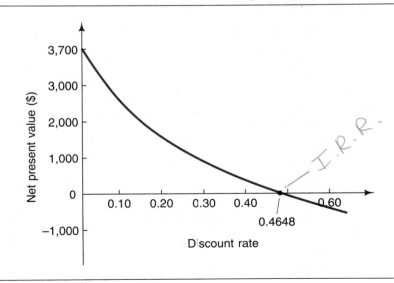

for normal projects. If the discount rate is 0, the NPV for the project equals the sum of all the positive cash flows minus the investment, or $3,700. In other words, for $r = 0$ no discounting is necessary. If the discount rate is 20 percent, the NPV is $1,393.39. If the cash flows are discounted at the IRR, the NPV of the project equals 0. If the discount rate exceeds the IRR, then the NPV is negative. For example, with the original cash flows, a discount rate of 60 percent gives an NPV of $-$406.33.

The NPV profile has several interesting general features. First, it intercepts the NPV axis at a value equal to the simple sum of all the cash flows of the project, because in that case the discount rate is 0. Thus, we have:

$$NPV(r = 0) = -I + \sum_{t=1}^{n} C_t$$

Second, the discount rate at which the NPV profile crosses the horizontal axis (the discount rate axis) is the IRR of the project. This follows from the fact that at that discount rate the NPV is precisely 0. Third, for very high discount rates, the NPV profile approaches the value $-I$, because as the rates increase, the present value of each cash flow is less and less. In the limit, the summation term in the NPV expression, Equation 14.1, vanishes. Thus:

$$NPV(r = \infty) = -I$$

The NPV profile in Figure 14.3 provides a graphical confirmation of the IRR rule. Indeed, the figure shows that whenever the IRR is greater than the appropriate discount rate, r, the NPV will be greater than 0. Consequently, for normal projects the NPV and IRR rules always produce the same accept or reject decision.

IRR COMPLICATIONS

The IRR has some pitfalls, so it must be handled with care. For example, some projects may have more than one IRR, and others may have none. The financial manager should be aware of these peculiarities to avoid making costly mistakes.

Projects with Multiple IRRs

In general, the maximum possible number of positive IRRs is equal to the number of sign changes in the project's cash flow stream. Consider the following cash flow pattern:

Year	Cash Flow
0	$-$2,000
1	$+$7,000
2	$-$6,000

We can find the IRR of this project by solving the following equation:

$$0 = -\$2,000 + \frac{\$7,000}{1 + IRR} - \frac{\$6,000}{(1 + IRR)^2}$$

To solve for the IRR, it is convenient to multiply this expression by $(1 + IRR)^2$. This results in:

$$0 = -2,000(1 + IRR)^2 + 7,000(1 + IRR) - 6,000$$

This is a quadratic equation that can be solved using some algebra. The general solution to an equation of the form $ax^2 + bx + c = 0$, is found from Equation 14.5:

$$x = \frac{-b \pm \sqrt{b^2 - 4ac}}{2a} \tag{14.5}$$

In our example, $a = -2,000$, $b = 7,000$, and $c = -6,000$. Also, in applying Equation 14.4 to solve for the IRR, $(1 + IRR)$ takes the role of x. Given this, the two IRRs of the project are:

$$(1 + IRR) = \frac{-7,000 \pm \sqrt{7,000^2 - 4 \times (-2,000) \times (-6,000)}}{2(-2,000)}$$

$$(1 + IRR_1) = 1.50$$
$$(1 + IRR_2) = 2.00$$

This calculation reveals that the IRRs of this project are 50 percent and 100 percent.

Figure 14.4 shows how the NPV of this cash flow stream varies with the discount rate. From the definition of the IRR we have NPV = 0 at discount

FIGURE 14.4 A Project with Multiple IRRs

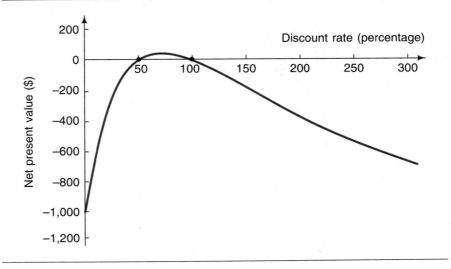

rates of 50 and 100 percent. The figure clearly shows that in this case it is erroneous to apply the IRR rule. Recall that the rule indicates that we should accept projects with an IRR greater than the appropriate discount rate. For example, if the appropriate discount rate is less than 50 percent, as is very likely, the rule would lead to acceptance of the project. However, in this case the project has a negative NPV for any discount rate less than 50 percent. In fact, this project should be accepted only when the appropriate discount rate for the project is between 50 percent and 100 percent.

Projects with No IRR

Consider a project with the following cash flows:

Year	Cash Flow
0	−$1,000
1	+1,500
2	−1,000

We can find the IRRs using Equation 14.5. Here, $a = -1,000$, $b = 1,500$, and $c = -1,000$, so the IRRs are equal to:

$$(1 + \text{IRR}) = \frac{-1,500 \pm \sqrt{(1,500)^2 - 4 \times (-1,000) \times (-1,000)}}{2(-1,000)}$$

$$(1 + \text{IRR}) = 0.75 \pm 0.66\sqrt{-1}$$

In this case the two solutions involve the square root of −1, which does not exist as a real number,[2] but is the unit of the imaginary numbers.[3] When we say that there is no real IRR, we mean that the IRR does not lie on the real number line. An important implication is that the NPV profile for the project will never cross the horizontal axis, because if it did, a real IRR would exist. Therefore, we have the interesting result that the NPV of a project with no real IRRs is either always above or always below the horizontal axis.

Since for projects with no real IRR the NPV is either always positive or negative, regardless of the value of the discount rate, the decision rule is extremely simple. For a project with no real IRRs, simply determine the NPV for a convenient discount rate, say, $r = 0$ percent, and if that NPV is positive, accept the project; otherwise, reject it. In the example, the NPV will

---

[2] In other words, there is no real number that, multiplied by itself, results in −1.

[3] The two IRR values are complex numbers. Complex numbers consist of a real part and an imaginary part. Whenever a project has complex IRRs, it will always have an even number of them. Each pair of IRRs arises from the positive and negative signs in Equation 14.5. Knowledge of this fact may help simplify the search for multiple IRRs. As an example, suppose you have already found two complex IRRs for a three-year project; then the remaining IRR is necessarily real, since complex roots can only come in pairs.

What a Sense of Humor!

Never mind trade issues: the U.S. and Japan can't even agree on what's funny. That culture gap was illustrated recently when a Japanese business-man on a United Airlines flight from Tokyo to San Francisco handed a flight attendant a trash-filled airsickness bag and claimed it was a bomb. His attempt at humor didn't go over very well with the crew, which placed the bag carefully in a protective box, dumped fuel, and headed back to Japan. [In April 1991] the prankster paid United a relatively small damage settlement of $29,000. An airline lawyer explained that after the man apologized, the company decided to take a "very Japanese action" and not sue for the total costs of the returned flight.

Source: David Ellis, "Can't You Yanks Take a Joke?" *Time*, April 15, 1991, p. 17.

always be negative, since for $r = 0$ we have NPV $= -\$1,000 + \$1,500 - \$1,000 = -\$500$. This project should be rejected regardless of the required discount rate.

The NPV profile for the project with no real IRRs is shown in Figure 14.5. We verify that the NPV is always negative, so the project should be rejected without further ado.

FIGURE 14.5   A Project with No IRRs

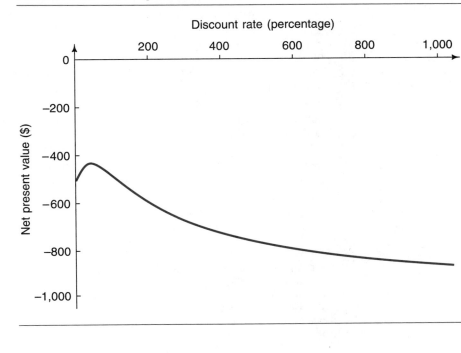

THE PROFITABILITY INDEX

☞ If the PI exceeds 1 when the cash flows are discounted at the appropriate rate, accept the project.

The profitability index (PI) is another capital budgeting technique based on present value rules. It measures the ratio of present value benefits to cost:

$$PI = \frac{PV \text{ of cash flows}}{PV \text{ of investment outlays}}$$

The present value of the cash flows is found by discounting them at the appropriate discount rate, just as we did in our discussion of NPV. For example, the present value of our original cash flows is $3,893.39 for a discount rate of 20 percent, and the investment is $2,500. Accordingly, the profitability index is:

$$PI = \frac{\$3,893.39}{\$2,500} = 1.5574$$

When the NPV is 0, the present value of the cash flows equals the present value of the investment cost. A 0 NPV corresponds to a PI of 1. If the PI is less than 1, the investment cost exceeds the present value of the cash flows, so the NPV would be negative. Finally, if the PI is greater than 1, the NPV will be positive. Here is a table of these correspondences:

NPV	PI
Negative	< 1
Zero	1
Positive	> 1

Now it is clear that we can formulate a rule for using the PI value that will give the same decisions as the NPV rule or the IRR rule:

PI RULE
**If the PI exceeds 1 when the cash flows are discounted
at the appropriate rate, accept the project.**

The NPV rule, the IRR rule, and the PI rule give the same accept-reject decisions for normal capital budgeting projects.

USING NPV, IRR, AND PI FOR RANKING PROJECTS

☞ The NPV, IRR, and PI ranking rules can give different rankings of project acceptability.

Firms often face the problem of mutually exclusive projects. For example, a given piece of land might be considered as a suitable location for a bakery or a service station, but not both. As another example, assume that the firm has enough investable resources to undertake only one of two profitable projects. Accepting one requires rejecting the other, so the financial manager must rank them. In some cases, there can be a number of mutually exclusively projects, and ranking is also important then.

We can state three rules for ranking projects that correspond to our three accept-reject rules:

NPV RANKING RULE
Of two mutually projects, choose the one with the higher NPV.

IRR RANKING RULE
Of two mutually exclusive projects, choose the one with the higher IRR.

PI RANKING RULE
Of two mutually exclusive projects, choose the one with the higher PI.

Although all three rules may give the same ranking, on some occasions the rankings differ. Consider the cash flows for a service station and a bakery that are candidates for the same land, so only one project can be accepted. Table 14.1 shows cash flows for the two projects, the IRRs, NPVs at a discount rate of 15 percent, and the PIs. Assuming a discount rate of 15 percent, both projects have a positive NPV and would be acceptable.

According to the NPV ranking rule, we should accept the service station because it has the greater NPV. According to the IRR ranking rule, however, we should accept the bakery because it has the higher IRR. Finally, according to the PI ranking rule, we should accept the bakery because it has the higher PI. Because the rules conflict, we must determine which one should be followed.

The reason for the conflicting rankings stems from the fact that the projects are of different scales. It is true that the bakery has a higher IRR, but because the service station is bigger, it accumulates a greater NPV at the required return of 15 percent. If the service station project were the same size as the bakery, the investment and all of the cash flows would be reduced by 60 percent, so it would require a $10,000 investment and would generate cash flows of $3,256. In that case the IRR would still be 23.29 percent, but the NPV for the "little" service station would be $2,328. Therefore, if the projects

TABLE 14.1 Service Station and Bakery Cash Flows

Year	Service Station	Bakery
0	−$25,000	−$10,000
1	8,141	3,431
2	8,141	3,431
3	8,141	3,431
4	8,141	3,431
5	8,141	3,431
6	8,141	3,431
IRR	23.29%	25.55%
NPV at 15%	$5,814	$2,986
PI	1.2326	1.2986

FIGURE 14.6   NPV Graphs for the Service Station and Bakery

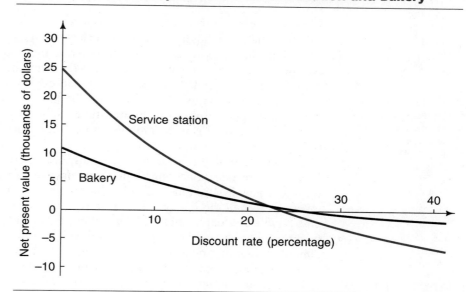

were of the same scale, the NPV and IRR criteria would give exactly the same ranking. From this we can see that the conflict emerges from the difference in scale.

Figure 14.6 graphs the NPV of the mutually exclusive projects. For low discount rates, the service station has the higher NPV, but for high discount rates, the bakery does. At a discount rate of 21.8 percent, the NPVs are equal at $912. Notice, however, that for discount rates above 21.8 percent, the NPV, IRR, and PI ranking methods all favor the bakery.

☞ When the ranking rules conflict, we should follow the NPV rule, because it ranks projects according to the amount of wealth they create for the firm.

When the ranking rules conflict, we should follow the NPV ranking rule, because it measures the difference between the benefits and costs of the project. The example of Table 14.1 helps us to see that more clearly. With the bakery, $10,000 is invested and an IRR of 25.55 percent is earned, but the wealth of the firm increases by only $2,985. If the firm accepts the service station, it invests $25,000 and earns only a 23.29 percent IRR. In spite of this, the service station has an NPV of $5,809, and choosing it gives $2,824 more wealth. Because the goal of the firm is to increase the wealth of its stockholders, we should follow the NPV ranking rule when there is conflict.[4]

[4] If you are still not convinced that the scale difference can distort the IRR criterion, consider the following example. Mr. Wimpy is desperate to eat some hamburgers, so he offers you two choices: give him $1 immediately, and he will gladly repay you $2 next Tuesday; or give him $100 today and he will gladly repay you $120 next Tuesday. In the first case the IRR is 100 percent, whereas in the second case it is only 20 percent. Nevertheless, with the second choice you will be a lot richer next Tuesday (and Mr. Wimpy will be a lot fatter) than with the first choice.

CAPITAL RATIONING

☞ In capital rationing, the correct solution is to choose the one collection of investment projects out of all possible collections that has the highest total NPV.

We saw that the firm should accept the service station and reject the bakery, but one apparent difficulty with this is the fact that the service station consumes $25,000 of the firm's investable funds, whereas the bakery uses only $10,000. Normally, this does not matter, because the firm should be able to obtain more investment funds from the capital markets if it has attractive projects.

Capital rationing is called for when the firm has a number of attractive investment opportunities but limited funds. The problem is to decide how the available capital is to be rationed among the projects. Once again we are faced with the necessity of ranking.

Capital rationing arises due to externally or internally imposed constraints. First, on rare occasions capital markets may be disturbed, preventing the raising of new funds. This might be due to action of the Federal Reserve or to some crisis in the markets. For example, when the Savings and Loan and junk bond crises exploded in the late 1980s, they resulted in a period of great disturbance in the market, the Fed tightened its controls, and many firms had difficulty obtaining debt financing. Second, a firm that believes market rates are too high may refuse to acquire new capital and instead limit its investment. It also might restrict the activities of various divisions of the firm to make them more rigorous in their budgeting.

Consider CapRat, Inc., a firm operating under capital rationing constraints with a total investment budget of $115,000. CapRat uses a discount rate of 16 percent for the projects in Table 14.2. The problem is to decide which ones to accept. All of them are acceptable, with positive NPVs and IRRs above 16 percent, and the capital required to undertake them totals $215,000. CapRat has a total capital pool of only $115,000, however.

One possible strategy is to accept the projects with the highest IRRs until the pool of capital is exhausted. If the firm follows that procedure, it will choose projects A, C, G, and B. For these, the investment totals $110,000 and no project with an IRR less than 18 percent will be accepted. Furthermore,

TABLE 14.2   Projects Available to CapRat, Inc.

Project	Investment	NPV	IRR	PI
A	$10,000	$ 3,000 (3)	0.24 (1)	1.30 (1)
B	30,000	6,000	0.18 (3)	1.20
C	40,000	10,000 (2)	0.22 (2)	1.25 (2)
D	60,000	15,000 (1)	0.16	1.25 (3)
E	25,000	5,000	0.17	1.20
F	20,000	4,000	0.16	1.20
G	30,000	6,500	0.18 (4)	1.22

Note: Numbers in parentheses indicate the projects' ranking order under each rule.

the total NPV of the projects will be $25,500. Of the $115,000 available, $5,000 will be left over because it is not enough to undertake any other project. As a second alternative, CapRat might rank projects by the PI. In this case, it would choose projects A, C, and D, for a total outlay of $110,000 and a combined NPV of $28,000. Again $5,000 would be left idle.

The IRR and PI ranking rules give an exact ranking to all of the projects, but they may not give the best solution to this problem. Because the firm is striving to maximize the wealth of its stockholders, it should choose the set of projects that gives the highest NPV. With only $115,000 available, it should choose D, C, and A. If it does this, its total investment will also be $110,000, but the total NPV will be $28,000. No other combination of investment of $115,000 or less creates as much wealth.[5]

The correct solution is to choose the one collection of investment projects out of all possible collections that has the highest total NPV. In the example of Table 14.2, this can be done fairly easily. When matters become more complex, firms sometimes use a technique called integer programming.

This technique of searching for the best set of projects can be implemented even when some of the projects in the set are mutually exclusive. Let us now assume that projects C and D are mutually exclusive. Under this circumstance, what is the best combination of the projects in Table 14.2? By having the computer search across all possible combinations that do not include both C and D and that do not exceed the available funds, we find that the best set of projects is A, D, E, and F, with an investment of $115,000 and a total NPV of $27,000. This shows that the technique of selecting the set of investments with the highest total NPV works for capital rationing even with mutually exclusive projects.

CASH FLOW IDENTIFICATION AND VALUATION

So far we have assumed that the investment and cash flows were known, and we explored techniques for evaluating and ranking projects. In actual capital budgeting applications, however, most of the work focuses on identifying the relevant cash flows. Once these are correctly specified, the mathematical analysis can be performed. We now concentrate on identifying cash flows and evaluating them properly.

Incremental Investment and Incremental Cash Flows

Almost all capital budgeting analyses are conducted assuming the framework of a functioning firm. Some investments have been made already and the firm already has some cash inflows. In a capital budgeting analysis, the entire focus

---

[5] Here the NPV and PI ranking rules give the same project selection, but that will not always be the case.

incremental cash flows
those cash flows that arise only if the investment is undertaken

☞ In capital budgeting analysis, the entire focus is on incremental cash flows.

is on new, or incremental, investment and **incremental cash flows.** In other words, it has to consider only those investments and cash flows that differ from the existing investments and cash flows, the latter being irrelevant to the decision. Only incremental investment and flows will be changed as a result of the capital budgeting decision. Therefore, the analysis must weigh the incremental investment against the incremental cash flows, with both in present value terms. Within this framework, we now turn to the cost of the investment.

The Cost of the Investment

In most capital budgeting projects the investment occurs at the outset, with cash flows coming later. For example, in constructing an office building, the builder pays the investment cost as the construction proceeds, but cash inflows begin only when the building is completed and the offices are rented. This makes it easier to identify the investment outlays than the cash flows.

The Investment Good and Installation Costs   In principle, the investment includes the full cost of the investment good and all outlays necessary to put it in working order. For example, assume you order a new lathe for a machine shop. The investment includes the price of the machine, shipping and insurance charges incurred in getting it to the work site, the installation cost, and any new electrical work required to make the lathe operable. In short, the cost includes all outlays incurred in obtaining the lathe and preparing it for operation.

☞ The market value of all goods already on hand used as part of an investment should be included in the cost of the investment.

opportunity cost
the value of a good used in a project that could be used elsewhere

Valuable Goods Already on Hand   In many instances, managers overlook some of the cost of an investment when they already own some part of the good to be invested. For example, for an office building to be built on land the firm already owns, should the land be included in the cost? The use of the land is part of the incremental cost, because by building on it, it cannot be sold or employed in some other manner. In general, the market value of all goods already on hand should be included in the cost of the investment, because that is the amount that could be realized if the goods were not employed in the investment. In other words, the market value is the **opportunity cost** that is being paid to use a good.

To see this more clearly, assume that the land for the office building was acquired 10 years ago for $100,000. Your best estimate of its current market value is $350,000. In calculating the cost of the investment, the land should be valued at $350,000, not $100,000, because its market value is the cash flow that is being sacrificed in using it for the office building. The amount originally paid is irrelevant to the cost of the investment.

sunk cost
a previously incurred cost that has no further value

Sunk Costs   A cost that was incurred previously and cannot be recovered is known as a **sunk cost.** Assume that immediately prior to considering the office building project the firm had installed a fence around the property at a cost of $15,000. If the office building is accepted, the fence must be removed. The removal cost is $4,000 and the fencing can be sold as scrap for $1,500. Which of these costs should be considered in evaluating the project?

First, the installation cost of $15,000 is irrelevant, because the existing fence has no use in the new project. To include that amount would be to commit the **sunk cost fallacy.** Second, if the office building is constructed, the firm must remove the fence at a cost of $4,000, so it is properly regarded as a cost of the project. Finally, the fence can be scrapped for $1,500, so this inflow must be deducted from the cost of the project. Therefore, as far as the fence is concerned in evaluating the project, the original cost should be disregarded, but the removal expense and the salvage inflow must be counted. The existence of the fence means that the office building will cost $2,500 ($4,000 − $1,500) more than otherwise.

New Investment in Working Capital   Virtually all major projects require an investment in **net working capital,** defined as current assets minus current liabilities, because they typically require an increase in cash balances, inventory, or accounts receivable. When projects are undertaken, funds must be found to finance the increased working capital, so this is a form of investment that projects require.

For example, consider a toy manufacturer with a successful Poison Ivy Patch doll. Last year the firm was unable to meet demand for the doll, so now it is considering building a new plant (no pun intended) to increase production. The firm estimates that inventories should be increased by 100,000 units at a production cost of $5 each. This means that its investment in inventories will increase by $500,000 if the project is undertaken.

The firm expects the itch for Poison Ivy dolls to last three years. After this time, the inventory will be sold off. This recapture of working capital is typical, but the funds are tied up in inventory for the duration of the project. In the capital budgeting analysis, we therefore include the increase in net working capital as part of the investment. The recapture of working capital is considered later.

Many projects require an increase in current assets, but they may also generate an increase in current liabilities. For example, a construction project may require more cash (a current asset) to pay for materials and labor. However, as materials are ordered and wages are accrued, there may be an increase in accounts payable, which is a source of financing for the firm. Therefore, we must pay attention to the change in net working capital, not just the change in current assets. Our new investment in working capital equals the increase in net working capital.

sunk cost fallacy
the error of including a sunk cost in a present value calculation—only incremental flows should be considered

☞ Sunk costs should be ignored in capital budgeting analyses. To include them is to commit the sunk cost fallacy.

net working capital
current assets minus current liabilities

☞ Most projects require investment in working capital or an increase in net working capital.

EXAMPLE 14.1

A large company is considering the fate of its small micro computer division that has operated for four years. During this time the firm has invested a total of $43 million in plant and equipment, and has sustained losses of $15 million. Now it has decided that it must sell off its existing plant and equipment for $10 million, and get out of the computer business or make another major commitment.

If the firm keeps the computer division alive, it will not sell its current facilities but it must buy four new $1 million computers to use in its development program and install these at a cost of $100,000 each. In addition, new investment of $8 million will be required for upgrading the plant. Part of the problem with the division so far was lack of inventory, so inventory will increase by 3,000 units at a cost of $1,000 each. What is the investment if the firm stays in the computer industry?

To answer this question we must decide what treatment should be given to the existing plant, the losses of the past four years, the new computers and their installation, the increase in inventory, and the new investment in upgrading plant and equipment. First, we know that the firm invested $43 million and suffered losses of $15 million over the last four years. For the decision about the future of the computer division, these past investments and losses are totally irrelevant. They are sunk costs, and no decision that the firm makes now can retrieve them.

Second, if the firm retains the computer division, it will not sell the plant and equipment, so it will forgo the $10 million sale price they would bring. Therefore, staying in the computer business must include this investment of $10 million. Third, the cash outlays associated with the four new computers are incurred only if the firm stays in the computer business, so this outlay of $4.4 million is part of the investment. Fourth, the new investment in plant is a new outlay directly associated with staying in the business, so this $8 million is part of the investment. Finally, the increase in inventory investment will occur only if the firm stays in the computer business, so this outlay of $3 million is also part of the investment. The following schedule gives the total investment if the firm decides to stay in the computer business:

Value of existing plant and equipment (net of any tax effects)	$10,000,000
New computers	4,400,000
New plant and equipment	8,000,000
Increase in inventory	3,000,000
	$25,400,000

Operating Cash Flows and Tax Effects   In any capital budgeting project, an investment is made in hope of receiving sufficient returns over its life to compensate for the outlay and give a return. Both the investment and the cash flows should be measured in present value terms.

Not all operating cash flows are relevant to the analysis, however. The capital budgeting decision should consider only those remaining after corporate income tax, because only they are available for distribution to the

TABLE 14.3   Calculating After-Tax Operating Cash Flows

Cash from sales	$300,000
— Cash outlays to generate sales	250,000
Operating cash flow	50,000
— Taxes	−15,000
After-tax cash flow	$ 35,000

Note: This table does not reflect possible tax shields.

☞ The capital budgeting decision should consider only the cash flows remaining after corporate income tax, because only the after-tax cash flows are available for distribution to the stockholders.

stockholders. In the case of the cost of the investment, this is accomplished with little effort; for the most part, all investment is made from after-tax funds. Even in the case of the investment outlays, however, there will be important tax effects. Because we measure the outlays on an after-tax basis, we must be careful to consider only the after-tax cash flows.

Another way to see why the after-tax cash flows are the relevant ones is to adopt the point of view of the stockholders. After all, it is their wealth the financial manager is trying to maximize, so their position has to be considered in laying down capital budgeting rules. For the stockholders, all of the dividends must come from after-tax earnings. Therefore, by focusing on the after-tax cash flows of a project, we measure the money available to reward the stockholders. We now consider the different kinds of operating cash flows and tax effects that the capital budgeting analysis must encompass.

After-Tax Operating Cash Flows   The after-tax operating cash flows in a given period depend on the cash received from sales, the cash outlays incurred to generate those sales, and the tax rate. For example, consider a manufacturer that sells 100,000 toys per year at $3 per toy. To produce and sell the toys, the firm incurs a number of cash outlays for raw materials, labor, other manufacturing costs, transportation, and marketing, and we assume that these come to $2.50 per toy. Furthermore, let us assume that the firm pays income taxes at the rate of 30 percent. With this information we can calculate the after-tax operating cash flows as shown in Table 14.3. The general structure is very similar to an income statement, but each item pertains to the actual cash flow rather than accounting income or expenses. The difference arises from those cases when accounting rules do not recognize cash flows as they occur.

depreciation
a reduction in accounting earnings intended to reflect the reduction in value of an income-producing asset

Depreciation

Depreciation is a reduction in accounting earnings intended to reflect the reduction in value of an income-producing asset. Because it is an accounting charge, we do not have to consider it in a capital budgeting decision. Even though depreciation is not itself a cash flow, it affects cash flow through taxes.

TABLE 14.4   The Effect of Depreciation on Cash Flow

	No Depreciation	*With Depreciation*
Total sales	$300,000	$300,000
— Cost of goods sold	250,000	250,000
Gross income	50,000	50,000
— Depreciation expense	0	15,000
Taxable income	50,000	35,000
Taxes at 30%	15,000	10,500
Net income	35,000	24,500
After-tax cash flow	35,000	39,500

depreciation tax shield
the change in taxes due to the depreciation charge

☞ Even though depreciation is not itself a cash flow, it affects cash flow through taxes.

As a result, every capital budgeting analysis must consider the **depreciation tax shield**—the change in taxes due to the depreciation charge. This shield is a cash flow because the cash outlay for taxes is reduced by its amount. For many projects, particularly real estate investment, it is a critically important cash flow.

The depreciation tax shield depends on the amount of the depreciation charge. The depreciation charge is determined by accounting rules made by the federal government, which allows firms to choose between accelerated and straight-line depreciation. For simplicity, and because the treatments are essentially the same for both methods, we assume throughout our discussion of capital budgeting that all depreciation is straight-line. However, we note that in actual practice, accelerated depreciation is used very often. We also note that land can never be depreciated.

☞ The existence of the depreciation expense gives a depreciation tax shield.

Calculating the Depreciation Tax Shield   For capital budgeting, depreciation is important only for its effect on cash flows, and this effect arises because the depreciation expense reduces taxes. Thus, the depreciation expense generates a depreciation tax shield.

To understand exactly how this occurs, consider our toy manufacturer of Table 14.3, with gross cash flow of $50,000. We will examine the firm with and without a depreciation expense of $15,000 for an air compressor. Table 14.4 calculates the tax bill for the firm in each case. If the firm is allowed a depreciation expense, it pays $4,500 less tax, which is the depreciation tax shield. The shield (S) equals the tax rate (T) times the amount of the depreciation (D):

$$S = T \times D \qquad (14.6)$$

For our example, we have $S = 0.30 \times \$15,000 = \$4,500$. This is the same result obtained previously. Notice that in Table 14.4 the after-tax cash flows

TABLE 14.5 Cash Flow Versus Accounting Income

	Accounting Income	Cash Flows
Total sales	$300,000	$300,000
— Cost of goods sold	250,000	250,000
Gross income	50,000	50,000
— Depreciation expense	15,000	Not cash
Taxable income	35,000	Not cash
Taxes at 30%	10,500	10,500
Net income	$ 24,500	$ 39,500

with and without the effect of depreciation differ by $4,500—the amount of the depreciation tax shield.

Income Versus Cash Flow It is important to mention that accounting income normally differs from cash flow. In actual practice, this is due to many reasons, notably the accrual method of accounting. For example, with accrual accounting, revenue from a sale may be recognized well before the sale generates any cash flow. Also, depreciation affects accounting income and cash flow differently. For our toy firm, we can see a difference between income and cash flow due solely to the treatment of depreciation.

Table 14.5 examines the computation of a year's income and a year's cash flow for the toy company. The first column computes the net income as $24,500. The second column computes the corresponding cash flow, ignoring the depreciation expense because it is not a cash flow. The tax payment is a cash flow, however, and it is the same under both circumstances. From Table 14.5 we see two equivalent ways of computing the cash flow:

1. Compute the net income and add back the depreciation.
2. Ignore the depreciation expense itself, but in computing the taxes, use the amount that will actually be paid as a result of the depreciation expense being included.

According to method 1, the cash flow is $24,500 + $15,000 = $39,500. The identical results of the second method are shown in the second column of Table 14.5.

EXAMPLE 14.2

Lightning Bolts, Inc. sells $5,000 worth of bolts per year and generates manufacturing costs of $2,500 per year to produce them, plus a $500 depreciation expense. If the firm pays taxes at the 25 percent rate, what is its after-tax cash flow?

The after-tax cash flow can be calculated by the first method:

Cash from sales	$ 5,000
— Operating costs	−2,500
— Depreciation expense	−500
Taxable income	$ 2,000
— Taxes at 25%	−500
Net income	$ 1,500

$$\text{Cash flow} = \text{net income} + \text{depreciation expense}$$
$$= \$1,500 + 500$$
$$= \$2,000$$

According to the second method:

Cash from sales	$ 5,000
— Operating costs	−2,500
— Depreciation expense	Not cash
Taxable income	Not cash
— Taxes	−500
Cash flow	$ 2,000

With each method, we find the same cash flow of $2,000

☞ Usually, the increase in net working capital is recaptured at the termination of the project.

Recapture of Working Capital Investment   In discussing the investment that the firm makes for a project, we noted that an increase in net working capital is often necessary to support accounts receivable and inventory. Typically, when a project is terminated, those inventories are drawn down, the receivables are collected, and the firm recaptures the investment in additional working capital. Capital budgeting analysis must reflect this cash inflow.

Because the increased net working capital is financed through the investment of after-tax dollars, the recaptured working capital is a cash flow that is not taxed. Generally, it is added to the final period's after-tax cash flow to compute that period's total after-tax cash flow. The relationship between the original investment in working capital and its recapture at the end of the project's life is illustrated in Figure 14.7, where it is assumed that the entire investment is recuperated.[6]

---

[6] This is a simplified account of the actual working capital cash flows. In practice, not all working capital is needed at time $t = 0$. Rather, it gradually increases over the initial years of the investment and gradually declines during the final years. Also, the assumption that all the investment in working capital is recaptured at the end of the project's life may not be appropriate, because some of the working capital may be lost. For example, some of the inventory may become obsolete, and some accounts receivable may not be paid.

FIGURE 14.7   Working Capital Cash Flows

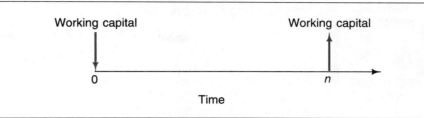

Terminal Value, Project Termination, and Salvage Value

Every capital budgeting analysis must examine a finite horizon, even if it does not capture the indefinite future that some project might have. For example, when the hula hoop was analyzed by its creators in the 1950s, the capital budget probably do not anticipate that the product would last so long with recurrent episodes of popularity. Because it is difficult to anticipate the distant future, capital budgeting analysis works under the assumption that the project will terminate at a given future date, so its value at that time must be estimated. The best way to evaluate this **terminal value**—the present value of the subsequent cash flows on the termination date of the analysis— is to assume that it occurs as a cash flow on the termination date. Often these estimates can be very uncertain. For example, if you were introducing the hula hoop today with a five-year capital budgeting horizon, how could you realistically estimate its terminal value five years from now?

Most capital budgeting projects require the acquisition of depreciable equipment, a manufacturing facility, or buildings. These items are expected to have some value and, together with the product's subsequent cash flows, they are treated as though they were sold on the termination date. Therefore, the money that their sale generates—the **salvage value**—must also be incorporated as a cash flow in the final period of the project's analyzed life.

The cash flow that is realized from the sale of a depreciated asset depends on the sale price relative to the book or depreciated value. The actual tax treatment of depreciated property can be complicated and quite variable. However, we can state the general principle behind the treatment and incorporate that into our analysis.

Recall that invested goods are purchased from after-tax funds. Therefore, if an asset is sold for an amount equal to its book value, the firm has merely recaptured its invested funds. In this case, the entire proceeds are an after-tax cash flow. If the firm sells an asset for more than its book value, it generally must pay tax on the difference. If an asset has a book value of $2,000 and is sold for $3,000, we would treat the $1,000 as taxable. Finally, if a firm sells an asset below its book value, it can recognize a loss on the asset. Assume that an asset with a $2,000 book value is sold for $1,500 by a firm in the 30 percent tax bracket. For tax purposes, the firm sustains a loss on that sale that it can use to offset other earnings. In this example, the loss of $500 would generate a tax savings equal to the tax rate times $500, or $150 ($500 × 0.30).

terminal value
the present value, at the termination date, of cash flows to be received after the termination date

salvage value
the price to be received for depreciated property on sale at the termination date of a project

FINANCE

TODAY

Fun-Loving Entrepreneurs

Near-billionaire Jack Kent Cooke was asked which business he would keep if he could have only one. Cable TV, worth at least $1 billion (including debt)? The $500 million in real estate holdings? Or the Washington Redskins, a money-losing team worth maybe $90 million?

"The Redskins," Cooke snapped. "Sports introduced me to a world that was 100 percent fun." If "fun" is the only incentive to owning a sports franchise, it must be a powerfully concentrated form of fun. In this age of million-dollar-a-year ballplayers and rocketing franchise prices, even the top-ranked teams can lose money. Yet when one comes up for sale, the bidding resembles a feeding frenzy in the shark tank. Much of the bidding is accounted for by members of the Forbes Four Hundred, 24 of whom own a team, or a significant hunk of one or more teams, as shown in the table.

Do rational businessmen really risk an investment of $90 million in a project just to have fun? Or is there something more to it? The following is a picture of the Redskins' financial performance. In 1988 the Redskins' operating revenues, flowing mainly from an estimated $11 million of net ticket income and $17 million of network television payments, ran about $30 million. The team's estimated operating expenses, led by $20 million in player costs, totaled roughly $32 million.

Now let's imagine Cooke puts the Redskins on the market for $90 million. Can a deal like this carry itself? It can, and let's see how.

The key is depreciation. Let's assume Cooke sells the Redskins for $90 million. About two-thirds of a franchise purchase price—mainly player contracts—can be written off over five years. For the Redskins, that's $12 million a year in depreciation. At a 34 percent corporate tax rate, the new owner can save more than $20 million in taxes over the five years, cutting the after-tax purchase price to around $70 million. With that investment and the projected $9 million operating profits (assuming it equals the cash flow), the NPV of the project is positive, as long as the interest rate is below 12.8 percent. The rich man's toy turns out to be a viable business after all.

In addition, the firm keeps the $1,500 as an after-tax cash flow. If we define S = sale price, B = book value, and T = tax rate, then we can summarize these treatments as follows:

Tax	After-Tax Cash Flow
$(S - B)T$	$S - (S - B)T$

Members of the Forbes Four Hundred Who Owned 30 Percent or More of a Major Sports Team in 1988

Name	Team (sport)	Estimated Worth (in millions of dollars)
Harvey "Bum" Bright	Dallas Cowboys (football)	$100
Ed DeBartolo	San Francisco 49ers (football)	100
Leon Hess	New York Jets (football)	100
Jack Kent Cooke	Washington Redskins (football)	90
William Clay Ford	Detroit Lions (football)	90
August Busch	St. Louis Cardinals (baseball)	85
Alex Spanos	San Diego Chargers (football)	85
Gene Autry	California Angels (baseball)	80
Eddie Gaylord	Texas Rangers (baseball)	80
Paul Allen	Portland Trail Blazers (basketball)	70
Edgar Bronfman	Montreal Expos (baseball)	70
Thomas Monaghan	Detroit Tigers (baseball)	70
Hugh Culverhouse	Tampa Bay Buccaneers (football)	65
William Davidson	Detroit Pistons (basketball)	65
Irwin Jacobs	Minnesota Vikings (football)	65
Joan Kroc	San Diego Padres (baseball)	65
Carl Pohlad	Minnesota Twins (baseball)	65
	Minnesota Vikings (football)	65
Ewing Kauffman	Kansas City Royals (baseball)	60
Robert Lurie	San Francisco Giants (baseball)	60
Ted Turner	Atlanta Braves (baseball)	60
	Atlanta Hawks (basketball)	60
George Argyros	Seattle Mariners (baseball)	57
David & Richard Jacobs	Cleveland Indians (baseball)	55
Herb & Mel Simon	Indiana Pacers (basketball)	55
Ted Arison	Miami Heat (basketball)	35

Source: John Merwin, "Dumb Like Foxes," *Forbes*, October 24, 1988, pp. 45–46.

The tax and after-tax cash flow expressions are valid whether $S = B$, $S > B$, or $S < B$. For example, if $S = B$, then this expression is $S - 0 \times T = S$.

Analyzing the Yuppie Nougat Project

In this section we state a more complex capital budgeting problem and perform a complete analysis. As such, the discussion provides a model for the solution to many capital budgeting problems that you might actually encounter.

The Bergen Candy Company has been studying an investment project calling for the manufacture and introduction of a new candy bar to be called Yuppie Nougat. The candy bar is designed to appeal to the yuppie market, so the firm expects to use the finest foreign chocolate and to price the bar very high relative to its cost of production and ingredients. Otherwise, no yuppie would even think of buying it. Part of the expense will require a vast marketing program, complete with endorsements by yuppie heroes, of course.

The project is expected to last eight years, after which time yuppies will be more interested in dentures than candy bars. The introduction of the candy bar requires 400 new machines costing $10,000 each. Installing each machine costs $100, and the machines will be depreciated straight-line over five years. The production facility will be located at a site Bergen already owns and that could have been rented for $200,000 per year. The firm must invest $1 million in year 1 to convert the facility to the Yuppie Nougat project.

Bergen expects to sell 2 million bars per year for the first three years and 1.5 million each year thereafter. The price will be $2.50 per candy bar, with a production cost of $0.50. The marketing expense per bar actually sold is scheduled at $1.00. Outlets have been chosen with yuppies in mind, the aim being to have Yuppie Nougat "available wherever Perrier is sold." Therefore, the firm expects to maintain large inventories of about 500,000 bars on average. No other increase in working capital is expected. When the project is terminated in eight years the machines should be worth $2,000 each, and the formula and name of the product can be sold for $500,000. Bergen has determined that the appropriate after-tax discount rate for Yuppie Nougat is 18 percent. Should Bergen conquer the yuppie world with Yuppie Nougat?

We begin by breaking the problem into small steps. First, we determine the cash flows associated with the investment, the operating flows, and the terminal value. At first, we do not consider taxes, but merely note which flows will be affected by taxes and which will not.

STEP 1: Determine the investment

At the outset of the project the firm buys 400 machines at $10,000 each plus an installation cost of $100 per machine. The installation cost may be treated as part of the machine cost, so the investment for the machines is $4,040,000 (400 × $10,100). We are also told that Bergen must invest $1 million in year 1 for certain modifications to the building. In addition, it must increase its investment in working capital because of the increase in inventory. For 500,000 bars at $0.50, the increased investment in working capital is $250,000. We value this not at the sales price, but at the manufacturing cost, which is the actual cash flow associated with creating the candy bar. Therefore the investment occurs partially right now (year 0) and partially next year, according to the following schedule. All of these flows are already on an after-tax basis.

Year	Year 0	Year 1
Machines	$4,040,000	
Working capital	$250,000	
Plant conversion		$1,000,000
	$4,290,000	$1,000,000

STEP 2: Determine the operating flows

For each candy bar sold, we have:

Sales price	$ 2.50
Production cost	−0.50
Marketing expenses	−1.00
Gross profit per bar	$ 1.00

We are also told that unit sales will be 2 million per year for the first three years and 1.5 million in years 4 through 8. Thus, we have:

	Years 1–3	Years 4–8
Sales	$ 5,000,000	$ 3,750,000
Production cost	−1,000,000	−750,000
Marketing expense	−2,000,000	−1,500,000
Gross profit	$ 2,000,000	$ 1,500,000

This gross profit will be subject to taxation, but it must first be adjusted by the depreciation expense. Because the machines are depreciated for five years straight-line, we have a depreciable amount of $4,040,000, a depreciation expense of $808,000 per year for the first five years, and nothing thereafter.

	Years 1–5	Years 6–8
Depreciation expense	$808,000	0

This depreciation expense will affect the taxable income, even though it is not itself a cash flow.

STEP 3: Identify the terminal value flows

Often the cash flows in the final year differ from the regular years. The Yuppie Nougat project is no exception, because Bergen expects to sell the machines and the rights to the candy bar. Also, the firm must reflect the recovery of its additional working capital investment. At year 8 the 200 machines are fully depreciated. If they are sold for $2,000 each, the result is a $440,000 inflow that is fully taxable. If the rights to the candy bar are sold for $500,000, that amount is also taxable. However, if $250,000 increased investment in working capital is recovered, this amount will not be taxable. Therefore, the terminal value cash flows at year 8 are as follows:

Taxable	$940,000
Nontaxable	$250,000

Having classified and identified the relevant cash flows, we now convert them to an after-tax basis. We proceed through each of the categories we have separated: the investment, the operating flows, and the terminal value flows.

STEP 4: Identify the after-tax investment flows

The investment cash flows are made from after-tax funds, so they are already expressed on an after-tax basis.

STEP 5: Identify the after-tax operating flows

In Table 14.6 we compute the after-tax cash flows for each of the years of the project. Because sales change after three years and the depreciation expense lasts

TABLE 14.6   The After-Tax Operating Cash Flows for the Yuppie Nougat Project

	Years 1–3	Years 4–5	Years 6–8
Sales	$5,000,000	$3,750,000	$3,750,000
— Production	1,000,000	750,000	750,000
— Marketing	2,000,000	1,500,000	1,500,000
Net sales	2,000,000	1,500,000	1,500,000
— Depreciation	808,000	808,000	0
Taxable income	1,192,000	692,000	1,500,000
Tax at 34%	405,280	235,280	510,000
Net income	786,720	456,720	990,000
+ Depreciation	808,000	808,000	0
After-tax operating cash flows	$1,594,720	$1,264,720	$ 990,000

for five years, we treat years in groups 1–3, 4–5, and 6–8. Within each group the operating flows are the same. Notice that we compute net income and then add the depreciation expense to compute the operating cash flow.

STEP 6: Identify the after-tax terminal value flows

We have already seen that some terminal value flows are taxable and some are not. The taxable $940,000 received for the sale of the machines yields $620,400 after taxes ($940,000 × 0.66). To this we add the nontaxable $250,000 recapture of our working capital investment for a total terminal value after-tax cash flow of $870,400.

STEP 7: Compute the total after-tax cash flows for each year

Table 14.7 sets out the after-tax cash flows for each year. It merely reports the sums of the results we have already achieved.

STEP 8: Compute the relevant measures of desirability and make the decision

First, we compute the present value of the flows for years 1 through 8 from Table 14.7, using the discount rate of 18 percent:

Year	Total After-Tax Cash Flows	NPV at 18%
0	−$4,290,000	−$4,290,000
1	594,720	+504,000
2	1,594,720	+1,145,303
3	1,594,720	+970,596
4	1,264,720	+652,329
5	1,264,720	+552,821
6	990,000	+366,727
7	990,000	+310,786
8	1,860,400	+494,937

The total NPV of the project at 18 percent is $707,499. Because Yuppie Nougat would increase the value of the firm by this amount, Bergen should accept it. It can also be verified that its IRR is 22.8433 percent.

Finally, we compute the profitability index of this project:

$$PI = \frac{PV \text{ of cash flows}}{\text{investment}} = \frac{\$4,997,499}{\$4,290,000} = 1.1649$$

The PI exceeds 1, which also signals acceptance.

TABLE 14.7 After-Tax Cash Flows for the Yuppie Nougat Project

Year	Investment Cash Flows	Operating Cash Flows	Terminal Value Flows	Total
0	$ −4,290,000			$ −4,290,000
1	− 1,000,000	$1,594,720		594,720
2		1,594,720		1,594,720
3		1,594,720		1,594,720
4		1,264,720		1,264,720
5		1,264,720		1,264,720
6		990,000		990,000
7		990,000		990,000
8		990,000	$870,400	1,860,400

FREQUENTLY ENCOUNTERED CAPITAL BUDGETING PROBLEMS

This section deals with some typical capital budgeting problems. By learning how to analyze them we can improve our capital budgeting skills and review the principles developed in this chapter.

The Machine Replacement Decision

☞ The machine replacement problem involves finding the best time to replace one machine with a new one of the same type.

In many industries, machines are purchased, used, and replaced by other identical machines. Almost any machine can be kept in service a little longer by incurring a higher operating cost often due to increased maintenance. As time goes on, however, operating cost becomes very high; at some time, high enough to justify replacing the machine. The financial manager has the job of determining when this is.

TABLE 14.8 Cash Outflows for Different Cycles of Machine Replacement Over a Six-Year Period

Year	Two-Year Cycle	Three-Year Cycle	Six-Year Cycle
0	$10,000	$10,000	$10,000
1	1,000	1,000	1,000
2	11,500*	1,500	1,500
3	1,000	11,800*	1,800
4	11,500*	1,000	2,100
5	1,000	1,500	2,500
6	1,500	1,800	3,000

* Includes $10,000 for machine replacement.

☞ The machine replacement problem is one of choosing the service life of the machine that minimizes the present value of the costs.

The machine replacement problem really has no cash inflows to consider. The machine is instrumental in generating some positive cash flows, but the cash flows do not form part of the decision about replacement because they are the same for both new and old machines. Instead, the problem considers only the investment cost of a new machine and the operating cost of keeping it running. Therefore, we must choose the service life of the machine that minimizes the present value of the costs. Just as with maximizing net present value, this contributes to the process of creating wealth.

To see the issues at stake, consider a machine that costs $10,000 and has the following operating costs in each year:

Year	Operating Cost
1	$1,000
2	·1,500
3	1,800
4	2,100
5	2,500
6	3,000
7	3,600
8	4,300
9	5,500
10	7,000
11	8,400

These include the general cost of running the machine and maintenance expenses. The purchase occurs at time $t = 0$, so the first operating outlay of $1,000 occurs one year later, and the schedule of operating costs rises with the age of the machine. When the old machine is replaced, it cannot be sold, due to its complete exhaustion.

To see more exactly the choices the firm is facing, consider a six-year period over which the firm can provide itself with a machine by following a number of replacement strategies. For example, it can replace the machine after two years or after three years, or it can keep it for the full six years.

Table 14.8 shows the exact cash flows the firm incurs for each of these strategies. For example, if the machine is replaced every two years, the operating cost is $1,000 for the first year and $1,500 for the second year. In addition, the firm must pay the purchase price for the replacement machine. For all three strategies, the machine is exhausted at the end of year 6 and is scrapped.

Because each of these three strategies covers exactly the same time span, they are directly comparable. The firm is trying to choose the correct replacement period, so it can decide by choosing the strategy with the lowest present value of costs over the six years. To decide among the alternatives, we need only compute the present value of the cash flows for each one.

INTERNATIONAL PERSPECTIVES

What the Brochures Don't Tell You

Sure, there are millions of consumers in East Europe craving Nikes and Walkmans, but setting up shop isn't easy. Even the most basic items such as telephone books, not to mention telephones, can be hard to come by. A few cautionary tales:

Getting a Dial Tone in Budapest

How can you spot an American in Hungary?

    Answer: He's the one who starts dialing as soon as he picks up the phone.

    For Hungarians, who often wait at least 20 seconds for a dial tone, this popular joke is no laughing matter. Hungary's telephone system is one of the worst in Europe, with static-filled lines, sudden cutoffs, and phones that won't ring or won't stop ringing.

    The waiting time for a new hookup is 5 to 10 years. The fastest way to get a line is to buy a mobile phone and a subscription for $3,000 from Westel Radiotelefon. Luckily, American Telephone & Telegraph's USADirect has an access number in Hungary, for placing collect and credit-card calls. That's if you can get a dial tone.

Secrets of Finding Office Space in Warsaw

Don't hunt for real estate agents if you need office space in Warsaw. They don't exist. Just start pumping every contact for tips about rentals before they hit the market. Once the word gets out, it's too late.

    Greasing palms still makes scarce items suddenly appear. But hire a good Polish "fixer" to handle the task, since local customs dictate a certain style in doling out bribes. Some executives help Warsaw landlords get a visa to the West in exchange for an office.

    Hang tough when negotiating your rent. If you don't appear savvy, landlords could hike the price of each square foot from $3 to $10. Comparison shopping is the key. Don't take no for an answer. And don't let your fixer out of your sight.

Landing a Lunch Table in Prague

Doing the proverbial deal on a napkin during a power lunch may be tougher than you think, at least in Prague. Most restaurants are still state-owned, and workers are paid a straight salary—regardless of service. Since many headwaiters prefer less work, walk-in customers are shooed away from nearly empty restaurants. Lesson one: Always make a reservation.

But that, too, may be harder than you would imagine. Floods of Western newcomers have taxed restaurant capacity. Another tip: Ask your prospective Czech partners to book at restaurants they like best. You may be in for a surprise treat. In the end, you might want to attach an eatery to your office—if you can find an office.

Knowing Who You're Up Against

It's Saturday morning in Prague, time to privatize. Since late January, nearly 90 auctions for small, state-owned businesses have been held. On this particular morning in a drafty room at the top of a dusty staircase in an old Communist Party community center, about 100 prospective buyers are competing for a dozen shops. The black-market money changers are the easiest to spot. They wear black leather jackets and gold chains.

On the block is a beer pub on the outskirts of town. Bidding starts at $3,178, doubles in no time, and then slowly floats to $12,300. "The beer will be flowing all the time," chatters the auctioneer. One more lurch to $13,500. Sold—to the man in the black leather and gold chains.

Paycheck? What's a Paycheck?

It's the ultimate checkless society. No plastic, either. Just cold cash. So to meet a payroll each month might mean loading up an armored truck with sacks of zlotys, forints, or korunas. Even if Western checks are issued, it could take weeks to process them at East Europe's outmoded state banks.

Most employees prefer to receive their pay in cash, anyway. But to get it from a state bank, they could have to wait in line for half a day. When they finally reach the teller's window, it takes forever for bank employees to count out the bills. The largest denomination in Hungary is worth $66, and in Czechoslovakia it's just $33. Instead, many companies open their own payment windows and dole out the cash themselves.

Source: "What the Brochures Don't Tell You," *Business Week*, April 15, 1991, pp. 52–53.

Capital Budgeting and Social Security

Many economists are concerned about how the social security system will be funded in the next century. Until recently, social security was almost entirely a pay-as-you-go system, in which current workers were taxed to pay retirees' benefits.

The system worked fine as long as the population grew smoothly. But serious problems result in such a system whenever the growth rates of different age groups differ substantially—as do the baby-boom generation, born in the years between 1948 and 1964, and the generation born since 1964. The decline in the birth-rate since 1964 implies that, around the period 2030–50, there will be more retirees per worker than ever before.

To accommodate this demographic change, the government has gradually raised the social security tax rate over time, producing a surplus in the social security fund that can be used to provide retirees with benefits in the years 2030 to 2050 without raising taxes substantially. Economists consider this type of tax-smoothing over time to be optimal.

The problem with this plan is that it requires building a surplus that can be drawn on in the future. Unfortunately, by counting the social security surplus in its unified budget, the government has offset the surplus in the social security fund with a larger deficit elsewhere. The existing social security surplus is being offset entirely by other government borrowing. If this is allowed to continue, we will see either a tremendous tax increase around the year 2030 or a drastic curtailment of social security benefits.

One problem with building a surplus for the next 40 years is that the accumulations needed (estimated at $12 trillion) may exceed the value of all federal debt by the year 2030. This situation would create a conflict because under current law the government cannot invest in the private sector. However, the analysis of government net worth and capital budgeting suggest a possible solution.

Part of the accumulation could be used to retire public debt, thus releasing funds to the private sector and allowing greater private investment. And if a capital-budgeting system were in place, we could also plan to increase government spending on capital projects, beginning today through the year 2030. This would enhance private productivity and provide returns in the future. When funds are needed to pay retirement benefits in the years after 2030, the government would enhance capital spending.

From 1990 to 2030 the social security surplus would be used to retire some government debt and to finance additional government investment spending. From 2030 on, government capital spending would be reduced to a lower level, while additional social security benefits are paid. This plan simply adjusts the timing of different types of government expenditure to smooth total expenditure and tax rates over time. The federal debt would be reduced, but it would not be eliminated completely.

Source: "Capital Budgeting and Social Security," *Business Review*, November–December 1990, p. 9.

Assuming an 18 percent discount rate, the present values are:

Two-year replacement	$26,640
Three-year replacement	$20,945
Six-year replacement	$16,308

Consequently, keeping the machine for six years is the best plan because it has the lowest cost.

Machine Replacement and the Equivalent Annuity Method

Although we know it is better to replace the machine after six years instead of after two or three years, we still cannot be sure that that is the overall best strategy. After all, we could replace the machine after five years, seven years, or some other amount of time. However, comparing the six-year with the seven-year replacement strategy is not so easy. To apply the same analysis we used above, we would have to consider operating the machine over 42 years. We could do this, but it is a very cumbersome procedure we would rather avoid.[7]

equivalent annuity method
a method that calculates the annuity with a present value equal to a set of costs associated with some enterprise over a specified period

We can solve the machine replacement problem with an alternative technique called the **equivalent annuity method.** This calculates the annuity that has a present value equal to the cost of operating the machine over a given number of years and is implemented by following these steps:

1. For any replacement strategy (one year, two years, etc.) calculate the present value of all costs incurred in operating a machine for that period.
2. Using the same discount rate employed in Step 1, find the value of the annuity of the same length that the present value in Step 1 will purchase.
3. Because this annuity amount is the effective annual cost of operating the machine under that strategy, choose the lowest annuity amount.

For example, consider the three-year replacement strategy. Operating the machine for three years involves the cash flows shown in Table 14.8. Applying our three-step procedure we find:

STEP 1:

$$\text{Present value} = \$10,000 + \frac{\$1,000}{1.18} + \frac{\$1,500}{1.18^2} + \frac{\$1,800}{1.18^3}$$

$$= \$13,021$$

---

[7] The period of analysis is the least common multiple (LCM) of the replacement strategies considered. For example, the LCM of 2, 3, and 6 is 6. This is why we chose a six-year period for the analysis in that case. Similarly, to analyze the six- and seven-year strategies, we must consider a period of 42 years since the LCM of 6 and 7 is 42.

STEP 2: This present value amount of $13,021 will purchase an annuity of $5,989 for three years, with an 18 percent discount rate:

$$\text{Annuity amount} = \frac{\$13,021}{PV(18, 3)}$$

$$= \frac{\$13,021}{2.174}$$

$$= \$5,989$$

Therefore, the annual cost of operating the machine with replacement every three years is $5,989.

STEP 3: Calculate the annuity amount for each replacement strategy. These equivalent annuities are shown in Table 14.9.

Each replacement strategy has its own annuity associated with it, and the one that gives the lowest amount is the best. The data in Table 14.9, which are graphed in Figure 14.8, show that the effective annual cost reaches a minimum when the machine is replaced after eight years.

An alternative method of finding the optimum replacement time is intuitively appealing. It is based on comparing two consecutive PV of costs; when the PV of costs increases from one period to the next for the first time, it has just reached a minimum. This process can be seen in the last column of Table 14.9. Since the formal analytical derivation of the rule is rather cumbersome, we provide only the final decision rule.

TABLE 14.9   Effective Annual Costs of Operating a Machine for Different Replacement Strategies

t (years)	C_t	PV(t)	Equivalent Annual Cost
1	1,000	10,847	$12,792
2	1,500	11,925	7,615
3	1,800	13,020	5,989
4	2,100	14,103	5,243
5	2,500	15,196	4,860
6	3,000	16,308	4,662
7	3,600	17,438	4,575
8	4,300	18,582	4,557*
9	5,500	19,822	4,610
10	7,000	21,159	4,708
11	8,400	23,622	5,073

* Minimum equivalent annual cost.

FIGURE 14.8   Effective Annual Costs for Different Machine Replacement Strategies

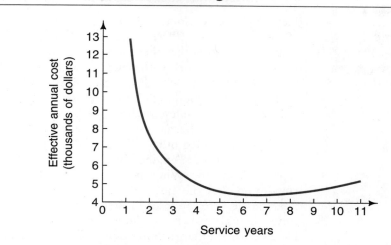

If the operating cost at time t is C_t, the present value of all costs, including the investment cost, up to time t is $PV(t)$, and the present value annuity factor is $PA(r, t)$, then the optimal replacement time, t, occurs when the following inequality is met for the first time:

$$C_{t+1} > \frac{PV(t)}{PA(r, t)} \qquad (14.7)$$

We can see that $C_8 = \$4,300$, $PV(7) = \$17,438$, and $PA(7, 18) = 3.8115$. Thus,

$$\$4,300 < \frac{\$17,438}{3.8115} = \$4,575.07$$

Since Inequality 14.7 is not met, we should wait more than seven years before replacing the machine. This result can come in very handy, since in this case it saves us the trouble of calculating any numbers for the possibility of replacing at any time before seven years.

If we repeat the calculations for $t = 8$ we have: $C_9 = \$5,500$, $PV(8) = \$18,582$, and $PA(8, 18) = 4.0776$. Applying these values to Inequality 14.7, we have:

$$\$5,500 > \frac{\$18,582}{4.0776} = \$4,557.13$$

Because the inequality is now met for the first time, the correct replacement time is eight years. Of course, this is the same result obtained with the

FINANCE TODAY

HP's Printer Unit: From Rule-Breaker to Role Model

Hewlett-Packard Co. isn't known for going out on a limb. But in the early 1980s, when then HP Vice-President Richard A. Hackborn and his team of engineers decided that there was a huge potential market for inexpensive laser printers to work with personal computers, they threw away the rule book. That worked so well that the Boise (Idaho)-based printer business now serves as something of a model for the rest of HP.

What was so different about the printer group? For one thing, it made decisions quickly because it wasn't hamstrung by the overlapping committees that then ruled other HP computer businesses. And, instead of building its own printer "engine," it struck a deal to buy the hardware from Japan's Canon Inc. When it came to marketing, the unit made a key decision: to go after the entire PC market, not just HP's own customers. Engineers made sure the laser printer worked with all IBM PC clones—at a time when HP's own computer division hadn't yet built an IBM-compatible PC. To ship large volumes quickly, they signed on hundreds of computer dealers, who eagerly stocked the printers.

Boise was allowed its independent attitude because the printers were stand-alone products that didn't have to fit into a corporate computer strategy. Because minicomputers and workstations did, they were subject to oversight by HP's committee structure.

But no one at the company's Palo Alto headquarters complained once they saw the results. Debuting in mid-1984, HP's LaserJet was the first successful desktop laser printer, basically a small office copier that uses a laser to etch the dots that form words and images on the copier drum. Even before Apple Computer Inc. promoted "desktop publishing" in 1985, HP was selling the original $3,495 LaserJets by the thousands to PC owners who wanted better output than noisy dot-matrix machines could provide. When desktop publishing came to PCs, sales accelerated. And in 1990, when HP started selling LaserJets designed for the Apple Macintosh, they

equivalent annuity method; the advantage clearly lies in the potential saving of many computations.[8]

Price Versus Quality in Machine Choice

The choice between price and quality is a familiar decision in everyday life. For example, consumers must choose between an expensive refrigerator that

---

[8] Choosing the time at which to test the inequality is really guesswork. It is usually best to choose a few relatively widely spaced times, and check for the sign of the inequality until you find two times at which the sign is different. The optimum replacement time lies between them.

sold like hotcakes. Seven years after the introduction of the LaserJet, Hewlett-Packard still has nearly 60 percent of the $3.6 billion market for laser printers.

HP's thriving, $2 billion-plus printer business—which now includes about a dozen models of low-cost, ink-jet, and laser printers—has presented to HP executives new alternatives for doing business. "LaserJet really blazed a trail here," says HP software group General Manager Bob Frankenberg.

And HP's laser printers have proven that HP can be nimble enough to keep ahead. Boise has brought out new models at an aggressive pace, giving competitors little opportunity to grab a bigger slice of the market. IBM, the nearest rival, has only an 11 percent share.

To keep pushing prices down, HP has continually cut costs with new manufacturing techniques. And managers have kept a tight lid on expenses, despite 40 percent annual revenue growth. "That is a major lesson for the rest of HP," says Hackborn.

As competition at the dealer level intensifies, HP is keeping pace. When it replaced the $2,695 LaserJet II with the LaserJet III a year ago, it added more features and cut the price to $2,395. Then, in February, HP dropped the price on its LaserJet IIP to $1,295 from $1,495—just in time to match Apple's new $1,299 Personal LaserWriter LS, introduced in March.

If not an out-and-out role model, the printer business has become something of an inspiration for HP managers. Last year, 150 HP executives crowded into a meeting to hear Hackborn share some of his management secrets. The most obvious lesson? Sometimes, it pays to break a few rules.

Source: Barbara Buell, "HP's Printer Unit: From Rule-Breaker to Role Model," *Business Week*, April 1, 1991, p. 79.

lasts longer and requires less energy, or the economy model that is cheaper but less efficient. Like the consumer, the financial manager faces a similar problem in choosing equipment for a plant. A given machine may cost more than another, but it may have a lower maintenance cost and may be able to produce more units. This section shows how to apply capital budgeting techniques to this frequently encountered problem. Notice that, because the "cheap" and "quality" machines are intended to produce the same item, they are mutually exclusive.

To see how to choose between the two strategies, consider the cash flows for the two machines shown in Table 14.10, which reflect the initial cost of the machines. The cheap machine lasts for three years and generates an after-tax cash flow of $7,000 per year. The quality machine lasts five years, gen-

TABLE 14.10   Cash Flows for the Cheap and Quality Machines

	Year					
	0	*1*	*2*	*3*	*4*	*5*
Cheap machine	−$12,000	$7,000	$7,000	$7,000		
Quality machine	−22,000	8,000	8,000	8,000	$8,000	$8,000

erating after-tax cash flows of $8,000 per year. These after-tax cash flows are net of operating expenses and also reflect differences in the productivity of the machines. We assume that the discount rate is 15 percent. Not only does the quality machine last longer, it also produces a better cash stream. On the other hand, the advantage of the cheap machine is that it costs less.

☞ Projects with different lives are mutually exclusive projects with different time horizons.

This direct comparison is complicated by the fact that the machines have different lives. Thus it is really not sufficient to determine which investment has the greater NPV due to that difference. The comparison of NPVs is meaningless because the firm is presumed to be operating over five years, but the cash flows from the cheap strategy are not even shown for years 4 and 5. If we assumed that the cheap machine was replaced after three years, that strategy would have cash flows for six years, whereas the quality machine would have them for only five years. One solution is to consider a sequence of cheap and quality machines over some identical time interval, in this case 15 years. Working with 15 years of data is a cumbersome way of solving this problem. Fortunately, choosing between a cheap and quality machine has some aspects of the machine replacement problem, and can be solved by applying the equivalent annuity method.

Using this method, we realize that the cheap machine generates a three-year annuity of $7,000 for an initial investment of $12,000. The quality machine produces a five-year annuity of $8,000 for a price of $22,000. Using the discount rate of 15 percent, we find that the present value of the cheap machine is $3,982 and that of the quality machine is $4,818. This makes it appear that we will be better off to purchase the quality machine. As we have seen, however, these NPVs are not directly comparable because they cover different time spans. In particular, this comparison is not fair because it neglects the cash flows from the cheap strategy in periods 4 and 5.

To put the same point in a slightly different way, the NPV of the quality machine is the reward for operating that machine for five years, whereas the NPV from the cheap machine is a reward that can be reaped every three years. The question then becomes, should the firm prefer an NPV of $4,818 every five years or of $3,982 every three years? To answer this question, we turn to the equivalent annuity method.

By adopting the cheap machine, we achieve an NPV of $3,982, which would buy a three-year annuity of $1,744:

$$\text{Annuity amount} = \frac{\$3,982}{PV(15, 3)}$$

$$= \frac{\$3,982}{2.2832}$$

$$= \$1,744$$

Because the cheap machine will be replaced every three years, following that strategy amounts to choosing a perpetuity of $1,744 per year.

The next task is to apply the equivalent annuity method to the five-year machine. Its net present value of $4,818 would purchase a five-year annuity of $1,437, with a 15 percent discount rate:

$$\text{Annuity amount} = \frac{\$4,818}{PV(15, 5)}$$

$$= \frac{\$4,818}{3.3522}$$

$$= \$1,437$$

This is effectively a perpetuity as well, assuming that the quality machine is replaced every five years.

Both machines are now on a comparable footing, because we are looking at the cash flow each of them can provide each year over the same horizon. From this it is clear that the firm should prefer the cheap machine with its annuity of $1,744 over the quality machine and its annuity of $1,437. Obviously, it is not always best to buy quality.

Investment Timing

Personal computers offer undeniable benefits for many potential purchasers. With the market now moving toward maturity, however, their prices are falling dramatically. Assume that a firm has carefully computed the cash flows that would come from buying a set of personal computers. Regardless of when the firm buys the computers, the decision will generate cash flows over the subsequent four years, as shown below:

Year After Purchase	After-Tax Cash Flow
1	$30,000
2	30,000
3	40,000
4	40,000

Notice that the timing of these cash flows is measured relative to the time the computers are purchased. For example, if the computers are purchased

FINANCE

TODAY

Is America Finally Ready For the Gasless Carriage?

If you think electric cars are a far-out dream, think again. The Impact, a two-seater from General Motors Corp., may hit the road in 1993. If it sells big, it's going to change driving—and walking, too. Look sharp at a crosswalk, because you won't hear an electric car coming.

GM won't let outsiders drive the Impact, but it should be like watching TV with the sound off. At a stop, no juice flows to the twin front motors, which saves energy and makes the car silent. When you start off—by pushing a button on the dash marked "F" for forward or "R" for reverse—the car is still nearly noiseless. On the highway, there's no sound from the tailpipe: The Impact doesn't have one. Even at 75 mph, you'll hear only the thrum of tires, the rush of wind, and the subtle whir of the front-wheel motors. As there's no gear-shifting, either, the motors spin at a dizzying 11,900 rpm—vs. about 4,000 rpm for ordinary engines.

The car is a leap forward in making electric cars palatable. It looks great, for one thing. John Schinella, formerly the chief stylist at GM's Advanced Concept Center in Newbury Park, Calif., and now a top GM designer in Michigan, gave the Impact a teardrop shape and low, sleek lines. This isn't just for looks. The sloped front end, along with the skirts that half cover the rear wheels, give the car a drag coefficient of 0.19—34 percent better than the slipperiest conventional car. The rounded windshield extends far ahead of the driver, while the rear window spans a spacious cargo area. A high center hump that runs the length of the car houses 32 10-volt lead-acid batteries. There is even air-conditioning and a sound system. Oddly, though, the windows crank down by hand—to conserve power.

Mash the pedal to the floor, and the Impact jumps instantly—unlike gas-powered cars, which hesitate briefly while their engines and transmissions kick in. It will go from 0 to 60 mph in 8 seconds—1.5 seconds faster

two years from now, the first cash flow of $30,000 will occur three years from now. With the discount rate of 12 percent, this positive cash flow stream has a present value of $108,580 when the computers are purchased.

The computers' current price is $100,000 and management makes the following forecast of prices for the next four years, as shown below:

Year	Computer Prices
0	$100,000
1	85,000
2	72,000
3	68,000
4	65,000

than Mazda Motor Corp.'s Miata. Thanks to an aluminum body and parts, the Impact weighs just 2,200 pounds, including 870 pounds of batteries, but it still meets U.S. safety standards. Its top speed is 100 mph, though GM will limit that to 75 with a governor. Take your foot off the accelerator, and the Impact slows quickly: Its motors automatically become generators, creating drag and slowing the car—while cranking out juice to help recharge its batteries.

Plenty of problems must be solved before the Impact becomes more than a curiosity. Under ideal conditions, it goes only 120 miles per charge. In stop-and-go traffic or with the air conditioner on, that goes way down. The car has a charger that plugs into a standard wall outlet—but it can take up to eight hours to replenish the batteries. The other hurdle is sticker shock: Auto magazines project a $20,000 to $30,000 price, though GM says it hasn't decided.

Will anyone pay that much? Skeptics point to the forgettable Electrovette, a version of the Chevrolet Chevette that GM announced in 1979. GM predicted then that electric buggies would be 10 percent of its production by 1990. Soon, plunging gasoline prices doused consumer interest, and the car was never built. This time, GM is being conservative. It will build the Impact in a small factory in Lansing, Mich., home of the discontinued Buick Reatta. The plant can build only 25,000 cars a year.

Still, "we're just crazy enough to think there are people out there who will like these things," says GM Chairman Robert C. Stempel. Given GM's modest expectations and the allure of its car, this time he may be right.

Source: David Woodruff, "Is America Finally Ready for the Gasless Carriage?" *Business Week*, April 8, 1991, p. 58.

☞ Investment timing is a technique used to determine the optimum time to undertake a project

Since the positive cash flows have a present value of $108,580, the firm captures an NPV of $8,580 if it purchases the computers now. However, it might do better by waiting for computer prices to fall. The goal is to choose the strategy with the greatest net present value as of today.

If the firm buys computers in year 1, the purchase price will be $85,000. The present value of the cash inflows, measured at the time of purchase, will still be $108,580. So, measured at $t = 1$ the project will have a net present value of $23,580. However, the firm has the goal of maximizing share price at the present. Therefore, it should buy now, at $t = 0$. To evaluate the present value of the project today of purchasing the computers at $t = 1$, the manager must discount the net present value of the project, as measured at $t = 1$ back to the present. Discounting $23,580 at 12 percent for one period gives a $t = 0$ present value of $21,054. Since the NPV of buying immediately is $8,580, it is preferable to wait at least one year to buy the computers.

367

TABLE 14.11   Net Present Values for Buying Computers at Different Times

Year	Purchase Price	NPV of Cash Flows at Time of Purchase ($108,580 − price)	NPV of Decision at $t = 0$
0	$100,000	$ 8,580	$ 8,580
1	85,000	23,580	21,054
2	72,000	36,580	29,161
3	68,000	40,580	28,884
4	65,000	43,580	27,696

Instead of waiting just one year, it might be better to wait longer. To explore this possibility, Table 14.11 presents the full data for this decision problem. Column 3 shows the present value of the cash flows that the firm receives, $108,580, minus the cost of purchasing the computer at that time. Therefore, this is a present value measured for the date of purchase.

Over the four years, considering the present value at the time of purchase, the present value continues to increase. However, we want to know the present value of all of these alternatives, as measured at time 0. Therefore, we must discount these figures, measured at various future dates, back to time 0, as shown in the final column. The greatest present value is $29,161 when the firm buys the computers two years from now. Therefore, the firm should wait for two years before purchasing the equipment.

An alternative way of calculating the optimum investment time is to evaluate the following inequality[9]:

$$I_t - I_{t+1} < r \times \text{NPV}_t \tag{14.8}$$

The optimum investment time, t, occurs when Inequality 14.8 holds for the first time. For the example of Table 14.11 we have for year $t = 1$:

$$\$85,000 - \$72,000 = \$13,000 > 0.12 \times \$23,580 = \$2,829.6$$

Since Inequality 14.8 does not hold, it is optimal to wait at least one year before investing in the computer project. For the possibility of investing at time 2 we have:

$$\$72,000 - \$68,000 = \$4,000 < 0.12 \times \$36,580 = \$4,389.60$$

In this case the inequality holds, so the firm should invest in the computers two years from now, a result which coincides with our previous answer.

---

[9] Inequality 14.8 is only an approximation. For example, it should contain the term $\ln(1 + r)$ instead of r. Nevertheless, it provides an excellent answer for most realistic scenarios.

SUMMARY

This chapter introduced capital budgeting, which is crucial because by making the correct capital budgeting decisions the firm creates wealth, thus fulfilling its basic function.

The most difficult part of capital budgeting analysis is estimating cash flows and converting them to an after-tax basis. As we have seen, operating flows, investment flows, and depreciation all receive different treatments. Once the cash flows are identified on an after-tax basis, they are discounted at the appropriate rate to determine the NPV of the project. If the project has a positive NPV, it should be accepted.

We have also considered some other capital budgeting techniques. The internal rate of return and profitability index are two techniques based on present value concepts. While both are useful for ranking projects, they must be employed with great care because of the possibility of false results. We considered other evaluation methods, but they are almost always inappropriate.

We also examined some more complex issues and frequently encountered problems in capital budgeting. The job of the financial manager is complicated by the fact that some projects are mutually exclusive with others. In such a situation, using the IRR to rank them may lead to an erroneous decision, so the manager should base the decision on the NPV criterion.

Similar difficulties arise in attempting to choose projects consistent with a limited amount of investable funds. When the firm must ration capital, some managers use the IRR for project ranking. However, because IRR does not take the size of the project into account, this can lead to a less than optimal selection. Instead, the manager should choose the set of projects that has the largest NPV without exceeding the investment budget.

The machine replacement problem requires choosing the best time to replace a machine with a new identical one. This is essentially a cost min-imization problem, and we developed methods to choose the correct moment. In capital budgeting, as in personal financial decisions, one must choose between a quality good and a cheap good. The two typically differ in cost, performance, and useful life. This chapter showed how to evaluate a choice in present value terms. Finally, we addressed the problem of investment timing. Sometimes a good investment becomes even better by waiting.

QUESTIONS

1. How do good capital budgeting decisions create or destroy wealth?
2. In a successful capital budgeting decision, how much wealth will be created?

3. Assume that I replace an old machine that has a book value of $1,000 with a new one. If I cannot sell the old machine and must discard it, how should its book value be treated in calculating the cost of the investment? Explain.

4. When I replace the old machine of Question 3 and sell it for $200, how do I treat this sale in calculating the cost of the investment?

5. Assume that I am planning to sell an old electric motor for $200 but that I find I can use it in a new investment project. Does this use of the old machine affect the investment outlay for the new project? Explain.

6. Assume that your firm has invested $100,000 in a project for each of the last three years by paying a research company. Also assume that there have been no cash flows from the project. Your firm is going to reevaluate the viability of the project. If the project is dropped, all of the previous expenditures will have no future value. How should you treat these outlays?

7. If working capital is recaptured at the end of a project, why is there investment in working capital?

8. Your current toy-making process is generating positive cash flows of $150,000 each year on an after-tax basis. If you invest $500,000 to modernize the process, the positive cash flows will increase to $250,000. Identify the cash flows that are relevant to making the capital budgeting decision.

9. React to the following statement: $1 of depreciation expense reduces the firm's earnings by $1 just as does any other expense. Therefore, it should be treated as any other expense in a capital budgeting analysis.

10. What is the depreciation tax shield?

11. Explain the difference between straight-line depreciation and MACRS.

12. Which depreciation method, straight-line or MACRS, is generally better for the firm? Why?

13. At the end of a project, assume that you recapture $10,000 of invested working capital. Is this treated as an operating flow? Explain.

14. Evaluate the following assertion: The main thing you need to know in making an investment decision is how soon you will get your original investment out of the project. This is a question that is exactly answered by the best capital budgeting technique—payback.

15. Evaluate the wisdom of the following analysis: Investors are presented with the firm's annual report and other accounting data. Because that is what they see, they must base their investment decision on it. Accordingly, the firm should choose projects that will improve reported financial results, in particular, those that will give the greatest ROI.

16. The payback period technique is frequently maligned because it disregards the time value of money and neglects cash flows beyond the payback period. Is this an airtight criticism? (*Hint:* Consider the rela-

tionship between the payback period and the IRR for an investment whose positive cash flows constitute a perpetuity.)

17. The NPV and IRR methods are based essentially on the same formula. Despite this, they are very different concepts. Explicitly state the differences.

18. Using the NPV profile technique, explain why the NPV and IRR rules will always result in the same accept or reject decision for a normal project.

19. Suppose that you have a 10-year project with an NPV of $100,000 with a discounted payback period of 9.5 years. What does this say about the amount and timing of the cash flows of this project?

20. For projects that are mutually exclusive, why is it necessary to rank them?

21. What is the pitfall in ranking mutually exclusive projects by the IRR?

22. If a firm does not face capital rationing, does it need IRR at all in ranking projects?

23. Explain why the firm should take the collection of projects with the highest combined NPV in those situations in which it faces capital rationing.

24. What is the purpose of the equivalent annuity method as applied to the machine replacement problem?

25. In choosing between high- and low-quality machines, what is the main criterion for making the choice?

26. Explain why people wait to buy items when they think that they will fall in price. Assume that buying an item now would have a positive NPV.

27. If two projects are mutually exclusive and require the same investment, will the IRR and NPV techniques give them the same ranking?

28. Projects A and B are normal. If the sum of all of the cash flows of A is greater than the corresponding sum for B, and if $IRR_A > IRR_B$, will the IRR and NPV techniques give them the same ranking?

29. You are considering a project in which the cash flows have a total of three sign changes. You wish to find all the real IRRs, and you have already determined that for $r = 0$ the NPV is $-\$2,000$, and that $IRR_1 = 20$ percent, and $IRR_2 = 37$ percent. Should you continue to look for the third possible IRR? Explain.

30. In Question 29 suppose that for $r = 0$ the NPV is $+\$1,300$. The two known IRRs are the same. Should you continue to search for the third possible IRR? Explain.

31. You are considering a project in which the cash flows have a total of four sign changes. You wish to find all the real IRRs, and you have already determined that for $r = 0$ the NPV is $5,000, and that $IRR_1 = 10$ percent, and $IRR_2 = 26$ percent. How many more IRRs should you look for—none, one, or two? Explain.

32. In Question 31 suppose that for $r = 0$ the NPV is $-\$2,300$. The two known IRRs are the same as before. How many more should you look for? Explain.

33. A three-year project has three sign changes in its cash flow stream. You have already found two complex IRRs. Is the other IRR real or complex? Explain.

34. In Question 34, if the third IRR were real, would it necessarily be positive?

PROBLEMS

1. Your investment project will require a microcomputer that costs $4,000 plus 5 percent sales tax. Delivery and setup is $150. Cables to connect the machine to the existing printers will cost $50. A cabinet will cost $200. Which of these expenditures should be included in calculating the investment outlay? What is the investment?

2. In Problem 1, assume that you have the cables on hand. Although used, they could be sold for $20. What effect does this have on the investment cost?

3. Your firm was considering raising alligators for the burgeoning specialty food market. Based on this plan, you snapped up 500 acres of swampland at $1,000 an acre in south Florida. Now you have abandoned that project and are considering one to bring outdoor ice skating to Florida. You could sell the land for $100 an acre. If you go ahead with the skating project, you may be on thin ice, but it would cost $1 million to install the necessary refrigeration equipment. Based on this information, what can you say about the investment in the ice skating rink?

4. The legendary Mr. Fishe is trying to salvage a Spanish galleon laden with gold off the Florida Keys. In his efforts to date, one of the salvage boats worth $200,000 already sank and Fishe is considering abandoning the effort. If he goes ahead, the project will require an additional outlay of $350,000. What is the investment amount that is relevant to his decision now?

5. Everyone knows that chinchilla breed only in the presence of skunks. For your pelt business, you accordingly bought 1,000 skunks five years ago for $10 each. Now you have learned that chinchilla will breed even if no skunks are present, so you want to sell the skunks, but the market stinks. Each skunk will bring only $1. What was the original investment for the chinchilla project? (Beware of the skunk cost fallacy!)

6. Consider the following outlays necessary to open your hardware store, and calculate the total investment: land with building, $200,000; necessary renovations, $15,000; shelving, $10,000; inventory, $225,000; first

year's property tax, $5,000; one month's wages for the staff, $5,000; air conditioning service contract for three years, $1,500; sign, $750.

7. In your ice cream store, you expect to sell 15,000 scoops with cones per month at an average price of $0.75. You pay $0.40 per scoop and $0.02 per cone. What is your gross operating cash flow per month?
8. You will depreciate the ice cream store building and equipment, and the depreciation expense will be $1,500 per month. If your tax rate is 35 percent, what will be your after-tax cash flow based on the information in this problem and Problem 7?

Use the following information for the next three problems. A firm buys a piece of capital equipment for an investment project at a price of $150,000 and pays $30,000 shipping, installation, and setup costs.

9. What is the investment outlay?
10. Assuming straight-line depreciation and a five-year life, what is the depreciation expense for year 3?
11. What is the depreciation expense in year 5 if the equipment is to be depreciated over 10 years?
12. A firm has $100,000 per year in sales, a tax rate of 0.28, and operating costs of $73,000, and shows a depreciation expense of $2,000 per year. Calculate the annual after-tax cash flow.
13. You are considering expanding your alligator wrestling show and have gathered the following data. The special alligator you need (with rubber teeth) costs $80,000. Annual receipts should be $150,000. Your operating expense will be $70,000 per year, including fish for the alligator and hospital expenses for you. You will have to buy a truck for $10,000. You can depreciate both the truck and the alligator on a straight-line basis over five years, at the end of which time the project will terminate. You expect the alligator and the truck to be worthless at the end of the five years. Calculate all of the before-tax cash flows associated with this project.
14. For the data of Problem 13, assume that your tax rate is 30 percent and calculate all of the after-tax cash flows from the project.
15. If you could earn 18 percent in an investment of risk equal to that of the alligator project, should you wrestle or not?
16. What if your discount rate is 22 percent? Should you wrestle in that case?
17. Using trial and error, find the IRR of the alligator wrestling project.
18. If the cash flows from alligator wrestling are discounted at 12 percent, compute its profitability index.

Use the following information for the next 20 problems. Assume that you run a photocopying service and that you are considering purchasing a larger, faster machine. The new machine costs $75,000, including installation and all setup. It will replace your old fully depreciated machine, which you can sell for $8,000. It also will use more power, raising your electric bill about $500 per year. The machine is expected to last five years and will be depreciated on a straight-line basis. If you go ahead with the project you will increase your normal copying business by 500,000 copies per year at an average sales price per copy of $0.05. In addition, you will be able to make specialized high-quality copies that you could not make before. These can be sold for $0.08 and you estimate selling 100,000 per year. Paper, toner, and all other supplies average $0.02 for the normal copies and $0.04 for the high-quality ones. Right now you hold supplies inventories of $1,500, but because your volume will increase, you expect to require inventories of $3,000. The new machine is faster, so you will have no increase in labor costs, which are now $25,000 per year. Your tax rate is 35 percent and your cost of capital is 16 percent. You may ignore any cash flows coming after year 5.

19. What is the amount of the investment, including the replacement of the old machine?
20. Is there any change in working capital? If so, what cash flows are associated with working capital investment?
21. What will sales be for the ordinary quality copies per year?
22. How much are you projecting in high-quality copy sales per year?
23. Prepare a table to present your before-tax cash flows and include those values calculated in the last four questions.
24. What are your operating costs associated directly with the ordinary copies? Enter these in the table.
25. What are your operating costs associated directly with the high-quality copies? Enter these in the table.
26. Compute all other operating costs associated with this project. Enter them in the table.
27. Calculate the depreciation expense for each year. Enter it in the table.
28. Now begin making a table of after-tax cash flows. Begin by computing your after-tax investment cost. Enter it in the table.
29. Compute the after-tax operating cash flow for each year. Enter it in the table.
30. Include the after-tax cash flows associated with working capital, if any. Enter them in the table.
31. Compute the depreciation tax shield. Enter it in the table.
32. Before going further, remember that only *incremental* cash flows matter. Review your treatment of the labor expense and the inventory.
33. Compute the after-tax cash flows for all five years.
34. Compute the NPV of the project's after-tax cash flows.
35. Compute the NPV of the project. Should you buy the new machine?
36. Compute the profitability index of the project.
37. What is the IRR of the project?
38. What is the NPV if you discount all of the after-tax cash flows at the IRR?

Use the following information for the next 14 problems. Some ice-making machines make solid cubes, others make crushed ice, which is rather porous. In your diner, you serve 120,000 16-oz. colas per year. With your current crushed ice machine you are putting an average of 12 oz. of cola into each cup. If you replace the crushed ice machine with the cuber, each cup will take only 9 oz. The cuber costs $15,000 and you can salvage the crushed ice machine for $2,500, which equals its book value. The cuber can be depreciated straight-line over three years. Ignore the salvage value of the cuber and any cash flows after the third year. You are paying $0.02 per ounce for the cola and $0.03 per cup. Both machines require $250 per year in electricity. The difference in the amount of water used is negligible, but the cuber costs $500 per year to maintain, whereas the crushed ice machine had expected maintenance costs of $300 per year. The after-tax discount rate is 9 percent and the tax rate is 40 percent.

39. What is the investment?
40. What new investment in working capital is required?
41. What are the positive operating flows from the project, if any, in each year?
42. What are the operating costs associated with the project in each year?
43. Calculate the depreciation expense for each year.
44. How will you treat the cups?
45. Prepare a table showing all of these before-tax items.
46. What is the after-tax investment?
47. Compute the total operating flows from the project and convert them to an after-tax basis.
48. Compute the depreciation tax shield.
49. Prepare a table showing these and any other after-tax cash flows.
50. What is the NPV of the project?
51. Compute the profitability index of the project.
52. What is the IRR of the project?

Use the following information for the next eight problems. Project A requires an investment of $1,000 and pays $1,000 per year for two years. Project B also costs $1,000 and pays $5,000 after five years. Project C costs $500 and pays $3,000 after five years. All of these cash flows are after taxes. Only one project can be selected.

53. What is the payback period for each project?
54. According to the payback method, which project is to be selected, if you can select only one?
55. What is the NPV of each project if the discount rate is 12 percent?
56. If only one project can be selected, which would be preferred according to the NPV rule?
57. What is the IRR of each project?
58. Which project would be selected if you used the IRR as the decision criterion?

59. Compare projects B and C. Why does the NPV technique choose the one it does?
60. Which decision criterion works best in contributing to shareholder wealth?
61. We argued in the text that for normal projects, the NPV and the IRR methods will always give the same accept or reject decision. Prove this assertion for any one-year project. (*Hint:* Show that if IRR $> r$, then we must necessarily have NPV > 0 for that project.)
62. Show that for projects with perpetuity cash flows the payback period, PP, is the inverse of the project's IRR.
63. Projects A and B have the same single cash inflow, C, and the same IRR. However, their initial investments differ. Also, project A pays the cash inflow C one year from now, whereas C is received two years from now with project B. What is the relationship between the two investments? For example, the relationship could be something like $I_A = I_B/C$.
64. You are considering opening a car dealership on a piece of land. The initial investment is $73 million and the cash inflows for years 1 through 5 are all equal to $26 million. What is the NPV for this project if the discount rate is 17 percent?
65. Compute the IRR for the car dealership project of Problem 64.
66. Another project that interests you is building a shopping mall. The initial investment is $90 million and the cash inflows for years 1 through 5 are $30 million. What is the NPV of this project if the discount rate is 15 percent?
67. Compute the IRR for the shopping mall project.
68. There is just one more problem with the two projects we have been considering. Both would use the same piece of land, so they are mutually exclusive. Which should be chosen, if either? Explain.

Consider the two projects shown below. The cash flows shown are all presented on an after-tax basis. Use these data to solve Problems 69 through 74.

	Cash Flows	
Year	Project A	Project B
0	−$75,000	−$55,000
1	30,000	22,000
2	18,000	13,200
3	50,000	36,667

69. If the discount rate is 18 percent, what is the NPV of project A?
70. If the discount rate is 18 percent, what is the NPV of project B?
71. Find the IRR of project A.
72. Find the IRR of project B.

73. Which project should you prefer?
74. If the discount rates are 20 percent and 18 percent for projects A and B, respectively, which project should you prefer?

You have analyzed the following projects and determined their NPVs, which are presented below. Use this information to solve Problems 75 through 77.

Project	NPV	Required Investment
Alpha	$10,000	$ 50,000
Sigma	20,000	90,000
Gamma	5,000	10,000
Beta	45,000	110,000
Epsilon	9,000	35,000
Nu	7,000	20,000
Tau	12,000	30,000
Phi	30,000	90,000

75. If you are limited to $70,000 in investable funds, which projects should you accept?
76. If you are limited to $130,000 in investable funds, which projects should you accept?
77. If you are limited to $250,000 in investable funds, which projects should you accept?

Cassidy the butcher is wondering how often he should replace his salami-slicing machines. Use the following information about the operating costs per machine to solve the next four problems.

Year n	Operating Cost	PA(12%, n)	PV of Operating Costs at 12%*
1	$ 700	0.89	$ 625.00
2	1,000	1.69	1,422.19
3	1,200	2.40	2,276.33
4	1,400	3.04	3,166.06
5	1,400	3.60	3,960.45
6	1,700	4.11	4,821.73
7	2,000	4.56	5,726.42
8	2,400	4.97	6,695.74
9	3,000	5.33	7,777.57
10	4,500	5.65	9,226.45
11	6,000	5.94	10,951.31
12	9,000	6.19	13,261.39

* This column gives the sum of the present value of operating costs up to year *n*, not including the initial cost of the slicer.

78. Assume that each slicer costs $20,000 and your cost of capital is 12 percent. How long should Cassidy keep a slicer?
79. Assume now that a slicer costs $10,000 and your cost of capital is 12 percent. How long before Cassidy should replace the machine?
80. If the discount rate is 12 percent, how little would the machine have to cost to make Cassidy replace it after nine years?
81. If the discount rate is 12 percent, how little would the machine have to cost to make Cassidy replace it after five years?

Down on South Fork Ranch, a little spread just outside Dallas, there is a herd of cattle. Your problem is to advise Mr. Ray Theon, the ranch owner, on the best time to liquidate the herd. The longer you wait, the higher will be the NPV at the time of liquidation. This increasing NPV is due to the growing size of the herd. However, the herd will grow at a slower rate as it gets larger, perhaps due to the emotional upsets that seem to abound in this corner of the world. At any rate, assume that Mr. Theon has a 15 percent cost of capital. The different liquidation points and the correspondent NPVs from liquidating the herd on those dates are shown below.

Year	NPV of Liquidation
0	$1,000,000
1	1,150,000
2	1,400,000
3	1,900,000
4	2,100,000
5	2,300,000
6	2,500,000

Assuming that Ray must liquidate no later than year 6, use this information to solve the next eight problems.

82. If your discount rate is 15 percent, would you rather liquidate immediately or at year 1?
83. If your discount rate is 18 percent, would you rather liquidate immediately or at year 1?
84. If your discount rate is 12 percent, would you rather liquidate immediately or at year 1?
85. If you have a discount rate of 15 percent, when will you liquidate?
86. If you have a discount rate of 20 percent, when will you liquidate?
87. If you have a discount rate of 8 percent, when will you liquidate?
88. If you have a discount rate of 12 percent, when will you liquidate?
89. If you have a discount rate of 30 percent, when will you liquidate?
90. Projects C and D are mutually exclusive. They have the same IRR and the same constant annual cash flows. However, the life of C is

twice the life of D. If D is preferable to C, how are the two investment outlays, the annuity cash flow, and the life of D related?

91. Consider projects A and B, where the positive inflows constitute annuities which start at time 1. Project A lasts for n_A years and B for n_B
years. Show that if $NPV_A > NPV_B$ and $n_A < n_B$, the equivalent annuity
for A is greater than that for B.

Risk in Capital Budgeting

In Chapter 14 we introduced the techniques of capital budgeting, but implicitly assumed that the project cash flows were known with certainty. In the real world, the future is uncertain and project cash flows are almost always risky. The financial manager must take this riskiness into account in making capital budgeting decisions.

This chapter considers some of the sources of risk affecting project cash flows. Some of these are under the control of managers, and others are not. The financial manager must understand both sources and manage risk whenever possible.

After introducing techniques for analyzing risk, the discussion focuses on two different types of leverage and how they affect the risk level of the firm. Both types arise from the introduction of fixed charges into the firm's financial plan. **Operating leverage** results from fixed operating expenses, whereas **financial leverage** arises from fixed financing expenses. Both affect the overall risk level of the firm and the stock price. As we will see, interactions between them are particularly important, because the two effects working together can have dramatic effects on risk and, therefore, on value.

The chapter concludes by integrating the perspectives of the financial manager and the shareholders to form one consistent vision of firm risk. In essence, we know that shareholders hold a portfolio of securities and are concerned with the risk of a particular capital budgeting project in a particular firm only as that project contributes to the risk of their entire portfolio.

operating leverage
leverage resulting from the use of fixed costs in operations

financial leverage
leverage resulting from the use of fixed costs in financing

SOURCES OF RISK IN CAPITAL INVESTMENT PROJECTS

☞ The discount rate is higher for a capital budgeting project with greater risk.

In any capital budgeting project, different factors affect its cash flows. Some of these are under the firm's control and others are not. Factors within the firm's control include the choice of safe or risky projects and the way in which a given project is implemented. Influences beyond the control of the firm may be changing social trends and government policies.

Sources of Risk Within the Control of the Firm

The major way in which a firm affects the risk of its cash flows is through its choice of projects. It is often tempting to choose risky projects because of

☞ The firm can affect its total risk by the projects it selects and by the technology it chooses to implement them.

their greater potential cash flows. As we have seen, however, a firm always prefers less risky projects if the expected cash flows are equal.

Even after a particular project is chosen the firm can partially determine the riskiness of its cash flows by the way it implements the project. For example, a firm can reduce risk by renting the production facility and manufacturing equipment and, if the project is successful, the firm can later buy its own facilities. On the other hand, if the project is unsuccessful, the firm has not invested great amounts. Many such risk-minimizing strategies are more expensive if the project is successful, however.

Sources of Risk Beyond the Control of the Firm

☞ Some risks are beyond the control of the firm, such as the condition of the general economy.

Social trends, government policy changes, and business cycles are beyond the control of the firm, yet can have a great impact on project cash flows. For example, firms in the high-fashion segment of the apparel industry are very subject to the whims of public taste. By contrast, the manufacturer of business shirts has a much more stable market.

Government action affects some projects dramatically. In the artificial sweetener and pharmaceutical industries, for example, a product could be completely destroyed overnight by governmental decree or the refusal to license a new drug. In the early 1970s, cyclamates were used extensively as an artificial sweetener, but based on evidence that they caused cancer, the government completely banned their use.

The cash flows of many projects vary as the market or the economy as a whole fluctuates. This means that some have a high degree of systematic risk. As we have seen in our discussion of security markets, this market risk is nondiversifiable and completely unavoidable.

Merely because some projects are riskier than others is not a valid reason always to prefer the low-risk ones. Otherwise, no one would drill oil wells or do research on new drug treatments. In fact, the greatest potential rewards come from the riskiest projects. In the capital budgeting process, the firm must weigh the risks against the potential rewards for each project. Because of this, the wise use of risk analysis techniques is extremely important.

The following sections discuss three familiar techniques of risk analysis: breakeven analysis, sensitivity analysis, and scenario analysis. Their main use is to provide the financial manager with a feel for the project's risk dimensions. Each method focuses on the total risk of the project. Later we consider systematic risk.

BREAKEVEN ANALYSIS

breakeven analysis
a technique for analyzing profitability as a function of investment and sales

The success of many capital budgeting projects depends on the ability to produce a certain number of units of a given product, whether a good or service. The profitability of a project can be analyzed for different levels of sales by using **breakeven analysis.** Virtually every project involves some **fixed cost**—the cost the firm incurs no matter how many units of a good or

fixed cost
the cost the firm incurs no matter how many units of a good or service are produced

variable cost
the cost that is incurred to produce each unit of a good or service

total cost
the sum of the fixed and variable costs

☞ Breakeven analysis can give information about the profitability of a project at different levels of sales, but it does not focus on NPV.

service are produced. It includes plant overhead, depreciation for equipment, utilities, and other expenses that do not vary with the level of production. For example, a pencil manufacturer's fixed costs include the facility and equipment for producing the pencils. In addition, the firm incurs a **variable cost,** the amount required to produce each unit of the good or service. In the case of the pencil manufacturer, the variable costs include wood, graphite, and labor. The **total cost** equals the sum of the fixed and variable costs.

Breakeven analysis focuses on the relationship between sales and fixed and variable costs. If the pencil manufacturer sells a pencil for $0.10 and the variable cost required to make it is $0.07, the firm covers its variable cost. However, it may lose money if it fails to sell enough pencils to recover all its fixed costs.

To see more clearly the kind of analysis involved, consider a firm that plans to manufacture computer switches to sell for $10 each, with a variable cost of $8 per switch. The fixed cost associated with this project will be $100,000. Figure 15.1 reflects these facts, showing fixed costs, total costs, and revenues. The firm incurs the fixed costs whether it manufactures one switch

FIGURE 15.1   Breakeven Analysis for the Computer Switch Project

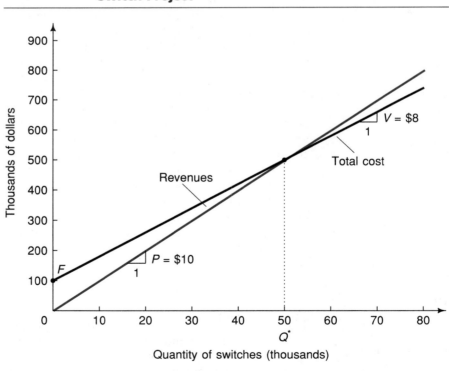

or one million. The total cost line reflects the fixed costs (F) plus the variable costs (V). For example, if the firm manufactures a quantity (Q) of 10,000 switches, its total cost (TC) will be $180,000:

$$TC = F + (V \times Q)$$
$$= \$100,000 + (\$8 \times 10,000)$$
$$= \$180,000$$

The firm's revenue (R) depends on the price (P) and quantity (Q). Sales of 10,000 switches generate revenues of $100,000:

$$R = P \times Q$$
$$= \$10 \times 10,000$$
$$= \$100,000$$

With production and sales of 10,000 switches, the company has total costs of $180,000 and revenues of $100,000, so it loses $80,000. As Figure 15.1 indicates, it incurs a loss at any level of production and sales below 50,000 switches.

breakeven point
the level of production
and sales at which the
revenue equals the total
cost

If the firm produces and sells exactly 50,000 switches it has neither a profit nor a loss. This is the **breakeven point**—the level of production and sales at which total revenue equals total cost. If the firm sells more than 50,000 switches, it makes a profit. In the graph, the revenue line lies above the total cost line for levels of production and sales greater than 50,000. The project breaks even when:

$$TC = R$$

Alternatively, if we separate the total costs and revenues into their components, the project breaks even when:

$$F + (V \times Q) = P \times Q$$

The breakeven point is the level of sales (Q) at which there is neither a profit or loss, so denoting the breakeven quantity as Q^*, we have:

$$Q^* = \frac{F}{P - V} \qquad (15.1)$$

For the switch company, we find the breakeven point to be:

$$Q^* = \frac{\$100,000}{\$10 - \$8}$$
$$= 50,000 \text{ switches}$$

Breakeven analysis can be used to evaluate the likelihood of making a profit with the switches, helping the financial manager to see the level of profitability or loss for various levels of sales. It also can help the manager choose between different technologies or manufacturing techniques for making the same product. For example, suppose there is another way to make exactly

FIGURE 15.2   Breakeven Analysis for the Switch Project with the New Technology

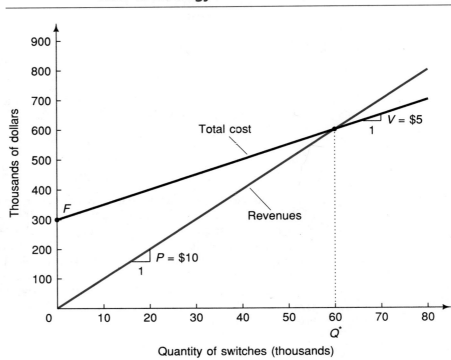

the same switch that employs new technology for which fixed costs are $300,000. In addition, the switches can be made at a lower variable cost of $5 each using the new technology. Because they are the same switches, they continue to sell for $10 apiece. Figure 15.2 presents a breakeven analysis with the new technology. We find the breakeven point (Q^*) using Equation 15.1:

$$Q^* = \frac{\$300,000}{\$10 - \$5} = 60,000 \text{ switches}$$

Due to the higher fixed cost, the firm has to sell 60,000 switches to break even, contrasted with the original breakeven point of 50,000. In spite of the higher breakeven point, the high-technology method may have some advantages. For example, if the firm can sell 100,000 switches, the profits vary greatly, depending on the choice of technology. If the old technology is

TABLE 15.1 Profits from the Switch Project at Various Levels of Sales for Old and New Technologies

Number of Switches Sold	Old Technology	New Technology
0	$ − 100,000	$ − 300,000
10,000	− 80,000	− 250,000
20,000	− 60,000	− 200,000
30,000	− 40,000	− 150,000
40,000	− 20,000	− 100,000
50,000	0	− 50,000
60,000	20,000	0
70,000	40,000	50,000
80,000	60,000	100,000
90,000	80,000	150,000
100,000	$ 100,000	$ 200,000

chosen, the profit will be $100,000, as shown below:

$$\text{Profit} = R - TC$$
$$= P \times Q - [F + (V \times Q)]$$
$$= \$10 \times 100,000 - [\$100,000 + (\$8 \times 100,000)]$$
$$= \$100,000$$

With the new technology and a sales level of 100,000 switches, the firm will do much better:

$$\text{Profit} = R - TC$$
$$= P \times Q - [F + (V \times Q)]$$
$$= \$10 \times 100,000 - [\$300,000 + (\$5 \times 100,000)]$$
$$= \$200,000$$

Under the new technology, the profit will be $200,000, or twice as much as with the old technology.

Which technology should the firm choose? The answer depends on its estimate of sales and its confidence about that estimate. For example, if it is sure it will sell no more than 55,000 switches, it should use the old method. If it is sure it can sell at least 100,000 switches, it should employ the new one because it will obtain a greater profit.

Table 15.1 shows the level of profit for different levels of sales under the two technologies, and Figure 15.3 presents the same information graphically. If the firm sells 66,667 switches, the two methods perform equally well. For any level of sales below that, the low-technology strategy is better, making either a greater profit or a smaller loss than the high-technology strategy.

FIGURE 15.3   Profit Comparison for the Switch Project with High- and Low-Technology Production

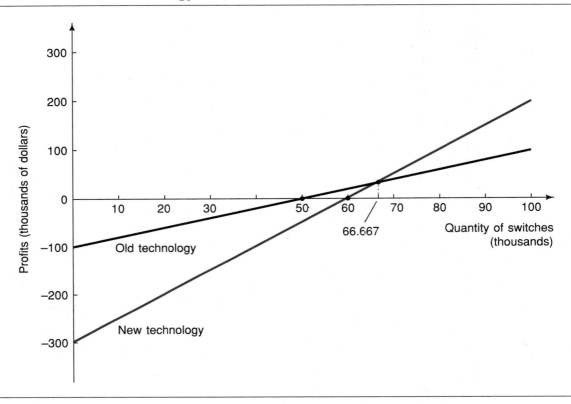

For higher levels of sales, the new method is preferable since it produces more profits. For example, we already noted that with sales of 100,000 switches, it gives twice the profit of the old method.

The two technologies have quite a difference in their mixture of fixed and variable costs. The proportion of fixed costs relative to variable costs is known as operating leverage. An operation with a high level of fixed costs relative to variable costs has high operating leverage. For the switch company, the high-technology strategy involves a higher degree of operating leverage than the low-technology strategy. If the firm is confident that it can sell a large number of switches, the breakeven analysis and profit comparison gives a strong reason to prefer the former.

Although breakeven analysis is a useful technique for examining operating risk in a given period, it does not evaluate present values. In particular, it considers only one period, and it does not reflect the present values of future

FINANCE TODAY

Cruel and Unusual Stupidity

The strategy was crafty but cruel. When Continental Can was trying to cut costs in its plants during the late 1970s, the company employed a secret computer program called BELL, a reverse acronym for Let's Limit Employee Benefits. Managers used the program to target and lay off employees just weeks or months before they were vested in the company pension plan. In that way, the company aimed to avoid millions of dollars in pension payments.

It was a costly mistake. The United Steel Workers of America filed a class-action suit in 1982 under the Employee Retirement Income Security Act. Federal courts ruled that the company had acted illegally and ordered Continental to compensate its retired workers. [In January 1991] Continental finally reached an agreement under which it [would] pay $415 million to 3,000 people, the largest settlement in the 17-year history of ERISA.

Source: "Too Slick with the Pink Slips," *Time*, January 14, 1991.

---

cash flows. It also does not consider the investment outlay. The next section discusses a modified version of the technique that focuses on the key decision variable—the net present value of the project.

DISCOUNTED BREAKEVEN ANALYSIS

discounted breakeven analysis
a modification of breakeven analysis that incorporates time value of money concepts

We know that the financial manager should use the NPV technique to evaluate projects. Although the traditional breakeven analysis focuses on the annual profits from a project, **discounted breakeven analysis** can be conducted by focusing on NPV. Consider a project that requires an investment of $I. As before, let the price of each unit be $P, the variable cost per unit be $V, and the fixed annual costs be $F. These fixed costs include the annual depreciation, D. The discount rate for the project is r percent, and the project has a life on n years. The firm estimates that it will sell Q units in each year of the project's life. For simplicity, suppose the firm does not pay taxes.

As Figure 15.4 shows, this project has an outlay of $I at time $t = 0$ and generates annual cash inflows equal to:

$$\text{Annual cash flow} = PQ - (F - D + VQ)$$

These equal annual cash flows constitute an annuity. Notice that to obtain the annual cash flow it is necessary to subtract the depreciation, D, from the fixed costs, F, because depreciation is not a cash expense. We can now calculate

FIGURE 15.4 Time Line for the Discounted Breakeven Analysis

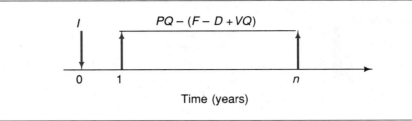

the expression for the net present value of this project:

$$\text{NPV} = -I + [PQ - (F - D + VQ)] \, \text{PA}(r, n)$$

The project breaks even when its NPV equals 0. Let the breakeven quantity when using the discounted breakeven method be Q_d^*. Then, setting the above expression to 0 and solving for the breakeven quantity, we obtain:

$$Q_d^* = \frac{F}{P - V} + \frac{I - D \times \text{PA}(r, n)}{(P - V) \, \text{PA}(r, n)} \tag{15.2}$$

We can see from Equation 15.2 that the discounted breakeven quantity will normally differ from the traditional breakeven quantity given in Equation 15.1. Consequently, we should be careful in using the traditional quantity, as it is likely to give an erroneous estimate of the breakeven that results from using discounted cash flow techniques.

To illustrate the difference between the traditional and the discounted breakeven methods, let us return to our example of the switch company, and assume that it uses the old technology. In that case, annual fixed costs are $100,000, variable costs per switch are $8, and the price of each switch is $10. Given these data, we determined that the traditional breakeven quantity is 50,000 units.

To use the discounted technique, we must know the amount of initial investment for the project, the annual depreciation, the life of the project, and the appropriate discount rate. Assume that $I = \$500,000$ and $n = 10$ years, so $D = \$50,000$.[1] Given this information, and assuming a discount rate of $r = 10$ percent, we calculate the discounted breakeven using Equation 15.2:

$$Q_d^* = \frac{100,000}{10 - 8} + \frac{500,000 - 50,000 \times \text{PA}(10\%, 10)}{(10 - 8) \, \text{PA}(10\%, 10)}$$

$$= 50,000 + 15,686$$

$$= 65,686 \text{ switches}$$

---

[1] For simplicity, we assume straight-line depreciation and a 0 salvage value at the end of the project's life.

This calculation clearly illustrates that the traditional breakeven quantity may seriously underestimate the true quantity, which is found using the NPV technique. The discounted quantity of 65,686 switches is much greater than the traditional breakeven of 50,000 switches. If the firm believes it can sell 60,000 switches each year, the traditional breakeven would indicate a profitable project. At that sales level, however, the project has a negative NPV and should be rejected. Only with sales estimates greater than 65,686 will the project generate wealth for the firm.

SENSITIVITY ANALYSIS

sensitivity analysis
a technique that measures the change in one variable as a consequence of a change in another

To determine whether a project should be undertaken, the financial manager must explore how the NPV varies with a change in sales. **Sensitivity analysis** is a technique measuring the change in one variable as a consequence of a change in another variable. Its purpose is to consider what happens to the NPV if the sales forecast is in error, or if other variables differ from their predicted values.

The uses of sensitivity analysis can be illustrated by continuing our example of the switch company. Let us assume that the firm estimates that sales will be 80,000 switches per year, and because of this it has elected to consider only the high-technology strategy. Furthermore, we assume sales are expected to be 80,000 for each of the next five years, after which the switch will be obsolete and the project will be terminated. In that case, the after-tax cash flows of the project, assumed here to be equal to net income, will be the same for each of the five years, and will equal $70,000 based on a 30 percent tax rate:

Revenue	$ 800,000
— Fixed cost	− 300,000
— Variable cost	− 400,000
Gross profit	100,000
— Taxes	30,000
Net income	$ 70,000
(assumed to equal cash flow)	

Suppose the initial investment is $200,000 and the discount rate is 12 percent. Under these assumptions, the NPV of the project is $52,336:

$$\text{NPV} = -\$200,000 + \frac{70,000}{1.12} + \frac{70,000}{1.12^2} + \frac{70,000}{1.12^3} + \frac{70,000}{1.12^4} + \frac{70,000}{1.12^5}$$

$$= \$52,334$$

Although $52,334 is the firm's best estimate of the NPV of the project, it clearly depends on a number of other estimates being correct. Most clearly, if sales differ from their forecast level, the NPV will differ. But NPV also changes if the cost estimates prove to be incorrect. If either fixed or variable costs differ from their forecasted values, NPV will be altered as well. The

TABLE 15.2   Switch Project Cash Flows Under Alternative Sales

SALES 10 PERCENT LESS THAN FORECAST (72,000 switches)

Revenue	$ 720,000
— Fixed cost	−300,000
— Variable cost	−360,000
Before-tax operating cash flow	60,000
— Taxes	18,000
After-tax annual cash flow	$ 42,000

SALES 10 PERCENT MORE THAN FORECAST (88,000 switches)

Revenue	$ 880,000
— Fixed cost	−300,000
— Variable cost	−440,000
Before-tax operating cash flow	140,000
— Taxes	42,000
After-tax annual cash flow	$ 98,000

financial manager has to know how sensitive the NPV estimate is to changes in these variables.

To examine the sensitivity of NPV to change in sales, let us recalculate what happens if the current forecast of 80,000 units is 10 percent too high and 10 percent too low. For each case, the new level of after-tax cash flow is recalculated in Table 15.2. First, if sales fall 10 percent below the forecast, annual sales will be 72,000 and total revenues will be $720,000. Fixed costs remain unchanged at $300,000, and total variable costs drop to $360,000. A 10 percent drop in sales makes the annual after-tax cash flow fall from $70,000 to $42,000. By contrast, if sales increase by 10 percent per year to 88,000 units, revenue increases to $880,000 and the annual after-tax cash flow is $98,000. From this, we can see that the annual after-tax cash flow is very sensitive to such a change. If sales fall just 10 percent below their predicted value, it falls by 40 percent. If sales are 10 percent larger than predicted, it increases by 40 percent. Again, we stress the convenient assumption that after-tax cash flow and net income are equal in this example.

The change in annual after-tax cash flow for a change in sales is as follows:

10% Sales Decrease (72,000 units)		Predicted Sales (80,000 units)		10% Increase (88,000 units)
$42,000		$70,000		$98,000
	−40%		+40%	

This sensitivity of cash flows to a change in the sales level is important, but the most critical consequence is the effect on the NPV of the project, which changes even more dramatically. If sales are 72,000 switches per year, the NPV is:

$$NPV = -\$200,000 + \frac{42,000}{1.12} + \frac{42,000}{1.12^2} + \frac{42,000}{1.12^3} + \frac{42,000}{1.12^4} + \frac{42,000}{1.12^5}$$

$$= -\$48,599$$

If sales are 88,000 switches per year, the NPV is:

$$NPV = -\$200,000 + \frac{98,000}{1.12} + \frac{98,000}{1.12^2} + \frac{98,000}{1.12^3} + \frac{98,000}{1.12^4} + \frac{98,000}{1.12^5}$$

$$= \$153,268$$

Figure 15.5 graphs the NPV as a function of the sales level and shows its sensitivity to a change in sales. If sales are just 10 percent less than forecast, the NPV of the project is −$48,599. On the other hand, a 10 percent increase above the forecast level increases the NPV to $153,268. If sales are 75,852 switches per year, the project has a 0 NPV.

Sensitivity analysis could also be conducted to determine the response of the NPV to a change in other variables, such as unexpected changes in variable costs, price, fixed costs, and the life of the project. It helps the financial manager choose the best projects or the best ways of implementing them. It allows the manager to ask "what if" questions.

In spite of its obvious usefulness and the fact that many firms employ it, the technique has some limitations. For example, it allows only one variable to change at a time. In particular, it does not readily allow for interactions between two or more variables. For example, we considered a 10 percent

FIGURE 15.5   The Sensitivity of NPV to a Change in Sales for the Switch Project

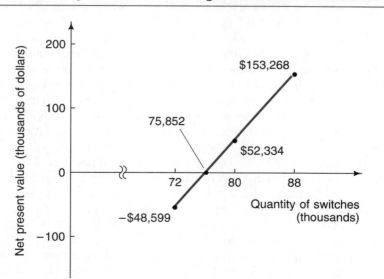

increase or decrease in both sales and price, but we assumed that one was fixed and the other varied. This, of course, is not the normal case. Typically, a price increase means that sales will fall. Sensitivity analysis does not allow this kind of interaction to be examined very easily.

SCENARIO ANALYSIS

scenario analysis
a technique that examines the firm's circumstances if a certain set of events, called a scenario, arises

Scenario analysis examines the firm's circumstances if a certain set of events, called a scenario, arises. The manager specifies a scenario and its likely effect on variables of key interest. By a particular specification, the manager can allow a number of variables to change simultaneously, thus examining their effect on a project's NPV.

Consider the computer switch project once more. Although the firm may have expectations regarding sales, variable and fixed costs, taxes, and after-tax cash flows, other developments may occur that could completely alter the cash flows from the project. For example, the computer market could slump, the switch could become obsolete much sooner than expected, or tax rates could rise. The specification of a scenario can take many such changes into account simultaneously.

With the diversity of possible outcomes in mind, assume the manager has developed three scenarios, which we will call "most likely," "pessimistic," and "optimistic." Under the pessimistic scenario, the manager fears the firm's tax rate will rise to 35 percent as the result of government action, and that the economy will suffer due to more money being pulled from the private sector for taxes. In addition, the firm could expect a 10 percent drop in sales. The optimistic scenario assumes the tax rate will not change, but that the economy will expand at a higher than expected rate. Thus sales would be 15 percent above their currently projected level of 80,000 units per year. In addition, the switch has a useful life of seven instead of five years, and fixed costs can be held to $285,000 per year instead of the currently projected $300,000. The most likely scenario provides after-tax annual cash flows of $70,000 and an NPV of $52,334. Table 15.3 examines the firm's cash flows and the NPV of the switch project under the three scenarios.

If the pessimistic scenario materializes, the tax rate rises and sales fall. The result of these two changes is dramatic, with annual cash flow being only $39,000 on an after-tax basis and the project's NPV falling to −$59,413. On the brighter side, if the optimistic scenario develops, sales will be 15 percent higher than the most likely level, the project lasts seven years rather than five, and fixed costs are only $285,000 per year; thus seven years of after-tax annual cash flows of $122,500 will give a net present value of $359,060.

In many respects, scenario analysis is similar to sensitivity analysis, but with some differences. With sensitivity analysis, the manager looks at the effect of a change in one variable on a project's NPV. With scenario analysis, the manager considers a situation in which a number of variables differ from their expected values. In this technique, the manager allows for interactions among the different factors, and can consider their total effect on NPV.

TABLE 15.3   Cash Flows and NPVs for the Switch Project Using Three Scenarios (I = $200,000; r = 12%)

	Pessimistic	Most Likely	Optimistic
Sales (per year)	72,000	80,000	92,000
Project life (years)	5	5	7
Tax rate	0.35	0.3	0.3
Fixed costs	$300,000	$300,000	$285,000
Revenue	$720,000	$800,000	$920,000
— Fixed cost	−300,000	−300,000	−285,000
— Variable cost	−360,000	−400,000	−460,000
Operating cash flow	60,000	100,000	175,000
— Taxes	14,000	30,000	52,500
After-tax cash flow	$39,000	$70,000	$122,500
Project NPV	−$59,413	$52,334	$359,060

However, it does not allow as many different outcomes to be considered as easily as sensitivity analysis. Each scenario must be carefully thought out in advance to include the significant changes that might be experienced.

OPERATING LEVERAGE AND THE VARIABILITY OF EBIT

The old and new switch-manufacturing technologies included quite a difference in the mixture of fixed and variable costs. The proportion of fixed costs relative to variable costs is operating leverage. An operation with a high level of fixed costs relative to variable costs has high operating leverage. In the switch company, the new strategy involves a higher measure of operating leverage than the old one.

We now examine the effect of operating leverage on the riskiness of the firm's operating profits; that is, the firm's earnings before interest and taxes, or EBIT. We focus on operating profits in order to separate the risk resulting from the firm's operations from that associated with its financing policy.

business risk
the variability of a firm's EBIT

We define **business risk** as the variability in a firm's EBIT, and show how operating leverage increases business risk. Table 15.4 shows the EBIT for different levels of sales, for both the old and new strategies. The breakeven point is higher for the new strategy because of its higher fixed costs, consistent with our previous findings. In addition, the table shows the greater variability of EBIT for the high-technology strategy.

To examine the effect of operating leverage more closely, assume the firm expects to sell 66,667 switches per year. At this level, the new and old technologies give the same EBIT of $33,334. Let us also assume that the standard deviation of sales is 10,000 units. This means there is about a 68

TABLE 15.4   Sales, Revenues, Costs, and Profits for the Switch Company

		Low-Technology		High-Technology	
Switches Sold	Revenues	Total Cost	EBIT	Total Cost	EBIT
10,000	$100,000	$180,000	$ − 80,000	$350,000	$ − 250,000
20,000	200,000	260,000	− 60,000	400,000	− 200,000
30,000	300,000	340,000	− 40,000	450,000	− 150,000
40,000	400,000	420,000	− 20,000	500,000	− 100,000
50,000	500,000	500,000	0	550,000	− 50,000
60,000	600,000	580,000	20,000	600,000	0
70,000	700,000	660,000	40,000	650,000	50,000
80,000	800,000	740,000	60,000	700,000	100,000
90,000	900,000	820,000	80,000	750,000	150,000

percent chance that actual sales will fall between 56,667 and 76,667, assuming sales are normally distributed.

For the expected sales of 66,667, the two strategies have the same expected EBIT. However, as sales move away from that figure, EBIT varies as well. For the old-technology/low fixed cost strategy, the variability is not so great. In fact, as Table 15.4 shows, a change of 10,000 units in sales causes only a $20,000 change in EBIT for the old strategy, compared with a $50,000 change for the new one. We conclude that the EBIT for the latter is much more susceptible to a variation in sales.

To measure the operating leverage, we compute the change in EBIT for a change in sales, on a percentage basis. The measure of operating leverage (MOL) is:

$$\text{MOL} = \frac{\text{Percentage change in EBIT}}{\text{Percentage change in sales}} \tag{15.3}$$

An equivalent expression is:

$$\text{MOL} = \frac{(P - V)Q}{(P - V)Q - F} \tag{15.4}$$

Equation 15.4 shows that the MOL will always be greater than 1 for any firm that has some fixed operating expenses, F. This is because the denominator is smaller than the numerator, so the entire fraction is greater than 1.

Consider again expected sales of 66,667 switches. With this figure and using the cost data for each strategy, we can compute the MOL. For the low operating leverage strategy we have:

$$\text{MOL} = \frac{(\$10 - \$8)\, 66,667}{(\$10 - \$8)\, 66,667 - \$100,000} = 4.0$$

For the high operating leverage strategy we have:

$$MOL = \frac{(\$10 - \$5)\ 66{,}667}{(\$10 - \$5)\ 66{,}667 - \$300{,}000} = 10.0$$

Both strategies employ some operating leverage because both have some fixed operating costs. As a result, both have MOL values greater than 1. However, using larger fixed operating costs increases the MOL significantly. The MOL of 10 obtained for the new strategy means that for each 1 percent change in unit sales from the base level of 66,667, the EBIT will change by 10 percent. Notice that the MOL depends on the base sales level chosen. For example, at the breakeven quantity of sales the MOL will always be infinite. This is not surprising, because it reflects the fact that at the breakeven point there are no operating profits, and any increase in sales will produce some operating profit, or EBIT; and a change from no profit to some profit represents an infinite percentage increase.[2]

Although operating leverage increases risk, we cannot conclude that the firm should minimize it. It merely means that the financial manager must choose the correct amount of operating leverage. As we have emphasized so many times, the financial manager must trade off the good (higher expected EBIT) against the bad (higher business risk).

FINANCIAL LEVERAGE AND TOTAL RISK

☞ For the firm, increasing financial leverage increases both total and systematic risk.

Financial leverage affects the firm in ways similar to operating leverage. However, whereas operating leverage results from fixed operating costs, financial leverage arises from fixed financing charges, that is, the interest and principal payments on debt. Just as operating leverage increases the expected EBIT and its variability, financial leverage increases the expected value and variability of the firm's earnings per share, or EPS.

For operating leverage, the manager must choose the correct level of fixed operating costs. For financial leverage, the manager must choose how much debt financing to use.

Because of its greater risk, it appears the firm should avoid debt financing. Instead, it might rely strictly on stock financing. However, using debt has some advantages. First, it may be cheaper because the debtholders have first claim on the assets of a firm. Therefore, the rate of return demanded by the bondholders will be less than that demanded by the stockholders. Second, the firm makes interest payments from EBIT. By contrast, it pays dividends

---

[2] It is a common misconception to assume that a change from 0 to 1 (in any variable) represents a 100 percent increase. For instance, a newspaper once reported a 100 percent increase in murders in a certain small town, relative to the previous year. Further reading revealed that there had been one murder that year. This had the intriguing implication that there had been 0.5 murders the previous year!

INTERNATIONAL PERSPECTIVES

The Bhopal Lesson

Bhopal is the capital of the state of Madhya Pradesh in central India. First inhabited in the eleventh century, Bhopal now has a population of more than 800,000. Among Bhopal's major points of interest is the nineteenth century Taj-ul-Masjid, the largest mosque in India.

On December 3, 1984, Bhopal suffered the worst industrial accident on record. In the early-morning hours, toxic gas began leaking from a storage tank at a Union Carbide pesticide plant. The noxious fumes spread through the city, killing more than 3,500 residents and leaving an estimated 200,000 others with a variety of injuries and ailments.

As a direct result of the accident, Union Carbide's stock dropped nearly 30 percent, losing about $1 billion literally overnight (see the figure). The reason for the precipitous stock price drop is clear: The market anticipated a series of costly lawsuits, which could potentially result in Union Carbide's bankruptcy.

The accusations went back and forth. Union Carbide claimed that a disgruntled Indian employee had caused the accident. The government of India charged that the plant design was poor and its maintenance was faulty. After years of litigation, on February 14, 1989, the Indian Supreme Court ordered Union Carbide to pay survivors $470 million in damages.

The Bhopal disaster reminds us that any project has risks associated with it, and that risk assessment is an essential element in any capital-budgeting decision. While terrible accidents such as the one in Bhopal, and later in Chernobyl, will probably occur from time to time, careful planning can minimize them.

Source: "Bhopal," *American Academic Encyclopedia* (New York: Grolier Electronic Publishing, Inc., 1990).

from after-tax earnings. This means that debt financing carries with it a tax deduction, which may make it an attractive source of funds.

As usual, a trade-off exists. To capture the benefits of debt financing the financial manager must increase the risk of the firm relative to financing only with common stock.

The Effect of Financial Leverage on EPS

To see the effect of financial leverage on EPS, let us extend our consideration of the switch company. Assume the firm has decided to employ the low-operating leverage strategy and requires $1 million to finance its operations. These funds may come from either debt or equity. Assume each share of stock trades in the market for $100. If the firm uses only stock, it will have

The Effect of the Bhopal Accident on Union Carbide Stock Price

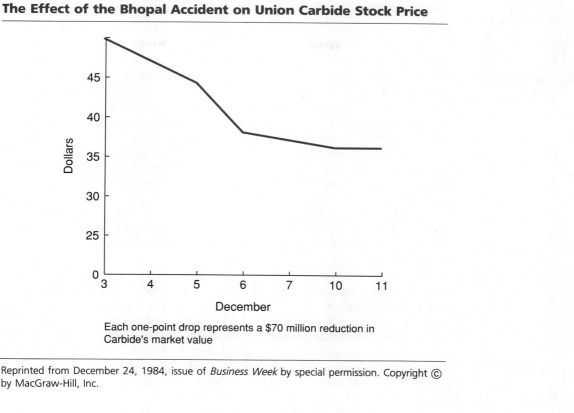

Each one-point drop represents a $70 million reduction in Carbide's market value

Reprinted from December 24, 1984, issue of *Business Week* by special permission. Copyright ©️ by MacGraw-Hill, Inc.

10,000 shares outstanding. Throughout, we assume that the firm pays a 30 percent tax rate.

To begin the analysis, we assume the firm uses 100 percent stock financing. We consider different sales levels to examine the effect on the EPS. As the base case, we use sales of 70,000 switches. Table 15.5 presents income statements at various sales levels, with the base case in the middle column. For example, with 70,000 switches sold, EBIT is $40,000. With 10,000 shares outstanding, net income is $28,000 and EPS is $2.80. In this first analysis, keep in mind that the firm has 0 financial leverage.

We now consider how EBIT and EPS vary with changes in the level of sales. If sales vary by 10,000 switches from our base level of 70,000, EBIT changes by $20,000, or 50 percent, and net income also changes by 50 percent. If sales are 60,000, net income drops by 50 percent, from $28,000 to $14,000.

FINANCE

TODAY

The Incentives for Innovation

There are essentially two types of technological innovations: *process* innovations, which are new production processes or improvements on existing technology, and *product* innovations, which are the creation of new products or improvements on existing products.* Both types of innovations are patentable. Because the economies of these two are essentially the same, the following discussion focuses on production innovation for simplicity.

Intellectual property has the unusual (although not unique) property that the knowledge it contains is not depleted with use. For example, no matter how many times the formula for aspirin is used, the formula itself (i.e., the knowledge contained in the patent) remains unchanged. As a result, the marginal cost of using this knowledge (that is, the formula for aspirin) is 0. For economic efficiency, this knowledge should be made available to anyone interested, because doing so does not diminish the stock of knowledge (or reduce the number of times aspirin can be made). Over time, however, such a policy would have some unfortunate consequences.

Generally, innovation is the result of investment expenditures on research and development (R&D). Because expenditures on R&D occur before a new product is created, the firm's decision to incur these costs involves considerable uncertainty. The expected rate of return on R&D, which is the present discounted value of the stream of net operating profits divided by the present value of the R&D costs, has to be at least as great as the opportunity cost of resources devoted to R&D—that is, the expected rate of return that would have been earned if the same resources allocated to R&D were invested elsewhere.

While the opportunity cost of capital is easy to determine (it is simply the interest rate), the rate of return on R&D is more difficult to ascertain.

---

* The economic reasons for copyright protection, essentially the same as those for patent protection, are not discussed separately. The reasons for protecting trademarks, however, differ from those for patents and copyrights, as trademarks are thought to provide information for consumers about the quality of a product. Protection of trademarks is intended to ensure that they have some informative value to consumers, rather than to protect an idea itself.

☞ Although increasing financial leverage increases risk, it may benefit the firm also by allowing it to capture the tax deductibility of interest.

The 10,000 change in unit sales also means a 50 percent change in EPS. If sales go from 70,000 to 60,000 units, EPS drops from $2.80 to $1.40. Table 15.5 details these changes.

Because there is no financial leverage, the change in net income and EPS is proportional to the change in EBIT. In order words, without financial leverage, a percentage change in EBIT causes the same percentage change

It depends on how much R&D must be spent before a new product is discovered and developed, how much demand there will be for the new product, and how much production costs will be. The return on R&D also depends on the time the firm can produce the product exclusively and therefore earn economic profits.

In the absence of government intervention, maintaining exclusive rights to an innovation for any period of time is often difficult. Given that the marginal cost of using the knowledge created by the innovation is 0, one could conclude that governments have no reason to award these rights. Without assigning exclusive rights to produce the innovation, however, the amount of time the innovating firm can produce the product is both less certain and likely shorter; any other firm that can figure out how to make the product could also produce it without changing the knowledge associated with the innovation. For example, a firm that did not discover the formula for aspirin but, instead, was able to produce it would reduce the return earned by the innovating firm. This is true even though entry by the noninnovating firm in this market does not diminish the innovating firm's ability to produce aspirin. This reduced return on the investment in R&D appears to increase efficiency by promoting competition; however, it also reduces the number of R&D projects that will be undertaken. If, however, the government assigns property rights to innovations (and enforces them), then the amount of time the product can be produced exclusively will increase, raising the rate of return on R&D, which in turn has a positive effect on the amount of innovation.

Of course, the world is not certain. There is no way of knowing in advance whether the R&D expenditures will produce an economically viable product. Intellectual property rights are a way of rewarding firms for incurring the risk associated with R&D by increasing the expected rate of return on R&D, thereby making more projects possible.

As long as innovation is considered desirable, assigning property rights to intellectual property is one way to encourage firms to innovate.

Source: "The Economics of Innovation," *Review of the Federal Reserve Bank of St. Louis,* November–December 1990, pp. 39–40.

in net income and EPS. However, if the firm uses financial leverage, the change in net income and EPS will be more than proportional to the change in EBIT.

To see how financial leverage increases the variability of net income and EPS, assume that the switch company gets 90 percent of its financing from stock and the remaining 10 percent from bonds that pay 4 percent interest.

TABLE 15.5   **The Firm's Income Statement with Zero Debt**

	Switches Sold		
	60,000	70,000	80,000
Sales	$600,000	$700,000	$800,000
Cost of goods sold	(480,000)	(560,000)	(640,000)
Fixed operating costs	(100,000)	(100,000)	(100,000)
EBIT	$ 20,000	$ 40,000	$ 60,000
Fixed financing expenses	0	0	0
Earnings before taxes	$ 20,000	$ 40,000	$ 60,000
Taxes (at 30%)	(6,000)	(12,000)	(18,000)
Net income	$ 14,000	$ 28,000	$ 42,000
Shares outstanding	10,000	10,000	10,000
EPS	$ 1.40	$ 2.80	$ 4.20

Because we assume the entire capitalization is $1 million, the firm has $100,000 in bonds outstanding. In addition, it has $900,000 in stock financing, or 9,000 outstanding shares with a market value of $100 per share.

For the case in which the firm uses 10 percent debt, Table 15.6 presents the income statements for alternative sales. To make these results comparable with those of Table 15.5, we use the same level of sales. Notice that changing financial leverage does not affect EBIT, so EBIT is the same in both tables. Important changes emerge in the lower portions of the income statement. First, we have financial leverage because the firm has fixed debt payments. Having borrowed $100,000 at 4 percent, the firm must make debt payments of $4,000, regardless of its sales. As a result, earnings before taxes become more variable. To see why, notice first that at a level of sales of 70,000 switches, EPS is still $2.80. This means that we can examine the variability in net income and EPS by observing how they change with sales. For example, in the 0 debt case in Table 15.5, sales of 60,000 switches resulted in a net income of $14,000 and EPS of $1.40. If the firm uses a 10 percent debt, that sales level means net income will drop to $11,200 and EPS will drop to $1.24, as shown in Table 15.6. Clearly, with financial leverage, a drop in sales causes net income and EPS to fall more than if the firm used no debt.

Just as net income and EPS drop more radically for a given drop in sales in the presence of debt, they also increase more for an increase in sales. Tables 15.5 and 15.6 illustrate this principle. If the firm sells 80,000 switches instead of 70,000, and if it is using no financial leverage, net income is $42,000 and EPS is $4.20. By contrast, with 10 percent debt financing, sales of 80,000 gives net income of $39,200 and EPS of $4.36.

Figure 15.6 highlights the relationship between EPS and sales for different levels of debt financing. The greater the percentage of assets financed by debt,

TABLE 15.6   The Firm's Income Statement with 10% Debt and Various Levels of Sales

	Switches Sold		
	60,000	*70,000*	*80,000*
Sales	$600,000	$700,000	$800,000
Cost of goods sold	(480,000)	(560,000)	(640,000)
Fixed operating costs	(100,000)	(100,000)	(100,000)
EBIT	$ 20,000	$ 40,000	$ 60,000
Fixed financing expense	(4,000)	(4,000)	(4,000)
Earnings before taxes	$ 16,000	$ 36,000	$ 56,000
Taxes (at 30%)	(4,800)	(10,800)	(16,800)
Net income	$ 11,200	$ 25,200	$ 39,200
Shares outstanding	9,000	9,000	9,000
EPS	$ 1.24	$ 2.80	$ 4.36

FIGURE 15.6   The Variability in EPS for Different Levels of Debt Financing

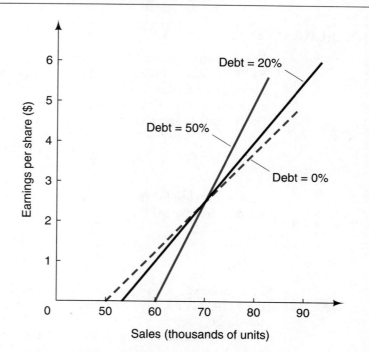

the more sensitive EPS is to any change in sales. The higher the level of debt, the steeper the slope of the line relating EPS and sales. Also, the higher the level of debt financing, the greater must be the level of sales to give a 0 EPS. On the other hand, if the firm has a high level of sales, financial leverage dramatically increases EPS.

The Effect of Financial Leverage on Liquidity

☞ Increasing financial leverage may impair the firm's liquidity.

So far, we have focused primarily on how financial leverage affects EPS. We noted how increasing reliance on debt financing makes EPS more variable and how financial leverage lets EPS increase very quickly when sales rise. In addition to these effects on EPS, financial leverage affects liquidity—the ability of the firm quickly and easily to amass disposable financial assets. The higher the level of financial leverage, the greater the fixed financial charges the firm must pay. Therefore, the firm may lack funds for emergencies because it has already committed them to pay debt.

The liquidity problem can be particularly severe in periods of low sales. A firm can easily have several years of negative earnings in a recession, and these difficult times can quickly erode its financial resources. With high leverage, however, the firm must make the normal debt payments no matter what its sales. In summary, with the fixed payments characteristic of leverage, it cannot vary its financial payments to fit its changing sales level. This can severely affect liquidity.

THE MEASURE OF FINANCIAL LEVERAGE

We measured operating leverage by examining the percentage change in EBIT resulting from a percentage change in sales. We construct a similar measure for financial leverage by examining the change in EPS for a given change in EBIT. This relation is known as the measure of financial leverage (MFL) and is given by:

$$MFL = \frac{\text{Percentage change in EPS}}{\text{Percentage change in EBIT}} \qquad (15.5)$$

As was the case for the measure of operating leverage, there is an equivalent formula for the MFL:

$$MFL = \frac{EBIT}{EBIT - i} \qquad (15.6)$$

In Equation 15.6, i represents interest payment. Note that the MFL, just as the MOL, will always be greater than 1 for any firm with some debt outstanding.

To illustrate the computation of the MFL, consider a 10 percent debt and a sales level of 70,000 switches. Table 15.6, which considers this situation, shows that a sales level of 70,000 switches results in an EBIT of $40,000. Using Equation 15.6 we compute an MFL of 1.11:

$$\text{MFL} = \frac{\$40,000}{\$40,000 - \$4,000} = 1.11$$

Therefore, with 10 percent financial leverage, the percentage change in EPS is 1.11 times greater than the percentage change in EBIT. In general, the higher the financial leverage of the firm, the greater its measure of financial leverage.

INTERACTIONS BETWEEN OPERATING AND FINANCIAL LEVERAGE

To this point we have considered operating and financial leverage separately. Because they both affect the firm's overall risk level in terms of its EPS, the financial manager has to consider them simultaneously to determine the best level of risk. The best level of risk is the level that maximizes shareholders' wealth.

Table 15.7 illustrates the combined effects of operating and financial leverage by considering different levels of sales and their effect on the firm's EBIT and EPS. In one case, we consider the old-technology strategy along with 0 financial leverage. In the second case, we have the new-technology strategy coupled with 20 percent debt financing. As the table shows, EPS varies much more when both operating and financial leverage are high. Figure 15.7 also demonstrates the higher variability of EPS by graphing the values from Table 15.7. The much steeper slope for the high-leverage strategy indicates the greater variability in EPS when the firm employs both financial and operating leverage. Clearly, the financial manager can greatly affect the riskiness of the firm by altering these policies. In making such a decision, it is important to remember that high operating leverage magnifies the effect of high financial leverage, and vice versa.

TABLE 15.7 Sales, EBIT, and EPS for the Switch Company with Alternative Operating and Financial Leverage

Switches Sold	Low Operating Leverage and No Financial Leverage		High Operating Leverage and 20% Financial Leverage	
	EBIT	EPS	EBIT	EPS
50,000	0	0	−50,000	−7.25
60,000	20,000	1.40	0	−1.00
70,000	40,000	2.80	50,000	3.68
80,000	60,000	4.20	100,000	8.05
90,000	80,000	5.60	150,000	12.43

FIGURE 15.7   The Combined Effects of Operating and Financial Leverage

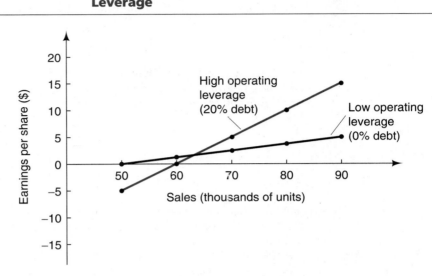

THE MEASURE OF TOTAL LEVERAGE

Recall that the MOL measures the percentage change in EBIT resulting from a 1 percent change in sales. Also, the MFL measures the percentage change in EPS for a 1 percent change in EBIT. Since both measures refer to percentage changes in EBIT, we can combine them to measure total leverage. We need a measure of the firm's total leverage because, as we have just seen, operating and financial leverage work together to determine the riskiness of the firm's earnings.

The measure of total leverage (MTL) considers the percentage change in EPS for a unit percentage change in sales. The general formula for the MTL is:

$$MTL = \frac{\text{Percentage change in EPS}}{\text{Percentage change in sales}} \tag{15.7}$$

We may also think of the measure of total leverage as the product of the measures of operating and financial leverage. If we multiply and divide the right-hand side of Equation 15.7 by the percentage change in EBIT, then we can express the MTL in terms of the MOL and MFL:

$$MTL = MOL \times MFL \tag{15.8}$$

We can apply the measure of total leverage for the switch company using the data in Table 15.7. We assume an initial sales level of 70,000 switches and measure the total leverage for the two strategies. For the low-leverage strategy the MFL is exactly 1 because there is no leverage. The MOL is found from Equation 15.4:

$$MOL = \frac{(\$10 - \$8)\ 70,000}{(\$10 - \$8)\ 70,000 - 100,000} = 3.5$$

For the high-leverage strategy we have an MOL of 7:

$$MOL = \frac{(\$10 - \$5)\ 70,000}{(\$10 - \$5)\ 70,000 - 300,000} = 7$$

Similarly, the measure of financial leverage for the high-leverage strategy is found from Equation 15.6:

$$MFL = \frac{\$50,000}{\$50,000 - \$8,000} = 1.19$$

We now compute the combined effect of operating and financial leverage to find the measure of total leverage. For the low-leverage strategy:

$$MTL = MOL \times MFL = 3.50 \times 1 = 3.50$$

For the high-leverage strategy:

$$MTL = MOL \times MFL = 7 \times 1.19 = 8.33$$

We interpret these measures as follows. For a 1 percent change in sales, the EPS changes by 3.50 percent for the low-leverage strategy and by 8.33 percent for the high-leverage strategy. This means that the higher operating and financial leverage of the latter makes EPS more than twice as sensitive to a change in sales.

LEVERAGE, TOTAL RISK, SYSTEMATIC RISK, AND THE REQUIRED RATE OF RETURN

In the preceding sections we explored the effect of operating and financial leverage on the total risk of the firm. However, from our discussion of securities markets we know that diversifiable risk does not affect the required rate of return. Some kinds of risks that firms bear are diversifiable. For example, the risk of fire or bad weather can be diversified by having geographically dispersed facilities. Diversifiable risks should not affect the required rate of return or the value of the firm, at least not in a perfect market. In essence, investors can diversify away such risks by holding securities from many firms. By contrast, both operating and financial leverage increase the firm's systematic risk.

Operating Leverage and Systematic Risk

☞ In both securities markets and capital budgeting projects, the required return depends largely on systematic risk.

For a project using a high degree of operating leverage, the cash flows not only have a larger standard deviation, they have higher systematic risk (higher beta). In our analysis of the switch project, we noted the effect of different levels of sales on EBIT. One of the main factors affecting sales is the general economic situation. Assuming that switch sales are positively correlated with

FINANCE TODAY

Simon & Schuster's *Nancy Reagan:* How Big a Blockbuster?

Credit Kitty Kelley for knowing her audience. *His Way: The Unauthorized Biography of Frank Sinatra* splattered mud all over the reputation of one of America's most beloved entertainers. But her 1986 book topped *The New York Times* best-seller list for two months. Kelley's new exposé is no less sensational. *Nancy Reagan, The Unauthorized Biography* accuses the former First Lady of drug use and meddling in White House policy. It even says she had a long affair with Sinatra—romantic White House lunches, that sort of thing.

At $24.95 a copy, people can't soak up the sleaze fast enough. The book's publisher, Simon & Schuster Inc., a subsidiary of Paramount Communications Inc., says it shipped its entire first printing of 600,000 copies within two days of its April 8 release. It has added an extra printing of 175,000 copies to fill reorders. Says Simon & Schuster Vice-President Jack McKeown: "This book is outpacing anything in recent memory, including Salman Rushdie's *Satanic Verses*."

McKeown had better hope the frenzy persists. Simon & Schuster is betting big that readers will want to rattle the skeletons in the Reagans' closet. The former President said in a terse statement that the book is filled with "flagrant and absurd falsehoods." Accurate or no, this much about the book is indisputable: *Nancy Reagan* must be a runaway best-seller if it's to turn a profit.

Tough Math.   The economics of blockbuster bookselling are risky. Here's how the figures work, according to several industry rivals: Simon & Schuster paid Kelley a $3.5 million advance. Production and marketing costs could total an additional $2 million. To cover that, readers must buy roughly 550,000 copies from bookstores, which pay the publisher about $10 a copy. On top of that, of course, S&S will reap profits from the paperback and other ancillary rights.

The publisher should break even relatively easily. It has already issued 775,000 copies and plans another printing. Bookstores routinely return un-

the economy as a whole, a high degree of operating leverage heightens the effect of shifting switch demand. This means that high operating leverage contributes to systematic risk; other things being equal, a project with high operating leverage has greater systematic risk.

The systematic risk of a project is measured by its beta. Unfortunately, project betas are notoriously difficult to estimate directly, because if the project is just beginning, one has no data to use in the estimation. There are some ways around this practical problem, as we discuss below. Systematic risk is extremely important (though difficult to measure), because the required return

sold 30 percent of the books they order, and such a return rate is probable even for this dynamite book. But that means S&S has to ship only 10,000 more copies to break even on the hardback.

Still, making a fat profit won't be a cinch. Although *Nancy Reagan* was launched with huge publicity, publishers predict sales will decline once the media glare fades. "The sales in the first week have been remarkable," says Peter Osnos, publisher of Times Books, a Random House Inc. imprint. "But publishers always have to hold their breath to see if a book has staying power."

Simon & Schuster is confident *Nancy Reagan* will continue to sell briskly. McKeown points out that it has started stronger than Kelley's Sinatra biography. The company could use a smash hit: It stands to lose millions on another pricey project—Ronald Reagan's memoirs. That book, *An American Life: The Autobiography of Ronald Reagan*, isn't selling well enough to recoup Reagan's $5 million advance. Trade journal *Publishers Weekly* says it was the ninth-best-selling nonfiction book of 1990, with gross sales of about 375,000 copies. But industry execs say Simon & Schuster needed to sell far more than that to break even. McKeown won't comment on sales, but he says: "We're proud of the job we did with it."

To be sure, Kelley's acid etching is selling far faster. Waldenbooks Inc., the nation's largest bookstore chain, estimated sales at 40,000 copies in the first week. And browsers at the Doubleday shop on New York's Fifth Avenue were another good sign. Most say the appetite for dirt on Nancy Reagan will linger after the first lust subsides. Then again, they may have been victims of subliminal advertising: From the store's stereo system came the unmistakable baritone of Frank Sinatra. He was singing *The Way You Look Tonight*.

Source: Mark Landler, "Simon & Schuster's *Nancy Reagan:* How Big a Blockbuster?" *Business Week*, April 22, 1991, p. 35.

for a project is a function of its systematic risk, not its total risk. The security market line (SML) equation applies to the project just as much as it applies to any stock or bond in the security market. The main principles relating operating leverage and required return are:

1. The required return on a project depends on its systematic risk.
2. Higher operating leverage increases both total risk and systematic risk.
3. Because of 2, higher operating leverage increases the required return of the project.

The Market Price of Risk and the Required Rate of Return

market risk premium
the extra compensation, above the risk-free rate, that investors require for investing in the market portfolio or in a firm with a beta of 1

To apply the SML equation in capital budgeting, we need estimates of r_f, beta, and the **market risk premium**, $r_m - r_f$. We may estimate r_f by using the yield on a T bill as a close proxy. We also need an estimate of the market risk premium, $r_m - r_f$. The average difference between the return on the market and the risk-free rate has historically been about 8.3 percent. There is no guarantee that the future will be like the past, but it appears that this is a reasonable estimate of the normal market risk premium. For the purposes of this book, we use it in all of the applications of the SML and CAPM to capital budgeting.

☞ For an all-equity firm considering an expansion project, the required return is given by the SML, using the beta of the firm's shares.

Finally, we need an estimate of the beta of the project. This beta depends on the correlation between the project's cash flows and those of the market, the riskiness of the project's flows, and the market's risk as well. As noted, project betas can be difficult to estimate because of lack of data; however, we have a number of ways to address this problem. We begin by assuming for the moment that our firm is an all equity firm; that is, it uses no financial leverage. Under this assumption, we consider several special cases of applied capital budgeting that also suggest ways of obtaining beta estimates.

The CAPM and an Expansion Project

One of the most straightforward kinds of capital budgeting problems is one in which a firm decides to expand its entire operation. For example, a retail chain store might open an additional store. In this case, based on past experience, it can often make good cash flow estimates, and have a very good idea of the correct discount rate to use.

Consider a chain drug store planning to open a new store with an initial investment of $1.5 million. It expects the store to remain in service for 20 years and to generate yearly after-tax cash flows of $285,000. The firm has been operating many other stores in the same area for a number of years, and knows that its overall beta is 0.8; so it is relatively low risk. Assume that the current interest rate on Treasury bills is 8.36 percent. Should management open the new store?

Given that we have the investment amount and the after-tax cash flows from the project, we have to estimate the required rate of return on such a project. We then use this estimate of the required rate of return to compute net present value. We estimate the required rate of return using the SML equation:

$$r_j = r_f + (r_m - r_f)\,\beta_j$$
$$= 0.0836 + 0.083 \times 0.8$$
$$= 15\%$$

The required rate of return on the project is 15 percent, assuming an all-equity firm, so the firm uses this rate to discount the after-tax cash flows.

Because the cash flows are all equal, they constitute a 20-year annuity. Therefore, the NPV of the project will be:

$$NPV = -\$1,500,000 + \$285,000 \times PA(15, 20)$$
$$= -\$1,500,000 + \$285,000 \times 6.2593$$
$$= \$283,900$$

Since NPV > 0, the firm should open the new store. In this case, it was able to estimate the beta of the project with some confidence because it had already conducted other similar projects.

The CAPM and Mutually Exclusive Projects

An Atlanta firm is considering two competing uses for a piece of prime downtown land. The first application is to build an office building and lease offices to corporate customers. Alternatively, it could build a department store and lease the entire building to a single customer over the long term.

If the firm builds the office building, it owns the building and merely leases the offices. The building will cost $18 million to erect and should have a life of 15 years. Expected after-tax cash flows from the leasing income are $4.3 million per year. If the firm opts for the department store, the building cost will also be $18 million. Because it would be such a long-term lease, covering the 15-year life of the building, the payments the firm will receive are expected to be only $3.5 million per year on an after-tax basis.

The difference between the two projects lies in the riskiness of the cash flows. If the firm leases the store for 15 years, the project will have very little risk, assuming the store is financially sound. As a consequence, the firm estimates the beta to be 0.60.

On the other hand, the office building would have a number of tenants, as use of office space is cyclical. In recent recessions, entire buildings have been left empty in many sunbelt cities. Thus, the cash flows are closely tied to the state of the economy, so they have a great deal of systematic risk. If the economy is booming, occupancy rates will be high; but in recessions, a large portion of the building will be unoccupied. As a consequence, the firm estimates the office building project has a beta of 1.45.

With the same investment, the difference between the two projects lies in differences in systematic risk and the cash flows. The cash flows can be treated as an annuity, so the first step is to compute the required rates of return for the two projects. Suppose the risk-free rate of interest is 11 percent. The required rate of return for the office project would be:

$$r_o = r_f + (r_m - r_f)\, \beta_o$$
$$= 0.11 + 0.083 \times 1.45$$
$$= 0.23$$

INTERNATIONAL PERSPECTIVES

Will It Be Over When the Fat Lady Sings?

Queen Elizabeth II opened the Sydney Opera House on October 20, 1973, as sixty thousand balloons rose into a sky rent by fireworks and tortured by screaming military jets. A thousand liberated pigeons cautiously made their way heavenward amidst the chaos.

The building, sometimes compared to "a nun in a windstorm" for its layers of superimposed triangular roofs, was to cost $6 million. Unfortunately, what with problems over the famous roof, extensive changes in the interior, and other odds and ends, the actual cost was a little higher—about $100 million.

But was all the money spent worth it? Well, the altered interior has, unfortunately, provoked many complaints. The acoustics are poor, not a very desirable characteristic in an opera house. The seats are cramped; visibility is spotty. Operating costs are so high that the operation loses around $10 million a year.

So the prime minister of New South Wales, where Sydney is located, has proposed to change the interior back to the original design. That little job, it is estimated, will come to $400 million at today's prices. So when the dust settles, the Opera House will have cost not $6 million but half a billion, quite aside from the accumulated operating losses. Of course, the $400 million price for changing back the interior may itself have been underestimated.

Source: John Train, *Famous Financial Fiascos* (New York: Clarkson N. Potter, 1985), p. 95.

The required rate of return for the department store would be:

$$r_d = r_f + (r_m - r_f)\ \beta_d$$
$$= 0.11 + 0.083 \times 0.60$$
$$= 0.16$$

We now apply these discount rates to calculate the NPV of both projects, assuming that we are still dealing with an all-equity firm, and treating the cash flows as an annuity in each case. For the office building:

$$\text{NPV} = -\$18,000,000 + \$4,300,000 \times \text{PA}(23, 15)$$
$$= -\$18,000,000 + \$4,300,000 \times 4.1530$$
$$= -\$142,100$$

For the department store:

$$NPV = -\$18,000,000 + \$3,500,000 \times PA(16, 15)$$
$$= -\$18,000,000 + \$3,500,000 \times 5.5755$$
$$= \$1,514,250$$

☞ Project ranking should be based on NPVs calculated with a required return reflecting the business risk of the project.

Based on this analysis, the firm rejects the office building and accepts the department store. In spite of the fact that the former has larger expected cash flows, these are not large enough to compensate for the higher systematic risk. Relative to the return demanded for the systematic risk, the department store is very attractive. Therefore, capital budgeting analysis cannot consider just the investment and project cash flows in choosing between two projects, but must also reflect the systematic risks. In particular, it may be inappropriate to use the same discount rate to evaluate different projects.

Figure 15.8 illustrates the importance of risk for analyses such as the one just completed. The SML shows the required rate of return for the market as 19.3 percent, which is equal to the risk-free rate of 11 percent plus the market risk premium of 8.3 percent. A project with a beta higher than that of the market (1.0) must have a higher required rate of return than the market. In the case of the office building, that required return was 23 percent; for the department store, it was 16 percent. The lesson is that the adequacy of a project must be measured relative to its required rate of return, which in turn depends on the systematic risk of the project.

FIGURE 15.8   The Importance of Risk Analysis

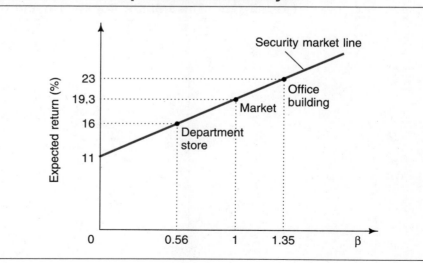

Capital Budgeting for a New Venture

In an attempt to respond to radically changing market conditions, a well-established college textbook publisher, Bookworm, is considering a move into computer software. It has focused exclusively on college textbooks for 30 years and is a leader in the field. Financed entirely with equity, the firm estimates its current beta to be 1.1.

☞ The firm can estimate systematic risk for a new project by using the systematic risk of firms in a similar business as a proxy.

Software for computers, and particularly for microcomputers, is a risky business. Like most products in the electronics and computer fields, demand for it is highly cyclical. Three other firms are also financed entirely with equity and specialize in the kind of software the publisher is considering. These software firms have betas as follows:

Firm	Beta
Macrohard	1.35
Nerdwhiz	1.40
Softbrain	1.38

Figure 15.9 shows the SML with a risk-free interest rate of 9.1 percent and the position of the four firms on the SML. Bookworm must determine the correct discount rate to apply to its cash flows from the software venture.

FIGURE 15.9   The SML for Bookworm and the Software Firms

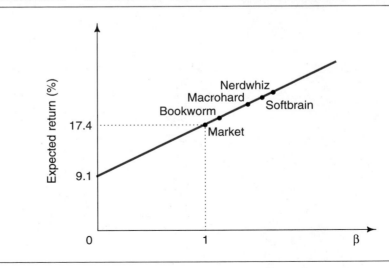

Its required return is 18.23 percent, based on its publishing enterprise:

$$r_b = 0.091 + 0.083 \times 1.1 = 18.23\%$$

The question that Bookworm must answer is whether it should use this rate or some other discount rate to evaluate the feasibility of the software project.

It is tempting to think that Bookworm has a competitive advantage relative to the other firms because its required return of 18.23 percent is lower than that of the software firms, which are calculated below:

Macrohard	$r_m = 0.091 + 0.083 \times 1.35 = 20.31\%$	
Nerdwhiz	$r_n = 0.091 + 0.083 \times 1.40 = 20.72\%$	
Softbrain	$r_s = 0.091 + 0.083 \times 1.38 = 20.55\%$	

Bookworm must be careful to use the right discount rate as it contemplates this change. Its beta on its publishing business is irrelevant to that on its projected software. The required rate of return depends on a project's beta, not on the firm's other lines of business.

As we can see from the data already presented, book publishing appears to have a systematic risk of 1.1. Software, by contrast, has betas in the range of 1.35 to 1.40, indicating a higher level of risk. For the capital budgeting decision, the discount rate depends on the systematic risk of the project's cash flows. Therefore, the discount rate for the new software project should be close to the required return for other similar projects. Based on the data presented for the software firms, the correct discount rate would appear to be about 20.5 percent, still assuming all-equity firms.

Figure 15.10 summarizes the principle developed here—that the discount rate must correspond to the systematic risk. The overall beta for Bookworm is 1.1, and that corresponds to a discount rate of 18.23 percent. That does not mean that the correct discount rate for any project that Bookworm might consider is 18.23 percent. For example, it might be considerably higher for a new venture such as the software project. By contrast, if the firm merely wishes to expand, it would be 18.23 percent, because the expansion would have the same systematic risk as the existing firm. At the low-risk end of the spectrum, the company might institute cost savings projects. For example, Bookworm might decide that it could save money on production costs by buying word processors for its editors. For cost savings projects, the cash flows are often very steady and certain, so they would deserve a low discount rate to match their low systematic risk. Whether the project has a low, medium, or high risk, the discount rate must reflect its systematic risk.

Financial Leverage, Systematic Risk, and Estimating Betas

As we have seen, increased operating leverage increases total risk, systematic risk, and, as a result, the required rate of return. Similar principles apply to financial leverage, but the risk-increasing effect of financial leverage operates

FIGURE 15.10   Risk Classes of Projects and Differing Required Rates of Return

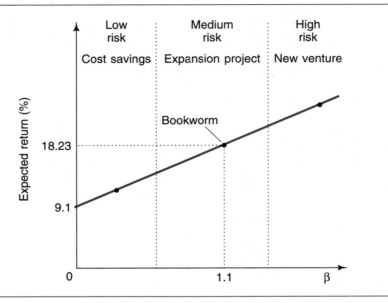

at the firm, not the project, level. As we noted, financial leverage increases the variability in EPS when sales levels change. Again, when sales are affected by the economy as a whole, financial leverage heightens that effect and contributes to the firm's systematic risk. Therefore, considering just the effect on systematic risk, a firm with higher financial leverage must have a higher required rate of return in the market than an otherwise identical low-leverage firm.

In the case of financial leverage, an important complication exists, however. Financial leverage does increase systematic risk, and for that reason should increase the required return on the firm's stock. But it also provides a tax shield due to the deductibility of interest payments. Its total effect on the required rate of return depends on both factors: (1) the higher leverage drives up systematic risk, but (2) it generates tax savings. Therefore, we cannot say with certainty that higher financial leverage increases the required rate of return. In fact, its effect on the firm's cost of capital is a disputed issue of great importance that we address in the next chapter.

This complication with financial leverage makes it more difficult to determine systematic risk. For example, we have just seen that we could estimate the systematic risk of a project by examining the systematic risk of an all-equity firm engaged in the same business. But what if the other software firms had used financial leverage? Then the beta of their stock would have depended partly on the risk of the software business and partly on the firms' financial leverage. This could lead to errors in estimates of systematic risk and the required return for the project.

Fortunately, the following relationship exists between the beta for a levered and an unlevered firm:

$$\beta_L = \beta_U \left[1 + (1 - T) \frac{D}{E} \right]$$
(15.9)

or
$$\beta_U = \frac{\beta_L}{1 + (1 - T) \dfrac{D}{E}}$$
(15.10)

where
β_L = beta for a levered firm
β_U = beta for an unlevered firm *with the same business risk*
T = the firm's tax rate
D = the market value of the firm's debt
E = the market value of the firm's equity

These equations show the relationship between the beta for a levered and unlevered firm, assuming the same business risk. In other words, the higher value for β_L is due strictly to the leverage difference, not to any differences in operating leverage or the riskiness of a project. The basic idea reflected by these equations is to take account of the increase in risk as the proportion of debt increases, a relation that is reflected by the debt/equity ratio in Equations 15.9 and 15.10. Partially offsetting this effect is the tax shield, which is reflected by the term $1 - T$.

☞ In any attempt to use another firm's systematic risk as a proxy for the business risk of a project, the financial manager must be careful to abstract from financial leverage considerations by de-levering the beta.

To understand the use of this formula, let us consider Bookworm's efforts once again. As we have seen, Bookworm looked at three all-equity firms in the software business to find a reasonable proxy for the beta it would face if it entered that field. Bookworm is considering one more firm as a proxy for its own beta, Bogus 1-2-3. Bogus has $3 million in equity outstanding and $1 million in debt, as measured in market value terms. Bogus has been paying taxes at a rate of 30 percent. Using market data, Bookworm estimates Bogus's beta to be 1.85. Because this estimate is taken from stock market data, it reflects the fact that Bogus uses financial leverage. Therefore, the beta for the software project must be less than this estimation, so Bookworm uses the formula given in Equation 15.10 to de-lever the beta. With the information for Bogus, we can compute the de-levered beta to be:

$$\beta_U = \frac{1.85}{1 + (1 - 0.3) \dfrac{1,500,000}{3,000,000}} = 1.37$$

This de-levered beta of 1.37 corresponds to the business risk of Bogus, because it eliminated the effect of the financial leverage on the systematic risk of Bogus's stock. Our estimate of 1.37 for the de-levered beta corresponds to the estimates derived from the other firms that were all-equity financed.

SUMMARY

This chapter introduced three techniques to analyze the cash flow from a project: breakeven analysis, sensitivity analysis, and scenario analysis. Breakeven analysis examines the relationship between a firm's level of sales and the profit from a project. We also discussed the discounted breakeven point, defined as the level of sales that results in 0 NPV. In sensitivity analysis, the reaction of a project's NPV to changes in different variables was explored. To reflect the potential for interaction among variables, we also introduced the technique of scenario analysis.

We then turned to leverage and its effect on the risk level of the firm. We considered both operating and financial leverage, and showed how both contribute to total risk and to systematic risk. The higher the degree of operating leverage, the more sensitive EBIT will be to a change in sales. Similarly, the higher the degree of financial leverage, the more sensitive EPS will be to a change in EBIT. To gauge the extent of both kinds of leverage, we developed measures for them as well as one for total leverage.

The chapter concluded by applying the concepts of the CAPM to capital budgeting, providing an integration of the markets for financial and real assets. By using the SML, the financial manager adopts discount rates that reflect the systematic risk of a project. The goal of capital budgeting then becomes the finding of projects that earn more than their required rate of return. Such projects have positive NPVs, and accepting them contributes to the wealth of shareholders.

QUESTIONS

1. How does breakeven analysis help the manager to assess the firm's business risk?
2. In traditional breakeven analysis, what does the slope of the total cost line represent?
3. In traditional breakeven analysis, what does the intercept of the total cost line represent?
4. In traditional breakeven analysis, what does the slope of the revenue line represent?
5. Why does the revenue line start at the origin of the traditional breakeven graph?
6. How are the traditional and the discounted breakeven analyses related?

7. If the variable cost and price of each unit increase by the same dollar amount, what happens to the traditional breakeven quantity?
8. If the variable cost and price of each unit increase by the same percentage, what happens to the traditional breakeven quantity?
9. If the fixed cost and the unit contribution margin $(P - V)$ increase by the same dollar amount, what happens to the traditional breakeven quantity?
10. If the fixed cost and the unit contribution margin $(P - V)$ increase by the same percentage, what happens to the traditional breakeven quantity?
11. Does high operating leverage affect EPS or only EBIT? Explain.
12. Does financial leverage have any effect on EBIT? Why or why not?
13. Are dividend payments to common shareholders a kind of fixed financial charge? Explain.
14. Are interest payments to bondholders a kind of fixed financial charge? Explain.
15. What is business risk?
16. Explain how high operating leverage contributes to business risk.
17. What is our measure of operating leverage (MOL)?
18. If a firm has no fixed operating cost, what is its MOL?
19. What is our measure of financial leverage (MFL)?
20. If a firm has no financial leverage, what will be its MFL?
21. If a firm has no financial leverage, what is the relationship between a change in EBIT and a change in EPS?
22. How do operating and financial leverage interact?
23. What is the measure of total leverage?
24. If you only know the MTL of some firm, what is the most you can say about its MOL and MFL?

PROBLEMS

Disko, a computer disk drive manufacturer, is expecting revenues next year of $100,000 if it sells 100 drives at $1,000. If Disko adopts technology A it will have fixed operating costs of $40,000 and a cost per drive of $400. With technology B it will have fixed costs of $20,000 and a cost per drive of $600.

1. For technology A, calculate the EBIT if sales are 80, 90, 100, 110, and 120 drives.
2. For technology B, calculate the EBIT if sales are 80, 90, 100, 110, and 120 drives.
3. For technology A, draw a graph showing the relationship between sales and EBIT.

4. For technology B, draw a graph showing the relationship between sales and EBIT.
5. What can you say about the choice of these two technologies? Can you confidently say which one Disko should choose?
6. Complete the following income statements for technology A assuming that Disko has no debt.

	Drives Sold		
	90	100	110
Sales	_____	_____	_____
Cost of goods sold	_____	_____	_____
Fixed operating costs	_____	_____	_____
EBIT	_____	_____	_____
Fixed financing expenses	_____	_____	_____
Earnings before taxes	_____	_____	_____
Taxes (40%)	_____	_____	_____
Net income	_____	_____	_____
Shares outstanding	1,000	1,000	1,000
EPS	_____	_____	_____

7. Using 100 drives as the base level of sales and the income statement of Problem 6, compute Disko's MOL.

8. Complete the following income statements for technology A, assuming that Disko has 900 shares outstanding worth $100 per share and that it also has $100,000 worth of long-term debt on which it is paying interest of 10 percent per year.

	Drives Sold		
	90	100	110
Sales	_____	_____	_____
Cost of goods sold	_____	_____	_____
Fixed operating costs	_____	_____	_____
EBIT	_____	_____	_____
Fixed financing expenses	_____	_____	_____
Earnings before taxes	_____	_____	_____
Taxes (40%)	_____	_____	_____
Net income	_____	_____	_____
Shares outstanding	900	900	900
EPS	_____	_____	_____

9. Using 100 drives as the base level of sales and the income statement of Problem 8, compute Disko's measure of financial leverage.
10. Using 100 drives as the base level of sales and the income statement of Problem 8, compute Disko's measure of total leverage.

11. Complete the following income statements for technology A, assuming that Disko has 800 shares outstanding worth $100 per share, and that it also has $200,000 worth of long-term debt on which it is paying interest of 10 percent per year.

	Drives Sold		
	90	100	110
Sales	_____	_____	_____
Cost of goods sold	_____	_____	_____
Fixed operating costs	_____	_____	_____
EBIT	_____	_____	_____
Fixed financing expenses	_____	_____	_____
Earnings before taxes	_____	_____	_____
Taxes (40%)	_____	_____	_____
Net income	_____	_____	_____
Shares outstanding	800	800	800
EPS	_____	_____	_____

12. Using 100 drives as the base level of sales and the income statement of Problem 11, compute Disko's measure of financial leverage.
13. Using 100 drives as the base level of sales and the income statement of Problem 11, compute Disko's measure of total leverage.

14. Complete the following income statements for technology B, assuming that Disko has no debt.

	Drives Sold		
	90	100	110
Sales	_____	_____	_____
Cost of goods sold	_____	_____	_____
Fixed operating costs	_____	_____	_____
EBIT	_____	_____	_____
Fixed financing expenses	_____	_____	_____
Earnings before taxes	_____	_____	_____
Taxes (40%)	_____	_____	_____
Net income	_____	_____	_____
Shares outstanding	1,000	1,000	1,000
EPS	_____	_____	_____

15. Using 100 drives as the base level of sales and the income statement of Problem 14, compute Disko's measure of operating leverage.

16. Complete the following income statements for technology B, assuming that Disko has 900 shares outstanding worth $100 per share, and that it also has $100,000 worth of long-term debt on which it is paying interest of 10 percent per year.

	Drives Sold		
	90	100	110
Sales	_____	_____	_____
Cost of goods sold	_____	_____	_____
Fixed operating costs	_____	_____	_____
EBIT	_____	_____	_____
Fixed financing expenses	_____	_____	_____
Earnings before taxes	_____	_____	_____
Taxes (40%)	_____	_____	_____
Net income	_____	_____	_____
Shares outstanding	900	900	900
EPS	_____	_____	_____

17. Using 100 drives as the base level of sales and the income statement of Problem 16, compute Disko's measure of financial leverage.
18. Using 100 drives as the base level of sales and the income statement of Problem 16, compute Disko's measure of total leverage.
19. Complete the following income statements for technology B, assuming that Disko has 800 shares outstanding worth $100 per share, and that it also has $200,000 worth of long-term debt on which it is paying interest of 10 percent per year.

	Drives Sold		
	90	100	110
Sales	_____	_____	_____
Cost of goods sold	_____	_____	_____
Fixed operating costs	_____	_____	_____
EBIT	_____	_____	_____
Fixed financing expenses	_____	_____	_____
Earnings before taxes	_____	_____	_____
Taxes (40%)	_____	_____	_____
Net income	_____	_____	_____
Shares outstanding	800	800	800
EPS	_____	_____	_____

20. Using 100 drives as the base level of sales and the income statement of Problem 19, compute Disko's measure of financial leverage.
21. Using 100 drives as the base level of sales and the income statement of Problem 19, compute Disko's measure of total leverage.
22. Complete the following table for Disko.

	Technology A with 0% Financial Leverage		Technology B with 20% Debt/Assets	
Sales	EBIT	EPS	EBIT	EPS
$ 80,000	_____	_____	_____	_____
90,000	_____	_____	_____	_____
100,000	_____	_____	_____	_____
110,000	_____	_____	_____	_____
120,000	_____	_____	_____	_____

23. Using the information completed in Problem 22, graph the relationship between sales and EBIT for technologies A and B. What can you infer from this graph?

24. Using the information completed in Problem 22, graph the relationship between sales and EPS for technologies A and B. What can you infer from this graph?

25. Using the definition of the measure of operating leverage given in Equation 15.3, and assuming a one unit change in sales, derive the expression for the MOL given in Equation 15.4.

26. Using the definition of the measure of financial leverage given in Equation 15.5, and assuming a $1 change in EBIT, derive the expression for the MFL given in Equation 15.6.

27. Consider a project such as the one in Figure 15.4. Show that if the firm uses linear depreciation and the project has no salvage value, the discounted breakeven quantity will always be greater than the traditional breakeven quantity.

28. Equation 15.4 expresses the MOL in terms of P, V, Q, and F. Find an equivalent expression in terms of $EBIT$ and F.

29. Using the result of Problem 28, find an expression for the measure of total leverage (MTL) in terms of $EBIT$, F, and the firm's interest payment (i).

30. A firm is financed entirely with equity and its shares have a beta of 1.12. Currently, the risk-free rate is 7.4 percent. Using our estimate of the market risk premium of 8.3 percent, what is the required return for an expansion project?

31. If a firm is in a business that has the same systematic risk as the market, but faces a 34 percent tax rate and is financed with $200,000 debt and $500,000 equity, what should the beta of its shares be?

32. What will the levered beta be if the firm issues $100,000 more debt?

PART 5

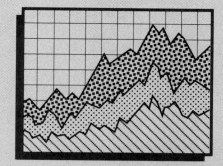

WORKING CAPITAL MANAGEMENT

Inventory Management

Inventories are assets of the firm, and as such they represent an investment. Therefore, managers must decide how much to invest in them. The investment character of inventories is very clear because if a firm holds a large inventory of, say, raw materials, the funds invested there will not be available for investment elsewhere. Because such investment requires a commitment of funds, managers must ensure that the firm maintains inventories at the correct level. If they become too large, the firm loses the opportunity to employ those funds more effectively. Similarly, if they are too small, the firm may lose sales. Thus there is an optimum level of inventories. This chapter considers the economic ordering quantity model for determining that level.

TYPES OF INVENTORIES

Holding inventory has both costs and benefits. As usual, the problem is to select the level that gives the greatest difference between them. This section explores the different kinds of inventories and some of the techniques used to manage them.

There are three basic types of inventories: raw materials, work-in-process, and finished goods. The raw materials inventory consists of the basic commodities that a firm purchases to use in its production process. Work-in-process inventory consists of goods in the production process; for example, in an automobile firm, this would be partially assembled autos. The finished goods inventory consists of completed items that are ready for sale.

BENEFITS AND COSTS OF HOLDING INVENTORIES

The benefits of holding inventories differ depending on the type of firm. A manufacturer must have some inventory of raw materials; otherwise, production would grind to a halt. Similarly, it cannot avoid some work-in-process inventory, because the production process takes time. Finally, it benefits from finished goods, which allow the firm to fill sales orders quickly.

Firms in the retailing industry may hold their entire inventory in finished goods because they generally purchase items in finished form from manufacturers and sell them to the public. Service industry firms are likely to have virtually no inventory, except those items used in creating their service. For example, a janitorial firm might hold only cleaning supplies. These items are not to be resold, but used to provide the janitorial service.

Given the clear benefits of holding inventories and the costs of running out of them, it might seem that firms should hold the greatest amount possible. That is costly, too, however, because funds invested there cannot earn a return elsewhere. Therefore, firms must manage their inventories carefully to get the best return from their capital. They must measure the benefit of holding inventory against the opportunity cost. The major costs are carrying costs and ordering costs.

Carrying Costs

Two basic carrying costs are associated with holding an item in inventory. First, there is the cost of storage, which for some items may be quite large. Examples are bulky commodities like wheat, and articles requiring special treatment, such as refrigeration. The second cost is that involved in financing the inventory. For example, if current interest rates are 12 percent, holding an item costing $100 in inventory for one year entails a $12 financing cost for the year. In other words, had the firm not held the $100 in inventory, it could have earned $12 elsewhere, say, in the bank. Together, the storage and opportunity costs of employing the funds elsewhere make up the total cost of keeping an item in inventory, or the **carrying cost.**

carrying cost
the total cost of keeping an item in inventory

Ordering Costs

Management must also consider the cost of ordering new items. For example, the manufacturer of bicycles requires an inventory of spokes for the wheels. The benefit of a supply of spokes is clear, since without them the firm cannot build bicycles. Holding too many spokes is wasteful, however, because the funds invested in them could be earning a return elsewhere.

To avoid holding too many spokes, the firm could order smaller quantities. At the extreme, it could buy them for each bicycle individually, in which case it would hold no extras. This extreme strategy has two obvious drawbacks. First, placing an order costs money. This **ordering cost** is the fixed expense in the preparation and execution of an order for goods, including paperwork and communication with the supplier. For the bicycle manufacturer, buying spokes for each bicycle would generate very large costs associated with ordering many times a year.

ordering cost
the fixed expense in the preparation and execution of an order for goods

A second problem with this strategy is with delays in receiving spokes. If the firm receives some orders late, it cannot complete bicycles according to schedule. Ideally, it would like to receive its new shipment as it exhausts the old supply; however, it runs a high risk of running out of spokes if shipments are delayed or if it uses spokes faster than anticipated. Therefore, inventory management requires planning for safety stocks.

safety stock
the planned number of items in inventory at the time the new inventory is received

The **safety stock** is the amount of an item the firm plans to have when it receives new inventory. It provides the firm enough of an item with which to keep going if shipment delays occur or if prices increase unexpectedly. Thus, it is designed to be available when unforeseen contingencies occur.

The firm must consider the benefits and costs of holding inventory, evaluate the cost of ordering new items, and plan for adequate safety stocks. Information plays a crucial role in these areas. The next section explores some techniques for controlling inventory and for gaining information about maintaining the optimum level.

INVENTORY MODELS

Inventory models vary from very simple to sophisticated and computerized ones, from the "look-and-see" approach to systems that record every sale and report it automatically and instantaneously to a computerized inventory-control program.

The Red Line Method

Imagine a bin full of spokes at the bicycle plant, from which workers withdraw the spokes as needed. As the level of spokes decreases, a red line painted on the inside of the bin becomes visible. When the level reaches the line, the firm orders more spokes. In this case, the red line indicates the **reorder point**, the level of inventory at which the firm reorders the item. Of course, the line should be drawn at a level that allows enough time for the new shipment to arrive, without depleting the current inventory.

reorder point
the level of inventory at which an inventory item should be reordered

This is one of the simplest inventory-control techniques we can imagine. Unfortunately, it has definite limitations. For example, it works only for items that are all stored in one place. In addition, although the position of the red line may reflect a good deal of thought and experience, the reorder point may not realistically reflect the expected rate of usage, the safety stock, the time for processing the order, and transportation time.

The ABC System

Because managerial time and effort are scarce and because some items in stock are more important than others, many firms use a system of priorities to manage their inventories. For example, it seems foolish to devote the same amount of managerial time to controlling the inventory of a small item with annual sales of $1,000 as to one with sales of $1,000,000 annually. The ABC system explicitly recognizes that some items are more important than others, and allocates management efforts in proportion to that importance.

FINANCE
TODAY

Drinking Your Inventory

You can have some fun buying wine and holding it in inventory until its value increases substantially, but don't take seriously anyone who says you can make money that way. Can you "invest" in wine by holding it in inventory over a long period of time? Only in the sense that you can "invest" in a dress at Bloomingdale's before its designer is widely acclaimed.

If you are a serious investor and want to realize your profits resulting from an increased value of your wine inventory, you have the option of auctioning the bottles in the two states that have legalized such auctions, Illinois and California. But figure on losing 30 percent of the sale price first to auctioneers' fees and then to shipping. Thus, you need about a 60 percent price appreciation on your precious inventory to just break even. When you allow for the time value of money, the appreciation necessary to break even may reach 100 percent or more; depending, of course, on the amount of time you hold the wine in your "cave." In other words, you'd have to double your inventory value within two to three years to earn any kind of return. Oh, and don't forget that as with any investment, your wine inventory may go up or down in value. Your safest bet may be to liquidate (literally) your wine at the dinner table. But remember that gasoline absolutely spoils wine, so please don't drink and drive.

Source: Peter Fuhrman, "Drinking Your Profits Is the Best Revenge," *Forbes,* June 25, 1990, pp. 270–272.

The ABC system classifies inventory items into three separate sets. The most important are classified as A, those of intermediate importance as B, and the least important as C. Managers monitor the items accordingly. For example, they might review A items monthly or even weekly, depending on the need, whereas B items might be reviewed quarterly, and C items only twice a year.

To illustrate in more detail how this system works, consider HammerHead, Inc., a very small hardware store. HammerHead sells only nine items, and has decided to classify them according to the ABC system. The two most important items belong to class A, the following three items to class B, and the final four to class C. In Table 16.1, the firm classifies its inventory according to unit purchase cost. Lawn mowers are the most expensive to purchase and nails the least expensive. Thus management will devote most of its efforts to controlling lawn mowers, and so on down the line.

The major problem with the unit cost is obvious in the revenue and profit columns. Because nails are a class C item, they receive very little attention.

TABLE 16.1 ABC Inventory for HammerHead, Classified by Unit Cost

Item	Unit Cost	Unit Price	Units	Revenues	Profit
Lawn mowers	$110.00	$260.00	120	$31,200	$18,000
Pumps	60.00	145.00	200	29,000	17,000
Lumber	10.20	19.00	2,400	45,600	21,120
Paint	7.00	15.00	2,000	30,000	16,000
Plants	4.50	7.90	1,700	13,430	5,780
Flashlights	3.75	6.90	300	2,070	945
Batteries	1.75	3.00	1,000	3,000	1,250
Fertilizer	1.70	5.50	400	2,200	1,520
Nails	1.60	3.15	9,000	28,350	13,950

However, they provide much more revenues and profits than, say, plants, which are a class B item. This problem may be solved by classifying items according to the annual profits they are expected to generate. Using this criterion, a new classification is obtained, as shown in Table 16.2. Notice that now the most important item is lumber, despite its relatively small unit cost. Similarly, the importance of nails increases.

Other more sophisticated criteria can be used to classify items using the ABC method. For example, the firm might set up a system that assigns a numerical value to the items according to their shipping times or according to their strategic importance to the firm. Whatever the method, the principle remains the same: managerial time is scarce, and should be assigned to items in accordance with their relative importance to the firm.

TABLE 16.2 ABC Inventory for HammerHead, Classified by Annual Profit

Item	Unit Cost	Unit Price	Units	Revenues	Profit
Lumber	$ 10.20	$ 19.00	2,400	$45,600	$21,120
Lawn mowers	110.00	260.00	120	31,200	18,000
Pumps	60.00	145.00	200	29,000	17,000
Paint	7.00	15.00	2,000	30,000	16,000
Nails	1.60	3.15	9,000	28,350	13,950
Plants	4.50	7.90	1,700	13,430	5,780
Fertilizer	1.70	5.50	400	2,200	1,520
Batteries	1.75	3.00	1,000	3,000	1,250
Flashlights	3.75	6.90	300	2,070	945

Computerized Inventory-Control Systems

Many firms use computers to control their inventory. This is especially efficient for those that hold large quantities of items.

point-of-sale system
a type of computerized inventory-control system

One type of computerized inventory control is the **point-of-sale system,** which is becoming very prevalent in retailing operations. With this system, the cashier keys the stock number of each item as it is sold into the cash register/computer, thus automatically updating the inventory.

bar code
an identifier printed on a product that is machine readable

Point-of-sale systems can also use electronic readers. For example, most major grocery stores use laser scanners to read the **bar codes,** the black-and-white striped identifiers printed on the products, on almost everything they sell. The operator passes the bar code in front of the laser, which reads the code and reports this sale to the computer. The computer records the item as sold and automatically signals the cash register to display the price.

With bar codes, many stores can avoid marking the price on each item separately. Also, when things are on sale, the store merely records the lower prices in the computer program one time and does not have to mark each article. Many stores use electronic wands that read stock numbers and function similarly to the bar code systems. These computerized systems dominate in stores with many different items on sale, most notably grocery and retail department stores.

A FORMAL INVENTORY MODEL

economic ordering quantity (EOQ) model
a mathematical model to determine the best size of an order for items in inventory

A method to assist in determining inventory-control policy is known as the **economic ordering quantity (EOQ) model,** because it establishes the most economical size of order to place. It depends on key variables such as the cost of carrying the good in inventory and its purchase cost, ordering cost, and rate of usage.

Like all formal models, the EOQ relies on certain simplifying assumptions, the main one being that the inventory is used at a known constant rate. That is, it follows the pattern shown in Figure 16.1. If the starting level of inventory is Q units, it falls at a constant rate from this initial point. With a constant level of usage, a starting level of Q units, and an ending level of 0 units, the average amount of inventory in stock will be $Q/2$ units.

☞ The EOQ model balances the cost of ordering against the cost of holding items in inventory, in order to find the most economical inventory strategy.

The goal of the EOQ model is to choose the ordering amount, Q, that gives the lowest total annual cost of maintaining the inventory. The model ignores safety stocks, which we consider later. The total cost of inventory depends on the two separate factors that we identified above: ordering and carrying costs. An item that is ordered very infrequently has a low annual ordering cost. However, more of the items must be ordered each time, so the Q will be larger. Also, because we assume the firm depletes its inventory at a constant rate, the average inventory, $Q/2$, will be larger the less frequently it is ordered. A policy of ordering only infrequently results in larger inventories and a higher carrying cost.

☞ Ordering costs decrease as the order size increases.

☞ Carrying costs increase in direct proportion to the order size.

Figure 16.2 shows the impact of these two costs on the total inventory cost. The line for the ordering cost shows that it will be smaller the larger

FIGURE 16.1   Inventory Level with a Constant Rate of Usage

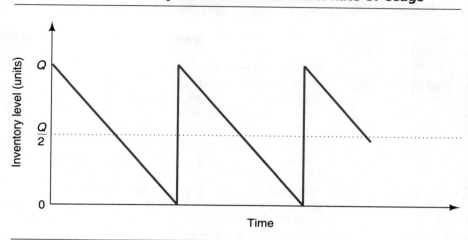

FIGURE 16.2   Inventory Costs

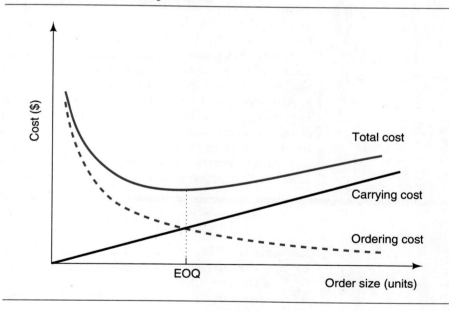

The Inventory-Performance Connection

John C. Psaltis, chief financial officer of electronic-connector maker Molex Inc.'s international operations, has every reason to be optimistic about the future. "Maintaining cash gives us the ability to grow our infrastructure even during downturns," says Psaltis. "We will continue to be strong in R&D and in capital expenditures since we feel we need to be in a position for the next upturn. If you have the strength to make it through, there will be great demand when you get there."

During the 1980s, Molex played its cards with a strong hand. Serving the notoriously cutthroat and globetrotting manufacturers of computers, business equipment goods, home appliances, and automobiles, Molex trounced competitors in part by offering agile product supply capabilities and superior on-site customer service. Molex's customers have moved from the United States to the Far East over the past two decades. The "next opening," says Psaltis, "will be in the Eastern bloc countries in Europe. They have a relatively cheap labor force, and they're pretty close to Europe, which is a substantial market."

Psaltis joined Lisle, Illinois–based Molex, in 1973 as its first international financial executive. Since then, Molex's international sales have grown from 11 percent to 73 percent of corporate sales of $594.4 million in 1990. Molex, which has 50 manufacturing sites in 20 countries, does more business in Japan than in the United States.

Molex has shown a remarkable ability to grow profitably over the last decade as it has expanded internationally and diversified its industry base. One smart move meant cutting its reliance on consumer electronics and appliances, which produced 40 percent of sales in 1990. Perhaps most noteworthy is that Molex is growing at a healthy clip while the electronic-connector industry is nearly stagnant, with 1 percent annual increases. In the first half of its 1991 fiscal year, ended December 31, 1990, Molex showed a 10 percent growth in sales to $344.4 million, compared with $289.5 million recorded during the same period of the 1990 fiscal year.

the order size. This makes sense, because fewer orders will be placed. By contrast, the carrying cost increases with the order size. This also makes sense, because we have already seen that the larger the order size, the larger will be the inventory. The job of the EOQ model is to find the optimum order size, or the economical amount to order. Ordering this quantity minimizes the total cost of inventory.[1]

---

[1] Notice that in Figure 16.2 the EOQ occurs at the order size where the curves for the carrying and ordering costs intersect. It can be shown that this must always be true.

Net income for the period rose 13 percent to $32.6 million in the first half, compared with $28.9 million in the previous year. Psaltis believes Molex is now well braced for the impact of recession. It currently has close to $150 million in cash and only $9 million worth of low-cost industrial revenue bond debt on its balance sheet.

Thanks to the business philosophy embraced by the founding Krehbiel family, which owns 40 percent of the company and occupies top management positions, Molex can take a long-term view of major financial decisions. The company, which has the highest cash flow per dollar of sales in the industry, has reinvested in research and development and plans to introduce 200 new products in 1991 on top of 233 new products added over the previous two years. That search for innovation has helped Molex maintain its reputation for high quality and service and develop a huge potential for growth. Molex is the second-largest electronic-connector manufacturer, but it controls only 4 percent of the market, which is expected to be worth $30 billion in 1999.

Molex's tack is to build manufacturing capability, rather than inventory. The company's inventory runs at half the industry norm, which surprisingly, Psaltis says, has resulted in improved delivery performance. That also translates into a sizeable backlog. At the end of the second 1991 quarter, Molex had a record backlog of $122 million, compared with $103 million a year ago.

Psaltis says his company's conservatism hasn't hindered operations. "We've forgone some go-go ideas because it would have leveraged us, but that hasn't stopped us from being innovative." Among those ideas were commercial bank proposals to use financial instruments to hedge Molex's currency exposures. "I do not see the necessity of paying out cash to report sales and profits differently from what actually comes through," says Psaltis.

Source: "Molex, Investing in the Future," *CFO*, April 1991, p. 30.

The total cost of inventory depends on the carrying cost and the ordering cost. To calculate the total cost, define the variables of the model as follows:

S = annual unit sales

P = purchase price of a unit for the firm

C = annual carrying cost as a percentage of the unit's price

F = fixed cost of placing an order

Q = the quantity ordered

We can express the total cost (TC) of inventory for a year as the sum of the carrying costs and the ordering costs:

$$TC = \frac{Q}{2} \times P \times C + \frac{S}{Q} \times F$$

The average value of the inventory over the year equals the average number of units in inventory, $Q/2$, times the purchase price of each unit, P. The yearly carrying cost equals the average value of the inventory times the annual percentage cost, C, of carrying \$1 in inventory. If the firm uses S units in a year and places an order of size Q each time it orders, then it must order S/Q times per year. For example, if a department store sells 1,000 television sets in a year and it orders 100 sets per order, it must order 1,000/ 100 = 10 times per year. If each order costs a fixed amount, F, the ordering cost for a year must equal the number of orders times the cost of each order, or $(S/Q) \times F$. With the help of calculus it is possible to derive the optimal order size, EOQ, which is given in Equation 16.1:

$$EOQ = \sqrt{\frac{2FS}{CP}} \qquad (16.1)$$

The firm minimizes its total inventory cost by ordering EOQ units each time. The EOQ depends on four variables, as shown in Equation 16.1. It increases as the fixed ordering costs and the annual sales level increase. This is because if the ordering costs increase, the firm orders less frequently, which means that it must order more units each time. By contrast, the EOQ falls as the percentage carrying cost and the purchase price increase. For example, if the carrying cost increases, the current inventory level becomes too expensive, and it is then better to order less each time. Of course, it will then be necessary to order more frequently.

EXAMPLE 16.1

A firm expects to sell twice as many units this year as it did five years ago. How much larger will its average inventory be?

Let S_{-5} and $EOQ_{-5}/2$ be the sales and average inventory levels five years ago. Similarly, let S_0 and $EOQ_0/2$ be the corresponding values for this year. Since $S_0 = 2S_{-5}$, we have

$$EOQ_0 = \sqrt{\frac{2FS_0}{CP}} = \sqrt{\frac{2F(2S_{-5})}{CP}}$$

$$= \sqrt{\frac{2FS_{-5}}{CP}} \times \sqrt{2}$$

$$= EOQ_{-5} \times \sqrt{2}$$

☞ The firm's inventory level is subject to economies of scale. If its sales double, the inventory level should increase by about 41 percent.

Thus, when unit sales double, the EOQ and the average inventory increase by a factor equal to the square root of 2, or by only 41.42 percent.

EXAMPLE 16.2

Consider our bicycle firm that orders spokes by the case. Assume each case costs $100 and the firm uses 1,000 cases per year. It stores spokes in a bin, so the only carrying cost is the financing cost, which is 12 percent per year. Ordering spokes costs $75 per order. Using these data, calculate the EOQ:

$$\text{EOQ} = \sqrt{\frac{2 \times \$75 \times 1,000}{0.12 \times \$100}} = 111.80 \text{ cases}$$

Therefore, the firm should order 112 cases per order. With this order size, it orders about nine times a year (1,000/111.8 = 8.94).

As we mentioned before, the EOQ model does not itself take safety stocks into account; however, we can use it in conjunction with safety stocks. Assume that our bicycle company wishes to have a safety stock equal to eight weeks' normal usage. This means it must order early enough so the safety stock can remain intact. Assume that the normal shipment period is two weeks.

Knowing the safety stock and the shipping time allows us to compute the order point. With 1,000 cases used per year and a safety stock equal to eight weeks' usage, the safety stock would be 154 cases (1,000 × 8/52 = 153.85). To be sure that it does not use the safety stock, the firm must order two weeks before the inventory falls to 154 cases. At its rate of usage, the firm uses 1,000/52 = 19.23 cases per week. Therefore, it should reorder when the inventory level reaches 192 cases. Since the shipment takes two weeks, the new spokes should arrive just when the inventory level reaches the safety stock. Therefore, the firm adopts 192 cases as the order point.

Figure 16.3 shows the inventory pattern the spokes should follow, based on our analysis. It reflects a safety stock of 154 cases and allows a two-week lead time for receiving orders. If the firm begins with a complete inventory of safety stock plus an order that it just received, it will have 154 + 112 = 266 cases on hand. As it begins to use these, it must reorder two weeks before it hits the level of the safety stock. This occurs on day 27 at the reorder point of 192 cases. Two weeks later the firm reaches the safety stock, but it then receives the shipment of spokes, which replenishes the inventory to 266 cases. With a policy of ordering nine times per year, the firm will order about every 40 to 41 days.

Under this policy, the firm should never have an inventory below the level of the safety stock, at least not in normal circumstances. If shipping is delayed or if the spoke maker goes on strike, there will be a delay in replenishing the items and the manufacturer will have to use some of the safety stock. After all, the only purpose of a safety stock is to absorb unforeseen circumstances. The eight-week safety stock seems quite generous for such a simple commodity as bicycle spokes.

FIGURE 16.3   The Inventory of Spokes Across Time

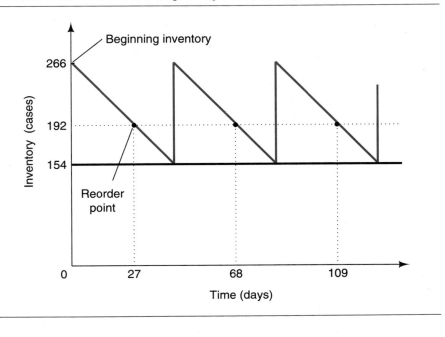

SUMMARY

This chapter examined the management of one of the most important kinds of working capital—inventory. Inventory represents a considerable investment of funds, and firms must pay close attention to it to be sure that they use it as effectively as possible. The major concern is to balance the benefits of having goods on hand versus the cost of securing the inventories. Depending on the type of inventory, the benefits may be the smooth running of the production process or the enhancement of sales. Ordering and carrying costs make up the total cost of the inventory.

Much of management focuses on gaining information about the state of the inventory and on minimizing the cost of maintaining a given level. This chapter reviewed some simple management techniques, including computerized methods. It concluded with a formal model called the economic ordering quantity model.

QUESTIONS

1. What are the three basic kinds of inventories?
2. Assume that your firm is a furniture manufacturer. What kinds of raw material inventories are you likely to have? What would happen to the firm if it cut its raw materials inventory to 0?

3. For the furniture manufacturer, what kinds of goods are in the work-in-process inventory? Could this type of inventory be eliminated?
4. What kinds of firms have little or no finished goods inventory?
5. What are the benefits of carrying an item in inventory?
6. What are the costs of carrying an item in inventory?
7. How do carrying costs behave as the order size increases?
8. How do ordering costs behave as the order size increases?
9. By what factor does the EOQ change if a firm's sales quadruple?
10. By what factor does the EOQ change if the unit purchase price doubles and, as a result, sales are reduced by half?

PROBLEMS

Use this information to solve all of the following problems. A microcomputer dealer purchases micros for $1,000 each. The cost of storing each computer is $100 per year, which does not include the financing cost of 12 percent. Placing an order costs $500, and the firm sells 900 computers per year.

1. What is the dollar cost of carrying a computer for one year?
2. What is the percentage cost of carrying a computer for one year?
3. If the firm orders 10 computers at a time, what will be the total ordering cost for a year's worth of sales?
4. If the firm orders 10 computers at a time, what will be the total carrying cost per year?
5. With an order size of 10 computers, what will be the total inventory cost per year?
6. If the firm orders 50 computers at a time, what will be the total ordering cost for a year's worth of sales?
7. If the firm orders 50 computers at a time, what will be the total carrying cost per year?
8. With an order size of 50 computers, what will be the total inventory cost per year?
9. If the firm orders 75 computers at a time, what will be the total ordering cost for a year's worth of sales?
10. If the firm orders 75 computers at a time, what will be the total carrying cost per year?
11. With an order size of 75 computers, what will be the total inventory cost per year?
12. If the firm orders 100 computers at a time, what will be the total ordering cost for a year's worth of sales?
13. If the firm orders 100 computers at a time, what will be the total carrying cost per year?
14. With an order size of 100 computers, what will be the total inventory cost per year?

15. From the preceding calculations, what can you determine about the best order size?
16. Graph the carrying cost of inventory relative to order quantity for orders of 10, 50, 75, and 100 computers.
17. Graph the ordering cost of inventory relative to order quantity for orders of 10, 50, 75, and 100 computers.
18. Graph the total cost of inventory relative to order quantity for orders of 10, 50, 75, and 100 computers.
19. Using the EOQ developed in this chapter, compute the optimum order size.
20. Assume that the ordering cost rises from $500 to $750 per order. How should that affect the EOQ? Compute the EOQ to confirm your hypothesis.
21. If the carrying cost drops to 10 percent, how should that affect the EOQ? Compute the EOQ to confirm your hypothesis.

The Management of Cash and Marketable Securities

marketable security
a financial obligation that can be converted into cash immediately, with little reduction in its value

Cash is critically important because the firm must meet its immediate obligations with cash payments. This chapter focuses on managing both cash and marketable securities, a close substitute. A **marketable security** is a financial obligation that the holder can convert into cash immediately, with little reduction in its value.

Holding some cash is essential to operating the firm, but holding too much is costly, because it does not earn any explicit return. As with the management of inventories, the central question is how much is the optimum amount to have on hand. Also, because money has a time value, the firm will want to collect cash owed to it as quickly as possible. Similarly, it wants to pay its obligations as slowly as possible. Naturally, the desire to collect cash quickly and to pay it slowly is subject to some constraints. For example, failure to make payments within a reasonable time may damage the firm's credit rating. The cash manager must know the techniques for speeding collections and slowing payments that are acceptable business practice.

Because holding large amounts of cash is costly, all firms prefer to put as much of it as they safely can into marketable securities. These earn a return, yet the firm can convert them into cash quickly. This chapter introduces the basic types of marketable securities and discusses the differences among them and their usefulness in managing the firm's working capital.

BENEFITS AND COSTS OF HOLDING CASH

transaction balance
cash held by a firm in order to pay for goods and services

Holding cash generates three kinds of benefits. First, the money is used to pay for goods and services. Cash held for these purposes constitutes a **transaction balance.** Without it, firms would have to obtain cash for each transaction that arose. The transaction balance acts as a pool of readily available money and benefits the firm by the convenience it offers.

precautionary balance
cash held to be sure the firm does not run out of cash

Because running out of cash is costly, firms keep an extra amount to avoid the penalties associated with running out. It is called a **precautionary balance.** If managers expect prices of securities to fall, it is better to hold

speculative balance
cash held in anticipation of falling security prices

☞ Holding cash does not generate an explicit monetary return, but it generates other kinds of benefits that have monetary value.

cash than to hold securities. This money is called a **speculative balance.** Firms essentially bet they will be better off holding cash, which does not earn a return, than holding a security that might fall in value. Firms do not normally hold the three types of cash balances in separate accounts. Instead, the point is to distinguish them as different reasons for holding cash.

Although a transaction balance generates convenience and a precautionary balance affords the firm a margin of safety, holding cash does not generate an explicit monetary return. So, it has costs as well as benefits, the main cost being the lost interest that it would otherwise earn. The goal of cash management is to maximize the difference between the benefits and costs.

CHOOSING THE RIGHT AMOUNT OF CASH

In this section we discuss two techniques for identifying the correct amount of cash for a firm to hold. The Baumol model relies on the same assumptions we used for the EOQ model in the previous chapter. In particular, it assumes that the rate of cash usage is constant and known with certainty. It is thus not surprising that the Baumol formula is a simple adaptation of the EOQ formula. The Miller-Orr model is more sophisticated, and assumes that net daily cash flows follow a random path.

The Baumol Model

Baumol model
a model of cash management based on the insight that cash is simply an inventory of money

The **Baumol model** considers cash to be a form of inventory. Just as a bicycle-manufacturing firm may hold an inventory of spokes, it may also hold a certain amount of cash; for the former, the unit is one spoke, and for the latter it is one dollar. Once this exact parallel is seen, the same technique used to derive an expression for the optimum inventory balance can be used to derive the expression for the correct cash balance.

As in the EOQ model, the Baumol model assumes that the firm uses cash at a known constant rate, and in doing so it incurs holding costs. Since these costs increase with the average level of cash, focusing on this factor alone would lead the firm to hold the least amount possible. However, as it depletes its cash, it must acquire new amounts, perhaps by liquidating some of its marketable securities. Each time the firm transacts in this way, it bears transaction costs, so it would want to transact as few times as possible during the year. This could be done by having a high cash level. As with the EOQ model, the correct balance is found by combining the holding costs and transaction costs so as to minimize the total cost of holding cash.

Let us assume that a firm has a maximum cash balance of C dollars. If it uses cash at a constant rate down to a level of 0, its average balance will be $C/2$. This is shown in Figure 17.1. If the firm is able to earn a yearly rate of return of r on its funds, the annual opportunity cost of holding cash can

FIGURE 17.1   Cash Level with a Constant Rate of Usage

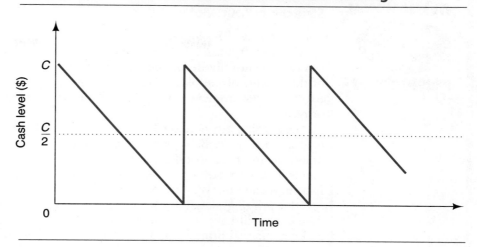

be computed as the average amount of cash held ($C/2$) times the rate of interest lost because the funds were held in cash and not invested elsewhere (r). Therefore, the cost of holding cash over a year is ($C/2$)r.

Suppose that over a year the firm will have a total need for cash equal to T. Since C are acquired each time cash balances are restored, then balances will be restored (T/C) times per year. If the cost of acquiring the cash is F, the total transaction cost for the period will be (T/C)F.

The Baumol model parallels the analysis for the derivation of the EOQ model. In particular, a close correspondence exists between their variables, as shown in Table 17.1.

Notice that the carrying cost of each dollar is the rate that could have been earned if the money had been invested, say, in marketable securities. This r is an example of an opportunity cost. In the EOQ model, the carrying cost, C, contains not only the forgone interest rate, but also other variable costs such as insurance.

TABLE 17.1   Correspondence Between the EOQ
                and Baumol Models

	EOQ Variable		*Baumol Variable*
S	annual unit sales	T	annual cash needs
F	cost of each transaction	F	cost of each transaction
C	carrying cost (%)	r	rate if cash is invested
P	unit purchase price	1	the price of $1

Stretching Your Money, Literally

Bank notes need no longer grow on trees, according to the Reserve Bank of Australia. Instead, let the world's currency notes be made of plastic— durable, beautifully decorated and, above all, hard to counterfeit. Because of the success of the plastic A$10 note introduced two years ago, the Australian government plans to eventually have all Australian bills made of plastic.

Displaying a commercial appetite almost unknown among central banks, the Reserve Bank hopes to exploit its plastic-note technology to grab a share of the world market for printing money for other governments. It has already produced a S$50 bill for Singapore; and another note is being issued for Western Samoa.

But printing money for anyone but tiny island states will not be easy. The bank will have to compete with a formidable range of government and commercial printers, most notably Britain's De La Rue, which makes the notes for about 80 of the world's central banks. The paper notes of rivals like De La Rue are cheaper, and everyone likes cheap money. If plastic catches on, De La Rue and others are certain to come up with versions of their own.

Nevertheless, in any such battle the Australian Reserve Bank will have a technological lead. It has spent two decades and A$20 million, or US$16 million, coming up with its plastic notes. Both the Isle of Man and, amazingly, Haiti produced plastic bank notes in the past. Their notes were more durable than paper, but just as easy to counterfeit. Australia's polymer-based substrate is much more high-tech: it comes with a transparent patch and a design which is raised slightly from the surface. In short, the technology defeats a forger with even the most sophisticated color photocopier.

The Reserve Bank's technology could also be valuable for travelers' checks and other security documents. But the biggest prize will be in America, where dollars are produced by a paper-maker called Crane and the Bureau of Engraving and Printing. Not only is the greenback— two colors and one size, whatever the denomination—the world's most popular currency (6.3 billion notes were printed in 1989), it is also among the easiest to counterfeit.

Source: "Spending Plastic" *Economist*, November 17, 1990.

Also notice that in the EOQ model the unit purchase price could be $2, $10.50, or any other amount. Because of this, we used the variable P to denote the purchase price of each unit of inventory. In the case of cash, the price of each unit is always $1.

Since we now know that the Baumol model parallels the EOQ model, it follows that the correct amount of cash to hold is given by:

$$C^* = \sqrt{\frac{2FT}{r}}$$ (17.1)

where C^* is the optimal C.

EXAMPLE 17.1

A firm has a total cash need of $500,000 for the coming year. The transaction cost for acquiring cash is $25 and the interest rate is 15 percent. Find the maximum amount of cash the firm should hold.

According to the Baumol model, the amount of cash to acquire each time, which is equal to the maximum cash level the firm will hold, is:

$$C^* = \sqrt{\frac{2 \times \$25 \times \$500,000}{0.15}} = \$12,909.94$$

Figure 17.2 graphs the transaction cost, holding cost, and total cost of holding cash. It shows that by acquiring more cash each time, the transaction cost decreases and the holding cost increases. The total cost reaches a minimum where the holding and transaction cost curves cross. Recall that this same result was also obtained when discussing the EOQ model.

FIGURE 17.2   Cash Balance Costs

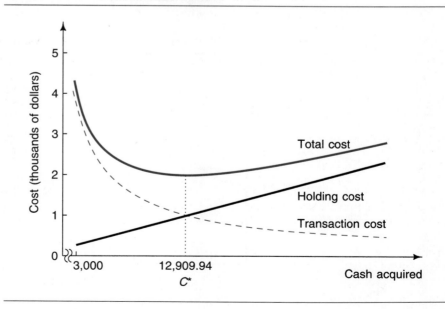

The Miller-Orr Model

The Baumol model relies on a very simple view of the way cash is used. For example, it assumes that the firm uses cash at a constant rate, starting from some initial holding, C. In practice, the actual usage pattern may be much more erratic. The **Miller-Orr model** explicitly incorporates the randomness feature of actual cash flow usage.

Miller-Orr model
a model of cash management that accounts for the fact that actual cash flows are random

The Miller-Orr technique is also known as the control limit method. The essential idea is that the cash level is allowed to fluctuate freely within an upper bound U and a lower bound L. Whenever the cash level reaches U, management reduces it to a predetermined target level Z, by investing the excess, usually in marketable securities. If, instead, the cash level reaches L, the firm increases it back to the target level Z, generally by selling marketable securities. In this way the cash flow will always fluctuate between U and L. This is depicted in Figure 17.3.

The problem facing the manager who uses this model is choosing the correct upper, target, and lower levels. Although the mathematical derivation of these levels is complex, the basic idea is quite simple. Essentially, Miller and Orr assumed that cash balance fluctuations are normally distributed, with a mean of 0. That is, the balance does not exhibit a tendency to increase or decrease over time. The lower limit is set by management, based on their willingness to let the firm run out of cash. For example, if management is willing to run out of cash with some frequency, they would set $L = 0$. The next step is to estimate the variance of the firm's daily cash flows, σ^2. Also, let F represent the fixed transaction cost, and $r_d = r/365$ be the daily interest rate. Based on this, the model gives the target cash balance, the upper control limit, and the average cash balance.

FIGURE 17.3   Cash Balances in the Miller-Orr Model

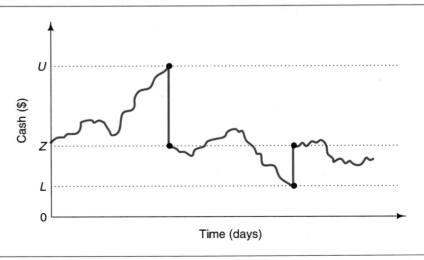

The target cash balance formula is:

$$Z = \sqrt[3]{\frac{3F\sigma^2}{4r_d}} + L \qquad (17.2)$$

The upper control limit formula is:

$$U = 3Z - 2L \qquad (17.3)$$

The average cash balance formula is:

$$ACB = \frac{4Z - L}{3} \qquad (17.4)$$

EXAMPLE 17.2

Suppose that Sandblast, Inc., knows that the cost of each cash transaction is $F = \$25$, that its opportunity cost of money is $r = 15$ percent per year, and that the standard deviation of daily cash flows is $10,000. Also suppose that management has set the lower control limit, L, at $100,000. Compute the target cash balance, Z, the upper control limit, U, and the average cash balance for Sandblast.

All we do is apply Equations 17.2 through 17.4:

$$Z = \sqrt[3]{\frac{3 \times \$25 \times (\$10{,}000)^2}{4 \times \left(\frac{0.15}{365}\right)}} + \$100{,}000 = \$116{,}585.17$$

$$U = 3 \times \$116{,}585.17 - 2 \times \$100{,}000 = \$149{,}755.50$$

$$ACB = \frac{4 \times \$116{,}585.17 - \$100{,}000}{3} = \$122{,}113.56$$

Notice that the target cash balance is not midway between the control limits. The same is true of the average cash balance. This is a curious feature of the Miller-Orr model.

TECHNIQUES OF CASH MANAGEMENT

☞ By collecting its accounts receivables early, the firm acquires additional cash that can be invested.

The control limit approach of the Miller-Orr model gives managers a guide in responding to cash surpluses or shortages. However, it gives no guidance about general cash-management policies for the firm's day-to-day operation. In particular, there are techniques for speeding the collection of money and for slowing its disbursement with which managers can conserve cash.

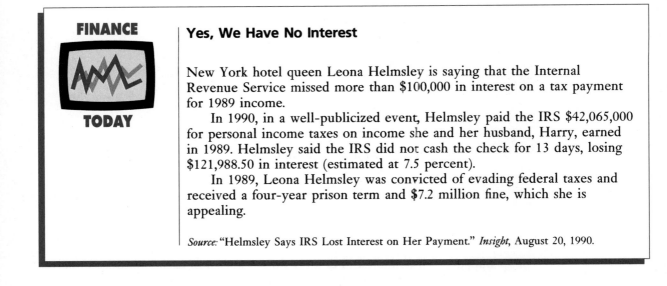

FINANCE TODAY

Yes, We Have No Interest

New York hotel queen Leona Helmsley is saying that the Internal Revenue Service missed more than $100,000 in interest on a tax payment for 1989 income.

In 1990, in a well-publicized event, Helmsley paid the IRS $42,065,000 for personal income taxes on income she and her husband, Harry, earned in 1989. Helmsley said the IRS did not cash the check for 13 days, losing $121,988.50 in interest (estimated at 7.5 percent).

In 1989, Leona Helmsley was convicted of evading federal taxes and received a four-year prison term and $7.2 million fine, which she is appealing.

Source: "Helmsley Says IRS Lost Interest on Her Payment." *Insight,* August 20, 1990.

Effects of Conserving Cash

If a firm pays $1 one day later or if it collects $1 one day earlier, it has the use of $1 for an extra day in both cases. The essential advantage of conserving cash in these ways is that the firm may invest it to earn a return. For example, if the interest rate is 12 percent and the firm collects $1 million a day early, the firm realizes a financial benefit equal to the one day's interest on that amount. In this case, it earns interest of:

$$\$1,000,000 \times \frac{0.12}{365} = \$329 \text{ per day}$$

There are many cases in which the sums saved are large or when the firm collects or pays small sums regularly. Then, attention to cash management can pay large dividends. For example, assume that your firm must deliver a cashier's check for $1 million in five days to a distant company. To get a cashier's check, you must actually pay the money when the check is cut. Consider two methods of delivering the check. First, you could obtain it today and mail it to reach the other company in five days. Second, you could wait five days, buy the cashier's check in the morning, and have someone fly to the receiver and deliver it personally.

If your firm hand-delivers the check, it can use the $1 million for five days. With an annual interest rate of 12 percent, the simple interest earned would be:

$$\$1,000,000 \times \frac{0.12}{365} \times 5 = \$1,643.84$$

This interest would be more than enough to pay the airline ticket and salary of the person delivering the check by hand. Therefore, that is definitely the better practice.

Actually, still better ways are available. Perhaps the manager should send the cashier's check by overnight mail and save even more money. Cash management has the very practical job of finding the best way to accelerate collections and delay payments, taking all costs and benefits into consideration.

Many firms face cash-management problems that are much more complex than our example. Consider a company like Sears with several million customers all over the country mailing in payments every month. Between the date the customer buys the goods in the store and the time Sears actually receives payment, a long time passes. During this time the customer benefits by having the good, but has not yet made payment. Sears, on the other hand, has only an **accounts receivable**—an amount owed to it. Figure 17.4 presents the two sides of this transaction.

From the sale date, Sears has an accounts receivable due to the sale. This receivable stays on the books until payment is available in its account. By contrast, the customer has the good long before paying. The time between the sale and the collection or payment is **float.** In this example, Sears has **negative float,** because it surrenders the good before it receives payment. By contrast, the customer has **positive float,** having received the good before paying.

Sears has a strong incentive to reduce the period of the float by collecting the accounts receivable early. If the company can do this, it gains the use of the money that much earlier. For the customer, the float is very attractive, as a result of having both the good and the use of the money that will eventually pay for it. Clearly, the customer benefits by extending the period of the float. This explains, in part, why credit cards have become so popular.

accounts receivable
obligations due to the firm from other parties that are expected to be collected within one year

float
the time between receipt of a good and payment

negative float
a float period in which a firm has made payment without receiving the good, or has relinquished an asset without receiving payment

positive float
a float period in which a firm has received a good without making a payment, or has received a payment without surrendering an asset

FIGURE 17.4   Float and the Collection Process

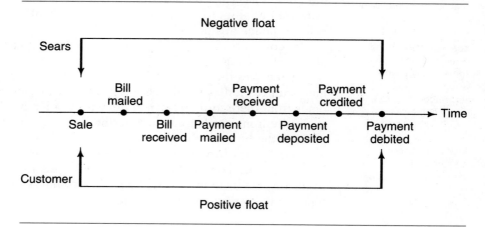

☞ The firm should strive to increase its positive float and reduce its negative float.

For a company like Sears, it is possible to calculate the normal amount of accounts receivable. This amount depends on the average daily amount of credit sales and the average collection period (ACP), in days, between the sale and the collection of funds.

$$ACP = \frac{\text{Accounts receivable}}{\text{Average daily credit sales}} \tag{17.5}$$

If Sears' credit sales are $10 million per day on average and the collection period is 82 days, it will have an investment in accounts receivable of $820 million:

Accounts receivable = $10,000,000 × 82 days = $820,000,000

If Sears could collect its funds tied up in accounts receivable faster, it would lower its investment in accounts receivable, and that money would be available to invest. For example, if Sears could reduce its collection period by just three days, the new level of accounts receivable would be:

Accounts receivable = $10,000,000 × 79 = $790,000,000

This implies having $30 million that could earn a return elsewhere.

Because the rewards of better cash management may be so great, well-developed techniques can improve collection and slow payments. The following section considers the costs and benefits of some of these techniques.

CONCENTRATION BANKING AND LOCK BOX SYSTEMS

☞ Banks offer systems such as lock boxes and concentration banking to aid firms in their cash-management programs.

The time between when a customer mails a payment and when the firm receives it means a frustrating delay for the firm in collecting cash. In the example of Sears, one way to collect payments is to have them all mailed to the home office in Chicago. Figure 17.5 shows average mail times in days from various cities to Chicago. Concentration banking and lock box systems help to reduce this period.

concentration banking
a technique in which customers mail payments to a regional collection center, rather than to a firm's home office

In **concentration banking,** the firm instructs customers to mail their payments to a regional collection center rather than to the home office. This way it receives the checks sooner and therefore can begin processing them more quickly. It deposits the checks in a local bank, and periodically transfers funds from there to the principal or concentration bank. It can do this electronically from one bank to another by a wire transfer, so the delay at this point of the process is negligible.

lock box system
a technique in which customers mail their payments to a post office box near their homes

With a **lock box system,** customers mail their payments to a post office box near their homes. The firm arranges with local banks to collect the payments, credit them to a local bank account as quickly as possible, and report the transactions to the home office.

FIGURE 17.5   Mail Time to Chicago: Hypothetical Example of a Lock Box Analysis

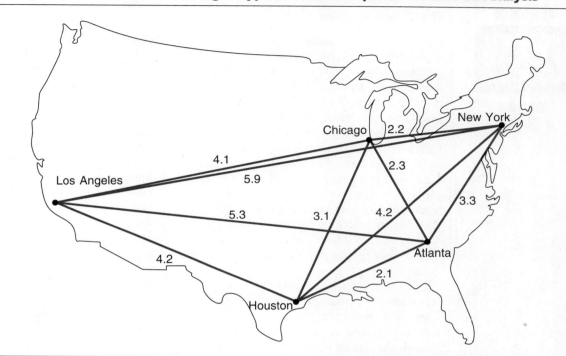

Source: From *Guide to Working Capital Management* by Keith V. Smith. Copyright © 1979 by McGraw-Hill Book Company. Reprinted by permission.

Evaluating the Two Systems

To see how to evaluate concentration banking and lock box systems, let us continue our example of Sears. We assumed that sales average $10 million per day, that the current period is 82 days, and that customers make all payments to the home office in Chicago. Suppose Sears has learned that it can establish a lock box system for an initial payment of $4 million and a yearly fee of $1 million. This will decrease the collection period by 1.5 days. As another alternative, Sears is considering a concentration banking arrangement that requires an initial payment of $6 million and a yearly fee of $1.5 million. This is more expensive, but it will cut the collection period by 2.5 days. Which system, if either, should Sears choose?

The solution depends on a direct comparison of the costs with the benefits. In both cases, the benefits are the reduction in the collection period and the freeing of cash for other uses. The lock box system reduces the collection period by 1.5 days. Given sales of $10 million per day, it will free $15 million

FINANCE

TODAY

The Check is in the Pail

The Federal Reserve System manages the clearing of checks through the banking system. Check clearing requires that any check that is written be returned to the check writer's bank so that funds may be withdrawn from the check writer's account and the check returned to the writer. As the following story from *Time* indicates, this is not always a smooth process:*

To the weekend cleaning woman at the Continental Illinois Bank of Chicago, the clear plastic bags on the floor of the computer room looked to be full of trash. She thereupon heaved them into a bin that was taken to a garbage-compaction area. But the following Monday, Continental's data processors discovered that they were short $227 million in checks that the bank had honored but not yet entered in its computers. A crew of janitors then began searching the immediate area, to no avail. Finally, after an anxious hunt, they located the documents in the compaction room amid bundles of wastepaper mingled with noxious cigarette butts and cardboard coffee cups.

If the checks had not been found, Continental would have faced the laborious job of straightening out a $227 million imbalance in its books. Last week, however, when the August 17 mishap came to light, bank officials maintained virtuously that such an outcome was impossible. Even though the bank's books are balanced daily, they said, paper trash is kept on hand for several days—just in case something important gets thrown out by mistake. Declared Eugene Croisant, a Continental executive vice president: "We provide for all contingencies." Even, apparently, for cleaning women.

* *Time*, September 8, 1986, p. 53.

for other uses. The concentration banking system reduces the collection period by 2.5 days, so it frees $25 million.

We must evaluate the costs associated with the two systems in present value terms. Assuming an interest rate of 12 percent, the lock box system costs $4 million plus the present value of a perpetuity of $1 million per year at 12 percent:

$$\text{PV of costs for lock box} = \$4,000,000 + \frac{\$1,000,000}{0.12}$$

$$= \$12,333,333$$

For the concentration banking scheme, the costs are an initial fee of $6 million and a yearly expense of $1.5 million:

$$\text{PV of costs for concentration banking} = \$6{,}0000{,}000 + \frac{\$1{,}500{,}000}{0.12}$$

$$= \$18{,}500{,}000$$

Because the benefits and costs are all in present value terms, we can compare them directly:

	Benefit	Cost	Net Benefit
Lock box	$15,000,000	$12,333,333	$2,666,667
Concentration banking	25,000,000	18,500,000	6,500,000

Since the concentration banking scheme gives a greater net benefit, the management of Sears should favor it over the lock box system.

ADVANTAGES OF DELAYING PAYMENTS

Just as collecting funds early has an advantage for a company, so does delaying payments. Basically, both strategies let the firm use cash longer to earn a return. Therefore, most firms consciously delay payments as long as they can without aggravating their suppliers.

☞ Firms should never make payments before they are due.

Firms should never pay their debts early and, within reason, it may actually be best to pay somewhat late. There are definite costs to being a perpetual late payer, however, including a bad credit rating and suppliers' unwillingness to make shipments. Whether firms should actually pay late as a matter of policy raises practical questions of whether the savings is worth the potential damage. It also raises ethical questions about whether it is right systematically to delay rightful payments to other parties.

A common technique is to use a distant bank for making payments. Figure 17.4 shows that the customer has the use of funds between the time Sears receives the check and the time the customer's account is debited. Because timely payment depends only on when the payee receives the check, firms should try to increase the time between payment received and payment debited. Many firms do this by using banks scattered over a wide location. Assume that a customer has bank accounts in both North Carolina and Oregon and thus might pay a North Carolina supplier with a check drawn on an Oregon bank. Normally, it takes longer for a check sent to a distant bank to clear. Part of this strategy also suggests that very small rural banks, which tend to be somewhat slower, might be best for increasing this portion of the float.

Strangling Cash

Firms with successful cash-management practices have a stranglehold on cash, holding it by the throat and releasing it only when they absolutely must. For example, National Distillers saves an extra $3 million per year and American Brands saves $5 million by controlling the payments they make to suppliers. One way that firms increase their float is by issuing checks from remote locations. Banks offer these services to their customers. For example, Chase Manhattan, located in New York City, issues checks from a Syracuse, New York, location, and Morgan Guaranty Trust, also of New York, issues checks from Delaware for its customers.

Using these locations increases the amount of time until the recipient can actually deposit and be credited with the payment. Until the check clears the issuer's account, the issuer has the use of the money. These differences are not always large. For example, the clearing time for a check drawn on one New York City bank and deposited in another bank is 1.14 days on average. However, if the check is drawn on a Syracuse bank, the average clearing time is 1.92 days. One of the most amazing things about the cash-management game is the importance of such apparently short amounts of time.

Some firms are extremely aggressive in maximizing their positive float. Levi Strauss, of blue jeans fame, uses a computerized system that reads the ZIP Code of the destination and automatically prints a check drawn on a remote bank with the greatest amount of clearing time.* The Federal Reserve System manages the nation's check-clearing system, so it is anxious to reduce float by speeding up check collection. Accordingly, it looks askance on systems designed to maximize float.

On occasion, firms become a bit too aggressive for their own good and can get into legal difficulties. The brokerage firm of E. F. Hutton was indicted and pleaded guilty to over 2,000 counts of bilking banks through its cash-management system. It is illegal to write checks without funds on deposit unless it is done with a bank's knowledge and agreement, as in a zero balance account system. E. F. Hutton managed to overdraw its combined bank accounts by more than $1 billion on some days without the knowledge of its banks.† As you can imagine, this practice generated considerable amounts of extra interest income.

The Federal Reserve is actively trying to speed check clearing by using jets and helicopters to move checks to clearing centers more quickly. For many firms, however, one thing will remain constant: they will still try to find ways to keep their hands on cash as long as possible.

* The preceding examples are drawn from Irwin Ross, "The Race Is to the Slow Payer," *Fortune*, April 18, 1983.

† Dexter Hutchins, "Post-Hutton Lessons in How to Manage Corporate Cash," *Fortune*, November 11, 1985.

Clearly, regulating cash flow in and out of the firm's bank accounts is a major concern. Sometimes, however, companies find themselves with more cash than they really need, in which case they generally invest the excess—that is, the money that they do not have to hold as a transaction, precautionary, or speculative balance—in marketable securities.

THE ROLE OF MARKETABLE SECURITIES

☞ Firms with excess cash can invest in marketable securities to increase their returns.

Cash earns no explicit return, so firms should maintain only necessary cash balances. However, cash needs are sometimes difficult to predict, and firms also must have a means of securing money on short notice. This also implies the availability of excess cash for short-term investment. Marketable securities play an important role in working capital management.

Marketable Securities as a Substitute for Cash

The great advantage of marketable securities is that they can be converted into cash immediately, yet they earn a rate of interest. Because of their quick convertibility, marketable securities often serve as a substitute for cash in working capital management. The firm can hold minimum levels of cash and can add to the amount as needed by selling the securities.

zero balance account
a checking account with a zero balance, used to be sure that no idle cash balances are maintained

Some firms employ an extensive policy of substituting marketable securities for cash by the use of zero balance accounts. As the name implies, a **zero balance account** is a checking account with no balance. Each day the firm totals all checks presented for payment against its account and transfers the amount to the account by selling marketable securities. Thus it uses the securities as a substitute for cash, because it holds all funds in this form until the moment of payment.

Temporary Investment in Marketable Securities

Although they earn a higher explicit return than cash, these securities typically provide a lower return than the firm can earn through investing in its own line of business. Therefore, it is generally unwise to invest in them on a long-term basis. However, on frequent occasions these securities can be used as a short-term investment medium.

First, sales may be unexpectedly large, generating an unexpectedly large amount of cash, so the firm can invest the excess in marketable securities to earn some return. Second, the company may have seasonal fluctuations in the amount of cash available. In such instances it will have the excess amount for only a short period, so it might invest that money in marketable securities. Third, firms often know in advance that they will soon need a large amount of cash, for example, to repay a bank loan. To accumulate the necessary funds before the repayment, they can invest the partially collected funds in marketable securities on a short-term basis.

INTERNATIONAL PERSPECTIVES

Fraudulent Fund Flows

It is widely accepted that funds transfer is now one of the most vulnerable areas for banks. Edgar Adamson, an agent with Interpol, reports that this is probably the most prevalent crime reported to the agency, and some of the transfers are not even through automated systems. Nevertheless, the speed at which enormous sums can disappear should give responsible bank officers cause for very serious thought.

The most recent evidence of the danger of insider abuse in the United Kingdom was disclosed when a bank officer in the funds-transfer department was able to plant a false document in the bank's computer. This instructed the correspondent to pass $107 million of bank funds it was receiving from Hill Samuel to accounts set up by a gang of fraudsters. The diversion was discovered within hours and the funds never left the correspondent bank.

Weekends are favorite times for fraud, to put the maximum period between theft and discovery. An officer in a funds-transfer department in Germany transferred funds over a long weekend to a Hong Kong bank. The loss was not discovered before the funds left the bank. However, investigators Kroll Associates pursued the fugitive bank officer across Southeast Asia from Hong Kong to Bangkok and to Kuala Lumpur. Eventually, says Kroll, the bank got its money back.

So too did the First National Bank of Chicago, which over a long weekend in 1988 had $70 million taken from three accounts. Each of the account holders responded quickly to the loss. The bank traced the transfers to two bank accounts in Austria and a stop was placed on the funds. A clerk in the funds-transfer department was arrested. It appeared another insider had corrupted him and he had handed over to an organized gang of fraudsters codes to trigger payments from the accounts. The clerk had also assisted in pretending to make the proper call-back procedures to the account holders, but he provided incriminating evidence by dialing only to his accomplices inside Chicago, rather than to the account holders, two of whom were outside the state. This became evident when the bank listened to tapes of the calls and conversations.

First National Bank says the crooks might have got away with the funds, but rather than wait to withdraw the money, they were "spending money before they had it, out buying Mercedes for the children." It adds:

Types of Marketable Securities

Whatever the reason for investing in marketable securities, there are many different types from which to choose. Governments, banks, and industrial corporations all issue them, and corporations use them as both an investment

"You can have the best procedures possible but you won't prevent inside collusion. We don't want to get to the situation where we are hampering productivity by installing so many procedures that we couldn't allow transfers to come through daily."

William List, a partner in Peat Marwick McLintock, says there are two aspects to the erroneous payment of outgoing monies. The first is a payment to the wrong person, the second a payment of the wrong amount. All systems use a code to identify the payee and if these codes are wrong, and yet do exist, the wrong payee will be paid. Most systems incorporate a positive check on the input of the code that it is correct. Few, however, incorporate checks to determine if these codes have been corrupted.

Paying the wrong amount is a fairly common occurrence and can happen purely as the result of an accident. But List says the risk is that such changes are made to payments in collusion with staff in the receiving institutions.

Ten warning signs to spot funds-transfer fraud:

1. lack of separation between authority to initiate a wire transfer and authority to approve
2. splitting transactions to bypass approval authorities
3. large or frequent transfers against uncollected funds
4. frequent payment errors by authorized system managers
5. inadequate security of the funds-transfer system, such as password
6. incoming transfers in which the account name and number do not match
7. absence of written funds-transfer agreements between institution and customer
8. the deposit of funds into several accounts which are then collected into a single account, followed by the transfer of those funds outside the country, when this type of requirement is not consistent with the customer's known business
9. a pattern of transfers of similar amounts both in and out of the customer's account on the same day or the next day
10. wire transfers by customers operating a cash business

Source: "The High Risk of Funds Transfer," *Euromoney*, November 1990, p. 53.

medium and a source of financing. We explored the various types of marketable securities used as financing vehicles in our discussion of the money market in Chapter 7. As we noted there, the most important are T bills, certificates of deposit, or CDs, commercial paper, repurchase agreements, and bankers' acceptances. The financial manager determines the firm's cash requirements and the amount available for temporary investment in marketable securities. These funds must then be allocated across different instruments with an eye to their risk level, liquidity, and maturity characteristics.

Risks in Marketable Securities

default risk
the risk that a debt obligation will not be paid as promised

Although marketable securities are very short-term instruments, they still have risks. First, there is **default risk** that the issuer will not pay as promised. This does not exist for U.S. Treasury issues, but other instruments such as CDs and commercial paper have a slight chance of default. In the early 1970s, for example, Penn Central stunned the financial marketplace when it defaulted on its commercial paper.

interest rate risk
the risk that a security's value will change due to a change in interest rates

Second, **interest rate risk** is the chance that the security's value will change due to a change in interest rates. When interest rates rise, the prices of all debt obligations, including marketable securities, fall. Similarly, a drop in interest rates causes a modest increase in the value of short-term marketable securities. Changing interest rates have less effect on prices of short-term than on long-term securities.

liquidity risk
the risk that a marketable security cannot be easily converted into cash

A third type of risk associated with all marketable securities is **liquidity risk,** the chance that the owner cannot convert a marketable security into cash. One of the reasons that firms invest in very short-term securities is for their great liquidity. Since the market for most of them is very robust, normally it is not difficult to sell securities for cash. It may be a problem sometimes, however, such as when a firm holds a CD of a bank undergoing reorganization. Again, these risks are relatively low.

Yield Relationships in the Money Market

The interest rates offered by different marketable securities differ to reflect the risk differences between them. Treasury bills offer the lowest rate since they have the best backing of all instruments, the full faith and credit of the U.S. Treasury. Commercial paper and bankers' acceptances typically have rates that are very close, with commercial paper issued by top industrial corporations having a slightly lower yield. Both commercial paper and bankers' acceptances lie below the yield of CDs. The difference between the commercial paper and CD rates reflects the greater creditworthiness of the best industrial corporations in relation to banks. A bankers' acceptance can offer a lower return than CDs because it is two-name paper, which gives the lender an added margin of security. Finally, Eurodollar CDs must pay a greater rate than domestic CDs because of their greater risk. While these relationships are the usual ones, there are occasional exceptions. Also, within each of the categories, yield differentials reflect the varying creditworthiness of the particular issuers.

One good source of information about current rates on marketable securities is the column "Money Rates," which appears daily in the *Wall Street*

FIGURE 17.6   Rates for Marketable Securities

MONEY RATES

Tuesday, April 30, 1991
The key U.S. and foreign annual interest rates below are a guide to general levels but don't always represent actual transactions.

PRIME RATE: 9%. The base rate on corporate loans at large U.S. money center commercial banks.

FEDERAL FUNDS: 6% high, 5¾% low, 5⅞% near closing bid, 5 15/16% offered. Reserves traded among commercial banks for overnight use in amounts of $1 million or more. Source: Babcock Fulton Prebon (U.S.A.) Inc.

DISCOUNT RATE: 5½%. The charge on loans to depository institutions by the New York Federal Reserve Bank.

CALL MONEY: 7½% to 8½%. The charge on loans to brokers on stock exchange collateral.

COMMERCIAL PAPER placed directly by General Motors Acceptance Corp.: 5.75% 15 to 57 days; 5.60% 58 to 64 days; 5.75% 65 to 270 days.

COMMERCIAL PAPER: High-grade unsecured notes sold through dealers by major corporations in multiples of $1,000: 5.90% 30 days; 5.90% 60 days; 5.90% 90 days.

CERTIFICATES OF DEPOSIT: 5.62% one month; 5.62% two months; 5.65% three months; 5.81% six months; 6.25% one year. Average of top rates paid by major New York banks on primary new issues of negotiable C.D.s, usually on amounts of $1 million and more. The minimum unit is $100,-000. Typical rates in the secondary market: 5.87% one month; 5.95% three months; 6.05% six months.

BANKERS ACCEPTANCES: 5.73% 30 days; 5.72% 60 days; 5.72% 90 days; 5.72% 120 days; 5.72% 150 days; 5.72% 180 days. Negotiable, bank-backed business credit instruments typically financing an import order.

Source: Wall Street Journal, May 1, 1991. Reprinted by permission of Wall Street Journal, © 1991 Dow Jones & Company, Inc. All Rights Reserved Worldwide.

Journal. Figure 17.6 presents this column, which gives a good idea of the kinds of yield differences that prevail among these securities.

SUMMARY

This chapter focused on the management of cash and its near substitute, marketable securities. Essentially, firms hold cash because of the great convenience it offers in making payments and avoiding default on obligations. Sometimes firms also hold cash in hopes of favorable changes in interest rates. Because it offers no explicit return, firms try to hold as little as possible. Sophisticated methods for determining the amount to maintain, such as the control limit approach of the Miller-Orr method, are widely used. Because firms can invest any excess, they have a strong motivation to collect money quickly and to pay it slowly. Various techniques exist to manage this cash flow, including concentration banking, lock boxes, remote banking facilities, and zero balance accounts.

This chapter also reviewed the different types of marketable securities that are available for investment, and considered the different types of risk associated with them. It concluded with a brief discussion of the normal yield relationships that prevail among marketable securities.

QUESTIONS

1. What are the three types of cash balances that firms hold?
2. What is the cost of holding cash as an asset?
3. In the Baumol method, by what factor does the average cash balance change if the annual cash needs, T, increase by a factor of three?
4. In the Miller-Orr method, why is there an upper control limit? In other words, why do firms not hold more cash than the amount indicated by this limit?
5. Would a firm be better off to collect $100,000 in an accounts receivable one day earlier or to pay an account payable of $100,000 one day later? Is there a difference?
6. What is the difference between positive and negative float?
7. If you are responsible for cash management, would you prefer to deal with a firm that has a longer or shorter collection period? Explain.
8. What is the difference between a concentration banking system and a lock box system?
9. How can marketable securities act as a substitute for cash?
10. Why are there so many different kinds of marketable securities?
11. If you had extra cash that your firm would not need for 90 days, would you consider investing it in Treasury bills or in a repurchase argreement? What factors would you consider?
12. What is the difference between interest rate risk and default risk? Do T bills have default risk? Do they have interest rate risk? Does a CD that matures immediately have default risk? Does it have interest rate risk?
13. Does a T bill have liquidity risk?
14. A close correspondence exists between the EOQ and the Baumol models. Is this a coincidence? Explain.
15. Although the two models are similar, the EOQ model considers the purchase price, P, of the inventory good, but the Baumol model does not seem to consider a corresponding variable. Is this true? Explain.
16. In the Baumol model, what is the value of the slope of the holding cost line? Refer to Figure 17.2.

PROBLEMS

1. Assume that interest rates are 12 percent and a firm collects $1 million 15 days earlier than it expected. What is the value of this early collection?
2. Your firm owes $1 million to a supplier. You could pay it now or you could wait for 15 days. If interest rates are 12 percent per year, what is the value of waiting?

3. Compare your answers to Problems 1 and 2. What does this indicate about the relative value of early collection and slow payment?

4. Firms sometimes actually use messengers to deliver and to collect payments. Your firm must make a payment of $500,000 in five days and interest rates are 10 percent. There are two ways of making the payment. First, you could mail it, but because mail times are uncertain you must mail it today to be sure it is there on time; however, you expect it to be there in two days. Second, you could wait four days and send it by overnight delivery for $20. Which should you choose? What is the expected savings of your alternative?

5. Your firm collects $10 million per year. If interest rates are 6 percent, what is the value of speeding your collections by one day?

6. Again assume that your firm collects $10 million per year and that interest rates are 6 percent. A bank is trying to sell you a cash-management system. A lock box system will cost $20,000 per year, but should speed your accounts receivable by three days on average. What would be the savings (or extra cost) of adopting the lock box system?

7. With $10 million in collections per year and interest rates of 6 percent, would your firm be interested in paying $100,000 per year for a concentration banking system that would speed your collection of accounts receivable by five days? What would be the extra savings or cost?

8. Compare the lock box and concentration banking alternatives of Problems 6 and 7. Which is preferable? Why?

9. For a large retailer, credit sales are typically $1 million per day and the collection period is 31 days. What is the average level of accounts receivable?

10. Assume that you can reduce your firm's average level of accounts receivable by $1 million and interest rates are 11 percent. What is the present value of the savings?

11. You owe $4,000 tax on your house and it is due on December 31. If you pay in November you will receive a 1 percent discount. If you pay in October you will receive a 2 percent discount. What specific days should you consider as possible payment dates?

12. For Problem 11, when should you pay if you are able to earn 11 percent per year on your funds? In this case, what is the cost (or benefit) of paying in October?

13. Again, when should you pay the tax if you can earn 15 percent per year on your funds? What is the cost of paying on the fifteenth of the month instead of the thirty-first?

14. You are a heavy credit card user, charging an average of $1,000 per month, but you always pay your monthly bill in full to avoid interest payments. Assuming you can earn 1 percent per month on your money, what would be the advantage of sending one payment ten days later than you normally do, but early enough to be on time? Assuming

that you go on charging $1,000 per month forever, what would be the present value of changing your policy to pay ten days later than you have been?

15. Interest rates are 15 percent per year, and you have an account with a $500,000 balance that earns no interest. Your banker wants to talk to you about a zero balance account instead. What is the largest fee per year that you would consider for such an account?

16. Your firm uses the Baumol model to determine the optimal cash balance. The interest rate, r, is 10 percent, the fixed cost, F, of acquiring new cash is $30 per transaction, and the total annual cash needs are $2 million. Construct a table showing the holding costs, the transaction costs, and the total costs for $20,000, $25,000, . . . , $45,000. Based on these numbers, give a close estimate of the maximum cash the firm should hold. Compare this estimate to the actual value using the Baumol formula.

17. A firm acquires $20,000 in cash each time it transacts, the holding costs are $2,000, and the transaction costs are $3,000. Find the average amount of cash, assuming the firm uses the Baumol model.

18. In the Miller-Orr model, show that the difference between the target cash level, Z, and the lower bound, L, is one-third of the difference between the upper and lower bounds.

CHAPTER 18

Accounts Receivable Management

accounts receivable
funds owed to the firm as a result of sales, but not yet collected

In this chapter we focus on the management of accounts receivable as we continue our discussion of techniques for managing working capital. **Accounts receivable** are funds owed to the firm as a result of sales. They arise naturally from the conduct of business. Essentially every sale the firm makes that is not for cash gives rise to an accounts receivable.

Most firms extend credit to customers for the period between the time the goods or services are delivered and the time the funds are collected. Managers must decide to whom, and under what conditions, credit should be extended, generally restricting it to individuals with a certain income level and specifying when they should pay. The management of accounts receivable also includes the management of collection procedures for customers who do not pay promptly.

MANAGING CREDIT

☞ Any sale with delayed payment generates an accounts receivable.

Any sale that is made without immediate payment generates an account receivable. In general, firms prefer immediate payment, but it is often impossible to avoid accounts receivable. Customary practice often requires firms to ship goods and allows the customer to pay later. In such cases firms will find it very difficult to demand immediate payment. Along the same lines, allowing a customer to defer payment for some period is often necessary to secure a sale.

The total amount the firm invests in accounts receivable depends on the annual credit sales, S, and on the average collection period, ACP, as follows:

$$\text{Accounts receivable} = \frac{S}{365} \times \text{ACP} \qquad (18.1)$$

☞ The credit policy must balance the value of increasing sales through credit with the costs of uncollectible accounts.

Suppose a firm has annual credit sales of $730,000 and allows its customers to pay in 30 days. It must make an investment in accounts receivable equal to:

$$\text{Accounts receivable} = \frac{\$730,000}{365} \times 30 = \$2,000 \times 30 = \$60,000$$

463

To understand why the investment must be $60,000, suppose the firm starts operating today. Since it sells $2,000 on credit every day and customers take 30 days to pay, after 30 days it will have a total of $60,000 in its accounts receivable. On day 31, and every day thereafter, the firm sells another $2,000 on credit, but the accounts receivable level does not increase because the first day's credit customers pay the $2,000 they owed. As a result, the new credit sales exactly offset the payment of the accounts due, and the accounts receivable level remains stable at $60,000, as long as the credit sales level does not change.

Because the firm makes a significant investment by extending credit to a customer, it must have a credit policy to control the investment. A **credit policy** is the set of principles that govern the extension of credit to customers. It must address three related issues. First, to whom will credit be granted? Through its **credit standards** the firm specifies the conditions that customers must meet. Second, for how long will credit be granted and in what amounts? The **credit period** is the time for which the firm grants credit. Third, what actions will be taken against customers who abuse credit? The **collections policy** is a set of guidelines that specifies the action to take against delinquent accounts. We consider each of these parts of the firm's credit policy.

Credit Standards

In granting credit, a firm takes a risk because there is a certain probability that the customer will not pay. In setting credit standards, the problem is to grant credit to the right customers, even though the firm lacks complete information about them. The initial tendency is to be very rigorous in applying high standards. If the firm restricts credit to customers whom it considers absolutely safe, it will not oblige many potentially valuable customers. Such a severe policy results in lost sales and lower profits. At the other extreme, if the firm sets its standards too loosely, it grants credit to many customers who will never pay and it will incur losses.

As usual in finance, the problem is one of balancing the benefit of profits from additional sales against the cost from increasing bad debts. In principle, the firm must choose standards that maximize the difference. This principle is clear, but the difficult task is to find the right set of credit standards.

Of course, the firm will grant credit to some customers and deny it to others, basing this decision on the probability that people will or will not pay. Again, it is not necessary or even convenient to be exceedingly strict in this matter. Some firms can afford to be more lenient than others, depending on the products they sell, the cost of money to them, and the credit period allowed.

To understand how these variables affect the decision, consider a customer who purchases a product worth S that the firm acquired for C. The cost of money for the firm is r percent per year, and the customer is allowed to pay T days after the purchase date. If the customer has a probability p of

---

credit policy
the set of principles that govern the extension of credit to the firm's customers

credit standards
the conditions that customers must meet in order to be granted credit

credit period
the length of time for which credit will be granted

collections policy
a set of guidelines that specifies the action to take against delinquent accounts

paying the S, and probability $(1 - p)$ of not paying at all at the end of the T days, the firm's expected revenue at the end of the credit period is:

$$E(\text{Revenue}) = S \times p + 0 \times (1 - p) = S \times p$$

To obtain this expected revenue, the firm must invest $\$C$ today. As with any investment decision, it expects the credit-granting decision to have a positive NPV, that is:

$$E(\text{NPV}) = -C + \frac{Sp}{1 + \left(\dfrac{rT}{365}\right)} > 0$$

This expression can be solved for the probability of payment, p, that is required to make the decision profitable for the firm:

$$p > \left(\frac{C}{S}\right)\left(1 + \frac{rT}{365}\right) \tag{18.2}$$

Inequality 18.2 provides insight into the main factors that determine the firm's credit-granting decision. It says that only customers deemed to have sufficiently high probability of paying will be allowed credit. Since the right-hand side of the inequality contains firm-specific variables, different companies will adopt different standards. For example, Inequality 18.2 states that a firm with a higher cost as a percentage of sales, C/S, will be stricter in granting credit than one with a lower value of C/S. This makes sense because firms with slim profit margins cannot afford to have too many of its credit customers default. Similarly, the higher a company's cost of money and the greater the credit period, the tougher it will be in granting credit.

EXAMPLE 18.1

Al wants to buy a washer and dryer on credit at Sears. The price of both machines is $S = \$800$, and their combined cost to Sears is $C = \$500$. Sears' cost of money is $r = 12$ percent, and the credit period is $T = 90$ days. If Al has a 60 percent probability of paying, should he be granted the credit?

According to Inequality 18.2, Sears should grant credit to any customer with a minimum probability of payment of 64.35 percent, as shown below:

$$p > \left(\frac{\$500}{\$800}\right)\left(1 + \frac{0.12 \times 90}{365}\right) = 64.35\%$$

Since Al does not meet this requirement, Sears should deny him credit.

Information and Credit Standards   We have seen that firms allow credit based on the perceived probability that the customer will pay. To estimate this probability and make better credit decisions, they gather information on

FINANCE TODAY

Your Credit Is Approved

Asked what it takes for a prospect to pass a credit check, a salesman at one of Urcarco Inc.'s used-car lots in Houston replies with a laugh, "A down payment." It's a funny line, unless you're a Urcarco shareholder.

The Fort Worth–based company's stock has been skyrocketing lately, giving it a market value of $640 million, and a price/earnings ratio of 33, more than twice the market's P/E ratio. Anyone surprised that the car business could be so good should remember that Urcarco is really a bank—or, more precisely, a pawnshop. It borrows money cheap and lends money dear, collateralized by personal property.

Urcarco's prospectus explicitly states that it welcomes customers with poor credit records and little cash. It requires modest down payments, usually $1,000 or less, and aims to more than offset its higher risks by marking up the cars a lot. However, since the small down payment mostly goes immediately out the door for sales tax, title and transfer fees, and insurance, Urcarco basically finances 100 percent of its sales.

A typical "note lot" used-car dealer—that is, one who does its own financing—might pay $1,500 to buy and fix up a used car and then sell it for maybe $3,000. Terms: a $1,000 down payment and a two-year loan for $2,000 at 22 percent per annum. That means the dealer has $500 in "money on the street," a key industry measure of exposure to risk. The $440 interest earned on the $500 investment is a very nice rate of return. That's the traditional way of doing business.

Here's Urcarco's way: they pay maybe $4,000 to buy and fix up a late-model used car, and then they resell it for $8,000. The down payment is still $1,000, but the loan runs for three years or more. So for a longer time,

☞ Gathering information helps the firm to establish better credit standards, but information is costly to acquire.

prospective credit customers. Information is costly to obtain, so companies must also weigh its benefits against its costs. For example, magazine publishers normally grant credit to subscribers without gathering any information on their creditworthiness. Why? Because the magazine and the subscription bill are sent at about the same time, so management can discover quite quickly which customers will not pay. The only risk exposure is the cost of a few magazines. If gathering information on subscribers costs more than the amount the firm is risking by granting the credit, it clearly does not pay to go after the information.

If the amounts involved are large and credit is likely to be granted repeatedly, it may be advisable for a firm to gather information about a potential customer. Standard & Poor's, a major financial publisher, specializes in obtaining and selling such data. In addition to purchasing information,

Urcarco has $3,000 in "money on the street"—several times the industry average.

According to some Texas dealers, Urcarco is using some extremely aggressive accounting policies, too. For example, to account for disappearing customers and cars, Texas dealers set aside 25 to 30 percent of sales. In contrast, Urcarco recently took a provision of just 18 percent of sales. Had Urcarco set aside 30 percent of sales, its earnings would have dropped significantly, and its P/E really would be a stratospheric 170.

Nearly half the assets of Urcarco are accounts receivable—the principal amount owed on the 20,000 or so cars Urcarco has financed to date. The company values these accounts receivable at $89\frac{1}{2}$ cents on the dollar. This contrasts with the normal figure of 80 to 90 cents for used-car dealerships. Urcarco's current repossession rate is between 22 and 33 percent, depending on who's talking.

Still in its development stage, Urcarco is not self-sustaining. Its latest prospectus says the company requires between $6 million and $8 million of cash each month "from sources other than its operations." That means borrowing money or floating stock. Without such sources, Urcarco would have been flat out of cash already. Clearly, the motivation is great to sell new stock issues. For example, a recent $100 million offering that successfully flogged across the United States and Europe was a bravura show. The company has already hinted broadly that the insiders, who control some 35 percent of Urcarco's stock, may sell at least some of their stakes as restrictions are lifted. If they can get even close to the stock's current price, it's a pretty good bet some insiders will take their money and run.

Source: William P. Barrett, "It's Legal, but Is It Smart?" *Forbes*, June 25, 1990, pp. 126–127.

firms often ask for information directly from potential customers. For instance, it is not unusual to ask a credit applicant to provide a financial statement or to complete a questionnaire.

credit scoring model
a statistically verified equation that predicts future payment performance

In many cases, particularly for consumer credit, firms use a **credit scoring model,** which is a statistically based equation that predicts future payment performance. The firm asks the potential customer to provide information about age, marital status, occupation, time at last residence, time at last job, income, home ownership, telephone number, and so on. Each answer contributes to a total credit score. If the score is large enough, the firm grants credit.

Analyzing Credit Firms should gather as much information as necessary to establish the probability of payment with a reasonable degree of accuracy.

Figure 18.1 presents an example of how to conduct credit analysis at three different levels. First, an applicant who has a good credit history may be accepted immediately, because the customer has a demonstrated high probability of payment. If the customer's credit history is insufficient to determine the probability of payment, the firm may ask for detailed information so that it can assess the risk more accurately. A person with a bad credit history may be turned down because the probability of payment is estimated to be below the minimum the firm requires. Regardless of the data it acquires, the company

FIGURE 18.1 Sequential Credit Analysis

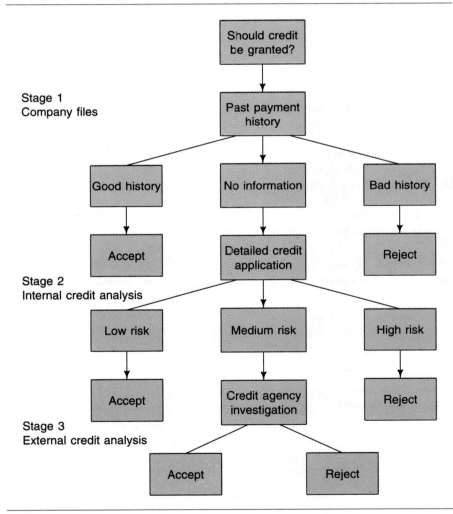

Source: Adapted from *Guide to Working Capital Management* by Keith V. Smith. Copyright © 1979 by McGraw-Hill Book Company. Reprinted by permission.

FINANCE

TODAY

Plastic Receivables

Thanks to the invention of the credit card, no American is too poor to acquire a small fortune in debt. U.S. consumers were carrying $279 billion in obligations on their credit cards as of February [1991]. To exploit that vast market, credit card companies are offering ever more imaginative inducements to pull out the plastic.

Latest example: Citibank, which [in April 1991] announced "Citibank Price Protection" for its 30 million MasterCard and Visa holders. The program guarantees that if you buy something with a Citibank card and see the item advertised at a lower price within 60 days, Citibank will refund the difference.

Not surprisingly, the deal comes with a number of restrictions. The lower price must be documented with a bona fide print advertisement, and Citibank's generosity has limits: no more than $250 for any individual claim or $1,000 in total claims in any year.

Will the come-on be expensive for Citibank? Maybe, but don't worry. According to the *Nilson Report*, a California-based industry newsletter, the company made $600 million in pure profit from its credit card business [in 1990], far more than from all its other operations combined. For competing issuers as well, credit cards are still so temptingly profitable that more customer-pleasing promotions are almost certainly on the way.

Source: "When the Price Isn't Right," *Time*, April 15, 1991, p. 45.

may accept low-risk applicants directly and reject high-risk applicants without further investigation.

The final step is to call for a credit investigation by an outside agency of applicants whose probability of payment is still uncertain. The firm takes this step only after it exhausts less expensive means of determining the applicant's creditworthiness, and if the potential profit from the sale justifies the cost of the investigation.

A Quantitative Approach to Granting Credit   As mentioned above, some firms use a credit scoring model to determine whether credit should be granted. Usually, this is a statistical method called discriminant analysis. Although the mathematical derivation of a discriminant score is fairly complicated, the idea is clear. The discriminant score should be used to discriminate between good payers and nonpayers. Given enough data on past payment performance and the characteristics of the potential customer, it is possible to compute a statistical model of the following form:

$$\text{Score} = a_1 F_1 + a_2 F_2 + \ldots$$

FIGURE 18.2   Discriminant Score Distributions for Good and Bad Payers

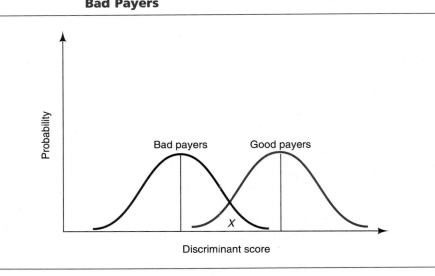

where a_i = a statistically determined weight for variable i

F_i = financial variable $i = 1, 2, \ldots$

In this model, the F_i terms are variables, such as the debtor firm's liquidity, debt equity ratio, or some other item that helps separate good payers from bad. The a_i terms are statistically estimated using the historical data on the two types of customers. Figure 18.2 shows how discriminant scores might be distributed. Good payers tend to have higher scores than bad payers, although there are clearly some exceptions. The lender's problem is to select an appropriate cutoff discriminant score on which the decision to grant credit will be based.

In Figure 18.2, the two distributions overlap. This means it is impossible to use the discriminant score to separate the good from bad payers with complete accuracy. In other words, no matter how hard the firm tries to discriminate, it will always make some mistakes. For example, a firm applying for credit with a score falling in the range denoted by X in the figure could be either a good payer with a low score, or a bad payer with a high score. Therefore the firm must attempt to assess the costs of two types of mistakes: granting credit to a bad payer and denying credit to a good payer. If these costs can be quantified, they can enter the statistical model directly to compute the optimum cutoff score for the credit decision. Otherwise, management must exercise subjective judgment in selecting a cutoff score. In general, the discriminant score has proved very useful in helping firms establish good credit standards.

The Credit Period

☞ A longer credit period will increase sales, but will require greater investment in accounts receivable.

The credit policy also sets a credit period. Often the firm couples the choice of a credit period with the offer of a discount for very prompt payment. For example, it may state its credit terms in the form "2/10; net 30," which means that it offers a 2 percent discount if payment is received within 10 days of the invoice date, and requires the customer to pay the full amount within 30 days—the credit period—if the discount option is not taken. Clearly, the firm offers the discount to induce prompt payment.

The credit period and the offer of a cash discount work together and should be established to give the desired effect. With credit terms of 2/10; net 30, the purchaser should pay either on day 10 and take the 2 percent discount or pay the net amount on day 30. The seller offers a 2 percent discount to encourage the purchaser to pay 20 days early, but it must ask itself whether it is really worthwhile to accept 2 percent less to receive the funds promptly.

Which customers are likely to pay early? To answer this question, consider a customer with a 10 percent annual cost of money who has made a credit purchase of $1.00 with 2/10; net 30 terms. If this customer forgoes the early payment option 10 days after purchase, it retains the use of $0.98 for another 20 days. By investing this $0.98 for 20 days at a 10 percent annual rate, at the end of the credit period the customer will have $0.98[1 + 0.10 × (20/365)] = $0.9854. Since at that time the payment must be $1.00, more than the amount of money the customer could make with the $0.98, forgoing the early payment is not a wise decision. It is not hard to see that only customers who earn a relatively high annual interest on their money should forgo the early payment. In this example, all customers with a cost of money lower than 37.24 percent should take the 2 percent discount. This is seen by solving the following inequality:

$$\$0.98\left[1 + r\left(\frac{20}{365}\right)\right] < \$1.00$$

$$r < \left(\frac{0.02}{0.98}\right)\left(\frac{365}{20}\right) = 37.24\%$$

Since the vast majority of firms in the United States have a cost of money lower than 37.24 percent, the discount appears to provide a strong incentive for early payment. In fact, it may be too strong, since it may represent an unnecessarily high cost to the firm. In this case, the cost to the firm is precisely 37.24 percent. In general, the annual interest rate, r, associated with credit terms of d/n; net T is equal to:

$$r = \left(\frac{d}{1 - d}\right)\left(\frac{365}{T - n}\right) \tag{18.3}$$

The intuition for Equation 18.3 is as follows. The first term on the right-hand side represents the rate of interest the firm is giving to customers who pay early; that is, the 20-day rate is $0.02/0.98 = 2.04$ percent. The second term represents the number of $(T - n)$-day periods contained in one year. For the example, the number of 20-day periods in a year is $365/20 = 18.25$. The product of these two terms is the annual interest rate the firm pays by offering the early payment discount. Thus, the firm pays an interest rate of $2.04 \times 18.25 = 37.23$ percent, which is the answer we had before, except for rounding error.

In addition to the discount, the selling firm must also pay close attention to the credit period itself. Customary practice is important in choosing this, as is competitive pressure within a given industry, but the seller must be aware of the cost of granting credit for differing periods.

For example, consider a company that currently offers its customers terms of 2/10; net 30 and is considering extending the terms to 2/10; net 60. With a credit period of 60 days, there are several likely effects. First, the liberal time will attract some customers, so sales should increase. Second, the firm incurs a cost from its present customers, because now they will wait until day 60 to pay, instead of day 30. Third, a higher proportion of customers will choose to pay the net amount instead of taking the discount by paying early because the implied rate of interest is substantially lower. For terms of 2/10; net 30 the interest rate is 37.24 percent. If the firm changes its terms to 2/10; net 60, the interest rate is reduced to 14.90 percent, and customers who earn greater rates will not take the discount. Using Equation 18.3, the calculation is:

$$r = \left(\frac{0.02}{0.98}\right)\left(\frac{365}{50}\right) = 14.90\%$$

COLLECTIONS POLICY

Every company will have, and should have, some difficulty with bad debt expenses. No matter how carefully it screens customers for creditworthiness, some bad risks will slip through. Furthermore, if a firm could make its credit standards so severe that it has no bad debt loss, it would be making a mistake, because it must be turning away some potentially good customers. Since some credit-granting decisions turn out to be mistakes, every firm must plan to collect late accounts.

The accounts receivable aging schedule is one technique to determine when to proceed with collecting past due accounts. It classifies accounts according to the amount of time they have been outstanding. Table 18.1 illustrates an aging schedule for a hypothetical customer.

If this customer received a credit period of 60 days, the account has $75 overdue. However, it appears that this customer, although somewhat slow in paying, may intend to pay in full, as suggested by the zero balance of any

INTERNATIONAL PERSPECTIVES

Trade Receivables

Many countries conduct a sizable portion of their international trade on credit, thus generating trade receivables. The importance of trade receivables has increased in both absolute and relative terms in the recent past. Indeed, for nonbanking businesses in the United States, trade receivables have grown from 24 percent of all claims on foreigners in 1986 to more than 40 percent at the end of 1990. During that same period, the total dollar value of receivables owed by foreigners to these same firms grew from about $8.8 billion to about $12.5 billion. It is also not surprising to find that over 95 percent of commercial claims, including trade receivables, are payable in U.S. dollars; this percentage has remained stable over the recent past. Given the volatility of foreign currencies and the economic strength of the United States, clearly it would be unwise for most U.S. businesses to engage in credit trade using foreign currencies.

The following table gives the actual levels of trade receivables and the total commercial claims on foreigners that were reported by nonbanking business enterprises in the United States. All of the figures are in millions of U.S. dollars at the end of the period.

	1986	1987	1988	1989	1990*
Commercial claims (total)[†]	$9,992	$10,600	$12,166	$13,748	$14,271
Trade receivables	8,783	9,535	11,091	12,140	12,471

* September data.
[†] Includes trade receivables, advance payments, and other claims.

Source: Federal Reserve Bulletin, March 1991, p. A66.

TABLE 18.1 Aging Schedule for a Hypothetical Customer

Age (days)	Amount
0–30	$360.00
31–60	280.00
61–90	75.00
>90	0.00

purchases made more than 90 days ago. Perhaps the firm should send a mild letter reminding the customer to pay soon. This is an inexpensive option and, in this case, is likely to be effective.

Any collection effort is costly, so the problem is choosing the correct level. As the effort and expense increase, bad debt losses should decrease. In principle, the firm should incur these expenses up to the point that the benefits from the effort just equal the cost. One potential cost is driving away customers who could be profitable, even if they are slow payers, as in the case of the one illustrated in Table 18.1.

☞ The firm should be willing to incur collection expenses up to the point that the benefits from the collection effort just equal the cost.

To control expenses and to avoid antagonizing customers, firms usually employ a sequence of steps of increasing severity. These go from the simple letter or telephone call to the very expensive legal action.

Letters and Telephone Calls

The first action the firm usually takes to collect a late account is to send a letter. Usually the first letter is extremely polite and merely tells the customer that a payment is past due. It might even apologize in case the customer has already sent a check. If this first step is unsuccessful, the firm sends more mild letters. If these do not produce the desired payment, later ones adopt increasingly harsher tones, eventually confronting the customer with the possibility of a collection agency or legal action. At this point, many late customers choose to send the payment.

If letters fail to produce results, the firm can call the customer directly. Calls, particularly to people at their place of employment, often produce results. In general, they are likely to be more effective for individuals than for firms. However, some laws limit the kinds of calls that can be made; for example, late-night harassment is not allowed.

Collection Agencies

Collection agencies specialize in collecting overdue accounts. For a percentage of the amount they obtain, they agree to take over the attempt to collect money due. They typically use letters, telephone calls, and even personal visits. They also can threaten to damage the late payer's credit rating. Collection agencies have a fearsome reputation; therefore, turning an account over to one can bring quick results. However, the firm must be aware that it probably means the permanent loss of a customer.

Legal Action

As a final step, the firm can employ, or threaten to employ, legal action to collect overdue accounts. Calls from a lawyer or the serving of legal papers can often bring payment from even very stubborn late payers. This is essentially the final and most expensive collection technique. Because of its expense, most firms use it only for large debts.

SUMMARY

This chapter examined the management of accounts receivable. Accounts receivable are almost certain to arise in the ordinary conduct of the firm's business. Because they represent an investment of funds and an extension of credit, these assets must be managed carefully.

In particular, the firm must develop a credit policy that includes setting standards, developing policies about the credit period, and employing methods to collect past due accounts.

QUESTIONS

1. If a firm has no explicit credit policy, does that mean it will have no accounts receivable?
2. What are the three components of a credit policy?
3. A manager for your company is arguing that the firm should extend credit only to customers who are 100 percent sure to pay as promised. Is this reasonable? Explain.
4. In your firm's discussion about its new credit policy, you suggest that you should acquire complete information on the creditworthiness of customers. Is this reasonable? Explain what attacks might be made on this position.
5. What is a credit-scoring model? Explain how it might be used in making decisions about automobile financing.
6. If a firm expresses its credit period as 1/10; net 90, what does that mean?
7. In Question 6, what is the credit period?
8. If a firm extends its credit period but keeps everything else the same, what should happen to credit sales? What should happen to accounts receivable?
9. If the average collection period increases by 10 percent and the daily credit sales simultaneously decrease by 10 percent, what happens to the firm's total investment in accounts receivable?
10. If the average collection period increases by one day and the daily credit sales simultaneously decrease by $1,000, what happens to the firm's total investment in accounts receivable?
11. Explain the intuition behind Equation 18.1.
12. Explain the intuition behind Equation 18.3.

PROBLEMS

1. The LousyWord Corporation has annual credit sales of $2 million. The cost of its word processing software is $70 and the selling price is $230. What is LousyWord's accounts receivable level if the average collection period is 65 days?

2. The Empty Nest Corporation classifies customers according to the probability, p, that they will pay their accounts receivable. The firm sells chocolates, which carry a fat margin. In fact, the cost of chocolates is only 40 percent of the sales price. Empty Nest allows customers 90 days to pay and has an annual cost of money of 15 percent. To which customers, in terms of their probability of paying, should the firm deny credit?

3. Pecatoribus, Inc., determines that it will grant credit to all customers with a probability of payment of at least 70 percent. The firm earns a 35 percent contribution margin on its sales and allows 120 days to pay. What rate of interest does the firm earn on its investments?

4. Lya's Wedding Cakes, Inc., provides 60-day credit to newlywed customers. However, believing that it is easier to collect before the honeymoon spell is over, Lya offers a 3 percent discount on the $400 cakes if payment is made 30 days after the wedding. If 40 percent of her customers pay early and the rest pay in 60 days, what is Lya's investment in accounts receivable? Assume that Lya sells 5 cakes each day.

5. MicroMouse, Inc., offers credit terms of 1/10; net 30. Describe which customers will pay early, based on the customers' cost of money.

6. Chubby's Electric Supply sells on credit, and 20 percent of the accounts receivable balance has an age between 0 and 30 days; 40 percent has an age between 31 and 60 days; and the rest has an age between 61 and 90 days. Given this limited information, what is your best estimate of Chubby's average collection period? Assume that daily sales are constant.

7. Lito Graph, Inc., is not sure whether to offer credit terms of 1/10; net 30 or 2/15; net 60. If Lito's objective is to entice as many customers as possible to pay early, which of the options should it choose?

CHAPTER 19

Sources of Short-Term Financing

Set of funds used in the day to day working operations of a firm

In the previous chapters on working capital we examined various kinds of assets. In this chapter the focus turns to the various ways of financing working capital. In many cases, especially when working capital fluctuates seasonally, it is financed through short-term liabilities.

Short-term financing is important to all firms, but it becomes critically important when interest rates fluctuate. Often, short-term interest rates are lower than long-term rates and this helps firms save money. Also, many companies have a varying need for financing and find it cheaper to use some short-term financing during periods of peak demand. It is not surprising that a wide variety of alternatives is available. Some of the opportunities arise spontaneously from the normal conduct of business, and others must be negotiated. This chapter explains how firms use short-term sources of financing their working capital and surveys the major sources of these funds.

→ when interest rates are low, more long-term bonds.

THE RATIONALE FOR SHORT-TERM FINANCING

Historically, and particularly in recent years, interest rates have shown a strong tendency to fluctuate, as depicted in Figure 19.1. The rates on both short-term and long-term financing sources vary, with the former having greater volatility and generally being lower than the latter.

For a firm seeking long-term financing, corporate bonds are a major source. However, if interest rates are high, issuing a long-term bond and promising to pay a high interest rate over that period can be expensive. Therefore, firms often use short-term financing to bridge the period of high interest rates. **Bridge financing** is the use of a short-term source to cover a temporary need.

Short-term financing also assists companies with seasonal needs. In preparation for an intense selling season, many firms build inventories beyond the normal level, but after the season they may be left holding an unusually high level of accounts receivable. This often requires extra financing until those accounts receivable are converted into cash. In retailing, for example, over 25 percent of annual sales frequently occurs between Thanksgiving and

☞ Short-term financing is often used when long-term interest rates are unusually high.

bridge financing
the use of a short-term financing source to cover, or bridge, a temporary financing need

FIGURE 19.1 Fluctuating Interest Rates

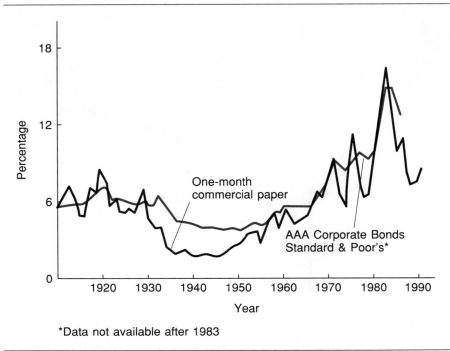

*Data not available after 1983

Source: Federal Reserve Historical Chart Book, 1989.

☞ Short-term financing is frequently used when a firm has certain seasonal financing needs.

Christmas. Rather than finance their pre-Christmas inventories with long-term sources, firms may use short-term financing to bridge this period of high need.

Figure 19.2 schematically depicts the asset structure of a firm with fluctuating levels of working capital. At the base are the long-term assets such as plant and equipment, which are constant through time. In addition it holds working capital, part of which is a permanent investment and is essential to the firm's operation. As we know, a certain level of cash, accounts receivable, and inventory is required for conducting normal business. The remaining working capital exhibits seasonal fluctuations and is the part that should be financed with short-term sources.

The firm must finance all of the assets shown in Figure 19.2, but it has a wide variety of strategies. For example, it can choose between long-term and short-term sources. It may be tempting to use a high proportion of short-term financing because it is often cheaper, but it involves risk as well. For example, if the firm uses a three-month loan it must renew that loan every three months. This raises the possibility that the firm might eventually be unable to secure the needed funds and thus be unable to meet its debt payment.

FIGURE 19.2   Firm Assets with Seasonal Fluctuation

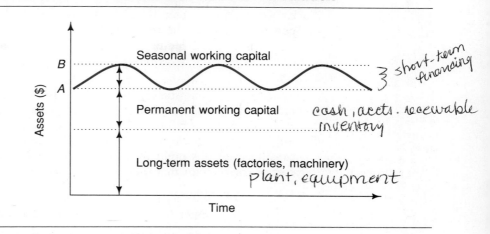

Handwritten notes: "short-term financing", "cash, accts. receivable inventory", "plant, equipment"

☞ The firm must determine the appropriate mix between short-term and long-term financing.

As a result, a major financing decision is to set the mix between short-term and long-term financing.

A very conservative policy uses long-term financing for all assets. In this case, the company would not face the potential embarrassment of having to secure short-term financing. This policy is represented in Figure 19.2 by the financing level B. A more aggressive policy, and one designed to achieve greater economy in financing cost, would be to finance all seasonal fluctuations of working capital with short-term sources. In this case, the amount of long-term financing is represented by point A.

In practice, very few firms follow the conservative strategy represented by point B. The two major reasons for this are that it is too expensive, and it ignores some of the cheap short-term sources that are readily available. For example, some sources arise spontaneously from the firm's normal operations, and the main question becomes how much to use. The answer depends largely on the firm's willingness to accept risk.

TRADE CREDIT

In Chapter 18 we noted that accounts receivable arise spontaneously in the conduct of business, because any credit sale generates a receivable. Whenever a firm has a receivable, it is extending credit to some other party. For every receivable that one firm has, some other firm has an account payable. Just as receivables arise spontaneously for each firm, so do accounts payable.

trade credit
credit that a firm receives when it buys a good or service without paying cash

An account payable is generated from **trade credit,** which a firm receives when it buys a good or service without immediately paying cash. Because it did not pay cash, it has the use of funds on credit from the time it receives the good until it makes final payment.

The Cost of Trade Credit

As we saw in Chapter 18, if the terms of the sale are d/n, net T, then the percentage cost of the trade credit is:

$$\text{Cost of trade credit} = \frac{d}{1-d} \times \frac{365}{T-n} \tag{19.1}$$

☞ Forgoing the discount offered on trade credit is equivalent to borrowing funds at the rate implied by the credit terms.

In most circumstances, taking the discount is better, unless short-term rates are very high or the firm direly needs short-term financing and is unable to secure a cheaper source. In any event, the manager should be aware that forgoing the discount for early payment usually carries a very high cost. We can illustrate this point by considering the following credit terms and the cost of trade credit that they imply:

Credit Terms	Annual Cost of Trade Credit
2/10; net 30	37.2%
1/10; net 30	18.4
2/10; net 45	21.3
2/10; net 60	14.9

Thus far we have seen that it is always wise to pay on either the last day of the discount period or the last day of the net period. Normally, it pays to take the discount, but this decision depends on the implied cost of trade credit relative to other sources of short-term financing. One other strategy requires consideration.

Stretching Accounts Payable

stretching accounts payable
delaying payment beyond the credit period

Some firms may not take the prompt payment discount and not pay the net amount by the due date. They may adopt a policy of **stretching accounts payable,** delaying payment beyond the credit period. In effect, this is a unilateral extension of the credit period against the wishes of the selling firm.

Consider a firm that buys goods on the terms of 2/10; net 30 and pays the full amount on day 90. In doing so, it violates the credit terms offered by the supplying firm, but it receives financing for the period from day 10 to day 90 by forgoing the discount. For such a firm, the implied cost of trade credit is 9.3 percent:

$$\text{Cost of trade credit} = \frac{0.02}{1-0.02} \times \frac{365}{90-10} = 9.3\%$$

Financing at a cost of 9.3 percent may be very attractive, but chronically paying late is certain to irritate suppliers. In extreme cases, the supplier may refuse to ship to the offending firm or require payment before shipping. The cost of bad relations with suppliers is difficult to quantify, but it is real.

FINANCE

TODAY

Lost and Not Found

Within limits, the stretching of accounts payable is clearly desirable. Delaying payments constitutes a form of financing, because the debtor has the use of funds while the payment is being delayed. Often firms adopt intentional payment-stretching practices. In other instances, the firm's creditors help by making it difficult for a firm with the best intentions to pay promptly.

Experts estimate that more than $1 billion is owed but unclaimed for stock dividends and bond interest. Estimates in this area are difficult to make with precision, but consider the recent experience of New York and California. After funds deposited with banks are left dormant for a certain period, the accounts typically revert to the state. For example, in California if an account shows no activity for seven years, the money in the account reverts to the state under "escheat requirements." In New York, the period is three years. In a recent year the government of New York received $162 million and California $50 million. These figures imply almost $1 billion of unclaimed funds in just these two states. The U.S. Treasury holds over $2.5 billion of matured non-interest-bearing debt securities on its books.

Often problems arise with bond interest payments and dividend payments. Owners move, die without leaving adequate records, cannot be found, and move without leaving a forwarding address. For example, Pacific Bell owes Richard Nixon $52.50 from 1979 but says it cannot locate him at his last known address in San Clemente.

Firms such as **Markham Company Research Services** of New York and **Keane Tracers** of Bala Cynwyd, Pennsylvania, exist to find people to whom money is owed and to help them get paid, in return for a commission. Markham employs 50 people to search for lost creditors and collects a commission as large as 50 percent of the recovered funds.

What happens to all of this money until it is finally paid to the rightful owner? Usually the debtor has use of the funds. Small wonder that debtor firms may not try too hard to find the payees. In the meantime, the funds that cannot be paid provide a very low-cost source of financing.

Source: Ben Weberman, "Finders, Keepers," *Forbes,* March 23, 1987.

Your Bankruptcy Is Preapproved

The government is deeply in debt, many corporations are deeply in debt, and the American consumer is in deep trouble. American consumers owe $3.2 trillion on credit cards, car loans, and mortgages; the average household owes about $35,000 a year. Nearly 18 percent of consumers' disposable income is eaten up servicing that debt.

Yet at a time when lenders are extremely wary of business borrowers, they are less reluctant to lend to consumers. Unsolicited offers for unsecured credit still arrive regularly. One such offer was recently mailed to a stockbroker in New England with this urging: "Apply and get up to $20,000 or more with just your signature—no collateral is needed."

Are consumers, spurred on by easy credit, spending themselves into personal bankruptcy? In 1990 a record 720,000 persons filed for personal bankruptcy, up nearly 17 percent over 1989. In part thanks to liberalized personal bankruptcy laws, the number of personal bankruptcies has been rising steadily since the early 1980s, even without a recession.

In 1988 personal bankruptcy losses totaled $12 billion, according to Kenneth Crone, director of Visa USA's bankruptcy recovery program. The number of bankruptcies should jump this year, and so will losses. For now, there's little lenders can do about it. Among the biggest consumer lenders are banks like Citicorp and Chase Manhattan. Citicorp's worldwide $110 billion (assets) consumer lending operations in 1990 generated an estimated $1.1 billion in profits, up from $842 million in 1989. Two-thirds of Citicorp's consumer profits in 1990 came from its credit cards. Chase's consumer operations earned about $350 million in 1990, up from $300 million the year before.

ACCRUED EXPENSES

accrued expense
an expense that has been incurred but has not yet been paid

Accrued expenses provide another source of spontaneous short-term financing. Arising from the normal conduct of business, they are expenses that have been incurred but have not been paid. One of the largest is likely to be employees' accrued wages. For an employee paid at the end of the month for work performed during that month, the firm has the use of those wages for the entire month. Assuming that an employee earns $2,000 per month, the firm holds $1,000 of those wages on average each month. With interest rates of 12 percent, the firm can earn $120 per year on this employee's accrued wages. If the firm paid this same employee a biweekly wage of $1,000, it would only hold an average of $500 in accrued wages for this individual. Then it could earn only $60 per year on the accrued wages. The pattern of

For some money center banks, consumer lending probably accounts for well over half their profits. On credit cards alone, banks with large loan portfolios can earn returns of 2 percent on assets, more than three times the profitability of business loans. However, this profitability will ebb as loan losses and delinquencies rise. Even American Express's high-quality credit card operations may feel some pressure: Amex's loan charge-offs could rise by $75 million in 1991.

All this is, of course, fodder for bill collectors. Two are publicly traded: Union Corp. and Payco American, each with over $70 million in revenues. Union's management expected 1991 to be a very good year but not necessarily a great year. Why? Because in a recession, recoveries decline, and with them the profits from dunning delinquents.

What do a beleaguered borrower's finances look like shortly before filing for bankruptcy? Darold Hoops, senior vice president of MasterCard International, undertook an analysis of the financial condition of 260 bankrupt borrowers three months before they filed for personal bankruptcy. Bankrupt borrowers carried three bank cards with a total of $7,775 outstanding, plus another 15 credit lines—such as retail credit, cars, gasoline and home equity loans. Each had a total debt balance of $46,000.

Most disquieting: The borrowers had been current on their loans for nearly six years on average. Then, with little warning, they filed for bankruptcy. That undercuts the widely held assumption that a mature consumer credit portfolio is pretty safe.

How many such bankrupts-to-be are out there today? No one knows. No wonder lenders are worried.

Source: Howard Rudnitsky, "An Excess of Plastic," *Forbes,* February 4, 1991, pp. 55–56.

accrued wages over time for monthly and biweekly payment is shown graphically in Figure 19.3.

For large companies, accrued wages constitute an important source of financing. For example, a firm that has 40,000 employees paid monthly, with an average salary of $2,000 per month, has the use of $40 million in accrued wages, on average. If it invests this average amount over one year at an interest rate of 12 percent, it will earn $4.8 million.

Usually, accrued expenses are not subject to much managerial manipulation. Switching employees from weekly to monthly pay would generate a larger amount of accrued wages but may prove costly by irritating employees. Although these expenses confer a benefit to the firm and are a readily available source of financing, it is very difficult to increase them as a financing source.

FIGURE 19.3   Accrued Wages with Monthly and Biweekly Payments

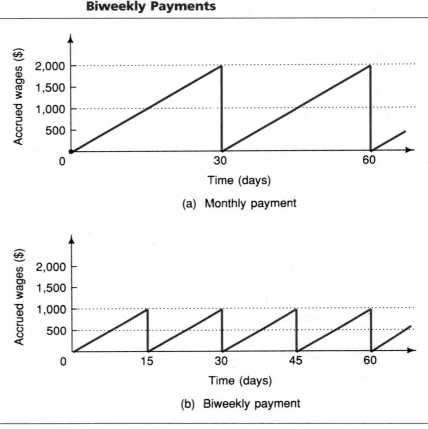

(a) Monthly payment

(b) Biweekly payment

UNSECURED SHORT-TERM BANK LOANS

unsecured loan
a loan made on the good credit of the borrower, without the borrower offering any special security to the lender

secured loan
a loan in which the borrower gives the lender the right to seize certain assets if payments are not made as promised

An important negotiated source of short-term financing comes in the form of unsecured bank loans. An **unsecured loan** is made on the good credit of the borrower, without the borrower offering any special security to the lender. By contrast, a **secured loan** is one in which the borrower gives the lender the right to seize certain assets if the borrower does not pay as promised.

To receive an unsecured loan, a firm must usually establish a good relationship with the bank by holding funds in the bank for checking accounts and other purposes. Also, a secured loan may often precede a request for an unsecured loan. For example, the bank may first finance some equipment, using the equipment itself to secure the loan. If the firm pays the loan satisfactorily, the bank may be willing to provide an unsecured loan in the future.

promissory note
a legal document in which a borrower promises to make certain payments for a loan

The borrower and the bank agree on the terms of an unsecured loan; that is, the amount, the time the loan is to be outstanding, the interest rate, and the exact payment terms. Once they agree, they execute a **promissory note,** which is a legal document that specifies all the terms of the loan.

COMPENSATING BALANCES

compensating balance
a proportion of a loan that a bank requires the borrower to maintain on deposit with the bank in a noninterest-bearing account

☞ The requirement of a compensating balance raises the effective cost of a bank loan.

Banks often require the borrower to maintain a portion of the loan amount on deposit in an account that does not earn interest. This deposit is a **compensating balance.** By requiring it, the bank raises the effective cost of the loan. For example, if a bank grants a borrower a one-year loan for $100 and requires that 10 percent be left as compensating balance, the borrower effectively receives $90; however, the borrower must still pay interest on the full $100. If the stated rate of the loan is 12 percent, then at the end of the year the borrower must pay $12 for the privilege of using $90 over one year. This represents an annual interest rate of $12/$90 = 13.33 percent.

In general, the effective rate of interest for a loan with a compensating balance is:

$$\text{Effective rate} = \frac{\text{interest rate } (\%)}{1 - \text{compensating balance } (\%)} \qquad (19.2)$$

We can use Equation 19.2 to solve this. As the following calculation shows, this results in an effective rate of interest of 13.33 percent, just as we found before:

$$\text{Effective rate} = \frac{0.12}{1 - 0.10} = 13.33\%$$

THE LINE OF CREDIT

Unsecured bank loans can be an expensive source of short-term funds, so firms try to avoid them. However, they can be an extremely important source of funds when unanticipated short-term financing difficulties arise. If the need for funds is acute, most firms are glad to know that money is available.

line of credit
a commitment by a financial institution to lend a certain amount of funds to a given borrower on demand

Many firms get around the need to use bank loans by establishing a line of credit. A **line of credit** is a commitment by a bank to lend to a firm a certain amount of funds on demand. Thus the company knows that it can borrow a given amount anytime it needs. Because this is a valuable service, and because being sure that the funds are available to lend is costly, banks charge a **commitment fee** for holding open a line of credit. Usually, it is a percentage of the loan amount and is charged even if the customer does not borrow any money. Normally, it is in the order of 0.5 to 1 percent of the committed amount.

commitment fee
a charge banks make for holding open a line of credit for a customer

How Treasury Bills Are Auctioned

Each week the U.S. Treasury uses the discriminatory auction to sell Treasury bills to major buyers. On Tuesday the Treasury announces, via the Federal Reserve Banks, the amount of 91-day and 182-day bills it wishes to sell on the following Monday and invites tenders (bids) for specified amounts of these bills. Tenders are due by 1:00 P.M. Eastern time on the Monday after the announcement, and the Treasury usually publicizes the results later that afternoon. The bills are issued to the successful bidders on Thursday.

Two different types of bids can be submitted in the T bill auction: competitive and noncompetitive. Competitive bidders include money market banks, dealers, and other institutional investors who buy large quantities of T bills. The tenders they submit indicate the amount of bills they wish to purchase and the price they are willing to pay. They are permitted to submit more than one tender. Noncompetitive bidders are usually small or inexperienced bidders who indicate the amount of bills they want to purchase (up to $1 million) and agree to pay the quantity weighted average of the accepted competitive bids.

After all bids are in, first the Treasury sets aside the amount of bills requested by the noncompetitive bidders. The remainder is allocated among the competitive bidders, beginning with those who bid the highest price, until the total amount is issued. The price paid by the noncompetitive bidders can then be calculated based on the competitive bids that were accepted.*

The Treasury bill auction is more complicated than the standard discriminatory auction since the noncompetitive bids are satisfied in full. Consequently, when submitting their bids, the major buyers do not know the exact amount being auctioned to them. During 1987, an average of around $14 billion of Treasury bills were auctioned each week.

* See James F. Tucker, *Buying Treasury Securities at Federal Reserve Banks* (Richmond, VA: Federal Reserve Bank of Richmond, February 1985), for further details.

Source: Business Review, March–April 1988, p. 7.

REVOLVING CREDIT AGREEMENTS

revolving credit agreement
an agreement under which a lender makes some amount of funds available to a customer on a continuing basis

Often a bank extends a **revolving credit agreement** in which it makes some amount of funds available to the customer on a continuing basis. For example, if the line of credit under a revolving credit agreement is $1 million and the firm borrows $800,000, it still has guaranteed access to $200,000. If the firm repays $500,000, reducing its debt to $300,000, it has $700,000 available.

In most respects, this agreement is similar to bank credit cards for consumers. These cards, such as Visa and MasterCard, typically work like a line of credit. The borrower cannot borrow more than the credit line, but is free to borrow up to that amount at any time. As the earlier loans are repaid, more of the line of credit is available for future borrowing.

SECURED SHORT-TERM FINANCING

collateral
assets pledged by a borrower as security for a loan

In addition to unsecured short-term borrowing, most firms have access to secured short-term financing. With a secured loan the borrower gives the lender a claim on some specific asset. This asset is the **collateral** for the loan.

In some cases, the lender may actually take possession of the collateral until the borrower satisfies the terms of the loan. This is common if the collateral is transportable and can be stored, such as stocks or bonds. In other cases, legal documents provide evidence of the claim. To obtain a secured loan, a firm must be able to pledge specific collateral of obvious value. Generally this is either receivables or inventory.

Accounts Receivable

Because of the obvious value of receivables, firms can use them as a way to obtain funds immediately. They can use accounts receivable in two basic ways: by pledging them as collateral, or by selling them outright.

pledging accounts receivable
using accounts receivable as collateral for a loan

Pledging Accounts Receivable   Using accounts receivable as collateral for a loan is **pledging accounts receivable.** To do this the firm must find a lender who can evaluate the quality of the receivables. Because the quality depends on the likelihood that the debtors will pay when promised, the lender typically is a financial institution with a credit department that can judge the risks associated with the receivables. It is helpful if the firm has had a continuing relationship with the lender, as this increases the likelihood that the lender is already familiar with the quality of the borrower's receivables.

When the borrowing firm pledges its receivables, it gives the lender a specific claim against those assets. It must also sign a promissory note, as in an unsecured loan, with the receivables acting as an extra guarantee that the funds will be repaid. Also, the borrower remains liable for the full payment of the loan even if it gives the receivables to the lender.

nonnotification basis
a method of pledging receivables in which the party owing the firm the receivables is not informed that the receivables have been pledged

notification basis
a method of pledging receivables in which the party owing the firm the receivables is informed that the receivables have been pledged

Pledging receivables can be a continuing process, with the firm presenting evidence of the receivables to the lender and receiving new funds periodically. The lender will lend only a fraction of the value of the receivables, thus ensuring that it will eventually receive full payment.

Although the lender has a claim on the receivables, ownership remains with the borrower. Only if the firm fails to pay on the loan as promised does the lender have the right to seize the collateral. Normally, a loan against the receivables is done on a **nonnotification basis.** That is, the lender does not inform the party owing the receivables that they have been pledged. If the loan is made on a **notification basis,** the lender informs the party owing the receivables that the borrowing firm has pledged the receivables, and that the borrower should send the payments directly to the lender.

factoring
the selling of accounts receivable

factor
the purchaser of accounts receivables in a factoring agreement

nonrecourse basis
a type of factoring agreement in which the factor purchases the receivables outright from the firm and bears the risk of collecting them

recourse basis
a type of factoring agreement in which the firm bears the risk of collecting the receivables

Factoring Accounts Receivable The firm can receive cash for its receivables by selling, or **factoring**, them. The purchaser is the **factor,** usually a financial institution. Often a bank will make a loan with the receivables as collateral or will be willing to act as a factor and buy them.

In purchasing the receivables, the factor pays some percentage of their full amount. Because the asset is a receivable, factoring typically involves both a sale of an asset and a loan. The factor receives title to the receivables, so this is a transfer of an asset. Although the firm expects to collect the receivables in the future, the factor pays immediate cash to the firm. Therefore, the transaction also involves aspects of a loan. The difference between the receivables due and the amount the factor pays for them depends on the quality of the receivables, the cost the factor expects to incur in collecting them, the time until the receivables are due, and the prevailing interest rate.

In a factoring arrangement a firm can sell receivables on a **nonrecourse basis;** that is, the factor buys the receivables outright from the firm and then collects them. Failure to collect them means a loss for the factor. With a nonrecourse agreement, the factor cannot demand any payment from the firm in the event that an account receivable is not paid, but bears the risk of collecting the receivables.

The firm can also sell receivables on a **recourse basis,** in which case it remains responsible for the receivables and, in effect, guarantees their collection. If the factor has difficulty collecting, it may have recourse to the firm to demand payment, so the firm continues to bear the collection risk. Naturally, there is a difference in the price the factor is willing to pay for the receivables, depending on whether the agreement is on a recourse or nonrecourse basis.

Inventory Loans

The attractiveness of inventory as collateral for a loan depends on how much real security it gives for the loan amount. If it can be converted into cash easily, it is more valuable as collateral than a less liquid inventory. Similarly, easily transportable inventory makes better collateral than inventory that is difficult to move. Finally, if it is easy to identify and control the inventory, it also makes better collateral. Because inventories are so diverse, there are several different ways to offer them as collateral.

lien
a claim against a set of assets

floating lien
a general claim against an entire class of assets, such as a certain type of inventory

Floating Lien A **lien** is a claim against a set of assets. With a **floating lien** the borrowing firm gives the lender a general claim against an entire class of assets. In inventory financing, this might include all inventory, present and future. A floating lien usually secures a loan when the items in inventory have small individual value and cannot be identified easily. It is also useful when items are moving in and out of inventory very rapidly. For example, the maker of electronic components may have thousands of circuit boards in stock that cannot be identified individually. If the boards are of little value individually and are going in and out of inventory rapidly, a floating lien would be the appropriate type of security agreement.

INTERNATIONAL PERSPECTIVES

A Brief History of Auctions

One of the earliest reports of an auction was by Herodotus, who described the bidding of men for wives in Babylon around 500 B.C.* This auction was unique, since bidding sometimes started at a negative price.† Some scholars interpret the biblical story of the sale of Joseph into slavery as an even earlier reference.‡ In ancient Rome, auctions were used in commercial trade and were held in the *atrium auctionarium*, where goods could be displayed prior to sale. Auctions were also used to liquidate property by Romans in financial straits. Caligula auctioned off family belongings to cover his debts and Marcus Aurelius held an auction of royal treasures to finance a state deficit. Plundered war booty was often sold at auction. The most notable auction in Rome was held in A.D. 193 when the Praetorian Guard put the whole empire up for auction. After killing the previous emperor, the guards announced they would appoint the highest bidder as the next emperor. Didius Julianus outbid his competitors, but after two months he was beheaded by Septimius Severus, who seized power (a winner's curse?). In China, auctions were used as early as the seventh century A.D. to sell the belongings of deceased Buddhist monks. In colonial America auctions were used to liquidate inventories, unload importers' unsold items at the end of the season, and sell secondhand furniture, farm equipment, and animals. Evidently the auction was considered a disreputable way of selling goods since the owner's name was usually concealed. The most infamous auctions in American history were the slave auctions held before the Civil War.

* Unless otherwise noted, the historical facts presented are from Ralph Cassady, Jr., *Auctions and Auctioneering* (Berkeley: University of California Press, 1967), Chapter 3.

† Martin Shubik, "Auctions, Bidding, and Markets: An Historical Sketch," in R. Engelbrecht-Wiggans, M. Shubik, and R. Stark, eds., *Auctions, Bidding, and Contracting: Uses and Theory* (New York: NYU Press, 1983), p. 39.

‡ Paul Milgrom, "Auction Theory," p. 1.

Source: "2,500 Years of Auctions . . . at a Glance," *Business Review*, March–April 1988, p. 4.

This example contrasts with that of a highway builder with several items of heavy equipment, such as bulldozers, that are easy to identify by their serial numbers. Furthermore, the equipment usually remains in inventory and each machine has a high value, so it is worthwhile to identify each one specifically. For the highway builder, the floating lien would not be the best security arrangement.

As these differences indicate, a floating lien is a relatively weak guarantee from the lender's point of view. If the lien is on items of relatively small individual worth, and if the items are hard to identify and easily transportable, the lender has little ability to enforce a claim on them. When possible, it is usually preferable to use another method of securing inventory as collateral.

Trust Receipts   When inventory items have serial numbers or are otherwise identifiable, the firm can use a trust receipt to guarantee a loan. A **trust receipt** is an agreement between the borrower and lender under which the borrower holds the goods in inventory and immediately forwards any proceeds from its sale to the lender.

Trust receipt financing is used extensively in the automotive industry, with the manufacturer acting as a lender to the dealer. The manufacturer knows that cars bearing certain serial numbers must be on the dealer's showroom floor, or the dealer must forward funds from the sale of the cars to the manufacturer. Because it is easier to inspect and enforce the collateral, this method of financing gives the lender a better form of security for an inventory loan than does a floating lien.

Warehouse Financing   Essentially, the greater control the lender has over inventory, the better the inventory can serve as collateral. We have already seen that trust receipts provide the lender with better collateral than floating liens. Of the prevailing kinds of collateral agreements for inventory financing, warehouse financing gives the lender the best collateral. Two basic types of warehouse financing agreements are available.

Under a **field warehousing agreement** the firm keeps the pledged inventory at the borrower's warehouse, but segregates it from other inventories. A warehouse company manages the segregation and then issues a **warehouse receipt** to verify that the pledged inventory resides in the warehouse and is stored separately. Only after the warehouse company issues the receipt does the lender advance funds. Furthermore, the warehouse company controls the pledged inventory and will not release it to the borrower until authorized to do so by the lender.

Compared with trust receipt financing, this kind of agreement gives the lender better control over the collateral because it is under the control of the warehouse company that acts as an agent of the lender. One drawback is the additional cost incurred by hiring the warehouse company.

Under this agreement the pledged inventory remains on the borrower's premises, even though it is under control of the warehouse company. The lender can have even more control over it by taking the collateral away from the borrower's premises. Under a **terminal warehousing agreement** the lender places the pledged inventory in a warehouse owned and operated by a warehousing company. Once it goes into the warehouse, the warehouse operator issues a receipt certifying that the specified goods are there. The lender then issues the loan funds to the borrower. The borrower cannot move the goods from the warehouse until the lender authorizes their removal. Thus the lender secures virtually complete control over the collateral and greatly increases the lender's safety. It is not surprising that lenders are willing to lend a greater percentage of the value of the inventory the more thoroughly they control it.

trust receipt
an agreement under which the borrower holds the goods in inventory and immediately forwards any proceeds from the sale of the inventory to the lender

field warehousing agreement
a security agreement for a loan in which the inventory is kept at the borrower's warehouse as security, but is segregated from the other inventories that are not pledged

warehouse receipt
a document verifying that pledged inventory is actually in the warehouse and is segregated from the company's other non-pledged inventories

terminal warehousing agreement
a security agreement in which the inventory that secures the loan is placed in a warehouse owned and operated by an independent warehousing company

Iraq's Stealth Financing

A grand jury investigation commenced in 1990 into the activities of Banca Nazionale del Lavoro's (BNL) Atlanta branch, in particular, agreements to grant $2.8 billion of unauthorized credits and guarantees to Iraq. The FBI, the Department of Agriculture (USDA) and the Office of the U.S. Attorney for the Northern District of Georgia took part in the investigation.

Investigations in Italy by the Italian secret service (SISMI) and by the Bank of Italy maintained that any illegal activity was confined to employees of the Atlanta branch, and did not involve either BNL headquarters in Rome or the BNL regional headquarters in New York. However, there were suggestions, one from the Italian finance minister Guido Carli, that this was not the whole story.

The Atlanta branch of BNL, which was headed by Christopher Drogoul, made unauthorized commitments and loans of $2.867 billion between the beginning of 1988 and the summer of 1989. This sum was on top of $900 million of authorized loans. The unauthorized loans were deliberately concealed from inspectors and auditors both inside and outside the bank. These funds took the form of loans to Iraqi banks, letters of credit to Western companies awarded contracts in Iraq, and direct transfers to other international banks for the same purpose.

About $720 million was disbursed to U.S. suppliers of agricultural produce to Iraq, almost all of which was guaranteed by the USDA's Commodity Credit Corporation (CCC). About $116 million worth of credits may have been used for arms purchases. The then vice president of the Atlanta branch, Paul von Wedel, alleged that Iraq planned to set up a bank in the United States or United Kingdom, financed by loans from BNL, to buy military technology.

Perhaps the most surprising aspect of the affair is the degree to which those responsible for arranging the credits managed to keep such a huge volume of business secret for so long. BNL's internal limits on global Iraqi exposure were exceeded several times over. New senior management was appointed at BNL, after president Nerio Nesi and director-general Giacomo Pedde resigned in August of 1989. From various accounts, the following points emerge:

- It was normal for trade-related business with Iraq to be passed through offices outside Italy even when the exporting companies were Italian. The reason was that some Iraqi customers had a record of nonpayment with Italian firms, and a number of cases had gone to court. BNL could not risk lending to these customers in Italy because of the danger that the courts would order the seizure of those customer's assets in the country. These would include any collateral held by banks against outstanding loans. It became routine, therefore, for enquiries concerning trade with Iraq to be passed to Atlanta.

(continued)

- Christopher Drogoul was an energetic and very able general manager, who had overseen a large increase in the volume of business handled by the Atlanta branch, which emerged as the most profitable in the United States. Trade finance was a target area of BNL internationally, and much of his effort was concentrated in that factor. The Iraqis were prepared to offer attractive interest rates, part of which BNL Atlanta was able to pass on to companies seeking export finance. Atractive terms helped to increase Atlanta's prominence. As a result, Drogoul was highly thought of by the BNL chiefs in Rome, and would have been given a relatively high degree of freedom.

- None of the major decision makers in the Atlanta branch were Italian, or had a record of long service with BNL. This increased the tendency to act unilaterally. Employees were also less likely to feel loyalty to the bank as a whole.

- BNL was overhauling its internal information and supervisory systems. These systems had been heavily criticized by inspectors from the Bank of Italy during the previous three years. The central bank complained in increasingly strong terms about the lack of precise information available, in particular about the activities of foreign branches, and BNL's long-term exposure.

- "Accounts were kept in such a way that they did not give the management an accurate picture of what the business of the bank actually was," said one Bank of Italy source. "A number of accounting and EDP [electronic data processing] procedures were put together at different times, so that the integration of all the different accounts had to be done manually, with a much greater chance of errors." In April 1989 the long-term credit operations of the bank were inspected, and found to be in chaos. "The examiners left the bank without making an assessment. They had to demand that the bank put things in order."

- BNL had attempted to address the situation, but the changes made to the internal reporting system at least temporarily made things worse. The Bank of Italy complained of "continuous delays in sending reports." All this made concealment easier.

- The Atlanta branch continued throughout this period to use computer and data-processing systems incompatible with those of the New York branch, despite several requests for them to update. This meant that Atlanta's records could not be readily accessed by the regional headquarters.

- Fund raising and lending were carefully synchronized to ensure that the large amounts of money moving from the interbank market to the Iraqi banks were not readily visible on BNL's books. While all other BNL branches in the United States (there are five in all) used Morgan Guaranty New York as their treasurer, BNL Atlanta used the local Morgan Guaranty branch. Money borrowed on the interbank market was paid into BNL Atlanta's correspondent account there, and then transferred on the same day to a BNL account in the name of the Central Bank of Iraq, which in turn would immediately pass on the funds to the final borrower. Both accounts therefore stood an excellent chance of being ignored by the inspectors, since they both reported a daily balance of 0. Bank of Italy investigators believe that documents coming in from creditor banks were systematically destroyed.

Given all the lengths to which the Atlanta branch went to conceal its Iraqi loans, it would seem illogical to suggest that BNL headquarters gave their assent to them, unless the intention was to fool the U.S. and Italian banking authorities. However, according to von Wedel, Drogoul assured him on at least one occasion that the business had been sanctioned in Rome. This statement is lent some support by the fact that a number of Italian companies supplying Iraq made enquiries at BNL's Rome headquarters about their trade finance arrangements with BNL Atlanta. Had these enquiries been examined, it would have been possible to see that Atlanta had exceeded its permitted limits on exposure to Iraq. However, given the administrative condition of BNL at the time, it is not beyond belief that this could have been missed.

Some $2.16 billion of credits remain outstanding on which Iraq is no longer paying interest. The bank is well enough provisioned to cope, but the loss of the principal would be less easy to swallow. The bulk of the loans will fall due around 1995.

Source: "Iraq's Unauthorised Billions," *Euromoney*, August 1990, pp. 32–34.

Electronic Paper

It wasn't all that long ago that corporate treasurers had to sign every commercial paper certificate by hand, before facsimile signatures became the norm. Now, the drive toward automation is taking a quantum leap forward: the certificates themselves are gradually being eliminated. The commercial paper market is making the long-awaited transition to a paperless, electronic book-entry system, with companies like AT&T, Boise Cascade, Borden, and Dow Chemical taking the lead.

Under a pilot program launched in October 1990 by The Depository Trust Co. (DTC), in New York City—the firm that developed electronic transfer for stocks and bonds—the majority of commercial paper transactions will slowly but surely be computerized over the following 12 to 15 months. By June of 1992, DTC expects to have roughly 60 percent of the market on-line.

So far, the actual transition to book entry has been pretty much "a non-event" from the issuer's side, says Richard H. Byrd, assistant treasurer at Borden Inc., in Columbus, Ohio. Issuers don't have to make any major changes to switch to book entry; they simply sign the DTC agreement to get into the system, sign an agreement with the issuing agent, and pay for a CUSIP (securities identification) number.

Nevertheless, the conversion to a book-entry system will eventually have considerable effect on both the issue and purchase of commercial paper, for companies of all sizes.

The Pilot Program   Electronic book entry will never be universal, notes James V. Reilly, the DTC vice president in charge of the pilot program. That's because the system will be restricted to issuers rated A-2/P-2 or better, as a means of limiting the chances that an issuer could become insolvent in the middle of the trading day. (In the unlikely event a default should occur, DTC has put other mechanisms in place to unwind or reverse an insolvent issuer's transactions electronically, right back to the start.) But even with tight restrictions on creditworthiness, Reilly believes that eventually some 75 to 80 percent of the market will join the book-entry system.

COMMERCIAL PAPER

commercial paper
a short-term debt obligation issued by corporations in the financial marketplace, backed solely by the promise of the firm to pay

The largest and most creditworthy industrial firms and banking firms have access to another important source of short-term financing called **commercial paper,** which is short-term debt issued by corporations in the financial marketplace. Firms back commercial paper solely by the promise of the firm to pay. To escape the requirement of registering with the Securities and Exchange Commission, the maturity of the commercial paper cannot exceed 270 days. The issuer promises to pay the holder a given fixed amount on a

For now, the program is being expanded in stages, because DTC is still working on bringing its disaster recovery time (in the event of computer failure) down to the three-hour maximum required by the Federal Reserve Bank. It will probably take DTC another 12 to 15 months to reach that goal. In the meantime, the company has set a series of caps or limits that will be raised quarter to quarter. At the program's start, the IPAs (issuing and paying agents) and dealers couldn't put more than 25 percent of their total commercial paper volume into book entry. By the end of June 1991, the cap will have moved up to 45 percent.

(The caps don't apply to issuers. Issuers, once accepted into the pilot program, conduct all subsequent commercial paper transactions on-line with book entry.)

Every quarter, as the program expands, the IPAs and dealers send a list of interested commercial paper clients to the DTC. Given current cap constraints, it's easier for the IPAs and the banks to fit smaller and mid-sized issuers in, since a very large issuer could easily take up an IPA's entire quota for the quarter.

Meanwhile, as the caps increase, volume on the system rapidly grows. By the end of June 1991, the book-entry system should be handling an average of $17 billion of issuances and maturities a day, up from $6.5 billion in January. In comparison, current average daily volume in the total commercial paper market is estimated at $50 billion to $60 billion.

With the volume of commercial paper issues growing by leaps and bounds, it "doesn't make sense for commercial paper to still be a paper-based market," says Borden's Byrd. After all, there are only so many hours in the day in which to process and deliver paper notes. The conversion to electronic book entry will cut the amount of time it takes to process transactions and allow the market to continue growing. And with fewer couriers speeding to deliver reams of certificates by 2:15, the streets of Manhattan should become a little safer in the process.

Source: Rosalyn Retkwa, "Commercial Paper Without the Paper," *CFO*, April 1991, p. 59.

certain future date. The commercial paper sells at a discount from that promised future payment. Figure 19.4 shows the growth in the commercial paper market. Financial companies tend to issue most of it.

After the debacle of Penn Central's default on its commercial paper in the early 1970s, the market has been limited to only very good credit risks. Nonetheless, as Figure 19.5 shows, there is a yield differential between commercial paper and T bills, reflecting the difference in creditworthiness and risk between the Treasury and the issuers of commercial paper.

FIGURE 19.4   **The Explosive Growth of the Commercial Paper Market**

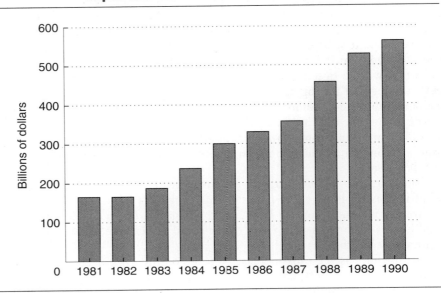

FIGURE 19.5   **The Yield Differential Between T Bills and Commercial Paper**

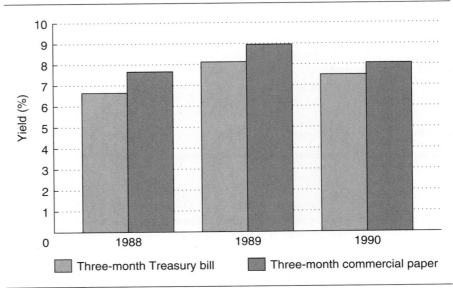

Source: Federal Reserve Bulletin, March 1991, Table 1.35.

SUMMARY

This chapter completes the discussion of working capital by focusing on sources of short-term financing. Firms have alternative strategies available to them in choosing the right mix between long-term and short-term financing. Conservative firms use a high proportion of long-term financing, whereas aggressive firms place greater reliance on short-term financing.

Whatever their attitudes toward risk, almost every firm uses some short-term financing. Some sources arise spontaneously from the normal conduct of business, such as accounts payable and accrued expenses, and can be of important magnitude. In addition, there are negotiated sources of financing, such as secured or unsecured loans. Commercial banks are a major source of unsecured loans. Because the loans are not secured, interest rates are often higher than the stated rate due to compensating balance requirements and commitment fees.

Secured short-term financing arises from the pledging of accounts receivable or inventories. Firms can convert accounts receivable into cash by pledging them as collateral for a loan or through factoring. When they do this on a recourse basis, they continue to bear the risk of collecting receivables. To avoid that risk, companies can factor their receivables on a nonrecourse basis.

Finally, firms can use their inventories as collateral to secure loans in several ways, for example, by pledging it as collateral under various warehousing arrangements. The choice of method depends on the nature of the inventory and the amount of control the borrower is willing to surrender to the lender. Generally, the more control the borrower surrenders, the larger the amount the lender will provide.

QUESTIONS

1. Assume that short-term rates are almost always lower than long-term rates. Would you finance your firm entirely with short-term funds? Explain.
2. Explain the purpose of using short-term financing as a bridge in periods of high interest rates.
3. If a firm has seasonal financing requirements, why doesn't it merely secure enough long-term financing to meet its total needs?
4. We noted that forgoing discounts usually implies that the purchasing firm will be borrowing, in effect, at a very high rate. What does this choice of credit terms say about the selling firm?
5. How do accrued expenses form a source of financing?
6. University professors are almost always paid monthly, but their salary for the academic year can be paid over 9 months or over 12 months. Which would you prefer? Why?

7. For short-term financing, would you expect the interest rate to be higher or lower for secured financing in comparison to unsecured financing?

8. How should the rate of interest on a short-term secured loan vary with the kind of goods offered as collateral? Specifically, would the liquidity of the security matter?

9. How are banks able to charge a commitment fee for a line of credit even though no credit has yet been extended? Should the bank be able to get away with this? Explain.

10. Explain why a MasterCard or Visa account is a type of revolving credit agreement.

11. When one party to an agreement has more information than the other, this condition is known as one of "asymmetric information." How does this concept apply to the factoring of receivables on a nonrecourse basis?

12. Pawnshops offer a source of secured financing. Explain how a pawnbroker would value the different types of collateral that might be offered. How would the amount the pawnbroker would be willing to lend vary with different types of collateral?

13. Is the operation of a pawnshop more like a field warehousing or terminal warehousing agreement? Explain.

PROBLEMS

1. You are considering credit terms of 2/15; net 45. What is the rate of interest implied by these terms?

2. What if the terms are 2/15; net 90?

3. Considering Problems 1 and 2, what does this show about the relationship between the length of the credit period and the cost of trade credit?

4. For a fixed credit period of 60 days and a discount period of 10 days, calculate the implied cost of trade credit for discounts of 1, 2, 3, 4, and 5 percent.

5. Prepare a graph of the implied cost of trade credit calculated in Problem 4.

6. For a fixed discount of 2 percent and a discount period of 10 days, calculate the implied cost of trade credit for net credit periods of 30, 60, and 90 days.

7. Graph the relationship between the cost of trade credit and the credit period as calculated in Problem 6.

8. For a fixed discount of 2 percent and a fixed credit period of 90 days, calculate the cost of trade credit for discount periods of 10, 20, 30, and 60 days.

9. Graph the relationship between the cost of trade credit and the discount period as calculated in Problem 8.

10. For an interest rate of 12 percent, calculate the effective rate of interest on a loan for compensating balance requirements of 5, 10, and 20 percent.

11. For a constant interest rate of 12 percent, graph the relationship between the effective rate of interest on a loan and compensating balance requirements using the calculations from Problem 10.

12. For a compensating balance requirement of 10 percent, calculate the effective rate of interest on a loan with interest rates of 6, 8, 10, 12, and 15 percent.

13. For a constant compensating balance requirement of 10 percent, graph the relationship between the effective rate of interest on a loan and the interest rate using the calculations from Problem 12.

14. Would you prefer a loan with a 12 percent rate of interest and a 10 percent compensating balance requirement, or one with a 14 percent rate of interest and no compensating balance?

15. Conway Tweety has to buy a $25,000 machine and his bank will provide the financing through a loan requiring a 10 percent compensating balance. How much money should Tweety borrow?

16. The formula to find the effective rate of interest for a loan requiring a compensating balance assumes that the loan must be repaid in one year. How would the formula change if the loan is to be repaid in six months, or in two years?

PART 6

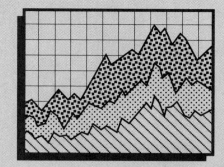

FINANCIAL ANALYSIS AND PLANNING

Financial Analysis

This chapter presents the basic techniques of financial analysis. The financial manager must have current information about the firm and how it is changing. Much of this information is derived from the firm's accounting statements: the balance sheet, the income statement, and the sources and uses of funds statement. The chapter introduces two important techniques for analyzing these statements: the percentage financial report, also known as common size analysis, and financial ratio analysis.

BASIC FINANCIAL STATEMENTS

balance sheet
a financial statement that presents all of the assets of, and claims against, a firm at a particular moment

income statement
a financial statement that summarizes the operation of the firm over a particular period

sources and uses of funds statement
a financial statement showing all the sources of funds for the corporation and how those funds were used

The three basic financial statements are the balance sheet, income statement, and sources and uses of funds statement.

The **balance sheet** presents all of the assets of the firm and claims against them at a particular time. Typical assets include cash, accounts receivable, inventory, and fixed assets. Typical claims include accounts payable, bank loans, and stockholders' equity. The balance sheet is like a financial snapshot, showing the firm's financial condition frozen at a specific time.

The **income statement** summarizes the operation of the firm over a particular period. It reports all the income of the firm and all the costs incurred to generate it. It differs from the balance sheet because it considers the flow of funds over a certain length of time, not merely the amount of funds at a particular moment. To continue our metaphor, the balance sheet might be like one frame from a film, but the income statement is the entire movie.

The third important financial statement is the **sources and uses of funds statement.** Its purpose is to show, over a given period, the sources from which the firm obtained its funds and how it put them to work. For example, over one year the firm may have obtained some funds from bank loans, some from an equity issue, and some from reducing its inventory levels. Those funds may have been used in part to buy new machinery, to increase the level of cash in the firm, and to reduce the accounts payable account. We consider each of these statements in detail in the following sections.

TABLE 20.1   Balance Sheets for Imaginary Products (thousands of dollars)

	Dec. 31, 1990	Dec. 31, 1991	Differ-ence		Dec. 31, 1990	Dec. 31, 1991	Differ-ence
				LIABILITIES AND NET WORTH			
ASSETS							
Cash	$ 175	$ 210	$ 35	Accounts payable	$ 325	$ 390	$ 65
Marketable securities	90	75	−15	Notes payable	225	530	305
Accounts receivable	560	520	−40	Accruals	50	40	−10
Inventory	330	670	340	Taxes payable	30	100	70
Current assets	1,155	1,475	320	Current liabilities	630	1,060	430
				Long-term liabilities	7,500	9,600	2,100
Plant and equipment	20,000	23,000	3,000				
Less accumulated depreciation	−7,500	−8,250	−750	**Total liabilities**	**8,130**	**10,660**	**2,530**
Total fixed assets	12,500	14,750	2,250	Common stock ($1 par; 1 million shares)	1,000	1,000	0
Total assets	**13,655**	**16,225**	**2,570**	Retained earnings	4,525	4,565	40
				Net worth	**5,525**	**5,565**	**40**
				Total liabilities and net worth	**13,655**	**16,225**	**2,570**

The Balance Sheet

The firm acquires assets by using the funds provided by investors. These investors have claims against the firm, which are set against the assets. The balance sheet summarizes the amounts and kinds of assets in the firm's possession. It also shows the claims made against those assets by investors. As the name implies, the balance sheet must balance. That is, the total value of the firm's assets must equal the total value of the claims against the firm. We can state this essential fact in the following equation:

$$\text{Total assets} = \text{total claims}$$

fiscal year
the firm's business year

Firms generally prepare their financial statements for the end of their fiscal year and for each quarter. The **fiscal year** is the business year, and it need not coincide with the calendar year.[1]

Table 20.1 shows a balance sheet for two consecutive years for Imaginary Products. The left portion shows the assets for each year. The assets fall into

---

[1] Firms sometimes have good business reasons for choosing a noncalendar year fiscal year. In retailing, for example, 25 percent of sales occur in a very short period before Christmas. If a retailing firm used the calendar year as its fiscal year, it would not be able to gather all the necessary information to make a timely report of its sales. Therefore, most retailers will prefer a later ending date for the calendar year, perhaps April 30.

two main categories—current and fixed. Thus, we have the relationship:

$$\text{Total assets} = \text{current assets} + \text{fixed assets}$$

current asset
an asset that can be converted into cash within one year

A **current asset** is one the firm will convert into cash within one year in its normal operation. For example, **cash** is clearly a current asset. Similarly, **marketable securities** are current assets because they are short-term assets that the firm can sell for cash very quickly. **Accounts receivable** are amounts due to the corporation from its customers, normally collected within a year. Therefore, these are current assets. **Inventory** is also a current asset, because most firms sell their inventory and receive cash from that sale within one year. In equation form we have:

marketable securities
financial assets maturing in less than one year

accounts receivable
amounts due to the corporation from its customers

$$\text{Current assets} = \text{cash} + \text{marketable securities}$$
$$+ \text{accounts receivable} + \text{inventory}$$

inventory
current assets used in the production process

fixed assets
long-term assets used in the production process

Fixed assets are more permanent assets that the firm will not normally convert into cash, at least not in the short run. For example, a refinery of Mobil's or an automobile assembly plant of Chrysler's would both be fixed assets. They are typically physical assets used in the basic process of the firm's operations. The balance sheet shows their initial value, plant and equipment, minus the accumulated depreciation charged against them. In equation form:

$$\text{Fixed assets} = \text{plant and equipment (cost)} - \text{accumulated depreciation}$$

historical cost
the amount actually paid for the asset

The balance sheet shows fixed assets at their **historical cost**; that is, the amount actually paid for them. The historical cost may differ from the market value or the replacement cost of the assets. The **market value** is the price at which the assets could be sold in the market today. The **replacement cost** is the cost of the assets if they were purchased new today.

market value
the current price of an asset in the open market

replacement cost
the price of an asset if it were acquired in the market today

The idea behind using the historical cost and subtracting the accumulated depreciation to arrive at the reported value of fixed assets is important. If the price of an asset did not change over time, and if the depreciation charged against it accurately reflected the falling value of the asset due to its use and age, the asset's balance sheet value would equal its market value. However, the reported value and the market value often differ, sometimes substantially.

book value
the value of the assets as shown in the financial books of the company

The value of the assets as shown in the financial reports and in the books of the company is the **book value.** Book value and market value may differ for several reasons. Consider the case of a personal computer. If the firm pays $5,000 for the computer and depreciates it 20 percent the first year, the book value will be $4,000 after one year of use. However, if developments in technology have made that machine obsolete, the computer may have a market value of only $1,500. Often, technological advancements make old equipment obsolete, so the book value can exceed the market value. In this case, the book value overstates the value of an asset relative to its market value.

It may also occur that the market value exceeds the book value. For instance, land is never depreciated, and accounting statements always reflect its original purchase price. Its market value may increase, however, and when this happens, the book value of the land is much less than its market value. In periods of high inflation, the book value of many assets can be less than their market value. In addition to land, this can happen for machinery that does not become obsolete so quickly.

Against the assets of the firm are claims of a variety of individuals and other firms. In the balance sheet, we can divide obligations into claims owed to creditors, or liabilities, and to the owners of the firm, or equity. Thus, we have:

$$\text{Total claims} = \text{total liabilities} + \text{equity}$$

Liabilities are either current or long-term. **Current liabilities** are those the firm reasonably expects to pay within the next year. **Long-term liabilities** are continuing ones the firm has undertaken that will not be completely repaid during the next year. The sum of current and long-term liabilities gives total liabilities:

$$\text{Total liabilities} = \text{current liabilities} + \text{long-term liabilities}$$

Accounts payable are current liabilities since they are short-term obligations that the firm has for goods or services it has received from others. For example, Imaginary Products may receive raw materials before paying for them. If, as normally occurs, the firm must pay within a year, the balance sheet shows those debts in the accounts payable category.

Many firms use short-term debt, usually from banks. **Notes payable** show the short-term debt that must be paid within the next year. Some other debts are **accruals.** One of the best examples of an accrual is the debt of the company to its employees. If the date of the balance sheet falls in the middle of a pay period, the firm will owe employees accrued salaries and wages. By the same token, firms do not pay their taxes everyday, but taxes accumulate. **Taxes payable** are owed but not yet paid. Summarizing, the current liability equality can be expressed as:

$$\text{Current liabilities} = \text{accounts payable} + \text{notes payable}$$
$$+ \text{ accruals} + \text{taxes payable}$$

Long-term liabilities consist of debts and leases. If a firm has sold a thirty-year bond, it has a long-term debt. Part of this debt may be due during the next year, and that portion is a current liability. Also, many firms use long-term **leases,** which are legal agreements to make a series of payments in exchange for the use of some asset.[2]

In addition to its liabilities to parties outside the firm, the corporation has obligations to its owners. The balance sheet presents these separated into common stock and retained earnings. The **common stock** account reflects the capital that has come from outside the corporation. The **retained earnings** account shows the accumulated effect of the firm's earnings since its inception.

---

[2] Leases are discussed in detail in Chapter 23.

---

current liabilities
liabilities that the firm must pay within one year

long-term liabilities
obligations that will not be completely repaid during the next year

accounts payable
amount owed by the firm to others

notes payable
the short-term debt that the firm expects to pay within the next year

accruals
current liabilities of the firm due for services such as wages owed but not yet paid

taxes payable
taxes owed but not yet paid

lease
an agreement to make a series of payments in exchange for the use of some asset

common stock
capital contributed by parties outside the corporation

retained earnings
accumulated earnings of the firm that have not been paid as dividends

equity or **net worth**
the sum of the common stock and retained earnings

Retained earnings are funds that the firm has earned and retained for use in the business instead of paying them to the shareholders. The sum of the common stock and retained earnings constitutes the **equity** or **net worth**:

$$\text{Equity} = \text{common stock} + \text{retained earnings}$$

Together, the firm's liabilities and equity must equal its assets. As discussed later in this chapter, the balance sheet supplies much of the information that is critical to successful financial analysis.

The Income Statement

sales
revenues generated by the firm from the sale of its products

cost of goods sold
the direct cost associated with the creation of the product

gross profit
the difference between sales and the cost of goods sold

The income statement details the firm's revenues and expenses during a particular period. Table 20.2 presents the income statement for Imaginary Products for two consecutive periods. It begins with a report of the dollar volume of the firm's **sales** for the period. Subtracting the cost of goods sold from sales gives the gross profit. The **cost of goods sold** (COGS) reflects the direct cost associated with creating the product. For a broom manufacturer, COGS would include the cost of materials and labor for making brooms. It would also include a portion of the factory cost, such as lighting for the building, maintenance, and repairs for equipment.

The **gross profit** is the difference between the sales and the cost of goods sold. The equation can be stated as follows:

$$\text{Gross profit} = \text{sales} - \text{cost of goods sold}$$

The firm also must recognize the depreciation expense to reflect the consumption of its capital and equipment. Similarly, the selling and administrative (S&A) expenses incurred by the firm also affect profit.

TABLE 20.2   Income Statements for Imaginary Products (thousands of dollars)

	1990	1991
Sales	$19,625	$25,280
Cost of goods sold	15,700	20,900
Gross profit	3,925	4,380
Depreciation	650	750
Selling and administrative expenses	2,425	2,615
Earnings before interest and taxes	850	1,015
Interest expense	725	940
Earnings before taxes	125	75
Taxes	47	28
Net income	**78**	**47**

After considering all sales and the costs of generating those sales, the result is the firm's **earnings before interest and taxes** (EBIT), which can be expressed as:

Earnings before interest and taxes = gross profit − depreciation
− selling and administrative expenses

In addition to depreciation and S&A expenses, the firm must pay interest on its debt. Interest is normally separated from the other expenses because it results from the debt-financing policies of the firm. By contrast, depreciation and S&A expenses are related to operating activities. Separating interest expenses facilitates comparison among firms. For example, two firms with identical operations would have the same EBIT, even if their debt policies differed. The EBIT is frequently used when measuring operating efficiency.

earnings before taxes (EBT)
earnings subject to income taxation

Subtracting interest expenses from EBIT gives the **earnings before taxes** (EBT):

Earnings before taxes = earnings before interest and taxes − interest

These are the earnings subject to income taxation. Subtracting taxes from EBT gives the firm's profit, or **net income** (NI). Net income, the proverbial "bottom line," is the amount that is actually available to the firm's owners after paying all other claimants, including the government.

net income
the firm's earnings after accounting for all expenses and taxes

Net income = earnings before taxes − taxes

The net income for the period is available to either reinvest in the company or to pay as dividends to shareholders. Thus,

Net income = retained earnings for the period + dividends

cash flow
actual payment of cash

In reading an income statement, we must remember the difference between the earnings the income statement reports and the cash the firm receives. **Cash flow** refers to the actual payment of cash. It is very important because only actual cash gives the firm the resources to meet its obligations. If a firm sells all its goods on credit, it can report large earnings for a period even when it receives no payments. In such an extreme case, the reported earnings might be large, but the cash flow would be zero.

depreciation tax shield
reduction in taxes created by the depreciation expense

Although depreciation is not a cash expense, it generates cash by reducing the firm's tax bill. This is known as the **depreciation tax shield.** To illustrate, consider a firm with earnings before taxes of $4,000 after deducting a depreciation expense of $1,500. For simplicity, suppose the firm pays a 34 percent tax rate on any EBT. The firm pays $4,000 × 0.34 = $1,360 in taxes. If depreciation were not a deductible expense, the EBT would be $5,500, and taxes in that case would be $5,500 × 0.34 = $1,870. The fact that depreciation is allowed as an expense shields the firm from paying $510 ($1,870 − $1,360) in taxes. In general, if T is the corporate tax rate, the depreciation tax shield can be calculated directly with the following formula:

$$\text{Tax shield} = \text{depreciation} \times T$$

Using this formula in the previous example, the depreciation tax shield is $1,500 × 0.34 = $510, just as we found before.

The Sources and Uses of Funds Statement

The sources and uses of funds statement shows how the firm acquires its funds in a given period and how it uses them. For example, if a firm borrows $1,000 from a bank and deposits it in its checking account, the loan is a source of funds that are used to increase the firm's cash account.

We have already seen that firms obtain funds by incurring obligations to debtholders and stockholders. Perhaps a less obvious example is a reduction of the firm's inventory level. This is a source of funds because it generates cash for the firm. Similarly, a use of funds might be the cash purchase of a delivery truck, or a reduction in accounts payable when cash is paid to suppliers.

Any firm essentially has three main sources and three uses of funds, as shown in Table 20.3, and they fall into pairs. As a source of funds, a firm can increase a liability account. By borrowing money, for example, it increases the funds available to it. Decreasing a liability account, that is, paying an existing debt, is a use of funds. Accordingly, an increase in a liability is a source of funds and a decrease in a liability is a use of funds.

If a firm increases an equity account, the increased obligation is a source of funds. For example, if a firm issues new stock, the sale of the stock would bring in new funds. Similarly, if a firm decreases an equity account, perhaps by buying its own stock in the market or by paying dividends, it uses funds. Reducing an asset account provides a source of funds. Reducing the plant and equipment account by selling some machines generates cash.

Constructing a sources and uses statement for one year requires balance sheets for two years. Table 20.1 provides all information necessary to construct the sources and uses statement for Imaginary Products for 1991. The right-hand column presents the difference in each account from one period to the next. Using this column and the rules given in Table 20.3 we can build the sources and uses statement.

TABLE 20.3   Sources and Uses of Funds

Sources	Uses
Increase in a liability account	Decrease in a liability account
Increase in an equity account	Decrease in an equity account
Decrease in an asset account	Increase in an asset account

TABLE 20.4   Sources and Uses of Funds Statement for Imaginary Products, December 31, 1990 to December 31, 1991 (thousands of dollars)

Sources		Uses	
Increase in long-term liabilities	$2,100	Increase in fixed assets	$2,250
Increase in notes payable	305	Increase in inventory	340
Increase in taxes payable	70	Increase in cash	35
Increase in accounts payable	65	Decrease in accruals	10
Net income from operations	47	Dividends paid	7
Decrease in accounts receivable	40	**Total uses**	**2,642**
Decrease in marketable securities	15		
Total sources	**2,642**		

Table 20.4 takes the amounts from the difference column in Table 20.1 and classifies each one as a source or a use of funds. The sources and uses of funds are ranked by dollar amount in Table 20.4. For example, the two major sources of funds in 1991 for Imaginary Products were an increase in long-term liabilities ($2.1 million) and an increase in notes payable ($305,000). Most of the funds were used to expand plant and equipment ($2.25 million) and to increase inventory ($340,000).

Note that all the information in Table 20.4 comes from the balance sheets of Table 20.1, with one exception. The sources and uses statement also reflects the cash dividend of $7,000 that Imaginary Products paid in 1991. We have seen that the net income of any corporation must go either to retained earnings or to pay dividends to the shareholders. On the balance sheets, the change in retained earnings for the year was $40,000. However, the income statement in Table 20.2 shows that the firm earned $47,000. The dividends paid to shareholders in 1991 do not appear on the balance sheet or the income statement, but they appear on the sources and uses statement. This allows a reconciliation of the three major financial statements.[3]

FINANCIAL ANALYSIS TECHNIQUES

financial ratio
the ratio of two balance sheet or income statement values designed to provide information about the firm's status or prospects

The remainder of this chapter explores two techniques of financial analysis. The first, the technique of percentage financial statements, allows a ready comparison of the performance of the firm over two periods or at two moments. It also allows comparisons among different firms.

The second technique, ratio analysis, investigates the firm's performance through financial ratios. A **financial ratio** is the ratio of two financial variables taken from the balance sheet or the income statement.

---

[3] Many firms call the sources and uses statement the statement of changes in financial position.

TABLE 20.5   Percentage Balance Sheets for Imaginary Products

	December 31, 1990	December 31, 1991		December 31, 1990	December 31, 1991
			LIABILITIES AND EQUITY		
ASSETS					
Cash	1.3%	1.3%	Accounts payable	2.4%	2.4%
Marketable securities	0.7	0.5	Notes payable	1.6	3.3
Accounts receivable	4.1	3.2	Accruals	0.4	0.2
Inventory	2.4	4.1	Taxes payable	0.2	0.6
Current assets	8.5	9.1	Current liabilities	4.6	6.5
			Long-term liabilities	54.9	59.2
Plant and equipment	146.5	141.8			
Less accumulated depreciation	−55.0	−50.9	**Total liabilities**	**59.5**	**65.7**
Total fixed assets	91.5	90.9	Common stock ($1 par; 1 million shares)	7.3	6.2
Total assets	**100.0**	**100.0**	Retained earnings	33.1	28.1
			Equity	**40.5**	**34.3**
			Total liabilities and equity	**100.0**	**100.0**

Percentage Financial Statements

☞ A percentage balance sheet expresses each balance sheet item as a percentage of assets.

Table 20.5 presents percentage balance sheets for Imaginary Products. We construct the balance sheet by dividing each asset and liability category by total assets. For example, at the end of 1991, 90.9 percent of the firm's assets were fixed assets.

The percentage balance sheet is particularly useful for identifying trends in the firm's asset and liability composition. Comparing the position of Imaginary Products at the end of the two years, we see that it increased its relative amount of current assets. Because the firm can convert current assets to cash, a high level of current assets reduces the chance that it will be unable to pay its bills.[4]

At year-end 1991, Imaginary Products was financing 6.5 percent of its assets with current liabilities, compared to 4.6 percent in 1990. Also, it increased

[4] As we will see in our later discussion of working capital, having a high level of current assets has both benefits and costs. The financial manager must find the best combination of the reduced risk that holding a higher level of current assets gives, while also paying attention to the higher cash flow that might be achieved by holding more fixed assets, rather than current assets. This trade-off illustrates once again that value depends simultaneously on cash, time, and risk.

TABLE 20.6   Percentage Income Statements for Imaginary Products

	1990	1991
Sales	100.0%	100.0%
Costs of goods sold	80.0	82.7
Gross profit	20.0	17.3
Depreciation	3.3	3.0
S&A expenses	12.4	10.3
EBIT	4.3	4.0
Interest expense	3.7	3.7
EBT	0.6	0.3
Taxes	0.2	0.1
Net income	**0.4**	**0.2**

☞ A percentage income statement expresses each income statement item as a percentage of sales.

long-term liabilities substantially. Together, the increases in relative amounts of current and long-term liabilities generated a large increase in the firm's reliance on debt. During 1991 the percentage of assets financed by some form of debt went from 59.5 percent to 65.7 percent. The relative decrease from 40.5 percent to 34.3 percent in the equity account also highlights the increasing reliance on debt financing.

A further examination of the position of Imaginary Products is possible by considering the percentage income statements of Table 20.6. To prepare this statement, we express the different income statement categories as a percentage of sales. For example, in 1991 the cost of goods sold was 82.7 percent of sales.

Table 20.6 shows a potentially large and dangerous increase in COGS over the two periods, from 80.0 percent to 82.7 percent. Although this may not appear large, it dramatically affects gross profit. The 3.4 percent [(82.7 − 80.0)/80.0] relative increase made the gross profit margin go from 20.0 percent to 17.3 percent, a relative drop of 13.5 percent [(17.3 − 20.0)/20.0]. For the financial manager analyzing the performance of Imaginary Products, this increase in COGS would be an immediate danger signal.

A second noticeable feature of the percentage income statements is the level of S&A expenses. These decreased from 12.4 percent of sales in 1990 to 10.3 percent of sales in 1991, despite the fact that their dollar amount increased. The reason for this relative reduction is that dollar sales increased even more than S&A expenses.

The percentage income statement also reveals the low profitability of Imaginary Products. For each dollar of sales, the firm earned only two-tenths of one cent on an after-tax basis in 1991. Unless these are particularly bad years, Imaginary Products could be heading for serious difficulties.

Financial Ratios

In addition to percentage financial statements, the financial manager will frequently use financial ratios to obtain an overview of some of the firm's key operating statistics. In addition, when following these measures over time, the manager can detect important trends in the firm's performance.

☞ Financial ratios summarize the firm's liquidity, profitability, leverage, and turnover characteristics.

This section presents the major financial ratios and shows how to calculate them using the financial statements of Imaginary Products. The four major groups are liquidity, profitability, leverage, and turnover ratios.

Liquidity Ratios   The two measures of liquidity managers use most widely are the current ratio and the quick ratio or acid test. The current ratio is defined by the following formula:

$$\text{Current ratio} = \frac{\text{current assets}}{\text{current liabilities}}$$

For Imaginary Products, at year-end 1991 the current ratio is \$1,475/\$1,060 = 1.39.

The acid test is defined as follows:

$$\text{Acid test} = \frac{\text{current assets} - \text{inventory}}{\text{current liabilities}}$$

For Imaginary Products, at the end of 1991 the acid test is (\$1,475 − \$670)/\$1,060 = 0.76.

These two ratios measure a firm's ability to meet its current liabilities with its current assets. The greater the amount of current assets relative to current liabilities, the safer the firm will be, other things being equal.

The acid test imposes a tough measure of firm liquidity—hence its name. In some cases it is not easy to convert inventory to cash because some of the inventory may be obsolete or, in some fraudulent cases, may not even exist. Because of these potential problems, the acid test ratio removes inventory from the calculation to see how many dollars the firm can generate from current assets to pay each dollar of current liabilities, without relying on inventory.

For Imaginary Products, the liquidity ratios are somewhat small. As a rule, many analysts think that a current ratio of 2.00 and a quick ratio of at least 1.00 are roughly correct. However, the best value for any of these ratios depends on the industry and the particular strategy of the firm.

These ratios are often most useful in identifying trends early, which is valuable because it allows the firm to take corrective action. For example, at the end of 1990 the current ratio for Imaginary Products was 1.83 and its quick ratio was 1.31. During 1991 both of these measures deteriorated substantially. This trend is clearly dangerous and deserves managerial attention.

Profitability Ratios   Three widely used accounting measures of profitability are the profit margin (PM), the return on assets (ROA), and the return on equity (ROE). The PM is calculated as follows:

$$\text{Profit margin} = \frac{\text{net income}}{\text{total sales}}$$

From the 1991 income statement for Imaginary Products, we have PM = $47/$25,280 = 0.19 percent.

The ROA ratio is given by:

$$\text{Return on assets} = \frac{\text{net income}}{\text{total assets}}$$

Using our example, this ratio is ROA = $47/$16,225 = 0.3 percent.

Finally, the ROE ratio is defined as follows:

$$\text{Return on equity} = \frac{\text{net income}}{\text{equity}}$$

For Imaginary Products we have ROE = $47/$5,565 = 0.84 percent.

Each of these profitability measures provides a slightly different gauge of a firm's operating success. The PM reveals how much profit a firm earns on each dollar of sales. By itself, it is not too meaningful because it varies so widely by industry and by firm. To interpret this measure, and most of the others discussed in this section, the manager has to know the trend of the measure over time for a given company or the industry norm for the ratio in question.

In contrast with the PM, the ROA and the ROE both determine the rate of return on some measure of investment. The ROA determines the return on all of the assets employed by the firm and the ROE focuses only on the investment contributed by the shareholders.

The performance of Imaginary Products is dismal by all of the measures. No investor can be happy when a firm earns less than 1 percent on equity. This poor performance also means that the firm will face great difficulties in attracting any new investment capital if potential lenders believe these ratios are indicative of future performance.

Leverage Ratios   Leverage ratios calculate the extent to which a firm relies on debt. Other things being equal, a higher leverage ratio indicates a riskier firm, because the debt payments are fixed even if the earnings of the firm fluctuate. As a result, should the cash flow diminish excessively, the firm might miss its debt payments deadline, putting it in technical default.

Four important measures of leverage are the times interest earned ratio (TIE), the debt to assets ratio (D/A), the debt to equity ratio (D/E), and the equity multiplier (EM). The TIE is given by:

$$\text{Times interest earned} = \frac{\text{earnings before interest and taxes}}{\text{interest expense}}$$

Times interest earned is calculated using the firm's earnings before interest and taxes because these are the earnings available to pay the interest. For Imaginary Products, in 1991 the TIE is $1,015/$940 = 1.08. This means that the firm is earning only $1.08 for each $1 of interest expense it pays, which is an extremely uncomfortable margin of safety. In 1990 the TIE was 1.17, so this measure has gone from bad to worse, and the financial manager should focus on this as a matter of great urgency.

The other leverage measures focus on the structure of the firm's long-term financing. The D/A ratio shows which portion of assets the firm finances with debt. The D/E ratio shows the relationship between the firm's debt and equity financing.

$$\text{Debt to asset} = \frac{\text{total debt}}{\text{total assets}}$$

For Imaginary Products in 1991 we have D/A = $10,660/$16,225 = 0.657.

$$\text{Debt to equity} = \frac{\text{total debt}}{\text{equity}}$$

The D/E ratio is $10,660/$5,565 or 1.916.

These two ratios convey essentially the same information. In fact, given one, we can calculate the other. For example, a D/A of 0.657 implies that the firm must finance 34.3 percent of its assets with equity. The ratio of debt to equity then equals 0.657/0.343, or 1.916, which is the D/E calculated above. In general, the relationship between the D/A and D/E is given by:

$$D/A = \frac{D/E}{1 + D/E}$$

The final leverage ratio we consider is the equity multiplier (EM), defined as the dollar amount of assets the firm uses for each dollar of equity.

$$\text{Equity multiplier} = \frac{\text{total assets}}{\text{equity}}$$

For Imaginary Products, in 1991 this ratio equals EM = $16,225/$5,565 = 2.92. Thus, for each dollar of equity the firm has 2.92 dollars of assets. The EM can also be expressed in terms of the D/E ratio. This is easily seen by noting that total assets = debt + equity. Thus, EM = 1 + D/E.

Turnover Ratios   The different turnover ratios measure managerial effectiveness in running the operations of the firm. Among the main ones are the average collection period (ACP), inventory turnover ratio (ITO), and asset turnover ratio (ATO). The ACP is calculated as follows:

$$\text{Average collection period} = \frac{\text{accounts receivable}}{\text{daily credit sales}}$$

From One Pocket to Another

The news that foreign companies operating in the United States have been grossly underpaying their federal taxes for the past 10 years has raised a considerable amount of political ire. Indeed, Congress is now proposing legislation that would force foreign corporations to stop what it considers abusive intercompany accounting practices that allow for the underpayment.

The prospect of additional paperwork—not to mention taxes—has chagrined global corporations operating in the United States. But there's an even greater reason for their concern. The U.S. action is part of a mushrooming trend among the industrialized countries toward closing such tax accounting loopholes. While European countries are just beginning to review the matter, Japan has already mandated stiffer standards. It has also adopted a preapproval accounting procedure, known as an "advance determination ruling," that might be the harbinger of the future—and a costly one.

The reports of tax underpayment in the United States came to light after a nine-month congressional investigation of 36 U.S. subsidiaries of foreign corporations—reportedly including Toyota, Toshiba, Sony, Fuji Bank, and Siemens—revealed that over the past decade, more than half paid little or no U.S. income tax. The investigation's results have been turned over to the Internal Revenue Service, whose own startling study showed that foreign corporations had a negative U.S. tax liability of $2 billion in 1986. At least two substantial IRS cases against foreigners are already pending: one against Japan's Yamaha Motors, for $27 million, and another against Daewoo, the Korean auto manufacturer, for $37 million, including back taxes.

By taking liberties with what accountants call the transfer pricing mechanism on a cross-border basis, global companies can shift taxable income from one country to another. In the case of the U.S. investigation,

In the case of Imaginary Products, the ACP in 1991 is $520/($25,280/365) = 7.51 days.

The ACP gives the average amount of time necessary to collect a bill. The figure of 7.51 days is extremely low for most firms that sell on credit. Either Imaginary Products is doing an extremely good job of collecting its bills, or a small proportion of the firm's total sales are made on credit. This stresses that improved collection measures should rely on annual credit sales and not total sales.

"the parent was charging the U.S. subsidiary inflated prices for products shipped over here," says Patrick Heck, assistant counsel for the U.S. Ways and Means oversight subcommittee that ran the investigation. "In many cases an almost identical product was being shipped to unrelated U.S. distributors at far less than the U.S. subsidiary was being charged," he adds.

For example, the subcommittee found that the U.S. distributor of a foreign corporation paid an average of $800 more than the parent's Canadian subsidiary paid when buying an identical car. In another case, he says, a foreign parent sold television sets to distributors for $150, while charging its U.S. subsidiary $250 for the same model. Other companies used excessive or illegal freight, insurance, interest, and other fees or charges to shift income from the United States. And while 18 foreign-owned electronics distributors reported $116 billion in gross receipts between 1979 and 1989, they paid only $654 million, or 0.5 percent of their revenues, in federal income tax.

Theoretically, corporations would use the transfer pricing mechanism to switch earnings from countries with high taxation to those with low taxation. But since the United States has lower absolute levels of corporate taxation than many of the home countries of the corporations cited—Japan and Germany, for example—a deliberate move by German or Japanese parent companies to shift income from the United States back home may seem counterproductive. But tax matters are seldom what they seem. As Heck points out, "tax rates may have nothing to do with what a company actually pays in taxes. Things like deductions and credits and differing accounting methods can motivate companies to shift income from one high-tax-rate country to another." In addition, the investigation found indications that the global companies were routing their profits through off-shore tax havens—thus avoiding taxes both at home and in the United States.

Source: Susan Arterian, "From One Pocket to Another," *Global Finance*, November 1990, pp. 56–61.

The ITO, which indicates how many times per year the inventory is sold or turned over, is defined as:

$$\text{Inventory turnover} = \frac{\text{cost of goods sold}}{\text{inventory}}$$

Notice that the ITO is defined in terms of the annual cost of goods sold and not in terms of annual sales. Since the inventory account is carried at cost, it must be compared against another cost. The ITO for Imaginary Products is ITO = $20,900/$670 = 31.19 times. The figure of 31.19 is very high for most firms, since it implies that the average item was in inventory for only 11.70 days. For a manufacturing firm, this would be unusual, because it requires a sizable stock of goods to meet incoming orders. For service firms, however, a high level of inventory turnover is not unusual.

The typical problem that arises with inventory is that it may become too large when sales are slow. To control this, it is often useful to determine the number of days of sales that the firm holds in inventory. This DSI measure is essentially the reciprocal of the ITO, and is defined as:

$$\text{Days of sales in inventory} = \frac{\text{inventory}}{\text{daily cost of goods sold}}$$

For Imaginary Products, in 1991 we have DSI = $670/($20,900/365) = 11.70 days. This same result is obtained by reasoning that if the inventory turns over 31.19 times in 365 days, the firm must have 365/31.19 = 11.70 days of sales in its inventory. Thus, ITO and DSI give essentially the same information.

The asset turnover (ATO) is given by:

$$\text{Asset turnover} = \frac{\text{sales}}{\text{assets}}$$

The ATO for Imaginary Products is $25,280/$16,225 = 1.56.

The ATO shows how many sales dollars are generated by each dollar of assets. It therefore measures how productively the firm uses its assets. For Imaginary Products, the ATO is 1.56 dollars of sales per dollar of assets. For a manufacturing firm, the 1.56 level is quite reasonable.

It is important to notice that several of these ratios are related to one another. We have already noted the relationship between the D/A and the D/E, but the most important one is between the ROE ratio and three of the other ratios. This is as follows[5]:

$$\text{ROE} = \text{PM} \times \text{ATO} \times \text{EM}$$

This relationship provides a connection among a profitability ratio (PM), a leverage ratio (EM), and a turnover ratio (ATO). It allows the financial manager to pinpoint the factors that lead to a given return on equity. For Imaginary Products, the ROE is 0.84 percent. This value can be broken down into its three components using the values computed previously. For Imaginary Products we have 0.84% = 0.19% × 1.56 × 2.92.[6] This clearly shows that the problem with the firm's very low return on equity lies in its dismal profit margin, and not in the productivity of its assets or in its use of leverage.

---

[5] This relationship is often referred to as the Du Pont equation. The student is asked to derive this relationship in an end-of-chapter problem.

[6] The product on the right actually gives 0.865 percent. The computational error is due to the rounding of each of the three ratios.

The Soviets Take Accounting 101

The concept of profit is just beginning to catch on in the Soviet Union. Houghton Mifflin is out to speed up the process. The Boston publisher's undergraduate accounting tome, the 1,300-page *Principles of Accounting,* will soon become the first Western accounting textbook sold in the Soviet Union.

On April 10 in Moscow, government-run publisher Finansy I Statistika signed an agreement with Houghton to translate and distribute the book to the country's 320,000 accounting majors. They should take particular note of Chapter 3, which is all about calculating business income.

Source: Harris Collingwood, "The Soviets Take Accounting 101," *Business Week,* April 22, 1991, p. 38.

This recognition should lead the financial manager to concentrate on urgently improving the firm's profit margin.

Summarizing, the preceding consideration of the percentage financial statements and the financial ratios for Imaginary Products shows clearly that the firm faces some problems. First, the gross profit margin is extremely low. The firm is simply not earning enough on its present volume of sales to survive and prosper. If the other firms in the same industry are behaving similarly, the poor performance of Imaginary Products could be due to the same factors that affect other firms. If other firms are earning a much better return on sales, however, problems may exist with the management of Imaginary Products. Whatever its source, the problem demands strong corrective action.

The second major problem confronting Imaginary Products is the low level of liquidity, as revealed by the TIE, current ratio, and ATO. There is a danger that the firm could soon have difficulty meeting its debt payments. This could lead to bankruptcy and the seizure of the firm's assets by creditors.

Limitations of Ratio Analysis

All of these ratios and the technique of percentage financial statements are meaningful only in conjunction with a firm's past performance or in comparison with other firms in the industry. Also, none of these measures has a "correct" value. For example, it might seem that a higher current ratio is always better. After all, the higher the ratio, the safer the firm is from default. However, managing a firm to ensure a high current ratio may lead to an inefficient use of resources. The firm might increase its current ratio by hoarding cash or by increasing its inventory way beyond normal levels. Since these assets by themselves do not generate any return, an exceedingly high current ratio would signal that management is too cautious, and probably underutilizing the firm's assets. As always, it is important to recognize not only the benefits but the costs of any financial decision.

When analyzing financial statements, we should always be on the lookout for "window dressing" tactics. For example, a simple way of improving the firm's liquidity ratios is to take out a long-term loan right before the end of the fiscal year, and repay it at the beginning of the next one. If the funds from the loan are kept in the form of cash, the current ratio will increase and may not accurately reflect the true liquidity of the firm. The moral is that ratios should be viewed as part of a whole, and not just in isolation.

SUMMARY

This chapter presented the three most important types of financial statements prepared by corporations: the balance sheet, the income statement, and the sources and uses of funds statement. It also discussed some of the analytical techniques that managers can apply to understanding these statements.

The balance sheet offers a financial snapshot of the firm at a given moment. In essence, it summarizes all of the assets and claims against those assets.

The income statement reports on the revenues and expenses of a firm over a given period. The ultimate purpose of the income statement is to show the amount of income available to reward common stock owners for their investment. This is the so-called bottom line.

The sources and uses of funds statement reports how new funds were acquired over a given period and how they were used. For example, a bank loan may be a source of funds used to buy a new machine.

We also considered some basic techniques of financial analysis. One is to present financial statements in percentage, or common size, terms. The other major technique is ratio analysis.

With percentage financial statements, the financial manager can compare the performance of a firm in other periods or with other firms. A percentage balance sheet presents each asset and liability category as a percentage of total assets. The percentage income statement shows each revenue and expense item on the income statement as a percentage of the firm's sales.

Ratio analysis is a technique commonly used to understand the firm's position. We can classify financial ratios into four major groups: liquidity, profitability, leverage, and turnover ratios. Each has its application to a particular management concern.

QUESTIONS

1. How do the income statement and balance sheet differ in their summary of the events in an accounting period?
2. What are the three major financial statements?
3. Explain why the sources and uses of funds must be equal.

4. If the firm spends cash to buy inventory, how does it affect the following categories:
   a. current assets
   b. working capital
   c. the firm's current ratio
   d. the firm's acid test ratio
5. What is the difference between market value and historical cost?
6. Will book value and historical cost be identical? If so, under what circumstances?
7. Will book value always equal market value? What could cause them to diverge?
8. If a firm uses cash to pay down its accounts payable, what is the effect on the following measures:
   a. current ratio
   b. acid test ratio
   c. long-term debt
   d. retained earnings
9. You examine the income statement for a firm for two successive years and notice that the cost of goods sold has increased. What could explain this?

PROBLEMS

Consider the balance sheets for Dismal Industries shown below and use the information contained there for the next six problems.

Balance Sheets for Dismal Industries (thousands of dollars)

	December 31, 1990	December 31, 1991		December 31, 1990	December 31, 1991
ASSETS			**LIABILITIES AND NET WORTH**		
Cash	$ 125	$ 100	Accounts payable	$ 250	$ 325
Marketable securities	45	50	Notes payable	225	340
Accounts receivable	310	570	Accruals	80	150
Inventory	400	200	Taxes payable	70	90
Current assets	880	920	Current liabilities	625	905
			Long-term liabilities	4,500	5,000
Plant and equipment	14,000	15,080			
Less accumulated			**Total liabilities**	**5,125**	**5,905**
depreciation	5,000	5,900			
Total fixed assets	9,000	9,180	Common stock	1,000	1,000
			Retained earnings	3,755	3,195
Total assets	**9,880**	**10,100**	Net worth	4,755	4,195
			Total liabilities and net worth	**9,880**	**10,100**

1. Calculate the current ratio for each year.
2. Calculate the quick ratio for each year.
3. Calculate the D/A for each year.
4. Calculate the D/E for each year.
5. Based on the calculations in Problems 1–4, what difficulties, if any, does this firm face? What other information might be helpful for analyzing the difficulties?
6. Using the balance sheets provided above, prepare a sources and uses of funds statement like that shown in Table 20.4.

Use the information from the income statement on the next page for Dismal Industries, in conjunction with the balance sheets given above, to solve Problems 7–14.

Income Statement for Dismal Industries for 1991 (thousands of dollars)

Sales	$8,000
Cost of goods sold	6,100
Gross profit	1,900
Depreciation	900
Selling and administrative expenses	350
Earnings before interest and taxes	650
Interest expense	400
Earnings before taxes	250
Taxes	100
Net income	**$ 150**

7. Compute the firm's profit margin.
8. What is Dismal's return on assets?
9. What is Dismal's return on equity?
10. What is the times interest earned ratio?
11. What is Dismal's average sales per day?
12. What is Dismal's average collection period?
13. What is Dismal's inventory turnover ratio?
14. What is Dismal's total asset turnover ratio?
15. For the Dismal Industries 1991 balance sheet, recast it as a percentage statement.
16. Prepare a percentage income statement for Dismal for 1991.
17. Using the income statement for Dismal and the 1991 balance sheet, consider the following. Assume that Dismal had sales of $9 million instead of $8 million and assume that the same percentage cost of goods

sold was maintained. Prepare an income statement that reflects those changes. In doing so, change only the items that must change.

18. Given the change in the income statement, how must the 1991 balance sheet change?

19. Go back to the income statement printed above and assume that the cost of goods sold was $7 million. Compute the new income statement based on that change.

20. What changes in Dismal's 1991 balance sheet are necessary given the new cost of goods sold presented in the preceding problem?

On January 1, 1992, Dismal borrows $1 million on a six-month loan and issues $5 million in debt. Both amounts it receives in cash. Assuming no other changes since December 31, 1991, solve the following four problems.

21. Compute the new current ratio.
22. Compute the new acid test ratio.
23. Compute the new D/A.
24. Compute the new D/E.

Dismal is planning to issue $5 million worth of stock and will receive that amount of cash, with each share having a $1 par value. The stock sells for $10 per share. Using Dismal's 1991 balance sheet printed above as your starting point, solve Problems 25–30.

25. What is the new value of common stock?
26. What is the new value of retained earnings?
27. What will Dismal's new current ratio be?
28. What will Dismal's new acid test ratio be?
29. What will Dismal's new D/A be?
30. Compute Dismal's new D/E.
31. Does the current ratio increase or decrease when current assets and current liabilities increase by the same dollar amount?
32. What happens to the current ratio when current assets and current liabilities increase by the same percentage?
33. A firm has just bought some inventory with cash. What effect does this transaction have on its current ratio?
34. The text provides an expression for the D/A in terms of the D/E. Find the expression relating the D/E in terms of the D/A.
35. Show that if a firm has a positive net income and uses some debt, its ROE will always be greater than its ROA.
36. Starting from the definition of ROE, show that ROE = PM × ATO × EM. (*Hint:* You can always multiply and divide any ratio by the same amount without affecting the result.)

CHAPTER 21

Financial Planning

Financial managers must be able to analyze the current position of their own firms as well as that of their competition. They must also plan for the company's financial future. In dealing with working capital, as we have seen, many firms seasonally build up their inventories and accounts receivable. Managers must anticipate these needs and seek the best financing before the funds are needed. Planning the financing of working capital is an important responsibility, and this chapter introduces some basic techniques.

One of the worst fates that can befall a corporation is running out of cash. When this happens the firm suffers financial embarrassment, and perhaps even bankruptcy, because it cannot pay its bills in a timely fashion. The financial manager is responsible for ensuring that the firm has enough cash for its needs. Naturally, this requires planning. A useful tool for planning future cash needs is the cash budget, and this chapter explains how to construct cash budgets and how to use them.

Financial managers must plan for the overall financial success of the firm, so they have to plan for continuing profitability. Profit planning typically uses a **pro forma statement,** which is a projected financial statement that reflects current forecasts of sales, costs, working capital, and other financial parameters. Financial managers might prepare a pro forma balance sheet for one year in the future, which will present the firm's expected financial position at that time. Based on those data, the firm can plan the necessary steps to achieve the projected position. This chapter explores the uses of pro forma financial statements.

In addition to the methods already mentioned, which concentrate on the financial statements of the firm, other planning methods are available. We consider these techniques in the closing section of this chapter.

pro forma statement
a projected financial statement reflecting current forecasts of sales, costs, and other financial parameters

THE CASH BUDGET AS A TOOL FOR FINANCIAL PLANNING

☞ A cash budget allows the firm to plan for the actual receipt and disbursement of cash.

Consider the case of Imaginary Products, first discussed in Chapter 20, with sales of $25,280,000 in 1991. Management is predicting a 7 percent increase in sales for 1992, or $27,050,000. Even if this projection is correct, if the firm offers credit some of these sales will not yield cash until the firm collects the payment. Also, sales during the year have seasonal peaks and valleys, and as a result, the firm's working capital level will fluctuate. Financial planning

TABLE 21.1 Balance Sheet for December 31, 1991, for Imaginary Products (thousands of dollars)

ASSETS		LIABILITIES AND NET WORTH	
Cash	$ 210	Accounts payable	$ 390
Marketable securities	75	Notes payable	530
Accounts receivable	520	Accruals	40
Inventory	670	Taxes payable	100
Current assets	1,475	Current liabilities	1,060
		Long-term liabilities	9,600
Plant and equipment	23,000		
Less accumulated		**Total liabilities**	**10,660**
depreciation	−8,250	Common stock	
Total fixed assets	14,750	($1 par; 1 million shares)	1,000
Total assets	**$16,225**	Retained earnings	4,565
		Net worth	**5,565**
		Total liabilities and net worth	**$16,225**

☞ Sales made for credit do not generate immediate cash flows, and the cash budget must take these delays into account.

must reflect these factors to determine what cash will be available at what times during the year.

Not only do cash inflows fluctuate over the year, demand for cash also varies with time. For example, the balance sheet for Imaginary Products for 1991 in Table 21.1 shows a total of $1,060,000 in current liabilities, which we know that the company must pay sometime during the next year. We do not know exactly when it must pay them, however. For example, if the liabilities are all due on January 1, 1992, Imaginary Products will be in deep trouble, because the balance sheet shows that it has only $210,000 in cash.

In addition to problems with fluctuating levels of cash inflows and outflows, there is also the chance that the firm may not realize its plans. While it expects that sales will increase by 7 percent, this may not happen. Often, firms seriously overestimate their sales for the forthcoming year. If Imaginary Products does this it could lead to a serious cash shortfall. Therefore, it must also plan to have a safety stock of cash.

cash budget
a plan for the cash inflows and outflows over a certain period of time, usually one year

Planning cash requirements and taking into account the inflows and outflows require a **cash budget,** which is a plan for the inflows and outflows over a certain period. It usually is prepared for each month of the coming year. Some firms use it to plan cash flows on a weekly or even on a daily basis, emphasizing the importance of cash for them.

PREPARING THE CASH BUDGET

As a first step in preparing the cash budget, the firm must estimate the sales for each period during the planning period. Table 21.2 shows the historical

TABLE 21.2   Monthly Distribution of Sales for Imaginary Products (thousands of dollars)

Month	Historical Sales	Actual Sales for 1991	Projected Sales for 1992
January	5%	$ 1,264.0	$ 1,352.5
February	7	1,769.6	1,893.5
March	10	2,528.0	2,705.0
April	12	3,033.6	3,246.0
May	16	4,044.8	4,328.0
June	22	5,561.6	5,951.0
July	7	1,769.6	1,893.5
August	7	1,769.6	1,893.5
September	5	1,264.0	1,352.5
October	2	505.6	541.0
November	4	1,011.2	1,082.0
December	3	758.4	811.5
Total	**100**	**$25,280.0**	**$27,050.0**

sales pattern for Imaginary Products on a monthly basis and the actual sales for 1991. It also shows the projected monthly sales in 1992.

Imaginary Products experiences a strong seasonal pattern in its sales, with highest amounts in the spring and early summer. For example, sales in June are 11 times greater than in October. This pattern might be typical of a swimsuit distributor or a firm selling patio furniture. Whatever the reason for Imaginary Products, cash inflows will be uneven over the course of the year. The widely varying sales makes planning cash requirements even more important. Failure to do so may result in serious problems.

Given the projected sales for each month, the second step in the preparation of the cash budget is to establish when those sales will actually generate cash. If the firm sells on credit, it will experience a delay in receiving payments. Imaginary Products has worked with its customers for a long time and can predict that they will pay within two months after the sales. Based on previous experience, the company anticipates the following distribution of payment for sales:

Payment Month	Percentage Paid
Month of sale	15%
Month after sale	35
Second month after sale	50

TABLE 21.3   Schedule of Cash Receipts for November 1991 Sales for Imaginary Products*

Month	Collected	Cash Amount
November 1991	15%	$151,680
December 1991	35	353,920
January 1992	50	505,600

* November 1991 sales were $1,011,200.

On December 31, 1991, when the firm is preparing its cash budget, it has not received full payment for its November or December sales. Consequently, cash inflows from these sales will affect the cash budget for 1992. To see this more clearly, consider the actual sales of $1,011,200 made in November 1991. According to the payment pattern shown above, the firm will capture cash for those sales according to Table 21.3. Knowing the projected amount of sales for each month and the pattern of payment gives the financial manager enough information to budget cash receipts.

The third step is to use the projected sales and payment pattern to prepare the projected cash inflows. Table 21.4 presents the projected cash inflows for Imaginary Products for the first four months of 1992. For March they are expected to be $1,746,000. This total results from collecting 15 percent of sales made in March, 35 percent made in February, and 50 percent made in January.

The fourth step is to make a schedule of disbursements. We have already observed that Imaginary Products had quite a bit of current liabilities at year end 1991. The timing of the payments the firm must make to fulfill those

TABLE 21.4   Projected Cash Receipts from 1992 Sales for Imaginary Products (thousands of dollars)

	January	February	March	April
Projected sales	$1,353	$1,894	$2,705	$3,246
Cash receipts				
Cash sales (15%)	203	284	406	487
Collections from preceding month (35%)	265	474	663	947
Collections from 2 months ago (50%)	506	379	677	947
Total	**$ 974**	**$1,137**	**$1,746**	**$2,381**

FINANCE

TODAY

Chaotic Forecasting

According to an old joke, Albert Einstein dies and goes to heaven, where he asks three archangels their IQs. "One hundred ninety-six, sir," replies the first. "Remarkable!" cries Einstein. "I look forward to talking with you about my theory of relativity." The second says 153. "Not bad," says Einstein. "We will have long talks about the prospects for international socialism and world peace." The third fellow grunts his IQ: "84." Einstein: "So, what do you think the economy will do next year?"

The record suggests that any economic forecaster who accurately predicts the future will do so out of luck. MIT's Nobel laureate Paul A. Samuelson frankly admits his profession is not good at calling the economic turns. "I don't believe we're converging on ever-improving forecast accuracy," he says. "It's almost as if there's a Heisenberg Indeterminacy Principle and God Almighty himself doesn't know what investment will be 18 months ahead."

God may know but economists seldom do. Way back in October of 1981, Evans Economics, a well-known forecaster, predicted a GNP growth rate of 3.3 percent for 1982. Wharton Econometric Forecast Associates, another established seer, predicted 2.2 percent growth. Chase Econometrics weighed in with a prediction of 2 percent. Disregarding the experts' opinions, the GNP then *dropped* 2.5 percent in the recession of 1982.

In January–February 1991, the stock market rose like a rocket in the midst of the Gulf War, gaining more than 18 percent between the start of the war on January 16 and its end on February 27. This amazing jump caught most forecasters by surprise, especially in light of the fact that the U.S. economy was in a recession at the time.

Atypical? A bit of bad luck, perhaps? Hardly. When the stock market crashed in October 19, 1987, most economists thought that the economy's growth would grind to a halt. Instead, during the last quarter of 1987, the economy continued expanding at a 6 percent–plus annual rate. In fact, a recession did not arrive until late 1990. "The three biggest features that the economic history books will describe for the Reagan era will be a high structural fiscal deficit, a chronic balance of payments deficit, and high real interest rates," says Paul Samuelson. "Not one of those three was predicted in 1979–80."

Part of the less-than-impressive prediction record is due to human nature. For example, the commercial relationship between forecasters and their clients often leads to the "tell 'em what they want to hear" syndrome. But let's face it—the greatest barrier to accurate forecasting is the increasingly complex and fast-changing nature of the world economy.

"When tomorrow is like today, you don't need a very elaborate model to predict," says Charles Wolf, dean of the Rand Corporation's graduate school.

Time was when forecasting was fairly simple. Lack of rain in the farm belt would cut the grain crop, which would reduce demand for railroad cars, which would cause the railroads to lay workers off and to cut their purchases of steel; a sharp recession would result. A single event would reverberate through the system in a predictable and dependable way. Not today. Today, for example, a bad grain harvest has little effect on the service sector, now 65 percent of GNP.

Are bigger computers and equations with more variables the answer? Or is long-term economic forecasting—accurate forecasting, that is—simply impossible? A growing number of economists believe it is impossible, in theory as well as in practice.

Economists are drawing many of their new insights from a hot branch of science and mathematics called "chaos theory." Physical scientists use chaos theory to understand and explain random, sudden, and massive events, such as earthquakes or avalanches. Biologists and meteorologists use chaos math to explain the rise and fall of animal populations, such as dinosaurs, and the branching patterns of lightning bolts. Now economists are using it, too.

According to the proponents of chaos, the real-world economy often adjusts through large discontinuous changes. The discontinuities occur, these economists argue, because the economy is inherently an unstable system. No outside shocks produce this turmoil. Examples of chaotic economic behavior include German hyperinflation in the 1920s, the stock market crash of October 19, 1987, and the loss of 190 points on Friday, October 13, 1989. All of these phenomena were sudden, massive, and utterly unpredictable. According to chaos-theorist and economist James B. Ramsey, "I strongly suspect that nothing, no single piece of information, precipitated October 19. What happened was that the system reached the point of instability." He adds, rather derisively, "It's easy to forecast when times are stable. It's just this year, plus 5 percent, plus a small error factor. No big deal."

What people really need is to be alerted to the kind of catastrophe—like the stock market crash in 1987—that can utterly upset their plans. But this is precisely what economics cannot provide. That hoary old Einstein joke makes a pretty good point.

Source: Ronald Bailey, "Them That Can, Do, Them That Can't, Forecast," *Forbes*, December 26, 1988, pp. 97–100.

TABLE 21.5   Projected 1992 Cash Disbursements for Imaginary Products (thousands of dollars)

	January	February	March	April
Payments to suppliers				
Cash	$ 75	$ 255	$ 380	$ 75
Lagged 1 month	60	80	435	95
Lagged 2 months	40	90	150	125
Wages and salaries	350	480	560	530
Rent expense	185	185	185	185
Tax payments			29	
Interest payments	40	40	520	
Notes due			450	
Total disbursements	**$750**	**$1,130**	**$2,709**	**$1,010**

obligations is the crucial question for the cash budget. Table 21.5 shows the projected cash disbursements that Imaginary Products anticipates it must make during the first four months of 1992. Due to the seasonal nature of its business, it will incur increasing costs for manufacturing supplies in those early months of the year, and to prepare the goods for the heavy spring and summer selling season, it will incur increased wage expenses.

If Imaginary Products is to have any cash problems, they are likely to arise in March. Then, sales receipts are still low from the winter, but the company has high materials cost and labor expenses as it prepares for the heavy selling season. In addition, March may be particularly problematic because tax payments are due, together with a large interest payment. Finally, a note is also due in March. Comparing the total cash inflows and outflows for the month we see that the outflows are $963,000 ($2,709,000 − $1,746,000) more than the inflows. If Imaginary Products is to overcome this and any other cash shortfall, it must make plans in advance.

As a fifth and final step in preparing the cash budget, the firm must assemble the projected receipts and disbursements, together with the cash available at the beginning of the period. In Table 21.6, for each month, line 1 shows the amount of beginning cash. For January this is simply the amount on the balance sheet for December 31, 1991. Line 2 shows the cash receipts the firm expects in each period (these figures are taken from Table 21.4). For any given month, adding the beginning cash and the cash receipts gives the total cash available to Imaginary Products. Line 3 shows the available cash; in February the firm will have a total of $434,000 + $1,137,000 = $1,571,000 to cover its cash disbursements.

Line 4 shows the projected cash disbursements that were calculated in Table 21.5. We must subtract that amount from the available cash to give the amount of cash the firm expects to have at the end of the month, given in line 5. We carry this ending cash figure forward as the beginning amount

TABLE 21.6   Cash Budget for Imaginary Products for 1992 (thousands of dollars)

	January	February	March	April
Beginning cash	$ 210	$ 434	$ 441	($522)
Cash receipts	974	1,137	1,746	2,381
Cash available	1,184	1,571	2,187	1,859
Cash disbursements	750	1,130	2,709	1,010
Ending cash	$ 434	$ 441	($522)	$ 849
Minimum cash balance	100	100	100	100
Excess (needed) cash	$ 334	$ 341	($622)	$ 749

of cash available for the next month. For example, January ended with an anticipated cash balance of $434,000, so this sum constitutes the beginning cash balance for February.

☞ Firms usually want to plan for some minimum cash balance to act as a cushion if the cash budget is not accurate.

In addition, the firm may wish to maintain a minimum cash balance as a precaution against planning errors. Imaginary Products keeps a cash balance of at least $100,000, as indicated in line 6. Therefore, we must subtract $100,000 from the ending cash total to find the excess cash, or the amount of cash the firm needs. If there is excess cash, Imaginary Products can invest it to earn a return. If there is not, the firm must acquire money to pay its debts and to maintain its minimum cash balance. Any excess or shortfall is shown in line 7 of Table 21.6.

In January 1992 Imaginary Products has a total of $1,184,000 available cash, out of which it expects to pay $750,000. This leaves an ending cash balance of $434,000. Out of this amount it will reserve $100,000 as a minimum cash balance for any unforeseen emergencies. Thus it has an excess of $334,000, which the company can invest to earn more profits .

Table 21.6 shows that Imaginary Products will have a cash shortfall in March 1992. Under the current plan, it does not have enough cash to pay its obligations and maintain its minimum cash balance of $100,000. According to the cash budget, the firm needs $622,000 in cash for March; however, this is a temporary shortfall because the cash budget shows a cash surplus for April. As a consequence, Imaginary Products has to arrange for a one-month loan to cover that temporary financing need.

☞ The cash budget allows the financial manager to identify periods of cash shortfall and to plan financing to cover the firm's cash needs.

The cash budget is crucial in uncovering the firm's cash needs. Without it, the manager might not have foreseen the need for financing in March, and Imaginary Products might not have had enough cash to meet its debts. Failure to pay the note that came due in March could have resulted in serious consequences for its credit standing and reputation. This, in turn, would almost certainly make its share price fall.

Not only is the cash budget essential for avoiding shortfalls, but it also identifies those periods when excess cash will be available for making other investments.

PRO FORMA FINANCIAL STATEMENTS

☞ Pro forma financial statements show the forecasted position of the firm.

A pro forma statement is a projected financial statement that reflects current forecasts of sales and expenses. It is useful in planning a firm's operation and in anticipating its future financial position. For example, a pro forma income statement for the next year will summarize the performance of the firm if it meets the current projections of sales and expenses. A pro forma balance sheet for next year will summarize the firm's expected financial position at that time.

In addition to using these statements for forecasting, the company can use them as management tools. If the manager prepares them based on current forecasts of sales and expenses and the result is not satisfactory, management knows that it has to alter its current plans to achieve a better result. This section illustrates the preparation of pro forma financial statements by continuing the example of Imaginary Products.

The Pro Forma Income Statement

Normally, the marketing department has a major role in determining what projected sales are reasonable. We have already seen that Imaginary Products is forecasting an increase in sales of 7 percent for 1992, from $25,280,000 in 1991 to $27,050,000 in 1992. One way of projecting future earnings and expenses is to assume that the future will resemble the past. In the pro forma income statement, this means assuming that the same ratio of expenses to sales that prevailed in the past will continue in the future. If no major changes in the firm's operations occur, this can be a reasonable assumption. Table 21.7 illustrates this technique, showing the actual income statement and the

TABLE 21.7   Income Statement for Imaginary Products for 1991 and Pro Forma Income Statement for 1992 (thousands of dollars)

	1991 Actual		1992 Projected
	Amount	Percentage	
Sales	$25,280	100%	$27,050
Costs of goods sold	20,900	82.7	22,370
Gross profit	4,380	17.3	4,680
Depreciation	750	3	812
Selling and administrative expenses	2,615	10.3	2,786
Interest expense	940	3.7	1,001
Earnings before taxes	75	0.3	81
Taxes	28	0.11	30
Earnings after taxes	47	N.A.	51

percentage income statement for 1991. In addition, the final column contains the projected income statement for 1992.

In this pro forma income statement, the forecasted sales are $27,050,000, reflecting the targeted 7 percent increase. The manager can construct the statement by assuming that the same operating ratios that prevailed previously will continue. In Table 21.7 the projected expense and profit items are constructed by applying the 1991 percentages, shown in the middle column, to the new projected sales figure of $27,050,000 for 1992.

☞ The pro forma income statement can often be created by using the firm's previous percentage income statement and the forecasted level of sales for the new period.

The financial manager should be very careful when applying the percentage of sales method to construct a financial income statement, because some accounts may not increase in direct proportion to sales. For example, in Table 21.7 we assumed that depreciation expenses would remain at 3 percent in 1992, the same as in 1991. This may be a reasonable assumption if the firm operated at full capacity in 1991; with production at full capacity, the firm must purchase additional machines to increase sales, which would result in an increased depreciation expense. However, if the firm had some slack capacity in 1991, it can increase sales in 1992 without investing in additional machines, and thus the depreciation expense would not increase in 1992. In fact, if the firm uses an accelerated depreciation method, the depreciation expense may actually decrease.

The Pro Forma Balance Sheet

☞ Preparation of a pro forma balance sheet requires the previous balance sheet and the pro forma income statement for the intervening period.

Preparation of the pro forma balance sheet requires information from a variety of sources, including the previous balance sheet and the pro forma income statement. This section illustrates the preparation of a pro forma balance sheet for Imaginary Products for December 31, 1992.

As the name implies, the essential requirement is that the balance sheet balance. Management can change many different asset and liability accounts to achieve this balance. We can simplify the process by making a few practical assumptions.

First, assume that Imaginary Products does not plan to issue any new common stock or long-term debt. Therefore, these accounts will be the same in the pro forma balance sheet as they were in the previous actual balance sheet of Table 21.1. Second, assume that management plans to adjust the marketable securities account to make the balance sheet balance from the asset side. For example, if it has more cash than required, it will invest the excess in marketable securities. If, on the contrary, the firm needs cash, it will have to sell some marketable securities. Also, management plans to adjust the notes payable account to allow the balance sheet to adjust from the liabilities side of the balance sheet. If the firm can reduce its notes payable, it will do so; conversely, it will increase its notes payable if it has to. Using these assumptions, we can construct the pro forma balance sheet by determining the planned level for each of the remaining asset and liability accounts. We consider each of them in turn.

**TABLE 21.8   Calculation of Accounts Receivable for the 1992
Pro Forma Balance Sheet for Imaginary Products**

Sales Month	Projected Sales	Uncollected on December 31	Contribution to Accounts Receivable
November	$1,082,000	50%	$ 541,000
December	811,500	85	689,775
Total			**$1,230,775***

* Rounding to the nearest $1,000, the total is $1,231,000.

Cash   If Imaginary Products uses the Baumol method of cash management described in Chapter 17, its level of cash on hand should increase with sales. However, the cash level does not increase linearly with sales. Instead, the Baumol model asserts that it should increase with the square root of sales. Since sales in 1992 will be 7 percent greater than in 1991, the cash level should increase by 3.44 percent.[1] With $210,000 at the end of 1991, the firm is expected to have $217,000 at the end of 1992, rounded to the nearest $1,000.

Accounts Receivable   We know that Imaginary Products collects 35 percent of its sales in the first month after the sale and 50 percent in the second month after the sale. Using this information, we can forecast the amount of receivables that the firm will have on December 31. For sales made in November, it collects 15 percent in November and another 35 percent in December, leaving 50 percent of receivables outstanding. Sales for November are forecasted to be $1,082,000, as shown in Table 21.2, and they will generate $541,000 in receivables as of December 31. In addition, since Imaginary Products collects 15 percent of its sales in the sales month, it must have 85 percent of its December sales left as receivables at the end of the month. The projected December sales of $811,500 implies receivables of about $690,000 at the end of the month. Table 21.8 summarizes these calculations, and shows that the total level of accounts receivable expected at the end of 1992 is about $1,231,000.[2]

---

[1] Notice that to find the increase in the cash level for 1992, you need to take the square root of 1.07, which is 1.0344. This means that if sales grow from $1.00 to $1.07 in the course of a year, the cash level will increase from $1.00 to $1.0344 in the same period of time. This represents an increase of 3.44 percent.

[2] Note that accounts receivable are expected to more than double during 1992. In December 1991 the actual level was $520,000, and it is expected to grow to $1,231,000 in December 1992. Such tremendous expected growth should be a matter of concern to the financial manager. In particular, one would expect an increase of only about 7 percent during the year, since accounts receivable should increase linearly with sales if the average collection period is unchanged. To explain this discrepancy, we assume that the receivables collection for the end of 1991 was unusually fast.

FINANCE TODAY

Sell Two Stocks and Call Me in the Morning

Small firms fail most often due to a crisis in short-term financial planning. Often they simply run out of cash and cannot pay their bills. Foothill Group, Inc., based in Los Angeles, has been in the business of helping such small firms with loans when commercial banks and other lenders were unwilling to take the risk.

For example, Preway, Inc., is a Wisconsin-based maker of fireplaces and grills, with sales of about $130 million per year. Due to planning difficulties, Preway suffered a cash shortage. Foothill offered Preway a $25 million line of credit. James Egan, chairman of Preway, said, "We were very pleased and surprised by Foothill's quickness and willingness to take on the risk. We still have a long row ahead of us, but we've gotten breathing room."

While Foothill played doctor to firms suffering from dreadful planning diseases, the doctor had contracted the same illness. Foothill played the oil boom in the early 1980s by investing heavily in Texas, where it had 25 percent of its assets. Failing to anticipate the incredible fall in oil prices of the mid-1980s, it lost $40 million in its Texas ventures.

At that point, Foothill sought help with its own doctor, Drexel Burnham Lambert. Drexel, famed for its ability to help firms with low credit ratings in issuing bonds (and at that time home to junk bond king Michael Milken), helped Foothill float a $40 million bond issue. While its management assured the public that Foothill was back on track, top management was selling shares very rapidly. Stockholders were not to worry, however, because the shares were being sold for "personal reasons." Honest.

By 1991, Drexel itself was bankrupt and "King Michael" was serving time in jail.

Source: Marc Beauchamp, "Taking the Cure," *Forbes,* May 5, 1986.

Inventory   If we assume that Imaginary products uses the EOQ method to manage its inventories, the inventory account level will increase in proportion to the square root of sales, as was the case with cash. With the projected 7 percent increase in sales, this means that the inventory level will increase by 3.44 percent, taking inventory at year end from $670,000 in 1991 to $693,000 in 1992.

Plant and Equipment   Imaginary Products is not planning any additions to plant and equipment is 1992, so we project that this asset category will remain at $23,000,000.

Accumulated Depreciation   The firm must depreciate assets on a fixed schedule determined when it places the assets in service. Therefore, we can project the accumulated depreciation at year end 1992 exactly. The depreciation for 1992 will be $812,000, which matches the figure on the pro forma income statement. This gives a total accumulated depreciation of $9,062,000.

Accounts Payable With the forecasted increase in sales, Imaginary Products expects to require more materials from its suppliers. If it maintains its present payment policies, its accounts payable at this same time next year should be approximately 7 percent greater than presently. This growth would parallel the anticipated increase in sales. If that is the case, the new level of accounts payable would be 7 percent greater than $390,000, or $417,000.

Accruals Just as Imaginary Products expects accounts payable to increase with sales, it plans the same increase in accruals, reflecting the greater number of workers that the firm requires to produce the higher volume of items that it plans to sell in 1992. A 7 percent increase in accruals gives a forecasted accruals account of approximately $43,000.

Taxes Payable Tax rates increase as income increases. Therefore, with its projected higher pretax profits, Imaginary Product's taxes may grow at a rate greater than 7 percent. Accordingly, even if the company follows the same policies regarding its tax payments, it expects to have 10 percent more in taxes payable in one year. This would mean taxes payable of $110,000.[3]

Retained Earnings We saw from the pro forma income statement that Imaginary Products expects earnings in 1992 of $51,000, which is a very low level of earnings for a firm with such a large asset base. Nonetheless, Imaginary Products plans a cash dividend of $0.03 per share. With 1 million shares outstanding, this is a total dividend of $30,000. Because the firm must devote after-tax earnings either to dividends or to retained earnings, it plans a $21,000 increase in retained earnings. This will increase retained earnings from $4,565,000 to $4,586,000.

Based on the forecast changes in each of the asset categories summarized above, Table 21.9 presents a partially completed pro forma balance sheet for December 1992. For all of the completed assets and liabilities, it shows total assets of $16,079,000 and total liabilities and net worth of $15,756,000. These numbers do not reflect the level of marketable securities or notes payable. Because the balance sheet must balance, we know that the following relationship must hold:

$16,079,000 + \text{marketable securities} = \$15,756,000 + \text{notes payable}$

Equivalently, we have

$\text{Notes payable} - \text{marketable securities} = \$323,000$

---

[3] Taxes payable are greater than the firm's earnings. This is possible if the firm owes taxes from previous years or if it must pay other types of taxes in addition to income taxes.

TABLE 21.9 Preliminary Pro Forma Balance Sheet for December 31, 1992, for Imaginary Products (thousands of dollars)

ASSETS			LIABILITIES AND NET WORTH		
Cash	$ 217		Accounts payable	$ 417	
Accounts receivable	1,231		Notes payable	?	Balancing item
Inventory	693		Accruals	43	
Marketable securities	?	Balancing item	Taxes payable	110	
Current assets	2,141	+ marketable securities	Current liabilities	570	+ notes payable
			Long-term liabilities	9,600	
Plant and equipment	23,000		**Total liabilities**	**10,170**	**+ notes payable**
Less accumulated					
depreciation	9,062		Common stock		
Total fixed assets	13,938		($1 par; 1 million shares)	1,000	
			Retained earnings	4,586	
Total assets	**$16,079**	**+ marketable securities**	**Net worth**	**5,586**	
			Total liabilities and net worth	**$15,756**	**+ notes payable**

The firm has the option of choosing any combination of the two balancing accounts, as long as their difference is $323,000. We assume that it prefers to have the lowest possible level of notes payable and will reduce its marketable securities to 0. It follows that it will have $323,000 in notes payable at the end of 1992. With these additional figures for marketable securities and notes payable, we can complete the pro forma balance sheet, which is presented in Table 21.10.

TABLE 21.10 Pro Forma Balance Sheet for December 31, 1992, for Imaginary Products (thousands of dollars)

ASSETS		LIABILITIES AND NET WORTH	
Cash	$ 217	Accounts payable	$ 417
Accounts receivable	1,231	Notes Payable	323
Inventory	693	Accruals	43
Marketable securities	0	Taxes payable	110
Current assets	2,141	Current liabilities	893
		Long-term liabilities	9,600
Plant and equipment	23,000	**Total liabilities**	**10,493**
Less accumulated			
depreciation	9,062	Common stock	
Total fixed assets	13,938	($1 par; 1 million shares)	1,000
		Retained earnings	4,586
Total assets	**$16,079**	**Net worth**	**5,586**
		Total liabilities and net worth	**$16,079**

Meltdown for the World's Nuclear Power Industry?

Risk is ever present, and the savvy financial manager must incorporate risk into the strategic planning of the firm. Unfortunately, the world's nuclear power industry does not seem to have been completely successful in this respect. After the nuclear reactor accident at Three Mile Island in 1979, the construction of new nuclear plants in the United States came to a grinding halt. The combination of safety problems and out-of-control construction costs made the feasibility of nuclear plants politically difficult and economically prohibitive.

Most analysts agree that the world dearly needs an alternative to oil as one of its main sources of energy. This was evident in the oil shocks of 1973 and 1979, and in the 1991 Gulf War between Iraq and the coalition of Arab and Western countries, leading to the liberation of the oil-rich Arab country Kuwait. While nuclear energy can theoretically provide abundant energy for the world, it is opposed by many on safety grounds. In Japan, a major importer of oil, a nuclear reactor at a plant about 200 miles from Tokyo had a close call in 1991 when radiation levels increased enormously. Fortunately, the cooling system worked, and a major disaster was averted. In contrast, the nuclear industry in France, a country with few conventional energy sources of its own, seems to enjoy a reasonable reputation and a solid safety record, at least thus far.

Perhaps more than the Three Mile Island incident, it is the nuclear meltdown at Chernobyl, USSR, on April 26, 1986, that has given nuclear energy a bad name. It seems that the cause of the Chernobyl accident was human error. Indeed, while the reactor was running and generating large amounts of heat, the emergency water-cooling system was turned off. One

FINANCIAL PLANNING AND PRO FORMA STATEMENTS

The pro forma balance sheet of Table 21.10 reflects an improvement in the firm's liquidity. It also reflects a decision to sacrifice modernization of plant and equipment. If Imaginary Products realizes the operating plans for 1992 it will greatly increase accounts receivable, and it will repay many of its outstanding notes. These measures will greatly increase its liquidity. The current ratio will increase from 1.39 at the end of 1991 to 2.40 in 1992. Therefore, the firm will go from being very illiquid to being sufficiently liquid.

With the appropriate liquidity currently being planned, management might decide to modernize the plant and equipment during 1992. It also has other alternatives for using its expected excess liquidity, for example, to pay a higher dividend, or even repurchase some of its outstanding shares.

miscalculation after another led to a neutron buildup in the nuclear core, where the nuclear reaction suddenly went out of control. This induced an explosion of the nuclear fuel, and another steam-induced explosion blew the lid off the reactor, whose containment structure was not designed for such tremendous pressures. A chemical explosion followed and the scattered fragments caused further local fires.

At first, the Soviet government tried to deny that anything had happened. However, monitoring in neighboring European countries soon revealed an unusual amount of radiation, and the USSR had to recognize the magnitude of the disaster.

Thirty-one persons were killed immediately or shortly thereafter and about 500 others were hospitalized. The force of the explosion and fire carried much of the radioactivity away from the site to high altitudes, where it spread across the Northern Hemisphere. Data on the worldwide effects of this fallout still remain inconclusive.

In the Soviet Union itself, authorities acknowledged in 1990 that several million people were still living on contaminated ground. Incidences of thyroid cancer, leukemia, and other radiation-related illnesses were higher than normal among this population. Similarly, in the animal population, the damage was tremendous. For example, soon after the accident, animals with two heads and horses with five or more legs were born.

Meanwhile, back at Chernobyl, the fateful reactor was entombed in concrete and the other reactors at the plant were back in operation. In a 1987 trial, six plant officials were convicted for gross safety violations.

Source: "Chernobyl," *Academic American Encyclopedia* (New York: Grolier Electronic Publishing, Inc., 1990).

☞ If the position of the firm revealed by the pro forma statements is not satisfactory, management knows that changes in its plans are required.

From the point that we have reached in our analysis, the managers of Imaginary Products might go on to consider additions to plant and equipment. The managers could incorporate some capital expenditures in a revised cash budget, and prepare new pro forma statements to reflect those plans. The essential point is that the firm can use pro forma statements and the cash budget to facilitate the planning process, thus offering management insights into the effects of various alternatives.

OTHER FORECASTING AND FINANCIAL PLANNING TECHNIQUES

Preparing cash budgets and pro forma statements can be a tedious process. Furthermore, their usefulness depends on the accuracy of the numbers that are used as input. Realizing these limitations, some important advances have been made in planning techniques.

Financial Planning Models

financial planning model
a computerized system expressing the different financial relationships for a firm

A **financial planning model** is a computerized system expressing different financial relationships using a firm's accounting statements as a base. In a typical model, changing one assumption about how long it will take to collect accounts receivable automatically affects the pro forma income statement and the pro forma balance sheet. For example, we based the cash budget for Imaginary Products on the assumption that the firm receives 15 percent of sales in the sales month, 35 percent the next month, and 50 percent the following month. The associated cash flows affect the balance sheet entries for cash and ultimately affect the profitability of the firm.

☞ With a financial planning model, managers can automate much of the preparation of the pro forma financial statements and cash budget.

A manager might wish to investigate the effect of collecting accounts receivable more quickly. For example, if Imaginary Products were able to collect 30 percent the first month, 40 percent the second month, and 30 percent the third month, how would this affect the cash account in the pro forma statement? In many financial planning models, we can determine the answer to this question by typing the three new percentages into the computer. The computer program would be able to calculate and print a new cash budget, a new pro forma income statement, and a new pro forma balance sheet in a matter of seconds. Such models can eliminate much of the drudgery and the chance of error from the preparation of the firm's pro forma statements. Another benefit is that it allows managers to check the effects of different management policies. They have been available for several years but, until recently, required access to a large mainframe computers. Now, many programs exist that operate on personal computers. Also, many spreadsheet computer programs make it very easy for managers to create their own financial planning models to fit their specific needs.

☞ With a financial planning model, the effects of prospective changes in sales or cash flows can be tested quickly.

Simulation Models

In discussing pro forma statements, we estimated the change in certain asset and liability categories by assuming that the same relationships that prevailed in the past would hold for the future. Such an assumption may work very well for some firms in some industries; however, it won't always. For example, one of the major expenses for an airline is fuel. Assuming that fuel cost is directly related to ticket sales is very dangerous. In many periods of high fuel cost, airline travel may actually decline due to general difficulties in the economy. In this instance, financial planning that assumes fuel costs to be a certain percentage of sales will be highly prone to error.

simulation model
a mathematical computer program expressing the relationship among several variables that allows the variables to change randomly

Simulation models are computer programs that express the relationship between two or more variables in mathematical terms. They allow the user to change one variable at random and to observe the effect of that change on other variables. A corporation might use a simulation model to gain a better understanding of the relationship between its performance and developments in the economy. For example, an airline might use it to try to predict the effect of an increase in oil prices on the economy and on its ridership. The change in oil prices would affect the company in several ways. First, it would have a direct effect by increasing its fuel costs. This effect would occur even if there was no change in the number of flights. However, with a major oil price increase, general economic activity might suffer. Because airlines rely very heavily on business travel, this could be particularly worrisome. The oil price increase could mean increasing fuel costs at exactly the time that ridership falls. This double-barreled effect could be very serious. Thus a simulation model could provide managers with a better picture of the vulnerability of their airline. More important, managers might learn what corrective action they could take to make their business less vulnerable to oil price increases.

☞ Simulation models allow managers to test the sensitivity of variables, such as cash flow, to random changes in other variables, such as changes in raw material prices.

Simulation models can be used to aid in the planning for many eventualities. Because they are usually quite complex and designed for specific applications, they tend to be used mainly by large firms. At the fast pace that computer technology is developing, however, we can expect to see more elaborate simulation models suitable for use on personal computers.

SUMMARY

This chapter explored some of the basic techniques of financial planning. The first of these concerns the cash budget. Every firm needs cash to survive. Failure to make a contractually obligated payment on time means technical insolvency, and can lead to bankruptcy and the dissolution of the firm. As a consequence, it is necessary to manage cash accounts to ensure that adequate funds are always available to pay obligations.

The cash budget is essentially a plan for the cash balances of the firm over a future period. Managers use it to highlight periods requiring additional cash and to identify those that generate excess cash.

The second major technique is the pro forma statement, which is a planned income statement for a future date. It relies on a forecast of revenues and expenses and provides a plan for firm operations over the coming period. A pro forma balance sheet is a planned balance sheet for a particular date in the future. Managers usually prepare it in conjunction with the pro forma income statement.

On occasion, pro forma statements give a picture that managers do not want to see, such as deterioration of the firm's liquidity. In such cases, preparation of the pro forma statements serves to highlight problem areas for management attention, and therefore is important in the planning process.

QUESTIONS

1. What is the difference between an income statement and a cash budget?
2. In preparing a cash budget, why does the financial manager have to know the level of sales and the collection pattern for sales?
3. Assume that you have prepared a cash budget for your firm and that you project a negative cash balance in one month. What responses are available to you?
4. Can you construct a pro forma balance sheet without a previous balance sheet? Why or why not?
5. When can you use financial ratios to guide the preparation of pro forma financial statements?
6. Can you construct a pro forma balance sheet without a pro forma income statement?
7. If a firm buys no new depreciable property during the period over which the pro forma statements are being prepared, is a pro forma income statement necessary to determine the accumulated depreciation on the pro forma balance sheet? Why or why not?
8. What is the difference between a financial planning model and a simulation model?
9. Assume that your firm is a large baker. If you wanted to test the sensitivity of its profitability to a wide variety of flour prices, would you be wiser to use a financial planning model or a simulation model? Why?

PROBLEMS

1. Assume that sales for November are $1.5 million. Of these sales, 30 percent are for cash, 20 percent are collected the next month, 20 percent the following month, 15 percent the following month, 10 percent the next month, and 5 percent the next month. Calculate the firm's cash inflow from these sales for each month.
2. For the same firm as Problem 1, assume that December sales are $1.2 million and follow the same collection cycle. Calculate the firm's cash inflows from these sales for each month.
3. Consider the following sales pattern observed in Sales Cycles, Inc., for the past year:

January	$150,000	July	$ 80,000
February	180,000	August	70,000
March	220,000	September	110,000
April	280,000	October	130,000
May	200,000	November	120,000
June	120,000	December	150,000

If Sales Cycles makes 40 percent of its sales for cash, collects 35 percent of its sales the following month, and the final 25 percent the next month, show the cash flows generated by the sales presented above.

4. In planning for next year, Sales Cycles expects sales to be 12 percent above last year's levels shown in Problem 3. Calculate the forecasted sales on a month-by-month basis for the next year.

5. Assume that Sales Cycles collects 60 percent of its sales in cash, 25 percent the following month, and the final 15 percent the next month. Based on the sales projected in Problem 4, calculate the firm's projected cash receipts for the next year.

We met Dismal Industries in Chapter 20. Its 1991 balance sheet and income statement are presented below. We will use Dismal to develop an integrated cash budget and pro forma statements.

Balance Sheet for December 31, 1991, for Dismal Industries (thousands of dollars)

ASSETS		LIABILITIES AND NET WORTH	
Cash	$ 100	Accounts payable	$ 325
Marketable securities	50	Notes payable	340
Accounts receivable	570	Accruals	150
Inventory	200	Taxes payable	90
Current assets	920	Current liabilities	905
		Long-term liabilities	5,000
Plant and equipment	15,080		
Less accumulated		**Total liabilities**	**5,905**
depreciation	5,900	Common stock	
Total fixed assets	9,180	($1 par; 1 million shares)	1,000
		Retained earnings	3,195
Total assets	**$10,100**		
		Net worth	**4,195**
		Total liabilities and net worth	**$10,100**

Income Statement for 1991 for Dismal Industries (thousands of dollars)

Sales	$8,000
Costs of goods sold	6,100
Gross profit	1,900
Depreciation	900
Selling and administrative expenses	250
Interest expense	400
Earnings before taxes	250
Taxes	100
Earnings after taxes	150

The sales pattern for Dismal for selected months usually follows the pattern given below:

	Percentage	Actual Sales for 1991
November	10%	$800,000
December	12	960,000
January	8	640,000
February	6	480,000
March	5	400,000

Dismal expects the same percentages to be maintained in 1992, but is looking for an increase in sales of 12 percent over the 1991 level.

6. Based on the information about sales, what is Dismal's total forecasted sales in 1992?
7. Based on the information presented, what is the forecasted level of sales for January, February, and March 1992?

Dismal collects 50 percent of its sales in cash, 30 percent the following month, and 20 percent the next month.

8. What collections will it make in the future (after December 31, 1991) from its 1991 sales? When will these amounts be collected?
9. For the January 1992 sales, what portions will be collected in January, February, and March?
10. For the February 1992 sales, what portions will be collected in February and March?
11. For the March 1992 sales, what portion will be collected in March?
12. Calculate the total cash inflows from sales for January, February, and March, based on your answers to the four preceding questions.
13. Dismal's balance sheet shows $905,000 in current liabilities, including $325,000 in accounts payable. It will pay off $25,000 of these accounts payable immediately, and pay the remainder evenly over January, February, and March. Prepare a schedule for the first three months of 1992 showing these disbursements.
14. Dismal plans to purchase $300,000 of supplies each month. It pays for 50 percent of these in cash, 25 percent the following month, and 25 percent the next month. Prepare a schedule for the first three months of 1992 showing the cash flows these purchases will generate.
15. Dismal must make its quarterly tax payment of $50,000 in March and principal payments on its notes payable of $150,000 in January and

March. Prepare a schedule for the first three months of 1992 showing the cash flows these disbursements will generate.

16. Dismal will pay 60 percent of its accruals in January and 40 percent in February, and will make wage payments of $150,000 in each month during the period January–March 1992. Prepare a schedule for the first three months of 1992 showing the cash flows these payments will generate.

17. Assemble all of the cash flows from the last four questions into a schedule of disbursements for Dismal Industries for the first three months of 1992.

18. Assemble the completed cash receipts and disbursement schedules into a cash budget for Dismal Industries for the first three months of 1992.

19. Using the income statement for Dismal Industries printed above, compute a percentage income statement.

20. Assume that Dismal's sales forecast for January–March 1992 is correct and that the same relative costs will be incurred. Using that information and the percentage income statement prepared in Problem 19, prepare a pro forma income statement for March 31, 1992.

We now turn to a preparation of a pro forma balance sheet for Dismal Industries. In the problems that follow, we will use the following assumptions. Dismal is not planning to issue any common stock or long-term debt. Dismal will use the cash and marketable securities accounts, together with the notes payable account, to force the pro forma balance sheet to balance. Inventory will expand at the same rate as sales.

21. Calculate the amount of accounts receivable Dismal should show on its March 31, 1992, pro forma balance sheet.

22. Calculate the amount of inventory Dismal should show on its March 31, 1992, pro forma balance sheet.

23. Assuming that Dismal purchases no new plant or equipment during this period, calculate the amount of plant and equipment it should show on its March 31, 1992, pro forma balance sheet.

24. Based on the pro forma income statement, what is the amount of accumulated depreciation that Dismal should show on its March 31, 1992, pro forma balance sheet?

25. Accruals should increase proportionally with sales, so what is the amount of accumulated accruals that Dismal should show on its March 31, 1992, pro forma balance sheet, assuming a sales increase of 12 percent?

26. Dismal expects taxes payable to increase by 15 percent over the pro forma period. What amount of taxes payable should it show on its March 31, 1992, pro forma balance sheet?

27. Dismal anticipates no dividend payments during the pro forma period, so what should it show on its March 31, 1992, pro forma balance sheet in the retained earnings account?

28. Using the data developed to this point, construct a pro forma balance sheet for Dismal Industries for March 31, 1992, leaving cash, notes payable, and marketable securities blank for future balancing.
29. Assuming no changes in marketable securities or notes payable, except for those in notes payable we have already considered, what is the value of the cash account?
30. If Dismal wishes to have the same ratio of cash to total assets on March 31, 1992, as it had on December 31, 1991, what action would you recommend?

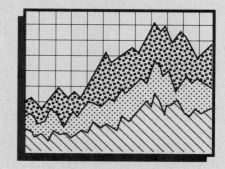

PART 7

STRATEGIC ISSUES IN CORPORATE FINANCE

Capital Structure and Dividend Policy

capital structure
the division of the firm's total capital needs among equity, debt, and other forms of financing

I n this chapter we consider two perennial problems of corporate finance: capital structure and dividend policy. **Capital structure** is the division of the firm's total capital needs among equity, debt, and other forms of financing. In setting capital structure, the manager must determine which sources of financing should be used, and in what quantities. In other words, the problem is how to structure the firm's capital in order to maximize shareholders' wealth. The pricing concepts developed in Chapter 10 emphasize the crucial role of dividends in share valuation. This chapter examines the role dividend policy plays in maximizing the value of the firm's shares.

perfect market
a market with no transaction costs and free information

The issues of capital structure and dividend policy are two of the murkiest and most controversial problems in corporate finance. We begin our analysis by examining their role in a world of zero taxes and perfect markets. A **perfect market** is one with no transaction costs and free information. In such an environment, neither capital structure nor dividend policy affects the value of the firm. After seeing why that is the case, we enrich our discussion to include both taxes and market imperfections.

CAPITAL STRUCTURE IN A WORLD OF PERFECT CAPITAL MARKETS AND NO TAXES

☞ If capital markets are perfect and if there are no taxes, the firm's choice of capital structure is totally inconsequential.

This section explores the famous argument of Modigliani and Miller,[1] which maintains that the choice of capital structure has no effect on the value of the firm if capital markets are perfect and there are no taxes. In essence, the argument runs as follows. If there are perfect capital markets and no taxes, capital structure cannot affect firm value because individual investors can alter their investment to any mix of debt and equity desired. If the firm uses leverage and the investor wishes an unlevered investment, the investor can undo the leverage by transacting in the financial marketplace. The same holds

---

[1] F. Modigliani and M. H. Miller, "The Cost of Capital, Corporation Finance and the Theory of Investment," *American Economic Review,* June 1958, pp. 61–297.

TABLE 22.1   Alternative Financing Plans

	Unlevered	Levered
Stock ($100 per share)	$1,000,000	$ 500,000
Bonds (10% interest)	0	500,000
Total financing	1,000,000	1,000,000

true if the firm uses no debt and the investor wishes a levered position. In this case, the investor trades to create "homemade leverage." In short, because the investor can create any capital structure desired, the choice of capital structure cannot affect the firm's value.

To explore their argument, consider a firm with assets worth $1 million that is considering two different plans for financing the assets. First, it can do this with 10,000 shares of common stock, each share costing $100. Alternatively, it might finance 50 percent of the assets with stock and 50 percent with debt. In that case, we assume the firm issues 5,000 shares of stock at $100 per share and issues debt of $500,000 at an interest rate of 10 percent. Table 22.1 summarizes the two plans.

If investors could not trade freely in the marketplace, they would be stuck with the degree of leverage chosen by the firm. However, with the ability to trade securities in a perfect market with no taxes, they can choose either capital structure, no matter what the firm does. To illustrate this idea, we assume first that the firm chooses the unlevered strategy and show how an individual investor trades to create homemade leverage. Second, we assume the firm chooses a levered strategy, and we show how the individual investor can unwind this leverage to create an unlevered position. Throughout our discussion, we assume the investor has a total capital of $100,000 to invest in this firm. Finally, we assume the firm's operating profit is uncertain, but it will be either $150,000 or $50,000.

The Investor and Homemade Leverage

We assume that the firm issues only common stock and that the investor wishes to create a position that is 50 percent stock and 50 percent debt. In that case, the investor borrows $100,000 at a rate of interest of 10 percent.[2] Combining the borrowed funds with the investor's own capital gives a total of $200,000, all of which is used to purchase funds in the unlevered firm, giving the investor 20 percent of the firm. If the argument is correct, this investment in the unlevered firm should perform exactly like a $100,000 investment in the levered firm.

---

[2] The borrowing rate is 10 percent because in a perfect market everyone can borrow at the same rate, so the investor's borrowing rate equals the firm's borrowing rate of 10 percent.

TABLE 22.2 Effects of Firm Leverage and the Effect of Homemade Leverage

	Operating Income			Operating Income	
	$50,000	$150,000		$50,000	$150,000
INVESTMENT OF $100,000* IN A LEVERED FIRM			**INVESTMENT OF $200,000 IN AN UNLEVERED FIRM** (homemade leverage)		
Firm's interest expense			Earnings to shareholders	$50,000	$150,000
(10% on $500,000)	−$50,000	−$50,000	20% claim on earnings	10,000	30,000
Earnings to shareholders	0	100,000	Investor's interest expense		
20% claim on earnings	0	20,000	(10% on $100,000)	−10,000	−10,000
			Total received	**0**	**$ 20,000**

* 20% of the equity.

☞ With perfect capital markets and no taxes, individual investors can create or eliminate leverage no matter what action the firm takes.

Table 22.2 shows the transactions necessary to create homemade leverage, and the outcomes for the investor. Remember that we are considering two different possibilities for the firm's operating income to show that the effects of the firm's leverage and homemade leverage are the same. First, the investment of $100,000 in the shares of the levered firm purchases 20 percent of the outstanding shares, because the total assets are worth $1 million and 50 percent is financed with debt. If the operating income for the firm is $50,000, then it has earned exactly enough to pay the bondholders their interest (10 percent of $500,000). This leaves nothing for the stockholders. Alternatively, if the operating income is $150,000, the firm pays $50,000 to the bondholders, leaving $100,000 for the stockholders. Our investor is entitled to 20 percent of that, or $20,000. In summary, for the direct investment of $100,000 in the levered firm, the investor receives nothing if the operating income is $50,000, and receives $20,000 if the operating income is $150,000.

Table 22.2 also shows the investment outcomes for the investor using homemade leverage. By borrowing $100,000 to supplement the capital of $100,000, the investor has $200,000 in the unlevered firm. Because the firm is unlevered, it has $1 million in equity, so the $200,000 gives the investor a 20 percent position in the firm. If the operating income is $50,000, our investor receives 20 percent of that, or $10,000. However, the investor must pay $10,000 interest on the borrowed funds, leaving 0. If the operating income is $150,000, our investor receives 20 percent, or $30,000. After paying $10,000 interest, $20,000 remains.

The direct investment in the levered firm gives exactly the same dollar payoff as investing in the unlevered firm when the investor uses homemade leverage. With $50,000 operating income, the investor receives nothing in both cases, but if the firm has $150,000 in operating income, the investor receives $20,000 in both cases. Therefore, the two positions are equivalent.

Look Ma, No Debt

Although most mature companies have some long-term debt on their balance sheet, some prefer to finance all their assets with equity only. According to capital structure theory, this must be the optimal course of action for these firms. One plausible explanation for this avoidance of debt is the perception that the firms' EBIT might become extremely volatile in the future. When volatility is excessive, the costs associated with financial distress and the risk of default may outweigh any tax-induced benefits of debt.

Here is a sampler of companies that recently reported no long-term debt on their balance sheets:

Firms with No Long-Term Debt

Company	52-Week Price Range*	P/E Ratio[†]
Anthem Electronics	$13–36	11
Dreyfus	22–38	9
Dun & Bradstreet	36–49	16
Logicon	14–20	11
Rollins	15–22	18
Skyline	12–18	23
Tootsie Roll	31–50	18
William Wrigley	44–59	19

* Prices rounded to nearest dollar.
[†] Price divided by past 12 months' per-share earnings, as of closing on January 29, 1991.

Source: Wall Street Journal, January 31, 1991.

Unwinding Firm Leverage

As an alternative, assume that the firm is levered and that the investor wishes to unwind or undo the effect of leverage. We have already seen that the investor can create homemade leverage, so unwinding firm leverage is exactly the opposite. In this case, the investor transacts to create an investment behaving like an investment in an unlevered firm.

Table 22.3 shows how an investment of $100,000 in an unlevered firm performs for operating income of either $50,000 or $150,000. With a $100,000 investment, our investor has a 10 percent claim, which pays either $5,000 or $15,000. If only a levered firm exists, can the investor invest in it in a way that makes the investment perform just as it would if funds were invested in an unlevered firm? In essence, the investor invests $50,000 in the stock of the

TABLE 22.3   Effects of Investing in Unlevered Firms and Unwinding Firm Leverage

	Operating Income			Operating Income	
	$50,000	$150,000		$50,000	$150,000
INVESTMENT OF $100,000* IN AN UNLEVERED FIRM			**UNWINDING THE LEVERAGE FOR AN INVESTMENT OF $50,000**		
Earnings to shareholders	$50,000	$150,000	Firm's interest expense		
10% claim on earnings	5,000	15,000	(10% on $500,000)	$ − 50,000	$ − 50,000
			Earnings to shareholders	0	100,000
			10% claim on earnings	0	10,000
			Interest received on		
			a loan of $50,000	5,000	5,000
			Total received	**$ 5,000**	**$ 15,000**

* 10% of the equity.

levered company, and lends the other $50,000 at the prevailing interest rate of 10 percent.

If the operating income is $50,000, the firm earns just enough to pay its interest expense, so the 10 percent claim on the firm's equity pays 0 to our investor. However, the interest earnings on the $50,000 pays $5,000, so our investor has a total dollar return of $5,000 if the firm's operating income is $50,000. As an alternative, if the operating income is $150,000, the firm pays its $50,000 interest expense, leaving $100,000 for the stockholders. With a 10 percent claim, the investor receives $10,000 and, in addition, the interest payment of $5,000, giving a total of $15,000.

No matter what the operating income, the investor's combined position of stock ownership and lending pays the same as the investment of $100,000 in the unlevered firm. Both positions pay $5,000 if operating income is $50,000 and $15,000 if operating income is $150,000. Therefore, the investor can undo the effect of the firm's leverage.

By these examples we have shown that the investor can create any kind of investment payoff that a firm could create through the selection of its capital structure. Because of the investor's ability to create or avoid leverage, the firm's choice of leverage cannot alter the payoffs available to investors. Therefore, the firm's leverage decision is irrelevant to the value of the firm.

Remember, though, we reached this conclusion under the assumptions of perfect capital markets without taxes. When we remove these assumptions, capital structure may affect firm value. However, if capital structure is irrelevant in a world of perfect markets and no taxes, we have shown that its

FINANCE

TODAY

The Debt Hangover

The role of corporate leverage has long been debated. Critics like American Airlines CEO Robert Crandall contend that growing indebtedness has hobbled companies and robbed them of their futures. The critics have a point. During the 1980s debt as a percent of total capital at nonfinancial companies grew from 34 percent to 49 percent. A more revealing measure is decreasing interest coverage, or times interest earned (TIE). In 1980 nonfinancial companies enjoyed a cushy interest coverage of 4.6. Today that margin of safety is estimated to be only 3.3.

While acknowledging that debt has risks, proponents of leverage argue that it has brought benefits too. During the 1980s stock prices rose 228 percent, due in no small part to cash flow improvements that higher borrowing helped generate. Higher debt has also improved companies' competitive position by lowering their cost of capital.

The use of debt clearly has advantages and disadvantages. Leverage, alas, is not a science, but an imponderable balance of math, intuition, fear, and greed. After the excesses of the 1980s, borrowers and creditors greeted the 1990s with a terrific debt-induced hangover.

It's no secret what debt can do for corporate performance. It boosts a company's return on shareholders' equity. But there was another reason managers chose to leverage up their firms: debt's privileged status in the corporate tax code. Interest payments to lenders are tax-deductible, whereas dividend payments to stockholders are not, making debt a far cheaper way to finance growth than equity. Hence, more debt, within limits, means a lower cost of capital.

Valuable though it is, there are limits to how much the tax break from leverage can do for shareholders. As a company increases its borrowing, it also increases its risk of default. At some point that differs for every company, the tax benefits are outweighed by the higher capital costs, and shareholder value begins to shrink. In other words, it's not worth risking the ranch by chasing deductions.

In the end, the lessons to be learned from the 1980s come down to two. The simplest and most painful is the one that many borrowers forgot: that debt is unyielding and unforgiving. Take on too much and there's a good chance you will be out of business. But lenders also forgot the second lesson: that interest yield is only one component of return—getting back the principal is the other.

Source: John J. Curran, "Hard Lessons from the Debt Decade," *Fortune*, June 18, 1990.

importance in the real world must depend on the existence of taxes and market imperfections.

DIVIDENDS IN A WORLD OF NO TAXES AND PERFECT MARKETS

In a separate contribution, Miller and Modigliani also argued that dividend policy is irrelevant to the value of the firm in a world with perfect markets and no taxes.[3] Just like investors can create homemade leverage, they can also create homemade dividends.

To see the recipe for homemade dividends, consider an all equity firm with assets of $1 million that is considering paying a cash dividend. Assume also that the firm has 10,000 shares outstanding and that a particular shareholder holds 1,000 shares, which is a 10 percent interest. Throughout this chapter, we assume that book and market values are identical. The firm is considering two alternative dividend policies:

1. Pay $100,000 as a cash dividend, leaving assets of $900,000, so each share will be worth $90 after the dividend is paid.
2. Pay no dividend, keeping all $1 million in assets, and the 10,000 outstanding shares will each be worth $100.

No matter which policy the firm follows, assume it earns 10 percent return on its assets during the next year of operations, as summarized in Figure 22.1. If it pays $100,000 in dividends, it will be smaller as a result of the dividend decision, holding only $900,000 in assets, but the stockholders will have $100,000 in cash. If the firm chooses not to pay a dividend, it will have $1 million in assets.

☞ If capital markets are perfect and there are no taxes, the dividend decision does not affect shareholder wealth.

We next consider the firm's position under the two policies after one year of operations, during which we assume the firm earned 10 percent on its assets. After that year of operations, it will have a total value of $990,000 if it paid a dividend, and $1.1 million if it did not.

The stockholder with a 10 percent original interest will have stock worth $99,000 if the firm paid the dividend, plus the $10,000 in dividends received, for a total wealth of $109,000. If the firm paid no dividends, the 10 percent ownership interest will be worth $110,000.

To show that the firm's dividend decision does not affect shareholder wealth, we have to see how the shareholder can undo the dividend policy by transacting in the marketplace. More exactly, if the firm pays a dividend, we will show how the stockholder can achieve the same position as if the firm had not done so. Similarly, if the firm chooses not to pay a dividend, we will show how the stockholder can achieve the same position as if it did.

---

[3] See Merton H. Miller and Franco Modigliani, "Dividend Policy, Growth, and the Valuation of Shares," *Journal of Business*, 34, October 1961, pp. 411–433.

FINANCE

TODAY

The Sky's the Limit

Government debt grew so dramatically in the 1980s that a taxpayer might well ask: "Now how much do I owe?" And perhaps more to the point: "Will my taxes go up to pay for it?"

It's true that the $150 billion average budget deficits of the 1980s tripled the national debt over the last 10 years, as shown in the figure. But that doesn't mean that the average taxpayer's debt burden is now three times as heavy. There are several mitigating factors.

First, population and prices have also increased, so the rise in real debt per capita has not been so dramatic. Second, real income per capita, and hence the average taxpayer's ability to pay a debt, have gone up too. And finally, the government has been accumulating assets, not just liabilities, over the years. Those assets can help the government rationalize the size of its debt.

But even so, some disturbing trends are beginning to emerge. The government is accumulating debt more rapidly than assets. If this trend continues, higher tax rates or reduced government services seem inevitable.

Nominal Federal Debt

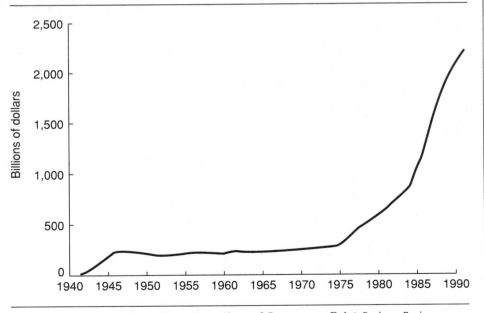

Source: Dean Croushore, "How Big Is Your Share of Government Debt? *Business Review,* November–December 1990, p. 3.

FIGURE 22.1 The Firm's Dividend Decision and Its Effects

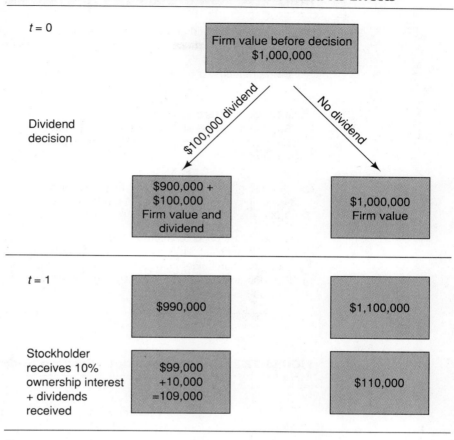

Table 22.4 shows the steps necessary for the stockholder to undo the firm's dividend decision. If the firm pays a dividend, as shown in the top half of the table, the shareholder merely uses the dividend received to buy more shares in the firm. With 10,000 shares outstanding and $900,000 in assets, each share sells for $90 so the shareholder can buy 111.11 shares with the $10,000 in dividends. Notice that this increases the shareholder's interest in the firm to 11.11 percent.

On the other hand, if the firm pays no dividend and the shareholder desires one, the transactions to create a homemade dividend are shown in the bottom of Table 22.4. In this case, the assets of the firm are $1 million, and with 10,000 shares outstanding each one will be worth $100. To receive a $10,000 dividend, the shareholder merely sells 100 shares. This leaves 900

☞ If capital markets are perfect and there are no taxes, the individual investor may transact privately to provide any kind of dividend policy.

TABLE 22.4 How to Undo the Firm's Dividend Policy

The firm pays a dividend and the shareholder doesn't want one:

Shareholder's position after dividend

1,000 shares at $90	$ 90,000
Cash dividend just received	10,000
	$100,000

Shareholder transacts to offset the dividend

Buy 111.11 shares at $90 per share for $10,000.

Now the shareholder owns 1,111.11 of 10,000 shares, or an 11.11% interest in the firm.

The firm doesn't pay a dividend and the shareholder wants one:

Shareholder's position after the no-dividend decision

1,000 shares at $100	$100,000

Shareholder transacts to create a dividend

Sell 100 shares at $100 for a total of $10,000.

Now the shareholder holds 900 shares at $100 per share for a total value of $90,000 and has an interest in the firm of 9%. In addition, the shareholder has $10,000 in cash.

FIGURE 22.2 The Shareholder's Position Under Alternative Plans

	Firm: Dividend paid (Firm value $990,000; Share price $99)	Firm: No dividend paid ($1,100,000; $110)
Shareholder: Did nothing	Stock $99,000; dividend received $10,000 } $109,000	Stock $110,000
Shareholder: Counteracted firm policy	Used dividend to buy 111.11 shares for a total of 1,111.11 shares at $99 = $110,000	900 Shares at $110 = $99,000; Proceeds from selling stock = $10,000 } $109,000

shares at $100 per share for an investment in the firm of $90,000. To see how these actions offset the firm's dividend policy, refer to the results summarized in Figure 22.2.

CAPITAL STRUCTURE IN THE REAL WORLD

The major complications of the real world that we neglected in our previous discussion are taxes and market imperfections. The existence of taxes makes it appear that firms should use a great deal of debt in their capital structures. By contrast, some market imperfections lead to the conclusion that firms must limit the amount of debt they use.

We begin our consideration of capital structure in the real world by considering the effect of taxes. The tax deductibility of interest suggests that firms should use a great deal of debt. To see why this is so, assume a firm has EBIT of $100,000 and faces a corporate tax rate of 30 percent. Borrowing costs are 10 percent. Under these assumptions, the firm has three claimants to its EBIT: stockholders, bondholders, and the government. To maximize its market value, the firm should reduce the government's tax bite wherever possible, and deliver a greater percentage of its EBIT to stock and bondholders. For a given set of assets and operating policy, the size of EBIT is fixed. However, the firm can change its allocation by modifying its capital structure.

Table 22.5 shows how capital structure can alter the allocation of funds to these three parties. If the firm has no debt and EBIT of $100,000, it pays $30,000 in taxes. However, as it begins to use leverage, the tax burden becomes smaller and smaller. With just 10 percent of the assets financed by debt, Table

TABLE 22.5   Capital Structure and the Division of a Firm's EBIT*

	Alternative Capital Structures			
	0% Debt	*10% Debt*	*20% Debt*	*70% Debt*
EBIT	$100,000	$100,000	$100,000	$100,000
Interest expense	0	−10,000	−20,000	−70,000
Earnings before tax	$100,000	$ 90,000	$ 80,000	$ 30,000
Tax (at 30%)	−30,000	−27,000	−24,000	−9,000
Earnings to stockholders	$ 70,000	$ 63,000	$ 56,000	$ 21,000
Shares outstanding	10,000	9,000	8,000	3,000
EPS	7.00	7.00	7.00	7.00
Percentage of EBIT paid in taxes	0.30	0.27	0.24	0.09
EBIT to bondholders and stockholders	$ 70,000	$ 73,000	$ 76,000	$ 91,000

* Assumptions: EBIT = $100,000   Corporate tax rate = 30%   Borrowing rate = 10%   Assets = $1,000,000
Share price = $100.

FIGURE 22.3   The Value of the Firm as a Function of Increasing Leverage, Assuming Perfect Markets

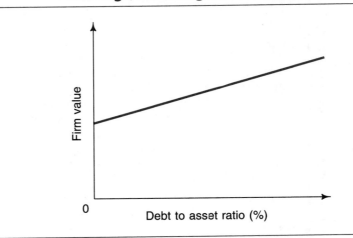

22.5 shows that $27,000 is paid in tax. By the time the firm has a debt/asset ratio of 70 percent, it pays only $9,000 in taxes. Therefore, the use of leverage reduces the portion of EBIT lost to taxes.

☞ Even if financial markets are perfect, taxes can make the capital structure decision important, because of the deductibility of interest payments.

With less being paid in taxes, the market value of the firm's outstanding securities should increase, because the cash available to reward stockholders and bondholders increases with the amount of leverage being used. This idea is represented in Figure 22.3, which shows the value of the firm increasing as leverage increases. This seems to imply that the firm should use virtually 100 percent debt financing. However, we must remember that this conclusion assumes that markets are perfect, except for the existence of taxes. In the next section we consider other kinds of imperfections that also affect the capital structure decision. As a consequence, we should *not* assume that firm value increases in lockstep with leverage in the real world.

☞ If financial markets are perfect, but there are taxes, it appears that firms should use 100 percent debt financing. This conclusion ignores the effect of increasing risk as more debt is employed.

In general, the total amount of cash available to bondholders and stockholders depends on the amount available, the corporate tax rate, T, the firm's borrowing rate, r_d, the amount of debt the firm does not use, CF_u, and the actual amount of debt the firm uses, D. The formula is:

$$\text{Cash to bond- and stockholders} = CF_u + T \times r_d \times D \qquad (22.1)$$

For example, when the firm uses 20 percent debt, or $200,000, the cash flow to bondholders and stockholders is $CF = \$70,000 + 0.30 \times 0.10 \times \$200,000 = \$76,000$. Clearly, according to Equation 22.1 and Table 22.5, the greater the use of debt, the greater the cash flow available to bondholders and stockholders. This suggests that the value of the firm should also increase in a similar fashion. This is indeed the case. The value of the levered firm equals the value of the unlevered firm plus a component that arises from the use of debt:

$$V_L = V_U + T \times D \qquad (22.2)$$

CAPITAL STRUCTURE, RISK, AND FINANCIAL DISTRESS

financial distress
any condition in which difficulties with the firm's financial obligations affect its operations

bankruptcy
a legally defined form of insolvency under the terms of the Federal Bankruptcy Act

☞ Financial distress, which may result from using too much financial leverage, has real costs.

A firm's value should increase with higher levels of leverage in the presence of taxes but with markets that are otherwise perfect, such as involving no transaction costs. Here we add more realism by considering other market imperfections; in particular, the risk of **financial distress**, including **bankruptcy.** Financial distress arises when the firm's financial obligations affect its operations. For example, if a company must sell productive equipment to meet its interest payments, it is in financial distress, because the financial obligations require an alteration of operating policy. There are many degrees of financial distress, the ultimate being bankruptcy leading to liquidation, a condition in which the firm is unable to meet its obligations and ceases operations.

By assuming in the previous section that markets were perfect except for taxes, we implicitly assumed that financial distress and bankruptcy were costless, in the sense that the firm's assets could be immediately sold at their fair market value and transferred to other productive employment without loss. This would be possible in a perfect market because there would be no transaction costs or delays of any kind. In the real world, however, financial distress is very costly. Assets cannot be sold and redeployed without a loss in value and efficiency. In bankruptcy proceedings, fees paid to accountants and lawyers are large, and these sums are lost to productive employment by the firm.

In Chapter 15 we observed how increasing financial leverage increases the riskiness of EPS. The higher the amount of leverage and the larger the promised debt payments, the greater the chance that the firm's EBIT will not be sufficient to make the promised payments to bondholders. For stockholders, the higher the degree of financial leverage, the greater the chance that the bondholders will not be paid and the greater the chance that the firm will go bankrupt, leaving them with nothing.

☞ The financial manager must weigh the advantage of saving taxes by using leverage against the increasing risk to the stockholders.

In spite of these dangers to the bond- and stockowners, there is an apparently undeniable advantage to using debt to avoid taxes. As a consequence, we have another of the ever-present trade-offs in finance. The financial manager must weigh the advantage of saving on taxes by using leverage against the increasing risk to the bond- and stockowners. It is necessary to select the correct amount of leverage to maximize the value of the firm, taking into consideration the trade-off between saving taxes and increasing risk.[4]

---

[4] Here we are assuming that the action that maximizes the firm's total value (the value of stocks plus bonds) is also the action that maximizes the value of its shares.

FIGURE 22.4   The Cost of Financial Distress and Increasing Leverage

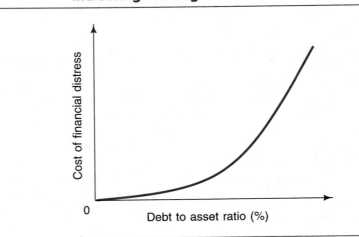

If we neglect tax effects and consider only financial distress, it appears that firms should use no debt.

Figure 22.4 shows how the cost of financial distress rises as leverage increases. As our measure of this cost we focus on the value of the firm. Very low levels of leverage have very little effect, because the use of a small amount of debt will not normally affect the probability of financial distress very much. As the amount of leverage increases, however, the cost of financial distress increases also, and the market value of the firm's outstanding bonds and stocks begins to fall. As the amount of leverage gets higher and higher, the cost of expected financial distress will increase dramatically, because increasing leverage increases the risk of financial distress at an increasing rate. For instance, a change in the debt to assets ratio from 0 to 10 percent might not change the risk of financial distress very much, but a change from 70 to 80 percent is likely to do so dramatically.

If we consider only the effect of financial distress, as shown in Figure 22.4, it appears the firm should use no debt financing. However, we must remember the trade-off. Figure 22.5 addresses those two offsetting effects explicitly by focusing on the changes in the firm's value as a function of financial leverage. The bottom half of the graph shows the negative effect on firm value due to the increasing chance of financial distress as leverage increases. In the top half we see the beneficial effect as a result of the taxes the firm saves, due to the interest deductibility feature of the tax law. The combined effects of tax savings and financial distress are shown in the dotted line of Figure 22.5. Initially, the total effect of leverage is positive, because the beneficial tax savings outweigh the negative financial distress effects. Eventually, however, the costs of financial distress become more important. This is reflected in the line showing the total effect, because it reaches a maximum value and then decreases as the amount of leverage is increased.

With low levels of debt, the tax savings usually outweigh the costs of financial distress.

With high levels of debt, the costs of financial distress may outweigh the benefit of tax savings.

FIGURE 22.5   The Effects of Tax Savings and Financial Distress as a Function of the Firm's Leverage

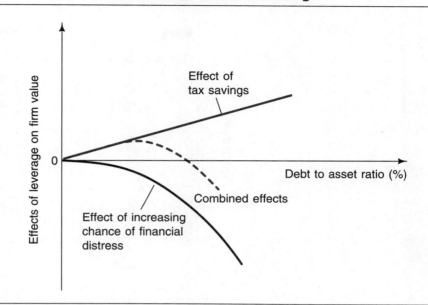

The financial manager should choose that level of leverage that maximizes value.

Capital structure had no effect on the value of the firm in an ideal world of no taxes and perfect markets. However, when we considered the effect of taxes alone, we reached the startling conclusion that a firm could always improve its position by using more debt, because it would reduce the government's tax bite, leaving more money to reward stock- and bondholders. Considering only taxes neglects another important kind of market imperfection—the fact that financial distress is costly. Increasing leverage increases the risk of financial distress with a negative effect on the value of the firm. The solution to this problem is to find the best trade-off between the benefit of saving taxes and the cost of increasing the risk of financial distress. That trade-off point maximizes the value of the firm and defines the appropriate level of leverage.

LEVERAGE AND THE FIRM'S COST OF CAPITAL

In our discussion of risk and return we saw that the investor's required rate of return depends on the systematic risk, or beta, of a project, as shown in the security market line of Figure 22.6. Because the firm's financing decision can affect its value, it also affects the required rate of return that the firm

FIGURE 22.6 The Relationship Between Beta and the Required Rate of Return (RRR) for a Project

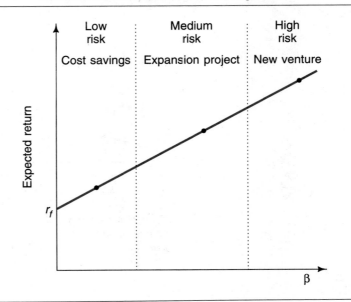

weighted average cost of capital (WACC)
the overall required rate of return for a firm that considers the cost of both debt and equity used by the firm; it is a weighted average because it reflects the proportions of both debt and equity used

must impose on its projects. This overall required rate of return is known as the **weighted average cost of capital (WACC)**. It considers the cost of both debt and equity, and is a weighted average reflecting the proportions of both as used by firm:

$$\text{WACC} = \frac{\text{equity}}{\text{assets}} r_e + \frac{\text{debt}}{\text{assets}} (1 - T)r_d \qquad (22.3)$$

where r_e = the market's required rate of return on the firm's shares
r_d = the market's required rate of return on the firm's debt
T = the company's tax rate

For example, consider a firm in the 30 percent tax bracket, with a required rate of return on its equity of 16 percent, and a required rate on its debt of 12 percent. If it uses 70 percent equity and 30 percent debt financing, its WACC is:

$$\text{WACC} = 0.7 \times 0.16 + 0.3 \times (1 - 0.3) \times 0.12$$
$$= 13.72\%$$

We can use this WACC measure to examine the effect of financial leverage on the firm's required rate of return and its value.

To examine the impact of leverage, assume the firm's operating policy and expected EBIT are fixed, and consider the effect on each component of

FINANCE TODAY

Dances with Debt

What movie studio wouldn't be dancing in the streets with films like *The Silence of the Lambs* and *Dances with Wolves* to its credit? Answer: Orion Pictures, the studio that released both hits. The Jodie Foster thriller and the Kevin Costner western come at the end of a losing streak that has lasted more than two years and helped run up $500 million of debt with such busts as *The Hot Spot, State of Grace,* and *Valmont.* So even though *Lambs* and *Wolves* together have grossed a stellar $230 million, Orion is struggling to keep the wolves from the door.

To attract new investors, the studio last week disclosed plans for a "major capital or financial restructuring" and an executive shake-up that pushed chairman and octogenarian co-founder Arthur Krim into an essentially powerless position. Such actions may not be enough. Orion's upcoming releases look weak—and the studio is so hungry for cash that [in March 1991] it sold its most promising new picture, a movie version of TV's cult hit *The Addams Family,* to Paramount at a loss.

Source: "Dances with Debt," *Time,* April 15, 1991, p. 45.

its financing as leverage is employed. In doing so, we assume that the tax rate is fixed. We have to consider:

1. The effect of increasing leverage on the different components of the WACC formula, namely r_e and $(1 - T)r_d$,
2. The effect on the overall cost of capital, or WACC, and
3. The effect on the value of the firm.

As we have seen, increasing leverage increases risk, so the required rate for both debt and equity should increase as leverage increases. What is the effect on the WACC? Because we are increasing both r_e and r_d it might appear that the WACC must increase also, but this is not necessarily the case. We must remember that we are also changing the proportions of debt and equity as we increase leverage. Therefore, the WACC may decrease even though both r_e and r_d increase.

Figure 22.7 illustrates the possibility that the WACC could decrease while r_d and r_e increase. Figure 22.7(a) shows how changing leverage affects both the equity/assets ratio and the required rate of return. In the bottom panel, the required rate of return of debt and equity are shown as a function of the debt/assets ratio. The required rate on the equity exceeds that of debt because the bondholders have first claim on the firm's cash flow. As the firm increases the proportion of debt, the required rate on both debt and equity increases, as Figure 22.7(b) shows. However, as the firm increases its use of debt, it obtains more and more financing from that source, which is cheaper

☞ The financial manager must find the correct level of debt to use, and this is defined as the level that gives the lowest overall cost of financing for a given operating plan.

FIGURE 22.7   The Effect of Increasing Leverage on r_e and r_d

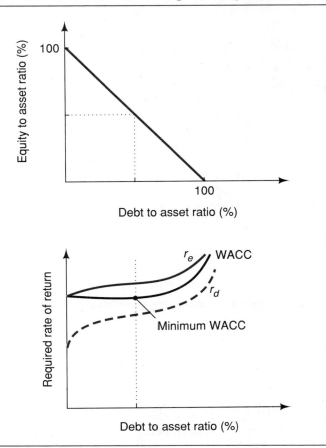

than equity. Therefore, in spite of the fact that the increasing use of debt makes the required rate for both debt and equity increase, the total financing cost, the WACC, can fall. This is also shown in Figure 22.7(b). At some point, however, the WACC begins to rise. Therefore, the financial manager must choose leverage to minimize it. The minimal WACC is shown in Figure 22.7(b) together with the corresponding degree of financial leverage. This indicates the optimum proportion of the debt the firm should use.

By using the level of debt that minimizes the WACC, the firm maximizes its value, as shown in Figure 22.8. It is no coincidence that this relationship obtains. Given a fixed operating plan, choosing the financing strategy that gives the lowest total WACC gives the highest market value for the firm's securities. The market value of the securities is just the present value of the cash flows to the owners, and if the cash flows are determined by the fixed operating plan, their present value will be maximized by adopting the financing plan giving the lowest WACC.

FIGURE 22.8   The Relationship Between Firm Value and the WACC

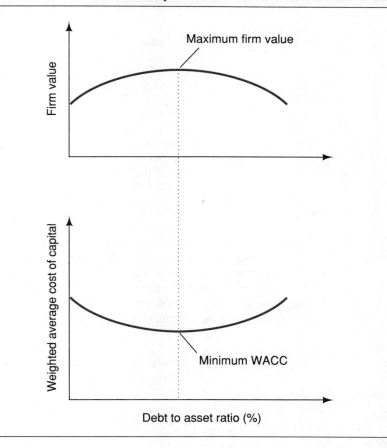

CAPITAL STRUCTURE PRACTICES

In real firms, chief financial managers invariably pay close attention to the capital structure decision. It is not merely a choice between issuing bonds or stocks, but among a wide variety of different kinds of financing vehicles.

Even assuming that a firm has made a basic decision to use, say, 60 percent equity and 40 percent debt, many issues remain. For example, what should be the maturity of the debt? Should any of it be convertible? For the short-term debt, should the firm use bank financing, or should it issue short-term notes in the market? A similar array of questions concerns equity. Should the firm issue preferred stock? If so, in what quantity and with what rate of preferred dividends?

While financial managers struggle with these issues, some underlying principles guide their conduct. For example, firms within a given industry

TABLE 22.6   Variation in Capital Structure Across Industries

Industry	Debt to Equity Ratio
Store, office, and bar equipment manufacturers	0.42
Wine and liquor distillers	0.38
Bakers	0.61
Clothing retailers	0.35
Restaurants, fast-food retailers	1.31
Fuel retailers	0.46
Recreation clubs	0.53
Thread manufacturers	0.41
Drug wholesalers	0.36

tend to have the same kind of capital structure. Firms in the electric utility industry use a great deal of debt financing, and those in the chemical industry tend to use relatively less debt, for instance. Table 22.6 illustrates the tendency for capital structure to vary across industries. By contrast, Table 22.7 highlights the tendency of firms within a single industry to have similar capital structures. This table shows the debt to asset ratios for some of the nation's major elec-

TABLE 22.7   Similarities in Capital Structure within the Electric Utility Industry

Firm	Debt to Asset Ratio	Dividend Yield
Consolidated Edison	34%	6.8%
Duke Power	43	7.6
Delmarva Power	45	7.2
General Public Utilities	46	0.0
Potomac Electric	47	6.9
Carolina Power & Light	48	9.0
Long Island Lighting	48	0.0
Allegheny Power	49	8.6
Pennsylvania Power & Light	50	8.9
Boston Edison	51	7.5
FPL Group, Inc.	51	7.2
Philadelphia Electric	52	12.7
Duquesne Light	53	12.7
Southern Co.	53	9.3
New England Electric	55	7.7
Savannah Electric	55	7.7
Average across all utilities	48	8.0

Source: Copyright © 1991 by Value Line Publishing, Inc.; used by permission.

tric utilities. Notice also that most of the firms have a high dividend yield (dividends/share price). This combination would be quite unusual for most industries, but is fairly normal for electric utilities, as the steady demand for electrical power means that they have very regular cash flows. Thus they can safely use a high level of debt.

INTERNATIONAL PERSPECTIVES

First a Lender, Now a Borrower Be

"When the U.S. deficit on current international transactions soared to record levels during the mid-1980s, some observers perceived a grave loss of U.S. competitiveness that was 'deindustrializing' America. Others warned of an imminent international financial crisis, predicting that the deficits would undermine confidence in the U.S. dollar (and in dollar-denominated assets) and induce a sharp drop in the dollar's foreign-exchange value and a sharp rise in U.S. interest rates. The heightened interest rates would precipitate a U.S. recession that would become worldwide—a 'hard landing.'"

Thus far, the landing has been far from hard. To be sure, the weighted average foreign-exchange value of the dollar did decline fairly steadily and significantly in real terms (adjusted for U.S. minus foreign inflation) during the years 1985 to 1987. But U.S. interest rates also generally declined, rather than rose, between the beginning and the end of this period, and both the U.S. and the world economies grew at a healthy pace. Between the end of 1987 and 1990, the real foreign-exchange value of the dollar changed relatively little, in spite of continued large U.S. current-account deficits; in fact, several central banks have on occasion sold large volumes of dollars in an effort to prevent the dollar from *rising* in the foreign-exchange markets! . . . The specter of a hard landing is invoked much less frequently in economic discourse."

The nonoccurrence to date of a hard landing does not prove that one will not take place. And even without a hard landing, the increasing U.S. indebtedness generated by the nation's current-account deficits will impose a growing burden on the U.S. economy. . . . "*

The following table gives the level of U.S. investment abroad, as well as the level of foreign investment in the United States, from 1970 to 1989. It is obvious from the last column of the table, and its graphical representation in the figure, that the United States has gone from a net lender of funds in the 1970s and early 1980s, to a net debtor since the mid-eighties. In fact, the United States has become the largest debtor on earth.

* Editor's note: The lengthy U.S. economic expansion finally gave way to recession late in 1990, but the consensus among prominent forecasters was that the recession would be brief and would not be worldwide.

(continued)

International Investment Position of the United States at Year End, 1970–89 (billions of dollars)

Year	U.S. Assets Abroad (1)	Foreign Assets in the United States (2)	Net International Investment Position of the United States (column 1 less minus column 2)
1970	$ 165.4	$ 106.9	$ 58.5
1971	179.0	133.5	45.5
1972	198.7	161.7	37.0
1973	222.4	174.5	47.9
1974	255.7	197.0	58.7
1975	295.1	220.9	74.2
1976	347.2	263.6	83.6
1977	379.1	306.4	72.7
1978	447.8	371.7	76.1
1979	510.6	416.1	94.5
1980	607.1	500.8	106.3
1981	719.6	578.7	140.9
1982	824.8	688.1	136.7
1983	873.5	784.5	89.0
1984	895.9	898.1	−2.2
1985	949.7	1,066.9	−117.2
1986	1,073.4	1,347.1	−273.7
1987	1,175.9	1,554.0	−378.1
1988	1,265.6	1,796.7	−531.1
1989	1,412.5	2,076.3	−663.7

Source: Survey of Current Business, June 1986, p. 28; June 1989, p. 43; June 1990, p. 59.

SUMMARY OF CAPITAL STRUCTURE

The major principles for choosing the right capital structure can be summarized in the following set of guidelines.

1. *If there are perfect markets and no taxes, choose any capital structure.* This is the setting analyzed by Modigliani and Miller. The investor can alter leverage at no cost, so the firm's choice of leverage cannot be important.
2. *If interest expenses are tax deductible, the greater the amount of leverage, the greater the tax savings, other things being equal.* Just considering the

International Investment Position of the United States

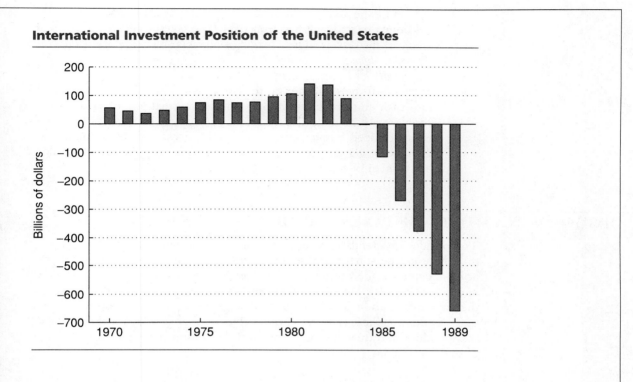

Source: Norman S. Fieleke, "The United States in Debt," *New England Economic Review*, September–October 1990, pp. 34–35.

effect of taxes, higher amounts of leverage mean lower taxes, giving a benefit to the firm.

3. *If interest expenses are tax deductible, the higher the tax rate, the greater the amount of tax savings, other things being equal.* Higher tax rates make it imperative for firms to avoid taxes. This means that the higher the tax rate, the greater the savings from using leverage. As a result, firms in a high tax bracket should use more leverage than other firms, other things being equal.

4. *The effect of financial distress reduces the value of leverage to a firm.* Using more leverage gives greater tax benefits, but it increases the

risk and expected cost of financial distress. The manager must consider the trade-off between rising tax savings and rising costs of financial distress as higher levels of financial leverage are used.

5. *The more difficult it is to liquidate the firm's assets, the greater is the potential penalty of financial distress.* For a firm with very liquid assets, financial distress will not be so costly, as it can convert those assets into cash quite readily without suffering a great loss of value. By contrast, a firm with illiquid assets, such as one that relies heavily on specialized human capital, will suffer greater costs of financial distress. In general, the less liquid a firm's assets, the lower should be its level of financial leverage.

DIVIDENDS IN A WORLD OF TAXES AND TRANSACTION COSTS

To consider dividends in a more realistic setting, we acknowledge the fact that there are personal taxes, in addition to corporate taxes, and that shareholders cannot trade costlessly to create their own dividends. For the moment, however, we continue to assume that everyone in the economy has the same information. The influences of taxes and transaction costs may mean that dividend policy can affect the value of the firm and the wealth of shareholders. We treat the problem from the points of view of the firm and of the shareholder.

Transaction Costs and the Firm

Consider again our firm with $1 million in assets that contemplates a $100,000 cash dividend to its shareholders, and assume that its investment plan requires $1 million in assets. If the firm pays no dividends, it has its assets already in place. By contrast, if it pays $100,000 in dividends, it must raise a new $100,000 in the capital market to pay for its investments. However, raising capital is costly, because the firm must pay flotation costs, which may be as large as 8 percent of the capital raised.

What should the firm do? If it pays the dividend and sells new stock to replace the $100,000, it will have to sell more than 1,000 new shares. For example, if the flotation costs are 6 percent, the firm would have to sell 1,064 shares at $100 per share, or $106,400 worth of stock, to raise the money. The difference would be siphoned off by the flotation costs, and neither the firm nor the shareholders would receive the benefits of this expense.

These flotation costs associated with raising new funds give firms an incentive not to pay dividends. In addition, a number of associated clerical expenses can be avoided if the firm does not pay dividends. In general, therefore, if the firm does not pay dividends it can avoid these expenditures and preserve more wealth for the shareholders.

FINANCE TODAY

Sticky Dividends

Many companies are becoming more generous to their shareholders; perhaps too generous. The average dividend payout ratio for Value Line's universe of 1,700 companies went from 33 percent in 1979 to over 54 percent in 1989, increasing every year except 1984. Although this is something for shareholders to cheer about, sometimes a high payout can do a company more harm than good. After all, paying out too much in dividends can jeopardize future growth by cutting back the money available for capital expenditures or research and development. Some firms even weaken their financial position to maintain high dividends.

"If they are paying out more dividends than their internal cash flow over a period of time, they'll dilute their financial position," says Wayne Stevens, director of research at Duff & Phelps. "They could actually borrow to make up the difference, but after a while, that becomes a constraint in terms of the ability of the company to borrow more."

One firm that continued to pay a dividend, even when cash flow could no longer cover the payment, was Church's Fried Chicken, the victim of a hostile takeover attempt by A. Copeland Enterprises. The chain of fast-food restaurants omitted its dividend after increasing it steadily for four years. The problem was that Church's net income declined by 78 percent, causing its payout ratio to leap to 100 percent.

"Generally, companies are loath to cut their dividends," says A. C. Moore, of Argus Research. "Companies tend not to cut the dividend until it becomes a matter of not being able to afford it and having to borrow. That's because cutting the dividend will usually cause a drop in the stock price." That's putting it mildly. Hell hath no fury like a shareholder whose dividend has been reduced without warning. Take chemical giant Union Carbide, for example. In May 1988, just when Carbide's stock was recovering from the Bhopal poison gas tragedy of 1984, the company announced a cut in its quarterly dividend from $0.38 to $0.20.

Wall Street, apparently taken by surprise, pushed Carbide's stock down from $22 to $18.75 in a single day. (In the next six months, Carbide's stock rebounded to $27.25, thanks to a 180 percent jump in earnings per share. The dividend remained unchanged.)

Lowering the dividend, comments Thomas Medcalf, portfolio manager of IDS Mutual Fund, is widely regarded by executives as an admission of failure. "It's sort of like walking around the country club with a huge catsup stain on your shirt."

Source: Ruthanne Sutor and Alexandra Ourusoff, "Dangerous Dividends," *Financial World,* February 21, 1989.

Personal Income Tax

☞ With personal income taxes, the dividends paid to individual shareholders are subject to taxation as ordinary income.

Dividend payments to individuals are subject to personal income taxation in the year received. By contrast, capital gains are not taxed until the shares are sold. By paying dividends, a corporation ensures that taxes are paid earlier, but by not paying dividends and allowing profits to accumulate in the value of the shares, the firm allows its shareholders to postpone paying taxes. In many cases, taxes can be deferred for many years if dividends are not paid.

Shareholders' Transaction Costs

☞ Because of market imperfections and taxes, the individual shareholder is unable to adjust cash flows costlessly through homemade dividends.

When a stockholder wants income from a stock portfolio, there are two ways to receive it: by receiving dividends and by selling part of the portfolio for cash. We have noted the undesirable tax consequences of receiving dividends, but there are also disadvantages to selling part of the portfolio.

When a stock is sold, the investor must pay transaction costs and also incurs a tax liability if the shares are sold at a profit. Selling stock may require a transaction cost in the neighborhood of 1 to 2 percent, so this diminishes the shareholder's wealth as well. If the firm is able to provide dividend income at a lower transaction cost, investors will prefer that.

Dividend Clienteles

dividend clientele
a group of investors favoring a particular kind of dividend policy

Shareholders have some reasons to avoid dividends and some reasons to seek them. An investor concerned about being taxed on dividends will prefer firms that pay little or no dividends. By contrast, an investor needing income may well prefer firms with a generous dividend policy. This suggests that firms with different dividend policies will appeal to different kinds of investors, or **dividend clientele**—a group of investors favoring a particular kind of dividend policy.

THE RESIDUAL THEORY OF DIVIDENDS

residual theory of dividends
the view that the firm should follow its investment policy of accepting all positive NPV projects, and paying out dividends when, and only when, funds are readily available

A number of conflicting pressures on the dividend policy of the firm stem from taxation and different kinds of transaction costs. An effort to sum up the influence of all of these different kinds of influences is known as the **residual theory of dividends.** According to the residual theory, the firm should follow its investment policy of accepting all positive NPV projects, paying out dividends only when funds are conveniently available. In this way, dividends are treated as a residual—the amount left over after the investment policy is satisfied. If the dividend is treated strictly as a residual, it can vary dramatically from period to period, depending on the firm's investment plan and operating results.

When we couple the existence of dividend clienteles with the residual theory, it appears that firms may be wise to operate under a slightly modified residual theory. A firm that attracts investors falling into a particular dividend clientele probably should maintain a fairly stable dividend policy. For example, one that attracts investors seeking high dividends will keep those investors happy only if it consistently pays fairly high dividends. If it lets dividends oscillate radically, both investors that seek dividends and those that wish to avoid dividends may avoid investing in the firm.

As a consequence, it appears that firms should maintain a fairly steady dividend policy in the short run, but in the long run they should attempt to treat dividends as a residual. In other words, according to this argument, dividends have to be managed in the short run, but should be determined as a residual in the long run. This seems to be the best conclusion about the importance of dividends if we consider the effects of taxes and transaction costs. However, one more important deviation from a perfect market must be considered before our discussion of the dividends can be complete.

DIVIDEND MANAGEMENT WITH COSTLY INFORMATION

☞ Because information is costly to gather and assess, dividends may be a useful signal of the future prospects of the firm.

We began our exploration of dividends under the assumption of perfect markets and zero taxes, and found that dividends were irrelevant to shareholder wealth. We relaxed these stringent assumptions and considered the effect of taxes and transaction costs. In that case, we found that firms were probably wise to manage their dividends in the short run to attract and keep a given dividend clientele. This conclusion was reached, however, under the assumption that all parties in the market have the same information about the firm. In this section, we consider a more realistic situation that recognizes the superior information held by some parties.

To say that everyone in the economy has the same information about the firm is to say that information is costless. In the real world, however, not everyone has the same information, and gathering it is costly in terms of both time and money.

asymmetric information
a situation in which two parties have different information about the same subject

Investors and management have different information about the firm's future cash flows. When two parties possess information about the same subject and that information has different value, they have **asymmetric information.** As a rule, managers are in a position to know much more about the firm than the typical investor. For instance, they know last month's sales before the investor does.

Let us assume that management has very favorable information about the firm that is not yet available to the investor. If this information is conveyed to the marketplace accurately, it will cause the firm's stock price to increase. However, investors know that management has an incentive to give false signals to the market, when it believes it will maximize the price of the stock.

This presents a problem. Management wants to send favorable news about the value of the firm to the market, but the market knows it should be skeptical of whatever good news management brings forth. After all, why should a

FINANCE TODAY

High Growth Dividends

The roaring stock market of the eighties kept investors hooked on the thrills of takeover plays. But in today's nervous market, a more sedate approach is gaining favor: investing for dividends. Investors can discover quality stocks that beat the 3.5 percent yield of the Standard & Poor's 500-stock index and that have good potential for dividend increases to boot.

If steady income is all you're after, there's no need to bother with stocks. Why not just buy Treasury bonds, which are yielding around 9 percent? With stocks, "there's the potential for higher future income and for capital gains, so the total return will be far superior to bonds," says Geraldine Weiss, editor of *Investment Quality Trends,* a newsletter that tracks dividend yields. And while Treasury rates are fixed, rising dividends help you keep pace with inflation.

Pfizer is a good example. Those who bought the drug stock in 1980, when it yielded around 4 percent, realized a 15 percent return on their original outlay because of increased dividends. Weiss notes that Pfizer's dividend grew 243 percent over the past decade, and its stock price grew 275 percent.

To find candidates for the Franklin Rising Dividends Fund, its president, William Lippman, checks for undervalued companies that have raised the dividend in 8 of the past 10 years, for a total of at least 100 percent. His picks pay out no more than 65 percent of earnings in dividends. He likes Wilmington Trust, a regional bank stock yielding 3.8 percent, which trades more than four points below the S&P average price-earnings ratio of 14.65. The bank has raised its dividend every year for nine years, for a total increase of 311 percent.

Utility stocks sport the highest yields. But "when you buy the highest dividend, you may sacrifice the growth of the dividend," says Lippman. In general, mature industries, such as the utility industry, tend to have a high dividend/payout ratio, but low growth; whereas industries with high growth potential will tend to pay very little dividends. Many high growth firms pay no dividend at all for many years.

Source: Suzanne Woolley, "Dividends: High Is Good, Room to Grow Is Even Better," *Business Week,* May 7, 1990.

signaling problem
the problem of transmitting information in a way to make it believable

simple good news announcement be believed on its own merit? The problem for management is to find a way to make the market accept the good news as being truthful. This is known as a **signaling problem**—transmitting information in a way to make it believable.

**dividend signaling
hypothesis**
the idea that dividend
changes convey believable
information to the market
about the firm's expected
future cash flows

Within this context, dividends may have a special relevance because of their ability to act as a credible signal. According to the **dividend signaling hypothesis,** dividend changes provide an effective way of allowing management to convey believable information to the market about the firm's expected future cash flows. In essence, management allows a higher dividend to do the talking.

OTHER CONSTRAINTS ON DIVIDEND POLICY

Three other factors that influence the dividend policy of the firm are cash flow, legal, and contractual constraints.

Cash Flow Constraints

Dividends are paid in cash. A firm without available cash cannot pay a dividend, no matter what its earnings. This emphasizes again the importance of cash flow rather than earnings in most financial contexts. Of course, even if the firm does not itself have cash on hand for the dividend, it may borrow funds. As we have seen, however, this requires incurring the costs of borrowing in order to incur the costs of paying the dividends, and may be unwise for that reason.

Legal Constraints

Laws govern permissible dividend practices and may constrain the firm's policy. To see the importance of such laws, consider the firm Wealth Transfer, Unlimited, operating under the slogan "We move wealth." In the absence of any legal prohibitions, Wealth Transfer might be true to its motto as follows: sell 10,000 shares of common stock for $10 each, for a total of $100,000, and issue bonds in the amount of $900,000. After these transactions that started the firm, the balance sheet of Wealth Transfer would appear as shown in Table 22.8. In the left half of the table, we see the balance sheet when the

TABLE 22.8   The Balance Sheet of Wealth Transfer

	At the Founding of the Firm				*After Paying a Large Dividend*		
ASSETS		**LIABILITIES**		**ASSETS**		**LIABILITIES**	
Cash	$1,000,000	Debt	$ 900,000	Cash	$0	Debt	$900,000
		Equity	100,000			Equity	−900,000
		Total liabilities and owners' equity				**Total liabilities and owners' equity**	
Total assets	**$1,000,000**		**$1,000,000**	**Total assets**	**$0**		**$0**

firm is first founded and is flush with cash. The $1 million in cash is offset by a large amount of debt and a small amount of equity.

Assume now that Wealth Transfer pays a dividend of $100 per share, paying out all of its cash. Each shareholder paid $10 per share and immediately receives $100 in dividends. This leaves the firm an empty shell as shown in the right half of Table 22.8. Now the firm has no assets and has equity of $-\$900,000$. At that point it declares bankruptcy. Because of the shareholders' limited liability, the missing $900,000 cannot be collected. Now you can see how brilliantly the firm is named, because Wealth Transfer achieves exactly what its name and slogan imply. It has transferred a considerable amount of wealth from the bondholders to the stockholders, and is out of business.

impairment of capital
the stripping of a firm's assets so that there is very little value of equity by paying a dividend

Although schematic, Wealth Transfer's behavior illustrates neatly a scheme that has been carried out all too often in the past. To curtail such unfair tactics, laws regulate dividend payments. In essence, they prohibit the **impairment of capital.** Capital is impaired when the firm strips itself of assets by paying a dividend. This is exactly what Wealth Transfer did. Usually these laws prohibit dividends that would exhaust the retained earnings shown on the firm's balance sheet. Clearly, the goal is to protect the bondholders from such games. In addition, bond convenants may further restrict the payment of dividends to protect bondholders even more, as discussed in the following section.

Contractual Constraints

bond indenture
the contract between the firm and the bondholders that defines the firm's conduct with respect to bonds that it issues

Bondholders know the tricks that management might use to transfer their wealth to shareholders. To prohibit this, bond indentures often restrict the kinds of dividends that firms can pay. The **bond indenture** is the contract between the firm and the bondholders that defines the firm's conduct with respect to its bond issues. It might typically restrict the payment of dividends to a certain percentage of earnings. In some extreme cases, it prohibits the payment of dividends altogether until the debt is repaid. Another kind of constraint in the bond indenture might prohibit dividend payments unless the firm's current ratio is sufficiently large. All of these restrictions are designed to ensure the firm will have enough funds to meet its obligation to bondholders.

TYPES OF DIVIDEND POLICIES

Faced with the constraints on dividends and the reasons for managing dividends, firms' dividend behavior generally falls into four distinguishable kinds of policies.

Constant Payout

In our discussion of stock price valuation models, we considered the possibility that some firms would pay dividends equaling a constant percentage of their earnings. For example, a firm having a 40 percent constant payout ratio and

FINANCE TODAY

Spending Other People's Money

Mario Kassar rose from film salesman to Hollywood movie mogul in a bit over a decade. Along the way, the chairman of Carolco Pictures Inc., of Rambo fame, has caused eyebrows to raise with his open-handed spending of company money—lavish even by the standards of Tinseltown. In 1990, at the Cannes Film Festival, as chieftain of this smallish moviemaker, Kassar paid about $200,000 to charter a 203-foot boat for 12 days. Few Carolco shareholders were there to share the fun.

The company has had more than its share of hits—the Rambo films with Sylvester Stallone and *Total Recall,* starring Arnold Schwarzenegger. In November 1990 it looked like an appealing property; at a share price of about $8, $1 less than the offering price in 1986, you could buy the whole common equity for around $240 million—about one year's revenues— small potatoes in the entertainment business. But don't jump to the conclusion that it is a bargain stock. Earnings have been erratic, and there are lots of questions about the way Kassar runs the company.

When it comes to rewarding its top executives, Carolco has few peers for companies of its size. In September 1990, for example, Carolco paid $13 apiece to buy back shares that Kassar bought for $9.50—an 80 percent premium over the market price, and almost 40 percent more than Kassar had paid for them the previous December. Thus, in a few quick months, Kassar netted over $11 million, about 80 percent of the company's net income for 1989.

While the bosses were gorging themselves on goodies, ordinary shareholders watched the value of their stock drop by half. Carolco says Kassar's premium was well worth it.

This isn't the first instance of the board's treating Kassar handsomely. During the eighties, Kassar and former co-chairman Andrew Vajna took loans from the company, repaying them on terms that ordinary mortals can only envy. In 1988 they paid back loans totaling $15 million, with 2 million shares of Carolco valued at their market price of $7.29.

The two executives also gave themselves a little sweetener. The pair took out another $8 million in loans around that time. The repayment terms? If the stock topped $11 at any time before August 1989, the new loan would be forgiven. In June the stock price hit $11, and the loan was wiped off the books. The stock dropped back again.

Although Kassar has indeed produced some megahits, Carolco's saga so far has been one of big rewards for the insiders, slim pickings for the shareholders.

Source: Lisa Gubernick, "Whose Money Is It, Anyway? *Forbes,* November 12, 1990.

earning $2 per share would pay a dividend of $0.80 per share. In fact, very few firms follow such a policy, and we can now see why. In general, earnings are quite volatile, fluctuating with changes in the economy and each firm's own special circumstances. If a firm follows a **constant payout policy,** the volatility in the dividends will match the volatility in earnings. For example, a 100 percent increase in earnings will require a 100 percent increase in dividends.

constant payout policy
a dividend policy according to which firms pay dividends that equal a constant percentage of their earnings

Given the existence of different dividend clienteles, a constant payout policy is likely to be a disaster for most firms. It would result in wildly fluctuating dividends, which would scare away all investors seeking a particular level of dividends, as they could not plan on a steady income. By the same token, investors interested primarily in capital gains would never know when they might receive a large dividend and the large tax liability that goes with it. As a consequence, very few firms follow such a policy.

Regular Dividends

regular dividend
a dividend policy according to which the firm pays a regular, steady dividend

The most popular kind of dividend policy is one that pays a **regular dividend.** For example, a firm that announces a dividend of $1.60 can generally be expected to maintain that level for a considerable amount of time. Furthermore, if it establishes the dividend at $1.60, it is generally a signal to investors that the firm believes the dividend to be sustainable. As a consequence, firms are generally careful to set the dividend at a sustainable level and to raise it only when the new level can be sustained.

Figure 22.9 illustrates this policy of regular dividends. At the beginning of the time period shown, the firm has a dividend of $1.60 per share, which is well below the maximum amount that the firm believes it can sustain. Thus

FIGURE 22.9 A Typical Regular Dividend Policy

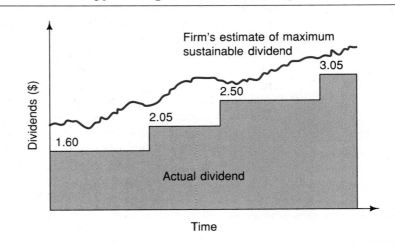

it has a cushion for error, in case it has been too optimistic in estimating the maximum sustainable dividend. In the graph, the firm prospers in the sense that its sustainable dividend level increases. However, it does not raise the dividend immediately, and when it does, it maintains a comfortable cushion between the amount and its estimate of the maximum it can sustain.

Under this kind of regular policy, the firm tries to make sure that the dividend acts like a ratchet. It may go up, but every effort is made to ensure that it does not go down, because a decrease in dividends is normally taken by the market as a very strong signal of financial distress. Naturally, this kind of policy requires the conservatism shown in Figure 22.9.

On occasion, firms err, and a dividend cut becomes unavoidable, as depicted in Figure 22.10. The firm begins with a dividend well below its estimated maximum sustainable level. At the outset, earnings are growing, so the firm believes that it can maintain a rather high dividend. Later, however, EPS drop and growth prospects are poorer than expected. Eventually, EPS even drops below the dividend level, but the firm does not immediately cut its dividend. So strong is the desire to avoid a cut that firms will maintain a dividend exceeding their current earnings; however, they cannot do this

---

FINANCE TODAY

Downsizing Dividends

S&P's *Outlook* reports that 409 corporations cut or omitted their dividends in 1990, the highest number since 573 companies were forced to take similar actions in 1982. Casualties in the first weeks of 1991 include Citicorp, Goodyear, Occidental Petroleum, McDonnell Douglas, and General Motors. Who's next?

Ford and Chrysler? A sharp slump in vehicle sales has contributed to lowered debt ratings for all three car companies. Some Chrysler debt is now rated as junk. Both these companies may find they have more urgent uses for the dividend money in running their businesses.

The Value Line Investment Survey database of 1,700 stocks was screened for heavily leveraged companies likely to reduce their payouts. The companies in the table were selected primarily on the basis of the "cash in/cash out" ratio listed in the last column. This is a measure of how well "cash flow," as Value Line defines it, covered dividends and capital expenditures for the latest reporting period. (The Value Line definition of cash flow does not take into account the effect on cash balances of fluctuations in inventory, receivables, and payables.) For the stocks below, the ratio is less than 1.

Unless business picks up, these companies are probably going to be faced with an unpleasant choice: cut or reduce the dividend or borrow money to pay it.

(continued)

Will These Payouts Last?

These steeply leveraged corporations are paying dividends they can ill afford. The cash in/cash out ratio for Preston, for example, is 0.33. The company takes in only 33 cents in net income plus depreciation for every dollar it pays out in dividends and capital expenditures.

Company	Recent Price	Latest 12 months EPS	Latest 12 months P/E	1991 Estimated EPS	Current Dividends*	Yield	Long-Term Debt/ Equity	Interest Coverage[†]	Cash In/ Cash Out[‡]
American Express	$24\frac{1}{2}$	$0.34	72.1	$2.88	$0.92	3.8%	194%	1.2	0.35
Boise Cascade	28	1.54	18.2	1.04	1.52	5.4	118	4.9	0.34
Chrysler	$12\frac{7}{8}$	0.30	42.9	−0.12	1.20	9.3	201	1.2	0.74
Dana	$31\frac{3}{8}$	2.22	14.1	2.52	1.60	5.1	141	3.1	0.77
Ford Motor	$29\frac{3}{4}$	4.65	6.4	1.64	3.00	10.1	362	1.8	0.77
Freeport McMoRan	$35\frac{1}{4}$	5.22	6.7	1.92	2.50	7.1	188	3.3	0.92
GTE	$30\frac{3}{8}$	2.26	13.4	2.26	1.65	5.4	121	2.9	0.96
GenCorp	$8\frac{3}{4}$	1.05	8.3	0.97	0.60	6.9	249	1.7	0.79
Ogden Corp	22	1.31	16.8	1.61	1.25	5.7	339	1.8	0.10
Pennzoil	$68\frac{3}{8}$	2.37	28.9	3.33	3.00	4.4	155	2.6	0.60
Preston	$9\frac{3}{4}$	−3.26	—	0.94	0.50	5.1	149	1.0	0.33
Southwest Gas	$15\frac{1}{8}$	1.53	9.9	1.77	1.40	9.3	242	2.3	0.60
Stone Container	$15\frac{5}{8}$	1.59	9.8	0.80	0.72	4.6	251	2.1	0.61
Whitman	22	−0.19	—	1.75	1.06	4.8	219	4.3	0.36
Williams Cos	$27\frac{1}{2}$	0.92	29.9	1.93	1.40	5.1	130	1.5	0.70

* Latest-quarter dividend multiplied by 4.
[†] Earnings before interest and taxes divided by interest charges.
[‡] Cash flow from operations (net income plus depreciation less preferred dividends) divided by outgo for common dividends and capital expenditures, based on latest reported figures.

Source: Value Line and *Institutional Brokers Estimate System* (a service of Lynch, Jones & Ryan), *via Lotus One Source.*

Source: Timothy Dodman and Gilbert Steedley, "Endangered Dividends," *Forbes,* March 4, 1991, p. 147.

for very long, or they will exhaust their cash resources.[5] This is exactly the problem faced by the firm in Figure 22.10. After EPS falls below the dividend level, its estimate of maximum sustainable dividend also falls, and eventually the firm realizes that it cannot maintain those payments indefinitely. Faced with this unhappy situation, Figure 22.10 shows that the firm cuts its dividend.

[5] As discussed previously, some firms may be prevented from paying out dividends in excess of their earnings in any given year.

FIGURE 22.10   A Typical Dividend Decrease

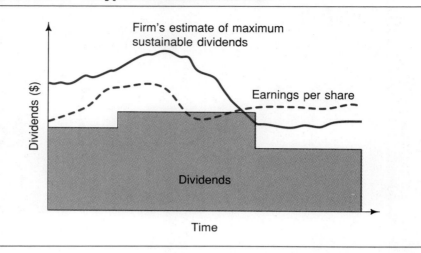

Because of the extremely unfavorable news it conveys to the market, firms generally hate to cut dividends. This reluctance is reflected in the size of dividend decreases. Since firms usually pay unsustainable dividends for as long as possible, when they finally do cut the dividends, they most frequently eliminate them altogether.

Multiple Increases

Some firms follow a policy of very frequent and very small dividend increases to give the illusion of movement and growth. The obvious hope behind such a policy is that the market rewards consistent dividend increases. At the very least, these **multiple increases** attract some attention.

multiple increases
the policy of making very frequent and very small dividend increases

Figure 22.11 shows the same stream of maximum sustainable dividends that we considered in Figure 22.9 and how dividends might be managed to show constant growth. Instead of waiting for a considerable period of time as the firm in Figure 22.9 did, this firm announces frequent, very small dividend increases. Some firms announce a dividend increase just about every year, so the same potential can be managed in two quite different ways. Which is better, and whether it makes a difference, is uncertain.

Extras

extra dividend
the portion of the dividend payment that will be made as circumstances permit

Some firms follow a policy of dividing their announced dividends into two portions—a regular and an extra dividend. The regular dividend continues at the announced level. The **extra dividend** is paid as circumstances permit. For example, a firm might have a regular dividend of $2 per year and announce an extra dividend of $0.30 this year. In the next year, the stockholder can expect at least a $2 dividend and perhaps an extra dividend as well. The firm

FIGURE 22.11 The Policy of Small Frequent Increases

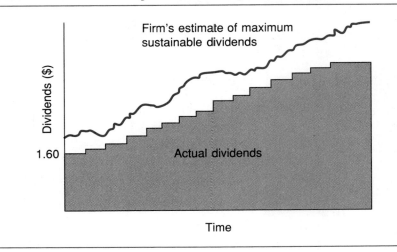

is not committed to paying an extra dividend, but if it does, the amount may vary.

The policy of extra dividends allows management to communicate with its shareholders, and shows how seriously management takes this communication through dividend announcements.

DIVIDEND PAYMENT PROCEDURES

Most firms pay their dividends quarterly, but there are some exceptions. Wrigley, Inc., the chewing gum company, pays a monthly dividend, but this is unusual. Because the procedure is so standardized, this section describes the normal payment system.

Shortly after the quarter's earnings are known, the board of directors of a firm meets to determine the next quarter's dividend. The day on which the firm announces the new dividend is the **dividend declaration date.** Let us assume that the declaration date is February 3. In this case the annoucement might be as follows: "The firm will pay a dividend of $1 per share for the next quarter to holders of record on March 15, with a payment date of April 12."

The dividend is to be paid in the future, and because stocks trade on a daily basis, it is uncertain who will receive it. The firm is saying in its announcement that the owner of the share, as shown on the books of the firm on the **holder of record date,** March 15, will receive the dividend. This still leaves a problem, because we cannot know how fast the transactions in the stock will reach the firm's books. For example, if you buy the share on March 12, will you be the holder of record on March 15 and receive the dividends? To eliminate such problems, the convention has been adopted of establishing

dividend declaration date
the time at which the next dividend is announced

holder of record date
the date on which a share must be owned in order to receive a given dividend

INTERNATIONAL

PERSPECTIVES

Stable Shareholders, Unite!

Compared with shareholders in the United States and Europe, those in Japan appear singularly docile. Ulrich Hocker, managing director of the German Shareholders Protective Association, has appealed to German companies' Japanese investors to attend association meetings to no avail. "We spoke to them, but they didn't want to get involved," he says.

Nonetheless a storm could be brewing in Japan. Japanese corporate earnings hit their highest levels ever in the fiscal year that ended in March 1990, but dividends in the following six months were the smallest they had been in 10 years. The result was a barrage of complaints in June at the annual shareholder meetings of some 1,600 corporations. In the past, Japanese shareholders had accepted low dividend ratios because they could be assured of capital gains in the ever-surging stock market. The market's 40 percent decline between January and November 1990 began to give them second thoughts.

Some 110 companies actually cut their dividends, despite some large gains in pretax profits. Typical is Nippon Road, which planned to cut its annual dividend from 15 yen ($0.12) per share to 9 yen in 1991, although it projected a 3 percent profit gain in that fiscal year.

Japanese companies apparently think they can get away with the low payout policy because of the widespread use of cross-shareholding—the retention by companies of shares in other companies with an understanding that the shares not be sold. In fact, the practice of stable shareholding has apparently strengthened in the last five years. According to a survey conducted by Japan's Commercial Code Research Center in February 1990, about 62 percent of companies surveyed said that 60 to 70 percent of their shares were held by stable shareholders. Five years earlier, 53 percent of those questioned gave this answer. Cross-shareholders receive such benefits as long-term sales or purchase agreements, discounts on products and access to loans in return for loyalty.

But a mini-revolt, if not sustained shareholder activism, may be in the offing. Life insurance companies are especially unhappy with the low dividend ratios. They pay policyholders out of income on their investments, and with individuals and corporations—especially banks—facing a liquidity squeeze, insurance companies are about the only source of money for new equity financing. Thus far, the insurance companies say, they don't plan to sell their shareholdings, but they aren't likely to buy more shares.

Source: Yoko Shibata, "A Mini-revolt over Dividends in Japan," *Global Finance,* November 1990, p. 71.

FIGURE 22.12   The Dividend Payment Process

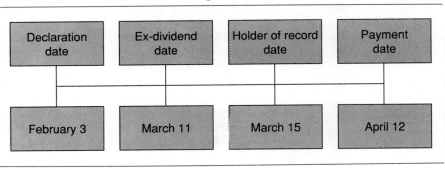

an ex-dividend date four business days prior to the holder of record date. The **ex-dividend date** is the date on which the stock begins trading without the right to receive the coming dividend. In our example, with a holder of record date of March 15, the ex-dividend date would be March 11.[6] If you bought the stock on the ex-dividend date or later, you will not get the dividend. It is customary to say that you bought the stock ex-dividend, which avoids any ambiguity about who will receive the payment.

ex-dividend date
the date on which the stock begins trading without the right to receive the coming dividend

The final date in the process is the **payment date,** the date the firm actually mails the dividend checks, in our example, April 12. The entire process is shown in Figure 22.12.

payment date
the date the firm actually mails the dividend checks

DIVIDEND SUBSTITUTES

Thus far we have focused strictly on cash dividends, actual payments of cash from the firm to the shareholders. We conclude by considering a dividend substitute, stock repurchases, which is a close substitute for a cash dividend.[7]

Stock Repurchases

stock repurchase
the purchase by a firm of its own shares

In a **stock repurchase,** a firm buys some of its own existing shares. This can be accomplished through a tender offer or an open market purchase. In a **tender offer,** the firm announces its intention to buy a certain number of shares at a stated price and allows shareholders to volunteer to sell their shares at that price. In an **open market purchase** the firm merely buys shares on the open market as any trader would.

tender offer
a way of purchasing shares in which a firm announces its intention to buy a certain number of shares at a stated price and allows shareholders to volunteer to sell their shares at that price

Whichever method of repurchase is used as an alternative to a cash dividend, the result is essentially the same from the firm's point of view. Consider an all-equity firm with a market value of its stock of $1 million, and assume that 10,000 shares are outstanding, each of which would trade

[6] Assuming that March 15 is a Friday.

[7] We considered stock dividends and stock splits in Chapter 13.

open market purchase
the purchase of shares in the marketplace following the same procedures as any trader would

☞ In most respects, a stock repurchase may be regarded as a substitute for dividends.

for $100. Assume also that the firm is considering a cash dividend of $10 per share or, alternatively, that it will buy 1,000 shares. Table 22.9 shows the position of the firm before any dividend or share repurchase.

The middle section of Table 22.9 shows the firm's position if it pays a dividend. If the firm pays a $10 per share dividend, it will distribute $100,000 in cash, so its assets will fall in value to $900,000. Correspondingly, each share must fall in value to $90. After all, the share was worth $100 before the dividend, and then it paid $10, so the form of wealth has been changed. Before the dividend, the owner had one share worth $100. After the dividend, the shareholder has $10 in cash and a share worth $90. The decision to pay a dividend cannot really create wealth, so the shareholders must be just as well off after the dividend as they were before.

The position of the firm electing to repurchase shares is shown in the right-hand section of Table 22.9. Again, with $100,000 spent to buy stock, the value of the firm's productive assets must fall to $900,000. Accordingly, the value of the outstanding shares must now have a total value of $900,000. But now 9,000 shares are outstanding and total assets are $900,000 so the shares continue to be worth $100 each.

These two alternatives are quite similar from the point of view of the firm. Both leave the firm 10 percent smaller than before, with total assets of $900,000. The only real difference is in the price and number of the shares outstanding. Shareholders who sold all their shares in a share repurchase have no further concern with the firm. Those who did not sell shares increased their ownership. For example, if you owned 500 shares before the repurchase, you would own 5 percent of the firm. If you kept them all, you would now own 500 of 9,000 shares or 5.56 percent of the firm. This shows that the main difference between cash dividends and share repurchases falls on the shareholders.

Advantages and Disadvantages of Share Repurchases

A share repurchase has certain advantages over a cash dividend, the most important being the tax effect for the shareholders. The strategy allows shareholders to choose whether they wish income now or not. If they do, they sell some fraction of their shares. If not, they merely hold their shares, receive

TABLE 22.9   The Position of the Firm with Dividends or Share Repurchase

BEFORE THE DIVIDEND OR REPURCHASE		AFTER A $10 PER SHARE DIVIDEND		AFTER REPURCHASING 1,000 SHARES	
Assets	Liabilities and owners' equity	Assets	Liabilities and owners' equity	Assets	Liabilities and owners' equity
$1,000,000	10,000 shares at $100: $1,000,000	$900,000	10,000 shares at $90: $900,000	$900,000	9,000 shares at $100: $900,000

INTERNATIONAL PERSPECTIVES

Dividend Yields Across Countries

The importance of dividends in long-term investment performance has been demonstrated in a number of studies. Of the 11.13 percent average annual total return provided by U.S. equities over the last six decades, 4.58 percent per year, or 41.2 percent of the total return, was collected in the form of dividends.

Over the 20 years ending in December 1989, the contribution of dividends to the total return of U.S. equities was 35.6 percent. Global equity investors registered a lower dividend contribution over the same 20-year period, with dividend yields averaging 26.2 percent of the total return of the market-capitalization-weighted Morgan Stanley Capital International World Index and 27.2 percent of the equally weighted World Index in local currencies. During this period, global equity markets, as measured by the market-capitalization-weighted MSCI World Index, provided a total annual compound return of 12.1 percent in local currencies; the total return of the equally weighted World Index was 15.5 percent. In U.S. dollar terms, global equity investors received a return of 13.3 percent and 16.7 percent, respectively, assuming reinvestment of dividends. The most important return measures for the MSCI World Index and selected countries over this 20-year period are shown in the table.

Given the fact the dividend returns are inherently less risky than capital returns, it would seem that investors should pay more attention to dividend yields and resist the urge to chase high-priced equities, which may provide excellent returns in the short run, but are also highly vulnerable to market corrections. The standard deviation of the annual capital return during the period between December 1929 and December 1989 was 21.3 percent, while the standard deviation of the annual dividend yield during the same period was only 1.5 percent. Over the 20-year period ending in December 1989, the standard deviation was 16.9 percent for the annual capital return and 0.9 percent for the annual dividend yield.

no income, and incur no tax burden. Therefore share repurchases should be preferred to cash dividends. At the very least, they conserve taxes.

Enter the IRS. The Internal Revenue Service knows about share repurchases and penalizes firms that use them regularly. The IRS frowns on attempts to help shareholders avoid taxes on dividends, although it has permitted occasional share repurchases without adverse tax consequences.

The decision to repurchase shares can be made for reasons other than taxes. For example, if a firm believes its stock is undervalued, it may repurchase its shares in the open market. This was the case with IBM and other firms immediately after the market crash of October 1987, when IBM repurchased some $1 billion of its own stock. As it turns out, it was probably a smart move, as the market recuperated from that slump rather quickly and proceeded

Return Characteristics in Local Currencies for Selected Countries and the MSCI World Index, December 31, 1969–December 31, 1989

	Average Quarterly Return	Average Quarterly Capital Gain	Average Quarterly Dividend Yield	Capital Gain (% of total return)	Dividend Yield (% of total return)
MSCI World Index Market-capitalization-weighted	3.22%	2.38%	0.85%	73.8%	26.2%
Equally weighted	3.97	2.89	1.08	72.8	27.2
Australia	3.42	2.34	1.08	68.4	31.6
Austria	3.12	2.35	0.77	75.3	24.7
Belgium	4.07	1.75	2.32	43.1	56.9
Canada	3.23	2.28	0.94	70.8	29.2
Denmark	4.19	3.12	1.07	74.4	25.6
France	4.05	2.78	1.26	68.8	31.2
Germany	2.61	1.55	1.06	59.5	40.5
Hong Kong	7.31	6.26	1.05	85.7	14.3
Italy	3.81	3.11	0.69	81.8	18.2
Japan	4.53	4.03	0.50	89.0	11.0
Netherlands	3.43	1.97	1.47	57.3	42.7
Norway	4.79	3.91	0.88	81.6	18.4
Singapore/Malaysia	4.90	4.27	0.63	87.2	12.8
Spain	3.55	1.83	1.73	51.4	48.6
Sweden	4.97	3.99	0.98	80.3	19.7
Switzerland	2.10	1.43	0.67	68.1	31.9
United Kingdom	4.50	3.22	1.28	71.5	28.5
United States	2.97	1.90	1.07	64.0	36.0

Source: A. Michael Keppler, "The Importance of Dividend Yields in Country Selection," *Journal of Portfolio Management,* Winter 1991, pp. 24–25.

to increase steadily over the following few years. Indeed, the Dow Jones industrial average surpassed the once stratospheric level of 3,000 for the first time on April 17, 1991.

SUMMARY

Most of the discussion in this chapter focused on the concepts behind the capital structure and dividend decisions. First, we traced the arguments of Miller and Modigliani for capital structure and dividends in a world of no taxes and no transaction costs. In each case, the value of the firm was independent of the manager's decision. This analysis helped us to see that any impact of capital structure or dividends on firm value depended on either market imperfections or taxes.

The existence of taxes creates an incentive for firms to use debt and to avoid paying dividends. However, neither effect is absolute because of market imperfections in the form of transaction costs. For capital structure, too much debt increases the expected cost of financial distress. For dividends, shareholder's transaction costs may provide a reason for the firm to provide dividends. In addition, we considered some of the practical procedures that managers actually follow in setting capital structure and dividend policies.

QUESTIONS

1. What is capital structure?
2. Why do different industries tend to have different capital structures?
3. What is the purpose of examining capital structure, assuming that there are no taxes and that financial markets are perfect?
4. What is the importance of the capital structure decision in a world of no taxes and perfect capital markets? Explain.
5. What is homemade leverage?
6. If we add just a little bit of realism and assume that there are corporate taxes but still assume that there are perfect capital markets, what is the importance of the capital structure decision, if any? What kind of capital structure should firms adopt in this case?
7. With corporate taxes and perfect capital markets, does a firm with twice the financial leverage of another have twice the value, assuming they both have the same value when they are unlevered?
8. What is the importance of financial distress and bankruptcy if there are perfect capital markets? Explain.
9. If we acknowledge that there are corporate taxes and that capital markets are not perfect, does the capital structure decision affect firm value? Explain.
10. Is there an optimum capital structure? If so, what factors determine it?
11. What is the weighted average cost of capital?
12. How does the cost of financial distress affect the value of increasing financial leverage?
13. What are the two outlets available for after-tax earnings?
14. What is the importance of the dividend decision in a world of perfect capital markets and zero taxes?
15. If a firm pays too little in dividends to suit you, how could you remedy this problem? Assume zero taxes and perfect capital markets.
16. If a firm pays dividends that are too large to suit you, how could you remedy this problem? Assume zero taxes and perfect capital markets.
17. How do your answers to the two previous questions change if there are taxes and imperfect capital markets?

18. Explain the reasoning that makes the residual theory of dividends attractive.

19. What is a dividend clientele? What kinds of clienteles would be attracted to utility stocks that normally pay very high dividends?

20. What kinds of dividend policies would you expect to be attractive to a yuppie with a very high income?

21. How do dividends perform as a signal? Why doesn't management just announce the information it is trying to convey?

22. Explain the relationship between share repurchases and the problem of asymmetric information.

23. What costs does a firm incur when it borrows to pay a dividend?

24. Why do bondholders place constraints on firms' dividend policies?

PROBLEMS

Use this information to solve Problems 1 through 17. A firm has a very simple capital structure of $50,000 of long-term debt with an interest rate of 10 percent. In addition, it has 1,000 shares outstanding with a market value per share of $50. This gives a total value of $100,000. Assume that capital markets are perfect and that any amount of new debt can be issued at 10 percent.

1. Assume that there are no corporate taxes and that you have $10,000 to invest. Explain how to transact to create an investment in this firm that is 75 percent debt. Note that the capital structure of the company itself does not change, but you are to use homemade leverage to create the desired leverage.

2. Assume that there are no corporate taxes and that you have $10,000 to invest. Explain how to transact to create an investment in this firm that is 25 percent debt. Note that the capital structure of the company itself does not change, but you are to transact in a way that allows you to unwind the firm's leverage in order to have an investment that is 25 percent debt.

3. If the firm has EBIT of $20,000, what are its net income, return on assets, and EPS?

4. If the firm has EBIT of $20,000 and you hold an investment in this firm that is 75 percent debt, what is your net income after all interest expense, and what is your return on assets?

5. If the firm has EBIT of $20,000 and you hold an investment in this firm that is 25 percent, what is your net income after all interest expense?

6. If the firm has EBIT of $30,000, what are its net income, return on assets, and EPS?

7. If the firm has EBIT of $30,000 and you hold an investment in this firm that is 75 percent debt, what is your net income after all interest expense, and what is your return on assets?

8. If the firm has EBIT of $30,000 and you hold an investment in this firm that is 25 percent debt, what is your net income after all interest expense?

9. If the firm has EBIT of $10,000, what are its net income, return on assets, and EPS?

10. If the firm has EBIT of $10,000 and you hold an investment in this firm that is 75 percent debt, what is your net income after all interest expense, and what is your return on assets?

11. If the firm has EBIT of $10,000 and you hold an investment in this firm that is 25 percent debt, what is your net income after all interest expense?

12. In Problems 3 through 11 we considered EBIT values of $10,000, $20,000, and $30,000. Assuming that these outcomes are equally likely, compute the standard deviation of EBIT and EPS for this firm.

13. Assume now that the required rate of return for the firm's equity is 15 percent and that the corporate tax rate is 30 percent. What is the firm's WACC?

14. If the firm changed its capital structure to be 75 percent debt, what would its WACC be?

15. If the firm changed its capital structure to be 25 percent, what would its WACC be?

16. Based on Problems 13 through 15, what appears to be the optimum capital structure for the firm in this case? (Continue to assume that financial distress is costless.)

17. If we acknowledge that capital markets are not perfect and that financial distress is not costless, how does the conclusion of Problem 16 change?

Use the following information to solve all of the problems below. A firm has earnings before tax of $100,000 and 10,000 shares of stock outstanding, with each share worth $100. Assume that you own 1,000 shares, that there are no taxes, and that capital markets are perfect.

18. What percentage of the firm do you own?

19. Assume that the firm pays no dividend. How could you transact on your own initiative to pay yourself a dividend of $5 per share?

20. After the transactions of Problem 19 are completed, how many shares do you own, and what percentage of the firm do you now own?

21. Assume that the firm pays a dividend of $10 per share. How could you transact to avoid the dividend altogether?

22. After the transactions of Problem 21, how many shares do you own and what percentage of the firm do you now own?

Forget all about dividends now, and assume that the firm will repurchase 10 percent of its shares.

23. After the repurchase, how many shares will be outstanding?
24. After the repurchase, what should be the value of each share?
25. If you do not sell any of your shares in the repurchase, what percentage of the firm do you now own?
26. If you do not participate in the share repurchase, how has your wealth been affected?
27. If you sold 50 percent of your shares in the share repurchase, what percentage of the firm do you now own?
28. If you sold 50 percent of your share repurchase, how has the percentage of the firm that you own changed?
29. If you sold 50 percent of your shares in the share repurchase, how has your wealth been affected?

Leasing and Mergers

lease
an agreement to rent an asset

lessor
the owner of an asset under a leasing agreement

lessee
the user of the leased asset

This chapter explores two strategic issues in finance: leasing and mergers. Leasing is essentially a financing decision, while merging is an investment decision, at least for the acquiring firm.

A **lease** is essentially the renting of an asset for some specified period. In leasing, the owner of the good is the **lessor** and the party that uses the good is the **lessee.** Either one may provide maintenance for the leased good. We focus primarily on leases in which the lessee undertakes the maintenance burden.

The lessee can either lease a good or borrow funds in the capital market and buy the good. In essence, the decision depends on the after-tax cash flows associated with each alternative. Assuming that the firm has already made the investment decision to acquire a good, we will analyze how this acquisition should be financed—by ownership or by leasing.

The United States is witnessing one of the largest waves of mergers in history. Firms frequently announce multibillion-dollar deals to take over another company. At the same time, many other corporations are selling portions of their businesses. To better understand these phenomena and how they affect shareholder wealth, we will first explore the terminology, methods, and recent history of mergers, and then consider how to evaluate a merger proposal. In a merger, there is an acquiring firm and an acquired, or target, firm. Evaluation techniques fall into two categories, depending on whether the acquiring firm pays cash or stock to the owners of the target firm. Numerous motives for mergers exist, some that are wise and others that are highly questionable.

This chapter concludes by examining the wealth effects of mergers on acquirers and targets. A merger always involves an exchange of assets between the shareholders of the acquiring and target firms. Does one side of the exchange benefit more, or does a merger usually constitute a fair exchange? Also, do these mergers serve the interests of society? The last sections of this chapter address these broader social concerns.

TYPES OF LEASES

In leasing, the lessor provides the asset to the lessee for a specified period in exchange for a series of payments. The length of the lease, the conditions

FIGURE 23.1 Flows of Assets and Funds in Leasing and Purchasing

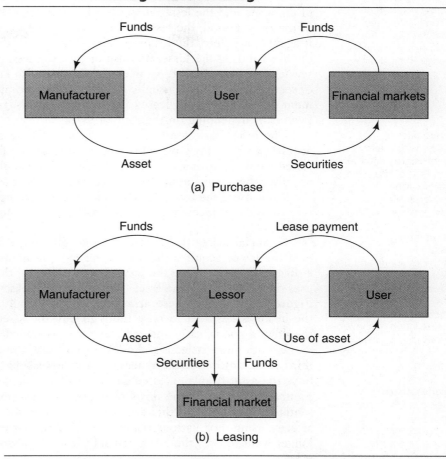

(a) Purchase

(b) Leasing

Source: Adapted from *Essentials of Managerial Finance* by John J. Pringle and Robert S. Harris. Copyright © 1984 by Scott, Foresman and Company. Reprinted by permission of HarperCollins Publishers.

for terminating it before the full term, the payments, and the party responsible for maintaining the asset are all determined by negotiation. Figure 23.1 summarizes the basic differences between purchasing and leasing. In a purchase, the party who will use the asset raises funds from the capital markets by issuing securities. These funds are then used to buy the asset from the manufacturer or distributor. In a lease, the lessor acquires funds from the securities markets and uses them to purchase the asset. The lessee acquires the use of the asset by paying a series of lease payments. The most important feature of the graph is the party who raises funds from the financial markets.

operating lease
a lease with a term that is considerably shorter than the life of the asset, and usually cancelable by the lessee on short notice

The lessee can engage in an operating lease or a financial lease. An **operating lease** typically has a term that is considerably shorter than the life of the asset, and the lessee may cancel it with fairly short notice. At the end of the lease period, the lessor expects to be able to sell the asset or to lease it again. Therefore, the lessor is very interested in the way the lessee treats the asset during the lease. Because of this, the lessor usually maintains and services the leased asset. An operating lease is also known as a maintenance or service lease. Lessees usually get automobiles, computers, and office equipment through operating leases. Operating leases usually have a life of one to five years, depending on the type of asset.

financial lease
a lease with a term that approximately equals the useful life of the asset, usually calling for a series of noncancelable lease payments over its life

The other basic kind of lease is a **financial lease,** in which the lessee acquires an asset for a period that is close to the useful life of the asset. The lessee contracts to make a series of payments over the life of the lease and usually provides maintenance services for the asset. At the end of the lease, the lessor owns the asset. As opposed to an operating lease, a financial lease is usually noncancelable, so the lessee commits to the full sequence of payments.

direct lease
a lease in which the lessor issues equity and uses the funds to purchase the leased asset

Financial leases themselves fall into different categories, depending on how the lessor acquires the asset. The most straightforward arrangement is a **direct lease,** in which the lessor issues equity in the financial markets and uses the funds to buy the asset. The lessor then leases the asset to the lessee. Figure 23.2 presents these arrangements graphically. In a **leveraged lease** the lessor issues debt to raise funds to buy the asset. Figure 23.2(b) shows the flow of goods, cash, and services for a leveraged lease.

leveraged lease
a lease in which the lessor acquires an asset by issuing debt, and perhaps some equity

In both a direct lease and a leveraged lease, the lessor buys the asset. A third basic type of financial lease is a **sale/leaseback,** in which the lessor buys the asset from the lessee and immediately leases it back to the lessee. Figure 23.2(c) shows the flows of goods and cash for a sale/leaseback. Essentially, the lessee in this arrangement retains the use of an asset it was already using. For various reasons, such as raising cash, the lessee may no longer want to own the asset, and sells it to the lessor and arranges to lease it back.

sale/leaseback
a lease in which the lessor acquires an asset from the lessee and leases it back to the lessee

LEASING VERSUS OWNING: THE BASIC DECISION

☞ The basic problem of leasing is whether to acquire a given asset by purchase or by leasing. Therefore, this is a financing decision.

Some firms sell an asset and then lease it back from the buyer. This raises an obvious question: if the firm has an asset and still wants to use it, why sell it and lease it back? Because the sale/leaseback is so common, it must have some important features.

The remainder of this chapter focuses on financial leases. The lease or buy decision is essentially a financing one. We assume the firm has already decided to use a given asset for a certain period based on a careful capital budgeting analysis. But should the firm finance the use of that asset by buying it or leasing it?

FIGURE 23.2 **Flows of Assets and Funds in Alternative Types of Financial Leases**

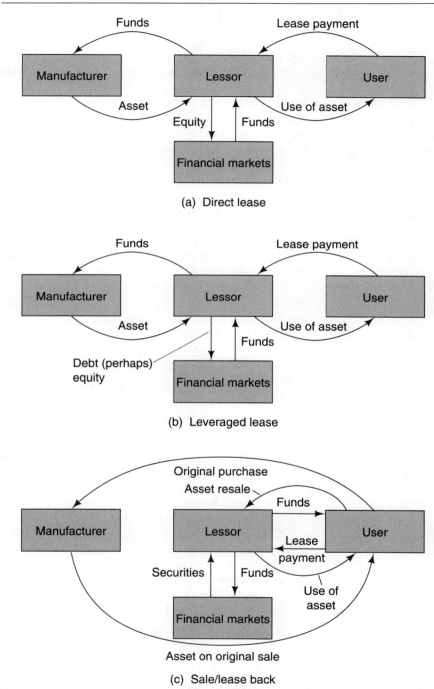

(a) Direct lease

(b) Leveraged lease

(c) Sale/lease back

Evaluating Leases

To evaluate leasing versus buying, we must keep two points in mind. The first concerns the principle of incremental cash flows, and the second focuses on assumptions about financial leverage.

☞ The lease versus borrow-and-buy analysis has to consider only the incremental cash flows resulting from the two financing alternatives.

Incremental Cash Flows   To choose between leasing and buying, we have to consider only the differential cash flows. For example, whether we buy the asset or lease it under a financial lease, we still will have to pay the maintenance costs, so we can ignore these. Presumably, the firm considered them in the original investment decision. For the financing decision, we have to consider only the incremental cash flows between the alternatives.

The Financial Leverage Effects   We know that financial structure can affect a firm's decisions. In deciding to lease or buy, we must be sure to consider any leverage effects of one alternative relative to the other. To be sure that we evaluate the alternatives on the same footing, we must hold the leverage effects constant.

☞ Leasing is equivalent to 100 percent debt financing, so the borrow-and-buy alternative should be evaluated on the assumption that the firm will borrow the full purchase price of the asset.

If we lease an asset, we commit ourselves to a series of contractually obligated payments, equivalent to the promised payments on a loan. Therefore, we may regard the leasing as a commitment to financing the asset with 100 percent debt. To make the buy alternative comparable, we must assume that we will buy the asset with funds derived entirely from debt. This is an important point, because it allows us to evaluate the tax effects of borrowing to buy the asset.

Identifying the Relevant Cash Flows

☞ The lease versus borrow-and-buy decision should be made on the basis of the after-tax NPV of the two financing alternatives.

Holding the financial leverage effects constant by assuming that we finance the purchase entirely by borrowing, which cash flows differ between the purchase and leasing alternatives? In answering this question, we must consider the various tax effects that the two alternatives generate. The lease requires only one type of cash flow, the lease payments themselves, and we must evaluate them on an after-tax basis.

If we buy, we can depreciate the asset, thereby gaining a depreciation tax shield. Also, if we buy the asset using debt financing, we receive some tax shields from the interest expenses. Finally, we can sell the asset at the end of its useful life for its salvage value. Table 23.1 summarizes the cash flows under the two alternatives.

Analyzing the Cash Flows

Suppose a firm will acquire a computer with an expected life of four years, a purchase price of $50,000, and an expected 0 salvage value. The firm is in the 30 percent tax bracket and uses straight-line depreciation. If it buys the computer, it can borrow the funds at a 12 percent rate of interest, which it

TABLE 23.1   Cash Flows with Leasing and Buying

Leasing	Buying
After-tax costs of the lease payments	Depreciation tax shield
	Interest payments
	Tax shield on the interest payments
	Principal payments on the debt
	Salvage value

would repay as an amortized loan. Alternatively, it can lease the asset for the four years by paying an annual lease payment of $15,000. Which alternative should the firm choose? To answer this question, we must consider all the payments that the firm will make under the two alternatives. In evaluating these flows, we must consider them strictly on an after-tax basis.

If the firm buys the computer, the actual outlay will be the $50,000 cost of the machine. Because we want our evaluation to be comparable with a lease, we assume that the firm borrows the entire $50,000. Because it uses an amortized loan, it repays it with four equal payments. Therefore, we may analyze the loan repayment as an annuity. For four years with a discount rate of 12 percent, the annuity factor is PA(12%, 4) = 3.037. This means that the annual loan repayment will be $16,461. In addition to the loan repayment amounts themselves, we must consider some important tax effects. First, interest on the loan payments is tax deductible, so the payments generate a tax shield. To calculate this in each period, we have to know which portion of the total payment is interest. Table 23.2 presents an amortization table with these calculations.

Because the loan is amortized, the payments remain constant, but the interest and principal vary with each one. In the first year, for instance, the interest due is $6,000 ($50,000 × 0.12), leaving $10,461 for principal repayment. As Table 23.2 shows, the interest decreases each year. Therefore, the

TABLE 23.2   Amortization of the Loan

Year	Payment	Interest	Principal Repayment	Balance
0	N.A.	N.A.	N.A.	$50,000
1	$16,461	$6,000	$10,461	39,539
2	16,461	4,744	11,717	27,822
3	16,461	3,338	13,123	14,699
4	16,461	1,763	14,697	2*

* The balance does not equal 0 because of rounding error.

Leasing Planes Is Not Plain Anymore

An airline buying planes used to follow a simple formula. It borrowed the purchase amount from commercial banks, which were short-term lenders; refinanced with insurance companies, which were long-term lenders; and used its retained earnings and funds generated by depreciation charges to make the payments.

That was in the good old days, when the industry was sheltered by an umbrella of regulation and guaranteed a profitable rate of return by federal decree. Fares were high and generally uniform, and competition was based on who offered the largest seats or, during the "sandwich wars," the best food. Deals for planes could be worked out on a golf course with a scoring pencil.

But the times they are a'changing. The relatively simple transaction of yesterday has evolved into a complex calculation with so many "what-if" assumptions that only computers can cope. In 1987, for example, Bankers Trust Co. made 30 computer runs, each using different assumptions, for an airline's management that was trying to decide whether to lease or buy.

A shiny, new fleet of jets does a lot for an airline. Usually, new planes reduce operating costs, helping to widen margins of profit. They burn less fuel and, in some models, require a cockpit crew of only two instead of the usual three. But the cost of new aircraft is becoming more difficult to bear, and airlines have found themselves in a financing squeeze. The first four-engine Boeing 707s, for example, had price tags of $5.5 million to $7 million when they were first rolled out in 1957. A twin-engine 737-300, the lowest-priced available commercial jetliner sold by the Boeing Co., went for $26 million to $33 million in 1988. Similarly, a Boeing 767 twin-jet can go for $51 million to $74 million, depending on the options it has.

With airplane prices sky-high, it is no wonder that many airlines find it nearly impossible to raise the money as capital. The likelihood, in fact, is that third parties, especially leasing companies, as well as commercial banks, investment banks, and independent investors, are becoming the jet makers' biggest customers.

Leasing firms are acquiring growing numbers of planes for various reasons. On one side, airlines want to stay as liquid as possible, unburdened by high capital costs, yet be able to change both the number and types of planes they fly in a highly competitive and quickly changing market. Leasing helps them do this. It also enables them "to shed aircraft and debt if serious economic downturns develop," says Donald P. Schenk, a Bankers Trust managing director for corporate finance.

On the other side, leasing firms are able to raise money more cheaply and, at times, more readily than airlines can. They also buy aircraft in large numbers and at prices lower than those available to the carriers. Leasing companies are also whizzes in the financial markets. International

Lease, for example, generates considerable cash from its operations, and it also borrows from a dozen commercial banks to finance its purchases. Since 1985 it has been able to borrow on an unsecured basis, and few of its planes are mortgaged. Its average cost of borrowing was 7.95 percent, at a time when the prime rate was 8.51 percent.

International Lease generally negotiates a lease with terms of 2 to 10 years, though most airlines prefer longer-term deals—as much as 18 to 20 years—for the sake of smaller installment payments. It has leased and sold aircraft to more than 50 of the world's 300 airlines, from the tiniest to the largest.

The lease payments may not return the full price of an aircraft to its lessor-owner, but an aircraft can be leased again or sold for its residual value—often at the price originally paid for it—at the lease's expiration. Some airlines, in fact, negotiate leasing deals in which the residual value goes to them. Whether to retain residual value, in fact, is one of the variables airline negotiators plug into their computers when considering new aircraft.

Another is taxation. "There's not a successful airline in the United States which does not reexamine its tax position on a regular basis to determine how it should finance its next plane," says Schenk. Airlines even try to determine whether they will actually be paying any taxes and if so, how much, in the years ahead. They also check the prospects for new tax legislation, searching for hints that will help them plan the structure of a lease.

An airline may contract to buy a jet when the delivery price is, say, $20 million. By the time the plane is delivered in a year or so, its fair market value may be $26 million. The airline then sells the craft at its fair market price and leases it back. One result of the transaction is an immediate cash infusion of $6 million.

At times airlines have structured financings in currencies they are "long" in as a result of their route structure. Australia-based Qantas Airways, for example, set up a deal in New Zealander dollars. Carriers with "a large revenue base in Japan," Schenk says, "arranged yen-denominated financings to offset their natural long position."

Mark E. Daugherty, an airline analyst at Dean Witter Reynolds, Inc., says that "leasing's here to stay." Some airlines, he says, are too deep in debt to borrow large sums to finance purchases. Leasing, he says, also enables airline companies to adapt to market changes with newer craft and are a reason for increased cash flows.

Leasing, says Schenk, is "the new magic of aircraft financing."

Source: Christopher Elias, "Aircraft Deals Are Anything but Plain Today," *Insight,* June 20, 1988, pp. 44–46.

TABLE 23.3   After-Tax Cash Flows for the Borrowing and Leasing Alternatives

| Year | Borrowing | | | Leasing |
	Loan Payment	Interest Tax Shield	Depreciation Tax Shield	After-Tax Lease Payment
1	−$16,461	$1,800	$3,750	−$10,500
2	−16,461	1,423	3,750	−10,500
3	−16,461	1,001	3,750	−10,500
4	−16,461	529	3,750	−10,500

tax shield due to the interest payment also decreases. The tax shield on the interest paid equals the amount of interest times the tax rate. In the first year, for example, the tax shield from the interest payment is $1,800 ($6,000 × 0.3). We must know these figures for each year, because they are an incremental cash flow of the decision to borrow funds to buy the computer. The first two columns of Table 23.3 show the loan payment and the interest tax shield for each of the four periods over the life of the loan. The loan payment has a negative sign, indicating that it is a cash outflow if the firm borrows and buys. The interest tax shield has a plus sign, showing the firm obtains the tax shield only if it borrows and buys.

Borrowing and buying also affects depreciation. Since depreciation is not a cash flow, it matters only because of the tax shield that it generates. For a computer costing $50,000 and 0 salvage value after four years, the annual straight-line depreciation expense is $12,500. The depreciation tax shield equals the depreciation expense times the tax rate, so borrowing and buying gives a depreciation tax shield of $3,750 each year. The plus signs in Table 23.3 reflect this benefit of borrowing.

The firm is also able to lease the computer for a yearly fee of $15,000. Because the full amount of the lease payment is deductible as a business expense, the after-tax lease payment is $10,500 ($15,000 × 0.7). Table 23.3 shows these after-tax lease payments in the last column.

Adding all of the cash flows for the two strategies gives the total after-tax cash flows for each alternative:

Total After-Tax Cash Flows

| | Period | | | |
	1	2	3	4
Buy	−$10,911	−$11,288	−$11,710	−$12,182
Lease	−10,500	−10,500	−10,500	−10,500

The choice between these two methods is a choice between two series of outflows. Because these are outflows, the firm should choose the method that gives the lower present value of outflows when the payment streams are discounted at the after-tax cost of debt. We saw that the firm could borrow for this project at 12 percent. Being in the 30 percent tax bracket means that its after-tax cost of debt is 8.4 percent ($12\% \times 0.7$). Therefore, we discount the flows at this rate.

Present value of the borrow-and-buy outflows:

$$PV = \frac{-\$10,911}{1.084} + \frac{-\$11,288}{1.084^2} + \frac{-\$11,710}{1.084^3} + \frac{-\$12,182}{1.084^4}$$

$$= -\$37,687$$

Present value of the lease outflows:

$$PV = \frac{-\$10,500}{1.084} + \frac{-\$10,500}{1.084^2} + \frac{-\$10,500}{1.084^3} + \frac{-\$10,500}{1.084^4}$$

$$= -\$34,470$$

net benefit of leasing (NBL)
the present value of the after-tax leasing outflows minus the present value of the after-tax borrow-and-buy outflows

In present value terms, leasing saves the difference in the two outflows, or $3,217. This difference is the **net benefit of leasing** (**NBL**).

$$NBL = PV \text{ of lease outflows} - PV \text{ of buy outflows}$$

In our example, we have:

$$NBL = -\$34,470 - (-\$37,687) = \$3,217$$

Because the NBL is positive, the firm should lease the computer, rather than buy it.

As an alternative, we can find the NBL by first combining the cash flows and then discounting:

$$NBL = PV \text{ (lease outflows} - \text{buy outflows)}$$

In our example, this would result in:

$$PV = \frac{\$411}{1.084} + \frac{\$788}{1.084^2} + \frac{\$1,210}{1.084^3} + \frac{\$1,682}{1.084^4}$$

$$= \$3,217$$

Just as before, the NBL is $3,217. Therefore, we can use either method to calculate the NBL.

EXAMPLE 23.1

Zerlina, Inc., will acquire a fleet of 20 cars to use for five years. Each automobile costs $10,000. The firm faces a 34 percent corporate tax rate. It has two alternative financing sources. First, it can borrow the funds at 10 percent and buy the fleet. If it borrows, it will pay only interest each year and repay all the principal in five years. The firm will depreciate the cars for five years on a straight-line basis. Alternatively, it can lease the entire fleet for $60,000 per year, including maintenance. The annual maintenance costs per vehicle would be $300. Should Zerlina lease or buy?

STEP 1: Identify the after-tax cash flows

Borrow and Buy   If Zerlina buys the cars, it will borrow $200,000. The firm must repay this principal in full after five years. With a 10 percent rate of interest, the firm pays $20,000 in interest each year. On an after-tax basis, this is $13,200 ($20,000 × 0.66).

If it buys the fleet, it will depreciate $200,000 over five years. This gives a straight-line depreciation expense of $40,000 per year. The depreciation tax shield is $13,600, which equals the depreciation expense times the tax rate ($40,000 × 0.34).

With a maintenance expense of $300 per car per year, the yearly maintenance expense is $6,000. On an after-tax basis this would be $3,960. We must charge this maintenance expense against the borrow-and-buy alternative because the lease expense already includes maintenance. This keeps the two alternatives on an even footing. The table on the next page specifies of these cash flows.

Leasing   With the lease alternative, the lease payment of $60,000 includes the maintenance, and the after-tax cost of the lease payment is $39,600. The table also shows these flows.

Borrowing

Year	Principal Payment	After-Tax Interest	Depreciation Tax Shield	Maintenance
1	—	−$13,200	$13,600	−$3,960
2	—	−13,200	13,600	−3,960
3	—	−13,200	13,600	−3,960
4	—	−13,200	13,600	−3,960
5	−$200,000	−13,200	13,600	−3,960

Leasing

Year	After-Tax Lease Payment
1	−$39,600
2	−39,600
3	−39,600
4	−39,600
5	−39,600

STEP 2: Determine the NPV of flows under each alternative

Borrow and Buy For each year, the total after-tax cash flows for the borrow-and-buy alternative are:

Year	Cash Flow
1	−$ 3,560
2	− 3,560
3	− 3,560
4	− 3,560
5	− 203,560

We have to discount these cash flows at Zerlina's after-tax cost of debt. With a 10 percent borrowing cost and a 34 percent tax rate, the firm's after-tax cost of borrowing is 6.6 percent. Using these numbers results in an NPV of −$160,047.

Leasing The NPV of the lease payments, using the cash flows found previously and an after-tax discount rate of 6.6 percent, is −$164,122.

STEP 3: Calculate the NBL and decide

In present value terms, the cost of leasing exceeds the cost of borrowing and buying the fleet. Because we want to minimize the NPV of the payments, we should prefer the borrow-and-buy alternative. The net benefit of leasing for this problem is NBL = −$164,122 − (−$160,047) = −$4,075. Since the net benefit of leasing is negative, it has no advantages. Zerlina should borrow and buy.

HOW LEASING CREATES VALUE

Normally, the firm's financing decision does not create value, at least in perfect markets with no taxes; for example, its capital structure is irrelevant. The same was true of the dividend decision.

☞ The benefits of leasing arise from market imperfections and the existence of taxes.

If markets are perfect and there are no taxes, then leasing must be a zero sum game between the lessor and the lessee. If the lease is a good deal for the lessee, it must be a bad deal for the lessor, and vice versa. In a world of perfect markets and no taxes, the choice between debt and leasing is irrelevant. However, leasing is big business, and its widespread use as a financing tool must be due to actual benefits for both parties. These benefits arise because of either taxes or market imperfections.

This section shows how such an arrangement can reduce taxes. When this occurs, the new wealth created may be divided between the lessor and the lessee. The next section considers other market imperfections that can also make leasing attractive.

FINANCE

TODAY

Please Re-Lease Me

A recent report in the press that General Electric is attempting "to limit its exposure to the aircraft industry" by selling half its stake in Polaris obviously was done without access to top management. Does it make sense for GE to bail out now just because the going is rough? "Absolutely not," says Gary C. Wendt, president and CEO of $55 billion-in-assets GE Capital (GECC). "We love the aircraft-leasing business. In fact, we're looking for another 20 percent increase in earnings this year."

That's good news for the tens of thousands of investors who, collectively, have over $1 billion tied up in commercial aircraft-leasing partnerships managed by GE Capital's subsidiary, San Francisco-based Polaris Aircraft Leasing. The client list of those six partnerships reads like a who's who of bankrupt and troubled U.S. airlines, such as Continental and Pan Am, which went Chapter 11 in 1990 and 1991, respectively. Investors are counting on GECC's global clout in the airline industry and Polaris's savvy in remarketing used planes to pull the partnerships through.

Including the 181 aircraft owned by the partnerships, GECC has a fleet of 405 commercial jet aircraft, 255 of which are owned or managed by Polaris. The remaining 150 are owned by GECC's Transportation and Industrial Funding Group. All of this makes GE the largest owner/manager of commercial jet aircraft, with about 5 percent of the world's fleet. As for aircraft leasing's current malaise, "we're confident that we'll come out of it on behalf of the funds and on behalf of our planes in good shape," says W. James McNerney, Jr., an executive vice president at GECC who oversees its aircraft-leasing operations.

Polaris's commercial aircraft investment partnerships were founded in the mid-1980s when domestic airlines were rapidly expanding. The company's strategy at the time was to capitalize on the airlines' need for used, narrow-body aircraft. Polaris's six publicly offered limited partnerships did just that. But, "the area in which Polaris partnerships specialized has been absolutely clobbered," says Philip Baggaley at Standard & Poor's. In addition to Polaris's leases to Continental and Pan Am, the partnerships rented planes to Braniff and Presidential Airlines, which both filed for Chapter 11 protection in the fall of 1989, as well as such troubled carriers as Midway, Hawaiian Airlines, TWA, and Emery Aircraft Leasing.

Currently, Income Fund I is the most troubled of Polaris's commercial aircraft limited partnerships, with seven of its 10 aircraft off lease. Fund I suspended cash distributions to limited partners in the first quarter of 1990 because of the Braniff default. Braniff leases accounted for about 84 percent of the fund's revenues. Last June, Fund I resumed payouts but at a reduced rate of $2.50 per limited-partnership unit—substantially less than the $33.76 distributed to investors for the first six months of 1989. When

Braniff defaulted on its lease agreement with Polaris, the fund repossessed its nine Boeing 737-200s from the airline but has only succeeded in re-leasing two. These new lease rates represent a 12 percent and a 30 percent decrease from the original lease agreements with Braniff.

While planes are off lease, the fund is liable for aircraft insurance, maintenance, storage, and other expenses. Worse still, because these planes are old—1968 and 1969 models—the partnership could incur substantial costs before it can re-lease the planes.

"The partnerships took a substantial position in Stage 2 aircraft, which are older, noisier, and less fuel-efficient planes," says Paul Turk of AvMark Inc., a Rosslyn, Va.-based consultancy specializing in the economics of the airline industry. "With the general malaise in the airline business, these are the planes that are being parked."

In a recent SEC filing, Polaris estimated that the cost of upgrading Fund I's fleet alone could exceed $10 million. And meeting tough new noise standards passed by Congress last October could cost tens of millions of dollars by the year 2000 if the funds are to keep their older planes in the air. GECC's McNerney says that some of those Stage 2 planes "will be at the end of their useful life."

Polaris's Fund II also has a plane off lease as a result of the Braniff bankruptcy. Another cause for concern is that 25 of the fund's 30 aircraft are leased by either Pan Am or TWA. All of Fund III's planes are leased to Continental, Midway, or TWA. Fund IV is heavily exposed to Emery and Continental. Together, Funds III and IV have a total of 31 aircraft on lease to Continental, which suspended its lease payments to the funds when it filed for bankruptcy last December. And to make matters worse, a controversial ruling by a judge in Continental's bankruptcy case in January is preventing Polaris from repossessing some of the aircraft. Virtually all of the leases for the aircraft belonging to the six funds come up for renewal within the next $2\frac{1}{2}$ years.

Will GECC, which has a very small investment in the troubled partnerships, come to the rescue? McNerney says that "just because our investment is less doesn't mean we aren't aggressively managing those planes."

What has sparked rumors that GE wants out of commercial aircraft leasing is GECC's search for partners to invest in Polaris. Outsiders have speculated that GE would unload the entire unit if it had the chance.

But it's a mistake to think all of Polaris looks as bad as the partnerships. Wendt points out that after buying Polaris, "we modified their strategy in two respects. We had them concentrate on new aircraft and we expanded their marketing operation on a truly global basis."

The result? Outside of the limited partnerships, Polaris and GECC have better planes on lease with healthier foreign carriers, such as British Airways. In fact, only 4 percent of GECC's investments are in planes over

(continued)

15 years old. That's because when Polaris and GECC purchase aircraft for their own accounts, they tend to acquire new, wide-body jets. "Our investment is skewed toward newer planes," says McNerney. That includes wide-body aircraft and Stage 3 narrow-body planes. More than 85 percent of the Transportation and Industrial Funding Group's leased planes are less than 10 years old. In contrast, the aircraft held by the partnerships date mostly from the late 1960s to the mid-1970s with few exceptions.

The fact that GECC upped its stake in Polaris from 81 percent to nearly 95 percent just last November supports GECC's claim that its game plan is not contraction in the guise of expansion, but rather expansion, pure and simple. "We think the aircraft financing industry is going to be huge over the next 10 years. Even GE may not be big enough alone to partake of that as much as our marketing capability will allow," says McNerney. Raising money through additional Polaris-sponsored partnerships is out of the question for now. In fact, Polaris closed its latest fund—Fund VI—prematurely on Jan. 22 largely because of a lack of investor interest.

The ideal partner would give Polaris access to additional financial and overseas markets. Not to mention favorable treatment under "foreign tax laws that we wouldn't normally have being a U.S. company," adds Wendt. So foreign investors must be high on GECC's list of prospects. The plan is for GECC to maintain its majority stake in Polaris.

How is the search progressing? Wendt hints that GECC is getting close on a couple of prospects, but insists he's in no hurry. "This is not one of those cases where I wake up in the morning and say, 'Holy cow. We've got to get rid of that Polaris stake today.' We don't."

Source: Alexandra Biesada, "Please Re-Lease Me," *Financial World,* April 16, 1991, pp. 66–67.

To see how leasing creates tax benefits, we consider an airline that buys and operates a plane. We then determine how the cash flows differ if the airline leases the plane instead. In this example, we assume that markets are perfect except for taxes. This means that the airplane costs the same for the airline or the lessor, and both have the same borrowing costs and maintenance costs.

☞ Differential income tax rates between the lessor and the lessee can make leasing attractive because it can generate more tax benefits.

The key assumption that makes leasing attractive in this case is a difference in the tax rates between the airline and the lessor. Airline profits are extremely volatile and some airlines often lose money. A firm that has a loss in a given year pays no taxes in that year. Furthermore, it can carry losses to subsequent years to offset future income. For example, if an airline has a $100 million

TABLE 23.4 After-Tax Financing Flows for the Airplane

	Airline	Lessor	Tax Collection
PLANE IS OWNED			
Depreciation tax shield	$ 0	$0	$0
Interest expense	−7,000,000	0	0
After-tax cash flow	−$7,000,000	$0	$0
PLANE IS LEASED			
Depreciation tax shield	$0	$1,700,000	−$1,700,000
Interest expense	0	−4,620,000	−2,380,000
Lease payment	−6,500,000	4,290,000	$2,210,000
After-tax cash flow	−$6,500,000	+$1,370,000	−$1,870,000
Advantage from lease	**$ 500,000**	**$1,370,000**	**−$1,870,000**

loss in 1991 and a $100 million profit in 1992, it will not pay taxes in either year. In 1991 it owes no tax because of its loss, and in 1992 it can offset its profits by the loss from 1991. As a result, the airline will be in the 0 percent tax bracket in both years.

Assume a plane costs $50 million and the firm can finance it with debt at a rate of 14 percent on a term loan. The firm will only pay interest on the loan for 9 years, and then make the final interest payment and repay the principal in year 10. We also assume that the full value of the plane is depreciated using the straight-line method over 10 years. We assume that the operating profit of the airline is 0, so the airline pays no taxes. The lessor is in the 34 percent tax bracket.

Table 23.4 sets out the after-tax cash flows resulting from the financing decision for both the airline and the lessor. These would be the same for years one through nine. In the tenth year, whoever owns the plane would repay the $50 million principal on the loan. We can focus on just the first nine years. The top panel of Table 23.4 shows the after-tax cash flows for the airline and for the lessor assuming the airline buys the plane. In that case, the lessor has nothing to do with the entire operation. The panel also shows that if the airline owns the plane, no tax is collected by the government because the airline has no profits.

If the airline owns the plane, it pays $7 million in interest each year. Because it has no income to shield, it cannot use the benefit of the tax shield on interest. Therefore, its after-tax cost for the interest expense is the full $7 million. If the airline had positive income, the depreciation expense of $5 million would provide a tax shield as well. Since it has no income, it receives no depreciation tax shield. In this top panel, the lessor plays no role, so all of its cash flows are 0.

The bottom panel shows the after-tax cash flows if the airline leases. In this case, the lessor buys the plane under the same terms available to the airline. The lessor pays $7 million in interest each year, which has an after-tax cost of $4.62 million per year. In addition, the lessor has a depreciation expense of $5 million, which generates a depreciation tax shield of $1.7 million. (Remember that the depreciation tax shield equals the depreciation expense times the tax rate, or $5,000,000 × 0.34 = $1,700,000.) With the leasing option, the airline makes a lease payment of $6.5 million. Again, because it has no income, the actual lease payment is its after-tax cost. The lessor receives the $6.5 million and pays taxes of 34 percent. This leaves the lessor with $4.29 million after taxes from the lease payment.

The decision to lease changes governmental tax collections. First, the lessor receives a depreciation tax shield of $1.7 million. Therefore, the government collects $1.7 million less than it would otherwise. Second, the interest payment of $7 million generates a tax shield of $2.38 million for the lessor. This tax shield reduces tax collections by the same amount. Finally, the lease payment is taxable. The government collects $2.21 million in taxes from this lease payment.

Summing all of the cash flows for the leasing option gives some interesting results. For each of the first nine years the airline has an after-tax cash outflow of $6.5 million and the lessor has a $1.37 million inflow. To see the advantage of leasing in this example, we must compare the position of the airline and the lessor with and without the lease. Under the lease, the airline does not have to repay the $50 million in the tenth year. However, it pays out $1.5 million more each year. The lease benefits the airline because it reduces its after-tax cost of using the plane by $500,000 in each year. The lessor reaps an after-tax inflow of $1.37 million each year. Between them, the airline and the lessor have a combined benefit of $1.87 million. This exactly equals the reduction in the government's tax collections. In this example, the government provides the funds to benefit the airline and the lessor.[1]

The entire benefit for the airline and lessor arose because the two firms were in different tax brackets. The party with the higher tax bracket normally is the lessor. The tax shields are more valuable the higher the tax bracket. Notice also in this example that taxes are the only market imperfection considered. Both the airline and the lessor had to pay the same price for the plane, and we assumed that the maintenance and operating costs would be the same for both. We now go on to consider other kinds of market imperfections that may also give an impetus to leasing.

---

[1] We did not fully consider the repayment of the $50 million principal that takes place after 10 years. The ultimate feasibility of this lease depends on the value of the plane at that time.

LEASING AND MARKET IMPERFECTIONS

☞ Leasing can also generate benefits if some parties can specialize in certain assets and thereby acquire a cost advantage over other parties.

To consider how market imperfections may affect the desirability of leasing, assume a firm specializes in managing a fleet of trucks and that this gives the firm a cost advantage. This advantage is a market imperfection that could make leasing a superior alternative to buying.

Convenience

Some advantages of leasing pertain to both operating and financial leases. Others come only to one kind of lease. For example, if a firm needs an asset for a short time, it may be better to rent or lease the item than to buy. A contractor might need a cement mixer for a particular job. The contractor could buy the mixer, use it on the job, and then sell it. However, the market for used cement mixers is imperfect, so the contractor cannot sell the mixer immediately for its true value. Because of the illiquidity of cement mixers, the firm that needs them temporarily will normally rent. That is better than getting stuck with (or in) a cement mixer.

Similarly, the fixed terms of financial leases may be very inconvenient. Imagine a firm that leases a manufacturing facility on a long-term financial lease. If technology changes, the firm might have to change the plant; however, this will be difficult if the plant is leased. The lessor may not permit the alterations; and the lessee may be unwilling to invest in making the changes anyway, since the lessor owns the plant. In either case, leasing the plant could result in loss of efficiency.

The Risk of Obsolescence

Aircraft manufacturers lease airplanes. Computer makers lease computers. The same is common for photocopier manufacturers. In these cases, the manufacturer has special expertise and knowledge about the product that make leasing more efficient than selling. Because the manufacturer also has superior knowledge about the future of the industry, it may be able to bear the risk of obsolescence better than the end user of the product. In this case, the manufacturer in effect sells a put option to the lessee, and the lessee pays for that risk protection in the form of higher lease payments.

The Ease of Financing

For many small companies, leasing may provide an easier and more convenient way to finance than debt. For example, if a firm needs a fleet of delivery vans, the van manufacturer will almost always have a financial subsidiary that specializes in leasing its products. Thus a small firm may find it more convenient to deal with the manufacturer/lessor than to borrow from a bank.

Leasing and Devaluation

Many firms in foreign countries are faced with the prospect of leasing equipment directly from a foreign manufacturer. For example, an airline in Latin America might not have the cash needed to purchase a new fleet of airplanes, and the local market may not be willing or able to lend the funds or provide leasing arrangements. In this example, the foreign airline will be forced to enter into a leasing agreement denominated in U.S. dollars, even though the bulk of its cash may be generated in the local currency.

Unfortunately, many of these same countries suffer from a chronic devaluation of their currency in relation to the U.S. dollar. The following example illustrates the high cost of such a state of affairs.

Suppose an airline from the hypothetical country of San Cristobal signs a leasing agreement with a U.S. airplane manufacturer, or with a third party acting as a lessor. The airline is obligated to make annual payments of US$10 million each year for the next 10 years. Assume that these payments are already on an after-tax basis. To simplify, the firm's cost of money is assumed to remain at 20 percent per year during the life of the lease, regardless of the rate of devaluation of the local currency—the peso.

If the annual devaluation rate of the peso relative to the dollar is d percent, then each successive year the airline will have to collect d percent more pesos in order to make the required US$10 million lease payment. Thus, if at the time of the first year's payment the exchange rate is 1 peso per dollar, then at the time of the nth payment $10,000,000(1 + d)^{n-1}$ pesos will be needed to purchase the dollars. This implies that, in terms of pesos, the sequence of payments made by the airline constitutes a growing

A larger firm may have similar advantages with leasing. In leasing high-priced items such as airplanes, the lessee can sometimes avoid the expenses associated with floating a bond issue. In other words, the legal and administrative costs of obtaining financing can be cheaper with leasing than with issuing debt. In some cases, leasing can increase liquidity. For instance, in a sale/leaseback arrangement, the lessee receives immediate cash.

The Effect on Financial Statements

At one time, one of the main alleged advantages of a financial lease was its effect on the firm's financial statements. As a result of a tightening of accounting rules, firms must now show financial leases on the firm's balance sheet and

annuity, which was discussed in Chapter 4. The present value of the cost of this deal in pesos is then:

$$PV = \frac{10,000,000}{0.20 - d}\left[1 - \left(\frac{1 + d}{1 + 0.2}\right)^{10}\right]$$

Using this equation, the following table illustrates the rising cost of the leasing deal to the airline, as the devaluation of the peso increases. Of course, the added costs arising from devaluation could be mitigated if, for example, the airline were able to raise ticket prices denominated in pesos.

DEVALUATION RATE	PRESENT VALUE OF LEASING COST (pesos)
0	41,924,720
2	44,618,090
4	47,558,270
6	50,769,150
8	54,276,800
10	58,109,610
12	62,298,520
14	66,877,180
16	71,882,150
18	77,353,170

Although this example is clearly a simplification of reality, it illustrates that a company entering into a leasing contract denominated in a foreign currency can expose itself to considerable risk if the local currency is expected to devalue substantially during the life of the lease.

off-balance sheet financing
financing that does not appear on the balance sheet

treat them as liabilities. Before the passage of this rule, FASB 13, leases provided **off-balance sheet financing** because firms did not show the contractual obligations of a financial lease on the balance sheet. Instead, the leases appeared only in the footnotes to the annual report. This advantage may have been more illusory than real, because it is doubtful whether this stratagem fooled investors. Now, with financial leases recorded on the balance sheet, this hiding game cannot work at all.

Firms can, however, arrange leases in a way that affects reported income. For example, they can structure a lease with small payments now and large payments in the future. This would give the effect of increasing current income, an effect that would be advantageous only if investors were ignorant of the real terms of the contract and were fooled by the inflated earnings figures.

MERGER TERMINOLOGY

merger or **acquisition**
the combination of two or more firms into a single independent company

In a **merger** or **acquisition,** two or more firms combine to form a single independent company. In essence, one firm buys and absorbs another. The buying firm is the acquirer and the company that is sold is the acquired firm. The merger may not change the name and operations of the target firm, but the target ceases to exist as an independent entity.

Horizontal and Vertical Mergers

horizontal merger
a merger between firms in the same industry

We may classify most mergers as horizontal or vertical. A **horizontal merger** occurs when the acquiring and target firms are in the same industry, and it can sometimes create important economies. Also, if the firms are complementary in certain ways, the merged firm can achieve significant advantages by improving economies of scale in purchasing or distribution. Usually, the acquiring firm dismisses the top management of the target firm.

antitrust legislation
legislation aimed at controlling the establishment of monopolies

One potential problem with horizontal mergers is that they may restrict trade or result in monopolies. **Antitrust legislation** attempts to prevent the establishment of monopolies. The Sherman Act of 1890 restricts mergers that result in a restraint of trade. The Clayton Act of 1914 limits mergers that may lessen competition or that may result in monopolies. Recent liberal interpretations by the courts, however, have allowed firms considerable freedom in completing horizontal mergers.

vertical merger
a merger between two companies specializing in different parts of the production chain

vertical integration
the integration or consolidation of the production chain into one firm

total integration
the owning of all phases of the production chain

A **vertical merger** occurs between two companies specializing in different parts of a given production chain. It gives rise to **vertical integration,** the consolidation of the production chain into one firm. Many mergers in the oil industry increase vertical integration. If we think of the oil business as consisting of exploration, refining, and distribution, we know that the firms in the industry will specialize in one area or the other. If a refiner and distributor merge, the resulting firm brings more of the production chain within its own control. Vertical integration can provide the oil refiner with an assured outlet for its refinery products and the distributor with an assumed supply of product. Some firms strive for **total integration,** the owning of all phases of the production chain, ranging from the acquisition of raw materials to the retailing of the final product.

Conglomerate Mergers

conglomerate merger
a merger between firms from unrelated industries

☞ Conglomerate mergers create no value because they do not affect competition or production efficiencies.

The **conglomerate merger** differs from both horizontal and vertical mergers in that it involves firms from unrelated industries. The merged firm achieves no operating economies, such as those that might arise from horizontal or vertical integration. Instead, the conglomerate essentially holds a portfolio of companies.

We can expect the total value of the firms after the merger to equal the sum of their premerge values. Some would argue that the combined firm is less risky than each of the separate firms due to its greater diversification and

☞ Conglomerate merg-
ers are essentially a form
of diversification by buying whole companies
instead of by holding a
diversified stock portfolio.

thus would be more valuable than the sum of the two individual firms. However, such an argument is fallacious because investors can merge the firms by simply buying each firm's stock and holding it as part of their portfolio. In other words, the investor realizes no diversification benefit from a conglomerate merger.

DIVESTITURES AND SPINOFFS

divestiture or **spinoff**
the disposal of some part
of a firm's operations in
the form of a newly
created company

Paralleling a dramatic increase in mergers, there has also been an increase in divestitures and spinoffs. In a **divestiture** or a **spinoff** a firm disposes of some part of its operations to form a new company. The largest ever was the split-up of AT&T in 1984, in which the communications giant spun off several regional operating units.

Although the fractioning of AT&T was mandated by the courts, many companies voluntarily decide to divest part of their holdings to achieve greater operating efficiency. This has happened with many of the financial operations of big companies such as General Motors, with its General Motors Acceptance Corporation (GMAC), and General Electric, with its General Electric Credit Corporation (GECC). These specialized companies deal only with the financing aspects of the business, and help increase sales by allowing more clients to obtain their products on credit.

MERGER PROCEDURES

negotiated takeover
a merger or acquisition in
which the acquirer nego-
tiates directly with the
management of the tar-
get firm

friendly takeover
a merger in which the
terms of the merger are
agreed on between the
management of the ac-
quiring and target firms

tender offer
an attempt to gain con-
trol of a target firm by
directly asking its shareholders to sell their shares
to the acquiring firm

Firms can initiate mergers in two basic ways. First, in a **negotiated takeover** the acquirer may negotiate directly with the management of the target firm. This is usually a **friendly takeover,** with the two parties agreeing to a set of terms. A second type is a **tender offer,** which arises without any direct negotiation with the management of the target firm. Instead, the acquiring firm approaches the shareholders directly and asks them to tender their shares to it. A shareholder who tenders a share promises to sell the share to the party making the offer at the tender price. To induce shareholders to tender their shares, the acquiring firm must offer a price above the current market price of the stock.

The acquiring firm chooses whether to proceed by negotiations or by making a tender offer. If the acquirer believes that the target firm would not be receptive to the former, it may opt for the latter. Firms generally prefer to negotiate. The management of the target firm may believe that the offer is not in the interest of the firm's shareholders and may reject the offer for that reason. Management may have less noble reasons for wishing to avoid a merger. We have already noted that the acquirer often fires the managers of the target company, so fear of being fired motivates management of the target firm to fight the takeover.

A target firm that finds itself in the grips of an acquiring firm may try to avoid the merger with that party. There are three basic strategies for avoiding a given acquirer, all with colorful names. First, the target firm may take a

TABLE 23.5 The Paying of Greenmail

Firm	Unwanted Shareholder	Premium Over Market Value
Blue Bell	Bass Brothers	$60.0
St. Regis	James Goldsmith	50.5
Castle & Cooke	Charles Hurwitz	14.0
Walt Disney	Saul Steinberg	60.0
Avco	Leucadia National	62.0

poison pill
an action taken by a target firm to destroy its attractiveness for the acquirer

poison pill.[2] It does this by taking some action that destroys its attractiveness for the acquirer. For example, firms with large amounts of cash are usually attractive takeover targets. One that finds itself a target may quickly dispose of its cash by buying some other firm. In fact, many companies use high leverage to make themselves less attractive as takeover targets.

A second technique is for the target to pay the acquirer to cease pursuit. Imagine a tender offer that is proceeding with an acquirer accumulating shares of the target in the marketplace. The management of the target may offer to pay the acquirer a higher than market price for the acquirer's shares, in return for which the acquirer agrees not to pursue the target firm. This practice is known as **greenmail.** For example, Carl Icahn initiated a hostile takeover attempt on Chesebrough-Pond. The attempt ended when Chesebrough bought back Icahn's shares at the market price, but also paid $95 million, or twice book value, for a company owned by Icahn. Some observers regarded this as paying off Icahn to drop the takeover attempt.[3] Another notorious case involves H. Ross Perot and General Motors. After GM acquired Perot's flagship company, Electronic Data Systems, Perot was granted a seat as a GM director. As GM's share of the auto market decreased, Perot's public chastising of GM's top management increased. Apparently, some directors couldn't take the heat, and negotiated with Perot to buy his shares for twice their market value, giving Perot a windfall profit on the order of $750 million. Many smaller GM investors were outraged, since they viewed the operation as a transfer of their wealth to Perot. Table 23.5 shows other famous greenmail payoffs.

greenmail
paying the acquirer a higher than market price for the acquirer's shares, in exchange for an agreement not to pursue the target

white knight
a friendly firm that acquires a firm being targeted by a hostile acquirer

A third way that target firms wriggle off the takeover hook is by finding a **white knight,** that is, a third firm that acquires the one being pursued by the hostile acquirer. In this case, the target still loses its independence, but its management may get a better deal or be more comfortable with the operating style of the white knight.

[2] No doubt this name is inspired by the presumed action taken by spies when they face imminent capture by the enemy.

[3] Colin Leinster, "Carl Icahn's Calculated Bets," *Fortune,* March 18, 1985; "The Raiders," *Business Week,* March 4, 1985.

TAX CONSEQUENCES OF MERGERS

☞ Mergers may create real economic benefits by creating tax savings.

Mergers may be either taxable or tax free. We already noted that the target firm ceases to exist in a merger, so its shares no longer exist. Essentially, a merger may treat the shares of the target firm as though they were sold or exchanged for shares of the acquiring firm. In the former case the shareholders must pay capital gains taxes on their shares. In the latter, the merger can be tax free if more than 50 percent of the target shareholder's compensation takes the form of shares of the acquiring firm.

HISTORY AND RECENT TRENDS

In the last 20 years the number of mergers has decreased; however, their dollar value and importance in the economy increased throughout the 1980s. The number of announced merger attempts fell from a high of about 6,000 in 1969 to a range of about 2,500 per year during the 1980s. It appears that in the early years of the 1990s enthusiasm for big mergers is reduced. This may be due in great part to the drying up of many of the traditional sources of money to conduct such massive transactions. Indeed, the entire banking industry faces a crisis in the 1990s that is at least comparable to the debacle suffered by the savings and loan industry during the latter part of the 1980s. Furthermore, many of the mergers occurred in the form of leveraged buyouts, or LBOs, which required immense amounts of borrowed money. With the virtual disappearance of the junk bond market after the demise of Drexel Burnham, LBOs have become an endangered species in the early 1990s.

MOTIVES FOR MERGERS

What is the motivation for mergers? First, we noted in our discussion that horizontal and vertical mergers may create important operating efficiencies. In a horizontal merger, the new firm may have market power or economies of scale that it lacked previously. A vertical merger may reduce firm risk by securing suppliers for production inputs and outlets for final products. Both may extend the scope of a superior management team over a larger enterprise.

In addition, there may be other motives for mergers, some valid and some of questionable worth. Three of these are the pursuit of tax benefits, the goal of portfolio diversification, and the desire to increase earnings per share.

Tax Benefits

tax-loss carry-forward
an accounting loss that the firm has not used to reduce taxes in the past and that can be carried forward to offset future income

On occasion, a merger can provide clear tax benefits. Consider a firm with a history of losses that has accumulated a large amount in tax-loss carry-forwards. A **tax-loss carry-forward** is an accounting loss that the firm has not been able to use to reduce taxes in the past, and that it can carry forward to offset future positive income. If the firm does not anticipate positive income soon, it will not be able to use the tax shelter and it will lose the tax shield

FINANCE TODAY

The Courageous Commodore

Cornelius Vanderbilt, when he died in 1877, left behind the first American fortune to reach $100 million. To put that century-ago fortune in current perspective, in those days a skilled worker earned $600 a year. Vanderbilt, who showed a young America what competition was, dominated the business scene of his day in a way that no person can even pretend to equal today.

Born May 27, 1794, on Staten Island, N.Y., the product of a century of sturdy, frugal Dutch farmers, he was a handsome, strapping boy, boisterous and brimming with energy. At 16, stirred by the procession of sails floating past the island, he borrowed $100 from his mother and bought his own small boat to hire out as a ferry to New York City. "I didn't feel as much real satisfaction," he reminisced years later, "when I made two million in that Harlem corner as I did on that bright May morning 60 years before when I stepped into my own periauger, hoisted my own sail and put my hand on my own tiller."

Cornelius thrived. He repaid his mother, invested his earnings in other boats, and earned a reputation as the best boatman in the harbor. By 1818 Cornelius had accumulated $15,000 and secured a solid future. He had also married a neighbor girl who bore him 13 children and endured his coarse, stubborn, overbearing manner. Most men of his time would have been content with that level of success, but something separated Vanderbilt from his stolid peers. Apart from energy, he possessed a clarity of vision and a creative, competitive drive that would not let him stop.

The first leap came in 1818, when he concluded that the future of shipping belonged to steam rather than sail. He sold his sailing vessels and hired on as captain of a ferry between New Brunswick, N.J., and New York City. He ignored the advice of friends who thought he was crazy to surrender his own ships and work for someone else. Cornelius was more concerned with learning the rules of the new game of steam.

He could not have picked a better time—or employer. Thomas Gibbons was an irascible jurist who went into the ferry business. Vanderbilt did a great job for Gibbons. He cut expenses, introduced tighter schedules, and built a reputation for reliability. He persuaded Gibbons to build a larger ferry, which Vanderbilt helped design and captained. Thus he learned the art of steamboat design.

Vanderbilt struck out on his own in 1829, on the New York–Raritan route, and wasted little time showing wealthier, more entrenched rivals his grasp of the game. He started with boats that were speedy yet comfortable, ran them with clockwork precision, trimmed costs but never service, and hustled business constantly.

When other lines admired his boats, Vanderbilt cheerfully sold them so he could design larger, faster, and more luxurious models. A rival line, richer but unable to compete against Vanderbilt, paid him a handsome sum to leave the Raritan route. Vanderbilt took the money and transferred his ships to the Hudson River. Here he confronted the powerful Hudson River Steamboat Association, which conspired to maintain rates on these routes and determined to crush the interloper.

But in the savage rate-slashing and reckless races that followed, Vanderbilt held his own. While the association had more resources, it also had more boats and bled more freely from the rate wars. It quietly offered Vanderbilt a bonus of $100,000 and $5,000 a year if he agreed to leave the Hudson for 10 years. Vanderbilt moved to Long Island Sound.

In the shipping wars, the most potent weapon was lower rates. The ideal boat was like his *Lexington*, which had a steam engine so effective her boiler consumed only about half the wood of a competing steamboat. Then, as now, in a competitive struggle, victory usually goes to the low-cost producer.

In 1848 the Commodore was, at 54, the envy of much younger men. Tall, erect, robust, the self-made millionaire still seemed as restless and hungry as the poor boy of 16 launching his first boat. Then the discovery of gold in remote California sent hordes of people on the interminable voyage around Cape Horn or the dangerous shortcut across the Isthmus of Panama, made nightmarish by malaria-infested jungle.

Vanderbilt was not the first to eye the nearer route across Nicaragua, or even to try it, but he was the man who moved boldly to develop it. This route saved 460 miles, but Vanderbilt saw how to shorten this even more: Build a canal.

At home Vanderbilt gradually sold off his other interests and said good-bye to the rivers and Sound. He was ready to try the open seas in an audacious project on a larger scale than anything he had ever attempted. In the end, he failed, but even in failing he made a new fortune.

After ordering new steam vessels designed for the Nicaraguan route, Vanderbilt went to London in search of financing, headed for Nicaragua, personally chose the port sites, and gave the sailors a few lessons in seamanship along the way. Back home, he formed the Accessory Transit Co. (ATC) to oversee the new line. In July 1851 Vanderbilt proudly sailed on the first voyage to ensure that all would go well.

The maiden voyage took 45 days, a saving of several days over the (precanal) Panama route, with fewer hardships and less exposure to tropical disease. The first return voyage eastward took only 29 days. Passengers flocked to the new line.

The Panama ships countered by lowering rates, a challenge the Commodore took up with relish. A stiffer blow came in August 1852 when British capitalists decided not to underwrite his proposed canal. Dejected,

(continued)

Vanderbilt resigned as president of ATC, sold his steamers to the company, and took a long vacation in Europe.

Vanderbilt returned in 1853 expecting to reclaim ATC from Garrison and Morgan, the two men running it, but they double-crossed him. The news sent Vanderbilt into a towering rage—he delivered his most famous and quotable blast: "You have undertaken to cheat me. I won't sue you, for the law is too slow. I'll ruin you."

Actually, he tried both. More ominous than his lawsuits were new ships he put on the Panama route at his now-familiar cut rates. This hurt both ATC and the Panama lines so badly that within a year they presented Vanderbilt with the familiar offer; Garrison and Morgan agreed to honor his claims from ATC, buy his new ships, and he was paid $40,000 a month to leave the isthmus. These were huge sums for a time when $10,000 would buy a good-size house.

Vanderbilt gradually withdrew from steamships. By 1860 he had accumulated a fortune of $20 million, and at 66 could took forward to a pleasant retirement.

Yet he did no such thing. Railroads were working a revolution in the transportation industry on land even more profound than his steamships had done on water. The Commodore had in fact dabbled in railroads in the 1840s and 1850s, picking up securities in several roads. The Harlem, for example, was widely regarded as one of the worst properties in the country, yet Vanderbilt saw that it possessed an invaluable route into the heart of New York City. Another road, the Hudson River, reached East Albany from New York, and farther north a third line, the New York Central, linked Albany to Buffalo. That was the gateway to the rapidly developing Midwest.

of the carry-forward. Enter a profitable company in a high tax bracket. If it acquires the company with the tax losses, the combined entity can use the carry-forwards of the target firm to offset its own income. Thus the merger can reduce the total sum of taxes.

Another way of making the same point is to realize that the tax-loss carry-forwards have value in the merger marketplace. Thus, a chronically unprofitable company may have value just because it can provide a tax shelter through its accumulated carry-forwards. Naturally those tax losses will be most attractive to potential acquirers in the highest tax brackets.

However, if the IRS believes the parties merged solely to cut taxes, it may prohibit the use of carry-forwards. This is particularly likely to happen if the acquiring firm immediately closes the operations of the target firm. This means that firms with tax-loss carry-forwards that have some decent

Vanderbilt was the first to grasp that the parts of these three warring roads would be infinitely more valuable as a whole. Out of them he forged what became the New York Central, a mighty trunk line second only to the Pennsylvania Railroad.

For his railroads, the Commodore watered the stock shamelessly—and then proceeded to make the water good by unifying operations, reducing costs, improving facilities, and running them well enough to pay dividends on even bloated capital. Seemingly he overpaid for the properties he acquired, but by running them more efficiently and at lower cost than the former owners, he made the thing work. It was an early example of what some leveraged buyout artists would try to do a century later.

During the depression that followed the panic of 1873, the Commodore astounded railroad men by adding another set of double tracks to the Central's line between Buffalo and Albany, at a cost of $40 million, making it the world's first continuous four-track road. He took active command in the savage rate wars being fought by the eastern trunk lines. Here again he established a basic rule of capitalism: In a price war, the low-cost producer almost always wins. He was still at it when death came in January 1877. He owned 60 percent of the New York Central; no other rail titan could boast of such complete control over the system he ruled.

Vanderbilt practiced capitalism on a scale on which it had never been practiced before and with a logical ruthlessness yet to be matched by the great captains of industry who made U.S. business the wonder of the world.

Source: Maury Klein, "The First Tycoon," *Forbes*, October 22, 1990, pp. 44ff.

prospects for the future are even more attractive, in which case the new firm may allow the target firm to continue operating. At any rate, merging firms must take care to avoid the wrath of the IRS. Subject to that danger, tax considerations provide a rational incentive for mergers.

The EPS Game

☞ Mergers may create the illusion of growth and excellent performance by increasing EPS.

Another incentive that was once very popular is known as the EPS (earnings per share) game. Under certain conditions a merger can increase a firm's EPS even without any change in the firm's operations. In the 1960s, firms found that they could dramatically increase their EPS by merging in a certain way.

We noted in our exploration of stock values that a high P/E ratio is often a signal of expected future high growth rates in earnings and dividends. In

TABLE 23.6   The EPS Game

	Earnings	Shares Outstanding	EPS	P/E Ratio	Share Price
BEFORE THE MERGER					
Hype Industries	$300,000	100,000	$3.00	30	$ 90
Dull Knife Corp.	300,000	100,000	3.00	10	30
AFTER THE MERGER*					
Dull Hype	600,000	133,333	4.50	30	135

* In the merger, Dull Knife shareholders receive one share of Hype Industries (market value $90) for every three shares they own.

the EPS game, a firm with a high P/E ratio acquires a low-P/E firm and convinces the market that the new combined firm deserves the acquirer's high P/E.

Here's how it works. Consider Hype Industries, a high-growth firm in a high-tech industry. Hype has a high P/E ratio and merges with Dull Knife Corp., a low-growth, low-P/E firm in a low-tech industry. The first two entries in Table 23.6 present financial data for these two firms before they merge. Both have the same earnings, the same number of shares outstanding, and the same EPS of $3. However, because Hype is a growth firm with high future expected earnings, the market values it at a higher multiple of its actual earnings. In fact, Hype has a P/E ratio of 30, giving its shares a price of $90. By contrast, the market expects no dramatic growth in the sales of Dull Knife. Therefore, Dull Knife has a P/E ratio of only 10, for a stock price of $30.

In a merger based on an exchange of stock, Hype gives one of its shares to Dull Knife and, in exchange, Dull Knife gives three shares to Hype. To acquire all 100,000 shares of Dull Knife, Hype issues 33,333 new shares, making a total of 133,333 shares outstanding.

The last entry of Table 23.6 shows the combined firm, which we will call Dull Hype. Earnings are $600,000, just the combined earnings of the two premerger firms. With 133,333 shares outstanding, the EPS increases to $4.50. Notice that this increase results simply from the merger. The only necessary condition for it to occur was that the P/E ratio of the shares given to Dull Knife had to be greater than that of Dull Knife's shares. The EPS magic is complete. Firms can create higher and higher levels of EPS just by merging.

Even though we have seen how to manufacture growing EPS with mergers, one more feature of the merger is worth exploring. If the firms can convince the market that the merged firm deserves the same high P/E ratio as the premerger Hype Industries, the share price of Dull Hype will go to $135.

Before the merger, the market values were as follows:

	Shares	×	share price	=	firm's market value
Hype Industries	100,000	×	$90	=	$9,000,000
Dull Knife	100,000	×	$30	=	$3,000,000

This gives a total premerger market value of $12 million. After the merger, based on the figures of Table 23.6 and the P/E ratio of 30 being applied to Dull Hype, the total market value would be $18 million, as follows:

	Shares	×	share price	=	firm's market value
Dull Hype	133,333	×	$135	=	$18,000,000

The total market value has gone up by $6 million. Thus, it appears that it it possible to manufacture $6 million of new wealth just by merging. This prospect seems too good to be true . . . and it is.

What is really going on here? If we step back and ask ourselves what the P/E ratio of the new firm should be, it seems fairly clear that the answer is 20, assuming that the premerger P/E ratios were correct. If we combine two firms with equal earnings one of which has a P/E of 30 and the other a P/E of 10, the P/E of the new firm should be 20, unless we convince the market that the merger enhances the growth prospects of the Dull Knife side of the firm.

For a time during the 1960s some conglomerates convinced the market that they could generate growth from newly acquired companies in unrelated lines of business. Accordingly, the market applied the high P/E of the acquiring firm to the earnings of the acquired low-P/E firm. Looking back on this period it appears to have been an incredible departure from good sense. However, the market actually responded in that way. A good example is the case of Automatic Sprinkler Corporation.

Between 1963 and 1968 the sales volume of Automatic Sprinkler Corporation (now called A-T-O, Inc.) rose by over 1,400 percent due solely to acquisitions. For example, in the middle of 1967, four mergers were completed in 25 days. These newly acquired companies were all selling at relatively low price-earnings multiples, and thus helped to produce a sharp growth in earnings per share. The market responded to this "growth" by bidding up the price-earnings multiple to over 50 times earnings in 1967. This boosted the price of the company's stock from about $8 per share in 1963 to $73\frac{5}{8}$ in 1967.[4]

In 1968, however, the game ended when one of the most respected conglomerates, Litton Industries, announced a downturn in EPS. This, together with federal investigations of conglomerate merger practices, brought

---

[4] Burton G. Malkiel, *A Random Walk Down Wall Street*, 2nd college ed. (New York: W. W. Norton, 1981), p. 65. This book is an excellent and highly readable introduction to the stock market.

TABLE 23.7   Stock Valuation During and After the EPS Game

Security	1967		1969	
	High Price	Price-Earnings Multiple	Low Price	Price-Earnings Multiple
Automatic Sprinkler (A-T-O, Inc.)	$73\frac{5}{8}$	51.0	$10\frac{7}{8}$	13.4
Litton Industries	$120\frac{3}{8}$	44.1	35	14.4
Teledyne, Inc.	$71\frac{1}{2}$*	53.8	$28\frac{1}{4}$	14.2
Textron, Inc.	55	24.9	$23\frac{1}{4}$	10.1

* Adjusted for subsequent split.

Source: Reproduced from *A Random Walk Down Wall Street*, Second College Edition, p. 67, by Burton G. Malkiel, by permission of W. W. Norton & Company, Inc. Copyright © 1981, 1973 by W. W. Norton & Company, Inc.

a selling wave of conglomerates and a general fall in P/E ratios from which conglomerates never recovered. Table 23.7 shows the before and after picture of some of the best-known of these companies.

With the advantage of hindsight, it is easy to see the problem. The EPS game appears to create value from nothing, but by now we should be very suspicious of such illusions.[5] More fundamentally, we know that the basic concern of the manager should be to maximize share prices, not EPS. Of course, share price is related to the firm's income stream, so managers might attend to earnings to raise the share price. Nonetheless, when they attempt to manage earnings, it should be to increase the share price. Accordingly, undue concentration on EPS does not benefit shareholders. Because the EPS merger game creates no real value, we may reject the desire to increase EPS as a valid reason for a merger.

CONGLOMERATE MERGERS AND PORTFOLIO DIVERSIFICATION

In addition to a desire to increase EPS, we noted above that conglomerate mergers often create a portfolio of firms. Does this create a diversification benefit for mergers? The justification for this kind of merger stems directly from portfolio theory.

---

[5] Perhaps the most widespread illusion is that wealth can be created by simply printing more and more money. Unfortunately, many countries continue to fall into this trap. Rather than creating wealth, however, they have created runaway inflation.

We have seen that it is possible to combine two risky, but poorly correlated, securities to form a portfolio that is less risky than either of the individual securities. A conglomerate merger applies the same principle to firms. It might merge two firms with poorly correlated cash flows to make a portfolio of firms. In fact, we may view a conglomerate as a portfolio of firms. In such a company, management usually allows the component firms to operate independently; however, the stock ownership is in the conglomerate itself.

Management can allow the units to operate independently because it has little to gain by operating them all together if they are in very different businesses. For example, Beatrice, one of the better-known conglomerates, has units in both phosphate mining and Mexican food. It is difficult to imagine what advantages it can gain by operating these two units together. (Perhaps Beatrice can serve salsa and tortillas at the mine?)

The diversification rationale for conglomerate mergers is as weak as the desire for higher EPS. The real question is whether the firm should create a diversified portfolio or whether the shareholder can do the job better. A conglomerate diversifies by actually buying and operating firms in unrelated lines of business. However, the acquisition of firms in mergers is costly. In addition, a conglomerate merger may actually interfere with the smooth operation of the acquired firm. In comparison, a stockholder can easily create a diversified portfolio of firms merely by holding the shares of many companies. This form of diversification is much easier, cheaper, and more flexible than actually buying and operating the companies. As a consequence, we may reject the desire for diversification as an appropriate motive for mergers. Table 23.8 summarizes the valid and invalid motives for mergers.

TABLE 23.8   Valid and Invalid Motives for Mergers

Valid	Invalid
Achieving economies of scale By becoming larger, usually through a horizontal merger, a firm can achieve operating economies in purchasing raw materials and in building its distribution network. These economies of scale can also be financial, so that the new larger firm has better access to financial markets.	**Increasing EPS** Increasing EPS is not a valid reason for a merger or for any other financial decision. The goal of financial decisions should be to increase share price, not to manufacture EPS.
Access to resources Through a vertical merger a firm can often succeed in acquiring access to necessary elements in the production chain, such as raw materials or distribution outlets.	**Achieving diversification** Because shareholders can achieve diversification in the financial markets faster and more cheaply than a firm can through mergers, the desire to achieve diversification is not a valid motive for a merger.
Tax considerations Some mergers bring clear tax benefits that justify them.	

INTERNATIONAL PERSPECTIVES

The Great European Merger

Just as mergers can benefit companies, so too can they benefit nations. In this regard, the European Community [formerly the European Economic Community] has been a model for many other groups of countries in the world, such as the Commonwealth, the Central American Common Market, and the Andean Pact.

Full economic integration has been a European goal for 30 years, with Europe 1992 the most recent and most ambitious initiative. Below is a brief review of the history of European integration, including a chronology with key dates.

In 1951 the European Coal and Steel Community established the framework for European integration. The original six members of the Community—Belgium, the Federal Republic of Germany, France, Italy, Luxembourg, and the Netherlands—subsequently signed the Treaty of Rome in 1957, which formally established the European Community (EC). The principal aims of the treaty were to preserve and strengthen peace; to create a region with the free movement of goods, people, services, and capital; and ultimately to form a political union.

Following the signing of the Treaty of Rome, barriers to trade began to fall. Tariffs between EC member countries were eliminated by 1968, 18 months ahead of the schedule in the Treaty of Rome. And, while not the sole reason, eliminating tariff barriers probably contributed to Europe's strong economic performance over the next 15 years. From 1958 to 1972 the EC's economy expanded nearly 5 percent per year, while intra-European trade grew about 13 percent per year (measured in constant dollars).*

The period from 1973 to the early 1980s, in contrast, was a difficult one for European integration. The oil price shocks in 1973–1974 and 1979 led to numerous problems, most important, a slowdown in economic growth. Real gross domestic product growth averaged 2.4 percent from 1972 to 1979 and 1.4 percent from 1979 to 1985. Partly in response to slower economic growth, integration slowed, or even reversed, as member states levied new border taxes, reintroduced trade quotas, increased subsidies, and established implicit barriers against both outside countries and other EC countries.

The movement toward integration resumed in the 1980s. Europeans became convinced that raising trade barriers did not improve economic growth and that low growth resulted from inefficient and inflexible econ-

* The Commission of the European Communities, the European Community (Brussels, 1987), p. 7.

omies. Moreover, the stubbornly high unemployment rates of the 1980s—relative to the 1960s and relative to the United States—provided additional incentive to integrate. Finally, increased international competition from the United States and Japan convinced Europeans of the need for economic integration.

In the mid-1980s the EC launched a systematic program to eliminate trade barriers and create a single European marketplace. The 1985 White Paper, officially known as "Completing the Internal Market," established the program to create a single European marketplace for goods and financial services. The White Paper included approximately 300 directives designed to eliminate barriers to the free movement of goods, people, services, and capital among the 12 EC member states. The Single European Act, ratified in 1986, adopted the White Paper, amended the Treaty of Rome, and set 1992 as the completion date of the internal market.

Key Dates in the History of the European Community

April 1951	The European Coal and Steel Community—the forerunner of the European Community—is formed by France, Germany, Italy, Belgium, the Netherlands, and Luxembourg.
March 1957	Treaty of Rome is signed by the same six countries, establishing the EC.
July 1968	All customs duties are removed for intra-EC trade; a common external tariff is established.
January 1972	Denmark, Ireland, and the United Kingdom join the EC.
March 1972	The "snake" exchange rate system is established, setting narrow margins for exchange rate movements among EC currencies, while maintaining fixed, but wider, margins against the dollar.
March 1979	The European monetary system (EMS) is established.
May 1979	Greece joins the EC.
January 1985	Spain and Portugal join the EC.
June 1985	The EC Commission submits the White Paper, "Completing the Internal Market."
February 1986	The Single European Act is signed.

Source: Thomas Bennett and Craig S. Hakkio, "Europe 1992: Implications for U.S. Firms," *Federal Reserve Bank of Kansas City, Economic Review*, April 1989, pp. 3–8.

THE FINANCIAL EVALUATION OF MERGERS

From our discussion of the legitimate motives, we know that we should pursue a merger only if it creates real economic value. Furthermore, such value must come from operating efficiencies of some kind, from better access to capital markets, from the acquisition of more certain sources of raw materials, from obtaining better distribution outlets, from tax benefits, or from some other source that translates into improved cash flows.

In a merger, the acquirer can pay the shareholders of the target firm with cash or with the acquirer's stock. The financial evaluation of a merger is different in the two cases.

The Analysis of a Merger Through a Cash Purchase

When a proposed merger has real economic benefits, the value of the merged firm equals that of the acquiring firm plus the value of the target firm plus the value of the merger benefit:

$$V_m = V_a + V_t + V_b \qquad (23.1)$$

where
V_m = the value of the postmerger combined firm
V_a = the value of the premerger acquiring firm
V_t = the value of the premerger target firm
V_b = the value of the merger benefits

The value of the merger benefits, V_b, equals the present value of the additional cash flows that the merger will generate.

From the acquirer's point of view, the most it should pay for the target firm is $V_t + V_b$. If the acquirer pays more, the merger will have negative NPV. From the target firm's point of view, it should never accept anything less than V_t, its value before the merger. Also, it should try to obtain as much as possible for its shareholders. From this, we can conclude that the merger price, P, must be greater than or equal to V_t and must be less than or equal to $V_t + V_b$:

$$V_t \leq P \leq V_t + V_b \qquad (23.2)$$

The price paid for the target firm, P, minus the premerger value of the target firm V_t, is the **merger premium:**

$$\text{Merger premium} = P - V_t \qquad (23.3)$$

merger premium
the price paid for the target firm minus the premerger value of the target firm

☞ One of the largest disputed points in a merger is the distribution of the merger benefit between the acquired and the acquiring firm.

If the premium is 0, the target firm's shareholders have no incentive to sell. If the premium is too large, greater than V_b, the acquiring firm has no incentive to buy. Therefore, the merger negotiation turns on how large the premium will be, or how any benefit will be split between the acquirer and the target firm.

As an example, consider firms A and T, the acquirer and target firms, respectively. Before the merger, firm A has 100,000 shares outstanding and a share price of $70, and firm T has 10,000 shares outstanding with a share price of $35. Let us also assume that the merger benefit will be $150,000. In summary, we have:

	Firm A	Firm T
Share price	$ 70	$ 35
Shares outstanding	100,000	10,000
Firm market value	$7,000,000	$350,000

In this case, the absolute minimum price acceptable to the shareholders of firm T is $35 per share. With any lower offer, the shareholders can merely sell their shares in the open market for $35 per share. Firm A cannot pay more than $50 per share, and if it pays that amount it receives none of the merger benefit. At any higher price, the merger has negative NPV for firm A. Accordingly, the price per share should be less than $50 and more than $35. If the parties agree on a price of $45, the premium is $10 per share, or $100,000. With a merger benefit of $150,000, $50,000 goes to firm A and $100,000 to firm T.

Thus far, we have been assuming that we know the premerger value of the target firm. Sometimes rumors of an impending merger circulate and the price of the target's shares rises in anticipation. This makes it very difficult for the acquiring firm to appraise the value of the target, independent of the merger taking place. Also, when merger talks are held, rumors of the negotiation leak out and other potential acquirers show an interest. Competition over the target can also cause the target firm's shares to increase in price.

As an example, assume firm T has a true value of $30 per share. Also assume that its share price increased from $30 to $35 because the market anticipated a merger. Let us continue to assume that the merger benefit is $150,000. If firm A pays $45 per share when the value of shares of firm T is $30 before any merger anticipation, the shareholders of firm T get the entire benefit. Because of the effect of rumors on the target firm's stock price, acquirers must be very discreet in their negotiations with potential targets. Later in this chapter we will see evidence on how merger benefits are typically distributed between the acquirer and the target.

The Analysis of a Merger Financed by Stock

☞ An acquired firm virtually always receives a merger premium.

When the acquirer pays the target firm's shareholders with stock of the combined firm, the analysis of merger prices becomes somewhat more complicated for two reasons. First, when the acquirer finances the merger by an exchange of stock, the number of its shares increases. Second, when the acquiring firm issues new stock to the target's shareholders, the ownership interest of its original stockholders falls.

To see the effects of the new shares and the changing ownership interest, let us use our example of firms A and T. Now, however, we assume that the shareholders of firm T receive stock instead of cash. The ratio of share prices between the two firms is 2 ($70/$35), so we assume that shareholders in firm T receive one share in exchange for two. Firm A will issue 5,000 new shares and the postmerger firm will have 105,000 shares outstanding. The market value of the postmerger firm should equal the sum of the market values of the two premerger firms plus the merger benefit, or $7.5 million. After the exchange of stock, each share should be worth the market value of the combined firm divided by the number of shares outstanding, or $71.43.

Because the shareholders of firm T received one share with a premerger value of $70 for two of their shares worth $35 each, it appears that they received none of the merger benefit. That is not the case, however. They received 5,000 shares, and we have seen that the postmerger share price would be $71.43. As a consequence, they received a total value of $357,150, or a merger premium of $7,150.

We know that the shareholders of firm T will not accept any amount of stock that is worth less than the original $350,000 value of the firm. Also, firm A will not offer any amount of stock greater than $500,000, which is the premerger value of firm T plus the merger benefit. We also know from Equation 23.1 that the value of the combined firm will equal that of the premerger firms plus the merger benefit. If the acquirer had S_a shares outstanding originally, and issues S_n new shares to the target company's shareholders, the merged firm will have S_m shares outstanding, where $S_m = S_a + S_n$. Therefore, the price of a new share, NS, will equal:

$$NS = \frac{V_m}{S_m} = \frac{V_a + V_t + V_b}{S_a + S_n} \tag{23.4}$$

The total compensation received by the shareholders of firm T is equal to the new shares, S_n, times the price of those shares, NS:

$$\text{Total compensation for firm T shareholders} = S_n \times NS \tag{23.5}$$

We know that this compensation must lie between the premerger value of firm T ($350,000) and the premerger value of firm T plus the entire merger benefit ($500,000):

$$V_t \leq S_n \times NS \leq V_t + V_b$$

Rearranging this expression, we get:

$$\frac{V_t}{V_m} \leq \frac{S_n}{S_a + S_n} \leq \frac{V_t + V_b}{V_m} \tag{23.6}$$

Equation 23.6 says that the percentage of the firm owned by the shareholders of the acquired firm $[S_n/(S_a + S_n)]$ must be equal to or greater than the ratio of the premerger target firm to the postmerger combined firm $[V_t/V_m]$, and less than or equal to the ratio of the value of the premerger

FINANCE TODAY

Takeover and Defense Tactics

There are numerous tactics for taking over corporations. Even more numerous are the modes of defense against takeovers. Following is a list of the major actions available to the offensive and defensive players of this increasingly popular enterprise, corporate takeover. The defensive tactics are grouped according to their impact on shareholder wealth, as indicated by research to date.

TAKEOVERS

- *Leveraged buyout:* heavily debt-financed buyout of shareholder equity, often by incumbent management.
- *Merger:* bidder negotiates with target management on the terms of the offer which is then submitted to a vote of the target's shareholders.
- *Proxy contest:* by a vote of the shareholders a dissident group tries to gain a controlling position on the board.
- *Tender offer:* bidder makes offer to shareholders for some or all of the target's stock.
  Friendly: offer supported by the target company's management.
  Unfriendly (hostile): offer opposed by target management.

DEFENSIVE TACTICS
(Shareholder approval required)

No Impact or No Evidence of Impact on Target Shareholder Wealth

- *Dual-class recapitalizations:* restructure equity into two classes with different voting rights with the goal of providing management or family owners with voting power disproportionately greater than provided by their equity holdings under a one-share, one-vote rule: typical dual class firm is already controlled by insiders and the recapitalization may also provide needed capital without dilution of control and without harm to the stock value.
- *Fair-price provision:* a supermajority provision which applies only to nonuniform two-tier hostile takeover bids; ensures that all shareholders selling within a certain time period receive the same price; the usual determination of fairness is the highest price paid by the bidder for any of the shares it has acquired in the target during a certain time period; has a low deterrence value and is not detrimental to stock values.
- *Rights of shareholders:* restricts rights of shareholders to vote on issues between annual meetings or at special shareholder meetings (e.g., only supermajority vote of the shareholders or the president of the board may call a special meeting).

(continued)

Positive Impact

- *Leveraged recapitalization or leveraged cash-out:* a change in capital structure and equity ownership, retaining a publicly traded company; financial leverage is increased significantly as the company replaces the majority of its equity with debt so that a raider cannot borrow against the assets of the firm to finance an acquisition; management (insiders) in essence receives a stock-split and proportional increase in ownership as all but inside shareholders receive a large one-time payout in cash or debt securities and continued equity interest in the restructured company.

Negative Impact on Target Shareholder Wealth

- *Change state of incorporation:* stringency of state antitakeover laws vary; may harm shareholders because it reduces takeover chances; may benefit states as they increase the likelihood of keeping jobs with strict state laws.
- *Reduction in cumulative voting rights:* increases management's ability to resist a tender offer but appears to reduce shareholder wealth. (Cumulative voting rights allow a group of minority shareholders to elect directors even if the majority opposes because each shareholder is entitled to cast a number of votes equal to the number of shares owned multiplied by the number of directors to be elected—thus one could accumulate votes for a particular director or group of directors.)
- *Staggered directors or classified board:* directors are broken into classes (usually three groups) with only one class being elected each year; works best with limit on number of board members; makes it difficult for a substantial shareholder to change all of the board at once without approval or cooperation of the existing board, but also makes any change of directors more difficult; also lowers the effectiveness of cumulative voting; has impact of significant negative abnormal returns.
- *Supermajority clause:* increases the number of votes of outstanding common stock needed to approve changes in control to two-thirds or nine-tenths from a majority of one-half (director must also be removed for cause); found to have significant negative stock-price effects around their introduction and on average they appear to reduce shareholder wealth; important to have an escape clause (provision allowing for simple majority vote) so that friendly offers are not also foreclosed; almost always combined with a lock-in provision.

- **Lock-in provision:** prevents circumvention of antitakeover provisions; most common provision requires a supermajority vote to change antitakeover amendments or limits the number of directors; has impact of a significant negative abnormal return.

DEFENSIVE TACTICS
(Shareholder approval not required)

Negative Impact on Target Shareholder Wealth

- **Litigation by target management:** a win by target may harm shareholders in that chances of acquisition may be lost or lowered—this may be reflected by a fall in share price, whereas the acquisition is likely to have increased share prices (examples: charges of securities fraud, antitrust violations, or violations of state or federal tender offer rules); delays control fight, yet also gives management time to find a friendlier deal.
- **Shareholder rights plans or poison pills:** do not require majority voting approval by shareholders; are triggered by an event such as a tender offer, or by the accumulation of a certain percentage of target's stock by a single stockholder; trigger allows target shareholders with rights to purchase additional shares or to sell shares to the target at very attractive prices; can be cheaply and quickly altered by target management yet makes hostile takeovers very expensive by diluting the equity holdings of the bidder, revoking his voting rights or forcing him to assume unwanted financial obligations; different types include: flip-over, flip-in, back-end, and voting plans; generally harmful to stock values; judicial approval of certain types of plans (e.g., flip-in and back-end) is still not clear.
- **Target block stock repurchases or greenmail:** target repurchases, at a premium, the hostile bidders block of target's stock; often results in substantial fall in stock returns for the target or reduced shareholder value from forgone takeover potential as opposed to normally positive stock price effects of a repurchase of stock by a nontargeted firm; yet evidence indicates that a net positive stock price may result from the initial hostile bidder purchase (positive impact) to the target repurchase (negative effect); benefits returns for bidder firm shareholders; practice is controversial and has been challenged in federal courts, congressional testimony, and SEC hearings.

Source: "Takeover and Defense Tactics," *Economic Perspectives*, January–February 1989, pp. 8–9.

target firm plus the merger benefit to the value of the postmerger firm $[(V_t + V_b)/V_m]$.

Substituting the values from our example into this expression, we have:

$$0.04667 \leq \frac{S_n}{100,000 + S_n} \leq 0.06667$$

Worst Case for the Target Firm's Shareholders   In the worst case for the target firm's shareholders, they receive only enough shares to compensate them for the premerger value of their firm, with none of the merger benefit. We can analyze the number of shares issued in this case as follows:

$$0.04667 = \frac{S_n}{100,000 + S_n}$$

$$S_n = 4,895 \text{ shares}$$

To see that this is correct, recall that the acquirer had 100,000 shares outstanding already. After the merger, there will be 104,895 shares in a firm worth $7.5 million. Therefore, each share will be worth $71.50. If the target firm's shareholders receive 4,895 of those shares, the total value received will be $350,000.

Best Case for the Target Firm's Shareholders   The best thing that can happen for the target firm's shareholders is to receive enough shares to compensate them for the premerger value of their firm and to allow them to capture the entire merger benefit. The number of shares issued in this case is given by:

$$\frac{S_n}{100,000 + S_n} = 0.06667$$

$$S_n = 7,143$$

The merged firm will have 107,143 shares outstanding, each worth $70. It will have a total value of $7.5 million. The target firm's shareholders receive 7,143 shares, or $500,000.

From this analysis, we see that the target firm's shareholders will receive at least 4,895 shares, or they won't accept the merger offer. The most they can hope to receive is 7,143 shares, because the acquiring firm will offer no more.

WHO BENEFITS FROM MERGERS?

If a merger is economically sound, the combined firm will be more valuable than the premerger target and acquiring firms. In such a case, value is to be split between the target and acquiring firms. How is that benefit divided? Does the target firm or the acquiring firm benefit? In some cases, mergers

FIGURE 23.3   The Performance of the Target Firm's Shares at the Time of the Merger Announcement

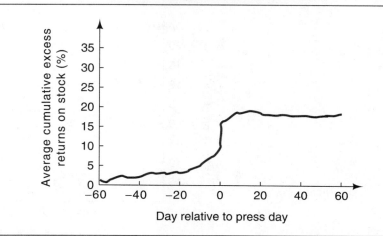

Source: P. Asquith, "Merger Bids, Uncertainty, and Stockholder Returns," *Journal of Financial Economics*, April 1983, pp. 51–83. Reprinted by permission of Elsevier Science Publishers.

take place even when they create no benefits. In other words, one or the other of the partners makes a mistake. What happens to target and acquiring firms?

These issues have been studied in detail. One approach is to examine the stock returns of the target and acquiring firms around the time the intention to merge becomes public. The best technique for doing this is to see how the stock prices compare to other firms of the same risk level. Figure 23.3 shows the performance of the target firm's shares just before and just after the announcement of a merger. The vertical scale shows the average performance of the shares relative to other shares of the same risk level in the market at the same time.

☞ Shareholders of target firms tend to benefit from mergers.

If the merger news gave the acquiring firm's shareholders no benefit, the bold line would be flat all the way across at the 0 percent level. The graph shows an important positive benefit for the target firm. About 20 trading days before the information becomes public, the stock price starts to move up and continues to do so until about 10 days after the announcement. By this time, there is almost a 20 percent gain on these shares relative to other stocks of the same risk level. Such a gain in 30 trading days is really spectacular.

☞ Acquiring firms seem to realize a small benefit from mergers.

How does this performance compare relative to the acquiring firm's shares? Figure 23.4 graphs the acquiring firm's shares and shows some, but very little, benefit for the acquiring firm. Other studies have found that acquiring firms, on average, actually lose value; however, whether they gain a little or lose a little is debated. In any case, it certainly appears that the target firms get most of the benefit.

FIGURE 23.4 The Performance of the Acquiring Firm's Shares at the Time of the Merger Announcement

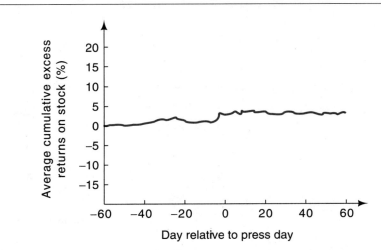

Source: P. Asquith, "Merger Bids, Uncertainty, and Stockholder Returns," *Journal of Financial Economics*, April 1983, pp. 51–83. Reprinted by permission of Elsevier Science Publishers.

MERGERS AND THE INTERESTS OF SOCIETY

☞ Mergers may serve society by contributing to production efficiencies, but may harm society by lessening competition.

While the target firm's shareholders appear to reap most of the benefit from the merger, it is still important to ask how society is affected by mergers, particularly in periods of heavy merger activity. If firms became so large that they were able to wield monopoly power over their markets, these mergers could harm the interests of society.

The effects of mergers on society are hotly debated. One of the factors that may alleviate the potential danger is that most mergers involve the acquisition of smaller firms. In such cases, there is relatively little danger of extreme market control. The recent merger wave, however, raises more serious concerns, because so many of the mergers have involved very large firms, with many of the largest mergers concentrated in crucial industries, such as oil.

In recent years, the concept of monopoly power has changed significantly because firms must compete in an increasingly global market in order to survive in the long run. Even if a company constitutes a monopoly in its home country, it must still compete with other international firms, not only at home, but in foreign markets as well.

Most analysts would agree that IBM had significant market power in the 1960s and 1970s. In fact, a long and unsuccessful legal process intended to break up the computer giant was started then. In the 1990s, however, few would argue that IBM has a comfortable position in the world market. While still dominant, IBM faces a fierce challenge from formidable Japanese and European rivals, as well as from U.S. competitors, such as Apple Computers and Compaq. It is not at all clear that IBM will remain a dominant world force in computers.

Another example involves the current attempt to force Microsoft Corporation, creator of the phenomenally successful Windows 3.0 and MS-DOS software programs, to spin off part of its operations. In fact, the firm is so successful that its creator, Bill Gates, is the youngest self-made billionaire in U.S. history. Microsoft has an unfair advantage over the competition in some areas, it has been argued, due to its detailed knowledge of the software used by so many personal computers. Despite these criticisms, Microsoft, like IBM, also faces very tough competition in world markets in the years ahead.

It is important to consider here whether society really benefits by having such giants spin off part of their holdings. Although the debate continues in the United States, many other countries seem to be at ease with their giant conglomerates. Examples abound: Michelin and Thomson Electronics in France; Shell and Philips in the Netherlands; Volvo in Sweden; Nestlé and Brown-Bovery in Switzerland; Bayer and Mercedes Benz in Germany; Fiat and Olivetti in Italy; Mitsubishi, Matsushita, and NT&T in Japan, to name just a few well-known firms. All of these firms share one common feature: They are extremely competitive in the global scene, even though they enjoy comfortable positions in their home markets.

SUMMARY

We began our review of leases by distinguishing operating and financial leases and noting that financial leases are really very similar to debt financing. Consequently, the choice of debt or leasing is basically a financing one. The principle for choosing a lease or debt is to evaluate the after-tax cash flows from each alternative and to choose the one with the lower net present value of costs.

We also noted that leasing can benefit both the lessor and the lessee, particularly when they have different tax rates. Other motivations for leasing arise from various other kinds of market imperfections. For instance, leasing may be more convenient than owning, it may help to avoid the risk of obsolescence, and it may make financing easier.

This chapter also explored the key features of mergers, the three types of which are horizontal, vertical, and conglomerate. The potentially valid motives for mergers include a desire to achieve greater economies of scale and a desire to secure a source of raw materials or an outlet for the finished product of a firm. Certain tax incentives may be important in mergers and can confer real benefits. Some spurious merger motives, such as the desire for EPS growth or diversification, propelled a wave of conglomerate mergers.

The financial evaluation of mergers differs depending on how the acquirer pays the target. The payment can take the form of cash or shares in the merged firm. In both cases bounds can be put on the compensation paid to the target firm. Essentially, the compensation must be at least as great as the premerger value of the target firm, but less than the merger benefit plus the premerger value of the target. Finally, we considered the allocation of the merger benefit between the acquiring and target firm, and the effects of mergers on society.

QUESTIONS

1. What is the difference between a financial lease and an operating lease?
2. What is the difference between a direct lease and a leveraged lease?
3. Explain how a sales/leaseback arrangement works.
4. Is the decision to lease or buy an investment decision, a financing decision, or both? Explain.
5. In evaluating lease versus buy, why should we assume that the buy decision finances the asset with 100 percent debt?
6. Leasing provides 100 percent debt financing. Is this claim true or false? Explain.
7. What tax benefits are typically relinquished by a firm if it leases rather than buys an asset?
8. What tax advantages does a firm acquire by leasing that it would not have if it bought an asset?
9. What is the net benefit of leasing (NBL)?
10. Explain how different tax rates between borrowers and lenders stimulate leasing.
11. Evaluate the following claim: Leasing may create some tax advantages, but the main advantage of financial leases for the lessee is that they allow the lessee to avoid the risk of obsolescence. For example, most airlines lease planes so that they can replace them with new models as soon as they come out.
12. What is the difference between a horizontal and a vertical merger?
13. If you were in charge of antitrust enforcement, what kinds of mergers would be of the greatest concern? Explain.
14. Explain why firms seek vertical integration and the role of vertical mergers in attempts to achieve this integration.
15. From an antitrust point of view, are conglomerate mergers problematic? Explain.
16. Explain the difference between achieving diversification through a conglomerate merger and through diversification in the stock market.
17. Is a tender offer likely to be used in a friendly or an unfriendly merger attempt? Explain.

18. If you owned shares in a company that pursued a policy of greenmail, what would you think about its management?
19. Explain why the managers of a firm might be willing to pay greenmail.
20. Why do managers try to use poison pills to avoid takeovers? How does this affect the interest of stockholders?
21. Based on the evidence presented in this chapter, do you think that stockholders need protection from merger attempts? Explain.
22. Why do managers of target firms seek white knights?
23. Explain how tax benefits can be created through mergers.
24. Are the tax benefits generated by mergers a creation of wealth for shareholders? Explain.
25. If we consider matters from the point of view of society as a whole, are the tax benefits generated by mergers a form of wealth creation? Explain.
26. In a cash purchase, what is the most that an acquiring firm should be willing to pay for a target?
27. In a cash purchase acquisition, what is the least that a target firm should accept?
28. What do we know about how merger benefits are usually distributed between the target and acquiring firm?
29. When a target is acquired by issuing stock, what happens to the ownership interest of the acquiring firm's shareholders?

PROBLEMS

Use the following information to solve Problems 1 through 9. Pisa Construction needs a new crane for its tower construction business. Pisa can buy one crane for $1 million and depreciate it straight line over five years to a $100,000 salvage value. It can borrow at 12 percent and is in the 35 percent tax bracket. If it borrows, Pisa will pay interest only for five years and repay the loan at the end of that time. Alternatively, it could lease the crane for the same five years for $180,000.

1. What is the annual after-tax cost of the lease payment?
2. What is the present value of the leasing alternative cash flows?
3. With the buy alternative, what is the annual depreciation expense?
4. With the buy alternative, what is the annual depreciation tax shield?
5. With the buy alternative, what is the annual interest?
6. With the buy alternative, what is the annual after-tax interest cost?
7. Compute the total after-tax cash flows for each year for the buy alternative.
8. What is the NPV of the buy alternative's cash flows?
9. Compute the NBL of leasing.

Use the following information to solve Problems 10 through 20. Abacus Software is a new firm that wants to furnish its offices. The furniture could be purchased for $180,000 or it could be leased. It should last about four years and have 0 salvage value at that time. Abacus can borrow for the furniture at 12 percent and would amortize the loan over four years. If it leases the furniture, the annual lease payment will be $40,000.

10. What is the annual payment on the loan option?
11. Make an amortization table for the loan.
12. Compute the interest tax shield for each year.
13. Compute the depreciation tax shield for each year.
14. Compute the after-tax lease payment for each year.
15. Based on the calculations that you have just made, create a table showing the principal payment, interest tax shield, depreciation tax shield, and after-tax lease payment for each year.
16. Compute the total after-tax cost of the borrow-and-buy alternative for each year.
17. Find the present value of the borrow-and-buy cash flows.
18. Find the present value of the leasing cash flows.
19. Compute the NBL.
20. Using the data from Problems 15 and 16, combine the annual cash flows from the borrow-and-buy alternative before discounting, and then find the NBL.

Use the following information to solve Problems 21 through 31. Deaf Leopard, a hard rock group specializing in the acoustic big band sound, has just blown its audio system out of existence. Now the group must replace the system, and its members are trying to decide whether to lease or buy. Drumbo, the group's trombonist, has suggested that the band lease the new system, since they're very likely to blow it out again. If Deaf Leopard buys an audio system, it will cost $240,000 and should last three years before it is obsolete and worthless from all the abuse. The band only knows about straight-line depreciation, so they will use that technique. The band has also been borrowing at 20 percent with amortized repayment and would finance its new system the same way, if it decides to buy. If it leases, the annual lease payment will be $75,000. Deaf Leopard is incorporated, and its marginal tax rate is 20 percent.

21. Evaluate Drumbo's suggestion.
22. What is the annual loan payment if Deaf Leopard buys?
23. Make an amortization table for this loan.
24. Compute the interest tax shield for each year.
25. Compute the depreciation tax shield for each year.
26. Compute the after-tax lease payment for each year.
27. Use the answers to Problems 22 through 26 to create a table showing

the principal payment, interest tax shield, depreciation tax shield, and after-tax lease payment for each year.

28. Compute the total after-tax cash flow for the borrow-and-buy alternative for each year.

29. Compute the present value of the borrow-and-buy cash flows.

30. Compute the present value of the leasing cash flows.

31. Compute the NBL.

Use the following information to solve Problems 32 through 48. Thirty microcomputers are available at a cost of $5,000 each and are expected to last five years and to have a 0 salvage value after that time. The same computers can be leased for five years with an annual fee of $28,000.

32. Your business school is planning to equip a microcomputer lab with 30 computers. The school can borrow the money for these computers at 10 percent and pay it back with a five-year amortized loan. The business school is tax exempt. Compute the annual payment for the loan.

33. Compute the business school's after-tax annual payment for the loan alternative.

34. What is the school's after-tax cost of the lease payment?

35. Compute the business school's after-tax present value of the borrow-and-buy cash flows.

36. Compute the business school's after-tax present value of the leasing cash flows.

37. Compute the business school's NBL.

38. Trumpet Castle, a struggling casino, is also considering acquiring 30 of the same computers. It can borrow at a rate of 15 percent to buy these computers and would depreciate them on a straight-line basis over five years. The firm is in the 40 percent tax bracket. Compute the annual payment for the loan, assuming a five-year amortized loan.

39. Prepare an amortization schedule for Trumpet's loan.

40. Compute Trumpet's annual after-tax cost of the loan payment. (Remember to treat the principal and interest payment separately.)

41. Compute Trumpet's annual depreciation expense.

42. Compute Trumpet's annual depreciation tax shield.

43. Compute Trumpet's after-tax cost of the lease payment.

44. Compute Trumpet's after-tax present value of the borrow-and-buy cash flows.

45. Compute Trumpet's after-tax present value of the lease cash flows.

46. Compute Trumpet's NBL.

47. Now consider the difference between Trumpet and the business school. Explain the difference in the NBL for the two concerns and explain how it might account for the widespread use of leasing.

48. By reflecting on the problems presented so far, what can you say about how tax-exempt institutions should acquire equipment such as computers?

Use the following information to solve the remaining problems. Duck Trucks (operating with the slogan, "We never get you stuck") has to add to its fleet of semis for its interstate duck hauling operations, and it has decided to expand its fleet of Muck Trucks. One Muck Truck costs 100,000 bucks and has a useful life of five years. If Duck purchases the truck, it will depreciate it over five years on a straight-line basis. Duck can borrow the needed bucks at a 10 percent rate of interest and will only pay interest for the first four years and repay all the principal in year 5. Alternatively, Duck can lease its Muck Trucks for 20,000 bucks each per year. Duck is in the 30 percent tax bracket.

49. Compute the annual interest expense for the borrow-and-buy alternative.
50. Compute the after-tax cost of the interest payments.
51. Compute the annual depreciation expense.
52. Compute the annual depreciation tax shield.
53. Create a table showing the principal repayment, after-tax interest cost, depreciation tax shield, and total after-tax cost for each year.
54. Compute the present value of the after-tax cash flows for the borrow-and-buy alternative.
55. Compute the after-tax cost of the annual lease payments.
56. Compute the present value of the lease alternative's cash flows.
57. Compute the NBL and determine whether Duck should lease or buy.
58. Using the data calculated in Problems 54 and 56, compute the NBL by consolidating the annual after-tax cash flows before discounting.

Use the following information to solve Problems 59 through 70. Iphagee Conglomerate has a P/E ratio of 27, a stock price of $81, and 1 million shares outstanding. Iphagee is considering acquiring Small Fry Fisheries. Small Fry has earnings of $1 million, 100,000 shares outstanding, and a P/E ratio of 5. Iphagee will exchange two of its shares for three shares of Small Fry, and it expects the postmerger firm to keep the P/E ratio of 27.

59. What is the total market value of Small Fry?
60. What is the price per share for Small Fry?
61. How many shares of Iphagee will be outstanding after the merger?
62. Assuming that this is strictly a conglomerate merger, what will be the postmerger earnings of Iphagee?
63. Assuming that this is strictly a conglomerate merger, what should be the market value of the postmerger firm if the EPS game does not work?
64. If Iphagee is correct and the new firm keeps the P/E ratio of 27, what will be the market value of the postmerger firm?
65. If the EPS game does not work, how much will the Small Fry shareholders receive for each of their shares?

66. If Iphagee is correct in its belief that the postmerger firm will have a P/E ratio of 27, how much will the Small Fry shareholders receive for each of their shares?
67. Should Small Fry accept the offer, assuming that no other offer is available?
68. If the EPS game does not work, what will happen to the value of a share of Iphagee due to the merger?
69. If the EPS game does work, and the postmerger Iphagee still has a P/E ratio of 27, what will have happened to the value of a share of Iphagee due to the merger?
70. If the market is wise to the EPS game, what should the P/E ratio of the postmerger Iphagee be?

Use the following information to solve Problems 71 through 78. A cattle feed lot firm, Standing Bull, is planning to buy Kansas in August, a large agribusiness concern specializing in corn production. Bull has 100,000 shares outstanding with a share price of $10. Kansas has 10,000 shares trading at $8 per share. Bull believes that the vertical integration from the purchase will give real benefits by providing a source of corn for the feed lot and a ready outlet for the corn production. Bull believes that the resulting firm should be worth $1.2 million.

71. What is the merger benefit?
72. What is the minimum price that Kansas should accept per share?
73. What is the maximum price that Bull should be willing to pay per share?
74. If Bull pays $10 per share, how is the merger benefit split between the two premerger firms?
75. If Bull pays $16 per share, how is the merger benefit split between the two premerger firms?

Consider the following additional information regarding the Kansas/Bull merger and use it to solve Problems 76 through 78. Kansas was trading at $8 per share before any rumors began circulating about the pending merger. Now, in anticipation, the stock of Kansas has gone up to $10 per share. Assume further that there are no other potential acquiring firms for Kansas.

76. In these new circumstances, what is the merger benefit?
77. In these new circumstances, what is the minimum price that Kansas should accept per share?
78. In these new circumstances, what is the maximum price that Bull should be willing to pay per share?

Use the following information to solve Problems 79 through 86. Prune Computer has been having trouble securing a steady source of computer chips for use in its microcomputer. It is considering acquiring a chip manufacturer, Chips Away, to solve this problem. Prune has 100,000 shares outstanding at $12 per share, while Chips has 15,000 shares trading at $8 per share. Prune estimates that the postmerger firm should be worth $1.5 million, and it plans to offer an exchange of shares to acquire Chips.

79. Compute the merger benefit.
80. If Prune offers two shares for three of Chips, how will the merger benefit be distributed?
81. What is the minimum number of shares that Chips should be willing to accept?
82. If the minimum number of shares is offered and accepted, how is the merger benefit distributed between the two premerger firms?
83. If the minimum number of shares is offered and accepted, how much of the postmerger firm will be owned by the shareholders of Chips?
84. What is the maximum number of shares that Prune should be willing to offer?
85. If the maximum number of shares is offered and accepted, how is the merger benefit distributed between the two premerger firms?
86. If the maximum number of shares is offered and accepted, how much of the postmerger firm will be owned by the shareholders of Chips?

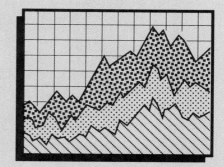

PART 8

FUTURES, OPTIONS, AND INTERNATIONAL FINANCE

645

27. INTERNATIONAL FINANCIAL MANAGEMENT

Entering a Foreign Market; Foreign Exchange; Geographical and Cross-Rate Arbitrage; Determinants of Foreign Exchange Rates; More Price Relationships; Hedging Foreign Exchange Risk; International Investment and Financing Decisions; International Financing; Summary

CHAPTER 24

The Futures Market

forward contract
a contract calling for the future delivery of some good at a price established at the initiation of the contract

Futures markets arose in the mid-1800s in Chicago and institutionalized an ancient form of contracting called forward contracting. A **forward contract** is an agreement reached at some time calling for the delivery of some commodity at a specified later date, at an established price. An agreement made today to deliver one ton of sugar one year from today at a price of $0.59 per pound, to be paid upon delivery, is a typical forward contract. Futures contracts are similar in many respects to forward contracts, but have specific features and a great deal more institutional structure.

This chapter explores the futures markets in the United States, beginning with a survey of the kinds of contracts and the institutional arrangements that are common to them. It also discusses futures market quotations and pricing principles, and strategies for speculating with contracts and using them to hedge risks.

Futures markets have a reputation for being incredibly risky and, to a large extent, this reputation is justified. As we will see, however, futures contracts may also be used to manage many different kinds of risks. As such, the futures markets play a beneficial role in society by allowing the transfer of risk and by helping to provide information about the future direction of prices on many commodities.

FORWARD CONTRACTS

☞ Forward contracts have unstandardized terms, which gives them flexibility but makes it costly to find a trading partner.

In a typical forward contract, two parties come together and agree to terms that they believe to be mutually beneficial. However, this kind of contract has a number of characteristics that may be drawbacks.

For example, in the sugar contract both parties must trust each other to complete the contract as promised. The price of $0.59 per pound is promised to be paid on delivery of the sugar in one year. At that time, however, the price of sugar will almost surely be different; let us assume that it will be

spot price
the price of a good for immediate delivery

$0.69. This is the cash price or the **spot price**—the price for immediate delivery of a good. In this event, the seller is obligated to deliver the ton of sugar and to receive only $0.59 per pound for it. In the open market, however, the sugar could be sold for $0.69 per pound. Obviously, the temptation exists for the seller to default on the forward contract obligation and to sell the sugar in the open market. The possibility of strong incentives to default are known in advance to both parties. Consequently, this kind of forward contract can reasonably take place only between two parties that know and trust each other to honor their commitments. Unfortunately, if we restrict ourselves to doing business only with people we trust, we are likely to engage in very little commerce.

A second problem with the forward contract is the difficulty of finding a trading partner. One party may wish to sell a ton of sugar for delivery in one year, but it might be difficult to find someone willing to enter into such a contract. Not only must both parties agree on the timing, but they must want to exchange the same amount of the good. These conditions can be quite restrictive and leave many potential traders unable to consummate desired trades.

A third and related problem is the difficulty fulfilling an obligation without actually completing delivery. Imagine that one party to the sugar contract decides after six months that it is undesirable to complete the contract by delivery. This trader has only two ways to fulfill the obligation: make delivery as originally agreed, or ask the partner to settle the contract now, by early delivery or the payment of cash, for example. This could be difficult to arrange unless the partner is willing to cooperate.

Because of these difficulties—establishing the contract terms, finding a trading partner, and the absence of a flexible means of settling the contract— forward markets have always been restricted in size and scope.[1] Therefore, futures markets have emerged to provide an institutional framework that copes with these deficiencies. The organized futures exchange standardizes contract terms and guarantees performance on the contracts to both partners. In the process, however, it has developed its own peculiarities that also have to be understood.

THE FUTURES EXCHANGE

A futures exchange is a nonprofit organization composed of members holding seats on the exchange. These seats are traded on an open market, so an individual wishing to become a member can do so by buying an existing seat from a member and by meeting other exchange-imposed criteria for financial soundness and ethical reputation. Prices for seats on the exchanges fluctuate quite radically, depending largely on the level of trading activity.

The exchange provides a setting in which futures contracts can be traded by its members and other parties who trade through a member. The members participate in committees that govern the exchange and also employ professional managers to execute their directives. So, although the futures exchange is itself a nonprofit corporation, it is constituted to benefit its members.

Each exchange determines the kinds of goods that it will trade and the contract specifications for each good. Table 24.1 lists the major world futures

[1] A notable exception is the forward market for foreign currency discussed below. This forward market is extremely large and overshadows the futures market for foreign exchange.

TABLE 24.1 World Futures Exchanges

	Date Founded	Principal Types of Contracts			
		Physical	Currencies	Interest Rates	Indexes
FUTURES MARKETS IN THE UNITED STATES					
Chicago Board of Trade (CBOT)	1848	✓		✓	✓
Chicago Mercantile Exchange (CME)	1919	✓	✓	✓	✓
Coffee, Sugar, and Cocoa Exchange (New York)	1882	✓			✓
Commodity Exchange, Inc. (COMEX) (New York)	1933	✓			
Kansas City Board of Trade (KCBT)	1856	✓			✓
Mid-America Commodity Exchange (Chicago)	1880	✓	✓	✓	
Minneapolis Grain Exchange	1881	✓			
New York Cotton Exchange, Inc.	1870	✓	✓		✓
Citrus Associates of the New York Cotton Exchange	1966	✓			
Petroleum Associates of the New York Cotton Exchange	1971	✓			
New York Futures Exchange (NYFE)	1979				✓
New York Mercantile Exchange	1872	✓			
Chicago Rice and Cotton Exchange	1976	✓			
PRINCIPAL FOREIGN FUTURES MARKETS					
International Futures Exchange (INTEX) (Bermuda)	1984	✓			✓
Bolsa de Mercadorios de Sao Paulo	1917	✓			
London International Financial Futures Exchange (LIFFE)	1982		✓	✓	✓
Baltic International Freight Futures Exchange BIFFEX (London)	1985				✓
Tokyo Financial Futures Exchange	1985		✓	✓	✓
Singapore International Monetary Exchange SIMEX (Singapore)	1984		✓	✓	✓
Hong Kong Futures Exchange	1977	✓			✓
New Zealand Futures Exchange	1985	✓	✓	✓	
Sydney Futures Exchange	1960	✓	✓	✓	✓
Toronto Futures Exchange	1984		✓	✓	✓
Kuala Lumpur Commodity Exchange	1985*	✓			

* Reorganized after default.

Source: Wall Street Journal, Futures Magazine, Intermarket Magazine, various issues, and Chicago Mercantile Exchange, 1985 Annual Report.

exchanges and the types of contracts traded by each. There is a great variety of goods traded, and some exchanges tend to specialize in certain segments of the industry.

FUTURES CONTRACTS AND FUTURES TRADING

According to its rules, each exchange provides a trading floor where all of its contracts are traded during official hours.

Typical Contract Terms

By specializing in a limited range of commodities, and by standardizing contract terms, the futures contract overcomes some of the difficulties of forward contracts. The difference between the two can be demostrated by examining the particular features of a futures contract. One of the oldest is the wheat contract traded by the Chicago Board of Trade. It calls for the delivery of 5,000 bushels of wheat, with delivery taking place in one of the designated delivery months of July, September, December, March, and May. Furthermore, only certain kinds of wheat are permitted for delivery, such as no. 2 Soft Red, no. 2 Hard Red Winter, no. 2 Dark Northern Spring, and no. 1 Northern Spring. The terms also control the manner of delivery. To deliver under this contract, the wheat must be in a warehouse approved by the Chicago Board of Trade, and a warehouse receipt is delivered to the purchaser. The warehouse receipt is a legal document of title to the wheat that is validated by the warehouse operator, who certifies that the wheat actually exists and is stored in the warehouse. This standardization of terms means that all of the traders will know immediately the exact characteristics of the good being traded, without negotiation or long discussion. In fact, the only feature of a futures contract that must be determined at the time of the trade is the futures price.

☞ Futures contracts are forward contracts traded in an organized exchange, with standardized terms.

Order Flow

Futures contracts are created when orders are executed on the floor of the exchange. The orders can originate with members of the exchange trading for their own accounts in pursuit of profit. Alternatively, they can originate with traders outside the exchange who enter orders through a broker, who has a member of the exchange execute the trade for the client. These outside orders are transmitted electronically to the floor of the exchange, where actual trading takes place in a **pit,** an area designated for the trading of a particular commodity. It is called a pit because it consists of an oval made up of different levels, like stairs, around a central area. Traders stand on the steps or in the central area, which allows them to see each other with relative ease.

pit
the area in which trading of futures contracts is conducted

FINANCE TODAY

The Pits: Conti Reads Its Own Ads

One of the largest commodity brokerage houses, ContiCommodities, a subsidiary of Continental Grain, for years ran huge ads in the newspapers that, in a subtle reverse pitch, printed descriptions of "mistakes" that commodity speculators were prone to make. The ads described types of speculators who should not enter this market (as though any should), and listed "rules" for doing well (as though this was even remotely likely). Here are some of the company's admonitions:

- "Keep reminding yourself on every position you take, 'My first loss is my least loss.'"
- "Do not overstay a good market—you are bound to overstay a bad one also."
- "Most people would rather own something (go long) than owe something (go short); it's human nature. The markets aren't human. So you should learn that markets can (and should) be traded from the short side."
- "Recognize that fear, greed, ignorance, generosity, stupidity, impatience, self-delusion, etc., can cost you a lot more money than the market(s) going against you, and that there is no fundamental method to recognize these factors."
- "Don't blindly follow computer trading. A computer-trading plan is only as good as the program. You know the old saying, 'Garbage in, garbage out.'"

Very nice! Unfortunately, someone in ContiCommodity believed their own ads. The company set up three commodity mutual funds, which were snapped up by an eager public.

All three lost so much money that they had to be closed down.

Source: John Train, *Famous Financial Fiascos* (New York: Clarkson N. Potter, Inc.), pp. 7–8.

☞ Unlike stock exchanges with their system of specialists, futures exchanges use a system of open outcry with many market makers.

This physical arrangement is important because it highlights a central difference between commodities exchanges and stock exchanges in the United States. In the stock market, there is a specialist for each stock, and every trade on the exchange for a particular stock must go through the specialist. In the futures market, any trader in the pit may execute a trade with any other trader. The rules require that any offer to buy or sell must be made by open outcry to all other traders in the pit. This gives rise to the appearance of chaos on the floor, because each trader is struggling to gain the attention of the others. Once a trade is executed, the information is communicated to the exchange officials who report the transaction over a worldwide electronic communication system. Also, the trader whose order was executed will receive confirmation of the trade.

The Clearing House and Its Functions

An outside party's trade must be executed through a broker, and the broker, in turn, must trade through a member of the exchange. Normally, the two parties to a transaction are located far apart and do not even know each other. This raises the issue of trust and whether the traders will perform as they have promised.

clearing house
the arm of a futures exchange that oversees and guarantees fulfillment of futures contract terms

☞ The futures clearing house oversees the delivery process and uses its financial resources to guarantee contract performance to all traders.

To resolve this uncertainty, each futures exchange has a **clearing house.** This is a well-capitalized financial institution that guarantees contract performance to both parties. As soon as the trade is consummated, the clearing house interposes itself between the buyer and seller, acting as a seller to the buyer and as a buyer to the seller. At this point, the original buyer and seller have obligations to the clearing house and none to each other. This arrangement is shown in Figure 24.1. The top part shows the relationship between the buyer and seller when there is no clearing house. The seller is obligated to deliver goods to the buyer, who is obligated to deliver funds to the seller. The lower part shows the role of the clearing house, which is to guarantee that goods will be delivered to the buyer and that funds will be delivered to the seller.

At this point, the traders need to trust only the clearing house, not each other. Because the clearing house has a large supply of capital and an impeccable reputation, there is no reason for concern. Also, as the bottom part

FIGURE 24.1   The Function of the Clearing House in Futures Markets

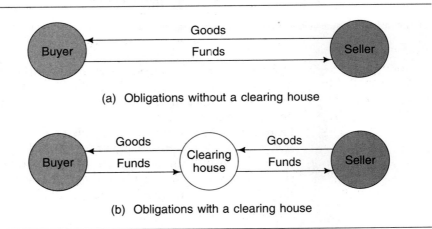

(a) Obligations without a clearing house

(b) Obligations with a clearing house

of Figure 24.1 shows, the clearing house has no net commitment in the futures market. After all the transactions are completed, it will have neither funds nor goods. It only guarantees performance to both parties.

The Clearing House and the Trader

Although the clearing house guarantees performance on all futures contracts, it now has its own risk exposure, because it will suffer if traders default on their obligations. To protect the clearing house and the exchange, traders must deposit funds with their brokers in order to trade futures contracts. This deposit, known as **margin,** must be in the form of cash or short-term U.S. Treasury securities, and acts as a good-faith deposit with the broker. If the trader defaults on the deal, the broker may seize the margin to cover any losses.

The margin, however, is usually quite small relative to the value of the goods being traded, normally having a value equal to only 5 to 10 percent of the goods. Because potential losses on the futures contract could be much larger than this margin, the clearing house must have other protection from potential default. Thus futures exchanges have adopted a system known as **daily resettlement,** or **marking to market,** through which futures traders realize their paper gains and losses in cash on the results of each day's trading. They may withdraw the day's gains and must pay the day's losses.

The margin deposit remains with the broker. If the trader fails to settle the day's losses, the broker may seize the margin and liquidate the trader's position, paying the losses out of the deposit. Thanks to this practice, the exchange has only limited exposure to loss from default, essentially losing only if the loss on one day exceeds the amount of the margin. This is unlikely to happen, and even if it does, the amount would probably be very small.

Fulfillment of Futures Contracts

After executing a futures contract, both the buyer and seller have undertaken specific obligations to the clearing house. They can fulfill those obligations in two basic ways. First, one party may actually make or take delivery as contemplated in the original contract. Second, if a trader does not wish to make or take delivery, the trader can enter a **reversing trade.** In fact, more than 99 percent of all futures contracts are settled by this means.[2] Actual delivery of a commodity is relatively rare in the futures market.

Delivery As indicated above, each futures contract has its own specific rules that cover the time of delivery, the delivery location, and the way in which the funds for the goods will change hands. Some investors who do not understand the futures market very well imagine that one could forget about a

---

[2] By contrast, more than 90 percent of foreign exchange forward contracts are completed by actual delivery.

margin
the good-faith deposit required before traders may enter futures contracts

☞ Unlike the stock market, in which the margin is a partial payment, the futures margin is merely a good-faith deposit.

daily resettlement or **marking to market**
the practice in the futures market of realizing gains and losses in cash each day

reversing trade
a trade that brings one's position in a futures contract to zero and completes all obligations in the contract

☞ Futures market contracts can be fulfilled by making or taking delivery or by a reversing trade.

INTERNATIONAL

PERSPECTIVES

Tarnished Silver

With little doubt, the Hunt manipulation of silver in 1979–1980 was the grandest futures manipulation of the twentieth century. At one time, the Hunts and their co-conspirators controlled silver worth more than $14 billion. The figure shows the price of silver for 1979 and 1980. At the beginning of 1979, an ounce of silver was worth about $6. In January 1980, the price briefly exceeded $50 during one trading day. In March 1980, the price of silver crashed, and silver fell to the $12 per ounce range. In 1990, silver traded for less than $5 per ounce.

In some ways, the silver manipulation was very simple, while in other ways it was incredibly complex. The manipulative efforts involved many other participants besides the flamboyant and well-known Hunts. These other conspirators included a number of very wealthy Saudis. In outline, the Hunts operated a corner on the silver market. They amassed gigantic futures positions and demanded delivery on those contracts as they came due. At the same time, they bought tremendous quantities of physical silver and held the physical silver off the market. Thus, they accelerated demand through the futures market as they restricted supply through the cash market. As a result the price of silver shot up.

As silver approached $50 per ounce in January 1980, the exchanges and the Chicago Futures Trade Commission took effective action by imposing liquidation-only trading. Under **liquidation-only trading,** traders are allowed to trade only to close an existing futures position; they are not allowed to establish any new positions. The next day, the price of silver dropped by $12 per ounce in one day. From January through February and into March, the manipulators struggled to support the price of silver. However, the exchanges also increased margins on silver. On March 19, the Hunts defaulted on their margin obligations. In a final desperate attempt to support the price of silver, the manipulators announced a plan on March 26, 1980, to issue bonds backed by their physical silver holdings. The market interpreted this ploy as an act of desperation and the market crashed again the next day." March 27, 1980, has become known as Silver Thursday because of this famous crash that ended the Hunts' effective domination of silver.

Minpeco, S.A., a Peruvian government-sponsored minerals marketing firm, was a major short trader in the silver market during 1979–1980.

futures position and wind up with pork bellies on the front lawn. In fact, the delivery process is more complicated.

As delivery approaches, the clearing house supervises the arrangements. First, it pairs buyers and sellers for the delivery and identifies the two parties to each other. Prior to this time, the two traders had no obligations to each other. Second, the buyer and seller communicate the relevant information

They sued the Hunts, their co-conspirators, and their brokers for $90 million of actual losses plus interest, plus trebled punitive damages. Minpeco won about $200 million in settlements and judgments against the defendants. This sum included a prejudgment settlement payment of $34 million by Merrill Lynch and Bache, two of the conspirators' largest brokers. The jury found that the three Hunt brothers, Bunker, Herbert, and Lamar, had indeed manipulated the silver market. After the verdict, Lamar Hunt, owner of the Kansas City Chiefs NFL team, paid $17 million in settlement. The full settlement was never collected from Bunker and Herbert, who sought protection in bankruptcy. Thus, these two brothers, who began the 1980s among the world's richest men, were bankrupt by 1990.

The Effect of the Hunt Manipulation on Silver Prices

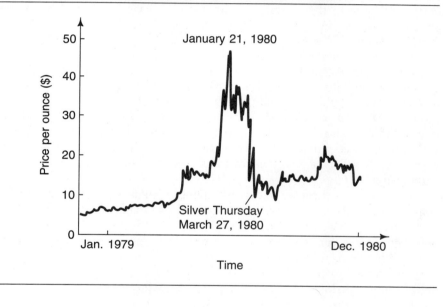

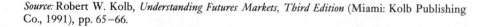

Source: Robert W. Kolb, *Understanding Futures Markets, Third Edition* (Miami: Kolb Publishing Co., 1991), pp. 65–66.

concerning the delivery process to each other and to the clearing house. Usually, the seller chooses the exact features of the delivered goods, for example, the kind of wheat, and the buyer must be notified of these conditions. The seller must also tell the buyer the bank account to which the funds are to be transmitted. Once the funds have been transmitted to the seller's account and this transaction has been confirmed by the seller's bank, the seller will deliver title of the goods to the buyer, usually in the form of a warehouse receipt.

As long as this transaction is proceeding smoothly, which is usually the case, the clearing house has little to do. It acts merely as an overseer. If difficulties arise, or if disputes develop, it must intervene to enforce the rules of the exchange.

Reversing Trades The delivery process can be quite cumbersome. For example, the seller may not choose to deliver the kind of wheat that the buyer wants. Also, the wheat may be stored in an approved warehouse that may be inconvenient for the buyer. If the buyer is a baker in Kansas who needs winter wheat, it may be very expensive and inconvenient to receive wheat of another type that is stored in Chicago. Because these physical commodities are bulky and difficult to transport, most futures traders fulfill their obligations by entering a reversing trade before delivery. Then, if they have to dispose of their supply of the good, or have to acquire the actual good, they do so in the regular spot market, outside the channels of the futures market.

Prior to the initiation of the delivery process, buyers and sellers are not associated with each other because the clearing house has interposed itself between them. This allows traders a means to end their commitment in the futures market without actually making delivery. Figure 24.2(a) shows the positions of three traders if there is no clearing house. At time 0, trader A buys a futures contract with trader B as the seller. Later, at time 1, which is still before delivery, trader A decides to liquidate the original position. Accordingly, A sells the identical contract that was purchased at time 0 to another trader, C.

In an important sense, trader A no longer has a position in the futures contract, but will just pass the goods from B to C and the funds from C to B. After time 1, price fluctuations will not really affect A. Traders B and C, however, have a very different perspective. Both have obligations to A and expect A to perform on the original contracts. This means that trader A is left with duties to perform in the delivery process. As a result, A still has obligations to perform, despite having no risk exposure anymore.

From the point of view of trader A, all of this is much simpler if there is a clearing house, as shown in Figure 24.2(b). Because the clearing house splits the original partners as soon as the trade is consummated, A can now execute a reversing trade to get out of the market altogether. After the trades are made, the clearing house can recognize that A has no position in the futures market, since A has bought and sold the identical futures contract. After time 1, trader C has assumed the position originally held by A. As a result, B's position is unaffected, and A has no further obligations.

It is important to recognize that the reversing trade must be for exactly the same futures contract as originally traded. Otherwise, the trader will have two futures positions rather than none. Also, it should be clear that any trader

FIGURE 24.2   The Mechanism of the Reversing Trade

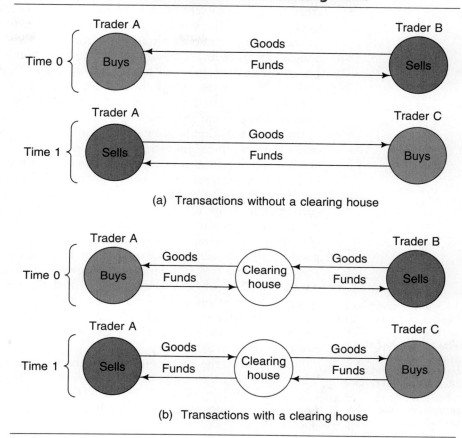

(a) Transactions without a clearing house

(b) Transactions with a clearing house

may execute a reversing trade at any time prior to delivery, which is exactly what most traders do, as delivery approaches. In Figure 24.2, trader C was new to the market, so the same number of futures contracts is still outstanding. However, if C had been executing a reversing trade also, the number of contracts outstanding would have decreased.

Futures Price Quotations

Futures price quotations are available daily in the *Wall Street Journal* and other newspapers. They are grouped by commodities and fall into four major groups: agricultural and metallurgical commodities, interest rate futures, foreign exchange futures, and stock index futures.

The agricultural and metallurgical commodities have been traded the longest, and include several grains, livestock, precious metals, petroleum products, and the famous pork bellies. The other three are all fairly recent creations. Foreign exchange futures are the oldest of the three, having begun trading in 1972. Stock index futures only began trading in 1982.

Interest rate futures contracts exist for several kinds of U.S. government obligations, including Treasury bills, notes, and bonds, and GNMAs, which are government-guaranteed mortgages on single-family dwellings. Foreign exchange futures are traded on the German marks, British pound, Japanese yen, Swiss franc, and Canadian dollar. Stock index futures are traded on several different indices, including the S&P 500, the Value Line Composite Index, the NYSE Composite Index, and a Major Market Index, which closely tracks the Dow Jones industrial average.

There are far too many different contracts to discuss each in detail, but their price quotations are all very similar. For illustrative purposes, we can use the corn contract traded by the Chicago Board of Trade (CBT). The corn quotations are presented in Figure 24.3. The first line of the quotation shows the commodity, followed by the exchange where the futures contract is traded, in this case the CBT. Next, the quotations show the amount of good in a single contract. In this case it is 5,000 bushels of corn. The last item in this first line is the method of price quotation. For corn the price is quoted in cents per bushel. Whereas all of this is important information, it is seriously incomplete. It reveals nothing about the quality of the corn or the places where delivery is permitted. As noted above, these factors are determined by the exchange, and any trader would want this information before trading.

nearby contract
the first maturing futures contract of a specific type

distant or **deferred contracts**
contracts that mature after the nearby contract

settlement price
the fair market price for a futures contract established by the settlement committee at the close of trading

The body of the quotation has a separate line for each contract maturity. The next contract to come due for delivery is called the **nearby contract**. Contracts with later delivery dates are **distant** or **deferred contracts**. The first three columns of figures show the open, high, and low prices for the day's trading.

The fourth column presents the **settlement price** for the day. In most respects, it is like a closing price, but it can have important differences. Because every trader marks to the market every day, it is important to have an official

FIGURE 24.3 Price Quotations for Corn Futures

	Open	High	Low	Settle	Change	Lifetime High	Lifetime Low	Open Interest
CORN (CBT) 5,000 bu.; cents per bu.								
May	258¼	259¼	257¼	258¾	+ 1½	306½	235	65,348
July	266	266½	264¾	266¼	+ 1¼	308¼	241½	88,701
Sept	265	265¾	264¼	265¾	+ 1	287½	240¼	18,148
Dec	264¾	265	263	264	− ¼	275	242½	55,185
Mr92	272¼	272¾	271	272¼	+ ¼	275¼	249	6,835
May	276¾	278¼	276½	278¼	+ 1	279½	258¼	1,285
July	280	281½	279	281½	+ 1¼	282	270¾	185

Est vol n.a.; vol Thur 46,325; open int 235,687, −460.

Source: Wall Street Journal, April 15, 1991. Reprinted by permission of Wall Street Journal, © 1991 Dow Jones & Company, Inc. All Rights Reserved Worldwide.

settlement committee
the committee, composed of exchange members, that determines the settlement price

open interest
the number of futures contracts obligated for delivery

price to which to mark. That is the settlement price and it is set by the **settlement committee** of the exchange. If the markets are active at the close of trading, the settlement price will normally be the closing price. However, if a particular contract has not traded for some time, the settlement committee may believe that the last trade price is not representative of the actual prevailing price. Thus the committee may establish a settlement price that differs from the last trade price. The "Change" column reports the change in the contract's price from the preceding day's settlement price. The next two columns indicate the highest and lowest prices reached by a contract of a particular maturity since it began trading.

The last column shows the open interest at the close of the day's trading. The **open interest** is the number of contracts currently obligated for delivery. If a buyer and seller trade one contract and neither is making a reversing trade, the open interest is increased by one contract. This is the case in the transaction shown in Figure 24.1, since neither party has any other position in the futures market.

Every contract begins and ends with no open interest. When the exchange first permits trading in a given contract maturity, there is no open interest until the first trade is made. At the end of the contract's life, all traders must fulfill their obligations by entering reversing trades or by making delivery; once this process is complete, there is no longer any open interest. Figure 24.4 shows the typical pattern that the open interest follows. When the contract is first opened for trading, open interest builds steadily, but as the contract nears maturity, it falls drastically. This is due to the fact that many traders enter reversing trades to fulfill their commitments without having to incur the expense and bother of actually making delivery.

The final line of the quotations shows the number of contracts that were estimated to have traded on the day being reported, and the actual volume

FIGURE 24.4 The Typical Pattern of Open Interest Over Time

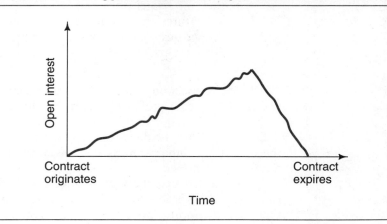

for the preceding day's trading. It also shows the total open interest, which is simply the sum of the open interest for all of the different contract maturities. The last item is the change in open interest since the preceding day.

FUTURES PRICING

One of the most important tasks of finance is to explain why prices in a market behave as they do and to specify as clearly as possible how they ought to behave. The basis plays a key role in our understanding of the factors that influence futures prices. This section begins with a discussion of the basis and then explores two models of futures prices.

The Basis

basis
the difference between the cash price and the futures price

☞ The basis must equal zero at the maturity of a futures contract.

The **basis** is defined as:

$$\text{Basis} = \text{cash price} - \text{futures price} \qquad (24.1)$$

Traders in the futures markets watch the basis very closely because its behavior is governed by certain rules. Also, the various pricing theories can be stated in terms of rules about how the basis will behave.

The first rule is that the basis must equal zero at the delivery date for the futures contract, to avoid arbitrage possibilities. To see why, assume that the following prices prevail the moment before delivery on the corn futures contract, and assume that there are no transaction costs:

Futures price of corn: 300 cents per bushel
Cash price of corn: 295 cents per bushel

Faced with these prices and the fact that delivery is at hand, a trader could make the following transactions to earn an arbitrage profit:

1. Buy 5,000 bushels of corn in the spot market at 295 cents per bushel, for a total price of $14,750.
2. Sell 1 futures contract for the immediate delivery of corn at 300 cents per bushel, for a total futures price of $15,000.
3. Deliver the purchased corn against the futures contract, and collect $15,000.

These transactions, all executed simultaneously, require no investment and produce a sure profit of $250. If the futures price had been less than the cash price, the trader could simply have bought the futures contract, taken delivery, and sold the delivery corn for a profit in the spot market. To avoid these arbitrage opportunities, the basis must be zero at the delivery date on the futures contract.

Prior to delivery, the futures price may be less than or greater than the cash price. If it is less than the cash price, the basis will be positive. Furthermore, the futures price and cash price must converge over the life of the

FIGURE 24.5   The Convergence of Futures and Cash Prices as Futures Contracts Approach Delivery

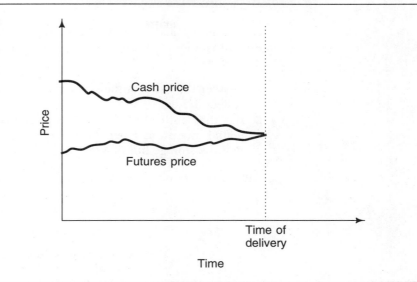

futures contract, because they must be equal at the delivery date. Figure 24.5 illustrates this convergence.

Two basic pricing factors are at work in the futures market. The first, and probably more important, is known as the cost-of-carry relationship. The second interprets futures prices as estimates of future spot prices. Together, they provide a good understanding of pricing in futures markets.

The Cost-of-Carry Relationship for Futures Prices

Imagine the following prices for corn:

Cash price: 250 cents per bushel
Futures price: 300 cents per bushel (for delivery in three months)

Also assume that it is possible to borrow funds at a rate of 1 percent per month, and that it costs $0.05 per month per bushel to store corn. These storage costs include the cost of the warehousing and insurance, for example. Faced with these facts, the following strategy appears viable:

1. Borrow $12,500 for three months at 1 percent per month.
2. Buy 5,000 bushels of corn in the cash market for 250 cents per bushel, for a total outlay of $12,500.
3. Store the corn for three months at $0.05 per bushel per month, to be paid at the end of the storage period, for a total storage cost of $750.

4. Sell a futures contract, calling for the delivery of corn in three months at a price of 300 cents per bushel, or a total price of $15,000.

All of these transactions would be implemented at the beginning of the three-month period. At the end of the period, the following transactions would be completed:

1. Deliver the 5,000 bushels of corn against the futures contract, and collect $15,000.
2. Pay the debt of $12,878.76 on the original loan, which reflects compound interest at 1 percent per month.
3. Pay the storage bill of $750.

After these transactions, the trader's net cash flows are as follows:

Time 0	Time 3 Months	
$0	Collect on futures contract	$15,000.00
	Pay debt	−12,878.76
	Pay storage costs	−750.00
		+$ 1,371.24

cost-of-carry relationship a pricing formula relating a futures price to the cash price of the same commodity

☞ The cost-of-carry model of futures pricing relates the futures price to the spot price through a no-arbitrage condition.

☞ The cost-of-carry includes all financing charges, storage costs, and insurance costs that would be incurred in storing a commodity.

This transaction reflects a successful arbitrage venture. The trader invested no funds and reaped a sure profit. In a market that performs efficiently, such a transaction would be impossible. This reasoning leads to the **cost-of-carry relationship:**

$$\text{Futures prices} \leq \text{cash price} + \text{cost-of-carry} \qquad (24.2)$$

where   cost-of-carry = storage costs + financing costs

Simply stated, this says that the futures price must be less than or equal to the cost of the commodity in the spot market, plus the cost of carrying the commodity forward in time to deliver against the futures contract. It includes both storage and financing costs. It must be noted that holding some goods may also yield certain advantages. For example, a financial instrument will have a financing cost to cover its price, but there may also be attractive interest payments on the instrument that will largely offset the cost. Therefore, the financing cost must be interpreted as the net financing cost. If Equation 24.2 does not hold, then there will be an arbitrage opportunity.

Is there a no-arbitrage condition if the trader decides to short-sell? To explore this question, consider prices of corn such as the following:

Cash price: 300 cents per bushel
Futures price: 250 cents per bushel (for delivery in three months)

With these prices and with unrestricted short selling, a trader could enter the following trades:

1. Sell short 5,000 bushels of corn at 300 cents per bushel and receive $15,000. (In this transaction, the trader borrows the corn and sells it, with the obligation to return the corn to its owner later.)
2. Invest the $15,000 for three months at 1 percent per month.
3. Buy one futures contract for the delivery of corn in three months.

At the end of three months the transactions would be completed as follows:

1. Take delivery of the 5,000 bushels of corn on the futures contract and pay 250 cents per bushel for a total of $12,500.
2. Return the corn to cover the short position.

The trader's cash flows would be as follows:

Time 0	Time 3 Months	
$0	Collect on investment	$15,454.52
	Pay for the delivery of the corn	− 12,500.00
	on the futures contract	+$ 2,954.52

In this case the trader would make a sure profit of $2,954.52, again without investment. As a consequence, with unrestricted short selling the following rule must also hold:

$$\text{Futures price} \geq \text{cash price} + \text{interest}$$

Having assumed the same borrowing and investment rates, we can put these two relationships together and obtain the following rule:

$$\text{Cash price} + \text{interest} \leq \text{futures price}$$
$$\leq \text{cash price} + \text{storage} + \text{financing costs}$$

This relationship assumes unrestricted short selling. For almost all commodities, however, there are restrictions on short selling. In this example we assumed that the trader had full use of the proceeds on the short sale. This is normally not the case. For some commodities, such as corn, it is virtually impossible to enter a short sale. It is possible for financial assets, but charges are incurred. Thus the cost-of-carry relationship implies the following:

$$\text{Futures price} \approx \text{cash price} + \text{storage costs} + \text{financing costs} \quad (24.3)$$

The relationship in Equation 24.3 does not hold as a strict equality because of the potential impact of costs or restrictions on short selling.[3]

---

[3] The practical effect of restrictions on short selling is discussed in more detail later in the section on interest rate futures in this chapter.

Spreads and the Cost-of-Carry

spread
the difference in price
between two futures
contracts

For a single commodity, a **spread** is the difference in price between two futures contracts of different maturities, such as the one between different pairs of corn futures contracts in Figure 24.3. Just as the cost-of-carry implies a price relationship between the futures price and the cash price, it also implies a relationship between futures prices for contracts with different maturities.

☞ Just as the cost-of-carry relationship determines the relationship between spot and futures prices, it also determines the relationship between two futures prices.

With unrestricted short selling, it must be the case that:

$$\text{Distant futures price} \approx \text{nearby futures price} + \text{storage costs} + \text{financing costs} \quad (24.4)$$

Equation 24.4 parallels Equation 24.3 very closely in form and spirit. To rule out arbitrage, prices must adjust so that it is impossible to sell a distant futures contract, accept delivery on a nearby futures, carry the delivered good to delivery on the distant contract, and make a profit. In this case, the storage and financing costs are to be incurred in the future. To make the investment opportunity riskless, the prospective arbitrageur must enter a forward or futures contract to establish the storage and financing costs at the outset. So the cost-of-carry relationship, with the assumption of unrestricted short selling, determines the relationship between the cash price and any futures price, and also determines the price relationship among all futures contracts.

Observed Futures Prices and the Cost-of-Carry Relationship

As we have seen, the cost-of-carry relationship expressed by Equation 24.3 must hold at every point in time if arbitrage opportunities are to be ruled out. However, it assumes that short selling is unrestricted. In many markets short selling is restricted by being costly; in some markets, it is almost impossible.

Although it is generally observed that the futures price exceeds the cash price, just as the cost-of-carry relationship with unrestricted short selling implies, that is not always true. Also, for most commodities the quoted prices for the more distant futures contracts are generally higher than prices for the nearby contract, just as we would expect from the cost-of-carry relationship. Again, there are exceptions to this rule. When deferred contract prices are greater than nearby prices, the futures market is said to be a **normal market**. When prices on deferred contracts lie below the nearby contract price, the futures market is said to be an **inverted market**. Figure 24.6 shows a recent inverted market for crude oil futures.

normal market
futures trading in which
the futures price exceeds
the spot price

inverted market
futures trading in which
the spot price exceeds
the futures price

An inverted price pattern is not what one would expect to observe, based on the cost-of-carry relationship. In fact, if unrestricted short selling were possible, arbitrageurs could make a fortune trading in an inverted market. From this we may conclude two things. First, serious barriers have been raised to short selling many commodities. Second, in markets where unrestricted

FIGURE 24.6 Price Quotations for Crude Oil

	Open	High	Low	Settle	Change	Lifetime High	Lifetime Low	Open Interest
Aug	409.0	409.0	404.0	406.0 +	1.0	523.0	363.0	455
Dec	421.0	422.0	414.0	416.0	....	575.0	374.0	1,489

Est vol n.a.; vol Thur 73; open int 6,437, +11.

CRUDE OIL, Light Sweet (NYM) 1,000 bbls.; $ per bbl.

	Open	High	Low	Settle	Change	Lifetime High	Lifetime Low	Open Interest
May	21.15	21.50	21.03	21.48 +	.59	32.70	17.20	63,087
June	20.70	21.03	20.63	20.97 +	.49	31.50	17.10	57,421
July	20.40	20.59	20.30	20.53 +	.36	30.40	16.80	33,841
Aug	20.14	20.30	20.04	20.25 +	.31	29.50	16.90	29,781
Sept	19.86	20.10	19.86	20.05 +	.29	28.72	16.90	24,342
Oct	19.72	20.10	19.72	19.92 +	.27	28.40	17.04	13,463
Nov	19.70	20.00	19.70	19.83 +	.24	28.10	17.20	8,855
Dec	19.68	19.85	19.62	19.77 +	.22	27.70	17.10	20,732
Ja92	19.55	19.70	19.55	19.71 +	.22	27.60	17.25	10,258
Feb	19.65	19.67	19.55	19.65 +	.21	27.00	17.50	5,626
Mar	19.65	19.65	19.55	19.62 +	.20	26.75	17.25	7,554
Apr	19.48	19.52	19.47	19.59 +	.20	26.50	17.50	11,569
May	19.57	19.57	19.57	19.57 +	.20	24.60	17.30	2,642
June	19.36	19.58	19.35	19.56 +	.20	24.50	17.70	6,832
July	....	....	....	19.56 +	.20	23.59	17.90	3,346
Aug	....	....	....	19.56 +	.20	19.65	17.75	1,773
Sept	....	....	....	19.56 +	.20	24.00	17.78	1,333
Oct	19.50	19.50	19.50	19.56 +	.20	19.45	18.85	219
Dec	....	....	....	19.56 +	.20	24.00	18.25	2,562
Mr93	....	....	....	19.56 +	.20	19.23	18.64	1,140
June	19.35	19.40	19.35	19.56 +	.20	23.00	18.80	6,245
Dec	....	....	....	19.56 +	.20	23.00	18.70	2,224

Est vol 83,208; vol Thur 102,930; open int 314,845, +12,-383.

Source: Wall Street Journal, April 15, 1991. Reprinted by permission of Wall Street Journal, © 1991 Dow Jones & Company, Inc. All Rights Reserved Worldwide.

short selling is not possible, the cost-of-carry relationship does not tell the whole story of futures prices. We still need some additional explanation of the observed prices for many futures contracts. The explanation brings the market's expectations regarding future cash prices into account.

Futures Prices and Expected Future Spot Prices

☞ To avoid attractive speculative opportunities, the futures price must be closely related to the expected future spot price of a commodity.

Traders in futures markets have expectations about the future cash prices for various commodities. It is not surprising that these expectations affect futures prices. Two questions are most important. First, how do futures market prices adjust to expectations about future spot prices? Second, how can traders' expectations about future spot prices have any effect on futures prices, given the cost-of-carry pricing relationship?

Figure 24.6 illustrates an inverted market for crude oil futures on April 15, 1991, which was a time of great turmoil in the world oil market. When the Gulf war ended faster than many analysts expected, the prospects for an excess supply of oil in the near future increased, as Kuwait could restore its production capacity, severely damaged as a result of Iraq's occupation from August 1990 to February 1991.

Assuming that the market was really expecting falling prices, these expectations should affect the prices at which traders are willing to buy and sell oil for future delivery. If futures prices are not consistent with the market's expectations, profitable trading opportunities will exist. They will not be arbitrage opportunities, but they can be expected to generate a profit. In Figure 24.6, for example, the futures price for the August 1991 delivery of crude oil is $20.25 per barrel, and this must be consistent with the market's expectation about the August 1991 spot price. To see why this must be so, assume that the expected spot price for August 1991 is $19.00. Faced with the actual futures price and the expected spot price, a trader could have sold the futures contract for a delivery price of $20.25 and planned to buy the oil in August for delivery at $19.00. If the trader's expectations were correct, this strategy would have yielded a $1.25 profit per barrel. If we ignore margin and daily resettlement cash flows, the trader could hope for this profit without even making an investment.

The traders in the crude oil futures market, in effect, get to vote on the future expected price of oil. They vote in proportion to the commitment they are willing to make by trading in the market. If the prevailing futures price does not equal the market's aggregate expectation, traders will continue to enter the market to try to capture profits. This action will have the effect of driving the futures price into equality with the market's aggregate expectation of the cash price at the time of delivery.

In the case of the heating oil futures contract, shown in Figure 24.7, the futures prices decrease for the months of May and June and increase until February, when they fall again. This behavior clearly reflects the seasonal demand for heating oil. If the crude oil and heating oil futures markets were dominated by the cost-of-carry relationship, we could not observe a pattern of falling prices over time, as in the case of the crude oil contract, or a pattern of rising and falling prices, as in the case of the heating oil contract.

If short selling in the oil market were unrestricted, the prices would have to exhibit a strictly increasing pattern, as we argued above. On the other hand, if short selling were totally impossible in a given market, the futures prices should equal the expected future spot price of the commodity in order to eliminate any opportunities to earn excessive speculative profits.

FIGURE 24.7 Price Quotations for Heating Oil

HEATING OIL NO. 2 (NYM) 42,000 gal.; $ per gal.							
May	.5590	.5620	.5560	.5605 +.0065	.8850	.4840	18,639
June	.5490	.5540	.5480	.5532 +.0080	.8575	.4800	12,763
July	.5470	.5540	.5460	.5533 +.0094	.8500	.4800	12,738
Aug	.5530	.5590	.5530	.5571 +.0091	.8507	.4900	8,183
Sept	.5675	.5700	.5670	.5696 +.0086	.8428	.5025	4,047
Oct	.5760	.5785	.5760	.5781 +.0081	.8500	.5130	2,292
Nov	.5860	.5860	.5850	.5866 +.0076	.7800	.5230	1,802
Dec	.5930	.5970	.5920	.5946 +.0076	.8262	.5330	13,495
Ja92	.5955	.5995	.5955	.5966 +.0076	.8200	.5340	2,900
Feb	.5830	.5835	.5830	.5846 +.0076	.5860	.5225	1,674
Mar	.5570	.5570	.5555	.5601 +.0076	.5620	.5415	595
Apr	....	....	....	.5401 +.0076	.5410	.5000	251
May	....	....	....	.5251 +.0076	.5350	.4875	381
Est vol 16,105; vol Thur 19,693; open int 79,836, +131.							

Source: Wall Street Journal, April 15, 1991. Reprinted by permission of Wall Street Journal, © 1991 Dow Jones & Company, Inc. All Rights Reserved Worldwide.

THE SOCIAL FUNCTION OF FUTURES MARKETS

Futures markets have often come under attack from different interest groups in society and from legislative bodies. The U.S. Congress actually forbade trading in onion futures, and at one point came very close to banning all futures trading. Currently, futures markets are thriving, partially in recognition of the two useful social functions that they serve. The first is the role of price discovery, and the second is assisting in the transference of risk in society.

Price Discovery

price discovery
the informational role of futures markets in which futures prices help observers discover likely future spot prices

☞ One of the main functions of futures markets is to provide information to the public about future spot prices.

Price discovery refers to the information contained in futures prices about future spot prices. In the absence of short selling, we argued that futures prices should equal expected future spot prices. If that were the case, futures prices would be a very good forecast of future spot prices, because they would be aggregating the opinions of many different traders. In fact, a number of studies have tested this theory. Although the forecast embodied in futures prices often has large errors, it does seem to perform very well on average. Furthermore, considerable evidence exists that futures prices perform better than professional forecasting services. They may not give good forecasts in some respects, but they do seem to perform better than most alternative indicators. Because of this, the role of the futures market in price discovery is very important, and some researchers think it is the most important social function that the market serves.

For example, imagine a broker preparing to bid on the delivery of a great deal of crude oil. The bid must be submitted now, but delivery is not to take place for nine months. As Figure 24.6 shows, the crude oil prices decrease steadily as the delivery date is more distant. If these futures prices are a good gauge of the spot prices to prevail at the time of delivery, it would be a mistake to submit a bid based on the current price. Instead, the bid should reflect the lower price of crude oil that is consistent with the futures prices at the time of delivery. In this case, the oil broker would be using futures prices as a guide to future spot prices, and could acquire a quality estimate at a very cheap price.

Risk Transference

☞ The second main function of the futures market is to provide a means whereby risk can be transferred among traders.

The second major social function is the opportunity that the futures market provides for risk transference. As we saw in our discussion of the CAPM, bearing risk is an important function in the capital markets that can be richly rewarded. As we have also seen, however, different investors have different degrees of risk tolerance. Therefore, a market that allows investors to modify the amount of risk that they must bear can be very useful. The futures market allows great latitude in the transference of risk from one trader who is unwilling to bear it, to others who will accept it in the hope of profit.

Futures Markets Adopt Today's Technology

In an effort to provide a secure audit record of all transactions and traders, the Board of Trade and the Mercantile Exchange, both in Chicago, will begin using hand-held devices and wireless technology to record their trades.

The exchanges will not, however, replace "open outcry," where traders shout and use hand signals, said Dale Lorenzen, chairman of the automated data input terminal (AUDIT) committee for the Board of Trade, and vice chairman of the Board of Trade.

The hand-held devices eventually chosen by the committee will transmit the trades via PC to a LAN, which in turn will be connected to a mainframe, according to Lorenzen.

Following a 1989 FBI investigation into trading practices, the two exchanges each committed $2.5 million to developing a prototype device that would use infrared or spread spectrum signals, weigh less than 1 pound, and record at least 30 trades per second per pit, Lorenzen said.

Traders currently record their trades on cards which are collected every 30 minutes and entered on a computer, Lorenzen said. The results are sent to a clearing house, which matches the trades with one another.

Under this system it is impossible to find out quickly whether or not any discrepancy exists between the two records of each trade. The AUDIT device will make it possible to know of a discrepancy within 1 minute, according to Lorenzen.

Three vendors have made it to the final cut: Spectrix, in conjunction with Panasonic; Texas Instruments, in conjunction with Omnipoint Data; and Synerdyne, in conjunction with Seiko.

Each device will undergo about 15 sessions of mock trading before being tried on the floor, Lorenzen said.

All traders who trade for their own accounts will use these devices by the end of 1992, Lorenzen said. Other futures exchanges may follow suit; the two exchanges have offered to share the technology with those in New York and Minneapolis.

Source: Louise Fickel, "Wireless Adds Its Voice to 'Open Outcry' at Futures Exchange," *Infoworld,* April 22, 1991, p. 31.

Assume that the broker who used the crude oil futures price to formulate the bid receives the contract. The actual price of that oil at the time of delivery is uncertain, so the broker has a considerable degree of risk. If prices rise unexpectedly, the oil must be purchased and delivered anyway, thus reducing profits. In this circumstance, the broker can choose between doing nothing and hoping that prices do not rise, thus bearing all the risk of the price fluctuation, and entering the crude oil futures market to reduce the risk.

Assume that the broker has to deliver 1 million barrels of crude in November 1991. To reduce the risk exposure, the broker could buy 1,000 contracts for November delivery at the current futures price of $19.83 per barrel. This transaction would have the effect of guaranteeing the price that must be paid for the crude oil and allow the broker to transfer the unwanted risk to some other party in the futures market. Possibly the trader opposite the broker is a crude oil supplier. The seller of the futures contract may be reducing risk as well by establishing the price to be received for the crude. In this case, it is not so much a matter of transferring risk, but the futures market would be allowing both the broker and the producer to reduce their risks. Once the broker enters this transaction, the price to be paid for oil is fixed. If the spot price in November is $20.00 per barrel, the broker will still pay $19.83. On the total of 1 million barrels, the broker saved $170,000 [($20.00 − $19.83) × 1,000,000]. Alternatively, if the spot price is $19.50 per barrel in November, the broker will still have to pay $19.83, in this case, paying $330,000 more by being in the futures market.

The point of this kind of transaction is not to ensure that a trader pays less for a good by entering the futures market, but to reduce risk. The broker had an initial risk position because the crude oil was needed. By transacting in the futures market, the broker offsets, or hedges, that risk. A hedge is simply a transaction that is designed to offset some risk. Once the broker has entered this hedge position, it is no longer uncertain how much will be paid for the crude oil.

This hedge is very important for society. For example, the broker might have been so risk-averse as to avoid even submitting a bid for the project unless it were possible to use the futures market to reduce the risk. Alternatively, the broker might have submitted a much higher bid that incorporated a risk premium component. In many cases, the physical realities of the production process involve risks, and those who carry out the process may not be the optimum risk bearers from the point of view of society. Others might be better able and more willing to bear certain risks. The futures market provides a means for transferring that risk to these parties.

SPECULATION WITH FUTURES

If numerous parties in the futures markets are receiving an important benefit by transferring their risk to others, who bears that risk and how are they compensated for these services? It is possible for the total risk in society to be reduced in the futures market. A wheat farmer might attempt to reduce risk by selling the crop through the futures market. Similarly, a cereal producer might reduce the risk associated with the need for wheat as a cereal ingredient by buying wheat in the futures market. In this happy example, the two are brought together and both reduce their risks, resulting in a net reduction of the risk undertaken by society.

• Many cases, however, do not provide opportunities for such mutual risk reduction. Then the risk that is transferred away from the hedger must be borne by a speculator. Speculators are often disparaged for their greed, but they actually play a very important role in futures markets. As we will see, different kinds of speculators provide different services in addition to bearing risk.

Kinds of Speculators

☞ Speculators benefit the futures market through their willingness to bear risk.

We can distinguish three different kinds of speculators by the length of time they usually hold a futures position: scalpers, day traders, and position traders. Scalpers have the shortest time horizon of all of the futures market speculators. It is not unusual for them to make a futures trade and then enter a reversing trade within a few minutes. They essentially attempt to make a profit by trading on the very short-term fluctuations in futures prices by sensing the immediate direction of the market. This approach requires that scalpers actually be in the pit, so that they can see how the trading is progressing and read the minds of the other traders. Scalpers generate a very high number of trades, and therefore must be in a position to have very low transaction costs. Even if they could sense the market developments from a position out of the pit, they certainly could not afford the costs that would be incurred in executing the transactions through a broker.

The scalper is hoping to make a profit out of a one- or two-tick fluctuation in the futures contract price. A tick is the minimum price movement on a contract that is permitted by the exchange, for most contracts $25 or less. For example, one tick on the Treasury bill futures contract is $25, and on the corn contract it is $12.50. Obviously, a scalper planning to make a profit out of such small price fluctuations must be on the floor in order to have low transaction costs. Typically, a round trip transaction charge for a contract is less than $1. A **round trip** is the purchase and sale of the contract.

round trip
the purchase and sale of a futures contract

Compared with scalpers, day traders are far-sighted: They may hold a position for a long time, maybe even two or three hours. The distinguishing feature of day traders is that they never maintain a position overnight. "Taking a position home" is just too risky in most cases, because sudden changes in the economic situation can have drastic effects on futures prices. With the market closed at night, traders have no way to abandon a losing position.[4]

To see the risk inherent in an overnight position, consider the orange juice concentrate futures contract. This contract is traded by the Citrus Associates of the New York Cotton Exchange, with 15,000 pounds of con-

---

[4] One interesting development is the new tendency for futures markets around the world to be linked. The Chicago Mercantile Exchange and the Singapore futures exchange now permit dual listing of certain contracts. Since they are on approximately opposite sides of the world, this allows trading in many more hours per day. Soon, futures contracts are likely to be traded 24 hours per day.

centrate per contract. Several times in the last decade the market was surprised by a sudden and unexpected freeze in the Florida orange groves. For traders holding a short position in orange juice, such a development can be disastrous. For this reason, day traders, by definition, always close their position by reversing trades before the end of the day's trading.

Speculators with the longest time horizon are position traders. They stake a position in the futures market that may be held for weeks or even months without adjustment. Position trades may be either outright positions or spreads. An **outright position** is simply buying or selling a given futures contract of a single maturity. Of all the futures strategies, this is probably the riskiest, and few position traders seem to be interested in this dangerous career.

Most position traders use spreads. That is, they take a position in two or more related contracts in a way that reduces the risk below the level that would be encountered in an outright position. Spreads may be for different contract maturities within a single commodity. As such, they are called time spreads or **intracommodity spreads.** Alternatively, traders may take a position in two related but different commodities; this is called an **intercommodity spread.**

For example, a trader might believe that the price of wheat is too high relative to the price of corn for a particular delivery month. A trade to capitalize on this belief would be to sell the wheat contract and buy the corn contract. Since the contracts traded are for two different goods, it is an intercommodity spread. The same factors tend to affect wheat and corn because they are substitute goods in many applications. For a transaction in two different commodities to be a spread, the price behavior of the commodities must be related. In a spread of any type, the trader is not trading on an absolute price movement for one futures contract, but is hoping that the price of one contract moves in a certain way relative to the price of another. Figure 24.8 shows how this kind of trade might be profitable. At the initial position, a relatively wide gap exists between the wheat and corn futures prices. The trader who believes the gap is too wide will sell the relatively overpriced wheat contract and buy the relatively underpriced corn contract.

As the figure shows, the prices of both goods fall, but as they do, the price gap closes over time. This generates a profit for the spread position that is equal to the difference in the gap at its initial position and the time the position is closed. Notice that the purchase of the corn futures alone would have resulted in a loss, even though the trader believed that it was relatively underpriced. An outright short position in wheat would have generated a much larger profit than the spread trade, however. In spread trading, traders sacrifice the greater gains that holding just one side of the trade might generate in order to limit risk. They anticipate a gain on one side and a loss on the other, with the gain being more than enough to offset the loss.

In a time spread, traders must believe that the futures prices are not correctly aligned. For example, a speculator might believe that the price of, say, lumber for the July contract may be high relative to the May contract

outright position
a position in a single futures contract, as opposed to a spread position, which would involve a position in two or more related futures contracts

intracommodity spread
a futures spread using two or more maturities of the futures contract on the same commodity

intercommodity spread
a futures spread using contracts on two or more different commodities

FIGURE 24.8   Price Movements for an Intercommodity Spread Between Wheat and Corn

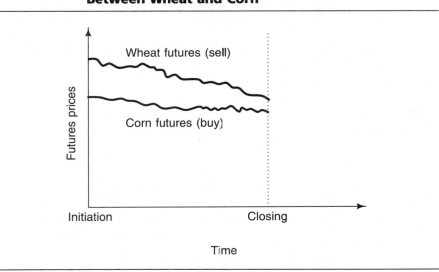

The Role of the Speculator

and low relative to the September contract. Trading on this belief, the speculator would sell the July contract and buy the May contract. This position will be profitable if the July price falls relative to the May price. Because both of the contracts traded are for the same commodity, this is a time spread.

The Role of the Speculator

In the futures markets, speculators serve a useful function by increasing the liquidity of the market. For example, the scalper's frequent trades make it much easier for hedgers to transact due to the increased liquidity. A result of a lack of liquidity is typically larger bid/ask spreads and lower market efficiency. This is not to imply that speculators trade in order to provide liquidity, but their profit-seeking behavior has that beneficial side effect.

The second major service that the speculator provides is bearing risk. Willingness to take on greater risk means that another party may be able to reduce risk. As discussed above, this makes it possible for risk-averse economic agents to undertake socially useful projects that they would otherwise be unwilling to consider.

Speculation and the Behavior of Futures Prices

Of course, speculators do not bear risk for free; they do so hoping to earn a profit. Earlier, we saw reason to believe that futures prices are good measures of future expected spot prices. If that is true, and if expectations on average are correct, speculators will not make any profit on average. However, they will be bearing risk. In other words, if futures prices equal expected future spot prices, and the expectations about future spot prices are correct, there is no way for speculators to make a profit, on average.

The great economists John Maynard Keynes and John Hicks proposed that the hedgers' needs usually require speculators to be buyers of futures contracts. If speculators take on long positions, they must be buying futures contracts at prices that are less than expected future spot prices. If this were not the case, the speculators would be buying futures contracts without the reasonable hope of gain. If the hypothesis of Keynes and Hicks is correct, and still assuming that expectations regarding future spot prices are correct on average, futures prices should rise over time, as the low futures price rises to meet the expected future spot price at the maturity of the futures contract. This process of futures prices rising over time is called **normal backwardation.**

normal backwardation
the pattern of futures prices rising over the life of a contract

If the hedgers' needs require speculators to be short in the aggregate, the futures price must lie above the expected future spot price if speculators are to be rewarded for their risk-bearing services. In this situation, the futures prices must fall over time so that they will equal the initially lower spot price at the maturity of the futures contract. This implies a pattern of falling futures prices over time, a price pattern known as **contango.** Figure 24.9 illustrates the two possibilities of normal backwardation and contango. For the sake of convenience, the expected spot price is shown as being constant.

contango
the pattern of futures prices falling over the life of a contract

FIGURE 24.9 Normal Backwardation and Contango in Futures Prices

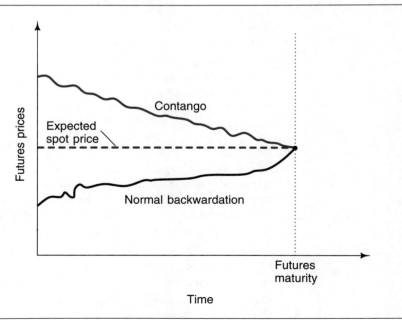

In spite of considerable research, neither of these hypotheses has been validated. Many studies continue to show that the futures price is generally equal to the observed cash price at maturity. If that is the case, speculators have little opportunity to make a profit on a consistent basis. This issue is of great importance for assessing the value of the futures market, because the amount the speculators earn determines the cost of risk transference for the hedger. The evidence to date is consistent with a low, or even no, cost of risk transference, because it does not appear that the speculators earn a consistent return.

One study explained this apparently strange result by considering the problem in the context of the CAPM. According to the CAPM, only the bearing of systematic risk is rewarded in the marketplace. Katherine Dusak advanced this argument and concluded that futures contracts tend to have no systematic risk. In the CAPM framework, this is consistent with her observed findings that futures prices tend to equal subsequent spot prices. According to her analysis, speculators have no return on the risky positions they assume because they are not bearing systematic risk. This makes them appear very much like gamblers. If Dusak's analysis is correct, speculators increase their risk by entering the futures market, but they are not paid for bearing this risk on a regular basis. This is like roulette players who take a risk by playing, but who earn no regular return because they are not providing the service of bearing systematic risk.[5]

INTEREST RATE FUTURES

The futures markets today trade a wide variety of goods with significantly different characteristics, ranging from pork bellies to financial instruments. These goods are also diverse with respect to their economic features, such as their storage potential and the quality of the markets for their short sale. Because of this tremendous diversity, it is impossible to cover all of the important features of these markets here.[6] Consequently, this section focuses on some key issues of financial futures.

Interest Rate Futures and the Yield Curve

As we saw in Chapter 9, the yield curve is extremely important for investing in bonds and managing bond portfolios. With different maturities of bonds with different yields, investors may commit their money for different periods of time in order to take advantage of a particular shape of the yield curve. We also saw how forward rates of interest play an important role in two

---

[5] See Katherine Dusak, "Futures Trading and Investor Returns: An Investigation of Commodity Market Risk Premiums," *Journal of Political Economy*, December 1973.

[6] For a treatment of futures markets in the United States, see Robert W. Kolb, *Understanding Futures Markets*, 3rd edition (Miami: Kolb Publishing Co., 1991).

theories of the term structure, the pure expectations theory and the liquidity premium theory.

☞ The prices of interest rate futures are consistent with the spot market yield curve.

In the interest rate futures markets, the exchanges have made a conscious effort to offer interest rate futures that cover the yield curve. For example, the International Monetary Market (IMM) of the Chicago Mercantile Exchange (CME) specializes in the shorter-maturity instruments. It currently offers interest rate futures contracts on Treasury bills, bank CDs, and Eurodollar deposits, all with maturities of about three months. By contrast, the Chicago Board of Trade focuses on the longer maturities. It trades a contract on long-term Treasury bonds, the most successful futures contract ever introduced, as well as on medium-maturity Treasury notes and on GNMAs.

To illustrate the connection between the yield curve and interest rate futures, we will focus on the IMM's Treasury bill contract. This calls for the delivery of $1 million face value of bills having 90 days to maturity at the time of delivery. The quotations for the T bill futures contract are presented in Figure 24.10. Prices are quoted according to a system known as the IMM index, which is simply the discount yield on the T bill futures subtracted from 100. For example, the quoted settlement value of 93.86 on the December 1991 contract means that the futures yield would be 6.14 percent. Converting these settlement figures back to yields gives us the values shown as the discount settlement yield in Figure 24.10. To contract for delivery of a 90-day T bill in April 1991 with delivery in December 1991, for example, a trader would have to agree to pay a price that was commensurate with a discount yield of 6.14 percent.

Interest rate futures' yields may be interpreted as forward rates of interest. In the case of the June 1991 T bill futures contract, its yield is the forward rate of interest for a 90-day T bill to run from June to September 1991. In other words, if we calculated from the spot market the forward rate for the same period as that covered by the June 1991 T bill futures contract, we should find a result that closely matches the yield on the T bill futures.

☞ Yields on futures contracts are very similar to forward rates of interest, with the differences stemming mainly from institutional features of the two markets.

If that were not the case, and markets were perfect, it would be possible to generate arbitrage profits by buying and selling spot market T bills and T bill futures to take advantage of the yield discrepancy. In fact, if markets were perfect, including the opportunity for unrestricted short selling, the forward rates of interest and the yield on the futures contract would have to

FIGURE 24.10   Price Quotations for Treasury Bill Futures

TREASURY BILLS (IMM)—$1 mil.; pts. of 100%

	Open	High	Low	Settle	Chg	Discount Settle	Chg	Open Interest
June	94.47	94.56	94.47	94.51	+ .06	5.49	− .06	35,101
Sept	94.31	94.31	94.26	94.29	+ .09	5.71	− .09	7,696
Dec	93.85	93.86	93.82	93.86	+ .09	6.14	− .09	954

Est vol 12,282; vol Thurs 6,721; open int 43,862, +169.

Source: Wall Street Journal, April 15, 1991. Reprinted by permission of Wall Street Journal, © 1991 Dow Jones & Company, Inc. All Rights Reserved Worldwide.

FIGURE 24.11   Observed Differences Between Forward and Futures Yields in the T Bill Market

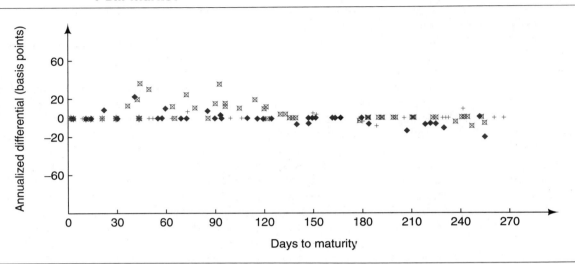

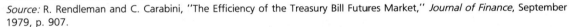

Source: R. Rendleman and C. Carabini, "The Efficiency of the Treasury Bill Futures Market," *Journal of Finance*, September 1979, p. 907.

be exactly equal. However, actual markets are not perfect, so the relationship would not have to hold exactly. If we take into account transaction costs, this still means that the difference between the forward rate of interest calculated from the spot market and the rate of interest implied by the futures contract would have to be very close.

This issue has been examined in great detail by a number of authors, but the definitive study was conducted by Rendleman and Carabini.[7] They attempted to determine the presence of arbitrage opportunities between spot and futures market T bills, given the fact that traders would have to pay transaction costs. One of these costs is the fact that short selling is constrained. These authors found that it cost about one-half of a percentage point, or 50 basis points, to sell a T bill short.[8] This meant that futures yields and forward rates of interest could differ by 50 basis points without giving rise to any arbitrage opportunities.

Using daily data for the years 1976–1978, Rendleman and Carabini tested for the presence of arbitrage opportunities, given the 50 basis point cost of short selling in the T bill futures markets. Figure 24.11 depicts their results

[7] See R. Rendleman and C. Carabini, "The Efficiency of the Treasury Bill Futures Market," *Journal of Finance*, September 1979. Rendleman and Carabini also review much of the previous research on this topic.

[8] Remember that short selling involves borrowing the good that is to be sold short. In this case, the 50 basis points is the charge imposed by the owner for lending the security.

graphically. For all 1,606 observations, a random sample of which are shown, they found that the difference in yields between the forward rate and the futures rate fell within 50 basis points from equality. In other words, there were no arbitrage opportunities, given the existence of transaction costs and the 50 basis point cost of short selling, since all of the points fall within 50 basis points of equality. Also, as the figure shows, most of their observations fell exactly on the line of perfect equality between the forward rate and the futures rate, implying no arbitrage opportunities even if short selling were costless.

SUMMARY

This chapter provided a general introduction to futures markets. We began by distinguishing futures and forward contracts. We then examined the institutional features of futures markets, including the flow of orders, the role of the clearing house, and the fulfillment of commitments in the futures market.

Futures pricing was also explored, and the importance of the basis was noted. Essentially, two models of the relationship between futures prices have wide acceptance. One uses arbitrage concepts to express a cost-of-carry relationship. If this relationship is violated, arbitrage opportunities will exist. The second model asserts that futures prices are equal to expected future spot prices, so market observers can use the futures market as a valuable information source. This price discovery is an important social function of futures markets. In addition, the markets help society by providing a mechanism to allow hedgers to transfer unwanted risk to speculators. Speculators play an important role because their trading activity generates liquidity for the market, and because they are willing to bear risk that is too great for hedgers.

QUESTIONS

1. What are the two major cash flow differences between futures and forward contracts?
2. What problems with forward contracts are resolved by futures contracts?
3. What are the two most important functions of the clearing house in a futures exchange?
4. What is the investment for a trader who buys a futures contract? Justify your answer.
5. What are the two ways to fulfill a futures contract commitment? Which is used more frequently? Why?
6. What is the difference between open interest and trading volume?
7. What is the basis and why is it important?

8. Explain why the futures price might reasonably be thought to equal the expected future spot price.

9. Assume that you believe the futures prices for corn are too low relative to wheat prices. Explain how you could take advantage of this belief.

10. Which is likely to have a greater variance—the basis or the cash price of a good? Why?

11. When hedgers transfer risk away to other traders, what group of traders accepts the risk? Is the risk merely transferred, leaving the total amount unchanged across all traders, or can the amount be reduced? Explain.

12. In previous chapters we noted that an upward-sloping yield curve generally implied that spot interest rates were expected to rise. If this is so, does it also imply that futures prices are expected to rise? Does this suggest a trading strategy? Explain.

13. Assume that you are a bond portfolio manager and that you anticipate an infusion of investable funds in three months. How could you use the futures market to hedge against unexpected changes in interest rates?

14. Assume that the spot corn price is $3.50, that it costs $0.017 to store a bushel of corn for one month, and that the relevant cost of financing is 1 percent per month. If a corn futures contract matures in six months and the current futures price for this contract is $3.95 per bushel, explain how you would respond. Explain your transactions for one contract, assuming 5,000 bushels per contract and assuming that all storage costs must be paid at the outset of the transaction.

The Options Market

option

the right to buy or sell a particular good for a limited time at a specified price

An **option** is the right to buy or sell a particular good for a limited time at a specified price. Its value is obvious. For example, if IBM stock is selling at $120 and an investor has the option to buy a share at $100, this option must be worth at least $20.

This chapter explores the options markets in the United States. Prior to 1973, options of various kinds were traded over the counter, but in 1973 the Chicago Board Options Exchange (CBOE) began trading them on individual stocks. Since that time the options markets have experienced rapid growth, with the creation of new exchanges and many different kinds of contracts. These exchanges trade options on goods ranging from individual stocks and bonds, to foreign currencies, to stock indices, to futures contracts.

These markets are very diverse, and have their own particular jargon. As a consequence, understanding them requires a grasp of the institutional details and terminology employed in the market. The chapter begins with a discussion of the institutional background of options markets, including the kinds of contracts traded and the price quotations for various options.

The successful options trader must also understand the pricing relationships that prevail. For example, how much should an option to buy IBM stock at $100 be worth if IBM is selling at $120? With IBM trading at $120, how much more would an option be worth if it required a payment of only $90? Fortunately, the pricing principles for options are well developed. Although the particular answers to these questions may sometimes be surprising, they are quite logical on reflection.

As in the futures market, much option speculation relies on techniques of spreading. This chapter examines some of the speculative strategies that investors use. However, options are also important for hedging, and their use to control risk is a well-defined area of study. For example, the new options contracts on stock indices have gained wide acceptance among managers as a potential tool for controlling the risk of their equity portfolios.

One of the most recent developments is the trading of options on futures contracts. Obviously, this is a complicated kind of instrument because it involves both options and futures contracts. Nonetheless, it has already received wide acceptance for some contracts.

As a result of the proliferation of these contracts, there are many ways to contract for the same good. This is very clear in the case of foreign currencies. For example, we have already mentioned futures contracts on foreign currencies, such as the deutschemark. There are also options on the marks, and even one on the mark futures contract. The chapter concludes with an exploration of foreign currencies, and an examination of the relationship among futures, options, and options on futures.

CALL AND PUT OPTIONS

call option
the right to buy a particular good at a certain price for a specified period of time

put option
the right to sell a particular good at a certain price for a specified period of time

☞ Ownership of any option gives the owner rights but no obligations. The purchase price of the option is the price paid for those rights.

The two major classes of options are call and put options. A **call option** gives the owner the right to buy a particular good at a certain price, with that right lasting until a particular date. A **put option** gives the owner the right to sell a particular good at a specified price, with that right lasting until a particular date. For every option, there is both a buyer and a seller. In the case of a call option, the seller receives a payment from the buyer and gives to the buyer the option of buying a particular good at a certain price, until a particular date. Similarly, the seller of a put option receives a payment from the buyer, who then has the right to sell a particular good at a certain price for a specified period of time.

In all cases, ownership of an option involves the right, but not the obligation, to make a certain transaction. The owner of a call option may, for example, buy the good at the contracted price during the life of the option, but has no obligation to do so. Similarly, the owner of a put option may sell the good under the terms of the option contract, which commits the seller to specific obligations. The seller receives a payment from the buyer, in exchange for which the seller must be ready to sell the given good to the owner. The discretion to engage in further transactions always lies with the owner of an option. Sellers have no such discretion, but are obligated to perform in certain ways if the owner so desires.

OPTION TERMINOLOGY

writer
the seller of an option

exercise or **striking price**
the price paid when an option is exercised

option premium
the price of an option

expiration date
the time at which an option matures

A great deal of special terminology is associated with the options market. The seller of an option is known as the **writer,** and the act of selling is called writing an option. The owner of the call may take advantage of the option by exercising it; that is, by buying a good under the terms of the option contract. Each contract stipulates the price to pay if the option is exercised; this is the **exercise price,** or **striking price.** In our example of the call option to buy IBM stock at $100 when it is selling at $120, the exercise price would be $100.

The price of the option is the **option premium.** Also, every option traded on an exchange is valid for only a limited period of time. It has no validity after the **expiration date,** or maturity. This terminology is used throughout the rest of this chapter.

OPTIONS EXCHANGES

As shown in Table 25.1, quite a few options exchanges in the United States trade a variety of goods. In many respects, options and futures exchanges are organized similarly. The options market, as the futures market, has a seller for every buyer, and allows offsetting trades. To buy an option, a trader simply has to have an account with a brokerage firm that is a member of the options exchange. The trade can be executed through the broker with the same ease as buying a stock. The buyer of an option pays for it at the time of the trade, so there is no worry about cash flows. For the seller, the matter is somewhat more complicated. The seller agrees to deliver the stock for a set price if the owner of the call so chooses, which means that the seller may require large financial resources. By representing the trader to the exchange, the broker is also obligated to be sure that the trader has the necessary financial resources to fulfill all obligations. For the seller, these obligations are not known at the time the option is sold. Accordingly, the broker must have financial guarantees from option writers. In the case of a call, the writer of an option may already own the shares of stock and deposit these with the broker; this is called a **covered call,** and it gives the broker complete protection, because the shares that are obligated for delivery are already in the possession of the broker. The writer who does not own the underlying stocks has written a **naked option.** In such cases, the broker may require substantial deposits of cash or securities to ensure that the trader has the financial resources necessary to fulfill all obligations.

covered call
a call option written on a good owned by the writer

naked option
a call option written on a good that the writer does not own

TABLE 25.1 U.S. Options Exchanges and Goods Traded

Options Exchange	Goods Traded
Chicago Board Options Exchange	Individual stocks
	General stock market indices
	Treasury bonds
American Exchange	Individual stocks
	General stock market indices
	Oil and gas index
	Oil index
	Transportation index
	Treasury bills
	Treasury notes
Philadelphia Exchange	Individual stocks
	Foreign currencies
	Gold and silver index
Pacific Exchange	Individual stocks
	Technology index
New York Stock Exchange	General stock market indices

Note: This listing does not include options on futures contracts.

☞ Every option can be described by its price, maturity, exercise price, and the good on which it is conferred.

The Option Clearing Corporation (OCC) oversees the conduct of the market and assists in making it orderly. As in the futures market, the buyer and seller of an option have no obligations to a specific individual, only to the OCC. Later, if an option is exercised, the OCC matches buyers and sellers, and oversees the completion of the exercise process, including the delivery of funds and securities.

Management of the exercise and standardization of contract terms are the largest contributions of the OCC. With standardized terms, traders can focus on their trading strategies without having to learn the intricacies of many different contracts. The benefits of the OCC in the marketplace are perhaps clearest in considering option quotations.

OPTION QUOTATIONS

No matter what the exchange or the good underlying the option, the quotations are similar. We will use the quotations for IBM to illustrate the basic features of the prices. Figure 25.1 shows the quotations for call and put options on individual stocks from the *Wall Street Journal*, and Figure 25.2 focuses on the quotations for options on IBM in particular. Options on IBM trade on the CBOE and the quotations pertain to the close of trading on the previous trading day.

Beneath the identifier "IBM," the quotations list the closing stock price for the day, and the second column lists the various strike, or exercise, prices available. The exercise prices are kept fairly near the prevailing price. As the stock price fluctuates, new striking prices are opened for trading at intervals of $5. As a consequence, volatile stocks are likely to have a great range of striking prices available for trading at any one time. Each contract is written on 100 shares, but the prices quoted are on a per share basis. On payment, the owner of the call would have the right to purchase 100 shares of IBM for the exercise price of, say, $100 per share until the expiration date. For the purchaser of the option, the total price to acquire a share of IBM would be the option premium plus the exercise price. The writer would receive the premium as soon as the contract is initiated. However the writer is obligated to sell 100 shares of IBM to the purchaser for $100 per share, if the purchaser chooses to exercise the option.

Obviously, the right to buy IBM at $100 per share is valuable when the market price is above $100. By contrast, we assume there is also a put option traded on IBM, which allows the owner to sell a share for $100. Investors are not willing to pay very much for the right to sell IBM at $100 through an options contract if they could sell it for more than $100 in the marketplace.[1]

---

[1] In the place of some prices, the letters *r* and *s* appear. An *r* indicates that a particular option was not traded on the day being reported. An *s* indicates that no option with those characteristics is available for trading by the exchange.

FIGURE 25.1 Quotations for Options on Individual Stocks

Friday, April 12, 1991

**Options closing prices. Sales unit usually is 100 shares.
Stock close is New York or American exchange final price.**

CHICAGO BOARD

Option & Strike
NY Close Price Calls-Last Puts-Last
Apr May Jun Apr May Jun

Option & Strike		Calls-Last			Puts-Last		
		Apr	May	Jun	Apr	May	Jun
AplMag	10	r	r	r	1/16	r	r
Baybks	15	r	r	2 3/16	7/16	r	1 1/4
	15 1/2	17 1/2	r	r	2	r	r
	15 1/2	20	r	r	r	r	4
BergBr	35	r	5/16	r	r	r	r
Blkbst	10	r	r	r	1/16	5/16	r
	11 3/4	11 1/4	s	s	1 3/8	s	s	r
	11 3/4	12 1/2	3/16	9/16	1 1/16	r	1	1 5/16
	11 3/4	15	r	r	5/16	r	r	3/8
BrMySq	65	s	s	r	s	s	1/4
	79 3/4	70	9 1/4	9 3/4	10 5/8	r	r	7/16
	79 1/4	75	4 1/2	5	6 1/2	1/4	13/16	1 1/4
	79 1/4	80	3/4	2	3 3/8	1 1/2	2 3/4	3 5/8
	79 1/4	85	r	3/4	1 3/8	r	r	r
Bruns	10	r	s	4 5/8	r	s	r
	14 5/8	12 1/2	1 7/8	r	r	r	r	r
	14 5/8	15	3/16	1/2	7/8	7/8	1 1/8	r
ChamIn	25	1 1/8	r	r	r	r	r
CompSc	60	r	r	r	r	r	5/8
	70 1/2	65	r	6 1/2	r	r	r	1 1/2
	70 1/2	70	r	3 3/8	4 1/2	r	r	r
ContBk	12 1/2	r	1	r	r	r	r
CypSem	17 1/2	r	2 5/8	r	r	r	r
	19 7/8	20	1/2	1 1/4	1 3/4	r	s	s
Dow Ch	40	s	s	r	s	s	s
	47 3/8	45	1 5/8	3	3 3/8	1/4	11/16	17/16
	47 3/8	50	1/8	3/4	1 3/4	2 3/4	3 1/2	3 7/8
	47 3/8	55	r	3/8	8 5/8	r	r	r
FtBkSv	17 1/2	1 3/4	r	r	r	r	r
FFB	25	7/16	1 7/8	r	r	r	r
	24 3/4	30	r	1/4	r	r	r	r
Ford	25	6 3/8	s	r	s	s	r
	31 1/2	30	2	2 3/4	3 3/16	11/16	1 3/8	r
	31 1/2	35	1/16	1/4	11/16	3 1/2	4	4 3/8
	31 1/2	40	r	1/16	r	r	r	r
FundAm	65	r	1 1/8	r	r	r	r
Fuqua	10	1 5/8	r	r	r	r	r
	11 1/2	15	r	s	3/8	r	s	r
Gap	35	s	s	24 1/2	s	s	r
	60 7/8	45	14 3/4	r	15 3/4	r	r	1/2
	60 7/8	50	8 1/2	r	12 7/8	r	r	1/2
	60 7/8	55	6 1/8	7 1/2	6 1/4	1/2	1 1/8	1 7/8

				Calls			Puts		
	69	75	r	7/8	2 1/4	r	6 7/8	r
	69	80	r	r	1 1/8	r	r	r
DiaSrk	25	r	r	2	r	r	r
DressB	10	1 1/8	r	r	r	r	r
	11	12 1/2	r	r	11/16	r	r	r
Dryfus	35	r	r	4 3/8	r	r	r
	38 1/4	40	r	1	r	r	r	r
E Kodak	40	1 3/4	2 5/8	3 1/8	1/4	13/16	1 7/16
	41 1/4	45	1/16	7/16	1	3 5/8	3 7/8	4 1/2
Eaton	55	r	r	r	r	1 7/8	r
Elan	35	1/4	r	3	r	r	r
	33 3/4	40	r	r	15/16	r	r	r
Engelh	25	r	1 9/16	2 1/4	r	r	r
Enron	50	6	r	r	r	r	r
	56 1/4	60	r	r	13/16	r	r	r
Everex	5	11/16	s	s	r	s	s
Exxon	50	10	s	9 7/8	r	s	r
	59 3/4	55	5	5 1/8	5 3/8	r	1/4	11/16
	59 3/4	60	9/16	1 3/8	2 3/8	3/4	r	2 3/8
	59 3/4	65	r	1/4	11/16	r	r	r
FedExp	25	r	s	r	r	s	1/2
	33	30	2 5/8	2 7/8	3 7/8	1/4	5/8	1 3/8
	33	35	r	5/8	2	2 3/8	2 3/4	4 1/4
	33	40	r	r	3/4	7 7/8	7 7/8	7 1/2
FstChi	17 1/2	r	s	r	s	s	3/8
	23 1/8	20	r	3 3/8	r	1/4	r	5/8
	23 1/8	22 1/2	1 1/16	1 3/4	r	5/16	1	1 1/2
	23 1/8	25	r	1/2	1 1/8	r	2 3/4	r
FIntste	30	r	r	r	r	r	1 3/4
	33	35	3/8	13/16	2	r	2 9/16	r
	33	40	1/8	s	7/8	r	s	r
Fluor	35	10 1/2	s	r	1/16	s	r
	45 1/4	40	5 3/8	s	r	1	s	r
	45 1/4	45	1 1/8	2 1/4	3 3/4	3/8	1 1/2	2 1/2
	45 1/4	50	1/8	3/4	1 3/16	4 5/8	r	5 1/2
	45 1/4	55	1/16	r	r	r	r	r
GrtWF	15	2 1/2	r	r	r	r	r
	17 1/2	17 1/2	7/16	1	r	r	r	r
Grumm	15	5/8	r	r	r	r	r
	15 3/4	17 1/2	1/16	r	1/2	r	r	r
Halbtn	35	r	s	8 3/4	r	s	3/4
	42 7/8	40	3 1/8	r	4 1/2	r	3/4	1 5/8
	42 7/8	45	3/16	1 1/4	2 1/2	2 5/8	3 5/8	3 7/8
	42 7/8	50	r	7/16	1	r	r	r
	42 7/8	55	r	1/2	r	r	1 3/8	r
Hitachi	90	2 5/8	4 3/4	r	r	r	r
Homfed	5	r	r	9/16	3/4	r	13/16
	4 3/8	7 1/2	r	r	3/16	r	r	r

				Calls			Puts		
	36 1/8	35	15/16	r	r	r	r	r
	36 1/8	40	r	r	r	5 1/2	r	r
LizCla	30	20	s	r	r	s	r
	49 1/2	40	9 1/8	r	r	r	s	r
	49 1/2	45	4 1/8	r	6 3/4	r	1	r
	49 1/2	50	3/4	1 7/8	3 3/8	r	r	r
Loral	35	3 3/4	r	r	r	r	r
	38 5/8	40	r	1 1/8	2	r	r	r
M C I	20	7 3/4	s	r	r	s	r
	27 5/8	22 1/2	5 3/8	5 3/8	r	r	r	r
	27 5/8	25	2 13/16	3 3/8	3 7/8	1/16	1/2	1 1/8
	27 5/8	30	1/16	1/2	1 7/16	2 1/2	3 5/8	r
	27 5/8	35	r	s	3/8	r	s	r
Mead	25	4 3/8	r	r	r	r	r
	29 5/8	30	1/2	r	1 11/16	12 1/16	r	r
	29 5/8	35	r	r	r	6 3/8	r	r
MedCre	45	r	r	r	r	1 1/8	r
Merck	80	28	s	28 1/2	r	s	r
	108 1/2	85	24	s	r	1/16	s	r
	108 1/2	90	19 1/8	s	20	r	s	1/2
	108 1/2	95	14	r	15 5/8	r	r	15/16
	108 1/2	100	8 3/4	r	11 3/4	r	5/8	1 7/8
	108 1/2	105	4 5/8	5 5/8	7 1/4	1/2	1 3/4	3 1/8
	108 1/2	110	1	2 7/8	4 3/4	2	3 3/4	5 5/8
	108 1/2	115	r	1 1/4	3	r	r	r
MGoRnd	25	r	r	7	r	r	r
	31	30	r	2 1/2	3 7/8	r	r	r
	31	35	r	5/8	r	r	r	r
Micron	15	3	r	r	r	r	r
	18	17 1/2	1 1/2	r	r	15/16	r	r
	18	20	1/16	5/8	r	r	r	r
MdwAir	5	r	3/16	r	1 5/8 11/16	r	r
	3 3/8	7 1/2	r	r	4 1/8	r	r	r
M M M	75	13 1/8	s	r	r	s	r
	88 1/8	80	8 1/4	s	r	r	s	r
	88 1/8	85	3 3/4	4 7/8	r	r	1 1/4	2
	88 1/8	90	1/2	17/16	2 7/8	1 3/4	2 7/8	4 5/8
	88 1/8	95	r	1/2	1 3/4	7	6 7/8	7 7/8
MIPS	12 1/2	7	s	r	r	s	r
	20 1/8	15	4 5/8	r	5 1/2	r	r	r
	20 1/8	17 1/2	2 7/16	3 3/8	3 7/8	r	r	r
	20 1/8	20	11/16	1 3/4	r	r	r	r
	20 1/8	22 1/2	s	r	1 3/4	s	3 3/8	r
Molex	30	r	2	r	r	r	r
Monsan	55	3 3/4	r	r	3 1/4	5/16	r
	59	60	1/4	r	2 3/4	2 1/8	r	3 7/8
	59	65	r	r	1 1/8	r	6 7/8	r
NWNL	30	r	1 1/4	r	r	r	r
Nucor	80	r	2 3/4	7	r	r	r
	79 7/8	85	r	1 1/8	r	r	6 3/4	r
PaineW	20	r	4	r	3 7/8	r	r
	23 7/8	22 1/2	1 5/8	1 7/8	2 1/4	r	r	r
	23 7/8	25	1/2	1	1 13/16	r	r	r
Pennz	70	3 1/2	4 1/4	r	r	r	r
	73 5/8	75	1/4	1 1/4	r	r	r	r
Pepsi	20	12 7/8	s	r	s	r	r

				Calls			Puts		
	19 1/2	20	1/8	9/16	1 1/8	r	r	r
	19 1/2	22 1/2	r	3/16	7/16	r	r	r
	19 1/2	25	s	1/16	s	s	r	s
OshK A	40	r	2 3/16	r	r	r	r
Pansph	10	r	2 3/4	3	r	r	r
	12 1/8	12 1/2	r	7/8	r	r	r	r
Pegsus	10	r	1 7/8	r	r	r	3/8
	11 7/8	12 1/2	r	r	r	r	r	7/8
PrecCs	35	r	5 7/8	r	r	r	3/16
	41 1/2	40	1 3/4	27/16	r	r	r	r
Promus	20	r	r	r	r	r	1 5/16
Raythn	75	5 3/4	r	8	r	r	2
	80 7/8	80	1 1/4	3 3/8	3 7/8	1 3/8	r	3 3/4
	80 7/8	85	r	1	2 7/8	r	r	r
Reuter	50	r	1 1/4	3 1/4	r	r	r
Slumb	50	s	r	s	r	s	1
	59	55	r	r	r	1/8	15/16	2 1/2
	59	60	11/16	1 7/8	3 5/8	2 3/4	3 1/4	4 3/4
	59	65	r	2	r	r	r	r
Shell	50	3 1/4	r	r	r	r	r
	53 5/8	55	r	r	2	r	r	r
SestBk	5	7 1/2	1 3/8 11/16	2	r	r	5/16	r
	6 1/4	7 1/2	7/8	1 1/16	1 1/8	r	1 3/4	2
Southn	30	r	r	r	4 1/4	r	r
Tribune	40	r	4 1/4	r	r	r	r
	43 5/8	45	r	1 1/4	2 3/4	r	r	3 3/4
UAL	110	s	42 3/4	r	s	r	r
	153 1/2	115	r	5	r	r	s	r
	153 1/2	120	32 1/2	32	r	r	r	1 1/2
	153 1/2	125	r	28 1/2	r	r	1/4	r
	153 1/2	135	r	19 1/4	22 1/2	r	r	r
	153 1/2	145	12 5/8	15	r	1/2	2 1/2	2
	153 1/2	150	5	r	r	r	s	4 3/4
	153 1/2	155	4	7 3/4	12 1/2	1	5	8 3/4
	153 1/2	160	5/8	3 1/4	10 1/4	3 1/2	6 5/8	r
UST	35	r	11 3/4	r	r	r	r
	46 1/8	40	r	6 1/4	r	r	r	r
	46 1/8	45	r	2 1/16	r	9/16	r	r
U Tech	45	r	4 1/8	r	5/16	7/8	r
	47 3/4	50	1/4	1 1/8	2 1/2	2 1/2	r	r
	47 3/4	55	r	r	r	r	r	r
Willms	30	2 7/8	3 5/8	r	r	r	r
	33	35	1/8	1/2	2	r	r	r
Call vol	313,112	**Open int**	3,316,382				
Put vol	191,067	**Open int**	2,097,930				

AMERICAN

Option & Strike
NY Close Price Calls-Last Puts-Last
Apr May Jun Apr May Jun

Option & Strike		Calls-Last			Puts-Last		
		Apr	May	Jun	Apr	May	Jun
Alcan	20	r	1 5/8	r	r	3/4	r
Amax	25	r	1 3/8	r	1 3/8	1 5/8
	24 7/8	30	r	r	3/8	r	r
AmBrnd	40	2	2 5/8	r	1/8	3/4	r

Source: Wall Street Journal, April 15, 1991. Reprinted by permission of Wall Street Journal, © 1991 Dow Jones & Company, Inc. All Rights Reserved Worldwide.

FIGURE 25.2 Quotations for Options on IBM Stock

I B M	95	r	s	s	1/16	s	s
108 3/8	100	8 5/8	s	11 3/4	3/16	s	2
108 3/8	105	4	5 5/8	7 3/4	1/2	2 1/8	3 5/8
108 3/8	110	13/16	2 3/4	5 1/4 2 3/16	4 1/2	6
108 3/8	115	1/8	1 1/8	3 1/8	6 5/8	7 7/8	9 1/4
108 3/8	120	1/16	7/16 13/16	11	12 1/8	13 1/4
108 3/8	125	1/16	1/4 11/16	16	16 1/2	17 3/4
108 3/8	130	1/16	3/16	5/8	20 3/4	r	22
108 3/8	135	1/16	1/16	7/16	26 1/4	r	27
108 3/8	140	1/16	s	3/8	r	s	r
108 3/8	145	r	s	1/4	r	s	r

Source: Wall Street Journal, April 15, 1991. Reprinted by permission of Wall Street Journal, © 1991 Dow Jones & Company, Inc. All Rights Reserved Worldwide.

☞ The lower the striking price, the higher the option price.

☞ The longer the time to expiration, the higher the option price.

A number of important features about options can be illustrated from the price quotations shown in Figure 25.1. First, for any given expiration, the lower the striking price for a call, the greater will be the price. Similarly, the longer the time to expiration, the higher will be the price. The same relationship holds true for put options. As we will see in the section on option pricing, there are very specific reasons why these kinds of pricing relationships must obtain in the marketplace.

OPTION PRICING

Option pricing affords one of the showcase triumphs of research in modern finance. The pricing models that have been developed for options perform very well and are useful for traders. In fact, traders on the options exchanges have immediate access to the information provided by option pricing models through computers located on the floors of the exchanges.

☞ The option price depends on five factors: the price of the underlying good, exercise price, maturity of the option, volatility of the underlying good, and interest rate.

As we will see, prices of options on stocks that do not pay cash dividends depend on five factors:

Stock price	S
Exercise price	E
Time until expiration	T
The volatility of the underlying stock	σ
The risk-free interest rate	r_f

Initially, it will be useful to consider the effects of just the first three factors; later we consider the more complicated situations that arise from taking into account different interest rate environments and different risk levels.

We can express the price of a call option as a function of the stock price, the exercise price, and the time until expiration using the compact notation $C(S, E, T) =$ option price. For example, the equation

$$C(\$120, \$100, 0.25) = \$22.75$$

says that a call option on a share trading at $120, with an exercise price of $100 and one-fourth of a year to expiration, has a price of $22.75.

Pricing Call Options at Expiration

If an option is not exercised before expiration, it expires immediately and has no value. The value of an option at expiration is important because many of the complications that ordinarily affect its prices disappear when it is about to expire.

With this terminology in mind, let us consider the value of a call option at expiration, when $T = 0$. We want to examine the relationship between the stock price (S) and the option's exercise price (E).

If the stock price is less than or equal to the exercise price ($S \leq E$), the call option is worthless and its owner should throw it away. To see why, consider a call option with an exercise price of $80 on a stock trading at $70. Since the option is about to expire, the owner may exercise it by paying $80, or allow it to expire. The owner then receives a stock trading in the market for $70, which represents a loss of $10. In this case it does not pay to exercise the option and the owner will allow it to expire. Accordingly, this option has no value and its market price will be 0. Employing our notation, we can say:

$$\text{If } S \leq E, \text{ then } C(S, E, 0) = 0$$

If a call option is at expiration and the stock price is less than or equal to the exercise price, the option has no value.

If the stock price exceeds the exercise price ($S > E$) at expiration, the value of the option equals the difference between the prices. The reason is that the owner can make an immediate profit of $S - E$ by paying the exercise price of $$E$ for the stock and selling the stock in the market for $$S$. In our notation we have:

$$\text{If } S > E, \text{ then } C(S, E, 0) = S - E$$

If the stock price exceeds the exercise price, the value of the call option equals the difference between the prices.

If this relationship did not hold, there would be an arbitrage opportunity. Assume for the moment that the stock price is $50 and the exercise price is $40. If the option sells for $5, an arbitrageur would make the following trades:

TRANSACTION	CASH FLOW
Buy a call option	$ −5
Exercise the option	−40
Sell the stock	50
Net cash flow	$ 5

As these transactions show, the arbitrageur will make an immediate profit of $5. Such a situation cannot persist for more than a fleeting moment in a well-functioning market.

If the value of the call option at expiration is greater than the difference between the stock price and the exercise price, there will also be an arbitrage opportunity. Continuing the example of a stock priced at $50 with an exercise price of $40, assume now that the call price is $15. Faced with these prices, an arbitrageur would make the following transactions:

TRANSACTION	CASH FLOW
Sell a call option	$ 15
Buy the stock	−50
Initial cash flow	−$ 35

The owner must immediately exercise this option or allow it to expire. If the owner exercises, these additional transactions take place:

TRANSACTION	CASH FLOW
Deliver stock	$ 0
Collect exercise price	+40
Net cash flow	+$ 5

In this case, the profit is $5. Alternatively, the owner may allow the option to expire. Then the arbitrageur simply sells the stock as soon as the option expires and receives $50, which is the same amount that was paid for the stock. In this case the profit is $15, since the arbitrageur keeps the option premium. Again, such a situation cannot persist in an efficient market.

From reflection on the case in which the stock price is less than or equal to the exercise price and the one in which the stock price exceeds the exercise price, we can state the first basic principle of option pricing:

$$C(S, E, 0) = \max(0, S - E)$$

At expiration, the value of a call option equals 0 or the difference between the stock price and the exercise price, whichever is greater.

This condition must hold to avoid arbitrage opportunities.

☞ At maturity, all options with positive intrinsic value should be exercised.

☞ At maturity, the option's value equals the maximum of the option's intrinsic value, or zero.

Option Values and Profits at Expiration

Consider both a call and a put option, each having a strike price of $100. Figure 25.3 shows their value at expiration for various stock prices. In Part

FIGURE 25.3   Values of Call and Put Options at Expiration When the Striking Price Equals $100

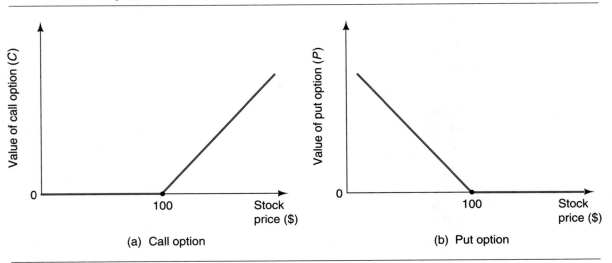

(a) Call option   (b) Put option

FIGURE 25.4   Profits for Call and Put Options at Expiration When the Striking Price Equals $100 and the Premium Is $5

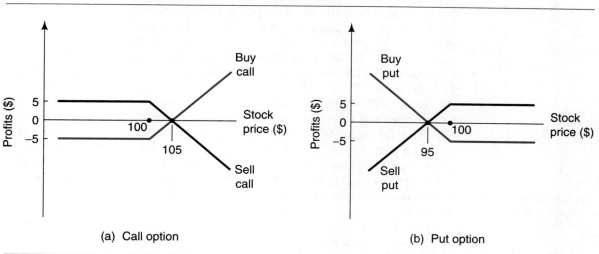

(a) Call option   (b) Put option

(a) the value of the call option is shown on the vertical axis and the stock price is shown on the horizontal axis. If the stock price is less than or equal to the exercise price of $100, the value of the call must be 0, as shown. For stock prices above the exercise price, the call price equals the difference between them. This is reflected by the fact that the graph of the call option's value rises at a 45-degree angle for stock prices above $100. Part (b) shows the same result for a put option. Although we have not discussed the pricing of put options in any detail, the reader can conclude that this is the correct graph by the same kind of argument given for call options.

Consider now the put and call options with exercise prices of $100, but assume that trades had taken place for them with premiums of $5 on both. Knowing that a price of $5 was paid allows us to calculate the profits and losses at expiration for the sellers and buyers. These outcomes are shown in Figure 25.4. Part (a) shows the profit and loss positions for the call option. The colored line pertains to the buyer of the call, and the black line to the seller.[2] For any stock price less than or equal to the exercise price of $100, the option will expire worthless and the purchaser will lose whatever was paid for the call. If the stock price exceeds $100, reaching $105, say, the owner will exercise by paying $100 for the share, receiving in exchange a share worth $105, thus breaking even. The total outflow of $105 is exactly

---

[2] Throughout this chapter, colored lines are used to indicate long positions and black lines short positions.

matched by the receipt of the share. For the owner, any stock price less than $100 results in the loss of the total amount paid for the option. For stock prices greater than the exercise price, the owner will exercise the option. Even then, however, the owner may lose money. In this example the stock price must be greater than $105 to generate any net profit.[3]

For the writer of the call, the profit picture is exactly opposite that of the owner. The best situation for the writer is for the stock price to stay at $100 or below. Then the writer keeps the entire option premium because the option will not be exercised. If the stock price is $105, the option will be exercised and the writer must deliver shares now worth $105 and receive only $100 for them. At this point, the loss on the exercise exactly equals the premium that was already received, so the writer breaks even. If the stock price is greater than $105, the writer will have a net loss. Notice that the buyer's profits exactly mirror the seller's losses, and vice versa, so the options market is a **zero sum game.** If we add up all of the gains and losses, ignoring transaction costs, the total will equal 0.

zero sum game
a game or market in which the total of all profits is zero

Part (b) of Figure 25.4 shows the profit and loss positions for put traders. By paying $5 for a put with an exercise price of $100, the buyer will break even at $95. The writer also breaks even at $95. These graphs indicate the wide variety of possible profit and loss patterns that traders may create using the options market. As we will see, this kind of graph is useful for analyzing a wide variety of market strategies.

Pricing a Call Option with a Zero Exercise Price and Infinite Time Until Expiration

☞ A call option on a stock with zero exercise price and an infinite time to maturity has the same value as the stock.

It may appear superfluous to consider an option with a zero exercise price and an infinite time until expiration, because it would not be traded in the options market. However, it represents an extreme that can be used to set boundaries on possible option prices. An option on a stock that has a zero exercise price and an infinite time to maturity can be surrendered at any time, without any cost, for the stock itself. Since such an option can be transformed into the stock costlessly, it must have a value as great as the stock itself. Also, an option on a good can never be worth more than the good itself. This allows us to state a second principle of option pricing:

$$C(S, 0, \infty) = S$$

A call option with a zero exercise price and an infinite time to maturity must sell for the same price as the stock.

Together, these first two principles allow us to specify the upper and lower bounds for the price of a call option as a function of the stock price,

---

[3] Strictly speaking, we need more than $105 to break even because money has time value. Nevertheless, it is customary to disregard this factor in discussing options.

FIGURE 25.5 Bounds for Call Option Prices

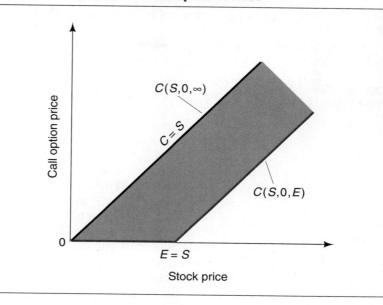

the exercise price, and the time to expiration. These boundaries are shown in Figure 25.5. If the call has a zero exercise price and infinite maturity, the call price must equal the stock price, and this upper bound is shown as the 45-degree line from the origin. Alternatively, if the option is at expiration, its price must lie along the heavy line running from the origin to the point at which the stock price equals the exercise price ($S = E$), and then upward at a 45-degree angle. Options in the real world, such as those with some time remaining until expiration and with positive exercise prices, would have to lie in the shaded region between these two extremes. To further our understanding of option pricing, we have to consider other factors that put tighter restrictions on the permissible amounts.

Relationships Between Option Prices

☞ An option with a lower exercise price than an otherwise identical option must have an equal or higher price to avoid arbitrage opportunities.

Numerous striking prices and expiration dates are available for options on the same stock. It is not a surprise that these prices must bear definite relationships to each other to prevent arbitrage opportunities. The first relationship is that if call options A and B are alike, except the exercise price of A is less than that of B, then the price of option A is equal to or greater than the price of option B:

$$\text{If } E_A < E_B, \text{ then } C(S, E_A, T) \geq C(S, E_B, T)$$

FINANCE TODAY

It's a Bond, It's a Stock, It's . . . a LYON?

Andrew D. Finger laughed the first time a Merrill Lynch & Co. broker tried to sell him a LYON. "I thought somebody had simply thought up a clever acronym," says the Cleveland accountant. But he got serious after doing research on Merrill's Liquid Yield Option Note, a variant on an old-style convertible that promises the guaranteed return of a zero-coupon bond and the potential capital appreciation of a common stock. In the past two years, Finger has put more than $100,000 in 12 LYONs.

Investors such as Finger are making zero convertibles—where the holder buys a bond that can be switched into equity—one of the hottest products on Wall Street. Merrill says that of the $1 billion raised in the largest zero convertible so far—Walt Disney Co.'s LYON in June—60 percent of the securities were gobbled up by 50,000 Merrill individual investors, with the rest bought by 200 institutions. In 1990, investors are expected to buy almost $4 billion worth of zero convertibles, compared with $5.2 billion from 1985 to 1989.

Here's how a zero convertible works: Investors buy the zero-coupon bonds at a large discount from face value. They get zero interest payments until the bonds mature, typically in 15 to 20 years, when the bonds are redeemed at face value. Because they are convertible into stock, LYONs accrue interest at a lower-than-market rate—now about 7.25 percent.

Handsome Fees.   The attraction for investors is that a LYON is convertible into stock at any time. If the stock should shoot up, the LYON suddenly becomes a lot more valuable. In the case of Morrison Knudsen Corp. bonds issued in April, investors paid $343 for one LYON when the stock was trading at $49\frac{1}{8}$. The company gives an investor the right to convert the LYON into 6.2 shares of Morrison Knudsen stock at any time. With the stock trading at $54\frac{3}{8}$ on July 24, the LYON was selling at $380. Indeed, the LYON has risen slightly more than the stock, 10.8 percent vs. 10.7 percent, because interest rates have fallen since April.

In this case the owner of each option may acquire the same share of stock during the same time period. However, the owner of option A may acquire the stock for a lower price than option B. Because of this clear advantage of A over B, A should have a greater value than B. Imagine two options that are alike, except the first has an exercise price of $100 and sells for $10, and the second has an exercise price of $90 and sells for $5. Figure 25.6(a) shows the profit and loss graphs for both. The option with the $90 exercise price

Merrill has underwritten more than $6.5 billion of the $7.5 billion in zero convertibles issued since 1985, and it has registered the term "LYON." But Salomon Brothers Inc. and First Boston Corp. are becoming competitors.

For the brokerage houses, these instruments can mean handsome fees. Disney paid Merrill $23 million. And issuing corporations can raise money from the public at below-market rates and also defer the interest payments for years.

Mauled.   The product isn't universally loved, though. Critics say buyers can be disappointed. "From the issuer's point of view, it's almost a no-lose proposition," says Robert Willens, a senior vice-president of Shearson Lehman Hutton Inc. "The stock has to keep going up at a rapid rate for investors to profit." He points to Du Pont Co.'s issue, where to profit from the equity play, the stock has to grow at a 13 percent compounded rate. If it doesn't go up, all the investor is left with is a below-market interest rate.

Indeed, one LYON has already mauled investors: an early zero convertible sold by Merrill in 1985 for Lomas Financial Corp., which is now in Chapter 11. That LYON has tumbled to $65 from $250.

Merrill's own LYON, also issued in 1985, is an example of how the investor is protected even if the stock falls. While Merrill's stock has declined by 33 percent in the past five years, its LYON has risen from $200 to $291 because Merrill, unlike Lomas, is sure to redeem the bonds at par, $1,000, when they mature in 2006.

The Street has grumbled for years about individuals' reluctance to buy common stocks. But the success of the Street's zero convertibles is proof that innovation plus a little protection can indeed attract the small investor.

Source: Jon Friedman and Larry Lights, "It's a Bond, It's a Stock, It's . . . a LYON?" *Business Week*, August 6, 1990.

has a much better profit and loss profile than the one with the $100 exercise price. No matter what the stock price, *S*, might be at expiration, it will perform better because it will produce a greater profit or suffer a smaller loss.

This price relationship is already an unsustainable result because it represents a disequilibrium in the market. With these prices, all smart traders would want the option with the exercise price of $90 and completely neglect the one with the $100 exercise price. This would cause the price of the latter

FIGURE 25.6   Relationship Between Prices of Options with Different Exercise Prices

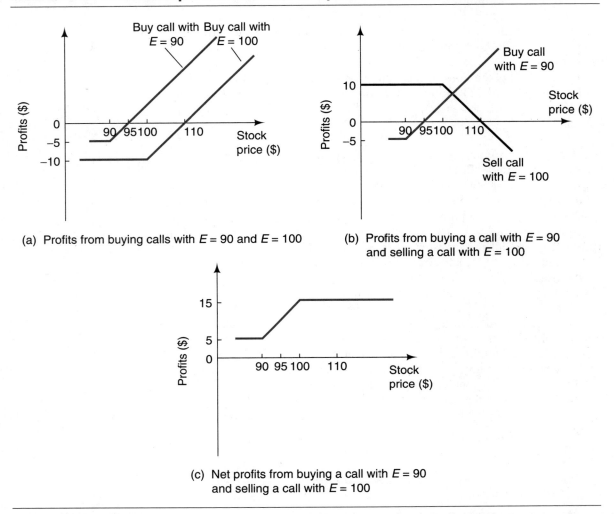

(a) Profits from buying calls with E = 90 and E = 100

(b) Profits from buying a call with E = 90 and selling a call with E = 100

(c) Net profits from buying a call with E = 90 and selling a call with E = 100

to fall until investors were willing to hold it too. We can see that the profit and loss possibilities shown in Figure 25.6(a) create an arbitrage opportunity by transacting as follows:

TRANSACTION	CASH FLOW
Sell the option with the $100 exercise price	$ 10
Buy the option with the $90 exercise price	− 5
Net cash flow	$ 5

TABLE 25.2   Profit or Loss on the Option Position

Stock Price at Expiration	E = $90	E = $100	Both Combined
80	−$5	+$10	+$5
90	−5	10	5
95	0	10	10
100	5	10	15
105	10	5	15
110	15	0	15
120	20	−5	15

The combined position is depicted in Figure 25.6(b), with the sale of the option with the $100 striking price shown by the black line. To see why this is a good transaction, consider the profit and loss position on each option and on the combination of the two for various expiration stock prices, as seen in Table 25.2.

For any stock price, some profit can be made by holding the two options. If the stock price is $90 or less, the profit will be $5 from the combined position, plus the net cash inflow of $5 received when the position was initiated. As the stock price at expiration goes from $90 to $100, the profit rises until it reaches the maximum of $15 at a stock price of $100. For stock prices at expiration above $100, the profit on the options position remains at $15. Figure 25.6(c) presents this result. This does not show the $5 inflow received when the trader entered the position. With the prices in the example, it is possible to trade to guarantee a total cash flow of between $10 and $20, depending on the stock price. We can accomplish this without risk or investment, so it constitutes an example of arbitrage. To eliminate the arbitrage opportunity, the price of the option with a striking price of $90 must be at least as large as the price of the option with the striking price of $100.[4]

A similar principle refers to the expiration date:

$$\text{If } T_A > T_B, \text{ then } C(S, T_A, E) \geq C(S, T_B, E)$$

If call options A and B are alike, except A has a greater time to expiration than B, then option A must sell for an amount equal to or greater than option B. This is true because the option with the longer expiration time gives the investor all the advantages of the one with a shorter expiration. In addition,

---

[4] An interesting result is to be noted here. If the prices are equal, a trader could buy the option with the lower striking price and sell the one with the higher striking price. This strategy would not guarantee a profit, but it cannot lose. Furthermore, in some cases it would pay off. For this reason, options with lower exercise prices almost always sell for higher, not just equal, prices.

the option that expires later gives the investor the chance to wait longer before exercising it. In certain circumstances, that extra time has some value.

If the option with the longer time to expiration sold for less than the one with the shorter time to expiration, it would create an arbitrage opportunity. To see how to conduct the arbitrage, assume that two options with a striking price of $100 are written on the same underlying stock. Let the first one have a time to expiration of six months and assume it has a price of $8. The second has three months to expiration and has a price of $10. The arbitrageur transacts as follows:

TRANSACTION	CASH FLOW
Buy the 6-month option for $8	−$ 8
Sell the 3-month option for $10	+10
Net cash flow	$ 2

By selling the longer-maturity option and buying the shorter-maturity one, the arbitrageur receives a net cash flow of $2. However, this transaction might seem risky if the three-month option is exercised. To see that the arbitrageur's position is secure, assume that the three-month option is exercised. In this case, the arbitrageur can simply exercise the six-month option, receive the underlying stock, and deliver it against the exercised three-month option. This guarantees $2 no matter what the stock price is; therefore, it is an arbitrage profit. Generally, the option with the longer time to expiration will actually be worth more than the one with the shorter time to expiration.

We have already seen that any option must be worth at least the difference between the stock price and the exercise price $(S - E)$ at expiration. If the stock price exceeds the exercise price $(S > E)$, the option is **in the money.** If the stock price is less than the exercise price $(S < E)$, the option is **out of the money.** If the stock price equals the exercise price $(S = E)$, the option is **at the money.** Before expiration, an option in the money generally is worth more than $S - E$. This difference is the **intrinsic value** of the option, the value if it is exercised immediately. Before expiration, we can expect an in the money option to be worth more than $S - E$ because being able to wait to exercise normally has some value. By exercising an option before expiration, the trader receives only the amount $S - E$. By selling the option in the market, the trader will get the market price, which normally exceeds $S - E$. Therefore, it generally does not pay to exercise early.[5]

Thus far we have set bounds for option prices and we have established relationships between pairs of options. In Figure 25.7, options C_1 and C_2 are alike except that C_1 has a lower exercise price. Accordingly, its price is more tightly bound than that of C_2. The two options in the second pair, C_3 and C_4, differ only by the time to expiration. Consistent with this fact, the price of the one with the longer time to expiration, C_3, has a higher price. Although

in the money
a call option with the price of the good exceeding the exercise price

out of the money
a call option with the exercise price exceeding the price of the good

at the money
an option with the price of the good equaling the exercise price

intrinsic value
for a call option, the price of the good minus the exercise price

---

[5] In the case of a dividend-paying stock, this is not always true.

FIGURE 25.7   Bounds on Option Prices and Permissible Relationships Between Pairs of Option Prices

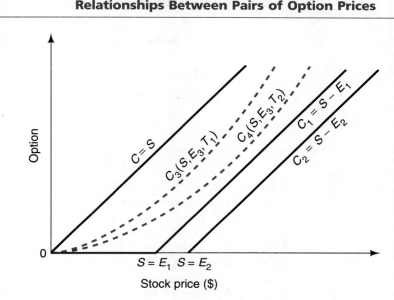

we can now put bounds on the overall price of options and can establish which should have the higher price, we have to be able to put further restrictions on the price of a call option. To do this, we must consider the impact of interest rates.

CALL OPTION PRICES AND INTEREST RATES

Assume that a stock sells for $100 and that over the next year its value can change by 10 percent in either direction. For a round lot of 100 shares, the value one year from now will be either $9,000 or $11,000. Assume also that the risk-free rate of interest is 12 percent, and that a call option exists on this stock with a striking price of $100 per share and an expiration date one year from now. With these facts in mind, imagine two portfolios constructed in the following way:

Portfolio A: 100 shares of stock with a current value of $10,000.
Portfolio B: 1. A $10,000 pure discount bond maturing in one year, with a current value of $8,929, which is consistent with the 12 percent interest rate.
                  2. One option contract, with an exercise price of $100 per share, or $10,000 for the entire contract.

TABLE 25.3   Portfolio Values After One Year

	Stock Price	
	+10%	-10%
Portfolio A		
Stock	$11,000	$ 9,000
Portfolio B		
Maturing bond	10,000	10,000
Call option	1,000	0

Which portfolio is more valuable, and what does this tell us about the price of the call option? In one year the stock price for the round lot will be either $11,000 if the price goes up by 10 percent, or $9,000 if the price goes down by 10 percent. This result is shown for portfolio A in Table 25.3. For portfolio B, we must consider both the bonds and the call option. As is also shown in the table, the bonds will mature in one year and will be worth $10,000 no matter what happens to the stock price. The stock price will have a strong effect on the value of the call option, however. If it goes up by 10 percent, the call option will be worth exactly $1,000, the difference between the stock price and the exercise price $(S - E)$. If the stock price goes down by 10 percent, the option will expire worthless. So if the stock price goes down, portfolio B will be worth $10,000, but if it goes up, B will be worth $11,000.

In this case, portfolio B is clearly the better one to hold. If the stock price goes down, it is worth $1,000 more than A. But if the stock price goes up, A and B have the same value. An investor could never do worse by holding portfolio B, and might have a chance of doing better. Therefore, the value of portfolio B must be at least as great as the value of portfolio A.

☞ The call price must be equal to or greater than the stock price minus the present value of the exercise price.

This tells us something very important about the price of the option. Since portfolio B is sure to perform at least as well as A, it must cost at least as much. Furthermore, we know that the value of A is $10,000, so the price of B must be at least $10,000. The bonds in B cost $8,929, so the option must cost at least $1,071. This means that the value of the call must be worth at least as much as the stock price minus the present value of the exercise price. In our notation, we have:

$$C \geq S - PV(E)$$

If the call did not meet this condition, any investor would prefer to purchase portfolio B rather than portfolio A. Furthermore, there would be an arbitrage opportunity.[6] Previously, we were able to say only that the price of the call

---

[6] The arbitrage transactions would involve buying portfolio B and selling portfolio A short. Assume that the price of the call option is $1,000, and try to work out the transactions and the arbitrage profit that must result.

must be either 0 or $S - E$ at expiration. Based on the reasoning from the example, we can now say that the call price must be greater than or equal to the stock price minus the present value of the exercise price. This substantially tightens the bounds that we can put on the value of a call option.

As the next example indicates, it must also be true that the higher the interest rate, the higher the value of the call option, other things held constant. In the example, the interest rate was 12 percent, and we were able to conclude that the price of the call option must be at least $1,071, because:

$$C \geq \$10,000 - \frac{\$10,000}{1.12} = \$1,071$$

For the same portfolio, imagine that the interest rate had been 20 percent. In that case, the value of the call option must have been at least $1,667, as shown below:

$$C \geq \$10,000 - \frac{\$10,000}{1.20} = \$1,667$$

From this line or reasoning, we can assert the following principle:

$$\text{If } r_{f1} > r_{f2}, \text{ then } C(S, E, T, r_{f1}) > C(S, E, T, r_{f2})$$

☞ The higher the interest rate, the higher the value of a call option.

Other things being equal, the higher the risk-free rate of interest, the greater the price of a call option.

CALL OPTION PRICES AND THE RISKINESS OF STOCKS

Surprisingly enough, the riskier the stock on which a call option is written, the greater will be the value of the option. Consider a stock trading at $10,000 that will experience either a price rise or decline of 10 percent over the next year. As we saw in Table 25.2, a call option on such a stock with an exercise price of $10,000 and a risk-free interest rate of 12 percent would be worth at least $1,071. Now consider a new stock trading at $10,000, that will experience either a 20 percent price increase or decrease over the next year. If we hold the other factors constant by assuming that interest rates are 12 percent per year, and focus on an option with a striking price of $10,000, what can we say about the value of the call option?

As discussed earlier, the call option on the stock that will go up or down by 10 percent must be worth at least $1,071. If the stock price goes down, it will be worth 0. If the stock price goes up, it will be worth $1,000, as shown in the left-hand columns of Table 25.4. In the right-hand columns, the stock will go up or down by 20 percent. If the stock price goes down, the call in this case will be worth 0, the same result as the call in the left-hand columns. If prices go up, the call in the right-hand columns will be worth $2,000, which is the difference between the exercise price and the stock price.

Any investor would prefer the option in the right-hand columns, because it cannot perform worse than the one in the left-hand columns, and it might

TABLE 25.4   Portfolio Values After One Year

	Stock Price			
	+ 10%	*− 10%*	*+ 20%*	*− 20%*
Portfolio A				
Stock	$11,000	$ 9,000	$12,000	$ 8,000
Portfolio B*				
Maturing bond	10,000	10,000	10,000	10,000
Call option	1,000	0	2,000	0

* In Portfolio B, the call option must be worth at least $1,071.

perform better if the stock price goes up. This means that its value must be at least as much as that of the call in the left-hand columns, but it will probably be worth more. The only difference between the two is the risk level of the stock. In the left-hand columns, the stock will move up or down by 10 percent, but the stock in the right-hand columns is riskier, because it will move 20 percent. By reflecting on this example, we can derive the following principle:

☞ The greater the volatility or riskiness of an underlying good, the greater the price of a call option.

$$\text{If } \sigma_1 > \sigma_2, \text{ then } C(S, E, T, r_f, \sigma_1) > C(S, E, T, r_f, \sigma_2)$$

Other things being equal, a call option on a riskier good will be worth at least as much as one on a less risky good.

CALL OPTIONS AS INSURANCE POLICIES

In Table 25.3 the call option will be worth either $1,000 or 0 in one year, and its current value must be at least $1,071. At first glance this is a terrible investment, to pay $1,071 or more for something that will be worth either 0 or $1,000 in a year. However, the option offers more than a simple investment opportunity because it also involves an insurance policy. The insurance character of the option can be seen by comparing the payoffs from portfolios A and B. If the stock price goes down by 10 percent, portfolio A will be worth $9,000 and portfolio B will be worth $10,000. If the stock price goes up by 10 percent, both will be worth $11,000. Holding the option ensures that the worst outcome from the investment will be $10,000. This is considerably safer than holding the stock alone. Under these circumstances it can make good sense to pay $1,071 or more for an option that has a maximum payoff of $1,000, because part of the benefit from holding the option portfolio is the insurance that the total payoff will be at least $10,000. This also explains the fact that the riskier the stock, the more the option will be worth, because the more valuable will be an insurance policy against particularly bad outcomes.

INTERNATIONAL PERSPECTIVES

Options on MYRA

Multiyear restructuring agreements, or MYRAs, are a common way of restructuring the foreign debt of less developed countries (LDCs). Lending banks are now adding option provisions to the restructuring deals. Three major option features are part of many recent agreements: an interest rate option, a currency option, and an option to convert debt into equity. For example, in the 1985 Mexican MYRA, banks were given an interest rate option: they could choose among a variable loan rate based on LIBOR, a variable rate linked to the U.S. six-month certificate of deposit rate, and a fixed loan rate with a comparable yield.

The interest rate option not only gives the lender a choice between two or more interest rates at the time of the restructuring, it also gives him a choice between a fixed or a floating interest rate. Usually, this decision must be made before the first interest payment is to be made.

The currency option usually allows the lender the right to choose between two or more currencies in which to receive loan repayments. Often the lender has the right to switch from the currency in which the loan was made, either into U.S. dollars or back into his own domestic currency. Usually, this option can be exercised at the time the loan was relent as part of the debt restructuring agreement, or on the first interest payment date. In the case of the 1985 Mexican MYRA, non-U.S. banks were given the option of switching at most one-half of their loans into the home country's currency.

The March 1987 rescheduling of loans to the Philippines was a slight variation on the currency option in that it included an equity conversion option. In this plan, the country hoped to fund part of its interest payments by persuading lenders to accept foreign currency notes in lieu of interest payments. These notes, denominated in non-Philippine currencies and sold at a price well below face value, could be redeemed at any time during their six-year life for their full face value in Philippine pesos. If converted, the pesos could then be used to buy government-approved equity investments.

In a few equity conversion options, such as the one used by Chile, lenders are allowed to convert their debts directly into local currency at full face value—even if such debt has been bought at a discount. These loans denominated in local currency may then be sold or exchanged for equity.

Although valuing these options is highly technical, the basic intuition is quite simple. The main determinant of value in all options is the volatility of the underlying variable. The higher the volatility, the higher the value of the option.

Source: Anthony Saunders and Marti Subrahmanyam, "LDC Debt Rescheduling: Calculating Who Gains, Who Loses," *Federal Reserve Bank of Philadelphia, Business Review,* November/December 1988, pp. 13–23.

Previously, we said that the price of the option must be at least as great as the stock price minus the present value of the exercise price. However, this formulation neglects the value of the insurance policy. If we take that into account, we can say that the value of the option must be equal to the stock price minus the exercise price, plus the value of the insurance policy. Or, if the value of the insurance policy is denoted by I, the value of the call option is given by:

$$C(S, E, T, r_f, \sigma) = S - PV(E) + I$$

However, thus far we have no way of putting a numerical value on the insurance policy, I. That task requires an examination of the option pricing model.

THE BLACK-SCHOLES OPTION PRICING MODEL

To this point, by reasoning about option prices and finding their boundaries, we have learned a great deal about them and their relationship to other variables. In the preceding discussion we identified five variables that affect the value of a call option. In the following list, a plus sign by a variable indicates that the price increases as the value of the associated variable increases:

+	Stock price	S
−	Exercise price	E
+	Time to expiration	T
+	Risk-free interest rate	r_f
+	Variability of the stock's returns	σ

We now know the basic factors that affect the prices of call options and the direction of their influence, but we still have a great deal to learn. For example, in exploring the bounds of option pricing we considered an example in which the stock price could move up or down by 10 percent in a year. This is obviously a great simplification of reality. In a given period of time, stock prices can take on a virtually infinite number of values. Also, stock prices change continuously for all practical purposes. To be able to put an exact price on a call option requires a much more realistic model of stock price behavior.

This is exactly the approach that was taken by Fischer Black and Myron Scholes as they developed the option pricing model (OPM).[7] Strictly speaking, their model applies to European options on nondividend-paying stocks, but it can be adjusted to deal with other cases.[8] The mathematics are complex,

[7] See Fischer Black and Myron Scholes, "The Pricing of Options and Corporate Liabilities," *Journal of Political Economy*, Vol. 81, No. 3 (May–June 1973), pp. 637–654.

[8] These adjustments and further developments of the OPM are beyond the scope of this text. The interested student should see Robert A. Jarrow and Andrew Rudd, *Option Pricing* (Homewood, Ill.: Richard D. Irwin, 1983), for a complete exposition of these and other developments.

FIGURE 25.8   One Possible Realization of a Wiener Process

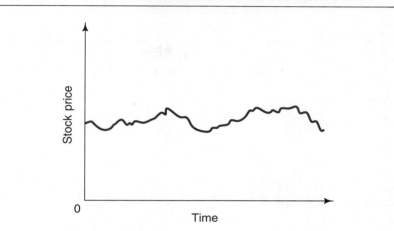

but the authors were able to derive their model by assuming that stock prices follow a path through time called a stochastic process. A **stochastic process** is a mathematical description of the change in the value of some variable through time. The particular one used by Black and Scholes is known as a Wiener process. The key features of the Wiener process are that the variable changes continuously through time, and the changes that it might make over any given interval are distributed normally. Figure 25.8 shows a graph of the path that stock prices might follow if they conform to a Wiener process.

Black and Scholes presented an explicit formula for the price of a call option. If we know the values of the five variables listed above, we can use the OPM to calculate the theoretical price of an option. Furthermore, whereas we cannot deal with the mathematics here, we can understand how to calculate option values, and the relationship between the OPM and the conclusions we reached in previous sections.

The formula for the Black-Scholes OPM is:

$$C = S \times N(d_1) - E \times e^{-r_f T} \times N(d_2)$$

where $$d_1 = \frac{\ln\left(\dfrac{S}{E}\right) + \left(r_f + \dfrac{\sigma^2}{2}\right)T}{\sigma\sqrt{T}}$$

$$d_2 = d_1 - \sigma\sqrt{T}$$

and $N(d_1)$ and $N(d_2)$ are the cumulative normal probability values corresponding to d_1 and d_2, respectively.

stochastic process
the mathematical description of the change in some variable through time

☞ The Black-Scholes option model assumes that stock prices follow a Wiener process and that arbitrage opportunities cannot exist.

☞ In spite of its apparent complications, the Black-Scholes option pricing model has received widespread use among investment professionals.

The most difficult part of this formula to understand is the use of the normal cumulative probability function. However, this is exactly the part of the OPM that takes account of the risk and allows it to give such good results for option prices. The best way to understand the application is with an example. Let us assume values for the five parameters and calculate the Black-Scholes value for an option. Assume the following:

$$S = \$100$$
$$E = \$100$$
$$T = \text{one year}$$
$$r_f = 12 \text{ percent}$$
$$\sigma = 10 \text{ percent}$$

The first task is to calculate values for d_1 and d_2:

$$d_1 = \frac{\ln\left(\frac{100}{100}\right) + \left(0.12 + \frac{0.01}{2}\right)^1}{0.1 \times 1} = 1.25$$

$$d_2 = 1.25 - 0.1 \times 1 = 1.15$$

The next step is to calculate the cumulative normal probability values of these two results. These values are the z-scores taken from the standard normal probability distribution shown in Figure 25.9. In this graph the two values of interest, 1.15 and 1.25, are shown. In calculating the cumulative normal probability values of $d_1 = 1.25$ and $d_2 = 1.15$, we simply have to determine the proportion of the area under the curve that lies to the left of the value in question. For example, if we were interested in a z-score of 0.00, we would know that 50 percent of the area under the normal curve lies to the left, because the normal probability distribution is symmetrical about its mean, and we know that the z-scores are standardized so that they have a mean of 0.00.

Because the standardized normal probability distribution is so important and so widely used, tables of its values are included in virtually every statistics textbook. A table of z-scores is found in the appendix. Using this table, we note that the probability of drawing a value from the standard normal distribution that is less than or equal to $d_1 = 1.25$ is 0.8944, so the two values we seek are:

$$N(d_1) = N(1.25) = 0.8944$$
$$N(d_2) = N(1.15) = 0.8749$$

Returning to the OPM, we can now make the final calculation:

$$C = \$100 \times (0.8944) - \$100 \times e^{-0.12 \times 1} \times (0.8749) = \$11.84$$

So, according to the OPM, the call option in this case should be worth $11.84. The value of this option using the OPM corresponds very closely to our

FIGURE 25.9   The Standard Normal Probability Function

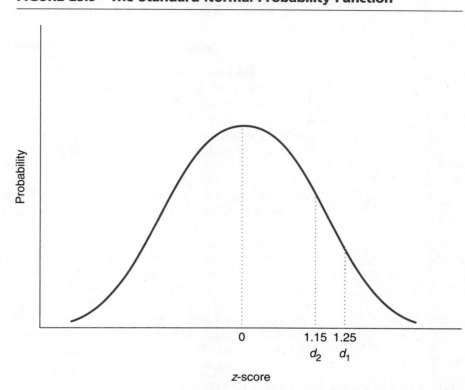

earlier example from Table 25.2. There we concluded that an option with similar characteristics must be worth at least $10.71. The result from the OPM is more precise, however. The difference between its value of $11.84 and the minimum of $10.71 is due to the value of the insurance policy that we were unable to pinpoint without the sophisticated approach of the OPM.[9]

Also, it should be clear that the OPM is very close to the result that we reached by just a process of reasoning. We were able to conclude that:

$$C = S - PV(E) + I$$

and the OPM says that

$$C = SN(d_1) - Ee^{-r_f T}N(d_2)$$

---

[9] Actually, part of the difference is due to the discounting method. Had our example used continuous discounting at 12 percent, we would have found that the value of the option had to be at least as great as $100 − $100(0.8869) = $11.31. This is much closer to the OPM value of $11.84.

The second term is simply the present value of the exercise price when continuous discounting is used, times $N(d_2)$. This means that the OPM can be written:

$$C = SN(d_1) - PV(E)N(d_2)$$

The terms involving the cumulative probability function are the terms that take account of risk. Coupled with the rest of the formula, they capture the value of the insurance policy. If the stock involved no risk, the calculated values for d_1 and d_2 would be very large (in fact, infinite) and then the calculated cumulative functions would both approach a value of 1. If $N(d_1)$ and $N(d_2)$ both equal 1, the OPM could be simplified to:

$$C = S - PV(E)$$

This is very close to the result we were able to reach without the OPM. However, it does not reflect the value of the insurance policy embedded in the option.

On first acquaintance with the OPM, many people think that it is too complicated to be useful. Nothing could be further from the truth. Of all of the models in finance, it is among those receiving the widest acceptance by actual investors. For example, machines on the floor of the CBOE give traders OPM prices for all options using instantaneously updated information on all of the parameters. Finally, the model has achieved such widespread acceptance that some manufacturers have even made special modules to allow their calculators to find OPM values automatically.

THE VALUATION OF PUT OPTIONS

put-call parity
the relationship between prices of put and call options on the same good

☞ By relating the price of a put to the price of a call through put-call parity, it is possible to find the value of a put option.

Although the OPM pertains specifically to call options, it can also be used to price put options through the principle of **put-call parity.**[10] Assume that an investor makes the following transactions:

Buy one share of stock: $S = \$100$.
Buy one put option with price $P = ?$, $E = \$100$, and $T =$ one year.
Sell one call option with price $C = \$11.84$, $E = \$100$, and $T =$ one year.

Assume also that the put and call options have the same underlying stock.

At expiration, the stock price could have many different values, some of which are shown in Table 25.5. The interesting feature about this portfolio is that its value will be the same, $\$100 = E$, no matter what the stock price is at expiration. This can be confirmed by examining Figure 25.10. Figure 25.10(a–c) shows the value of the short position in the call, the put, and the share of stock. In Figure 25.10(d) all of these instruments are aggregated, and the value of the entire portfolio is shown. Consistent with Table 25.5, no

[10] The put-call parity relationship was first derived by Hans Stoll, "The Relationship Between Put and Call Option Prices," *Journal of Finance*, December 1969, pp. 802–824.

TABLE 25.5   Possible Outcomes for Put-Call Parity Portfolio

Stock Price	Call Value	Put Value	Portfolio Value
$ 80	$ 0	$20	$100
90	0	10	100
100	0	0	100
110	− 10	0	100
120	− 20	0	100

matter what the stock price at expiration might be, the value of the entire portfolio will be $100 = E$. Holding these three instruments in the way indicated gives a risk-free investment that will pay $100 = E$ at expiration, so the value of the whole portfolio must equal the present value of the riskless payoff at expiration. This means that we have:

$$S - C + P = \frac{E}{(1 + r_f)^T}$$

FIGURE 25.10   The Put-Call Parity Values at Expiration

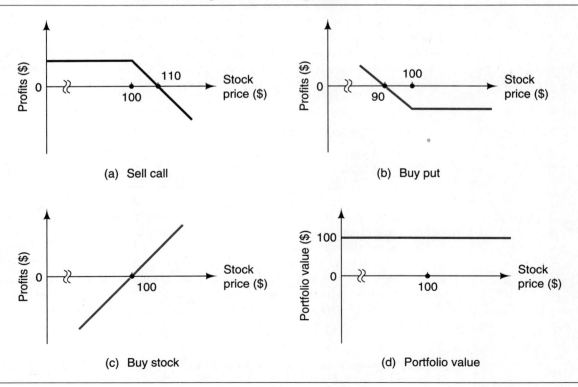

(a) Sell call

(b) Buy put

(c) Buy stock

(d) Portfolio value

The value of the put-call portfolio equals the present value of the exercise price discounted at the risk-free rate.

Since it is possible to know all of the other values, except for the price of the put, P, we can use this put-call parity relationship to calculate P. To see how this is done, let us assume as before that $r_f = 12$ percent and that the call value is $11.84, in accordance with the OPM. Rearranging the put-call parity formula gives the following:

$$P = \frac{E}{(1 + r_f)^T} - S + C$$

$$P = \frac{\$100}{1.12} - \$100 - \$11.84 = \$1.13$$

Under these circumstances, the put should be worth $1.13.

SPECULATING WITH OPTIONS

Many traders are attracted to the market by the exciting speculative opportunities of options. Relative to stocks, they offer a great deal of leverage. A given percentage change in the stock price will cause a great percentage change in the price of the option.

In our example of the option worth $11.84, consider the effect of a sudden 1 percent change in the price of the stock. If the stock price changes by 1 percent, the option price will change by 7.52 percent in the same direction. The call values shown below were calculated from the Black-Scholes formula, assuming that only the stock price had changed as indicated.

Original Values	1% Stock Price Increase	1% Stock Price Decrease
$S = \$100$	$S = \$101$	$S = \$99$
$C = \$11.84$	$C = \$12.73$	$C = \$10.95$

This leverage means that options can give investors much more price action for a given investment than simply holding the stock. Unfortunately, it also means that options can be much riskier than holding stock. Although they can be risky as investments, they need not be. In fact, they can be used to take very low-risk positions by using them in combinations. The possible combinations are virtually endless, including strips, straps, spreads, and straddles. To give an idea of the possibilities, we will consider a straddle.[11]

---

[11] For a discussion of these trading strategies, see Richard Bookstaber, *Option Pricing and Strategies in Investing* (Reading, Mass.: Addison-Wesley, 1981), Chapters 7–9.

TABLE 25.6 Payoffs for Calls, Puts, and a Straddle at Expiration

Stock Price at Expiration	Call Profit/Loss	Put Profit/Loss	Straddle Profit/Loss
$ 50	−$10	$43	$33
80	−10	13	3
83	−10	10	0
85	−10	8	−2
90	−10	3	−7
95	−10	−2	−12
100	−10	−7	−17
105	−5	−7	−12
110	0	−7	−7
115	5	−7	−2
117	7	−7	0
120	10	−7	3
150	40	−7	33

Note: Profit/loss figures reflect the amount paid for the instruments: call = $10; put = $7; straddle = call + put = $17.

Option Speculating with Straddles

straddle
the position consisting of a put and call option on the same good

A **straddle** is a position involving a put and a call option on the same stock. To buy a straddle, an investor purchases both. Consider a put and a call option and assume that both have an exercise price of $100. Assume further that the call sells for $10 and the put for $7. Table 25.6 shows the profits and losses for the call, the put, and the straddle as a function of the stock price at expiration. If the stock price equals the exercise price at expiration, both the put and the call expire worthless, and the loss on the straddle is $17, the entire premium paid for the position.

☞ For any anticipated stock movement, it is possible to devise an option strategy that will be profitable if that stock price movement occurs.

Any movement in the stock price away from $100 at expiration gives a better result. In fact, the value of the straddle increases $1 for every $1 movement away from $100 in the stock price at expiration. The straddle position breaks even if the stock price either rises to $117 or falls to $83. In other words, a $17 price movement away from the exercise price at expiration will cover the initial investment of $17. If the price of the stock differs greatly from the exercise price, there is an opportunity for substantial profit.

To view these possible results graphically, see Figure 25.11(a and b), which shows the profits and losses for the call and put, respectively. The profits and losses for buying the straddle position are shown in Figure 25.11(c) by the colored line. As this graph makes clear, the purchaser of a straddle is betting that the price of the stock will move dramatically away from the exercise price of $100, and will profit if the stock price goes above $117 or below $83. Figure 25.11(c) also shows the profit and loss position for the seller of a straddle with the black lines. The seller will profit if the stock price at

FIGURE 25.11 Put, Call, and Straddle Profits and Losses

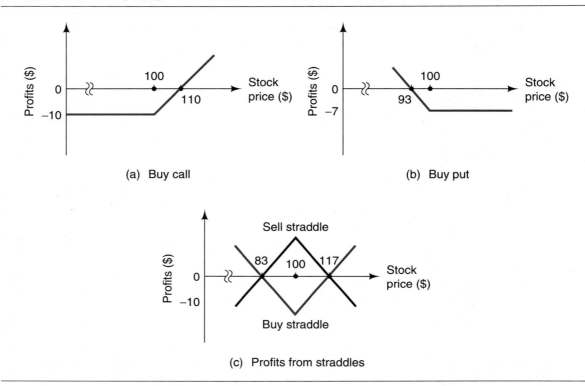

(a) Buy call

(b) Buy put

(c) Profits from straddles

expiration lies between $83 and $117. Obviously, the purchaser would be making a bet on a large movement in the stock price in some direction, while the seller would be betting that it remains reasonably close to the exercise price of $100. By using different combinations of long and short positions in call and put options, it is possible to construct an option portfolio with almost any imaginable set of payoffs.

HEDGING WITH OPTIONS

☞ In addition to speculating, options are useful for controlling the risk of a preexisting position through hedging.

As we saw with futures, very risky financial instruments can be used to control risk. One of the most important applications of options is their use as a hedging vehicle. Once again, the OPM gives important insights into this process.

To illustrate, let us use our original example of a stock selling at $100 and having a standard deviation of 10 percent. We saw that a call option with an exercise price of $100 and a time to expiration of one year would sell for $11.84. We also saw that a sudden 1 percent price rise in the stock from $100 to $101 would drive the price to $12.73. If the stock price and the option

TABLE 25.7   A Hedged Portfolio

	Original Portfolio *S = $100; C = $11.84*	*Stock Price Rises by 1%* *S = $101; C = 12.73*	*Stock Price Falls by 1%* *S = $99; C = $10.95*
8,944 shares of stock	$ 894,400	$ 903,344	$ 885,456
A short position for options on 10,000 shares (100 contracts)	− 118,400	− 127,300	− 109,500
Total value	**$ 776,000**	**$ 776,004**	**$ 775,956**

price are so intimately related, it should be possible to use options to offset the risk inherent in the stock.

This possibility is shown in Table 25.7. Consider an original portfolio comprised of 8,944 shares of stock selling at $100 per share, and assume that a trader sells 100 call option contracts, or options on 10,000 shares, at $11.84 each. In the table, this short position in the option is indicated by a minus sign. That entire portfolio would have a value of $776,000. Now consider the effect of a 1 percent change in the price of the stock to $101. The shares will be worth $903,344, and the option price will increase from $11.84 to $12.73. But this portfolio involves a short position in 10,000 options, so this creates a loss of $8,900. After these two effects are taken into account, the value of the whole portfolio will be $776,044. This is virtually identical to the original value.

On the other hand, if the stock price falls by 1 percent, the loss on the stock will be $8,944. The price of the option will fall from $11.84 to $10.95, and thus the entire drop in price for the 10,000 options will be $8,900. Taking both of these effects into account, the portfolio will then be worth $775,956. As this example indicates, the overall value of the portfolio will not change no matter what happens to the stock price. If the stock price increases, there is an offsetting loss on the option. If it falls, there will be an offsetting gain on the option.

☞ The Black-Scholes option pricing model indicates the exact option position to hold in conjunction with a stock to give a perfect hedge.

In this example, holding 0.8944 shares of stock for each option sold short will give a perfect hedge. The value of the entire portfolio will be insensitive to any change in the stock price. How can we know exactly the right number of options to trade to give this result? The careful reader might recall the number 0.8944. When the value of this call option was calculated, we saw that $N(d_1) = 0.8944$. This value gives the appropriate hedge ratio to construct a perfect hedge, and the principle can be summarized by the following rule: A portfolio comprised of a short position of one option and a long position of $N(d_1)$ shares of the stock will have a total value that will not fluctuate as the share price fluctuates. Alternatively, to hedge a long position of one share in a stock, sell a number of options equal to $1/N(d_1)$. This hedge will hold for infinitesimal changes in the stock price. In the preceding example, the hedge was not quite perfect because the change in the stock price was sizable.

Actually, the value of the portfolio fluctuates by only 0.0057 percent. Also, a change in the stock price will change the value of $N(d_1)$ because d_1 will change. This means that the hedge must be adjusted as the stock price changes, if it is to be kept perfect.

SUMMARY

This chapter presented an overview of options markets in the United States. Option trading on organized exchanges began in 1973 with the introduction of options on individual stocks. Since that time, options markets have expanded greatly, with options on metals, stock and other indices, foreign currencies, and futures contracts.

Options can be classified as put or call. Ownership of a call confers the right to buy a given good at a specified price for a specified period of time. Selling a call confers those same rights to the owner in exchange for a payment from the purchaser. Ownership of a put permits the sale of a good at a specified price for a specified period of time. Selling a put gives those rights to the buyer in exchange for a payment.

Starting merely from the assumption that options should be priced in a way that allows no arbitrage opportunities, it is possible to bound option prices very closely. It can be shown using the no-arbitrage condition that call option prices are a function of five variables: stock price, exercise price of the option, time to expiration, interest rate, and risk level of the good underlying the option. In addition, Black and Scholes developed a model that gives an exact price for a call option as a function of those variables. Although their model is theoretical, it has been shown to accord very well with actual option prices.

Options are useful financial instruments for both speculation and hedging. For example, an investor expecting a stock price to increase can profit from being correct by buying a call or selling a put on that stock. Furthermore, by speculating with options, it is possible to achieve more leverage than by merely trading the stock itself. Options are useful for controlling risk as well, because the careful combination of options and positions in the underlying good can give virtually any degree of risk that is desired. Combinations of options themselves widen the range of payoff possibilities available to the investor.

QUESTIONS

1. Respond to the following claim: Buying a call option is very dangerous because it commits the owner to purchasing a stock at a later date, and at that time the stock may be undesirable.
2. Comment on this claim: Buying a call option gives the right to acquire a stock, and selling a put option means that you may buy a stock as well. Therefore the two are the same.

3. Explain the difference between the option premium and the striking price.
4. On what five factors does the value of a call option depend?
5. On what factors does the value of an option at expiration depend?
6. Why should call options be worth more the lower the exercise price?
7. Why should options be priced in a way to eliminate arbitrage opportunities?
8. I bought a call option with an exercise price of $110 on IBM when IBM was at $108, and I paid $6 per share for the option. Now the option is about to expire and IBM is trading at $112. There's no point in exercising the option, because I will wind up paying a total of $116 for the shares—$6 I already spent for the option plus the $110 exercise price. Is this line of reasoning correct? Explain.
9. Why is the option market a zero sum game?
10. Why does the value of a call option increase with interest rates?
11. Why does the value of a call option increase with the volatility of the underlying good?
12. Why is the value of a call option at expiration equal to the maximum of zero or the stock price minus the exercise price?
13. Explain how a call option includes an insurance policy.
14. Two call options are identical except that they are written on two different stocks with different risk levels. Which one will be worth more? Why?

PROBLEMS

1. What is the value of a call option on a share of stock if its exercise price is $0 and its expiration date is infinite? Explain.
2. A call option is at expiration and has a striking price of $100. The stock on which it is written has a market value of $103. Assume that you paid $5 for the option. What is its value? Should you exercise? What is your profit or loss on the entire transaction if you do not exercise? If you do exercise?
3. A call option is at expiration and has a striking price of $80. The stock on which it is written has a market value of $75. Assume that you paid $8 for the option. What is its value? Should you exercise? What is your profit or loss on the entire transaction if you do not exercise? If you do exercise?
4. Two call options on the same stock have the following features. The first has an exercise price of $60, a time to expiration of three months, and a premium of $5. The second has an exercise price of $60, a time to expiration of six months, and a premium of $4. What should you do? Explain exactly, assuming that you transact for just one option. What is your profit or loss at the expiration of the nearby option if the stock is at $55, $60, or $65?

5. Assume the following: A stock is selling for $100, a call option on the stock with an exercise price of $90 is trading for $6 and matures in one month, and the interest rate is 1 percent per month. What should you do? Explain your transactions.

6. Two call options on the same stock expire in two months. One has an exercise price of $55 and a price of $5. The other has an exercise price of $50 and a price of $4. What transactions would you make to exploit this situation?

7. Option A has an exercise price of E_a, and the price of the underlying stock is S_a. The two corresponding values for option B are 10 percent greater than for option A. In all other respects, the two options are identical. According to the Black-Scholes model, how are their prices related? (For example, the price of option A might be twice that of option B.)

8. In the chapter we argued that the price of a call option with infinite maturity and zero exercise price must be equal to the stock price ($C = S$). Using the Black-Scholes model, show that $C = S$ even if the exercise price is not zero.

9. In the chapter we argued that the price of a call option at expiration should equal the difference between the stock price (S) and the exercise price (E), whenever $S > E$. Show this result using the Black-Scholes model.

10. Suppose the exercise price of a call option is set so that $E = S \times exp(r_f T_0)$, where T_0 is the time to maturity when the option is written, and $exp(x) \equiv e^x$. Using the Black-Scholes model, show that the original price of this option must equal $[2N(d_1) - 1]$ percent of the price of the underlying stock.

11. If the stock underlying a call option is sure to maintain its price over the life of the option, how much is the option worth?

Risk Management Using Futures and Options

Ｔhis chapter extends the discussion begun in Chapters 24 and 25 by treating futures and options as risk management tools. In the two preceding chapters we discussed basic hedging for futures and options; this chapter explores the concept in more detail. First, we analyze the use of the futures market for hedging. Futures are extremely useful in managing risk. We develop two methods for establishing a futures hedge and track their results in fairly realistic examples. Our discussion assumes that the goal is to reduce risk as much as possible.

When options are combined with other financial instruments or with other options, it is possible to change the payoff characteristics of investments dramatically. Our discussion shows exactly how different payoff patterns can be achieved and how they translate into different distributions of returns for the investment.

The chapter concludes by extending option concepts to develop an understanding of other kinds of instruments that corporations offer. For example, we will see that the common stock of the firm has important dimensions that make it act like a call option, that corporate bonds have a payoff pattern like a short position in a put option, and that convertible bonds behave like a combined short put and long call.

HEDGING WITH FUTURES

☞ The portfolio approach to hedging attempts to reduce risk by forming a portfolio of a risky position in the cash good and a risky position in the futures contract.

In this section we explore the use of futures to reduce risk by hedging agricultural commodities using the portfolio approach, which is one of the most highly respected techniques for hedging risk in many commodities. It is based on a stable relationship for commodities between the prices of the cash good and the price of the futures contract. The risk is reduced by forming a portfolio of a risky position in both the cash good and the futures contract.

Assume an owner operates a mill for crushing soybeans to obtain soybean oil, a prime ingredient in salad dressings and many other foodstuffs. The miller already has a supply of beans on hand that will be crushed during the next month, but the price to be received for the oil is uncertain. The miller wishes to use the futures market to hedge the risk of that uncertain future price.

713

FIGURE 26.1   Soybean Oil Prices During October

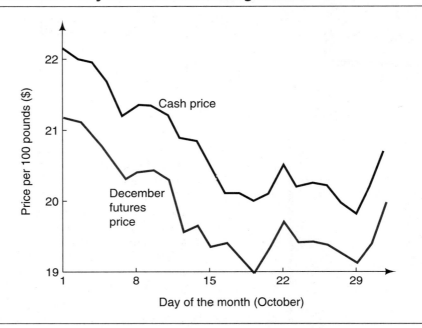

The Chicago Board of Trade trades a contract for soybean oil calling for the delivery of 60,000 pounds at a price quoted in dollars per 100 pounds. Assume that today is November 1 and the miller expects to have 1.5 million pounds of soybean oil ready to sell at the end of the month. The price of the oil today is $20.73, but the miller is not sure what it will be at the time of delivery. Accordingly, the miller decides to use the futures market to ensure a price today for the delivery of the oil at the end of the month.

On November 1 the December soy oil futures contract trades at $20.15, so the miller faces these prices:

December futures	$20.15
Cash	20.73
Basis (cash − futures)	0.58

This situation is somewhat unusual, with the futures price lying below the cash price, but prices have been falling recently. The graph of Figure 26.1 shows daily prices for soy oil and the daily prices for December soy oil futures during October. Notice the close relationship between the cash price and the futures price. As a result of this correlation, the basis has been quite stable, fluctuating around $1.5 to $0.75 per 100 pounds, as shown in Figure 26.2.

The miller, being a producer, can establish the future price of the soybean oil by selling the futures contract. Accordingly, with 1.5 million pounds, it might seem that the miller should sell 25 (1,500,000 pounds/60,000 pounds

FIGURE 26.2   Soybean Oil Basis in October

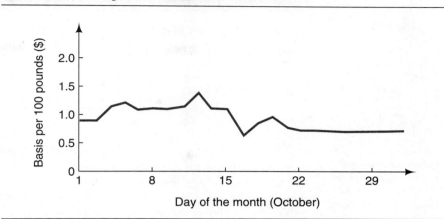

per contract) December contracts. In executing these transactions, the miller sells one pound in the futures market for each pound of oil that will be produced. However, this is not always the best strategy, particularly if the hedger wishes to minimize risk, measured by the variance of changes in the cash position. For example, what if the futures were more volatile than the cash price? The futures price might move $1.25 for each $1.00 move in the cash price. If so, 25 futures contracts would be too many.

Techniques have been developed for minimizing the risk exposure. By selling the futures contract against the oil that is being produced, the miller has essentially a two-asset portfolio. To make matters simpler, assume that there is only one pound of oil and the futures contract is for one pound of oil as well. The problem then is to choose the number of futures contracts, b, to minimize the risk exposure. In this case the portfolio consists of:

Long 1 pound of oil
Short b futures contracts

The miller's problem is to choose b to minimize the variance of the portfolio. It can be shown using linear regression analysis that the correct b to choose, b^*, is given by the following regression:

$$\text{Spot} = \alpha + b^* \times \text{futures} + \varepsilon$$

This is the correct hedge ratio in this model because it is the one that minimizes the risk as measured by the variance.

The miller uses the data shown in Figure 26.1 and performs the regression, finding:

$$\alpha = -0.018$$
$$b^* = -0.836$$
$$R^2 = 0.775$$

TABLE 26.1   The Miller's Position on November 1

Cash Market	Futures Market
Anticipates having 1.5 million pounds of soy oil by month's end	Sells 21 December soy oil contracts at $20.15
Current price: $20.73	

☞ In the portfolio approach to hedging, the investor finds the hedge ratio that minimizes the variance of the combined cash good and futures contract position.

These regression results indicate that the miller should sell 0.836 futures units for each unit of the spot commodity in order to minimize risk. Notice that the negative sign for the b^* coefficient indicates that the futures position should be short. With 1.5 million pounds of oil, hedging one-to-one implied selling 25 contracts. Now, however, the risk-minimizing strategy suggests selling 21 contracts ($25 \times 0.836 = 20.9$). Therefore our miller sells 21 futures contracts on November 1 at the prevailing price of $20.15, and plans to close the position at the end of the month. Table 26.1 summarizes the position on November 1 after these transactions.

Figure 26.3 shows the behavior of prices during November. Although both futures and cash prices had a negative trend, the basis was extremely stable, as shown in Figure 26.4. On November 29 prices stood as follows:

December futures	$19.12
Cash	19.61
Basis (cash − futures)	0.49

FIGURE 26.3   Soybean Oil Prices During November

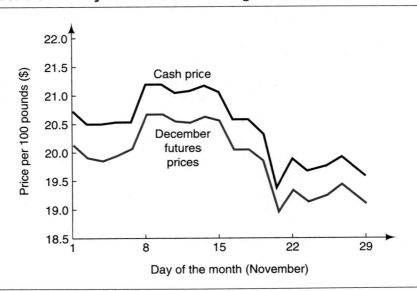

FIGURE 26.4   Soybean Oil Basis in November

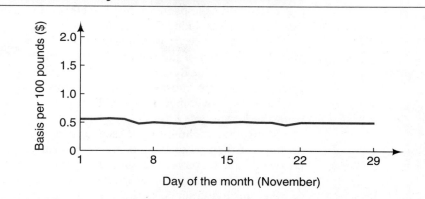

In accordance with the original plan, on November 29 the miller sold the newly produced soy oil at $19.61 and entered a reversing trade for 21 December futures contracts at $19.12. By entering the reversing trade, the miller is out of the futures market.

How did the miller fare with this hedge? Table 26.2 presents the entire transaction and the results for both the cash and futures markets. In the cash market, the final sale price was $19.61 per hundredweight. As 1.5 million pounds of oil have 15,000 hundredweights, the total result in the cash market was a loss of $16,800 from November 1 to November 29. In the futures market, the price fell as well, so the 21 contracts that were first sold and then covered involved 12,600 hundredweights and yielded a profit of $12,978. As

TABLE 26.2   The Miller's Position on November 29

Cash Market	Futures Market
NOVEMBER 1	
Anticipates having 1.5 million pounds of soy oil by month's end	Sells 21 December soy oil contracts at $20.15
Current price: $20.73	
NOVEMBER 29	
Sells 1.5 million pounds of soy oil at the market price of $19.61	Buys 21 December soy oil contracts at $19.12
Cash Result	*Futures Result*
Loss = 15,000 × ($19.61 − $20.73)	Gain = 12,600 × ($20.15 − $19.12)
= −$16,800	= −$12,978

Total Result: Futures gain − cash market loss = $12,978 − $16,800 = −$3,822

calculated in Table 26.2, the net loss was $3,822. Had there been no hedge, the loss would have been the full $16,800 of the cash price effect. This means that the hedge shielded 77 percent of the loss [(16,800 − $3,822)/$16,800].[1]

In this example, it would have been better, in hindsight, to have sold more futures. Part of the reason for this is the fact that the basis fell over the period of the hedge by $0.09, due at least partially to the fact that the futures price and cash price must be equal at maturity. However, given the information available on November 1, the miller made a good decision and benefited from the hedge.

Many other techniques are used for hedging with futures, but the emphasis on most of them is to reduce risk significantly. Futures can also be used to change the payoff patterns of different kinds of investments. However, options are usually a much better instrument for altering the payoff characteristics of different investments, as the next section explains.

ALTERING PAYOFF AND RETURN CHARACTERISTICS WITH OPTIONS

In the market today, futures and options contracts are traded on a variety of stock market indices, such as those discussed in Chapter 7. For example, Figure 26.5 shows quotations from the *Wall Street Journal* for futures, options, and options on the futures contract for the S&P 500 index. In this section, we show how to control the payoffs from a stock market index using options.

For all of the option analyses that follow, we make some simplifying assumptions:

1. There are no transaction costs.
2. The initial value of the index is $100.
3. The index pays no dividends.
4. The index is expected to return 15 percent over the next year.
5. The standard deviation of the index's return is 10 percent.
6. The returns on the index are normally distributed.
7. All options expire in one year.
8. The risk-free rate of interest is 6 percent.

Under these assumptions, we consider three call options and three put options with different exercise prices, as Table 26.3 shows. These are the Black-Scholes prices for options on the index.

---

[1] In an important sense, the expectation of the cash price should not have been $20.73, the price on November 1. The December futures price was already below the current spot price, so the miller should have expected a month-end spot price less than the current one. With the December futures at $20.15 and the November 1 cash price at $20.73, the miller might have expected a November 29 cash price somewhere between the two, perhaps about $20.45.

FIGURE 26.5   Quotations for Futures, Options, and Options on Futures for the S&P 500 Stock Market Index

FUTURES

S&P 500 INDEX (CME) 500 times index

	Open	High	Low	Settle	Chg	High	Low	Open Interest
June	382.00	383.75	378.20	382.40	+ 1.30	386.00	300.90	14,0676
Sept	385.00	386.30	381.00	385.05	+ 1.15	387.75	304.00	4,034
Dec	....	....	....	387.75	+ 1.05	390.60	316.50	1,857

Est vol 52,679; vol Thurs 50,909; open int 146,587, +215.
Indx prelim High 381.07; Low 376.89; Close 380.40 +2.77

OPTIONS

S&P 500 INDEX-$100 times index

Strike Price	Calls—Last			Puts—Last		
	Apr	May	Jun	Apr	May	Jun
330	....	....	53	....	....	1⅛
335	....	....	47¾	....	....	1½
340	....	....	42	....	....	1 13/16
345	35⅝	....	....	⅛	....	....
350	....	....	....	⅛	1⅛	2⅞
355	....	24	....	⅛	1⅝	3¼
360	....	20¼	22⅞	¼	2	4
365	15¾	....	....	⅜	2¾	5⅛
370	10⅞	14½	16⅞	¾	3½	6
375	7⅜	11	14⅛	1½	4⅞	7½
380	3½	6⅞	11⅛	3	6¾	9¼
385	1⅞	5⅜	8⅝	6	....	12
390	¾	3½	5½	....	....	14⅛
395	5/16	1 15/16	....	....	....	....
400	....	1¼	3¼	22¼	22¾	20⅜
425	....	....	7/16	....	....	....

Total call volume 20,578   Total call open int. 411,741
Total put volume 18,567   Total put open int. 442,284
The Index: High 381.07; Low 376.89; Close 380.40, +2.77

FUTURES OPTIONS

S&P 500 STOCK INDEX (CME) $500 times premium

Strike Price	Calls—Settle			Puts—Settle		
	Apr-c	May-c	Ju-c	Apr-p	May-p	Jun-p
370	12.95	15.55	17.95	0.55	3.25	5.75
375	8.50	11.90	14.50	1.10	4.55	7.20
380	4.85	8.75	11.50	2.45	6.35	9.10
385	2.30	6.15	8.85	4.90	8.70	11.40
390	0.95	4.15	6.65	8.55	....	14.10
395	0.45	2.65	4.85	13.05	....	17.25

Est. vol. 6,640; Thurs vol. 2,610 calls; 1,721 puts
Open interest Thurs; 27,595 calls; 45,664 puts

Source: Wall Street Journal, April 15, 1991. Reprinted by permission of Wall Street Journal, © 1991 Dow Jones & Company, Inc. All Rights Reserved Worldwide.

TABLE 26.3   Options in the Analysis

Calls		Puts	
Exercise Price	Initial Price	Exercise Price	Initial Price
$ 95	$11.16	$ 95	$0.78
100	7.46	100	1.80
105	4.55	105	3.61

FIGURE 26.6   Profit Graph for the Index Itself (Initial price = $100)

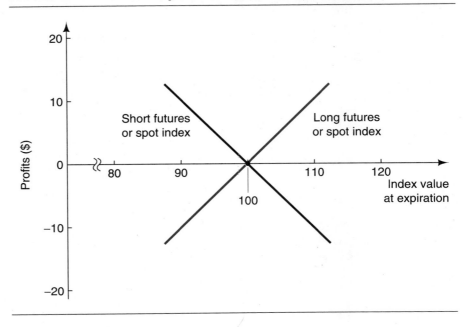

Basic Payoff Patterns

We now have a rich set of instruments to illustrate the different techniques that can be employed. Figure 26.6 shows the profits and losses for the index itself. The colored line shows the profit or loss incurred if the index or a futures on the index were bought at the current price of $100 and held until expiration.[2] That is, if the price of the index at expiration were $110, a long position would show a profit of $10. The black line shows the position of the short trader. Black lines are used throughout to indicate a short position.

Profits, Losses, and Returns for Single Options

As discussed in Chapter 25, the payoffs for options at expiration depend on the value of the underlying good. Figure 26.7 shows the profits and losses for the call option with an exercise price of $100 as a function of different values for the index at the expiration of the option in one year. Notice that the graph reflects the $7.46 premium and shows both long and short positions.

Figure 26.8 shows the profit graph for the put option with an exercise price of $100 and reflects the $1.80 price of this option. The put option breaks

---

[2] Because we assume that the index pays no dividends, the option and futures option behave similarly. Also, we assume that we hold the option to expiration. At expiration, the futures and index price must be equal. These assumptions allow us to focus on the index itself and on an option on the index.

FIGURE 26.7   Profit Graph for a Call Option (E = $100)

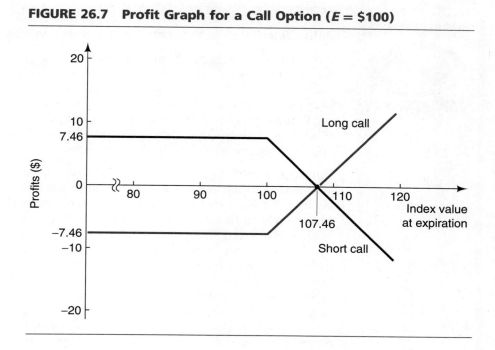

FIGURE 26.8   Profit Graph for a Put Option (E = $100)

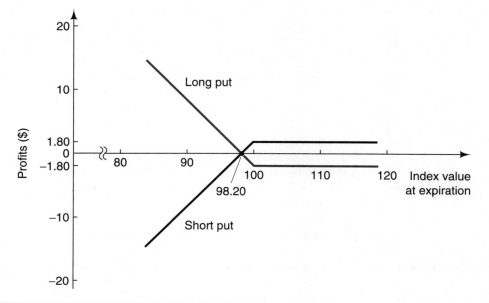

INTERNATIONAL PERSPECTIVES

With Wine Futures, You Can Always Swallow the Losses

It was hot and dry in the Bordeaux region of France this summer—just the kind of climatic conditions that can produce a wonderful vintage. And now that it's harvest time, connoisseurs and investors are wondering whether they should lock in prices by buying Bordeaux wine futures.

Futures are contracts that cover the price of a specific number of cases of wine for delivery 18 to 24 months after harvest. Wine merchants offer futures in the spring following the vintage.

Buying Frenzy.   Contracts for 1989 Bordeaux have been incredibly popular. Indeed, there was a buying frenzy after some experts began describing it as the vintage of the century. At Sherry-Lehmann Inc., a New York wine merchant, futures on '89 Château Haut-Brion were first offered last May at $850 a case. Now they're $895.

Of course, in part this reflects the depreciation of the dollar against the franc. Still, there's no doubt that wine futures represent the lowest price, because wine appreciates in price once it's bottled. For example, futures on '82 Château Latour were first offered in the spring of 1983 at $495 a case. The same 12 bottles currently go for $1,679 at retail in New York.

Although futures are available for many wines, investors and oenophiles covet the rich, expensive reds of Bordeaux. Investors often limit themselves to the region's top chateaux, including such stars as Latour, Margaux, Mouton-Rothschild, Haut-Brion, and Cheval Blanc.

Still, there are risks in wine futures—even for these blue-chip labels. Futures are first offered when the wines are in their infancy, so it's hard to judge whether they will turn out to be first-class. Although you may not lose money, your profits may suffer. For example, a Haut-Brion Graves from 1983, a so-so year, was first offered at $440 a case in 1984; in 1986, the retail case price was only $540.

Five Years.   Also, wine investing takes patience. Most experts advise holding on to your wine for at least five years before selling. Even so, it won't be easy to cash in on your investment. Most states prohibit individuals from selling wine without a liquor license. That often means having to employ an auction house.

And what of the 1990 vintage? While many are singing its praises, there's already some dissent. Wine critic Robert Parker, Jr., publisher of the *Wine Advocate*, thinks the grapes may be of uneven quality. It may have been *too* hot and dry in Bordeaux.

Source: John Meehan, "With Wine Futures, You Can Always Swallow the Losses," *Business Week*, October 15, 1990, p. 128.

even if the index value falls to $98.20 at expiration. If the index price is below $98.20, the long position makes a profit and the short position makes a loss.

Profits on Option Combinations

Having surveyed the options considered singly, we now turn to combinations of options the investor might choose. We illustrate a straddle, a bull spread, and a bear spread.

straddle
an option position consisting of a call and a put option with the same expiration and the same striking price

A **straddle** consists of a position in a call and a put option with the same expiration and the same striking price. To buy a straddle the investor purchases both a put and a call option, and the seller has a short position in both. Figure 26.9 shows the profits and losses from a straddle with an exercise price of $100. Such a straddle costs the price of the call ($7.46) and the put ($1.80), or a total of $9.26. If the index has an expiration value of $100, both the put and the call expire worthless and the total loss is 100 percent . However, if the index is above $100 at expiration, the call can be exercised. For example, if the index is $110 at expiration, the option has an exercise value of $10, the $110 index value minus the $100 exercise price. This $10 exercise profit would cover the cost of the straddle and leave a profit of $0.74.

☞ A straddle is a bet that the price of the underlying good will move dramatically away from its exercise price.

On the other hand, if the index falls in value the put can be exercised. For example, if the index has a value of $91 at expiration, the put has a value of $9 ($100 − $91), leaving a loss of $0.26 on the straddle. Figure 26.9 shows

FIGURE 26.9   Profit Graph for a Straddle (*E* = $100)

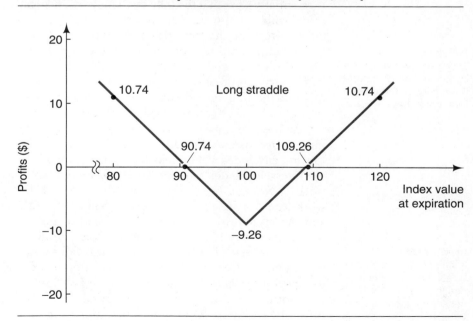

FIGURE 26.10   Profit Graph for a Bull Spread

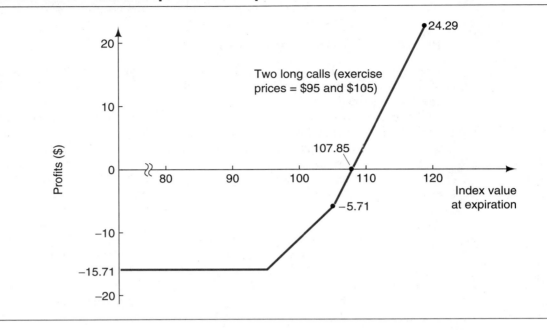

the breakeven points for the straddle. As it indicates, the purchase of a straddle is essentially a bet that the index will move dramatically away from its exercise price, which is also the current price of $100. If the index moves enough in either direction, the straddle earns a profit.

bull spread
a long position in two call options designed to profit if the price of the underlying good rises

A **bull spread** is a long position in two call options designed to profit if the price of the underlying good rises. An investor might buy a call option with a striking price of $95 and another with a striking price of $105. The price of the bull spread would be the price of the two call options, $15.71 ($11.16 + $4.55). Figure 26.10 shows the profits and losses from the bull spread.

As the profit graph shows, this strategy profits very handsomely if the index price rises. (After all, it is a bull spread.) Notice that it gives a total loss for any index value below $95, because both of the options will expire worthless. For index values between $95 and $105, the call with the exercise price of $95 can be exercised, but the one with the $105 exercise price is worthless. For index prices greater than $105, both options are exercisable and the profits rise even faster. If the index moves to $107.85, the strategy breaks even; any higher index price gives a profit.

bear spread
a long position in a combination of put options designed to profit if the underlying good falls in value

If an investor believes the index will fall in value, it might be better to enter a **bear spread**, which is a long position in a combination of put options designed to profit if the underlying good falls in value. Consider a combined long position in a put with a striking price of $105 and another with a striking price of $95. Figure 26.11 graphs the profits and losses from this bear spread.

FIGURE 26.11   Profit Graph for a Bear Spread

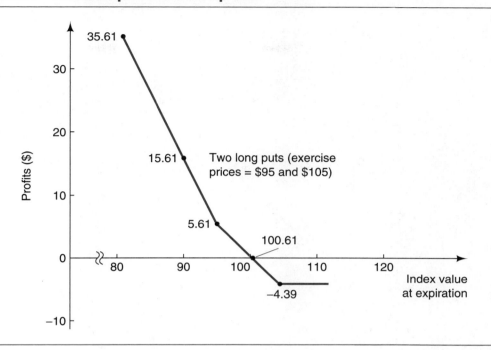

This spread is relatively cheap, $4.39, due to the low prices of the two options involved ($0.78 + $3.61). For any index price above $105, both puts expire worthless. In the $95 to $105 range, the put with the exercise price of $105 will be valuable and the other put will expire worthless. If the index value is less than $95, both can be exercised profitably. The angles of the profit line in Figure 26.11 reflect these different factors.

Holding the Index with Options

☞ Options can be used in conjunction with the underlying good to provide almost any probability distribution of returns the investor desires.

In Figure 26.6 we observed the profit graph of returns for holding the index itself. For many investors, the index may not provide the desired payoff characteristics. Options can be used in conjunction with the index to provide almost any kind of pattern the investor desires.

writing a covered call
writing call options on a spot good that the writer owns

Holding the Index and Selling Calls   One popular strategy is to hold some good and to write calls against it. This is called **writing a covered call,** because the investor already owns the underlying good. Figure 26.12 shows the profits and losses from writing one call on one unit of the index with an exercise price of $100. The investor receives an immediate payment of $7.46 from the buyer of the call.

FIGURE 26.12   Profit Graph for a Synthetic Put ($E = \$100$)

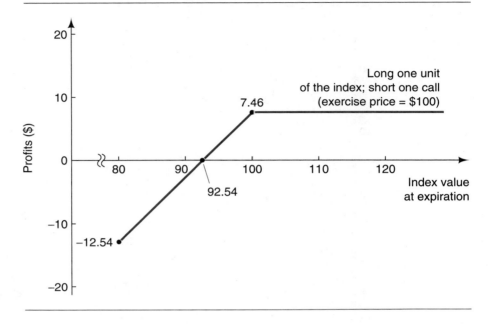

It is instructive to compare this graph with the profit graph for the index itself in Figure 26.6. If the index price is $100 at expiration, the index itself shows no profit. By contrast, if the investor writes a covered call and the index has a value of $100, the profit is $7.46. The investor gets to keep the option premium because the call expires worthless, so its buyer will not exercise it. However, the writer of the covered call has sold the chance to profit if the index increases above $100. Figure 26.12 shows that the total profit for the holder does not increase if the index value increases above $100. In short, writing a covered call amounts to selling the upside potential on the underlying good; in this case, it was sold for $7.46.

☞ Writing covered calls reduces both the risk and the expected return of the position in comparison with the underlying good.

Another interpretation of Figure 26.12 arises if we look at the structure of the profit graph. The payoff pattern is exactly the same as a short position in a put option with an exercise price of $100 and a premium of $7.46. This is clear from comparing Figures 26.12 and 26.8. Figure 26.13 presents both positions. Observe that the striking price for the simple put option is only $1.80, not the $7.46 of this new **synthetic put** consisting of the underlying good plus a short position in the call. What accounts for the difference?

synthetic put
a combination of a long position in the underlying good and a short position in the call

Notice that the synthetic put always pays $5.66 more than the simple put, as shown in Figure 26.13. Because of this difference, we see that the regular put and the synthetic put differ only by a riskless component. For example, assume that you sold the put and received $1.80. If you took this

FINANCE TODAY

Floor Exercises

When Laura Pedersen won a seat on the American Stock Exchange in January 1986—at the tender and record-setting age of 20—a colleague offered some encouraging words. In *Play Money*, her fast-paced, amusing trading-floor memoir, she recalls him saying: "You've got a great future in options. You can scream loud, jump high, think fast, and count without using your fingers."

And sure enough, in the four-odd—very odd—years during which she traded options, Pedersen screamed, jumped, slugged, spat, and cursed her way to $5.3 million in profits for her employer, Spear Leeds Kellogg/ Investors Co. At one point, her annual income topped $800,000. But by the time she called it quits, in October 1989, she was left with a sushi-raw throat, impaired hearing, strained vision—and a feeling of disillusionment. After the crash of October 1987—when she lost $1.3 million for her firm—the thrill was gone. "As did millions of other amateur players, I'd concluded that the sport had gone out of the game," writes Pedersen.

In fact, Pedersen was a consummate pro—a market-maker in index options, which are bets on the direction of the overall market. They are a favorite of portfolio managers, who use them to hedge against market swings. Serious stuff. Pedersen, however, aims not for the cerebellum but the funny bone, emphasizing the wacky pranks and peccadillos of her former colleagues.

My favorite is the anecdote—apocryphal, I hope—about Gary, the trader who just had to get to work one morning when his car became stuck on an icy street. In his trunk was the urn "conveniently" housing his grandmother's ashes. Pedersen relates: "Slightly wincing while scattering them under the tires, he reminded himself aloud: 'She always said for me to do everything I possibly could to get ahead in the business world because that's where the money is.'"

Source: Gary Weiss, "Floor Exercises," *Business Week*, April 29, 1991.

$1.80, and $92.54 more, you could buy a bond for $94.34. With rates at 6 percent this bond would pay interest of $5.66 in one year, so it would have exactly the payoff pattern of the synthetic put. In short, the cost of this position is $92.54.

If two investments have exactly the same payoff distribution, they must have the same price, assuming efficient markets. The price of the synthetic put is the price of the index minus the money received for shorting the call: $100 − $7.46 = $92.54. This is exactly the price of the synthetic put.

FIGURE 26.13   The Simple Put (E = $100) and a Synthetic Put

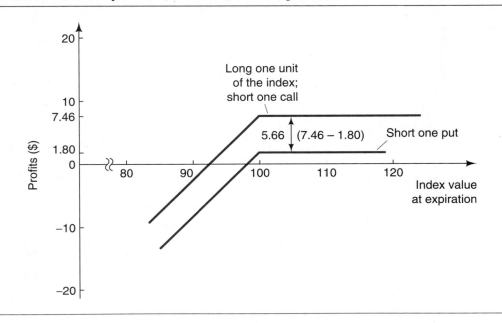

For this synthetic put, the maximum return is 8.06 percent. To see this, note that the maximum profit is $7.46, as shown in Figure 26.12, and that the investment for this position equals the cost of the index, $100, minus the option premium of $7.46. Therefore, the maximum return is $7.46/($100 − $7.46) = 8.06%.

Portfolio Insurance

portfolio insurance
the alteration of a portfolio's returns distribution to simulate a call option

Although the term "portfolio insurance" is used in many ways, it essentially refers to an alteration in the returns distribution of a portfolio that reduces the risk of large losses at the expense of also reducing the maximum returns. For our purposes, we define **portfolio insurance** as the alteration of a portfolio to simulate a call option. The portfolio is transformed by holding a long position and buying puts.

Consider a position that is long the index and long one put with a striking price of $100. Figure 26.14 shows the profit graph for this position. The put costs $1.80, so if the price of the index stays at $100, there is no profit or loss on the index and the put expires worthless, for a total loss of $1.80. A fall in the index below $100 gives a loss on the index, but it gives an exercisable

FIGURE 26.14   Profit Graph for an Insured Portfolio

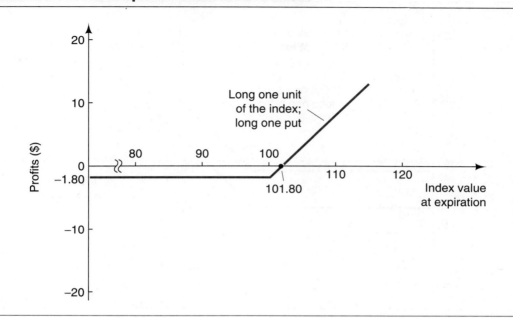

value of an equal amount on the put. For example, if the price of the index at expiration is $95, there is a $5 loss on the index, but the intrinsic value of the put is also $5, offsetting that loss exactly. For this reason, any terminal index value of $100 or less gives a $1.80 loss on the combined position. If the index value exceeds $100, the put expires worthless and the index gives a profit.

In Figure 26.14, the risk of large losses on the index is eliminated by the put. This is clear from the figure itself and from a comparison with Figure 26.6. In fact, the portfolio insurance position gives a payoff that is exactly like a call option with a striking price of $100 and a premium of $1.80. However, we know that such a call would cost $7.46, so the payoffs from the insured portfolio are like a call with a striking price of $7.46 plus a bond.

☞ An insured portfolio is similar to a call option because it insures against large losses and has exactly the same payoffs as a call option plus a risk-free bond.

We have already seen that a straight call with a striking price of $100 has a premium of $7.46. The fact that the insured portfolio behaves like a call with a striking price of $1.80 means that it also has elements of a bond. Figure 26.15 shows the profit graph for both investment opportunities. The insured portfolio pays off $5.66 more than the simple long call, no matter what the index value may be. If we buy the call with a premium of $7.46 and buy a risk-free bond for $94.34 that pays $5.66 interest in one year, we will have a portfolio with exactly the same payoff as the insured portfolio.

FIGURE 26.15   Profit Graph for an Insured Portfolio and a Simple Call ($E = \$100$)

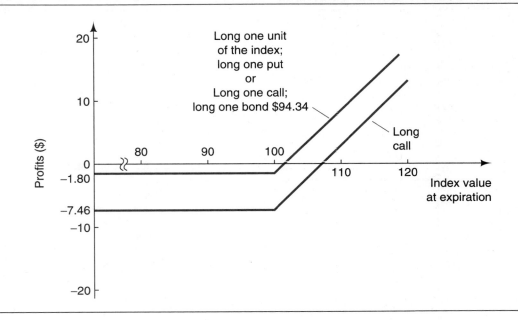

The following positions are exactly equivalent:

Call + Bond	Insured Portfolio
Buy 1 call with $E = \$100$ for $7.46	Hold a long position in the index for $100
Buy 1 risk-free bond for $94.34 paying 6% interest	Buy 1 put with $E = \$100$ for $1.80
Total cost: $101.80	**Total cost: $101.80**

Not surprisingly, the two positions with exactly the same payoffs have the same price. Also, we saw in Chapter 25 that a call option has elements of an insurance policy. An insured portfolio is similar because it insures against large losses and has exactly the same payoffs as a call option plus a risk-free bond.

A certain amount of profit is sacrificed in order to avoid the large losses, however. Assume the index value at expiration is $110. For a simple long position in the index, the profit would be $10. For the insured portfolio, it is $10 − $1.80 = $8.20. For all ending values of the index in excess of $100 the insured portfolio pays $1.80 less than a long position in the index alone.

In exchange for giving up that extra $1.80 in profit, the insured portfolio offers complete protection against losses of more than that amount.

Tailoring the Risk of a Long Position

We have seen that most option positions give payoffs that limit the maximum profit or loss. Options can also be useful for an investor who likes the profit graph of the simple long position in the option but finds it too risky. This section considers a position that is long one unit of the index, and that holds a short position in the call and a long position in the put as well. All of the options have a striking price of $100.

First, consider the profit graph from the following position:

Long 1 unit of the index
Short 0.25 calls with $E = \$100$
Long 0.25 puts with $E = \$100$

ratio position
a combination of a position in the underlying good plus some fractional value of options being held for each unit of the good

Because only some fractional value of options is held for each unit of the index, this is called a **ratio position.** Figure 26.16 shows the profits and losses that would be incurred with this combined position for various terminal values of the index. If we compare Figures 26.16 and 26.6, we notice that the slope

FIGURE 26.16   Profit Graph for a Position Long the Index, Short 0.25 Calls, and Long 0.25 Puts ($E = \$100$)

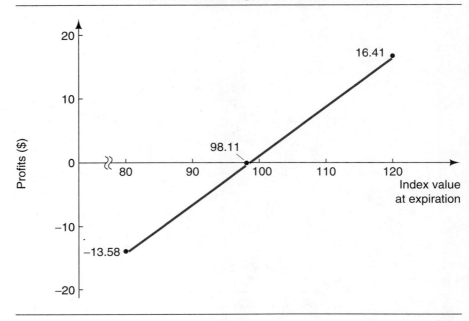

of the graph in Figure 26.16 is less. This means that a change in the value of the index does not affect the combined position as much as it affects the simple index position.

To see more clearly how the combined position reduces risk, assume now that the option positions are larger relative to the single unit of the index. In particular, assume that an investor holds the following combined position:

Long 1 unit of the index
Short 0.75 calls $E = \$100$
Long 0.75 puts $E = \$100$

Figure 26.17 shows the profit graph for this combined position, in which the slope of the graph is much smaller. Here the index value must fall below $83 to show a loss. For the simple position in the index the slope equals 1, because the profit changes $1 for every $1 change in the index. In the figure the slope is 0.25 because a change in the index of $1 makes the profit of the combined position change by only $0.25.

We conclude this section by showing how to hold the index and an option position to eliminate risk entirely. Suppose you make the following

FIGURE 26.17   Profit Graph for a Position Long the Index, Short 0.75 Calls, and Long 0.75 Puts ($E = \$100$)

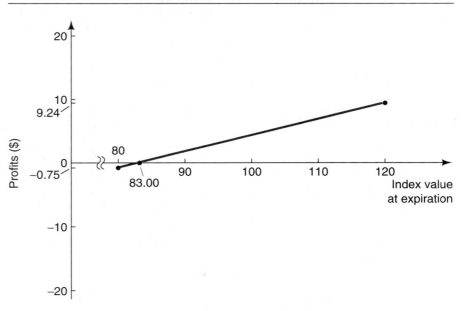

combination of investments:

Long 1 unit of the index with a price of $100
Short 1 call with $E = \$100$ and a premium of $7.46
Long 1 put with $E = \$100$ and a premium of $1.80

The total cost of this position is $94.34 ($100 − $7.46 + $1.80). What is the payoff? If the index is $100 at expiration, both options expire worthless, so the total payoff is $100. If the index is worth $105 at expiration, the put expires worthless and the call provides a loss of $5, for a total payoff of $100. If the index has a final price of $95, the payoff on the index is $95, the call option expires worthless, and the put can be exercised for $100 to deliver the index worth $95. This gives a total payoff of $100. In fact, no matter what the final index value might be, the combined position gives a total payoff of $100.

Because the combined position costs $94.34 and pays $100 no matter what the index value might be, the profit will always be $5.66, as shown in Figure 26.18. In fact, we have created a riskless investment costing $94.34. A riskless investment must earn the risk-free rate of 6 percent in an efficient

FIGURE 26.18   Profit Graph for a Position Long the Index, Short 1 Call, and Long 1 Put ($E = \$100$)

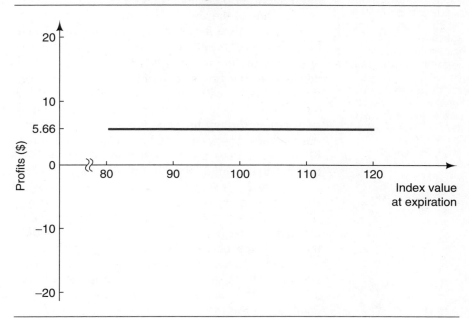

market, so we would expect it to give a profit of $5.66 ($94.34 × 0.06), or a total payoff of $100. This is exactly what we have.

By holding the index, shorting one put, and buying one call, we have managed to create a riskless portfolio. Obviously, it would be easier to merely buy the risk-free bond if all we want is the risk-free rate, but this result helps us understand the relationships among all of these financial instruments.

SPECIAL USES OF OPTION PRICING THEORY

Since the original development of option pricing theory, its ideas have been applied to improve our understanding of a number of different financial instruments. In the previous section we saw how options can be combined with the underlying good to create a variety of different payoff patterns. This section uses option principles to improve our understanding of other kinds of financial instruments. First, we can analyze stock in a firm as a call option. Second, owning a bond in the firm has the same payoff characteristics as a short position in a put option. Finally, owning a convertible bond gives the same type of payoff as a combination of a short put and a long call with different striking prices.

Similarity Between Stocks and Call Options

☞ The shares in a corporation have a payoff pattern that is similar to a call option on the firm with an exercise price equal to the amount owed the bondholders.

☞ The bonds of a corporation have a payoff pattern that is similar to a short position in a put.

Consider a firm with one share of stock and one bond promising to pay $100 in the next period. It issues no other securities. We examine the stock value as a function of the value of the firm to show that it behaves like a call option.

The due date for the bond payment corresponds to the expiration date for the option. On this date either the stockholder must pay the bondholder, or the bondholder receives title to the firm. The action the stockholder takes depends on the firm's value. First, assume it is worth $90. In this instance, the stockholder will not pay the bondholder the $100, but will allow the bondholder to take the firm. As a consequence, the stock will be worthless, as it will be for any terminal firm value of $100 or less. If the value is $110, the stockholder pays the $100 to the bondholder and has $10 left, so the value of the stock equals $10. For any firm value above $100, the stock price equals the firm value minus the $100 owed to the bondholder.

Figure 26.19 shows the value of the stock as a function of the value of the firm, with the characteristic shape of a long position in a call option. In this case the stock is a call option on the firm, and its expiration date is the due date of the bond. At expiration, the stockholder must exercise the call by paying the bondholder and taking title to the firm, or must allow the bondholder to seize the firm. In the latter case the option expires worthless; equivalently, the firm is bankrupt and the stock has a zero price. At expiration, any call will be worth the maximum of zero or the price of the underlying good minus the exercise price. Similarly, the stock will be worth zero or the value of the firm minus the payoff to the bondholder.

FIGURE 26.19   The Value of a Share at Maturity as a Function of the Firm's Value

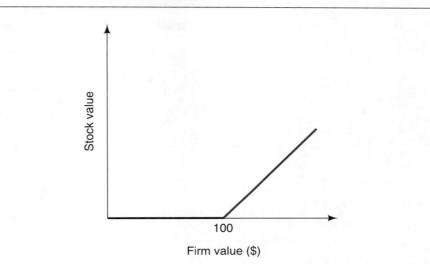

Similarity Between Owning Bonds and Short Positions in Put Options

Let us now consider the same case from the point of view of the bondholder. The stockholder has promised to pay the bondholder $100 on the due date. If the stockholder fails to pay, the bondholder seizes the firm. We observed that the stockholder will pay the bondholder if the firm has a value equal to or exceeding the promised payment. Therefore, the value of the bond on the due date will be $100 if the firm's value is $100 or more. However, the bond value can never exceed $100 because the stockholder will never pay more than the promised $100.

If the firm is worth less than $100, the stockholder will sacrifice it to the bondholder, who receives whatever it is worth. For example, if it is worth $80 on the due date, that is the amount the bondholder receives. Figure 26.20 graphs the value of the bond as a function of the firm's value. Notice that the bond has the characteristic payoff pattern of a short position in a put option.

The exercise price in this case is the promised payment of $100 because the stockholder has the option to put the firm to the bondholder and keep the $100. Like a short position in the put option, the value of the bond falls $1 for each dollar the underlying good is less than the exercise price. For example, if the firm price falls $10 below the exercise price of $100, the bond value will be $90.

FIGURE 26.20   The Value of a Bond's Maturity as a Function of the Firm's Value

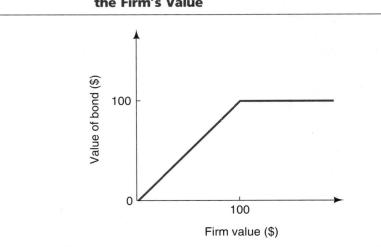

Option Pricing and Convertible Bonds

☞ A convertible bond has a payoff pattern that is like a combination of a regular bond and a call option on the equity of the firm.

A convertible bond is a complex security with characteristics of both debt and equity. Normally, it has a stated coupon rate and pays interest semi-annually. However, at the option of the bondholder, the bond can be surrendered in exchange for shares of common stock. When this occurs, the firm issues new stock, so more shares will be outstanding after the conversion than before. This means that ownership in the firm will be diluted.

To see how a convertible bond is like a combination of a regular bond and a call option on the equity of the firm, consider the following example. A firm issues a convertible bond today for $90, maturing in one year. At maturity, the firm promises to pay $100 to retire the bond, or the owner may surrender the bond in exchange for one share of stock. At the time of issuance of the convertible bond, only one share of stock was outstanding.

The bondholder has three payoff possibilities. First, at the maturity of the bond, the firm may be worth less than the promised payment of $100. In this case, the firm defaults and the bondholder takes it over as in the case of a straight bond. Second, the firm might be worth more than $200. In this case, the owner surrenders the bond and receives one share of newly issued stock. In that case, each of the two outstanding shares will be worth more than $100. Third, the firm might be worth between $100 and $200. In this case, the bondholder prefers to receive the promised $100 payment rather than convert, because each of the two shares would be worth less than $100. In this case, the shareholder would pay the bondholder the $100 and retain title to the firm.

FIGURE 26.21   The Value of a Convertible Bond at Maturity as a Function of the Firm's Value

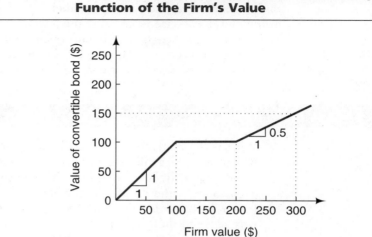

Following our discussion, Figure 26.21 graphs the possible values of the convertible bond on the due date as a function of the value of the firm. Notice that the value of the bond falls $1 for every $1 in shortfall of firm value below $100. By contrast, if the firm's value exceeds $200, the convertible bondholder receives only 50 percent of the excess, having only 50 percent of the outstanding shares after conversion. Also notice that the bond's payoffs are the combination of the straight bond's and the stock's payoffs, because for low firm values the convertible behaves like a straight bond, but if the firm value is high, the bondholder has a call option on one-half of the firm by forcing conversion. Also, Figure 26.21 shows that owning this convertible bond is like having a short put position with a striking price of $100, and one-half of a long call with a striking price of $200.

SUMMARY

This chapter extended our knowledge of risk control with options and futures. First, we discussed the portfolio approach to hedging and showed how to choose a hedge position in the futures market that should minimize the risk of an existing position in a physical asset.

The focus then turned to an exploration of options and their payoff and return distributions. First, we considered various puts and calls individually. Second, we examined how the payoff patterns could be altered by holding combinations of options. Third, we explored the way in which the payoff and returns distribution of an underlying good could be altered by holding the good in combination with different options.

Option theory has been applied to a number of different instruments. In this chapter we saw how common stock is analogous to owning a call on the firm with the exercise price being the payment promised to the bondholders. We also saw that a corporate bond has a payoff pattern with the same shape as a short position in a put. Finally, we noted that a convertible bond has payoffs similar to a short put combined with a long call.

QUESTIONS

1. What is the motivation behind the portfolio approach to hedging?
2. If you buy a straddle, what option or options do you purchase?
3. If you buy a straddle, what must happen to the price of the underlying good to make the position profitable?
4. If you believed that the price of an underlying good would remain very close to the exercise price on an option, what transactions would you make to profit from this belief?
5. If you purchase a bull spread, what options do you purchase?
6. If you purchase a bear spread, what options do you purchase?
7. What is the purpose of writing a covered call?
8. Compare the variance of a long position in an underlying good with that of a covered call position on that good.
9. What is a synthetic put?
10. What is the relationship between the payoffs of a put and a corresponding synthetic put at expiration of the option?
11. Why might traders engage in portfolio insurance?
12. What is the difference between holding a portfolio of the underlying good and holding such a portfolio that is insured?
13. Which has a higher expected return, the underlying good or the insured portfolio constructed on that underlying good?
14. If you have a long position in an underlying good, what option position would you enter to create a total portfolio with no variance?
15. Why is owning a stock like owning a call option on the firm?
16. If we interpret a stock as a call option on the firm, what is the striking price?
17. How is owning a bond issued by a corporation like having a short position in a put option?
18. Into what simpler instruments can we decompose a convertible bond? Explain.
19. What has a greater chance of an extremely large payoff, the underlying good, or a long position in a call option on the good?
20. What has a greater chance of a total loss, the underlying good, or a long position in a call option on the good?
21. What has a greater chance of a total loss, the underlying good, or a combined position of the underlying good with a short position in a call option on the good?

CHAPTER 27

International Financial Management

This chapter introduces the major issues in international corporate finance, beginning with the different ways in which a firm can enter a foreign market, a choice that depends largely on the nature of the good and the characteristics of the market.

Every firm operating in the international environment faces problems with foreign exchange—the exchange of foreign currencies into the home currency. Generally, the firm's foreign operations earn income denominated in foreign currency. Shareholders, however, expect payment in their home currency, so the firm must convert the foreign currency. Because the value of one currency relative to another is constantly changing, this conversion is risky. We call this **foreign exchange risk,** and its management is one of the big issues of international finance.

Operating in a foreign environment also creates special investment and financing difficulties, as well as gives firms access to attractive investment and financing opportunities. The chapter concludes with a brief exploration of these issues.

foreign exchange risk
risk resulting from the change in the value of one currency relative to another

ENTERING A FOREIGN MARKET

licensing agreement
an agreement under which a firm in the home country allows a firm in a foreign country to use its technology or brand name

direct foreign investment (DFI)
the owning and operating of physical assets by a firm in a foreign country

multinational firm
a firm engaged in direct foreign investment

A firm that considers entering a foreign market must choose one of three methods of doing business. First, it can export; that is, manufacture goods in its home country and ship them to the foreign country. A second strategy is licensing. In a **licensing agreement** a firm in the home country allows a firm in a foreign country to use its technology or brand name. The foreign firm plays an essential role in the manufacturing or distribution process. The third strategy is to enter a foreign market through **direct foreign investment (DFI);** that is, own and operate physical capital in a foreign country. A firm that engages in DFI is regarded as a **multinational firm.** Firms may use one or more of these methods, and some use all three.

On first examination, it appears that a firm can never profit from DFI. In comparison to a local firm, a foreign one always faces severe disadvantages that arise from differences in culture, language, and knowledge of the local market. Firms engage in DFI to capture some benefits they cannot capture through exporting or licensing, by exploiting some imperfection in the market for input into its production process or for its final product. Due to market

appropriability theory
the view that firms engage in DFI in order to appropriate the benefits that they have created through patents they hold or production processes they have developed

☞ The three ways for a firm to enter a foreign market are exporting, licensing, and direct foreign investment.

☞ The feasibility of direct foreign investment depends on the ability to exploit some kind of market imperfections.

imperfections, firms are unable to capture the full benefits of the products they have created unless they enter a foreign market through DFI. Thus they engage in DFI to appropriate the potential benefits of the patents they hold or the production processes they have developed. This is the **appropriability theory.**

Some examples will clarify this line of reasoning. Today we observe U.S. electronics firms that manufacture abroad and import the finished product into the United States. Labor is an important input for these products, and labor costs are substantially higher in the United States than in many other countries. Firms establish their manufacturing facilities abroad to take advantage of this wage differential. Because the same unit of labor costs more in the United States than abroad, the labor market is imperfect.[1] This imperfection provides a strong incentive for firms to consider DFI. If labor costs were uniform across national boundaries, U.S. firms would manufacture locally and save the cost of importing goods.

As another example, consider a firm that creates knowledge through its research program and wants to control the knowledge for its own benefit. Assume that it has developed a special production process and wants to use it to produce goods for a foreign market. Assume also that the firm cannot effectively export into the foreign market, perhaps due to trade barriers. The firm has two choices: it can license its technology to a local firm in the foreign market, or it can engage in DFI itself and build and operate a plant abroad. With the first option, the firm puts itself in a very risky position because the knowledge is no longer under its control. The licensee in the foreign country must learn the details of the technology to operate successfully, and there is nothing to stop it from taking that knowledge and using it for its own benefits. Although laws prohibit such a practice, they are very difficult to enforce effectively. To avoid this danger, the firm should decide to operate its own plant in the foreign country. Thus the desire to appropriate for itself the benefits of the knowledge it created leads to DFI.

The exact combination of methods firms use to enter a foreign market depends on the specific nature of the product and the position of the firm. Firms that engage in DFI are more fully involved in the international scene than those that merely export or license. We focus on the problems of the multinational firm in the remainder of this chapter.

FOREIGN EXCHANGE

In the foreign exchange market, it is important to realize that every price, or exchange rate, that is quoted is relative. To say that $1.00 is worth DM2.5 also implies that DM1 is worth $0.40. All foreign exchange rates are related

---

[1] We are assuming that the quality of the labor, including productivity, is the same. In some cases this may not be true.

FIGURE 27.1 Foreign Exchange Quotations

CURRENCY TRADING

EXCHANGE RATES

Friday, April 12, 1991

The New York foreign exchange selling rates below apply to trading among banks in amounts of $1 million and more, as quoted at 3 p.m. Eastern time by Bankers Trust Co.and other sources. Retail transactions provide fewer units of foreign currency per dollar.

Country	U.S. $ equiv. Fri.	U.S. $ equiv. Thurs.	Currency per U.S. $ Fri.	Currency per U.S. $ Thurs.
Argentina (Austral) ...	.0001052	.0001052	9506.00	9506.06
Australia (Dollar)	.7843	.7830	1.2750	1.2771
Austria (Schilling)	.08428	.08503	11.87	11.76
Bahrain (Dinar)	2.6532	2.6532	.3769	.3769
Belgium (Franc)				
Commercial rate	.02885	.02910	34.66	34.36
Brazil (Cruzeiro)	.00412	.00414	242.50	241.53
Britain (Pound)	1.7750	1.7875	.5634	.5594
30-Day Forward	1.7662	1.7780	.5662	.5624
90-Day Forward	1.7498	1.7628	.5715	.5673
180-Day Forward ...	1.7296	1.7435	.5782	.5736
Canada (Dollar)	.8692	.8696	1.1505	1.1500
30-Day Forward	.8666	.8669	1.1540	1.1535
90-Day Forward	.8619	.8623	1.1602	1.1597
180-Day Forward ...	.8560	.8564	1.1682	1.1677
Chile (Peso)	.003045	.003038	328.40	329.12
China (Renmimbi)	.191494	.191494	5.2221	5.2221
Colombia (Peso)	.001747	.001747	572.33	572.33
Denmark (Krone)	.1549	.1560	6.4574	6.4107
Ecuador (Sucre)				
Floating rate	.000966	.000966	1035.51	1035.51
Finland (Markka)	.25387	.25387	3.9390	3.9390
France (Franc)	.17553	.17684	5.6970	5.6547
30-Day Forward	.17506	.17638	5.7123	5.6697
90-Day Forward	.17415	.17549	5.7423	5.6982
180-Day Forward ...	.17294	.17427	5.7823	5.7382
Germany (Mark)	.5931	.5979	1.6860	1.6725
30-Day Forward	.5917	.5964	1.6901	1.6768
90-Day Forward	.5887	.5934	1.6988	1.6851
180-Day Forward ...	.5843	.5891	1.7115	1.6974
Greece (Drachma)	.005464	.005533	183.00	180.75
Hong Kong (Dollar) ...	.12837	.12835	7.7900	7.7910
India (Rupee)	.05048	.05048	19.81	19.81
Indonesia (Rupiah)	.0005255	.0005255	1903.02	1903.02
Ireland (Punt)	1.5860	1.5975	.6305	.6260
Israel (Shekel)	.4579	.4581	2.1839	2.1829
Italy (Lira)	.0007994	.0008065	1251.00	1240.00
Japan (Yen)	.007334	.007339	136.35	136.25
30-Day Forward	.007321	.007326	136.59	136.50
90-Day Forward	.007301	.007306	136.97	136.87
180-Day Forward ...	.007329	.007287	136.45	137.24
Jordan (Dinar)	1.5029	1.5029	.6654	.6654
Kuwait (Dinar)	z	z	z	z
Lebanon (Pound)	.001066	.001066	938.00	938.01
Malaysia (Ringgit)	.3652	.3650	2.7385	2.7400
Malta (Lira)	3.0628	3.0628	.3265	.3265
Mexico (Peso)				
Floating rate	.0003352	.0003352	2983.00	2983.03
Netherland (Guilder) ..	.5265	.5309	1.8995	1.8835
New Zealand (Dollar) .	.5900	.5900	1.6949	1.6949
Norway (Krone)	.1527	.1537	6.5500	6.5052
Pakistan (Rupee)	.0439	.0439	22.78	22.78
Peru (New Sol)	1.7062	1.7062	.59	.59
Philippines (Peso)	.03676	.03676	27.20	27.20
Portugal (Escudo)	.006915	.006876	144.62	145.44
Saudi Arabia (Riyal) ..	.26752	.26752	3.7381	3.7381
Singapore (Dollar)	.5688	.5688	1.7580	1.7580
South Africa (Rand)				
Commercial rate	.3681	c.3674	2.7168	c2.7218
Financial rate	.3028	.3003	3.3030	3.3300
South Korea (Won) ...	.0014052	.0014052	711.66	711.66
Spain (Peseta)	.009615	.009699	104.00	103.10
Sweden (Krona)	.1657	.1656	6.0360	6.0380
Switzerland (Franc) :.	.7000	.7075	1.4285	1.4135
30-Day Forward	.6985	.7059	1.4317	1.4167
90-Day Forward	.6959	.7033	1.4370	1.4219
180-Day Forward ...	.6930	.7004	1.4430	1.4278
Taiwan (Dollar)	.037341	.037453	26.78	26.70
Thailand (Baht)	.03945	.03945	25.35	25.35
Turkey (Lira)	.0002684	.0002704	3726.00	3698.01
United Arab (Dirham) .	.2723	.2723	3.6725	3.6725
Uruguay (New Peso)				
Financial	.000557	.000557	1795.01	1795.01
Venezuela (Bolivar)				
Floating rate	.01868	.01849	53.53	54.08
SDR	1.36420	1.35981	.73303	.73540
ECU	1.23391	1.22754	....	....

Special Drawing Rights (SDR) are based on exchange rates for the U.S., German, British, French and Japanese currencies. Source: International Monetary Fund.

European Currency Unit (ECU) is based on a basket of community currencies. Source: European Community Commission.

z-Not quoted. c-Corrected.

Source: Wall Street Journal, April 15, 1991, p. C10. Reprinted by permission of Wall Street Journal, © 1991 Dow Jones & Company, Inc. All Rights Reserved Worldwide.

to each other as reciprocals, which is apparent in Figure 27.1, showing foreign exchange quotations as they appear daily in the *Wall Street Journal*. Each set of quotations shows the rates for the current day and the preceding business day. This makes it possible to focus only on the two columns pertaining to the current quotation. The first point to notice is that the rate in one column has its reciprocal in the other column. The value of $/DM is just the reciprocal of the value of DM/$. For some countries, Figure 27.1 shows only the spot rate, the rate at which the currency can be exchanged into dollars at the moment.

For many of our major trading partners, such as Germany, England, Japan, and Canada, forward rates are quoted for periods of 30, 90, and 180 days into the future. The 30-day forward rate, for example, indicates the rate at which a trader can contract today for the delivery of some foreign currency 30 days hence, when the actual transaction and payment take place.

Large banks in the U.S. and abroad comprise the main foreign exchange market. As is typical of forward markets, there is no physical location where trading takes place. Instead, banks around the world are linked electronically through their trading rooms. Such a room may have access to 60 telephone lines and 5 or more video quotation screens.[2] The market has no regular trading hours and is always open somewhere in the world. In addition to large banks, some large corporations have access to the market through their own trading rooms.

☞ Foreign currencies are traded in a very active and sophisticated world-wide market.

Regional banks are unlikely to have trading rooms. Instead, they clear their foreign exchange transactions through correspondent banks with whom they have arrangements. Corporations, as well as individuals, that are too small to have trading rooms engage in foreign exchange transactions through their own banks.

GEOGRAPHICAL AND CROSS-RATE ARBITRAGE

geographical arbitrage
when one currency sells for two prices in two markets

cross-rate arbitrage
when the implied rate between two assets in one market does not match the rate between them in another market

☞ Foreign exchange prices are governed by the condition that they not allow arbitrage opportunities.

A number of pricing relationships exist in the foreign exchange market whose violation would create an arbitrage opportunity. The first two to be considered involve **geographical arbitrage** and **cross-rate arbitrage.**

Geographical arbitrage occurs when one currency sells for two prices in two different markets. As an example, consider the following prices that were quoted in New York and Frankfurt for the exchange rate between deutsche-marks (DM) and U.S. dollars (these are 90-day forward rates):

New York	$/DM	0.42
Frankfurt	DM/$	2.35

The New York price, quoted as $/DM, implies a DM/$ price equal to its inverse:

$$DM/\$ = \frac{1}{0.42} = 2.381$$

In New York the DM/$ rate is 2.381, but in Frankfurt it is 2.35. This discrepancy indicates that a geographical arbitrage opportunity exists. The example shows that to test for this, one simply takes the inverse of the price prevailing in one market and sees if it matches the price quoted in another market.

The next step is to determine the market in which a given currency is relatively cheaper. To make an arbitrage profit, the currency will be purchased in the market where it is cheap and sold in the market where it is expensive. Since a trader receives more marks per dollar in New York than in Frankfurt, the DM is cheaper in New York. To exploit this pricing difference, the trader

---

[2] One such trading room was featured in the film *Rollover*, starring Kris Kristofferson and Jane Fonda. In this story of international financial intrigue and panic, Kristofferson played the brilliant, hard-nosed manager of the trading room who saves the world from financial collapse.

FIGURE 27.2   Geographical Arbitrage

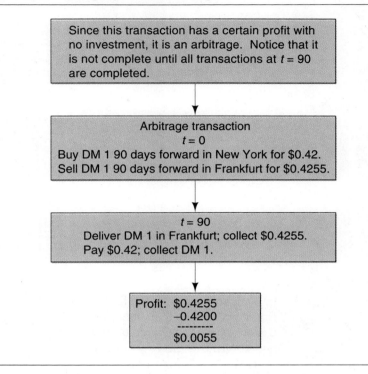

Since this transaction has a certain profit with no investment, it is an arbitrage. Notice that it is not complete until all transactions at $t = 90$ are completed.

Arbitrage transaction
$t = 0$
Buy DM 1 90 days forward in New York for $0.42.
Sell DM 1 90 days forward in Frankfurt for $0.4255.

$t = 90$
Deliver DM 1 in Frankfurt; collect $0.4255.
Pay $0.42; collect DM 1.

Profit: $0.4255
−0.4200

$0.0055

can enter the arbitrage transactions shown in Figure 27.2. These transactions represent the exploitation of an arbitrage opportunity, since they ensure a profit with no investment. At the outset, there is no cash flow. The only cash flow involved in the transactions occurs simultaneously when the commitments initiated at time $t = 0$ are completed at time $t = 90$ days. The profit, however, was certain from the time of the initial transactions.

The second kind of arbitrage opportunity involves cross-rates. In a given market, exchange rates for currencies A and B and for currencies A and C imply an exchange rate, called a cross-rate, between currencies B and C. If the rate implied for B and C does not match the actual rate between them in some other market, an arbitrage opportunity exists. The cross-rate is an implicit rate, since the rate for B in terms of C will not be stated explicitly in the market. As an example, assume we observe the following rates, where SF indicates Swiss francs, and all of the rates are 90-day forward rates:

New York	$/DM	0.42	2.3
	$/SF	0.49	2.04
Frankfurt	DM/SF	1.20	

FIGURE 27.3   Cross-Rate Arbitrage Transactions

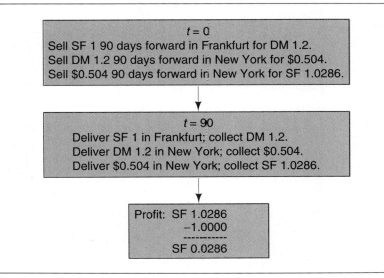

In New York, rates for the DM/SF or SF/DM are not stated. It is not surprising that currency rates in the United States are stated in terms of dollars and traders express the value of foreign currencies in dollars, just as shown in the quotations. But the two rates shown in New York imply a cross-rate for the DM/SF:

$$\text{DM/SF} = \frac{1}{\$/\text{DM}} \times \$/\text{SF}$$

$$= \frac{1}{0.42} \times 0.49 = 1.167$$

Since the rates for DM/SF differ in New York and Frankfurt, an arbitrage opportunity exists.

To exploit the arbitrage opportunity, one can trade only the exchange rates actually shown. For example, in New York there may not be a market for DM in terms of the Swiss franc.[3] To convert DM to SF in the New York market involves two transactions, first from DM to US$, and then from US$ to SF. To know how to trade, one must know which currency is relatively cheaper in a given market. In New York one receives DM1.167 per SF, but in Frankfurt SF1 is worth DM1.2, so the DM is cheaper in Frankfurt than in New York. Figure 27.3 shows transactions that exploit this arbitrage opportunity.

---

[3] Actually, in major foreign exchange centers, such as New York, some traders make markets in the major cross-rates. For many currencies in many markets, however, a separate quotation is not available for cross-rates.

DETERMINANTS OF FOREIGN EXCHANGE RATES

As the fundamental factors of supply and demand determine the price of agricultural commodities, similar factors shape the exchange rate that prevails between the currencies of two countries. These are numerous and quite complex, with entire books being written on them. Consequently, the brief discussion that follows merely indicates some of the most important influences.

One way of thinking about currencies is to regard them as essentially similar to other assets, subject to the same basic laws of supply and demand. When a particular currency is unusually plentiful, we might expect its price to fall. Of course, the price of a given currency in terms of some other currency is merely the exchange rate between them.

balance of payments
an accounting measurement of flows of goods and capital among nations

In foreign exchange, the flow of payments between one country and the rest of the world gives rise to the concept of a **balance of payments.** The balance of payments is generally calculated on a yearly basis. If a country's expenditures exceed its receipts, it has a balance of payments deficit; if receipts exceed expenditures, it has a balance of payments surplus. The balance of payments encompasses the flow of all kinds of goods and services among nations, including real goods, services, international investment, and all types of financial flows.

To understand how the balance of payments influences exchange rates, consider the following simple example. A country, Importeria, trades with other countries and always imports more goods than it exports. Therefore, there is always a net flow of real goods into Importeria. Importeria must pay for these goods in some way, so assume that the government simply prints sufficient additional currency to pay for them. This cannot go on for long without causing a change in the exchange rates between Importeria and its trading partners. As the trading partners continue to send more and more goods to Importeria, they collectively have fewer and fewer real goods themselves, but have a growing supply of the currency of Importeria.

☞ A continued policy of allowing imports to exceed exports should result in the fall in value of currency.

As the world's supply of Importeria's currency swells, it becomes apparent that it has only a few uses. Holders can use it to buy other currencies or to buy goods from Importeria. However, the accumulation of the currency continues until there is an excess supply at the prevailing exchange rate, so its value must fall. Just as Importeria cannot continually import more than it exports without the value of its currency falling, no country can continually consume more than it creates without the same result.

Fixed Exchange Rates

The kind of adjustment that a country such as Importeria might suffer in the value of its currency depends on the exchange rate system that is in effect. For most of its history the United States has used a **fixed exchange rate.** That is a stated exchange rate between two currencies at which anyone may transact. A country might import more than it exports for quite some time without causing a fixed exchange rate to change. However, even fixed exchange

fixed exchange rate
an exchange rate policy that requires stable prices for one currency in terms of another

The 'Shadow Bank of Japan' Strikes Again

For three days in mid-March, Shigeru Kita whipsawed the Tokyo currency market with $3 billion deals, buying and selling dollars for yen. In the process, the 65-year-old president of Hanwa Co., a steel-trading house, sparked outrage—and pocketed a swift $23 million profit.

Kita is one of the biggest remaining players of *zaitech,* the financial games practiced by cash-rich companies during the high-speed '80s in Japan. Most players have long since been scared off by the depressed stock market, the drop in real estate prices, and Japan's sputtering economy. Not Kita—at least, not so far. "For me, there's no beginning or end to *zaitech,*" he says. Kita's monthly trading, which has gone as high as $8 billion, now averages $5 billion.

Off Guard.   Kita first got a taste of currency trading when his brokers botched Hanwa's hedging strategies in 1983. Kita dove in, demanding that his dealers called him every 15 minutes until 11 P.M., after the New York market opens. Their preprogrammed phone numbers included those of his golf club, favorite restaurant, and singing teacher. By last year, only 29 percent of Hanwa's pretax profits of $243 million came from its $4.9 billion steel business. The rest came from *zaitech.* His ability to move currency rates has earned him the nickname of "shadow Bank of Japan."

In his March 11–13 foray, Kita called in eight employees from the accounting department to help his two full-time currency dealers. Using banks Hanwa regularly trades through, they bucked unspoken market etiquette by simultaneously placing huge orders, up to $300 million each. On

---

devaluation
a decrease in the value of a country's currency relative to other currencies

revaluation
a rise in the value of a country's currency relative to other currencies

rates are fixed only in the short run. The continual excess of imports over exports puts pressure on the value of Importeria's currency as the world's holdings of it continue to grow. Eventually, the fixed exchange rate between Importeria's currency and that of other nations will be adjusted. Importeria's currency will fall in value, or be **devalued.** Equivalently, the value of other currencies will increase relative to Importeria's currency, so those currencies are **revalued.**

Under a fixed exchange rate regime, exchange rates change only when a currency is under great strain to adjust to a new level. It may seem perplexing that the value of Importeria's currency would not adjust smoothly over time as the country continued its program of excess imports. Rates are fixed through the intervention of countries' central banks. As excess supplies of Importeria's currency accumulate in the world, central banks may use their reserves of other currencies to buy Importeria's. This buying eases the imbalance between

Monday, they bought the dollar, and on Tuesday, they sold, helping force it from above 138 yen to below 136. On Wednesday morning, they bought greenbacks at around 135, pushing the dollar up one yen within minutes. As the one setting off the market gyrations, Kita was able to cash in. But caught off guard were Japanese banks, which lost about $30 million as a result of his moves.

Burned.   The banks are now giving Hanwa the cold shoulder, quoting it unfavorable rates and spreading rumors that Kita got a tongue-lashing from the Finance Ministry. In fact, as a trading company, Hanwa is outside the ministry's jurisdiction. Kita has no fear that the banks will cut Hanwa off. "For 10 years, they have made huge profits off me," he says.

Hanwa borrows big to feed its high-risk habit: Debt runs as much as 12 times its equity. Hanwa has $5 billion in commercial paper outstanding and bank loans worth $11 billion. But it also owns land worth $2.9 billion.

Expanding his horizons, Kita is turning to the United States. Once burned by a misreading of the market for U.S. Treasury bonds, he shies away from fancy instruments such as futures and options. But he has some $1.5 billion in time deposits, mortgage-backed securities, and junk bonds.

For now, Kita is lying low in Japan. No more fireworks, he says—at least until the new fiscal year begins in April. After that, "I may do it again," he chuckles. To anyone who trades currency, those are fighting words.

Source: Karen Lowry Miller, "The 'Shadow Bank of Japan' Strikes Again," *Business Week,* April 8, 1991, p. 48.

supply and demand that would arise at the fixed level of rates. In effect, central banks sop up the excess supply of Importeria's currency, which would otherwise exist at the fixed level of exchange rates.

If the pressures against the currency of Importeria are not too severe, such action by the central banks may preserve the fixed level of exchange rates. However, the excess supply may become overwhelming, and central banks would be unable, or unwilling, to hold all of it. Thus Importeria would be forced to devalue its currency and set a new official rate of exchange. If the value of the Importeria unit of currency was one-tenth of a U.S. dollar before the devaluation, it might be reset at one-twelfth of a dollar after the devaluation. Then the procedure of trying to defend the new exchange rate would start anew. However, if Importeria persists in importing much more than it exports, it can expect to undergo another devaluation in the foreseeable future.

☞ With a fixed exchange rate system, changes in the value of a currency relative to others are infrequent, but are large and sudden when they do occur.

One obvious, and apparently disadvantageous, feature of a fixed exchange rate system is that when changes in the rates occur, they are rather large. The system has considerable advantages, however. First, it simplifies exchange transactions. If we can count on a fixed exchange rate for the next year, we do not have to control the risk of its changing, and this promotes international trade. Second, for multinational firms, a fully functioning fixed exchange rate system means that rate fluctuations do not affect accounting income. Third, it may constitute a form of discipline for economic policies, since participating countries would eventually realize that pursuit of certain policies leads to devaluation.

Perhaps for these reasons, and also as a signal of financial probity, the industrialized West pursued a fixed exchange rate policy from the end of World War II until 1971. Even stronger than a fixed exchange rate, the dollar was convertible into gold at a rate of $35 per ounce, according to the Bretton Woods Agreement. Other major currencies fixed their value in reference to the U.S. dollar, and until August 1971 the dollar remained as good as gold. At that time, faced with a weakening dollar and a soaring balance of payments deficit, the United States went off the gold standard. Attempts to reestablish some semblance of a fixed rate system, notably the Smithsonian Agreement of 1971, failed. March 1973 witnessed a new era in international foreign exchange. Most currencies were allowed to float, with daily fluctuations in exchange rates becoming the norm.

Other Exchange Rate Systems

This new system of exchange rates, or free market, prevails today, but the foreign exchange trader must consider a number of important exceptions and variations. With the breakdown of the Bretton Woods system and the failure of the Smithsonian Agreement, countries adopted a variety of exchange rate strategies, including free floats, managed or dirty floats, pegs, and joint floats.

freely floating rates
exchange rates that are allowed to fluctuate without government interference

managed or **dirty float**
floating exchange rates with government intervention

pegged float
fixing the value of one currency in terms of a second, with the value of the second being allowed to float

A currency is **freely floating** if it has no system of fixed exchange rates and if the central bank of the country in question does not attempt to influence its value. Few countries have truly freely floating exchange rates, as central banks seem unable to resist the temptation to intervene. When the central bank of a country engages in market transactions to influence the exchange value of its currency, but the rate is basically a floating rate, the policy is called a **managed float** or a **dirty float.** Opposed to this floating system, a number of countries continue to use a **pegged float** as a system of exchange rates. The value of one currency might be pegged to the value of another currency that itself floats. For example, Importeria might try to maintain a fixed exchange rate with the dollar, but the dollar itself floats against most of the world's currencies. In such a case Importeria pegs its currency to the dollar. Currencies can be pegged to a single currency or to a basket or portfolio of currencies.

joint float
when a group of currencies have a fixed exchange value in terms of each other, but the group floats in relation to currencies outside the group

☞ Today most major currencies are allowed to float, with occasional market intervention by central banks.

One other policy for exchange rate management is the **joint float.** In a joint float, currencies in a particular group have a fixed exchange value in terms of each other, but the group of currencies floats in relation to other currencies outside the group. The prime example comes from the European Community (EC), or European common market. The member nations formed the European monetary system (EMS) in 1979 and created the European currency unit (ECU). The basic strategy of the EMS agreement is to maintain very narrowly fluctuating exchange rates among the currencies of the participating countries. The ECU is expected to increase in importance with the advent of the virtual European unification in 1992.

In theory, a joint float system requires that the values of the currencies of the participating countries be fixed relative to one another, but float relative to external countries, such as the United States. This has important implications for speculation and hedging in all of these currencies. Recent experience has shown that some countries may be forced to devalue their currency relative to those of the group. Italy has faced the problem several times since the inception of the EMS. More recently, France has devalued several times.

MORE PRICE RELATIONSHIPS

☞ The interest rate parity theorem states the relationship among exchange rates and interest rates necessary to prevent arbitrage.

The geographical or cross-rate arbitrage opportunities, we noted before, occur when foreign exchange rates are aligned improperly. The examples in Figures 27.2 and 27.3 arose from a pricing discrepancy in the foreign exchange rates for a forward maturity of 90 days. Other price relationships are equally important and determine the permissible spreads that may exist between forward contracts of differing maturities. These are expressed as the interest rate parity theorem (IRP) and the purchasing power parity theorem (PPP).

The Interest Rate Parity Theorems

interest rate parity
a theorem that asserts that interest rates and exchange rates form an interconnected system

The **interest rate parity** theorem asserts that interest rates and exchange rates form an interconnected system. A change in interest rates will affect the exchange rate, and vice versa. The basic principle is that a trader will earn the same rate of return by investing in risk-free instruments of any currency, assuming that the proceeds from investment are converted back into the home currency by a forward contract initiated at the outset of the holding period. To illustrate interest rate parity, consider the rates of Table 27.1. If interest rate parity holds, the trader must earn the same return by following either of these two strategies:

Strategy 1 Hold an investment in the United States for 180 days.
Strategy 2 (a) Convert funds from US$ to DM at the spot rate.
　　　　　　(b) Invest for 180 days in Germany, and simultaneously purchase a 180-day forward contract to convert DM into US$ at a stated exchange rate.

(c) Convert the proceeds of the investment in DM back into dollars by means of the forward contract initiated in step (b).

If we adopt strategy 1 we could make the following transactions, assuming daily compounding. From Table 27.1, the 180-day interest rate in the United States is 20 percent per year, so an investment of $100 in the United States for 180 days yields:

$$\$100\left(1 + \frac{0.20}{365}\right)^{180} = \$110.36$$

In strategy 2 we would first exchange $100 for marks at the spot rate of $0.42 per mark, giving us $100/0.42 = 238.10$ marks. We would then invest these marks at the German 180-day interest rate of 29.9 percent per year. At the end of the 180 days the German mark proceeds are:

$$DM238.10\left(1 + \frac{0.299}{365}\right)^{180} = DM275.91$$

Simultaneous to the purchase of the marks, we engage in a 180-day forward contract, which will allow us to convert the marks into dollars at a rate of $0.40 per mark.

As the third step of strategy 2 we would arrange to convert our proceeds of DM275.91 back into dollars by using our forward contract. This would give us total dollar proceeds of:

$$DM275.91 \times 0.40 \; \$/DM = \$110.36$$

The IRP theorem says that the proceeds from these two strategies must be equal. In fact, we verify that the two strategies do yield the same proceeds of $110.36.

Let us now consider the same relationship, but for a 90-day horizon. Repeating the same operations as before for the new maturity gives:

Strategy 1   Invest $100 in the United States for 90 days = $104.80.
Strategy 2   Convert $100 to DM, invest in Germany for 90 days, and use a forward contract to convert DM into US$ after 90 days = $102.56.

covered interest arbitrage
a type of arbitrage transaction designed to take advantages of misaligned interest rates and foreign exchange rates

Strategy 1, investing in the United States, gives a higher return than investing the $100 in Germany. This means that an arbitrage opportunity is available. It is clearly better to invest funds in the United States than in Germany. Figure 27.4 shows the transactions necessary to take advantage of this discrepancy. This is known as **covered interest arbitrage,** because the position in the DM investment is covered by the forward contract to convert the proceeds back into dollars. The transaction is a genuine arbitrage opportunity because it makes possible a sure profit without risk and without investment.

TABLE 27.1 Interest Rates and Exchange Rates to Illustrate Interest Rate Parity

		Interest Rates	
Horizon	$/DM	United States	Germany
Spot	0.42	N.A.	N.A.
90-day	0.405	0.19	0.25
180-day	0.40	0.20	0.2990

Simply stated, interest rate parity asserts that such opportunities cannot exist in a well-functioning market. If they did exist, money-hungry traders would exploit them by making the transactions shown in Figure 27.4. This exploitation would go on at a frantic pace as long as the arbitrage opportunities were available. As the arbitrageurs borrowed more and more marks, they would drive up the interest rate in Germany, and as they bought bonds in the United States, the interest rate there would be driven down. This process would stop only when there were no further arbitrage opportunities. But if no arbitrage opportunities existed, the IRP theorem would hold. Thus, the very existence of arbitrageurs ensures that the theorem will hold.

FIGURE 27.4 Covered Interest Arbitrage

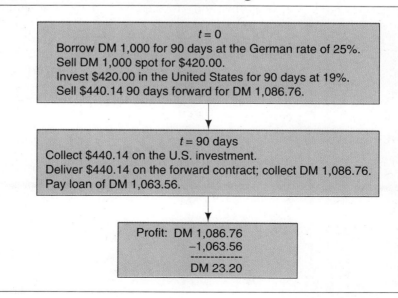

t = 0
Borrow DM 1,000 for 90 days at the German rate of 25%.
Sell DM 1,000 spot for $420.00.
Invest $420.00 in the United States for 90 days at 19%.
Sell $440.14 90 days forward for DM 1,086.76.

t = 90 days
Collect $440.14 on the U.S. investment.
Deliver $440.14 on the forward contract; collect DM 1,086.76.
Pay loan of DM 1,063.56.

Profit: DM 1,086.76
     −1,063.56

     DM 23.20

The European Currency Unit

In Rome in October 1990 the heads of state of the European Community (EC) specified, for the first time, that the ECU will be the EC's single currency, thus confirming the ECU as the financial numeraire of the single European market. In the next few years, an economic superpower will probably emerge, with a set of financial markets to match—the ECU markets.

Since it emerged in 1981, the ECU bond market has experienced three distinct phases: initial steps; dramatic expansion in 1985; and subsequent stagnation. The year 1990 seemed to mark the beginning of a phase of renewed growth—new issue volume could be nearly double that of 1989. Correspondingly, the ECU proportion of new international bond issuance has risen from the 4 to 6 percent range of recent years to 10 percent in the first half of 1990. This issue activity has led to a powerful growth in outstandings—to more than ECU55 billion by mid-1990. Market turnover has also risen substantially—secondary activity doubled in 1990.

The distinction between the traditional corporate market and the emergent ECU bond market of EC governments becomes apparent when the issue size is analyzed. The new government issues—ranging from ECU500 million to ECU2.1 billion—dwarf the traditional issues of ECU100 million. This distinction is critical, because it demonstrates the different target audience. The traditional ECU corporate bond is issued in small size and is locked up by the "Belgian dentist" type of investor for whom secondary market liquidity is not of prime importance. Major institutional investors are therefore unwilling to commit a serious volume of assets to such a market.

The new government market has begun to break this vicious cycle by offering issues of such large size that there is manifest liquidity—a classic characteristic of a properly developed government bond market relative to private sector issues.

At the end of the European monetary union process will be the single currency—the ECU subject to a single monetary policy run by the European Central Bank. Interest rates will be uniform throughout the EC, except for credit differentials that reflect the riskiness of different borrowers. There will be *no* "risk-free" interest rate, a crucial but little-recognized change. Even governments will have a credit risk, because they will have given up the power to print money to repay their bonds—the vital component of their risk-free credit standing in their existing national currencies. Giving up the power to debase the currency will be welcomed by the savers of Europe. Moreover, fiscal sovereignty will remain unfettered while borrowing remains responsible.

Only about 40 percent of EC governments' debt is in the form of bonds that are traded in the public markets. Once these are denominated in a single currency—the ECU—they will be only a little smaller than the size of the U.S. Treasury's marketable securities. Therefore, any move towards greater reliance on market debt by EC governments should make the ECU bond market of the European governments substantially larger than that of the U.S. Treasury. This is just one reflection of the financial power that will accompany the emergence of the world's leading economic superpower.

Composition of the ECU (in number of units)

Currency	Jan. 1, 1979 to Sept. 16, 1984	Sept. 17, 1984 to Sept. 20, 1989	Since Sept. 21, 1989
Deutsch mark	0.82800	0.71900	0.62420
French franc	1.15000	1.31000	1.33200
Pound sterling	0.8850	0.08780	0.08784
Italian lira	109.00000	140.00000	151.80000
Dutch guilder	0.28600	0.25600	0.21980
Belgian franc	3.66000	3.71000	3.30100
Luxembourg franc	0.14000	0.14000	0.13000
Danish krona	0.27700	0.21900	0.19760
Irish punt	0.00759	0.00871	0.00855
Greek drachma	—	1.1500	1.44000
Spanish peseta	—	—	6.88500
Portuguese escudo	—	—	1.39300

Source: "ECU Bonds, Pioneer of Currency Union," *Euromoney*, January 1991, pp. 71–76.

The Cost of a Mac Attack

The Economist magazine publishes the Big Mac index, a medium-rare guide to whether currencies are at their "correct" exchange rate. The McDonald's standard is based on the theory of purchasing power parity (PPP), which argues that in the long run, the exchange rate between two currencies should equate the price of an identical basket of goods and services in the respective countries. In this case, the "basket" contains only a Big Mac, which has the virtue of being made locally in more than 50 countries and of tasting virtually the same from Paris to Moscow.

In America the average price of a Big Mac (including tax) is about $2.20. In Tokyo you would have to fork out 370 yen for this gastronomic delight. Dividing the yen price by the dollar price gives an implied PPP of 168 yen/dollar, compared with the current exchange rate of 159 yen/dollar. So even after the recent slide in the yen, the dollar still looks to be 5 percent undervalued against the yen on PPP grounds. It also looks 14 percent undervalued against the D-mark, with a Mac-PPP of DM1.95.

Economists who have calculated PPPs by more sophisticated means come up with remarkably similar results. Professor Ronald McKinnon of Stanford University, one of the leading proponents of the theory of purchasing power parity, comes up with midpoint estimates for the dollar's PPP of Y165 and DM2.00.

Mac-currencies are now becoming truly global. The opening of the first McDonald's in Moscow has allowed the addition of the ruble to the sample. Muscovites have to pay the equivalent of $6.25 (converting at the official exchange rate) for a Big Mac, which makes it the most expensive hamburger in the sample. In other words, the ruble is overvalued against the dollar to a greater degree than any other currency, with an implied PPP of 1.70 rubles, compared with an official rate against the dollar of 0.60 rubles.

The Purchasing Power Parity Theorem

purchasing power parity a theorem stating the relationship among exchange rates, price levels, and inflation rates necessary to prevent arbitrage

Purchasing power parity is intimately tied to interest rate parity. The **purchasing power parity** theorem asserts that the exchange rates between two currencies must be proportional to the price level of goods in the two currencies. Violations of PPP lead to arbitrage opportunities, as shown in Figure 27.5. To simplify, assume that transportation and transaction costs do not exist and that there are no trade barriers between countries, such as quotas or tariffs.

Suppose the French franc is worth $0.10 and the cost of a croissant in Paris is FF 1, as shown in Figure 27.5. Also, a croissant sells for $0.15 in New York. This situation leads to the arbitrage opportunity that a trader can exploit by engaging in the transactions shown in the figure. The only price that can

Yet this overlooks one crucial fact: In Moscow fast food comes slow, with two- to three-hour queues. If this time is valued at average Soviet hourly wages, then the true cost of gorging on a Big Mac is roughly double the cash price. This implies a "queue-adjusted" Mac-PPP of 3.40 rubles. Indigestion, Mikhail?

Big MacCurrencies (hamburger prices)

Country	Local* Price	Implied PPP[†] of the Dollar	Actual Exchange Rate, April 30, 1990	Over- or Under-Valuation of Dollar
Australia	2.30	1.05	1.32	26%
Belgium	97.00	44.00	34.65	−21
Britain	1.40	0.64	0.61	−5
Canada	2.19	1.00	1.16	16
France	17.70	8.05	5.63	−30
Italy	3,900.00	1,773.00	1,230.00	−31
Japan	370.00	168.00	159.00	−5
Soviet Union	3.75	1.70	0.60	−65
United States[‡]	2.20			

* Price in local currency. Prices may vary between branches.
† Purchasing power parity: foreign price ÷ dollar price.
‡ Average of New York, Chicago, San Francisco, and Atlanta.

Source: McDonald's; Economist correspondents.

Source: "The Hamburger Standard," The Economist, May 5, 1990.

be charged for a croissant in New York that is consistent with the other values is $0.10.

The intimate relationship between the PPP and the IRP theorems originates from the link between interest rates and inflation rates. According to the analysis of Irving Fisher, the **nominal rate of interest** is composed of two elements, the **real** and **expected inflation rates.** We can express this relationship as follows:

nominal rate of interest
the rate of return in monetary terms

real inflation rate
the rate of return in terms of purchasing power

$$(1 + r_n) = (1 + r_r)[1 + E(i)] \qquad (27.1)$$

where r_n is the nominal interest rate, r_r is the real rate of interest, and $E(i)$ is the expected inflation rate. Since the expected inflation equals the expected change in purchasing power, we may interpret purchasing power parity as a

FIGURE 27.5   Croissant Arbitrage

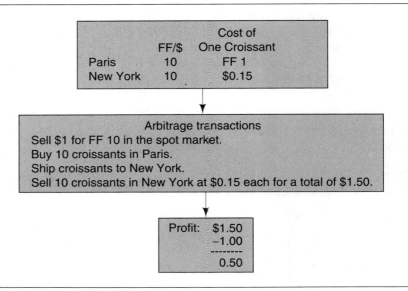

expected inflation rate
the expected rate of increase in the general level of prices

view about the linkage between exchange rates and relative inflation rates. Differences in nominal interest rates between two countries are probably due to differences in expected inflation. This means that interest rates, exchange rates, and inflation rates form a single integrated system.

HEDGING FOREIGN EXCHANGE RISK

☞ Firms can use foreign exchange futures and forward contracts to mitigate foreign exchange risk.

Many firms, and some individuals, face foreign exchange risk. Firms that import and export, for example, often have to make commitments to buy or sell goods for delivery at some future time, with the payment to be made in a foreign currency. Similarly, multinational firms operating foreign subsidiaries receive payments from the subsidiaries in a foreign currency. A wealthy individual may plan an extended trip abroad and may be concerned about the chance that the price of a particular foreign currency might rise unexpectedly. All of these parties are potential candidates for hedging unwanted currency risk.

☞ Translation exposure is a type of foreign exchange risk arising when the value of a currency must be restated in the currency of another country.

Hedging Transaction Exposure

The simplest kind of example arises in the case of someone like Moncrief Snobbody, who plans a six-month trip to Switzerland. He plans to spend a considerable sum during this trip, enough to make it worthwhile to attend to the exchange rates, assumed to have the values shown below. With the

TABLE 27.2   Moncrief Snobbody's Swiss Franc Hedge

Cash Market	*Futures Market*
January 12	
Moncrief plans to take a 6-month vacation in Switzerland, to begin in June, and to cost about SF250,000.	Moncrief buys SF250,000 180 days forward at 0.5134 for a total cost of $128,350.
June 16	
The $/SF spot rate is now 0.5211, giving a dollar cost of $130,275 for SF250,000.	Moncrief delivers $128,350 and collects SF250,000.
Savings on the hedge	$130,275 − 128,350 = $1,925

more distant rates lying above the nearby rates, Moncrief fears that the actual rates may be even higher in the future, so he decides to lock into the existing rates by securing the future delivery of Swiss francs at the currently available prices. Since it is now January and he plans to depart for Switzerland in June, Moncrief buys SF250,000 180 days forward at a price of 0.5134 $/SF. He anticipates that the SF250,000 will pay for his six-month stay, as Table 27.2 shows.

☞ Transaction exposure is a type of foreign exchange risk arising when a currency must be actually converted into another currency.

Hypothetical Swiss Exchange Rates in January

Spot	0.4935
Forward 90-day	0.5034
Forward 180-day	0.5134

By June 6, Moncrief's fears have been realized, and the spot rate for the Swiss franc is now 0.5211. Moncrief consequently delivers $128,350 and collects his SF250,000. Had he waited and transacted in the spot market on June 6, the SF250,000 would have cost him $130,275. By hedging his foreign exchange risk he saved $1,925, which is enough to finance an extension of his stay in Switzerland for a day or two.

Moncrief had a preexisting risk in the foreign exchange market, since it was already determined that he would acquire the Swiss francs. By trading in the foreign exchange market he guaranteed a price for himself of $0.5134 per franc. Had he waited, the price would have been higher; but it just as easily could have been lower. By entering the foreign exchange market, Moncrief eliminated the uncertainty regarding the price that he would have to pay to acquire francs. Of course, the foreign exchange market can be used for purposes even more serious than reducing the risk surrounding Moncrief Snobbody's Swiss vacation.

Hedging Import-Export Transactions

Consider the case of a small import-export firm that is negotiating a large purchase of Japanese watches. The Japanese executives, being notoriously tough negotiators, demand payment in yen on delivery of the watches. (If the contract had called for payment in dollars rather than yen the Japanese firm would bear the exchange risk.) Between the present and the delivery date is a six-month delay. However, the price per watch is agreed today to be yen 2,850, and the transaction will be for 15,000 watches. This means that the purchaser will have to pay yen 42,750,000 six months down the road. Hypothetical exchange rates for May 11 are given below. With the spot rate of $0.004173 per yen, the purchase price for the 15,000 watches is $178,396. If we treat the forward price on May 11 as a forecast of future exchange rates, we expect the dollar to lose ground against the yen. With the 180-day forward trading at 0.004237, it seems that the actual dollar cost might be closer to $182,329. If delivery and payment occur in November, the importer might reasonably estimate his actual dollar outlay in the $182,000 range instead of the $178,000 range.

Foreign Exchange Rates for $/Yen, May 11

Spot	0.004173
Forward 90-day	0.004200
Forward 180-day	0.004265

To avoid any worsening of his exchange position, the importer decides to hedge the transaction by trading in the foreign exchange market. Delivery is expected in November, so the importer buys yen 42,750,000 in the forward market at the forward price of 0.004265. Table 27.3 shows the transactions involved.

TABLE 27.3   The Importer's Hedge

Cash Market	Forward Market
May 11	
The importer anticipates a need for yen 42,750,000 in November to purchase a batch of watches.	The importer buys yen 42,750,000 180 days forward at a price of 0.004265. This gives a total dollar commitment of $182,328.75 due in 6 months.
November 11	
The importer pays yen 42,750,000 and receives the watches.	The importer pays $182,328.75 and receives yen 42,750,000. The spot price of yen is 0.004285.
Savings on the hedge	$183,183.75 − 182,328.75 = $855

On November 10 the watches arrive and the importer pays dollars to obtain the yen required. Now the spot price for yen is 0.004285 per dollar. If the importer had waited to purchase yen, they would have cost $183,183.75 (42,750,000 × 0.004285). Because the importer hedged, they cost only $182,328.75, thus saving $855. Even more important, using the forward market gave the importer a firmly established price for the watches.

INTERNATIONAL INVESTMENT AND FINANCING DECISIONS

In previous chapters we considered the firm's investment and financing decisions and learned techniques for making correct decisions. However, those discussions assumed a domestic firm operating in a domestic environment. We now consider special problems of capital budgeting and fund raising that arise in an international setting.

International Capital Budgeting

☞ In international capital budgeting, the relevant cash flows to discount are those coming back to the ultimate investor, usually the parent country.

In studying capital budgeting we learned that discounted cash flow techniques provide the best way to analyze prospective investments. In particular, we noted that accepting projects with a positive NPV contributes to the wealth of the shareholders. Determining the present value of a project depends on estimating the after-tax cash flows from the project and discounting those cash flows. The discount rate must reflect the systematic risk of those cash flows.

In the international setting, the same general principles hold, but several special issues also exist, most of which center around determining and evaluating cash flows. The typical multinational firm consists of a parent and several subsidiaries. A **subsidiary** is a firm owned by another firm. Usually a foreign subsidiary undertakes the foreign investment project. The subsidiary receives the cash flows from the project and the parent firm receives cash from the subsidiary.

subsidiary
a firm owned by another firm

Cash Flows of Subsidiaries Versus Parent Companies

☞ Cash flows from international capital budgeting projects should be measured in the home currency of the ultimate investor.

Which cash flows are relevant for the capital budgeting decision, the subsidiary's or the parent's? The two can be quite different, so the issue is of considerable practical concern, and it has a clear solution: the return from any project is due to the investor. Generally, the parent is the ultimate investor, because it provides capital to the subsidiary. In fact, it often wholly owns the subsidiary, in which case the subsidiary's cash flows are irrelevant. Only the cash flows back to the parent matter.

The Effect of Taxes

As in domestic capital budgeting, after-tax cash flows are the flows of concern. In the international capital budgeting environment, taxation becomes quite complicated. The subsidiary often pays tax in the foreign country and then

FINANCE TODAY

Frothy Trade

The beer brewing industry has been undergoing a process of internationalization for the past 25 years. This box examines the roles that three types of international transactions—merchandise trade, licensing agreements, and foreign direct investment—have played in this internationalization. As in other industries, a few general economic factors explain much of the increase in international brewing activity. What makes beer brewing a particularly interesting case study is that it provides an opportunity to demonstrate how certain economic factors, such as economies of scale and trade barriers, can affect the internationalization of an industry.

Merchandise Trade.   As with other goods, world merchandise trade in beer has expanded rapidly over the past 25 years (see the figure). Much of the increase in world beer trade—and in world trade in general—can be attributed to such factors as lower trade barriers, more efficient communication and transportation technology, and growth in real personal incomes. The value of world beer trade increased from $149 million in 1965 to $2.08 billion in 1987, a 14-fold increase; at the same time, world trade in all goods increased to more than 12.5 times its 1965 value. In more recent years, between 1980 and 1987, world trade in beer expanded 83.8 percent, while total world trade grew only 23.4 percent. Despite its rapid growth, trade in beer in 1987 accounted for less than one-tenth of 1 percent of total world merchandise trade.

On a volume basis, world trade in beer has nearly tripled since 1965, growing at an average annual rate of 6.5 percent between 1965 and 1987. The largest exporters of beer in this growing market, ranked by volume, are the Netherlands, West Germany, Czechoslovakia, Belgium, and Canada (see the table).* The largest importers are the United States, the United Kingdom, France, Italy, and West Germany.

Beer imports as a percent of total consumption (IPC) and exports as a percent of production (EPP) are larger for some of the smaller exporters and importers than they are for some of the larger exporting and importing countries. As the table shows, among 25 importers, beer IPC ranges from a low of 0.2 percent in Norway to 16.4 percent in Italy. The percent of beer consumption accounted for by imports in the largest beer importing country, the United States, is about 5 percent.

Similarly, among exporters, figures for EPP range from 0.4 percent in the United States to 41.6 percent in Ireland. The export numbers as a percent of production for such countries as the Netherlands and Luxembourg, however, are questionable as these countries do a significant amount of re-exporting to other countries (that is, much of the beer reported as exports

* The FAO *Trade Yearbook* indicates that Mexico was the world's third-largest exporter of beer in 1987.

World Trade of Beer and Other Goods

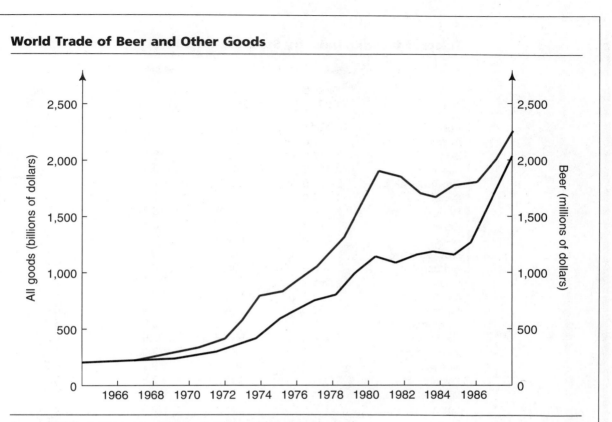

Source: FAO Trade Yearbook and *International Financial Statistics Yearbook.*

may simply be imported and then re-exported for consumption elsewhere).[†]

Few of the countries listed in the table are strictly importers or exporters of beer. Most of the countries that export beer also import some beer and vice versa. This pattern of trade is known as intra-industry trade. An examination of the IPC and EPP statistics in the table show that intra-industry trade in beer is more important to some countries than to others. The largest exporter of beer, the Netherlands, imported only 4.3 percent of the beer it consumed in 1987.[‡] Similarly, the two largest importers of beer, the United States and the United Kingdom, exported only 0.4 percent and 1.9 percent of their beer production in 1987. Ireland, on the other hand, exported nearly 42 percent of its production, while importing more than 12 percent of beer consumption.

[†] It has been noted that the Netherlands has a long history of re-exporting imported goods.

[‡] Re-exported goods from the Netherlands may not be included in the country's import figures.

(continued)

Selected Brewing Industry Statistics for 1987

	Exports 1,000 HL*	Imports 1,000 HL*	Exports as Percent of Production	Imports as Percent of Consumption
Australia	728.3	70.0	3.9%	0.4%
Austria	361.0	285.0	4.0	3.2
Belgium	2,537.0	565.5	18.1	4.7
Canada	2,415.8	448.0	10.5	2.1
Czechoslovakia	2,698.0	0.0	12.1	0.0
Denmark	1,934.0	20.8	22.8	0.3
West Germany	5,706.0	1,301.6	6.2	1.5
Finland	22.8	13.9	0.7	0.4
France	672.0	2,445.9	3.4	11.3
East Germany	N.A.	N.A.	N.A.	N.A.
Hungary	0.0	1,290.0	0.0	12.6
Ireland	2,066.0	415.0	41.6	12.5
Italy	73.1	2,162.8	0.7	16.4
Japan	293.3	224.0	0.5	0.4
Luxembourg	270.3	42.2	40.9	9.8
Netherlands	5,724.2	534.9	32.6	4.3
New Zealand	83.2	70.5	2.0	1.7
Norway	19.2	405.0	0.9	0.2
Poland	327.1	106.2	2.8	0.9
Portugal	74.5	34.3	1.5	0.7
Spain	121.0	735.0	0.5	2.8
Sweden	44.9	344.4	1.1	7.9
Switzerland	36.7	435.9	0.9	10.5
USSR	N.A.	900.0	N.A.	1.7
United Kingdom	1,140.0	4,093.1	1.9	6.5
U.S.A.	919.7	10,991.1	0.4	5.0

* 1 HL = 100 liters = 26.4 gallons.

Source: Derived from information in the Brewers Association of Canada's *International Survey: Alcoholic Beverage Taxation and Control Policies.*

Source: Jeffrey D. Karrenbrock, "The Internationalization of the Beer Brewing Industry," *Review of the Federal Reserve Bank of St. Louis,* November–December 1990, pp. 3–6.

tax credit
a subtraction of some amount directly from the tax bill

remits the remaining proceeds to the parent. The parent must then pay taxes on these proceeds as well. Often the parent receives a **tax credit** for taxes paid by subsidiaries in other countries; that is, a subtraction of some amount directly from the tax bill. For example, a $10,000 tax credit reduces the tax bill by $10,000.

Foreign Versus Home Currency

☞ In general, the expected cost of financing to the parent, measured in the parent's home currency, should be independent of the currency chosen for the actual financing.

If a firm takes a project in a foreign country, it almost certainly generates cash flows in the foreign currency. However, the investors in the parent normally contribute capital denominated in the parent's currency. Which currency should the firm use to calculate the NPV of the project? For the parent, financial managers must focus on the return they can pay to their investors. These investors are interested in changes in their own purchasing power as a result of their investment. This means that they must be concerned with the purchasing power of the investors. Because that depends largely on the value of the home currency, managers must consider the home currency cash flows that the project generates. These are the cash flows that will interest their investors, so they must be the correct ones to consider in making a capital budgeting decision. Financial managers must consider the problem of converting the foreign currency back into the home currency.

INTERNATIONAL FINANCING

A multinational firm often has broader financing opportunities than a strictly domestic firm. If the parent operates subsidiaries in foreign countries, a subsidiary may raise its own capital in the country in which it operates. Alternatively, the parent can raise capital and channel it to the subsidiary in the form of debt or equity. In addition, well-known multinational firms have access to world capital markets, as well as financial markets in their own countries.

Without special tax considerations or other market imperfections, the firm should expect to pay the same ultimate cost for capital no matter where it is raised. As we saw earlier in this chapter from our discussion of purchasing power and interest rate parity, the ultimate cost of funds should be the same no matter where funds are raised. As a general principle, we should expect the cost of financing to be independent of the country and currency in which funds are raised.

Certain factors can arise that make the cost of funds depend on where the firm raises them. Often, governments are anxious to attract DFI. It means more employment and tax income for the host country, so some countries actively seek DFI from multinationals by offering incentives such as special tax rules. On some occasions, host countries offer a **tax holiday,** a time during which they impose no taxes on multinational operations. As another incentive, some governments offer special training programs for workers in the area where a firm will invest. The host country also may provide financing for the subsidiary's operations.

tax holiday
a time during which the host country imposes no taxes on a foreign firm's operations

No matter how the host country encourages foreign firms to invest, it provides an incentive for investment that is specific to a particular location. This is clearest when the government actually finances the operations with debt. However, training programs, concessions on land costs, and tax holidays all substitute for the firm's own capital.

In this case the investment decision and financing decision become closely related. In perfect markets, investment and financing decisions are independent. This is not so when a government offers special incentives, because those incentives actually affect the cash flows from the project. The effect of these special financing sources makes the investment and financing interdependent, thus rendering the evaluation of international investments much more complicated.

SUMMARY

This chapter introduced some of the special issues that financial managers face when entering the international arena. The strategies for entering a foreign market are exporting, licensing, and direct foreign investment. No matter how a firm enters a foreign market, it confronts problems of foreign exchange. We considered how foreign exchange rates are quoted, the factors that determine exchange rates, and some arbitrage principles that govern the relationships among exchange rates, interest rates, and inflation rates. Finally, we discussed special problems financial managers face in managing exchange risk, capital budgeting projects, and the firm's financing of its foreign operations.

QUESTIONS

1. How can companies enter foreign markets?
2. Why do firms engage in direct foreign investment despite the disadvantages of doing so?
3. Explain the basic ideas of the appropriability theory.
4. Explain the imperfections in the labor market that may lead to direct foreign investment.
5. What is geographical arbitrage?
6. What is a cross-rate?
7. What is the balance of payments?
8. What is a fixed exchange rate policy?
9. What is the attraction of a fixed exchange rate policy?
10. What is the major difficulty with a fixed exchange rate policy?
11. What is the difference between freely floating rates and a dirty float?
12. Explain the basic idea of the interest rate parity theorem.
13. Explain the basic idea of the purchasing power parity theorem.
14. What is the difference between transaction and translation exposure?
15. In international capital budgeting, which cash flows are relevant to the decision?
16. Respond to the following claim made by a financial executive of a U.S. firm: Interest rates in the United States today are 12 percent, but only 7 percent in Germany. Obviously, we can save 5 percent if we borrow in Germany.

PROBLEMS

Use the following quotations to solve Problems 1 through 6.

	Exchange Rates				Interest Rates	
	New York		Frankfurt			
	$/£	$/DM	DM/£	DM/$	$	DM
Spot	1.6640	0.3879	4.3064	2.5880	—	—
30-day	1.6647	0.3887	4.2828	2.5727	10%	7.31%
90-day	1.6674	0.3905	4.2699	2.5608	11	8.57
180-day	1.6717	0.3935	4.2583	2.5413	12	8.83

1. Find a geographical arbitrage opportunity in these quotations.
2. Explain the exact transactions you would make to exploit the arbitrage opportunity.
3. Find a cross-rate arbitrage opportunity in these quotations.
4. Explain the exact transactions you would make to exploit the arbitrage opportunity.
5. Find a covered interest arbitrage opportunity in these quotations.
6. Explain the exact transactions you would make to exploit the arbitrage opportunity.

Use the following quotations to solve Problems 7 through 12.

	Foreign Currency Prices				Interest Rates		
	New York		Paris	Frankfurt	United States	France	Germany
	$/FF	$/DM	FF/$	DM/FF	$	FF	DM
Spot	0.105	0.30	9.5238	0.3500	N.A.	N.A.	N.A.
30-day	0.107	0.30	9.3458	0.3567	50%	1.5%	50%
90-day	0.109	0.30	9.1743	0.3633	60	37.78	60
180-day	0.11	0.30	9.0909	0.3650	65	50.20	65

7. Find a geographical arbitrage opportunity in these quotations.
8. Explain the exact transactions you would make to exploit the arbitrage opportunity.
9. Find a cross-rate arbitrage opportunity in these quotations.

10. Explain the exact transactions you would make to exploit the arbitrage opportunity.
11. Find a covered interest arbitrage opportunity in these quotations.
12. Explain the exact transactions you would make to exploit the arbitrage opportunity.
13. For his vacation, Irving buys 1,000 German marks in the forward market and pays $0.40 per mark. When Irving arrives in Berlin, the exchange rate is $0.45 per mark. How much does he save or lose by transacting in the forward market?
14. For her vacation, Alice buys 1,000 German marks in the forward market and pays $0.40 per mark. When she arrives in Munchen, the exchange rate is $0.38 per mark. How much does she save or lose by transacting in the forward market?
15. What conclusion can you draw from Problems 13 and 14?

Appendix

TABLE A.1   Present Value of $1

Period (n)	Interest Rate (r)								
	1%	2%	3%	4%	5%	6%	7%	8%	9%
1	0.9901	0.9804	0.9709	0.9615	0.9524	0.9434	0.9346	0.9259	0.9174
2	0.9803	0.9612	0.9426	0.9246	0.9070	0.8900	0.8734	0.8573	0.8417
3	0.9706	0.9423	0.9151	0.8890	0.8638	0.8396	0.8163	0.7938	0.7722
4	0.9610	0.9238	0.8885	0.8548	0.8227	0.7921	0.7629	0.7350	0.7084
5	0.9515	0.9057	0.8626	0.8219	0.7835	0.7473	0.7130	0.6806	0.6499
6	0.9420	0.8880	0.8375	0.7903	0.7462	0.7050	0.6663	0.6302	0.5963
7	0.9327	0.8706	0.8131	0.7599	0.7107	0.6651	0.6227	0.5835	0.5470
8	0.9235	0.8535	0.7894	0.7307	0.6768	0.6274	0.5820	0.5403	0.5019
9	0.9143	0.8368	0.7664	0.7026	0.6446	0.5919	0.5439	0.5002	0.4604
10	0.9053	0.8203	0.7441	0.6756	0.6139	0.5584	0.5083	0.4632	0.4224
11	0.8963	0.8043	0.7224	0.6496	0.5847	0.5268	0.4751	0.4289	0.3875
12	0.8874	0.7885	0.7014	0.6246	0.5568	0.4970	0.4440	0.3971	0.3555
13	0.8787	0.7730	0.6810	0.6006	0.5303	0.4688	0.4150	0.3677	0.3262
14	0.8700	0.7579	0.6611	0.5775	0.5051	0.4423	0.3878	0.3405	0.2992
15	0.8613	0.7430	0.6419	0.5553	0.4810	0.4173	0.3624	0.3152	0.2745
16	0.8528	0.7284	0.6232	0.5339	0.4581	0.3936	0.3387	0.2919	0.2519
17	0.8444	0.7142	0.6050	0.5134	0.4363	0.3714	0.3166	0.2703	0.2311
18	0.8360	0.7002	0.5874	0.4936	0.4155	0.3503	0.2959	0.2502	0.2120
19	0.8277	0.6864	0.5703	0.4746	0.3957	0.3305	0.2765	0.2317	0.1945
20	0.8195	0.6730	0.5537	0.4564	0.3769	0.3118	0.2584	0.2145	0.1784
21	0.8114	0.6598	0.5375	0.4388	0.3589	0.2942	0.2415	0.1987	0.1637
22	0.8034	0.6468	0.5219	0.4220	0.3418	0.2775	0.2257	0.1839	0.1502
23	0.7954	0.6342	0.5067	0.4057	0.3256	0.2618	0.2109	0.1703	0.1378
24	0.7876	0.6217	0.4919	0.3901	0.3101	0.2470	0.1971	0.1577	0.1264
25	0.7798	0.6095	0.4776	0.3751	0.2953	0.2330	0.1842	0.1460	0.1160
26	0.7720	0.5976	0.4637	0.3607	0.2812	0.2198	0.1722	0.1352	0.1064
27	0.7644	0.5859	0.4502	0.3468	0.2678	0.2074	0.1609	0.1252	0.0976
28	0.7568	0.5744	0.4371	0.3335	0.2551	0.1956	0.1504	0.1159	0.0895
29	0.7493	0.5631	0.4243	0.3207	0.2429	0.1846	0.1406	0.1073	0.0822
30	0.7419	0.5521	0.4120	0.3083	0.2314	0.1741	0.1314	0.0994	0.0754
31	0.7346	0.5412	0.4000	0.2965	0.2204	0.1643	0.1228	0.0920	0.0691
32	0.7273	0.5306	0.3883	0.2851	0.2099	0.1550	0.1147	0.0852	0.0634
33	0.7201	0.5202	0.3770	0.2741	0.1999	0.1462	0.1072	0.0789	0.0582
34	0.7130	0.5100	0.3660	0.2636	0.1904	0.1379	0.1002	0.0730	0.0534
35	0.7059	0.5000	0.3554	0.2534	0.1813	0.1301	0.0937	0.0676	0.0490
36	0.6989	0.4902	0.3450	0.2437	0.1727	0.1227	0.0875	0.0626	0.0449
37	0.6920	0.4806	0.3350	0.2343	0.1644	0.1158	0.0818	0.0580	0.0412
38	0.6852	0.4712	0.3252	0.2253	0.1566	0.1092	0.0765	0.0537	0.0378
39	0.6784	0.4619	0.3158	0.2166	0.1491	0.1031	0.0715	0.0497	0.0347
40	0.6717	0.4529	0.3066	0.2083	0.1420	0.0972	0.0668	0.0460	0.0318

Interest Rate (r)

10%	11%	12%	13%	14%	15%	16%	17%	18%
0.9091	0.9009	0.8929	0.8850	0.8772	0.8696	0.8621	0.8547	0.8475
0.8264	0.8116	0.7972	0.7831	0.7695	0.7561	0.7432	0.7305	0.7182
0.7513	0.7312	0.7118	0.6931	0.6750	0.6575	0.6407	0.6244	0.6086
0.6830	0.6587	0.6355	0.6133	0.5921	0.5718	0.5523	0.5337	0.5158
0.6209	0.5935	0.5674	0.5428	0.5194	0.4972	0.4761	0.4561	0.4371
0.5645	0.5346	0.5066	0.4803	0.4556	0.4323	0.4104	0.3898	0.3704
0.5132	0.4817	0.4523	0.4251	0.3996	0.3759	0.3538	0.3332	0.3139
0.4665	0.4339	0.4039	0.3762	0.3506	0.3269	0.3050	0.2848	0.2660
0.4241	0.3909	0.3606	0.3329	0.3075	0.2843	0.2630	0.2434	0.2255
0.3855	0.3522	0.3220	0.2946	0.2697	0.2472	0.2267	0.2080	0.1911
0.3505	0.3173	0.2875	0.2607	0.2366	0.2149	0.1954	0.1778	0.1619
0.3186	0.2858	0.2567	0.2307	0.2076	0.1869	0.1685	0.1520	0.1372
0.2897	0.2575	0.2292	0.2042	0.1821	0.1625	0.1452	0.1299	0.1163
0.2633	0.2320	0.2046	0.1807	0.1597	0.1413	0.1252	0.1110	0.0985
0.2394	0.2090	0.1827	0.1599	0.1401	0.1229	0.1079	0.0949	0.0835
0.2176	0.1883	0.1631	0.1415	0.1229	0.1069	0.0930	0.0811	0.0708
0.1978	0.1696	0.1456	0.1252	0.1078	0.0929	0.0802	0.0693	0.0600
0.1799	0.1528	0.1300	0.1108	0.0946	0.0808	0.0691	0.0592	0.0508
0.1635	0.1377	0.1161	0.0981	0.0829	0.0703	0.0596	0.0506	0.0431
0.1486	0.1240	0.1037	0.0868	0.0728	0.0611	0.0514	0.0433	0.0365
0.1351	0.1117	0.0926	0.0768	0.0638	0.0531	0.0443	0.0370	0.0309
0.1228	0.1007	0.0826	0.0680	0.0560	0.0462	0.0382	0.0316	0.0262
0.1117	0.0907	0.0738	0.0601	0.0491	0.0402	0.0329	0.0270	0.0222
0.1015	0.0817	0.0659	0.0532	0.0431	0.0349	0.0284	0.0231	0.0188
0.0923	0.0736	0.0588	0.0471	0.0378	0.0304	0.0245	0.0197	0.0160
0.0839	0.0663	0.0525	0.0417	0.0331	0.0264	0.0211	0.0169	0.0135
0.0763	0.0597	0.0469	0.0369	0.0291	0.0230	0.0182	0.0144	0.0115
0.0693	0.0538	0.0419	0.0326	0.0255	0.0200	0.0157	0.0123	0.0097
0.0630	0.0485	0.0374	0.0289	0.0224	0.0174	0.0135	0.0105	0.0082
0.0573	0.0437	0.0334	0.0256	0.0196	0.0151	0.0116	0.0090	0.0070
0.0521	0.0394	0.0298	0.0226	0.0172	0.0131	0.0100	0.0077	0.0059
0.0474	0.0355	0.0266	0.0200	0.0151	0.0114	0.0087	0.0066	0.0050
0.0431	0.0319	0.0238	0.0177	0.0132	0.0099	0.0075	0.0056	0.0042
0.0391	0.0288	0.0212	0.0157	0.0116	0.0086	0.0064	0.0048	0.0036
0.0356	0.0259	0.0189	0.0139	0.0102	0.0075	0.0055	0.0041	0.0030
0.0323	0.0234	0.0169	0.0123	0.0089	0.0065	0.0048	0.0035	0.0026
0.0294	0.0210	0.0151	0.0109	0.0078	0.0057	0.0041	0.0030	0.0022
0.0267	0.0190	0.0135	0.0096	0.0069	0.0049	0.0036	0.0026	0.0019
0.0243	0.0171	0.0120	0.0085	0.0060	0.0043	0.0031	0.0022	0.0016
0.0221	0.0154	0.0107	0.0075	0.0053	0.0037	0.0026	0.0019	0.0013

TABLE A.2 Future Value of $1

Period (n)	Interest Rate (r)								
	1%	2%	3%	4%	5%	6%	7%	8%	9%
1	1.0100	1.0200	1.0300	1.0400	1.0500	1.0600	1.0700	1.0800	1.0900
2	1.0201	1.0404	1.0609	1.0816	1.1025	1.1236	1.1449	1.1664	1.1881
3	1.0303	1.0612	1.0927	1.1249	1.1576	1.1910	1.2250	1.2597	1.2950
4	1.0406	1.0824	1.1255	1.1699	1.2155	1.2625	1.3108	1.3605	1.4116
5	1.0510	1.1041	1.1593	1.2167	1.2763	1.3382	1.4026	1.4693	1.5386
6	1.0615	1.1262	1.1941	1.2653	1.3401	1.4185	1.5007	1.5869	1.6771
7	1.0721	1.1487	1.2299	1.3159	1.4071	1.5036	1.6058	1.7138	1.8280
8	1.0829	1.1717	1.2668	1.3686	1.4775	1.5938	1.7182	1.8509	1.9926
9	1.0937	1.1951	1.3048	1.4233	1.5513	1.6895	1.8385	1.9990	2.1719
10	1.1046	1.2190	1.3439	1.4802	1.6289	1.7908	1.9672	2.1589	2.3674
11	1.1157	1.2434	1.3842	1.5395	1.7103	1.8983	2.1049	2.3316	2.5804
12	1.1268	1.2682	1.4258	1.6010	1.7959	2.0122	2.2522	2.5182	2.8127
13	1.1381	1.2936	1.4685	1.6651	1.8856	2.1329	2.4098	2.7196	3.0658
14	1.1495	1.3195	1.5126	1.7317	1.9799	2.2609	2.5785	2.9372	3.3417
15	1.1610	1.3459	1.5580	1.8009	2.0789	2.3966	2.7590	3.1722	3.6425
16	1.1726	1.3728	1.6047	1.8730	2.1829	2.5404	2.9522	3.4259	3.9703
17	1.1843	1.4002	1.6528	1.9479	2.2920	2.6928	3.1588	3.7000	4.3276
18	1.1961	1.4282	1.7024	2.0258	2.4066	2.8543	3.3799	3.9960	4.7171
19	1.2081	1.4568	1.7535	2.1068	2.5270	3.0256	3.6165	4.3157	5.1417
20	1.2202	1.4859	1.8061	2.1911	2.6533	3.2071	3.8697	4.6610	5.6044
21	1.2324	1.5157	1.8603	2.2788	2.7860	3.3996	4.1406	5.0338	6.1088
22	1.2447	1.5460	1.9161	2.3699	2.9253	3.6035	4.4304	5.4365	6.6586
23	1.2572	1.5769	1.9736	2.4647	3.0715	3.8197	4.7405	5.8715	7.2579
24	1.2697	1.6084	2.0328	2.5633	3.2251	4.0489	5.0724	6.3412	7.9111
25	1.2824	1.6406	2.0938	2.6658	3.3864	4.2919	5.4274	6.8485	8.6231
26	1.2953	1.6734	2.1566	2.7725	3.5557	4.5494	5.8074	7.3964	9.3992
27	1.3082	1.7069	2.2213	2.8834	3.7335	4.8223	6.2139	7.9881	10.2451
28	1.3213	1.7410	2.2879	2.9987	3.9201	5.1117	6.6488	8.6271	11.1671
29	1.3345	1.7758	2.3566	3.1187	4.1161	5.4184	7.1143	9.3173	12.1722
30	1.3478	1.8114	2.4273	3.2434	4.3219	5.7435	7.6123	10.0627	13.2677
31	1.3613	1.8476	2.5001	3.3731	4.5380	6.0881	8.1451	10.8677	14.4618
32	1.3749	1.8845	2.5751	3.5081	4.7649	6.4534	8.7153	11.7371	15.7633
33	1.3887	1.9222	2.6523	3.6484	5.0032	6.8406	9.3253	12.6760	17.1820
34	1.4026	1.9607	2.7319	3.7943	5.2533	7.2510	9.9781	13.6901	18.7284
35	1.4166	1.9999	2.8139	3.9461	5.5160	7.6861	10.6766	14.7853	20.4140
36	1.4308	2.0399	2.8983	4.1039	5.7918	8.1473	11.4239	15.9682	22.2512
37	1.4451	2.0807	2.9852	4.2681	6.0814	8.6361	12.2236	17.2456	24.2538
38	1.4595	2.1223	3.0748	4.4388	6.3855	9.1543	13.0793	18.6253	26.4367
39	1.4741	2.1647	3.1670	4.6164	6.7048	9.7035	13.9948	20.1153	28.8160
40	1.4889	2.2080	3.2620	4.8010	7.0400	10.2857	14.9745	21.7245	31.4094

Interest Rate (r)

10%	11%	12%	13%	14%	15%	16%	17%	18%
1.1000	1.1100	1.1200	1.1300	1.1400	1.1500	1.1600	1.1700	1.1800
1.2100	1.2321	1.2544	1.2769	1.2996	1.3225	1.3456	1.3689	1.3924
1.3310	1.3676	1.4049	1.4429	1.4815	1.5209	1.5609	1.6016	1.6430
1.4641	1.5181	1.5735	1.6305	1.6890	1.7490	1.8106	1.8739	1.9388
1.6105	1.6851	1.7623	1.8424	1.9254	2.0114	2.1003	2.1924	2.2878
1.7716	1.8704	1.9738	2.0820	2.1950	2.3131	2.4364	2.5652	2.6996
1.9487	2.0762	2.2107	2.3526	2.5023	2.6600	2.8262	3.0012	3.1855
2.1436	2.3045	2.4760	2.6584	2.8526	3.0590	3.2784	3.5115	3.7589
2.3579	2.5580	2.7731	3.0040	3.2519	3.5179	3.8030	4.1084	4.4355
2.5937	2.8394	3.1058	3.3946	3.7072	4.0456	4.4114	4.8068	5.2338
2.8531	3.1518	3.4785	3.8359	4.2262	4.6524	5.1173	5.6240	6.1759
3.1384	3.4985	3.8960	4.3345	4.8179	5.3503	5.9360	6.5801	7.2876
3.4523	3.8833	4.3635	4.8980	5.4924	6.1528	6.8858	7.6987	8.5994
3.7975	4.3104	4.8871	5.5348	6.2613	7.0757	7.9875	9.0075	10.1472
4.1772	4.7846	5.4736	6.2543	7.1379	8.1371	9.2655	10.5387	11.9737
4.5950	5.3109	6.1304	7.0673	8.1372	9.3576	10.7480	12.3303	14.1290
5.0545	5.8951	6.8660	7.9861	9.2765	10.7613	12.4677	14.4265	16.6722
5.5599	6.5436	7.6900	9.0243	10.5752	12.3755	14.4625	16.8790	19.6733
6.1159	7.2633	8.6128	10.1974	12.0557	14.2318	16.7765	19.7484	23.2144
6.7275	8.0623	9.6463	11.5231	13.7435	16.3665	19.4608	23.1056	27.3930
7.4002	8.9492	10.8038	13.0211	15.6676	18.8215	22.5745	27.0336	32.3238
8.1403	9.9336	12.1003	14.7138	17.8610	21.6447	26.1864	31.6293	38.1421
8.9543	11.0263	13.5523	16.6266	20.3616	24.8915	30.3762	37.0062	45.0076
9.8497	12.2392	15.1786	18.7881	23.2122	28.6252	35.2364	43.2973	53.1090
10.8347	13.5855	17.0001	21.2305	26.4619	32.9190	40.8742	50.6578	62.6686
11.9182	15.0799	19.0401	23.9905	30.1666	37.8568	47.4141	59.2697	73.9490
13.1100	16.7386	21.3249	27.1093	34.3899	43.5353	55.0004	69.3455	87.2598
14.4210	18.5799	23.8839	30.6335	39.2045	50.0656	63.8004	81.1342	102.9666
15.8631	20.6237	26.7499	34.6158	44.6931	57.5755	74.0085	94.9271	121.5005
17.4494	22.8923	29.9599	39.1159	50.9502	66.2118	85.8499	111.0647	143.3706
19.1943	25.4104	33.5551	44.2010	58.0832	76.1435	99.5859	129.9456	169.1774
21.1138	28.2056	37.5817	49.9471	66.2148	87.5651	115.5196	152.0364	199.6293
23.2252	31.3082	42.0915	56.4402	75.4849	100.6998	134.0027	177.8826	235.5625
25.5477	34.7521	47.1425	63.7774	86.0528	115.8048	155.4432	208.1226	277.9638
28.1024	38.5749	52.7996	72.0685	98.1002	133.1755	180.3141	243.5035	327.9973
30.9127	42.8181	59.1356	81.4374	111.8342	153.1519	209.1643	284.8991	387.0368
34.0039	47.5281	66.2318	92.0243	127.4910	176.1246	242.6306	333.3319	456.7034
37.4043	52.7562	74.1797	103.9874	145.3397	202.5433	281.4515	389.9983	538.9100
41.1448	58.5593	83.0812	117.5058	165.6873	232.9248	326.4838	456.2980	635.9139
45.2593	65.0009	93.0510	132.7816	188.8835	267.8635	378.7212	533.8687	750.3783

TABLE A.3   Present Value of an Annuity of $1

Period (n)	Interest Rate (r)								
	1%	2%	3%	4%	5%	6%	7%	8%	9%
1	0.9901	0.9804	0.9709	0.9615	0.9524	0.9434	0.9346	0.9259	0.9174
2	1.9704	1.9416	1.9135	1.8861	1.8594	1.8334	1.8080	1.7833	1.7591
3	2.9410	2.8839	2.8286	2.7751	2.7232	2.6730	2.6243	2.5771	2.5313
4	3.9020	3.8077	3.7171	3.6299	3.5460	3.4651	3.3872	3.3121	3.2397
5	4.8534	4.7135	4.5797	4.4518	4.3295	4.2124	4.1002	3.9927	3.8897
6	5.7955	5.6014	5.4172	5.2421	5.0757	4.9173	4.7665	4.6229	4.4859
7	6.7282	6.4720	6.2303	6.0021	5.7864	5.5824	5.3893	5.2064	5.0330
8	7.6517	7.3255	7.0197	6.7327	6.4632	6.2098	5.9713	5.7466	5.5348
9	8.5660	8.1622	7.7861	7.4353	7.1078	6.8017	6.5152	6.2469	5.9952
10	9.4713	8.9826	8.5302	8.1109	7.7217	7.3601	7.0236	6.7101	6.4177
11	10.3676	9.7868	9.2526	8.7605	8.3064	7.8869	7.4987	7.1390	6.8052
12	11.2551	10.5753	9.9540	9.3851	8.8633	8.3838	7.9427	7.5361	7.1607
13	12.1337	11.3484	10.6350	9.9856	9.3936	8.8527	8.3577	7.9038	7.4869
14	13.0037	12.1062	11.2961	10.5631	9.8986	9.2950	8.7455	8.2442	7.7862
15	13.8651	12.8493	11.9379	11.1184	10.3797	9.7122	9.1079	8.5595	8.0607
16	14.7179	13.5777	12.5611	11.6523	10.8378	10.1059	9.4466	8.8514	8.3126
17	15.5623	14.2919	13.1661	12.1657	11.2741	10.4773	9.7632	9.1216	8.5436
18	16.3983	14.9920	13.7535	12.6593	11.6896	10.8276	10.0591	9.3719	8.7556
19	17.2260	15.6785	14.3238	13.1339	12.0853	11.1581	10.3356	9.6036	8.9501
20	18.0456	16.3514	14.8775	13.5903	12.4622	11.4699	10.5940	9.8181	9.1285
21	18.8570	17.0112	15.4150	14.0292	12.8212	11.7641	10.8355	10.0168	9.2922
22	19.6604	17.6580	15.9369	14.4511	13.1630	12.0416	11.0612	10.2007	9.4424
23	20.4558	18.2922	16.4436	14.8568	13.4886	12.3034	11.2722	10.3711	9.5802
24	21.2434	18.9139	16.9355	15.2470	13.7986	12.5504	11.4693	10.5288	9.7066
25	22.0232	19.5235	17.4131	15.6221	14.0939	12.7834	11.6536	10.6748	9.8226
26	22.7952	20.1210	17.8768	15.9828	14.3752	13.0032	11.8258	10.8100	9.9290
27	23.5596	20.7069	18.3270	16.3296	14.6430	13.2105	11.9867	10.9352	10.0266
28	24.3164	21.2813	18.7641	16.6631	14.8981	13.4062	12.1371	11.0511	10.1161
29	25.0658	21.8444	19.1885	16.9837	15.1411	13.5907	12.2777	11.1584	10.1983
30	25.8077	22.3965	19.6004	17.2920	15.3725	13.7648	12.4090	11.2578	10.2737
31	26.5423	22.9377	20.0004	17.5885	15.5928	13.9291	12.5318	11.3498	10.3428
32	27.2696	23.4683	20.3888	17.8736	15.8027	14.0840	12.6466	11.4350	10.4062
33	27.9897	23.9886	20.7658	18.1476	16.0025	14.2302	12.7538	11.5139	10.4644
34	28.7027	24.4986	21.1318	18.4112	16.1929	14.3681	12.8540	11.5869	10.5178
35	29.4086	24.9986	21.4872	18.6646	16.3742	14.4982	12.9477	11.6546	10.5668
36	30.1075	25.4888	21.8323	18.9083	16.5469	14.6210	13.0352	11.7172	10.6118
37	30.7995	25.9695	22.1672	19.1426	16.7113	14.7368	13.1170	11.7752	10.6530
38	31.4847	26.4406	22.4925	19.3679	16.8679	14.8460	13.1935	11.8289	10.6908
39	32.1630	26.9026	22.8082	19.5845	17.0170	14.9491	13.2649	11.8786	10.7255
40	32.8347	27.3555	23.1148	19.7928	17.1591	15.0463	13.3317	11.9246	10.7574

			Interest Rate (r)					
10%	*11%*	*12%*	*13%*	*14%*	*15%*	*16%*	*17%*	*18%*
0.9091	0.9009	0.8929	0.8850	0.8772	0.8696	0.8621	0.8547	0.8475
1.7355	1.7125	1.6901	1.6681	1.6467	1.6257	1.6052	1.5852	1.5656
2.4869	2.4437	2.4018	2.3612	2.3216	2.2832	2.2459	2.2096	2.1743
3.1699	3.1024	3.0373	2.9745	2.9137	2.8550	2.7982	2.7432	2.6901
3.7908	3.6959	3.6048	3.5172	3.4331	3.3522	3.2743	3.1993	3.1272
4.3553	4.2305	4.1114	3.9975	3.8887	3.7845	3.6847	3.5892	3.4976
4.8684	4.7122	4.5638	4.4226	4.2883	4.1604	4.0386	3.9224	3.8115
5.3349	5.1461	4.9676	4.7988	4.6389	4.4873	4.3436	4.2072	4.0776
5.7590	5.5370	5.3282	5.1317	4.9464	4.7716	4.6065	4.4506	4.3030
6.1446	5.8892	5.6502	5.4262	5.2161	5.0188	4.8332	4.6586	4.4941
6.4951	6.2065	5.9377	5.6869	5.4527	5.2337	5.0286	4.8364	4.6560
6.8137	6.4924	6.1944	5.9176	5.6603	5.4206	5.1971	4.9884	4.7932
7.1034	6.7499	6.4235	6.1218	5.8424	5.5831	5.3423	5.1183	4.9095
7.3667	6.9819	6.6282	6.3025	6.0021	5.7245	5.4675	5.2293	5.0081
7.6061	7.1909	6.8109	6.4624	6.1422	5.8474	5.5755	5.3242	5.0916
7.8237	7.3792	6.9740	6.6039	6.2651	5.9542	5.6685	5.4053	5.1624
8.0216	7.5488	7.1196	6.7291	6.3729	6.0472	5.7487	5.4746	5.2223
8.2014	7.7016	7.2497	6.8399	6.4674	6.1280	5.8178	5.5339	5.2732
8.3649	7.8393	7.3658	6.9380	6.5504	6.1982	5.8775	5.5845	5.3162
8.5136	7.9633	7.4694	7.0248	6.6231	6.2593	5.9288	5.6278	5.3527
8.6487	8.0751	7.5620	7.1016	6.6870	6.3125	5.9731	5.6648	5.3837
8.7715	8.1757	7.6446	7.1695	6.7429	6.3587	6.0113	5.6964	5.4099
8.8832	8.2664	7.7184	7.2297	6.7921	6.3988	6.0442	5.7234	5.4321
8.9847	8.3481	7.7843	7.2829	6.8351	6.4338	6.0726	5.7465	5.4509
9.0770	8.4217	7.8431	7.3300	6.8729	6.4641	6.0971	5.7662	5.4669
9.1609	8.4881	7.8957	7.3717	6.9061	6.4906	6.1182	5.7831	5.4804
9.2372	8.5478	7.9426	7.4086	6.9352	6.5135	6.1364	5.7975	5.4919
9.3066	8.6016	7.9844	7.4412	6.9607	6.5335	6.1520	5.8099	5.5016
9.3696	8.6501	8.0218	7.4701	6.9830	6.5509	6.1656	5.8204	5.5098
9.4269	8.6938	8.0552	7.4957	7.0027	6.5660	6.1772	5.8294	5.5168
9.4790	8.7331	8.0850	7.5183	7.0199	6.5791	6.1872	5.8371	5.5227
9.5264	8.7686	8.1116	7.5383	7.0350	6.5905	6.1959	5.8437	5.5277
9.5694	8.8005	8.1354	7.5560	7.0482	6.6005	6.2034	5.8493	5.5320
9.6086	8.8293	8.1566	7.5717	7.0599	6.6091	6.2098	5.8541	5.5356
9.6442	8.8552	8.1755	7.5856	7.0700	6.6166	6.2153	5.8582	5.5386
9.6765	8.8786	8.1924	7.5979	7.0790	6.6231	6.2201	5.8617	5.5412
9.7059	8.8996	8.2075	7.6087	7.0868	6.6288	6.2242	5.8647	5.5434
9.7327	8.9186	8.2210	7.6183	7.0937	6.6338	6.2278	5.8673	5.5452
9.7570	8.9357	8.2330	7.6268	7.0997	6.6380	6.2309	5.8695	5.5468
9.7791	8.9511	8.2438	7.6344	7.1050	6.6418	6.2335	5.8713	5.5482

TABLE A.4 Future Value of an Annuity of $1

Period (n)	1%	2%	3%	4%	5%	6%	7%	8%	9%
1	1.0000	1.0000	1.0000	1.0000	1.0000	1.0000	1.0000	1.0000	1.0000
2	2.0100	2.0200	2.0300	2.0400	2.0500	2.0600	2.0700	2.0800	2.0900
3	3.0301	3.0604	3.0909	3.1216	3.1525	3.1836	3.2149	3.2464	3.2781
4	4.0604	4.1216	4.1836	4.2465	4.3101	4.3746	4.4399	4.5061	4.5731
5	5.1010	5.2040	5.3091	5.4163	5.5256	5.6371	5.7507	5.8666	5.9847
6	6.1520	6.3081	6.4684	6.6330	6.8019	6.9753	7.1533	7.3359	7.5233
7	7.2135	7.4343	7.6625	7.8983	8.1420	8.3938	8.6540	8.9228	9.2004
8	8.2857	8.5830	8.8923	9.2142	9.5491	9.8975	10.2598	10.6366	11.0285
9	9.3685	9.7546	10.1591	10.5828	11.0266	11.4913	11.9780	12.4876	13.0210
10	10.4622	10.9497	11.4639	12.0061	12.5779	13.1808	13.8164	14.4866	15.1929
11	11.5668	12.1687	12.8078	13.4864	14.2068	14.9716	15.7836	16.6455	17.5603
12	12.6825	13.4121	14.1920	15.0258	15.9171	16.8699	17.8885	18.9771	20.1407
13	13.8093	14.6803	15.6178	16.6268	17.7130	18.8821	20.1406	21.4953	22.9534
14	14.9474	15.9739	17.0863	18.2919	19.5986	21.0151	22.5505	24.2149	26.0192
15	16.0969	17.2934	18.5989	20.0236	21.5786	23.2760	25.1290	27.1521	29.3609
16	17.2579	18.6393	20.1569	21.8245	23.6575	25.6725	27.8881	30.3243	33.0034
17	18.4304	20.0121	21.7616	23.6975	25.8404	28.2129	30.8402	33.7502	36.9737
18	19.6147	21.4123	23.4144	25.6454	28.1324	30.9057	33.9990	37.4502	41.3013
19	20.8109	22.8406	25.1169	27.6712	30.5390	33.7600	37.3790	41.4463	46.0185
20	22.0190	24.2974	26.8704	29.7781	33.0660	36.7856	40.9955	45.7620	51.1601
21	23.2392	25.7833	28.6765	31.9692	35.7193	39.9927	44.8652	50.4229	56.7645
22	24.4716	27.2990	30.5368	34.2480	38.5052	43.3923	49.0057	55.4568	62.8733
23	25.7163	28.8450	32.4529	36.6179	41.4305	46.9958	53.4361	60.8933	69.5319
24	26.9735	30.4219	34.4265	39.0826	44.5020	50.8156	58.1767	66.7648	76.7898
25	28.2432	32.0303	36.4593	41.6459	47.7271	54.8645	63.2490	73.1059	84.7009
26	29.5256	33.6709	38.5530	44.3117	51.1135	59.1564	68.6765	79.9544	93.3240
27	30.8209	35.3443	40.7096	47.0842	54.6691	63.7058	74.4838	87.3508	102.7231
28	32.1291	37.0512	42.9309	49.9676	58.4026	68.5281	80.6977	95.3388	112.9682
29	33.4504	38.7922	45.2189	52.9663	62.3227	73.6398	87.3465	103.9659	124.1354
30	34.7849	40.5681	47.5754	56.0849	66.4388	79.0582	94.4608	113.2832	136.3075
31	36.1327	42.3794	50.0027	59.3283	70.7608	84.8017	102.0730	123.3459	149.5752
32	37.4941	44.2270	52.5028	62.7015	75.2988	90.8898	110.2182	134.2135	164.0370
33	38.8690	46.1116	55.0778	66.2095	80.0638	97.3432	118.9334	145.9506	179.8003
34	40.2577	48.0338	57.7302	69.8579	85.0670	104.1838	128.2588	158.6267	196.9823
35	41.6603	49.9945	60.4621	73.6522	90.3203	111.4348	138.2369	172.3168	215.7108
36	43.0769	51.9944	63.2759	77.5983	95.8363	119.1209	148.9135	187.1021	236.1247
37	44.5076	54.0343	66.1742	81.7022	101.6281	127.2681	160.3374	203.0703	258.3759
38	45.9527	56.1149	69.1594	85.9703	107.7095	135.9042	172.5610	220.3159	282.6298
39	47.4123	58.2372	72.2342	90.4091	114.0950	145.0585	185.6403	238.9412	309.0665
40	48.8864	60.4020	75.4013	95.0255	120.7998	154.7620	199.6351	259.0565	337.8824

			Interest Rate (r)					
10%	*11%*	*12%*	*13%*	*14%*	*15%*	*16%*	*17%*	*18%*
1.0000	1.0000	1.0000	1.0000	1.0000	1.0000	1.0000	1.0000	1.0000
2.1000	2.1100	2.1200	2.1300	2.1400	2.1500	2.1600	2.1700	2.1800
3.3100	3.3421	3.3744	3.4069	3.4396	3.4725	3.5056	3.5389	3.5724
4.6410	4.7097	4.7793	4.8498	4.9211	4.9934	5.0665	5.1405	5.2154
6.1051	6.2278	6.3528	6.4803	6.6101	6.7424	6.8771	7.0144	7.1542
7.7156	7.9129	8.1152	8.3227	8.5355	8.7537	8.9775	9.2068	9.4420
9.4872	9.7833	10.0890	10.4047	10.7305	11.0668	11.4139	11.7720	12.1415
11.4359	11.8594	12.2997	12.7573	13.2328	13.7268	14.2401	14.7733	15.3270
13.5795	14.1640	14.7757	15.4157	16.0853	16.7858	17.5185	18.2847	19.0859
15.9374	16.7220	17.5487	18.4197	19.3373	20.3037	21.3215	22.3931	23.5213
18.5312	19.5614	20.6546	21.8143	23.0445	24.3493	25.7329	27.1999	28.7551
21.3843	22.7132	24.1331	25.6502	27.2707	29.0017	30.8502	32.8239	34.9311
24.5227	26.2116	28.0291	29.9847	32.0887	34.3519	36.7862	39.4040	42.2187
27.9750	30.0949	32.3926	34.8827	37.5811	40.5047	43.6720	47.1027	50.8180
31.7725	34.4054	37.2797	40.4175	43.8424	47.5804	51.6595	56.1101	60.9653
35.9497	39.1899	42.7533	46.6717	50.9804	55.7175	60.9250	66.6488	72.9390
40.5447	44.5008	48.8837	53.7391	59.1176	65.0751	71.6730	78.9792	87.0680
45.5992	50.3959	55.7497	61.7251	68.3941	75.8364	84.1407	93.4056	103.7403
51.1591	56.9395	63.4397	70.7494	78.9692	88.2118	98.6032	110.2846	123.4135
57.2750	64.2028	72.0524	80.9468	91.0249	102.4436	115.3797	130.0329	146.6280
64.0025	72.2651	81.6987	92.4699	104.7684	118.8101	134.8405	153.1385	174.0210
71.4027	81.2143	92.5026	105.4910	120.4360	137.6316	157.4150	180.1721	206.3448
79.5430	91.1479	104.6029	120.2048	138.2970	159.2764	183.6014	211.8013	244.4868
88.4973	102.1742	118.1552	136.8315	158.6586	184.1678	213.9776	248.8076	289.4945
98.3471	114.4133	133.3339	155.6196	181.8708	212.7930	249.2140	292.1049	342.6035
109.1818	127.9988	150.3339	176.8501	208.3327	245.7120	290.0883	342.7627	405.2721
121.0999	143.0786	169.3740	200.8406	238.4993	283.5688	337.5024	402.0323	479.2211
134.2099	159.8173	190.6989	227.9499	272.8892	327.1041	392.5028	471.3778	566.4809
148.6309	178.3972	214.5828	258.5834	312.0937	377.1697	456.3032	552.5121	669.4475
164.4940	199.0209	241.3327	293.1992	356.7868	434.7451	530.3117	647.4391	790.9480
181.9434	221.9132	271.2926	332.3151	407.7370	500.9569	616.1616	758.5038	934.3186
201.1378	247.3236	304.8477	376.5161	465.8202	577.1005	715.7475	888.4494	1103.4960
222.2515	275.5292	342.4294	426.4632	532.0350	664.6655	831.2671	1040.4858	1303.1253
245.4767	306.8374	384.5210	482.9034	607.5199	765.3654	965.2698	1218.3684	1538.6878
271.0244	341.5896	431.6635	546.6808	693.5727	881.1702	1120.7130	1426.4910	1816.6516
299.1268	380.1644	484.4631	618.7493	791.6729	1014.3457	1301.0270	1669.9945	2144.6489
330.0395	422.9825	543.5987	700.1867	903.5071	1167.4975	1510.1914	1954.8936	2531.6857
364.0434	470.5106	609.8305	792.2110	1030.9981	1343.6222	1752.8220	2288.2255	2988.3891
401.4478	523.2667	684.0102	896.1984	1176.3378	1546.1655	2034.2735	2678.2238	3527.2992
442.5926	581.8261	767.0914	1013.7042	1342.0251	1779.0903	2360.7572	3134.5218	4163.2130

TABLE A.5   Cumulative Probability for the Standard Normal Distribution

	0.00	0.01	0.02	0.03	0.04	0.05	0.06	0.07	0.08	0.09
0.0	0.5000	0.5040	0.5080	0.5120	0.5160	0.5199	0.5239	0.5279	0.5319	0.5359
0.1	0.5398	0.5438	0.5478	0.5517	0.5557	0.5596	0.5636	0.5675	0.5714	0.5753
0.2	0.5793	0.5832	0.5871	0.5910	0.5948	0.5987	0.6026	0.6064	0.6103	0.6141
0.3	0.6179	0.6217	0.6255	0.6293	0.6331	0.6368	0.6406	0.6443	0.6480	0.6517
0.4	0.6554	0.6591	0.6628	0.6664	0.6700	0.6736	0.6772	0.6808	0.6844	0.6879
0.5	0.6915	0.6950	0.6985	0.7019	0.7054	0.7088	0.7123	0.7157	0.7190	0.7224
0.6	0.7257	0.7291	0.7324	0.7357	0.7389	0.7422	0.7454	0.7486	0.7517	0.7549
0.7	0.7580	0.7611	0.7642	0.7673	0.7704	0.7734	0.7764	0.7794	0.7823	0.7852
0.8	0.7881	0.7910	0.7939	0.7967	0.7995	0.8023	0.8051	0.8078	0.8106	0.8133
0.9	0.8159	0.8186	0.8212	0.8238	0.8264	0.8289	0.8315	0.8340	0.8365	0.8389
1.0	0.8413	0.8438	0.8461	0.8485	0.8508	0.8531	0.8554	0.8577	0.8599	0.8621
1.1	0.8643	0.8665	0.8686	0.8708	0.8729	0.8749	0.8770	0.8790	0.8810	0.8830
1.2	0.8849	0.8869	0.8888	0.8907	0.8925	0.8944	0.8962	0.8980	0.8997	0.9015
1.3	0.9032	0.9049	0.9066	0.9082	0.9099	0.9115	0.9131	0.9147	0.9162	0.9177
1.4	0.9192	0.9207	0.9222	0.9236	0.9251	0.9265	0.9279	0.9292	0.9306	0.9319
1.5	0.9332	0.9345	0.9357	0.9370	0.9382	0.9394	0.9406	0.9418	0.9429	0.9441
1.6	0.9452	0.9463	0.9474	0.9484	0.9495	0.9505	0.9515	0.9525	0.9535	0.9545
1.7	0.9554	0.9564	0.9573	0.9582	0.9591	0.9599	0.9608	0.9616	0.9625	0.9633
1.8	0.9641	0.9649	0.9656	0.9664	0.9671	0.9678	0.9686	0.9693	0.9699	0.9706
1.9	0.9713	0.9719	0.9726	0.9732	0.9738	0.9744	0.9750	0.9756	0.9761	0.9767
2.0	0.9772	0.9778	0.9783	0.9788	0.9793	0.9798	0.9803	0.9808	0.9812	0.9817
2.1	0.9821	0.9826	0.9830	0.9834	0.9838	0.9842	0.9846	0.9850	0.9854	0.9857
2.2	0.9861	0.9864	0.9868	0.9871	0.9875	0.9878	0.9881	0.9884	0.9887	0.9890
2.3	0.9893	0.9896	0.9898	0.9901	0.9904	0.9906	0.9909	0.9911	0.9913	0.9916
2.4	0.9918	0.9920	0.9922	0.9925	0.9927	0.9929	0.9931	0.9932	0.9934	0.9936
2.5	0.9938	0.9940	0.9941	0.9943	0.9945	0.9946	0.9948	0.9949	0.9951	0.9952
2.6	0.9953	0.9955	0.9956	0.9957	0.9959	0.9960	0.9961	0.9962	0.9963	0.9964
2.7	0.9965	0.9966	0.9967	0.9968	0.9969	0.9970	0.9971	0.9972	0.9973	0.9974
2.8	0.9974	0.9975	0.9976	0.9977	0.9977	0.9978	0.9979	0.9979	0.9980	0.9981
2.9	0.9981	0.9982	0.9982	0.9983	0.9984	0.9984	0.9985	0.9985	0.9986	0.9986
3.0	0.9987	0.9987	0.9987	0.9988	0.9988	0.9989	0.9989	0.9989	0.9990	0.9990
3.1	0.9990	0.9991	0.9991	0.9991	0.9992	0.9992	0.9992	0.9992	0.9993	0.9993
3.2	0.9993	0.9993	0.9994	0.9994	0.9994	0.9994	0.9994	0.9995	0.9995	0.9995
3.3	0.9995	0.9995	0.9995	0.9996	0.9996	0.9996	0.9996	0.9996	0.9996	0.9997
3.4	0.9997	0.9997	0.9997	0.9997	0.9997	0.9997	0.9997	0.9997	0.9997	0.9998

Glossary

accounting earnings the earnings reported on the firm's financial statements

accounting profits the earnings reported on the firm's income statement

accounts payable obligations that the firm has for goods it has received from others

accounts receivable obligations due to the firm from other parties that are expected to be collected within one year

accrual accounting an accounting method that recognizes expenses and revenues when committed, rather than when the associated cash flows actually occur

accruals current liabilities of the firm due, not for goods received, but for services, such as wages, owed but not yet paid

accrued interest on a coupon bond, the interest earned since the last coupon payment that has not yet been paid

acquired or **target firm** the firm that is bought in a merger or acquisition

acquirer the buying firm in a merger or acquisition

acquisition the absorption of one firm by another, basically a type of merger

aggressive portfolio a portfolio with a beta greater than 1.0

alpha the intercept of the characteristic line

amortized loan a loan with payments of equal size that consist of both principal and interest

annual compounding a type of interest calculation in which interest is added to the principal annually

annuity a series of equal cash flows made at regular intervals

annuity due an annuity with the first cash flow occurring immediately

annuity method a method for choosing between projects with different lives that calculates the annuity that has a present value equal to the cost of operating the machine over a given number of years

antitrust legislation legislation aimed at controlling the establishment of monopolies

appropriability theory the view that firms engage in direct foreign investment to appropriate the benefits that the firm has created through the patents they hold or the production processes they have developed

arbitrage the act of making a riskless profit without investment

arbitrage pricing theory a new theory of equilibrium security pricing that is derived from the principle that there can be no arbitrage opportunities

asymmetric information the situation arising when two parties possess information about the same subject and that information has different value

at-the-money option in the options market, an option with an exercise price equal to the cash price of the underlying good

average tax rate the amount of tax paid on a given amount of income divided by that income amount

balance sheet a financial statement that presents all of the assets of the firm and claims against the firm at a particular moment in time

balloon payment the final large payment on a partially amortized loan

bank holding company a nonbank corporation owning one or more commercial banks

banker's acceptance a financial security showing evidence that a bank has accepted the obligation to make a payment for a customer

bankruptcy a legally defined form of insolvency under the terms of the Federal Bankruptcy Act

bar code a unique, machine-readable product identifier printed on a product

basis the value of an asset on the firm's books that is important for calculating depreciation and capital gains or losses when the asset is sold; in the futures market, the cash price minus the futures price

beating the market to consistently earn a rate of return in excess of the market's equilibrium risk-adjusted rate of return

beta a measure of the systematic risk of a given security relative to the market as a whole

bid-asked spread the difference between the price at which one is willing to sell (the asked price) and the price at which one is willing to buy (the bid price)

block trade a trade of 10,000 or more shares of stock

board of directors a group of individuals responsible for the operation of a corporation

bond a financial security issued by a corporation or government entity that shows proof of indebtedness by the issuer and that calls for payments to the owner

bond contract or **bond indenture** a legal document stating in precise terms the promises made by the issuer of a bond and the rights of the bondholders

bond discount for a bond with a market price less than the par value, the par value minus the bond's price

bond equivalent yield a type of yield used for pure discount bonds to put them on a comparable basis with coupon bonds

bond market the market for debt obligations with original maturities of more than one year

bond trustee an individual or firm charged with the responsibility of protecting the rights of the bondholders and monitoring the performance of the issuer to assure that all promises are kept

book value the value of the assets as shown in the financial reports and in the company's books

break-even analysis a technique for analyzing profitability as a function of investment and sales

break-even point the level of production and sales at which the revenue equals the total cost

broker a person who executes orders to buy or sell for a client

broker's call rate the rate charged by banks for loans to brokerage houses on loans secured with securities

business risk the variability of the firm's EBIT

call option the option to buy a good at a specified price for a specified period of time

call price the price the issuer must pay to retire a callable bond when it is called

callable bond a bond that may be retired at the discretion of the issuer, usually subject to certain constraints

capital asset pricing model (CAPM) an economic model that expresses the equilibrium relationship between expected return and systematic risk for a security or portfolio

capital budgeting the process of evaluating projects and committing funds for investment in those projects

capital gain or **capital loss** the gain or loss in the value of an asset over an investment period

capital market the market for long-term commitments of investable funds

capital market line a line expressing the equilibrium relationship between expected return and risk for well-diversified portfolios

capital rationing the allocation of investment funds among a set of projects requiring more financing than is available

capital structure the division of a firm's financing between the ownership claims of stock and the debt claims of bonds

carrying cost the total cost of keeping an item in inventory

cash budget a plan for the cash inflows and outflows over a certain period of time, usually one year

cash dividend a cash payment made to the owners of a share of stock

cash flow a receipt or a payment of cash

cash management the management of the timing of cash receipts and payments

certificate of deposit (CD) a certificate issued by a bank stating that funds are on deposit with that bank

characteristic line a line showing the relationship between returns for a given security or portfolio and a market index

clearing house in the options or futures market, the corporation that is responsible for matching buyers and sellers and for ensuring that traders fulfill their performance obligations

closed-end investment company an investment company that issues a number of shares at creation, allows those shares to trade in the market at whatever price the market permits, and issues no new shares over the life of the company

collateral trust bonds bonds secured by financial assets

commercial paper an instrument of the money market issued on a discount yield basis

common stock equity capital contributed by parties outside the corporation

company analysis the analysis of a particular company in order to assess the future price performance of its securities

composition a form of financial distress in which the creditor agrees to accept some reduced amount as payment in full

compound interest interest paid on both the principal and previous interest that was earned

concentration banking a cash management technique in which customers are instructed to mail their payments to a regional collection center, rather than to a firm's home office, in order to speed collection

conglomerate a firm composed of many subunits in unrelated fields of business

conglomerate merger a merger between firms from unrelated industries

consolidated tape the consolidated report of stock trading activity from a number of exchanges

constant growth model a stock valuation model, consistent with the dividend valuation model, which can be applied when dividends grow at a constant rate

constant payout policy the policy of paying a fixed percentage of a firm's earnings as dividends in each period

consumer loans loans made to individuals

contango the tendency of futures prices to fall during their trading lives

control limit method a statistical cash management technique, also known as the Miller-Orr method

conversion premium the additional amount per share of stock that one pays to obtain the share by converting the bond rather than by buying the stock in the marketplace

conversion price   the price paid for each share of stock, assuming that the bond is converted, which equals the market price of the convertible bond divided by the conversion ratio

conversion ratio   the number of shares to be received for each convertible bond when it is converted

convertible bond   a bond that gives the bondholder the option of surrendering the bond and receiving in return a specified number of shares of common stock, thereby converting the bond into stock

corporation   a business firm with numerous owners who own stock in the firm and whose liability for loss is limited to the amount of their investment

correlation   a measure of the tendency of two variables to be above or below their means at the same time

correlation coefficient   a statistic measuring the tendency of two variables to change together

cost-of-carry relationship   the cost of storing or carrying a commodity from one period to another, which includes the financing, insurance, storage, and transportation that might be incurred

cost of goods sold (COGS)   the direct cost associated with the creation of the product

coupon bond   a bond making a series of regular payments, called coupon payments, throughout its life

coupon payment   the periodic payment made by coupon bonds in fulfillment of debt contracts

coupon rate   the ratio of the annual coupon payment on a bond to its par value

covariance   a statistic measuring the tendency of two variables to change together

covered call   a call option sold by an investor owning the underlying good

credit period   the length of time for which credit will be granted

credit policy   the set of principles that govern the management of the extension of credit to the firm's customers

credit-scoring model   a statistically verified equation that predicts future payment performance

credit standards   the conditions that customers must meet in order to be granted credit

cumulative preferred stock   a type of preferred stock requiring that any dividend payments that the firm misses must be paid later, as soon as the firm is able, and before common stockholders receive dividends

current asset   an asset that can be converted into cash in the normal operation of the firm within one year

current liabilities   those liabilities that the firm must reasonably expect to pay within the next year

daily resettlement   in the futures market, the practice of realizing the gains and losses from each day's trading in cash on that day

day-of-the-week effect   the tendency of returns on particular days of the week to differ from those on other days

day order   an order to trade given to a broker that is effective only on the day it is given

day trader   in the futures market, a trader who maintains a speculative position for the period of a single trading day only

debenture   a bond with no specific pledge of particular assets as security

debt to equity ratio (D/E)   the ratio of the dollar amount of debt outstanding to the value of equity outstanding

deep discount bond   a bond that has a price much lower than its face value

default   the failure of a debt issuer to make one or more debt payments as promised

default risk   the chance that one or more promised payments on a security will be deferred or missed altogether

defensive portfolio   a portfolio with a beta less than 1.0

deferred contract   in the options market, the contracts that have expiration or maturity dates after the next contract to mature

deflation   a decrease in the general level of prices

depreciable value   the cost of an asset minus the expected salvage value

depreciation   a reduction in accounting earnings intended to reflect the reduction in value of an income-producing asset

depreciation tax shield   the change in taxes due to the depreciation charge

direct foreign investment (DFI)   the ownership and operation of physical assets by a firm in a foreign country

direct lease   a lease in which the lessor issues equity in the financial markets and uses the funds acquired to purchase the asset, which is to be leased

discount   for a closed-end investment company, the percentage that the price of a closed-end investment company share lies below the net asset value per share; for a debt security, the difference between the promised future payment and the price

discount bond   a bond with a price below its par value or face value

discount broker   a broker who will execute clients' trade orders at rates below those charged by full-service brokers

discount yield   a yield calculated according to the discount method, which is commonly used for money market instruments

disintermediation   the process of direct contact between surplus and deficit spending units, without the help of a financial intermediary

distribution network   the system employed by the investment bankers for distributing a newly issued security

diversifiable risk, nonsystematic risk, or **unique risk**   the risk that can be avoided through diversification

diversification   the allocation of investable funds to a variety of investments in order to reduce risk

divestiture or **spinoff**   the disposal of some part of a firm's operations in the form of a newly created company

dividend   a cash payment made to the owner of a share of stock

dividend clientele   a group of investors favoring a particular kind of dividend policy

dividend declaration date   the time at which the next dividend is announced

dividend policy   the policy regarding the payment of cash dividends to stockholders

dividend/price ratio   the ratio of dividends per share to the share price, a measure of the yield of a stock; also known as the dividend yield

dividend signaling hypothesis   the hypothesis that dividend changes provide an effective way of allowing management to convey believable information to the market about the firm's expected future cash flows

dividend valuation model   a stock valuation model that expresses the value of a share as the present value of all future dividends to come from the share

dominance a security dominates another if it provides a risk/return combination that is preferred by all risk-averse investors

double taxation the taxation of corporate earnings distributed as dividends as both corporate income and as individual income

Dow Jones Industrial Average a stock market index based on thirty of the largest industrial firms

dual regulatory system a system of bank regulation at both the Federal and the state level

dumbbell strategy a strategy for managing bond portfolios in which investment is concentrated in very short and very long maturities

duration a measure of the sensitivity of the price of a bond to a change in the interest rate

earnings after taxes (EAT) or **net income** the value of the firm's earnings after all taxes and other obligations have been met

earnings before taxes (EBT) earnings eligible for income taxation

earnings per share (EPS) the accounting earnings of a firm divided by the number of shares outstanding

economic earnings for a given period, the amount of funds that may be withdrawn from a firm without changing its future cash flow generating ability

economic ordering quantity (EOQ) model a mathematical model to determine the best size of an order for items in inventory

effective rate of interest the simple interest equivalent of a compounded interest rate

efficient frontier the graph in expected return/risk space of all nondominated securities and portfolios

efficient market a market that fully reflects all of the information in a given information set

efficient set the set of all portfolios and securities that is not dominated by any other

equipment trust certificate a debt obligation using particular equipment, usually railroad cars, as collateral

Eurobond a debt obligation issued by a country but sold outside that country and denominated in a currency other than that of the issuer

Eurodollar a dollar-denominated bank deposit held outside the United States

ex-dividend date the date on which the stock begins trading without the right to receive the coming dividend

exercise price or **striking price** in the options market, the price that will be paid if the option is exercised

exercising an option taking advantage of the privilege to buy or sell a good that is guaranteed by ownership of an option

expected value the mean or average value of a random variable

expiration date or **maturity** the date after which the option has no validity

export the manufacture of goods in one country and the sale in another

extra dividend the portion of the dividend payment that will be made as circumstances permit

face value the par value of a bond or the price the bond would sell at if the coupon rate and the yield to maturity were equal

Federal agency debt debt issued by an arm of the Federal government other than the Treasury

Federal Deposit Insurance Corporation (FDIC) a Federal bank regulatory agency also charged with insuring bank deposits

Federal Reserve Bank a bank that is a member of the Federal Reserve system

filter test   a test of market efficiency that attempts to determine whether mechanical trading rules can beat the market

financial asset   a good that promises future benefits in the form of monetary payments

financial distress   any condition in which difficulties with the firm's financial obligations affect its operations

financial intermediary   a firm acquiring funds from one group of investors and making those funds available to another economic unit

financial lease   a lease with a term that approximately equals the useful life of the asset, usually calling for a series of noncancelable lease payments over the life of the lease

financial leverage   leverage resulting from the use of fixed costs in financing

financial market   a market in which funds are committed in exchange for obligations of future monetary payments

financial planning model   a computerized system expressing the different financial relationships for a firm

financial ratio   the ratio of two balance sheet or income statement values designed to provide information about the firm

finished goods inventory   those completed items that are ready for sale

first-in/first-out (FIFO) accounting   an accounting technique for inventories that assumes the first item put into inventory is the first item withdrawn from inventory

first mortgage bond   a bond that offers the bondholders the first claim against specific pieces of property owned by the corporation in the event of default

fiscal policy   the policy of the government with respect to taxation and expenditures

fiscal year   the business year chosen for the firm, which may or may not coincide with the calendar year

fixed assets   assets used in the production process and held by the firm on a long-term basis, such as machinery

fixed cost   the cost the firm incurs no matter how many units of a good or service are produced

float   the time between receipt of a good and payment

floating rate notes (FRN)   debt obligations whose rate of interest fluctuates with changes in market rates of interest

floor broker   a broker on the floor of an exchange who executes orders for customers

flotation   the initial sale of a security

flotation cost   the total cost of issuing a new security

foreign bond   a bond issued in a foreign currency and sold in the country of the currency of denomination

foreign currency   money issued by a foreign government

foreign exchange   the currency of a foreign country

foreign exchange risk   risk resulting from the change in the value of one currency relative to another

foreign tax credit   a direct credit against U.S. taxes equal to the amount of taxes paid to foreign governments

forward contract   a contract calling for the delivery of some good at a date in the future at a price determined at the time of contracting

forward rate   a rate of interest implied by spot instruments that pertains to a period in the

future; according to some theories, the forward rate is a good predictor of future interest rates

fourth market   a market for stocks in which the trading parties execute the trades without any intermediary such as a broker or a stock exchange

friendly takeover   a merger in which the terms of the merger are agreed upon between the management of the acquiring and target firms

full-service broker   a broker who provides order execution and investment research and who charges full commissions for order execution

fully amortized loan   an amortized loan with payments large enough to fully repay both principal and interest

fundamental analysis   the search for superior-performing securities based on the examination of publicly available information

funded pension plan   a pension plan in which the sponsor of the plan places assets under the management of a pension plan trustee to manage in a way to provide future benefits for employees covered by the pension plan

future value   the value of the payment if the payment were made at some point in the future

futures   a type of contract in which parties contract for the future sale or purchase of some good, with the price being determined in advance

futures market   an organized exchange specializing in the trading of futures contracts

general obligation bond   a municipal bond backed by the full taxing power of the issuing entity

general partner   a partner with unlimited liability

Government National Mortgage Association (GNMA)   a Federal government agency active in the stimulation of the housing market that issues debt

greenmail   an agreement by the management of the target firm to pay the acquirer a higher-than-market price for the acquirer's shares in exchange for an agreement from the acquirer not to pursue the target firm

gross profit   the difference between sales and the cost of goods sold

growth rate   the rate at which a firm's dividends grow

growth stocks   the stocks of firms expected to enjoy a rapid increase in earnings or value

hedge ratio   in the options market, the number of contracts to trade per unit of a spot position in order to offset the price variability in the spot position

historical cost   the amount actually paid for the asset

holder-of-record date   the date on which a share must be owned for the shareholder to receive a given dividend

holding period return   for an investment, the end-of-period wealth divided by the beginning wealth; a measure of profit

holding period yield   the percentage change in the value of an investment over a specified investment horizon or holding period

homogeneous expectations   the assumption used in capital market theory that all investors have identical expectations about the future

horizontal merger   a merger between firms in the same industry

immunization   the strategy of managing a bond portfolio in such a way that the value of the portfolio does not change with changes in interest rates

impairment of capital   the stripping of a firm's assets so that there is very little value of equity by paying a dividend

in-the-money option   an option that could be exercised profitably immediately

income statement   a financial statement that summarizes the operation of the firm over a particular period

incremental cash flows of an investment those cash flows that will differ if the investment is undertaken

indenture   the agreement between the issuer and the bondholder that governs a bond issue

indifference curve   a line connecting points, usually in expected risk/return space, that are equally preferred by an investor

industry analysis   the analysis of factors specific to an industry that may affect securities prices for firms in that industry

industry life cycle hypothesis   the theory that industries follow a natural progression of birth, growth, maturity, and decay

inflation   the change in the general price level over time

informationally efficient market   a market in which prices respond quickly to new information

initial margin   in margin trading for securities, the percentage of the value of securities that one can borrow

inside director   a member of the board of directors who is also a member of top management

insider   a person with special knowledge about the operation of a firm

insider information   information that is not publicly available but that might be possessed by individuals with positions of trust in a corporation

insider trading   the illegal trading of securities based on information not available to the public

interbank market   the market for currencies and debt obligations conducted among major banks

interest rate risk   the risk that a security's value will change due to a change in interest rates

internal rate of return   the discount rate that makes the net present value of a set of cash flows equal to zero

intrinsic value   the true worth of a security, which may differ from the market price

inventory   current assets used in the production process and held by the firm

inverted market   in the futures market, a situation in which futures contracts have prices lower than the cash price for the same good

investment bank   a firm specializing in helping governments and firms issue new securities

investment banking   the industry engaged in assisting firms to issue new securities

investment company   a firm that pools funds from investors and uses those funds to buy a portfolio of securities, with each investor owning a fraction of those shares proportional to the investment; investment companies may be mutual funds or closed-end funds

lagging indicator   an economic variable that changes after the economy as a whole

lead bank   the primary investment bank in a consortium of investment banks attempting to sell a new security

leading indicator   an economic variable that changes before the economy as a whole

lease   a contractual agreement calling for the renting of an asset for some specified period of time

leasing   a form of financing in which a firm acquires an asset to use for a specified period of time and agrees to make a series of payments

lessee   the party to a leasing agreement that uses the leased asset

lessor   the owner of an asset who provides the use of the asset under a leasing agreement

leverage   the use of fixed charges in the firm's operations

leveraged lease   a lease in which the lessor acquires the needed funds to purchase the asset by issuing debt, and perhaps some equity, in the financial markets

licensing agreement   an agreement under which a firm in the home country allows a firm in a foreign country to use its technology or brand name

limit order book   the record of orders awaiting execution at particular prices

limited liability   the principle that stockholders' financial liabilities are limited to the value of their stock

limited partner   a partner with limited liability, usually taking no active role in the management of the firm

limited partnership   a partnership with one or more limited partners

liquid market   one in which an asset can be sold easily for a price that approximates its true value

liquidity risk   the risk that a marketable security cannot be converted easily into cash

load   the sales charge imposed by some mutual funds on new investments

lock box system   a cash management technique in which customers are instructed to mail their payments to a post office box near their homes in order to speed collection

long-term capital gain or **long-term capital loss**   the gain or loss on the sale of an asset held longer than six months

long-term liabilities   continuing obligations the firm has undertaken that will not be completely repaid during the next year

lower control limit   the cash balance at which the firm should replenish its cash balances according to the Miller-Orr method

machine replacement problem   the problem of finding the best time to replace an aged capital item with an identical new one

maintenance margin   in the stock market, the minimum fraction of the traded shares value that must be on deposit with the broker

margin   in the stock market, the partial payment for a security made by an investor who is borrowing the rest of the funds necessary to undertake an investment

margin call   the demand from a broker for an investor to deposit additional margin funds with the broker

margin trading   the practice of trading securities using borrowed funds to finance a portion of the investment transaction

marginal productivity of capital   the rate of return earned on the next unit of capital equipment to be employed

marginal tax rate   the tax rate to be applied to the next increment of income

market anomaly   a departure, or apparent departure, of security pricing from the equilibrium risk/return relationship

market indices   summary measures of market performance

market makers   traders who trade for their own account in specific securities

market order   an order to execute a transaction at the prevailing market price at the time of the order

market portfolio a portfolio in which each asset available in the market is included in proportion to its market value

market risk, systematic risk, or **nondiversifiable risk** that portion of a security's risk that depends on the market, and therefore cannot be diversified away in a portfolio

market risk premium the extra compensation, above the risk-free rate, that investors require for investing in the market portfolio or in a firm with a beta of 1

market value the price an asset can command in the open market at the present time

marketable security a financial obligation that can be converted into cash immediately, with little if any reduction in its value

marking to market in the futures market, the required realization of gains and losses for each day's trading

maturity the time remaining until a bond matures

merger or **acquisition** the combination of two or more firms, with the result being a single, independent company

merger premium the price paid for the target firm minus the premerger value of the target firm

Miller-Orr method a statistical technique used to calculate the optimal cash level a firm should have

minimum risk portfolio among the assets available, the combination that has the lowest possible risk

Modified Accelerated Cost Recovery System (MACRS) a depreciation method in which a stated percentage of the asset's value is allowed as the depreciation expense for the year, with the Federal government establishing rules to govern ACRS

monetary policy the policy of the government with respect to monetary variables, such as the growth in the money supply

money center banks the very largest commercial banks such as Citibank, Chase Manhattan, and Manufacturers Hanover

money market the market in which securities are traded that have one year or less until their maturity

mortgage market the market for the sale and purchase of mortgage debt

multibank holding company a nonbank corporation owning more than one bank

multinational firm a firm engaged in direct foreign investment

multiple increases the policy of making very frequent and very small dividend increases

municipal bond a debt obligation issued by a state or local government agency that is usually free from Federal taxation and that is generally free from certain state and local taxes as well

municipal debt the debt incurred by a town, state, or some other form of local government that is normally free of Federal income taxation

mutual fund a type of investment company which pools investments from individuals to purchase a portfolio and gives to investors fractional ownership of the created portfolio; a mutual fund also redeems investors' shares at the net asset value of the shares

mutually exclusive projects two projects, both of which cannot be accepted

NASDAQ the automated price quotation service of the National Association of Securities Dealers

National Association of Securities Dealers (NASD) a trade association that helps to regulate the performance of the over-the-counter securities market

negative float   a float period in which a firm has made payment without receiving the good or has relinquished an asset without receiving payment

negotiated takeover   a merger or acquisition in which the acquirer negotiates directly with the management of the target firm

net asset value (per share)   the value of the securities underlying one share in an investment company

net benefit of leasing (NBL)   the present value of the after-tax leasing outflows minus the present value of the after-tax borrow-and-buy outflows

net present value of a project   the difference between the present value of the cash flows from the project and the investment

net working capital   current assets minus current liabilities

New York Stock Exchange Composite Index   a stock market index reflecting the performance of all stocks listed on the New York Stock Exchange

no-load fund   a mutual fund that imposes no initial load, or sales, fee

nominal rate   an interest rate reflecting only the promised dollar payments without reference to the expected purchasing power of the payments

nondiversifiable risk, systematic risk, or **market risk**   the risk that cannot be avoided through diversification

nonmarket risk, unsystematic risk, or **diversifiable risk**   that portion of a security's risk that does not depend on the market, and therefore can be diversified away in a portfolio

normal market   in the futures market, a situation in which futures contracts have prices that are higher than the cash price for the same good

note   a bond that typically has a short or medium (ten-year) maturity when issued

notes payable   the short-term debt that the firm must reasonably expect to pay within the next year

odd lot   a set of shares of one company with a number different from a round lot (usually 100 shares) or a multiple of a round lot

odd lot trader   a trader who trades in odd lot amounts

off-balance-sheet financing   financing that does not appear on the balance sheet; recent regulations no longer allow this reporting technique

one-bank holding company   a nonbank corporation owning one bank only

open interest   in the futures market, the number of contracts obligated for delivery at a certain time

open market operation   transactions by the Federal Reserve in the market for U.S. Treasury securities in order to implement monetary policy

open market purchase   the purchase of shares in the marketplace following the same procedures as any trader would

operating lease   a lease with a term that is considerably shorter than the life of the asset, with the lease usually cancelable by the lessee on fairly short notice

operating leverage   leverage resulting from the use of fixed costs in operations

operationally efficient market   a market that performs well in order execution

option   a financial contract that allows the owner to buy (a call option) or sell (a put option) a particular good at a specified price for a specified period of time

option writer   another name for the seller of an option

ordering cost   the fixed expense in the preparation and execution of an order for goods

out-of-the-money option   an option that cannot be exercised profitably immediately

outside director   a member of the board of directors who is not employed by the corporation

over-the-counter market   a market for the sale of securities that has no central exchange, but that operates by electronic communication over diverse geographical areas

par bond   a bond with a market price equal to its par value or face value

par value or **face value**   for a pure discount bond, the amount that is promised to be paid upon maturity; for a coupon bond, the principal amount of the bond

partially amortized loan   an amortized loan with payments that only partially repay the principal over the life of the loan

partition of risk   the separation of the risk of a security or portfolio into its systematic and unsystematic components

partnership   an organization of two or more persons for the purpose of engaging in some line of business

payback period   the time until the positive operating cash flows from a project equal the amount of the investment

payment date   the date the firm actually mails the dividend checks

pension fund   a fund created for the purpose of paying pensions to retired employees

perfect market   a market with no transaction costs, no taxes, and full information on the part of all participants

perpetuity   a bond that pays a coupon forever and never matures

point-of-sale system   a type of computerized inventory control system

poison pill   some action taken by a target firm designed to destroy the attractiveness of the firm for the acquirer

portfolio   a collection of different securities held by a single investor

portfolio theory   the theory of how to combine risky investments into a portfolio giving the best combination of risk and expected return

position trader   in the futures market, a trader who takes a speculative position and maintains it for a period longer than one day

positive float   a float period in which a firm has received a good without making a payment or has received a payment without surrendering an asset

positive net present value project   a project with a present value of cash flows that exceeds the present value of the investment

precautionary balance   cash held to be sure the firm does not run out of cash

preemptive right   the right of common stockholders to buy new shares before the shares are offered to others

preferred stock   a security issued by corporations with features of both equity and debt that usually calls for the payment of a fixed dollar amount

premium   in the options market, the price of an option

premium bond   a bond with a market price greater than its par value or face value

present value   the value of a payment if the payment was made immediately

price/earnings (P/E) ratio   the ratio of a share price to the earnings per share for the same stock

primary market   the market for the original issuance of securities

principal   the value of the initial investment in any kind of project

private placement   the selling of an entire security issuance to a single buyer or small consortium of buyers, without the issues ever being made available to the public

pro forma statement   a projected financial statement reflecting current forecasts of sales, costs, and other financial parameters

probability distribution   a function specifying the probability of different values for a random variable

progressive tax rate   a tax rate that increases as the amount of taxable income increases

prospectus   a legal document describing a planned security and the operating and financial condition of the issuing entity

proxy   a statement giving another party the right to vote one's shares

proxy fight   the struggle to gain voting rights from shareholders who will not be attending the annual meeting

public offering   the issuance of a new security that is offered for sale to the public at large

pure discount bond or **zero coupon bond**   a bond that makes no intermediate payments between its issue date and its maturity date

pure discount instrument   a debt instrument paying no coupons, but which pays its par value upon maturity

put option   an option giving the owner the right to sell a particular good at a specified price, with that right lasting until a particular date

random variable   a variable that takes different values with some probability

random walk hypothesis   a statistical hypothesis about the movement of stock prices that, if true, would imply that future security prices are totally unpredictable from past security prices

raw materials inventory   the basic commodities that a firm purchases to use in its production process

real good   a physical or tangible good

real rate of interest   the expected change in purchasing power necessary to induce investors to postpone consumption

real return   the percentage change in purchasing power earned on an investment

registered bond   a bond with the owner's identity registered and reported to the tax authorities

registration statement   a legal document that must be filed with the Securities and Exchange Commission prior to the public offering of securities

regular dividend   a dividend policy according to which the firm pays a regular, steady dividend

reinvestment rate   the rate at which funds paid from one investment can be reinvested

reorder point   the level of inventory at which an inventory item should be reordered

replacement cost   the price of replacing an asset if it had to be acquired on the market today

residual claim   a claim that is to be satisfied only after other claims, such as the claim of the common stockholders on the firm

residual theory of dividends   the view that the firm should follow its investment policy of accepting all positive NPV projects, and paying out dividends when, and only when, funds are readily available

restricted branching   the practice of allowing banks to establish branch offices only under certain restrictions

retained earnings   the accumulated earnings of the firm that have not been paid as dividends

return on assets   the ratio of accounting earnings to the book value of assets

return on equity   the ratio of accounting earnings to the book value of equity

return on a security   the change in price of the security plus any payments made by the security during the time period the security is held, divided by the amount originally paid for the security

revenue bond   a bond issued by a state or local government agency that promises to pay the bondholder only out of the revenues earned by some specific project

reversing trade   in the futures market, a trade that brings an investor's net position in a particular futures contract back to zero

risk aversion   the tendency of individuals or firms to avoid risk unless it is compensated

risk differential   the difference in yields between two bonds due to differences in default risk

risk-free asset   an asset free of risk of default, usually conceived as a U.S. Treasury security

risk-free return   the yield on a risk-free asset

risk neutrality   an investor's indifference to risk

risk/return trade-off   in the securities market, the relationship that shows increasing return to require increasing risk

risk structure of interest rates   the difference in yields between bonds of different quality rankings, or levels of default risk

runs test   a test of market efficiency that tests whether prices tend to have "runs" of price increases or price decreases, rather than having mixed increases and decreases

safety stock   the planned number of items in inventory at the time the new inventory is received

sale/leaseback   a lease in which the lessor acquires the asset from the lessee and then leases it back to the lessee

sales   the revenues generated by the firm from the sale of its products

salvage value   the amount for which the asset can be sold at the end of its useful life

scalper   in the futures market, an individual who trades on the very short run price fluctuations

scenario analysis   a technique that examines the firm's circumstances if a certain set of events, called a scenario, arises

secondary market   the market for the exchange of existing financial claims

security market line (SML)   an equation expressing the expected return on a security as a function of r_f, the beta of the security, and the expected return on the market

selling group   the group of investment bankers with primary responsibility for helping to sell a newly issued security

semistrong form efficiency   the hypothesis that security prices fully reflect all publicly available information

sensitivity analysis   a technique that measures the change in one variable as a consequence of a change in another

separation theorem   the theorem that asserts that the choice of the portfolio of risky assets is separable from the choice of the risk level to be borne

serial bond   a bond that provides for the retirement of a portion of bonds each year in a period before the maturity of the bond issue

serial correlation test   a test of market efficiency that tests whether successive price changes are so strongly correlated that they allow for mechanical trading rules that could beat the market

shelf registration   the registration of a planned security offering that allows for the postponement of the security's issuance and that allows for the issuance of multiple securities under the same registration with the Securities and Exchange Commission

short sale   the sale of a borrowed security executed in the hope that the price of the security will fall

short-term capital gain or **short-term capital loss**   gain or loss on an asset held less than six months

signaling problem   the problem of transmitting information in a way to make it believed

simple annuity   an annuity with the first cash flow occurring in one period

simple interest   interest computed on the assumption that any interest itself does not earn interest

simulation model   a mathematical computer program expressing the relationship between two or more variables that allows one variable to be changed randomly in order to study the effect on other variables of interest

sinking fund   a fund set aside by the bond issuer for the orderly retirement of bonds

sole proprietorship   a business owned by a single individual

sources and uses of funds statement   a financial statement showing all the sources of funds for the corporation and how those funds were used

specialist   on a stock exchange, the member assigned to make a market in a given security, including holding shares in inventory, and keeping a record of all orders awaiting execution

speculative balance   cash held in anticipation of falling security prices

spread   the difference between the buying and selling price for a trader

standard deviation   a measure of variability or risk equal to the square root of the variance

Standard & Poor's 500   500 of the largest and most important stocks in the U.S. market; the name of a stock market index measuring the performance of those 500 stocks

statement of changes in financial position   the statement that focuses on working capital or cash, designed to report the liquidity position of the firm

sticky issues   new securities that are difficult to sell

stochastic process   the statistical description of the movement of a variable through time

stock   a financial security that evidences ownership in a corporation

stock dividend   the issuance to existing shareholders of additional shares in proportion to their original holdings in a firm when the proportion is less than 25 percent

stock exchange   an organization for trading stocks, in which the trading of stocks takes place under rules created by the exchange at the physical facility provided by the exchange

stock market   the market in which ownership claims on firms are traded

stock repurchase   the purchase by a firm of its own shares

stock split   the distribution of new shares to existing stockholders, when the amount of increase in the number of shares is greater than 25 percent

stop order   an order to buy or sell a given security when the price reaches a certain level

straight-line depreciation   a technique in which the depreciation expense is the depreciable value divided by the number of years in the depreciation period

street name   the holding by a broker of a customer's share in a general account

striking price   in the options market, the price that must be paid to exercise an option

strong form efficiency   the hypothesis that security markets fully reflect all information, both public and private

subchapter S corporation   a corporation with no more than 25 stockholders that elects to be treated as a partnership for tax purposes

subordinated debenture   a debenture that has a claim that is inferior to other outstanding debentures

subsidiary   a firm owned by another firm

sunk cost   a previously incurred cost that has no further value

sunk cost fallacy   the error of including a sunk cost in a present value calculation; only incremental flows should be considered

syndicate members   investment banking firms that have committed themselves to assisting in the flotation of a given security

syndicated loan   a loan to a single lender made by an organized group of lenders

tax credit   an amount that is allowed to be subtracted directly from the tax bill

tax holiday   a period of time during which a foreign country imposes no taxes on the operations of a multinational firm

tax-loss carry-back   the amount of a business loss that can be used to offset tax liabilities in previous years

tax-loss carry-forward   an accounting loss that the firm has not been able to use to reduce taxes in the past and that can be carried forward to offset future income

taxes payable   taxes that are owed, but that have not yet been paid

technical analysis   the attempt to forecast securities prices by relying on historical price and volume data

technical insolvency   the failure to make a scheduled promised payment on time

tender offer   an attempt to gain control of a target firm in which the acquiring firm approaches the shareholders, directly asking them to sell their shares to the acquiring firm

term loan   a loan with an initial maturity spanning a number of years that is arranged with a single lender or a consortium of lenders

term structure of interest rates   the relationship between term to maturity and yield to maturity, which is depicted by a yield curve

term to maturity   the amount of time remaining until a bond matures

third market   a market for the exchange of stock that uses the services of brokers, but that does not use a stock exchange

tick   the minimum allowed fluctuation in a security's price

time series model   a statistical model that expresses the value of an economic variable as a function of past values of that variable

time value of money   the principle that $1 received (or paid) today has a greater value than $1 received (or paid) in the future

total cost   the sum of the fixed and variable costs

total integration the owning of all phases of the production chain, ranging from the acquisition of raw materials to the retailing of the final product

total risk the unsystematic plus systematic risk of a security or portfolio, usually measured by the standard deviation or variance of returns

transaction balance cash held by a firm in order to make necessary payments for goods and services

trend analysis the attempt to predict the future value of an economic variable by examining its past trend

trust services the service of managing funds for individuals and businesses that have entrusted their funds to the trust department of a bank or other financial institution

trustee for a bond issue, the agent charged with the responsibility of protecting the rights of the bondholders and monitoring the performance of the issuer to assure that all promises are kept

unfunded pension plan a pension plan in which the sponsor has pension obligations but has not yet put aside any specific funds for meeting those obligations

U.S. Treasury bill a pure discount obligation of the U.S. Treasury with initial maturity of less than one year

U.S. Treasury bond a bond issued by the U.S. Treasury

underwriter an investment bank that buys an entire issue of securities from the issuing firm and assumes the risk of selling the securities

unit banking state a state in which each bank may have only one office

unlimited liability the principle holding an owner of certain kinds of businesses responsible for losses exceeding the value of the firm

unrestricted branching the practice of allowing banks to establish branch offices anywhere within a given state

upper control limit the cash balance at which the firm may reduce its cash balance according to the Miller-Orr method

utility the satisfaction achieved from some source

Value Line index a stock market index based on approximately 1,700 stocks that is published by *Value Line Investment Survey*

variable cost the cost that is incurred in producing each unit of a particular good or service

variance a measure of the dispersion of a random value from its expected value

vertical integration the integration or consolidation of the production chain into one firm

vertical merger a merger between two companies specializing in different parts of the production chain

voluntary bankruptcy a bankruptcy arising when a bankrupt petitions the court for a judgment that it is bankrupt

warrant a long-term call option on the stock of the firm which is created by the firm's calling for the delivery of a new share of stock instead of an existing share

weak form efficiency the hypothesis that security prices fully reflect all historical price and volume data

weighted average cost of capital (WACC) the overall required rate of return for a firm; it considers the cost of both debt and equity used by the firm and it is a weighted average because it reflects the proportions of both debt and equity that are used

white knight a friendly firm that acquires a target firm, allowing the target firm to escape a hostile acquirer

work-in-process inventory   goods in the production process

working capital   the set of funds used in the day-to-day operation of the firm, usually including all assets that will be converted into cash within one year

writing an option   selling an option

yield   the percentage rate of return on an investment

yield approximation formula   a formula used to approximate the yield to maturity on a bond

yield curve   the graph of the relationship between interest rates and maturity for bonds that are similar in other respects

yield to maturity   the yield on a bond, assuming that all promised payments are made, calculated according to the Bond Pricing Formula

zero balance account   a checking account with a zero balance, used to be sure that no idle cash balances are maintained

zero coupon bond   a bond with no coupon payments that promises to pay only its face value upon maturity

Answers to Selected Problems

CHAPTER 2

1. $1,909.09 **2.** $2,100 **6.** $1,000 **8.** $2,200
11. $38.18

CHAPTER 3

2. $13,000 **4.** $11,038 **5.** $31,179.46
7. $42,570 **9.** $42,930 **11.** $28,035.11
13. $27,643.77 **17.** 14.93%
18. 14.49% **20.** 12.55% **23.** $731.19
25. 18.92% **28.** 46.67% **29.** $635,518.08
31. 16.24 years **32.** 6 years **33.** 6 years
34. $1 + r_A = (1 + r_B)^{1.26}$ **36.** $g = 0.36\%$ per year
38. 1,259.97 years **40.** 229.40 years

CHAPTER 4

1. $319.47 **3.** $222.51 **6.** $93.50 **8.** $953.30
10. 4.6069 **14.** $6,483.85 **15.** $13,388.67
17. $3,077.81 **19.** $972.19 **22.** $5,667,797.62
23. $4,182,888.43 **24.** $19,437,619.14
25. 77.05 times **26.** $13,281.00 **28.** $267.86
29. 25% **31.** $(1 + r)^n = 2$ **32.** $117,647.06
34. 11.11% **35.** inflation rate > 0.5976%
36. $6,293.66

CHAPTER 5

1. $47.52 **2.** $8.42 **4.** $26,235 **6.** $119,000
8. $1,300 **9.** $222.22 **10.** 7 years

CHAPTER 9

1. $620.92; $593.45; $649.93 **2.** $926.69
4. $r_{1,2} = 19.14\%$ **6.** $r_{3,4} = 16.05\%$ **8.** $929.59
10. $1,000 **12.** 10% **14.** YTM > 8.21%
15. YTM < 9.17%

CHAPTER 10

1. $P_0 = \$2.85$ **2.** $20 **4.** $24.48; $33.32
7. $54.55 **8.** $46.15 **9.** $70.54 **10.** $74.21

12. 10.64% **14.** 14.87% **16.** $25.71
17. $387.89

CHAPTER 11

1. 11.33% **2.** 12% **3.** Variance = 338.24
7. $\text{Var}_Q = 52.67$; $\text{Var}_R = 8.67$; $\text{cov}(Q, R) = 18.67$
12. 12.67% **13.** $p = \frac{3}{8}$ **14.** $\rho = -\frac{1}{2}$
15. $\sigma = 8.29\%$

CHAPTER 12

1. 12.5% **2.** 16.61% **5.** 0.9412 **7.** 0.8 **9.** 0.18
11. $67,046 **13.** $16,562,336 **15.** −$1,275
17. 0.7 **18.** 5.33% **19.** 17%

CHAPTER 14

1. $4,600 **5.** $10,000 **7.** $4,950 **10.** $36,000
15. NPV = $100,757 **16.** NPV = $84,682
17. IRR = 61.63% **18.** PI = 2.44 **21.** $25,000
22. $8,000 **34.** $57,277 **35.** NPV = − $11,223
36. PI = 0.8362 **37.** IRR = 8.8154%
39. $12,500 **41.** $7,200 **46.** $12,500
48. $2,000 per year **50.** NPV = $3,194.03
51. PI = 1.2555 **52.** IRR = 22.8442%
54. Project A **56.** Project B **58.** Project A
61. $\text{NPV} = C\dfrac{\text{IRR} - r}{(1 + \text{IRR})(1 + r)}$ **63.** $I_A = C \times I_B$
65. 22.9287% **69.** − $6,217 **71.** 13.21%
75. gamma, nu, and tau **78.** 10 years
79. 9 years **80.** $16,207.43 **81.** $2,159.55
86. year 3 **87.** year 6 **89.** now
90. $I_C - I_D > nX$

CHAPTER 15

1. $8,000; $14,000; $20,000; $26,000; $32,000
7. 3.0 **9.** 1.999 **10.** 5.997 **15.** 2.0 **17.** 1.994
18. 3.993 **28.** $\text{MOL} = \dfrac{\text{EBIT} + F}{\text{EBIT}}$
29. $\text{MTL} = \dfrac{\text{EBIT} + F}{\text{EBIT} - i}$ **30.** 16.70%
32. 1.396

CHAPTER 16

1. $220   **3.** $45,000   **5.** $46,100   **7.** $5,500
9. $6,000   **11.** $14,250   **13.** $11,000
19. 63.69 units   **21.** 94.87 units

CHAPTER 17

1. $4,931.51   **2.** $4,931.51   **4.** $390.96
6. $-$15,068.49   **9.** $46,500,000   **12.** $7.66
15. $75,000   **16.** $35,000; $34,641.02
17. $12,247.45

CHAPTER 18

1. $356,164.38   **2.** $p < 41.48\%$ **3.** 23.40%
4. $96,000   **5.** $r < 18.43\%$ **6.** 51 days
7. 16.55%

CHAPTER 19

1. 24.83%   **2.** 9.93%   **4.** 7.37%; 14.90%; 22.58%;
30.42%; 38.42%   **6.** 37.24%; 14.90%; 9.31%
8. 9.31%; 10.64%; 12.41%; 24.83%   **10.** 12.63%;
13.33%; 15.00%   **12.** 6.67%; 8.89%; 11.11%;
13.33%; 16.67%   **14.** 13.33%   **15.** $27,777.78

CHAPTER 20

1. 1.408; 1.017   **2.** 0.768; 0.796   **3.** 0.5187; 0.5847
4. 1.0778; 1.4076   **7.** 0.0188   **8.** 0.01485
9. 0.0358   **11.** $22.22   **12.** 25.65 days
13. 40   **21.** 3.6325   **24.** 2.3838   **27.** 6.54
29. 0.3311   **30.** 0.5438

CHAPTER 21

1. November, $450,000; February, $225,000;
April, $75,000   **3.** May, $233,000; September,
$88,500   **5.** July, $120,960; October, $129,920

7. Total = $1,702,400   **9.** January, $358,400
11. $224,000   **13.** $100,000 each month
17. February total = $535,000   **19.** EAT = 1.88%
21. $331,520   **23.** $8,955,000   **25.** $168,000
27. $3,188,424   **29.** $185,880

CHAPTER 22

3. NI = $15,000; ROA = 15%; EPS = $15
7. ROA = 20%   **8.** ROA = 40%   **10.** ROA = 10%
12. σ_{EBIT} = $14,142; σ_{EPS} = $14.14   **14.** 9%
18. 10%   **20.** 9.5%   **23.** 9,000 shares
27. 5.5556%

CHAPTER 23

1. $117,000   **3.** $170,000   **5.** $108,000
8. $-$661,176   **10.** $59,262   **13.** $13,500
14. $28,000   **17.** $-$135,644   **19.** $43,724
20. $43,704   **22.** $113,934   **25.** $16,000
29. $-$204,065   **31.** $69,312   **34.** $28,000
36. $-$106,142   **38.** $44,747   **41.** $30,000
43. $16,800   **46.** $37,976   **49.** $10,000
52. $6,000   **56.** $-$57,402.76   **58.** $17,995
59. $5 million   **61.** 1,066,667   **63.** $86 million
65. $80.62   **70.** 21.5   **71.** $120,000   **73.** $200,000
76. $100,000   **78.** $200,000   **81.** 8,696 shares
83. 8%   **86.** 20%

CHAPTER 25

1. $C = S$ **3.** $C = 0$ **5.** Arbitrage profit = $4
7. $C_b = 1.1\,C_a$ **11.** $C = S - E \exp(-r_f T)$

CHAPTER 27

1. DM in the spot market   **3.** DM/£, 180 days,
New York/Frankfurt   **7.** FF, 180 days,
New York/Paris   **9.** DM/FF, 180 days,
New York   **13.** saved $50   **14.** lost $20

Acknowledgments

Chapter 1, p. 6 "America's Most Admired Corporations" by Alison L. Sprout, *Fortune,* February 11, 1991. Copyright © 1991 The Time Inc. Magazine Company. All rights reserved. **p. 9** "Clear the Court of Economists, Please," *Business Week,* April 22, 1991. Reprinted from Business Week by special permission, copyright © 1991 by McGraw-Hill Inc.

Chapter 2, p. 20 "Will Counterfeit Bucks Stop Here?" *Business Week,* April 8, 1991. Reprinted from Business Week by special permission, copyright © 1991 by McGraw-Hill Inc. **p. 26** "The Good Central Bankers' Guide" from *The Economist,* March 2, 1991.

Chapter 3, p. 46 "These Piggies Went to Market" from *Time,* March 18, 1991. Copyright © 1991 The Time Inc. Magazine Company. Reprinted by permission.

Chapter 4, p. 68 "LDC Debt Rescheduling: Calculating Who Gains, Who Loses" by Anthony Saunders and Marti Subrahmanyam, *Federal Reserve Bank of Philadelphia Business Review,* November/December 1988.

Chapter 5, p. 80 "One Company's Taxes" by Laura Saunders, adapted by permission of *Forbes* magazine, January 9, 1989. Copyright © Forbes Inc., 1989. **p. 84** "Lies of the Bottom Line" by Dana Wechsler Linden, adapted by permission of *Forbes* magazine, November 12, 1990. Copyright © Forbes Inc., 1990. **p. 88** "Look into Your Heart and Pay" from *Time,* March 18, 1991. Copyright © 1991 The Time Inc. Magazine Company. Reprinted by permission. **p. 90** "Is This Kid for Real?" from *Time,* February 25, 1991. Copyright © 1991 The Time Inc. Magazine Company. Reprinted by permission. **p. 92** "White House to IRS: Hands Off the Rich" from *Time,* April 1, 1991. Copyright © 1991 The Time Inc. Magazine Company. Reprinted by permission.

Chapter 6, p. 104 "Name-Dropping on Wall Street, No Longer What It Used to Be," *Wall Street Journal,* February 22, 1991. Reprinted by permission of the Wall Street Journal. **p. 110** "Buying A Little Insurance Insurance," *Business Week,* December 10, 1990. Reprinted from Business Week by special permission, copyright © 1990 by McGraw-Hill Inc.

Chapter 7, p. 117 "Hefner Dresses Up Her Stock," *Fortune,* June 18, 1990. Copyright © 1990 The Time Inc. Magazine Company. All rights reserved. **p. 127** "Where Pennies Still Count," *Fortune,* February 25, 1991. Reprinted by permission of Fortune magazine. **p. 133** From "Dave Barry Turns 40" by Dave Barry. Copyright © 1990 by Dave Barry. Reprinted by permission of Crown Publishers, Inc. **p. 140** "Don't Get Mad, Go Short" by Frederick E. Rowe, Jr., adapted by permission of *Forbes* magazine, June 25, 1990. Copyright © Forbes Inc., 1990.

Chapter 8, p. 148 "Why Bears Drive Volvos" by Frederick E. Rowe, Jr., reprinted by permission of Forbes magazine, January 21, 1991. Copyright © Forbes Inc., 1991. **p. 156** "A Share in the Colony" from *The Economist,* December 8, 1990.

Chapter 9, p. 166 "J. P. and the Bond Covenant" taken from "Burlington Northern Tries to Break Its Bonds" by Gelvin Stevenson and Brenton Welling, *Business Week,* June 10, 1985. Reprinted from Business Week by special permission, copyright © 1985 by McGraw-Hill Inc. **p. 176** "A Tale of Two Credit-Rating Agencies," *The Economist,* March 30, 1991.

Chapter 10, p. 198 "Squeeze Play" by Robert McGough, adapted by permission of *Forbes* magazine, November 19, 1984. Copyright © Forbes Inc., 1984. **p. 206** "Stakes, Shares and Digestible Poison Pills," *The Economist,* February 2, 1991. **p. 210** "Shuffling the Chrysler Board," from *Time,* March 25, 1991. Copyright © 1991 The Time Inc. Magazine Company. Reprinted by permission. **p. 216** "Why the Brokers Own Yachts," by Mark Hulbert. Reprinted by permission of *Forbes* magazine, January 21, 1991. Copyright © Forbes Inc., 1991.

Chapter 11, p. 232 "Retirement Outlook," from *Personal Investor,* January 1991. Reprinted by permission of Personal Investor Magazine, Plaza Communications, Irvine, CA. **p. 245** "Tough Times? Yippee!" *Business Week,* January 14, 1991. Reprinted from Business Week by special permission, copyright © 1991 by McGraw-Hill Inc. **p. 247** "Thanks, Boone" by Eric Schmuckler, adapted by permission of *Forbes* magazine, November 26, 1990. Copyright © Forbes Inc., 1990. **p. 249** " Country Risk and the Gulf Crisis" by Hania Forham from *Euromoney,* September 1990. Reprinted by permission of Euromoney Publications.

Chapter 12, p. 272 "Sliding Seats" from *The Economist,* November 10, 1990. **p. 282** "An Incentive a Day Can Keep Doctor Bills at Bay," *Business Week,* April 29, 1991. Reprinted from Business Week by special permission, copyright © 1991 by McGraw-Hill Inc.

Chapter 13, p. 289 "Maybe the Market Isn't So 'Efficient' After All," *Business Week,* October 30, 1989. Reprinted from Business Week by special permission, copyright © 1991 by McGraw-Hill Inc. **p. 294** From *Famous Financial Fiascos* by John Train. Text copyright © 1985 by Bedford Research, Inc. Reprinted by permission of Clarkson N. Potter, Inc., a division of Crown Publishers, Inc. **p. 297** "Investment Swindles: How They Work and How to Avoid Them" from the National Futures Association, 1987. Reprinted courtesy of National Futures Association. **p. 314** "Insider Trading," by Mark Hulbert. Reprinted by permission of *Forbes* magazine, December 24, 1990. Copyright © Forbes Inc., 1990.

Chapter 14, p. 328 "The CRIBs Age" by Lawrence Minard, adapted by permission of *Forbes* magazine, November 18, 1985. Copyright © Forbes Inc., 1985. **p. 334** "Can't You Yanks Take a Joke?" by David Ellis from *Time,* April 15, 1991. Copyright © 1991 The Time Inc. Magazine Company. Reprinted by permission. **p. 348** "Dumb Like Foxes," by John Merwin, adapted by permission of *Forbes* magazine, October 24, 1988. Copyright © Forbes Inc., 1988. **p. 356** "What the Brochures Don't Tell You," from *Business Week,* April 15, 1991. Reprinted from Business Week by special permission, copyright © 1991 by McGraw-Hill Inc. **p. 358** "Capital Budgeting and

Social Security" by Dean Croushore, *Federal Reserve Bank of Philadelphia Business Review,* November/December, 1990. Reprinted by permission of the Federal Reserve Bank of Philadelphia. **p. 362** "HP's Printer Unit: From Rule-Breaker to Role Model," *Business Week,* April 1, 1991. Reprinted from Business Week by special permission, copyright © 1991 by McGraw-Hill Inc. **p. 366** "Is America Finally Ready for the Gasless Carriage?" *Business Week,* April 8, 1991. Reprinted from Business Week by special permission, copyright © 1991 by McGraw-Hill Inc.

Chapter 15, p. 387 "Too Slick with the Pink Slips" from *Time,* January 14, 1991. Copyright © 1991 The Time Inc. Magazine Company. Reprinted by permission. **p. 398** "The Economics of Innovation," insert to an article by Alison Butler, "The Trade-Related Aspects of Intellectual Property Rights: What Is at Stake?" Reprinted by permission from the *Review of the Federal Reserve Bank of St. Louis,* November/December 1990. **p. 406** "Simon & Schuster's *Nancy Reagan:* How Big a Blockbuster?" *Business Week,* April 22, 1991. Reprinted from Business Week by special permission, copyright © 1991 by McGraw-Hill Inc. **p. 410** From *Famous Financial Fiascos* by John Train. Text copyright © 1985 by Bedford Research, Inc. Reprinted by permission of Clarkson N. Potter, Inc., a division of Crown Publishers, Inc.

Chapter 16, p. 430 "Drinking Your Profits Is the Best Revenge" by Peter Fuhrman, adapted by permission of *Forbes* magazine, June 25, 1990. Copyright © Forbes Inc., 1990. **p. 434** From "Molex: Investing in the Future." Reprinted from the April 1991 issue of *CFO, the Magazine for Senior Financial Executives,* Copyright © 1991 CFO Publishing Corporation.

Chapter 17, p. 444 "Spending Plastic" from *The Economist,* November 17, 1990. **p. 448** "Helmsley Says IRA Lost Interest on Her Payment." Reprinted with permission from *Insight,* August 20, 1990. Copyright © 1990 Insight. All Rights Reserved. **p. 452** "The Check Is in the Pail" from *Time,* September 8, 1986. Copyright © 1986 The Time Inc. Magazine Company. Reprinted by permission. **p. 454** "Post-Hutton Lessons in How to Manage Coporate Cash" by Dexter

Hutchins. From *Fortune*, November 11, 1985. Copyright © 1985 The Time Inc. Magazine Company. All rights reserved. **p. 456** "The High Risk of Funds Transfer," from *Euromoney*, November 1990. Reprinted by permission of Euromoney Publications.

Chapter 18, p. 466 "It's Legal, But Is It Smart?" by William P. Barrett, adapted by permission of *Forbes* magazine, June 25, 1990. Copyright © Forbes Inc., 1990. **p. 469** From "When the Price Isn't Right," *Time*, April 15, 1991. Copyright © 1991 The Time Inc. Magazine Company. Reprinted by permission.

Chapter 19, p. 481 "Finders, Keepers" by Ben Weberman, adapted by permission of *Forbes* magazine, March 23, 1987. Copyright © Forbes Inc., 1987. **p. 482** "An Excess of Plastic" by Howard Rudnitsky, adapted by permission of *Forbes* magazine, February 4, 1991. Copyright © Forbes Inc., 1991. **p. 486** "How Treasury Bills Are Auctioned" by Loretta J. Mester, *Federal Reserve Bank of Philadelphia Business Review*, March–April 1988. Reprinted with permission from the Federal Reserve Bank of Philadelphia. **p. 489** "2,500 Years of Auctions . . . at a Glance" by Loretta J. Mester, *Federal Reserve Bank of Philadelphia Business Review*, March–April 1988. Reprinted with permission from the Federal Reserve Bank of Philadelphia. **p. 491** "Iraq's Unauthorised Billions" from *Euromoney*, August 1990. Reprinted by permission of Euromoney Publications. **p. 494** "Commercial Paper Without the Paper" by Rosalyn Retkwa. Reprinted from the April 1991 issue of *CFO, the Magazine for Senior Financial Executives*. Copyright © 1991 CFO Publishing Corporation.

Chapter 20, p. 516 "From One Pocket to Another" by Susan Arterian from *Global Finance*, November 1990. Reprinted by permission of Global Information, Inc. **p. 519** "The Soviets Take Accounting 101," *Business Week*, April 22, 1991. Reprinted from Business Week by special permission, copyright © 1991 by McGraw-Hill Inc.

Chapter 21, p. 528 "Them That Can, Do, Them That Can't, Forecast" by Ronald Bailey, adapted by permission of *Forbes* magazine, December 26, 1988. Copyright © Forbes Inc., 1988. **p. 535** "Taking the

Cure" by Marc Beauchamp, adapted by permission of Forbes magazine, May 5, 1986. Copyright © Forbes Inc., 1986.

Chapter 22, p. 554 "Hard Lessons from the Debt Decade" by John J. Curran from *Fortune*, June 18, 1990. Copyright © 1990 The Time Inc. Magazine Company. All rights reserved. **p. 556** "How Big Is Your Share of Government Debt?" by Dean Croushore, *Federal Reserve Bank of Philadelphia Business Review*, November/December, 1990. Reprinted with permission from Federal Reserve Bank of Philadelphia. **p. 565** "Dances with Debt" from *Time*, April 15, 1991. Copyright © 1991 The Time Inc. Magazine Company. Reprinted by permission. **p. 569** "The United States in Debt" by Norman S. Fieleke from *New England Economic Review*, September/October, 1990. Reprinted by permission of the Federal Reserve Bank of Boston. **p. 573** "Dangerous Dividends" by Ruthanne Sutor and Alexandra Ourusoff from *Financial World*, February 21, 1989. Copyright © 1989 by Financial World. All rights reserved. **p. 579** "Whose Money Is It Anyway?" by Lisa Gubernick, adapted by permission of *Forbes* magazine, November 12, 1990. Copyright © Forbes Inc., 1990. **p. 581** "Endangered Dividends" by Timothy Dodman and Gilbert Steedley. Reprinted by permission of *Forbes* magazine, March 4, 1991. Copyright © Forbes Inc., 1991. **p. 585** "A Mini-Revolt Over Dividends in Japan" by Yoko Shibata from *Global Finance*, November 1990. Reprinted by permission of Global Information, Inc. **p. 588** "The Importance of Dividend Yields in Country Selection" by A. Michael Keppler from *The Journal of Portfolio Management*, Winter 1991. This copyrighted material is reprinted with permission from Institutional Investor, Inc.

Chapter 23, p. 600 "Aircraft Deals Are Anything but Plain Today" by Christopher Elias. *Insight*, June 20, 1988. Reprinted with permission from Insight. Copyright © 1988 Insight. All Rights Reserved. **p. 606** "Please Re-lease Me" by Alexandra Biesada. Reprinted from *Financial World*. Copyright © 1991 by Financial World. All rights reserved. **p. 618** "The First Tycoon" by Maury Klein, adapted by permission of *Forbes* magazine, October 22, 1990. Copyright

© Forbes Inc., 1990. **p. 626** "Europe 1992: Implications for U.S. Firms" by Thomas Bennett and Craig S. Hakkio from *The International Finance Reader,* ed. by Robert W. Kolb, Kolb Publishing Company, 1991. **p. 631** "Takeover and Defense Tactics" by Paul R. Krugman from *Economic Perspectives,* Jan–Feb. 1989, pp. 8–9. Reprinted by permission of the Federal Reserve Bank of Chicago.

Chapter 24, p. 651, From *Famous Financial Fiascos* by John Train. Text copyright © 1985 by Bedford Research, Inc. Reprinted by permission of Clarkson N. Potter, Inc., a division of Crown Publishers, Inc. **p. 654** "The Hunt Silver Manipulation" from *Understanding Futures Markets* by Robert W. Kolb. Reprinted by permission of Kolb Publishing Company. **p. 668** "Wireless Adds Its Voice to 'Open Outcry' at Futures Exchanges," *Infoworld,* April 22, 1991. Reprinted by permission of Communications Inc. Further reproduction is prohibited.

Chapter 25, p. 690 "It's a Bond, It's a Stock, It's ... a LYON?" by Jon Friedman and Larry Light, *Business Week,* August 6, 1990. Reprinted from Business Week by special permission, copyright © 1991 by McGraw-Hill Inc. **p. 699** "LDC Debt Rescheduling: Calculating Who Gains, Who Loses" by Anthony Saunders and Marti Subrahmanyam, *Federal Reserve Bank of Philadelphia Business Review,* November/December, 1988. Reprinted with permission of Federal Reserve Bank of Philadelphia.

Chapter 26, p. 722 "With Wine Futures, You Can Always Swallow the Losses" by John Meehan, *Business Week,* Oct. 15, 1990. Reprinted from Business Week by special permission, copyright © 1990 by McGraw-Hill Inc. **p. 727** "Floor Exercises" by Gary Weiss, *Business Week,* April 29, 1991. Reprinted from Business Week by special permission, copyright © 1991 by McGraw-Hill Inc.

Chapter 27, p. 746 "The 'Shadow Bank of Japan' Strikes Again" by Karen Lowry Miller, *Business Week,* April 8, 1991. Reprinted from Business Week by special permission, copyright © 1991 by McGraw-Hill Inc. **p. 752** "ECU Bonds, Pioneer of Currency Union" from *Euromoney,* January 1991. Reprinted by permission of Euromoney Publications. **p. 754** "The Hamburger Standard" from *The Economist,* May 5, 1990. **p. 760** "The Internationalization of the Beer Brewing Industry" by Jeffrey D. Karrenbrock. Reprinted by permission from the *Review of the Federal Reserve Bank of St. Louis,* November/December, 1990.

Index

Future Value of $1

				Interest Rate (r)					
Period (n)	1%	2%	3%	4%	5%	6%	7%	8%	9%
1	1.0100	1.0200	1.0300	1.0400	1.0500	1.0600	1.0700	1.0800	1.0900
2	1.0201	1.0404	1.0609	1.0816	1.1025	1.1236	1.1449	1.1664	1.1881
3	1.0303	1.0612	1.0927	1.1249	1.1576	1.1910	1.2250	1.2597	1.2950
4	1.0406	1.0824	1.1255	1.1699	1.2155	1.2625	1.3108	1.3605	1.4116
5	1.0510	1.1041	1.1593	1.2167	1.2763	1.3382	1.4026	1.4693	1.5386
6	1.0615	1.1262	1.1941	1.2653	1.3401	1.4185	1.5007	1.5869	1.6771
7	1.0721	1.1487	1.2299	1.3159	1.4071	1.5036	1.6058	1.7138	1.8280
8	1.0829	1.1717	1.2668	1.3686	1.4775	1.5938	1.7182	1.8509	1.9926
9	1.0937	1.1951	1.3048	1.4233	1.5513	1.6895	1.8385	1.9990	2.1719
10	1.1046	1.2190	1.3439	1.4802	1.6289	1.7908	1.9672	2.1589	2.3674
11	1.1157	1.2434	1.3842	1.5395	1.7103	1.8983	2.1049	2.3316	2.5804
12	1.1268	1.2682	1.4258	1.6010	1.7959	2.0122	2.2522	2.5182	2.8127
13	1.1381	1.2936	1.4685	1.6651	1.8856	2.1329	2.4098	2.7196	3.0658
14	1.1495	1.3195	1.5126	1.7317	1.9799	2.2609	2.5785	2.9372	3.3417
15	1.1610	1.3459	1.5580	1.8009	2.0789	2.3966	2.7590	3.1722	3.6425
16	1.1726	1.3728	1.6047	1.8730	2.1829	2.5404	2.9522	3.4259	3.9703
17	1.1843	1.4002	1.6528	1.9479	2.2920	2.6928	3.1588	3.7000	4.3276
18	1.1961	1.4282	1.7024	2.0258	2.4066	2.8543	3.3799	3.9960	4.7171
19	1.2081	1.4568	1.7535	2.1068	2.5270	3.0256	3.6165	4.3157	5.1417
20	1.2202	1.4859	1.8061	2.1911	2.6533	3.2071	3.8697	4.6610	5.6044
21	1.2324	1.5157	1.8603	2.2788	2.7860	3.3996	4.1406	5.0338	6.1088
22	1.2447	1.5460	1.9161	2.3699	2.9253	3.6035	4.4304	5.4365	6.6586
23	1.2572	1.5769	1.9736	2.4647	3.0715	3.8197	4.7405	5.8715	7.2579
24	1.2697	1.6084	2.0328	2.5633	3.2251	4.0489	5.0724	6.3412	7.9111
25	1.2824	1.6406	2.0938	2.6658	3.3864	4.2919	5.4274	6.8485	8.6231
26	1.2953	1.6734	2.1566	2.7725	3.5557	4.5494	5.8074	7.3964	9.3992
27	1.3082	1.7069	2.2213	2.8834	3.7335	4.8223	6.2139	7.9881	10.2451
28	1.3213	1.7410	2.2879	2.9987	3.9201	5.1117	6.6488	8.6271	11.1671
29	1.3345	1.7758	2.3566	3.1187	4.1161	5.4184	7.1143	9.3173	12.1722
30	1.3478	1.8114	2.4273	3.2434	4.3219	5.7435	7.6123	10.0627	13.2677
31	1.3613	1.8476	2.5001	3.3731	4.5380	6.0881	8.1451	10.8677	14.4618
32	1.3749	1.8845	2.5751	3.5081	4.7649	6.4534	8.7153	11.7371	15.7633
33	1.3887	1.9222	2.6523	3.6484	5.0032	6.8406	9.3253	12.6760	17.1820
34	1.4026	1.9607	2.7319	3.7943	5.2533	7.2510	9.9781	13.6901	18.7284
35	1.4166	1.9999	2.8139	3.9461	5.5160	7.6861	10.6766	14.7853	20.4140
36	1.4308	2.0399	2.8983	4.1039	5.7918	8.1473	11.4239	15.9682	22.2512
37	1.4451	2.0807	2.9852	4.2681	6.0814	8.6361	12.2236	17.2456	24.2538
38	1.4595	2.1223	3.0748	4.4388	6.3855	9.1543	13.0793	18.6253	26.4367
39	1.4741	2.1647	3.1670	4.6164	6.7048	9.7035	13.9948	20.1153	28.8160
40	1.4889	2.2080	3.2620	4.8010	7.0400	10.2857	14.9745	21.7245	31.4094